COLLEGE ENGLISH AND COMMUNICATION

Fifth Edition

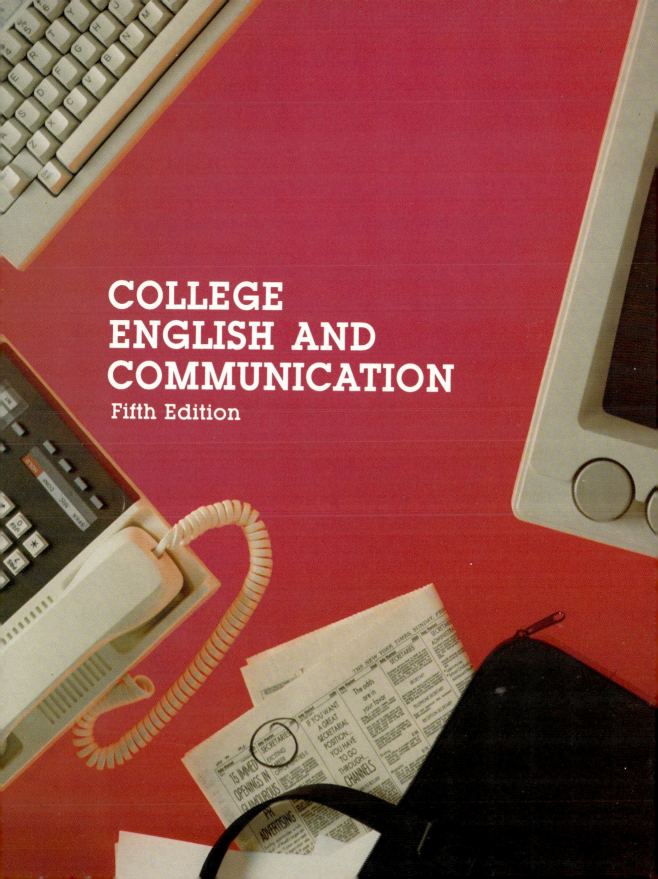

COLLEGE ENGLISH AND COMMUNICATION

Fifth Edition

MARIE M. STEWART, Ph.D.
Late Head of the
Business Education Department
Stonington High School
Stonington, Connecticut

KENNETH ZIMMER, Ed.D.
Professor Emeritus of
Business Education and Office Administration
School of Business and Economics
California State University
Los Angeles, California

SUE C. CAMP
Assistant Professor
Broyhill School of Management
Gardner-Webb College
Boiling Springs, North Carolina

Gregg Division
McGRAW-HILL BOOK COMPANY

New York Atlanta Dallas St. Louis San Francisco
Auckland Bogota Guatemala Hamburg Johannesburg
Lisbon London Madrid Mexico Montreal New Delhi
Panama Paris San Juan São Paulo Singapore
Sydney Tokyo Toronto

Sponsoring Editor: Marion B. Castellucci
Editing Supervisor: Larry Goldberg
Cover/Text Designer: Nancy Axelrod-Sharkey
Production Supervisor: S. Steven Canaris

Photo Editor: Rosemarie Rossi
Cover Photograph: Interactive Graphics, Inc./Sulpizio Design, Inc.
Technical Studio: Fine Line, Inc.

Photo Credits
Jules Allen/Vision Fotos, page 33 *(bottom)*. Courtesy of AT&T: pages 36
(bottom), 40. John P. Cavanagh, page 39 *(top)*. Richard Hackett, pages 33 *(top)*,
34, 35, 36 *(top)*, 38, 39 *(bottom)*, 297, 298, 300, 397, 398, 399 *(bottom)*, 400,
465–468, 565, 566, 567 *(top)*, 568. Courtesy of NCR Corporation: page 37.
Bob Rogers, pages 299, 399 *(top)*, 567 *(bottom)*.

Library of Congress Cataloging-in-Publication Data

Stewart, Marie M., (date)
    College English and communication.
    Includes index.
    1. English language—Business English.   2. English language—
Rhetoric.   3. English language—Grammar—1950–
4. Communication in management.
I. Zimmer, Kenneth, (date).   II. Camp, Sue C., (date).   III. Title.
PE1479.B87S73   1986   808'.066651   86-31
ISBN 0-07-072854-2

The letters and memos in this book were created electronically.

COLLEGE ENGLISH AND COMMUNICATION,   Fifth Edition

3 4 5 6 7 8 9 0   VNHVNH   8 9 3 2 1 0 9 8

ISBN 0-07-072854-2

PREFACE

The modern business world is highly competitive and performance-oriented. To improve productivity and profitability, companies across the country spend millions of dollars hiring the best new employees and upgrading the skills of their present employees. No matter what job you want and what specific skills you have—typing or operating word processing equipment, for example—to succeed in business, you need effective communication skill.

Why do employers demand communication skill from every employee? Experienced managers know that most business workers spend the greater part of each workday communicating—writing letters, listening to instructions, speaking to coworkers, and reading correspondence. Workers whose reading, writing, listening, and speaking skills are poor will perform poorly in most business environments because faulty communication leads to misunderstandings and errors. Workers who communicate effectively, on the other hand, generally do well on the job.

THE *COLLEGE ENGLISH AND COMMUNICATION* PROGRAM

The fifth edition of *College English and Communication* provides a comprehensive program to help you develop the proficiency in writing, listening, speaking, and reading that you will need for career success. It is designed to help you master the fundamental principles of communication, and it achieves this goal through its carefully planned, step-by-step presentation.

Business Communication and Technology. Because understanding the communication process is fundamental to effective writing, speaking, listening, and reading, Chapter 1 offers an introduction to communication in business. Chapter 1 also describes how communication affects human relations and how the new electronic office technologies affect communication.

Listening and Reading. As a follow-up to the introduction to communication in Chapter 1, Chapter 2 helps you develop your listening and reading skills—skills that are as important on the job as they are in the classroom. In Chapter 2 you will begin a long-range program for improving your listening and reading skills.

Proofreading and Editing. Chapter 3, new to the fifth edition, will give you an understanding of the proofreading and editing processes and their importance in producing error-free communications. The ability of word processing equipment to facilitate proofreading and editing is discussed, and common proofreaders' marks are introduced.

Grammar, Punctuation, and Style. Chapters 4 and 5 provide a thorough discussion of the principles of grammar, punctuation, and style—principles that you must master if you wish to write and speak effectively. Many examples are given to illustrate proper usage, and "Memory Hooks" are provided as aids to memorizing correct usage. "Checkup" exercises provide immediate practice and reinforcement of the principles covered in these chapters.

Words.   The effective communicator must, of course, be able to use words skillfully both in writing and in speaking, and *College English and Communication,* fifth edition, provides a continuing program to expand and refine your vocabulary. Chapter 6 will introduce you to the reference tools that will make your writing less difficult and, at the same time, more effective. In this chapter you will learn techniques for using words precisely and for achieving variety in word usage. In addition, Chapter 6 offers some basic methods for improving spelling.

The Craft of Writing.   Understanding the rules of grammar and having a wide vocabulary do not, of course, guarantee effective writing. Letters, memos, and reports must be planned if they are to achieve their goals, and Chapter 7 presents the techniques for planning and organizing messages. This chapter also discusses writing techniques that will help transform average writing into forceful communication.

Memos.   The most common form of business writing is the interoffice memorandum, and an entire chapter is devoted to this topic in this edition. Chapter 8 covers different memo styles as well as writing techniques.

Letters.   Chapter 9 offers you the opportunity to apply all the writing techniques you've learned. This chapter covers letter formats and specific letter types—requests, claim and adjustment letters, public relations letters, and social-business letters. In addition, a section on the use of form letters and boilerplate text concludes the chapter. The text provides ample opportunity to learn about and practice writing each type of letter.

Reports and Special Communications.   Reports are important, commonly used business communications, and they are treated in detail in Chapter 10. Besides memorandum reports and long reports, this chapter discusses minutes of meetings, news releases, and telecommunications.

Oral Communication.   Speaking to coworkers, customers, and others is an important part of the business day for most people, and Chapter 11 presents the basic information that you must know to speak effectively in one-to-one and group situations.

Communicating for Career Success.   During employment interviews and on the job, all the communication skill that you have developed will be tested. In Chapter 12 you will discover how you can apply your communication skill to find a job and to make your interviews more effective. In this chapter you will also learn techniques for handling your communication duties on the job.

Communication Projects.   As mentioned above, the text offers Checkup exercises within the sections in Chapters 4 and 5; in addition, it offers a variety of "Communication Projects" at the end of each section.

- Practical Application exercises reinforce the principles presented in each section and review principles covered in previous sections.
- Editing Practice exercises help you acquire the ability to detect—and to correct—errors in English usage.
- Case Problems generally emphasize the human relations aspects of successful business communication. They will help you develop your ability to make sound decisions in typical on-the-job situations.

Electronic Office Glossary.   A handy new reference tool, the Electronic Office Glossary offers brief definitions of terms frequently encountered in the modern office.

SUPPLEMENTARY MATERIALS

Besides the text, the *College English and Communication* program includes a workbook of communication activities for students, instructor's editions of text and workbook, test masters, and a microcomputer test bank.

The Workbook.   A comprehensive book of skill-building activities, *Communication Problems Correlated With College English and Communication,* fifth edition, provides additional exercises to improve communication skills. The exercises provide excellent reinforcement of the text principles section by section, as well as periodic reviews of preceding sections.

Instructor's Edition of the Text.   New to this edition, *College English and Communication* offers a page-for-page instructor's edition of the student text. Short teaching suggestions and short exercise solutions appear, in color, right on the page to which they refer. In addition, grouped at the back of the instructor's edition are explanations of how to use the program; additional detailed section-by-section teaching suggestions; and longer solutions to exercises in the text, carefully cross-referenced to the actual exercises.

Instructor's Edition of the Workbook.   Another new teaching aid is the instructor's edition of the workbook. Not only does it include a page-for-page facsimile key of all the workbook exercises, but it also includes objective tests for the students (see below).

Tests.   Test masters are included at the back of the instructor's edition of *Communication Problems Correlated With College English and Communication.* Twelve tests cover all the chapters of the text. In addition, an inventory test for use at the beginning of the course and a final examination for the end of the course are included. A facsimile key to the tests follows the tests at the back of the instructor's edition of the workbook.

A new microcomputer test bank offers instructors additional test questions. Tests can be generated on a random, nonrandom, or alternating-question basis, and instructors can edit as well as add questions.

ACKNOWLEDGMENTS

We would like to thank the following educators for their invaluable comments on the manuscript for this program: Marie-Louise Brauch, The Berkeley School, Waldwick, New Jersey; Tommie L. Pierce, Shreveport-Bossier Vocational Technical Institute, Shreveport, Louisiana; Marcia K. Shallcross, Palomar College, San Marcos, California; Arlene K. Sinding, Hillsborough High School, Belle Mead, New Jersey; and Dr. Mildred M. Whitted, St. Louis Community College at Forest Park, St. Louis, Missouri.

KENNETH ZIMMER
SUE C. CAMP

CONTENTS

CHAPTER

ONE

COMMUNICATING IN BUSINESS

THE COMMUNICATION PROCESS

Communication, very simply defined, is the exchange of messages. Most people, except for an occasional hermit or recluse, communicate on a daily basis.

Very early in life, we learn to communicate our needs to others. A baby, for example, learns that crying makes parents respond quickly with attention, a dry diaper, food, or all three. During the development period from infancy to adulthood, communication becomes more complex. Speaking, writing, listening, reading, and observing become part of the communication spectrum.

KINDS OF COMMUNICATION

Communication is divided into two main categories: verbal and nonverbal. Verbal communication uses words to exchange the message. This includes both spoken and written words. Nonverbal communication completes the message exchange without the use of words. This includes gestures, expressions, and body movements. Both verbal and nonverbal communication techniques are combined by good communicators to make their communication more effective.

This important combination, or, even more so, the lack of it, is readily observable. Have you ever listened to a speaker who is an authority on a subject but who lacked expression? It is difficult to look beyond the nonexpressive personality to find the message content.

EFFECTIVE COMMUNICATION

Effective communication is essential to successful family, social, and business relationships. A communication breakdown can lead to misunderstandings and serious problems in our personal and business lives. Good communication skills can positively affect most aspects of our relationships with others.

Communication is effective if:

1. It enables the receiver to interpret the message exactly as the sender intended.
2. It evokes the desired response from the receiver.
3. It develops favorable relations between the sender and the receiver.

PURPOSES OF COMMUNICATION

No matter what the specific content of a message, its sender has at least one of the four main purposes for communication in mind. All messages are sent for one of these reasons:

To inquire. "What kind of computer do you recommend?"
To inform. "The auction will begin at noon."
To persuade. "Buy your airline tickets before the price increases."
To develop goodwill. "Thank you for opening an account with us."

COMPONENTS OF COMMUNICATION

Five basic components are needed to exchange messages:

1. *Message sender*. The sender composes the intended message.
2. *The actual message*. The actual message is the one transmitted. It may or may not be what the message sender intended.
3. *Message transmission*. The message can be transmitted in a variety of ways including conversation, computer, letter, memo, telephone, or a combination of these.
4. *Message receiver*. The actual message is received.
5. *Message interpretation*. The receiver interprets the message.

Ideally, the intended message, the actual message, and the message interpretation are the same. Miscommunication is the result when these three components do not agree. Consider the following example.

Sal Bartauski, a college freshman, was upset with his semester grades but knew he must write to his parents. He transmitted this *actual message* by letter to his parents: "I got only one D this semester." They received the message and interpreted it this way: "Sal got only one D this semester. This is much better than the four Ds he got last semester." Everything seems clear. Right? Wrong!

Miscommunication occurred. In his haste, the actual message sent did not convey the intended message. Sal received only one D this semester, but he also received three Fs. Sal's parents wanted him to do well; therefore, they interpreted his message in a positive way.

Miscommunication and communication breakdowns can often be avoided by using the "feedback" technique. In the process of transmitting a message, the sender uses devices to determine if the receiver is interpreting the message correctly. The feedback technique is easier in face-to-face communication than it is in situations where sender and receiver are separated by time and place, as in written communication.

In face-to-face conversation, feedback can be immediate. The sender can observe the receiver's expressions that signal whether the message is clear or confusing. The sender can ask questions to determine whether the message is being received accurately. The receiver can question content that is unclear.

With most written communication, feedback cannot be achieved so easily because receiver response is not usually immediate. The wrong response, questions from the receiver, or no response may indicate a temporary breakdown in communication.

FACTORS THAT INFLUENCE COMMUNICATION

Although the sender of a message knows the goals he or she seeks to achieve, the sender must keep in mind that there are many factors that influence the communication either favorably or unfavorably. Senders who are aware of the factors control them so that they will have a favorable effect on the communication process. Among the major factors that influence the communication process are (1) the background of the receiver, (2) the appearance of the communicator or the communication, (3) the communication skills of the sender and the receiver, and (4) distractions.

Background of the Receiver

Background refers to these four elements:

1. The *knowledge* already possessed by the receiver as related to the facts, ideas, and language used in the message.
2. The *personality* of the receiver, particularly the emotions, attitudes, and prejudices that are likely to influence the way the message is interpreted.
3. The *experiences* the receiver has had relative to the message content.
4. The *interest and motivation* of the receiver regarding the subject of the message.

These background factors play an important role in determining the reaction of the receiver to the message. For example, suppose you receive a letter from a brokerage firm explaining an investment opportunity. You have not made this kind of investment previously. Your *knowledge* about securities is very limited. Thus your reaction would be different from that of the person who is knowledgeable about many kinds of investments. Your *personality* is extremely conservative. In fact, all your prior investments have been insured.

However, your *experience* with this brokerage firm has been good, and your *interest and motivation* grew when you saw the tax advantages available with this investment opportunity.

Obviously, the communicator who weighs all these factors before preparing the message stands a greater chance that the message will be accepted by the receiver than the person who ignores these factors.

Appearance of the Communicator or Communication

What do these three have in common? (1) An unkempt speaker or salesperson, (2) a receptionist or telephone operator who does not speak distinctly, (3) a sloppy letter filled with erasures. They all transmit communications in an unfavorable way. Each communication has the opportunity to be a goodwill ambassador and to achieve a positive reaction. Appearances do make a difference.

Communication Skills of Sender and Receiver

The tools of language include selecting words accurately and spelling or pronouncing them correctly to express meaning. How well the message sender uses the tools and how well the message receiver interprets their use are major determinants of message effectiveness. Using the wrong word, making a grammatical error, or misusing a punctuation mark may change the intended meaning of the message. Even if the receiver understands the message, the receiver's opinion of the message sender is certain to suffer. For example, a receiver may not do business with a company because of a carelessly written sales letter. The receiver may feel that a company that is careless about its letters will also be careless about filling an order.

Although each of these tools of language is discussed much more thoroughly in later sections of this book, you should be aware that there is a very definite relationship between these tools and reading, listening, and speaking—not just a relationship to writing. If the communication process is to be successful, the message sender must be an effective writer and speaker and the receiver must be an effective reader and listener. Because all of us are sometimes senders and sometimes receivers, we must strive for efficiency in using the basic tools of language for reading, writing, listening, and speaking.

Distractions

Under what environmental conditions is the written or oral message received? Is the room noisy? too warm or too cold? poorly lighted? Is the message receiver more concerned about some personal event at the time the message is received? All of us are subject to distractions that draw our attention away from what we are reading or hearing. As we read or listen, many thoughts may pass through our minds. Sometimes these thoughts are triggered by something we read, hear, or see. Whatever the reason, the result is that we do not concentrate on the message and may miss important information that can cause us to reach erroneous conclusions.

Distractions are easier to prevent when speaking to someone because the environment can often be controlled. However, when writing a communication, the message sender has little control over the receiver's environment but can prevent at least one distraction, a sloppy-looking letter.

YOU AS A BUSINESS COMMUNICATOR

Effective communication is essential for successful relationships. Although this book is concerned primarily with effective communication in the business world, you should keep in mind that improving your communication techniques will favorably affect all aspects of your life—not just your business life.

Language Facility

Because every employee is involved in some form of communicating, you must have facility in using the language to both send and receive messages. A skilled communicator must be able to communicate facts, ideas, opinions, and instructions with a minimum of effort and with clarity, confidence, and knowledge. Therefore, you must know how to use language correctly. You must command a broad vocabulary, which involves not only the ability to spell and pronounce words but also the ability to select words precisely. You must be able to speak and write without error, with as much clarity and in as few words as possible. Not only must you be familiar with the many media available for communication, but also you must have the ability to select the best medium to convey a particular message. Also, you must be able to read and to listen with understanding.

In recent years, business people and the general public have become increasingly aware of the need for improving every business worker's communication skills—particularly the skills of workers who come in contact with the public. Today, courses in effective speaking and writing, as well as in reading improvement, are offered not only by colleges and universities but also by companies themselves. Businesses know that the time and money spent to improve the communication skills of their employees represent dollars saved in time and understanding in day-to-day business operations.

Acquiring Knowledge and Using It

You must study communication skills and practice them. Everyone can improve these skills. In addition to taking courses, one of the best ways to improve communication skills is by observing and critically analyzing the communications you receive. You can learn much from the successes and mistakes of others.

COMMUNICATION SKILLS AND YOUR FUTURE

Perhaps the best way to prove your ability to accept leadership responsibilities is through communication. You can convince others of your merits through the skillful use of verbal and nonverbal messages.

Communication skills play an important role in your business future. The time you spend now is an investment in your career and contributes to your own personal advancement.

COMMUNICATION PROJECTS

Practical Application

A. Define *communication* and list its five basic components.

B. The two main categories of communication are verbal and nonverbal. Successfully combining the two enhances message effectiveness. It is possible to transmit mixed signals to your message receiver when your words say one thing and your actions and expressions say something different. Give an example of how such conflicting messages can be transmitted simultaneously.

C. What is the feedback technique? Give some examples of feedback in face-to-face communication. In non-face-to-face communication, what responses might indicate a communication breakdown?

D. Name the factors that influence communication. Describe each briefly.

E. Interview a business executive about communication. Ask the executive questions such as these:

1. Are written and spoken communications a big part of your job?
2. What communication problems do you see often?
3. Has communication been important in your career advancement?
4. What does your company do to improve the communication skills of employees?
5. What recommendations do you have for me as a student of business communication?

Editing Practice

Spelling Alert! Write each of the following sentences, correcting the spelling errors. A sentence may have more than one misspelled word.

1. Anthony wrote a recommendation letter to the personel manager.
2. Please give me your answer as soon as posible.

3. What time are you planing to leave for Houston?
4. He leisurly finished the report yesteday.
5. Sheila shiped the order last week. We recieved it today.

Case Problem

Hiring a Receptionist. You are going to hire a receptionist for your company. The job description lists the main responsibilities as answering the phone and greeting customers. During any spare time, the receptionist will type letters, memos, and reports. What communication skills would you expect the good applicants to have?

2

COMMUNICATING AND HUMAN RELATIONS

Human relations involves the ability to understand and to deal with people in such a way that a favorable relationship is maintained. People who lack human relations skills will have great difficulty in achieving success in their jobs.

Even with the many innovations in communication technology, effective communicators still use human relations techniques. Carefully evaluating each situation, they take time to consider the needs and feelings of those involved and apply human relations techniques. Whether they are sending messages by letter, traditional telephone, or sophisticated satellite-transmitted teleconference, human relations is the key to successful communication.

EXTERNAL AND INTERNAL COMMUNICATION

Human relations is a vital factor in *external communication* (communication that goes outside the organization). Such communication must often persuade receivers to respond favorably. A sales letter, for example, tries to get a potential customer to buy from your company. A letter lacking human relations techniques will likely land in the trash can.

Human relations is also very much a part of all levels of *internal*

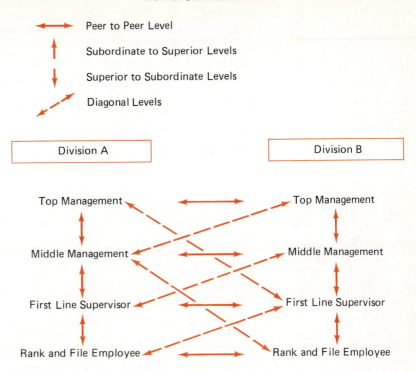

Internal Communications

Peer to Peer Level

Subordinate to Superior Levels

Superior to Subordinate Levels

Diagonal Levels

Division A

Division B

Top Management

Top Management

Middle Management

Middle Management

First Line Supervisor

First Line Supervisor

Rank and File Employee

Rank and File Employee

communication (communication within the organization). Management uses communication to accomplish company objectives. Management must, for example, let employees know when and how a specific job must be done. Nonmanagement personnel use communication for understanding and clarifying when and how a specific job must be done. They also use it to convince management that their knowledge and personal attributes qualify them for pay increases or promotions. Both management and nonmanagement personnel use communication for feedback purposes.

Internal communication is based on four sender-receiver-level relationships: peer to peer, subordinate to superior, superior to subordinate, and diagonal (between different levels from different departments). The diagram shown above illustrates these levels and shows how a person can be a superior in one communication situation and a subordinate in another. Please note that communication should go two ways—not just one.

UNDERSTANDING HUMAN NEEDS

To be an effective communicator, you must first understand the needs of the message receiver. A famous psychologist, Abraham Maslow, divided human needs into five levels:

1. *Physical needs.* Physical needs are those basic needs that are essential to life. They include such things as food, clothing, and shelter. Until these basic needs are satisfied, it is difficult to think of anything else.
2. *Security needs.* Security needs represent our desire to be safe from mental abuse and physical harm. Most people want to avoid unpleasant confrontations and dangerous situations.
3. *Social needs.* Social needs are evident in our wanting to be part of a group. These needs can be met through family, social, employment, or other groups.
4. *Esteem needs.* Esteem needs are met through a feeling of self-importance, self-respect, prestige, power, and recognition. Being the fastest runner, winning a baking contest, being the captain of the team—all of these help meet our esteem needs.
5. *Self-actualization needs.* Self-actualization needs are met through a sense of achievement, competence, creativity, and helping others to meet their needs. People who reach the top of their fields often want to use their abilities and resources to benefit others. They may also want to help others attain similar success.

NEEDS CAN CHANGE

To communicate effectively, you must examine carefully each situation and assess the needs of the receiver. Needs motivate people to act or react in a certain way. Some theorists believe that a satisfied need is not a motivator. If you had just finished two cheeseburgers, an order of fries, and a large milkshake, food would not be a motivator. If you had just been on a restricted diet, food could definitely be a motivator.

At various times, the first three needs levels (physical, security, and social needs) can be fully satisfied. However, the last two (esteem and self-actualization) always have room for more satisfiers. Situations and receivers must be evaluated with each communication to determine the best motivator for the desired action. Empathy is a good name to describe this process. *Empathy* is the psychological projection of yourself into another person's situation.

APPLYING HUMAN RELATIONS TECHNIQUES TO COMMUNICATION

Becoming an effective communicator takes knowledge, effort, and practice. Below are some very practical human relations techniques that will help you improve your communication skills.

Evaluate Each Communication Situation

1. Determine the needs and special circumstances your receiver may have.

2. Decide what would best motivate your receiver to respond favorably.
3. Visualize your receiver.
4. Use empathy.

Demonstrate a Positive Attitude

1. Build relationships with peers, superiors, subordinates, and those outside your company.
2. Be enthusiastic about your job, your company, and your product.
3. Control your emotions.
4. Dress appropriately.
5. Cooperate with others.
6. Establish a favorable reputation for your business.

Be Productive

1. Do a good job.
2. Use your time well.
3. Be neat and well-organized.
4. Be punctual.
5. Look for ways to reduce cost and improve quality.

Be a Good Listener

1. Listen carefully and let the speaker know you are interested.
2. Take notes.
3. Ask questions when you are unsure of the message content.
4. Encourage others to participate in the conversation or discussion when it is appropriate.
5. Respect the opinions of others.

Be Confidential

1. Release information to authorized personnel only.
2. Release information at the appropriate time—not early and not late.
3. Do not spread rumors—even if they are true.

Be Considerate of Others

1. Be courteous, honest, and patient.
2. Be tactful and diplomatic.
3. Treat others as you would like to be treated.
4. Use words and terms that your receiver understands.
5. Be prompt in answering correspondence and returning phone calls.

COMMUNICATION PROJECTS

Practical Application

A. Define the following terms:

1. Human relations

2. External communication
3. Internal communication
4. Empathy
5. Diagonal communication

B. Tell which needs level each of the following represents:

1. A burglar alarm system for your home
2. A jogging suit with school name and colors
3. A jacket with your company emblem
4. Health foods
5. Election as president of an organization
6. A successful recording artist's giving an unknown singer a chance
7. A smoke detector
8. A request for you to design and paint a mural in a public building
9. Owning an expensive car or boat
10. Basic clothing

C. For each numbered item, select the letter of the human relations technique each situation violates.

    a. Evaluate each communication situation.
    b. Demonstrate a positive attitude.
    c. Be productive.
    d. Be a good listener.
    e. Be confidential.
    f. Be considerate of others.

1. Katrina has something bad to say about her supervisor at least once a day. She also criticizes the product her company makes.
2. Julio monopolizes every conversation. He always asks questions about matters that have just been discussed.
3. Ms. Alvarez directed a sales letter on vacation condominiums to high school students.
4. Mr. Salverno told the staff about a proposed pay increase for them.
5. Raquel consistently arrives late and leaves early. She usually takes extra time for coffee and lunch breaks.
6. Raymond lacks tact when talking to the people who work for him. He is also impolite in dealing with customers.
7. Bob always has the "scoop" on what is happening. He gladly shares this information (some true and some not true) at coffee breaks.
8. Lana seldom returns phone calls the same day she receives them. Sometimes she waits a month to answer her correspondence.
9. Mrs. Sanchez listens attentively, but she never takes notes. Thus she has to have details repeated frequently.

10. The office manager loses his temper when anyone disagrees with him.

Editing Practice

Using Tact. Each of the following items lacks tact. Rewrite each one to correct the problem.

1. We can't ship the suit you ordered (catalog #3654) until you send us the size. Don't delay your order further. Send the size today.
2. In our recent sales campaign, we sold 6000 blenders. Your complaint is the only one we received. Even though 5999 people were completely satisfied, we are shipping you a new blender today.
3. The terms on our invoice were clearly stated. We offered a discount if payment was received within 10 days. You took 30 days to pay; therefore, send us the $35 balance.

Case Problem

A Positive Attitude. Susan Williams is beginning her first job after finishing college. Her academic background is excellent. Her employer said, "Susan, you have potential for advancement. If you do a good job and show us a positive attitude, you will get your first promotion in six months."

Susan will definitely do a good job. How can she convey to her employer that she has a positive attitude?

3
COMMUNICATING IN THE ELECTRONIC OFFICE

Technology has definitely had an impact on business communication. For years, the only equipment used in an office was the typewriter, the telephone, and the calculator. Now, the electronic office has sophisticated typewriters that can calculate, telephone systems that can transmit typed messages, and calculators that can talk.

Technology has drastically changed the ways messages are originated, transmitted, and received. However, technology has not lowered the standards for business communication. Effective communication must still be clear, complete, concise, consistent, correct, and courteous; and human relations techniques must be applied.

THE TRADITIONAL OFFICE

To understand fully why the electronic office was needed, we must first look at the traditional office.

Organizational Structure

Most offices were composed of secretaries, typists, and clerks who handled the paperwork for a business. Each executive had a full-time secretary who did a variety of tasks such as typing, filing, and duplicating. Work loads varied considerably. For example, one secretary might have been extremely busy while the secretary in the adjoining office might have had idle time. Idle time was especially a problem when the executive was away from the office. When a secretary was temporarily away, work would pile up.

Environment

Even though some authorities were predicting a paperless office, there was a paper explosion. The availability of convenience copiers and the ease of getting computer printouts seemed to encourage businesses to create mounds of paperwork—some of it necessary and some not. Filing cabinets were filled to capacity. Computer printouts were stacked on every available surface.

Desks were cluttered with correspondence, folders, message pads, and a variety of error correction material (erasers, correction tape, and correction liquid).

Productivity

There were enough people, but they were not turning out enough work. Office costs were rising, but the amount and quality of work were at best remaining constant. Information was not readily available for executives, and this hampered decision making.

THE ELECTRONIC OFFICE

The need for improved organization, environment, and productivity caused management to look for ways to improve the office. Many innovations found their way into the office.

Organization

Management often restructured the organization to provide for adequate supervision. Office personnel were given new titles and responsibilities that did not tie them to a specific executive. This new structure allowed them to progress through career paths that were visible and accessible.

Environment

Technology improved the environment. *Word processing* equipment provided an easier way to produce correction-free communications that eliminated the various correction materials. *Electronic storage systems* (tapes, disks, etc.) reduced the number of filing cabinets, the stacks of computer printouts, and the proliferation of unnecessary copies. *Electronic distribution systems* were used to deliver messages within the office, to branch offices, and to other destinations. For example, *voice mail* was used to solve the telephone tag problem (repeated failure to make contact by phone even though both parties are trying). Voice mail stores the actual voice. *Facsimile copiers* were used to transmit exact copies of already completed handwritten and typewritten information as well as graphs, illustrations, and pictures.

Productivity

Information systems helped managers make decisions by making the necessary data readily available. One innovation that saves time and increases accessibility is the *executive workstation*. The executive workstation is sometimes a microcomputer operating independently, but more often it is a computer terminal linked to the company's main computer. Without leaving the office, an executive can examine information and make the calculations necessary to provide an informed, timely decision. Automated equipment simplified tasks and increased the amount of work completed by executives and other office personnel.

BUSINESS COMMUNICATION TECHNOLOGY

During the last thirty years, technology has provided major developments for the electronic office: information processing, word processing, and telecommunications. In some offices, these three developments are operated independently. However, the trend is to merge them into a total system—an information processing system.

Information Processing

Information processing is the manipulation of data by electronic means to collect, organize, record, process, distribute, and store information for decision-making purposes. It performs numerical calculations, which makes it useful in keeping accounting, inventory, and sales records. It helps to schedule operations and control costs.

Information processing can relieve office personnel of routine, time-consuming, repetitive work. It can, for example, provide a list of past-due accounts. It can sort information from a marketing survey to provide a list of potential customers. The possibilities are seemingly unlimited. One of the major functions of information processing is word processing.

Word Processing

Even though the term *word processing* is new, office personnel have been processing words for years. They have taken written, typed, and spoken words and produced them in final typewritten form. Today, however, technology has simplified the production of the final form. The concept of word processing is taking ideas and using automated equipment to produce them in final form. Once the idea is entered into the equipment, it becomes a *document*.

Word processing equipment evolved from the automatic typewriters that appeared on the market in the 1960s. Since that time, there have been many improvements and developments by different vendors. One of the main benefits of word processing equipment is that it has text-manipulation capabilities. In other words, text can be added, deleted, moved, corrected, and revised before the final document is printed.

Word processors have keyboards that are very similar to typewriter keyboards. Information is entered using this keyboard. Simultaneously, the document appears on a screen. The operator can read the document and make needed changes. When sure that the document is correct, the operator initiates a print command. The revised document is printed at a speed very much above that of superior typists. Because changes were made before printing, there are no messy corrections in the final copy.

The word processing function is accomplished by dedicated word processors, microcomputers with word processing software, and a company's main computer. *Dedicated word processors* are designed and used primarily for word processing applications; however, some of them have calculating functions. *Microcomputers* have word processing capabilities usually through a *software program*—a set of instructions—that was written specifically for that purpose. Some companies use computer terminals to access word processing functions in their main computer.

Word processing improves productivity by reducing costs and improving the quality of written communications.

Telecommunications

Telecommunications is the transmission of information by telephone lines, satellites, or networks. Because of rising postage costs and the need to speed up message delivery, many companies are using telecommunications of various types to transmit information. The telephone call is a simple but familiar form of telecommunications. However, voice is not the only way that data can be transmitted electronically. Today printed words and graphic images may also be sent electronically.

LINKED EQUIPMENT. The ability of two pieces of electronic equipment to communicate has facilitated the transfer of information from one place to another. The automated office does not consist of isolated equipment operating independently. Communication lines link computers to other computers, word processors, printers, and data bases. These communication networks can be set up within an organization for internal communications, or they can be used to communicate with other organizations that have compatible equipment.

ELECTRONIC MAIL.   About 2 million messages a day are sent by electronic mail. Messages are relayed from the sender's terminal through a central computer to the receiver's terminal, where they are stored until read. The advantages of electronic mail are that it eliminates the need for the sender and receiver to communicate at the same time, as the telephone requires, and it eliminates the time needed by the postal or other delivery service to deliver a message in paper form.

TELECONFERENCING.   Teleconferencing allows a group of people in different locations and even different time zones to meet and confer electronically. Teleconferencing offers text, audio, and video capabilities. By means of teleconferences, executives can reduce the time and cost of traveling to meetings. Companies can deliver training and development seminars to employees in different locations.

COMMUNICATION SECURITY

Much of the information processed and stored in a computer is either confidential or necessary for the continued success of company operations. Imagine the consequences of new product designs being "electronically leaked" to competitors or the accounts receivable records being accidentally destroyed.

Management should protect company records from accidental security breaks, from unintentional destruction, and from unauthorized access. Many states are passing laws covering electronic "snooping."

BUSINESS COMMUNICATION AND YOU

If you have not already embarked upon a career, you will soon do so. Whether you choose to be an accountant, secretary, computer programmer, sales representative, doctor, lawyer, teacher, or engineer, you must acquire a thorough knowledge of your field. You must also be an effective communicator.

Communication plays an important part in achieving success. Make an investment in your future by beginning a personal communication development program.

COMMUNICATION PROJECTS

Practical Application

A. Contact three companies that sell word processing equipment. Ask them to send you advertising brochures describing their equipment. If you were an author working on a novel, which one would you choose? If you needed to produce letters and mailing lists, which would you select? Be sure to consider the functions you would need and the price.

B. Interview someone who has work experience in both the traditional office and the electronic office. Report the interview in dialogue form as follows:

Student:	What kinds of equipment did you use in the traditional office?
Office Employee:	I used a typewriter, a telephone, and an adding machine.

C. Review an article on business communication technology. Write a one-page summary.

D. List the people with whom each of these professionals might be communicating: doctors, lawyers, teachers, and secretaries.

Editing Practice

Spelling Alert! Rewrite the paragraph below, correcting the problems with numbers.

Too secretaries wanted two trade their to typewriters four won word processor that they would share. They felt this would work because each secretary types only for hours per ate-hour day. Each secretary works four five executives. The tin executives agreed two the trade.

Case Problem

The Personal Touch. Alex Dupree is graduating from college in May. He is preparing his application letter and résumé, which he will be sending to many different companies. Some parts of his résumé will change before graduation. He would like to send original letters and résumés to each prospective employer. How can word processing equipment help him?

CHAPTER
TWO

DEVELOPING
LISTENING
AND
READING SKILLS

THE LISTENING PROCESS

We all know how important reading skill is in today's world. In every aspect of our personal lives, we encounter many written records: birth certificate, diploma, driver's license, marriage license, and so on. Most business records also must be in written form: bills, checks, receipts, letters, and contracts, just to mention a few of the many written documents used every day in the business world. With so many vital communications in written form, we can see why reading skills are essential to each of us. What you may not realize is that listening plays an even greater part in daily life.

WHY LISTENING SKILL IS NEEDED

You may be surprised to learn that listening skill is equally as important as reading skill. Surveys reveal that the majority of business people spend most of their communication time in listening activities.[1] The average business employee spends approximately 70 percent of the working day in spoken communication. Although half this time is spent listening, research reveals that most of us listen with only 25 percent efficiency.[2]

HOW ACTIVE AND PASSIVE LISTENING DIFFER

There are two types of listening: active listening and passive listening. When we listen passively, we absorb just enough of the speaker's words to keep the conversation flowing, but actually we understand little of what the speaker is saying. We probably can tell from the speaker's inflection and tone of voice when we should react by nodding, smiling, shaking the head, or saying, "I see." We are at-

[1] William F. Keefe, *Listen, Management,* McGraw-Hill Book Company, New York, 1971, p. 9.
[2] Ralph G. Nichols and Leonard A. Stevens, *Are You Listening?* McGraw-Hill Book Company, 1957, pp. ix, 6, 8.

tempting to reassure the speaker that he or she has our attention (though not much of it). With friends and relatives, passive listening sometimes meets the demands of social conversation—but such is not always the case. Remember, a nod here and a smile there can sometimes indicate unintentional agreement!

The world of business requires a great deal more of a listener—it requires *active* listening. Active listening means concentrating on what is being said and mentally participating. Business conversation is sprinkled with facts—names, dates, places, and prices—and each is important. The salesclerk must hear the customer's wishes; the bank teller must hear amounts and denominations of currency; the travel agent must hear the traveler's destination, the mode of travel, and other details that are important to the traveler. And the best way that the listener can actively participate is to mentally summarize what the speaker is saying.

HOW TO IMPROVE YOUR LISTENING SKILL

When we are reading, we may sometimes let our attention wander from the message the writer is trying to communicate because we know that we can return later to read what we missed. Imagine what would happen if the written word vanished immediately after being read! We could never return for a rereading. All that would survive from our reading would be whatever was left in our memories—and that is all!

Of course, the spoken word really does vanish immediately after it has been said. Therefore, we cannot afford to let our attention wander when we are listening, because we get only one chance to absorb the speaker's words. Yet it is so much easier for the listener's attention to wander than for the reader's. A major reason is that the average person speaks between 125 and 150 words a minute, but a good listener can comprehend about 300 words a minute.[3] Perhaps the listener's mind realizes that it is necessary to listen only half the time and therefore does so. Unfortunately, missing a sentence or even a single word can so alter the speaker's message that it is changed or destroyed. Since the listener has no way of knowing exactly when the most important parts of a spoken message will come, the listener must concentrate on every word.

Whatever the reasons for poor listening, listening is a skill that can be improved. All good communication programs, whether they be in schools or in businesses, devote some time to the improvement of listening skills.

Determine Your Listening Strengths and Weaknesses

Everyone has both listening strengths and listening weaknesses. The first step toward improving your listening skill is to determine what

[3] Ibid., p. 78.

weaknesses need to be eliminated. Your answers to the following questions will help you decide where to begin your listening-improvement program.

1. Have you recently had your hearing tested?
2. Do you try to screen out distracting outside sights and sounds when you listen to someone speak?
3. Do you make it a point not to interrupt before a speaker finishes a thought?
4. Do you avoid doing something else (reading, for example) while trying to listen?
5. When people talk to you, do you concentrate on what they are saying rather than think of other things at the same time?
6. Do you listen for ideas and feelings as well as for facts?
7. Do you look at the person who is talking to you?
8. Do you believe that other people can contribute to your knowledge?
9. If something is not clear to you, do you ask the speaker to repeat or reexplain the point?
10. Do you avoid letting the speaker's words and phrases prejudice you?
11. When someone is talking to you, do you try to make the person think that you are paying attention even if you are not?
12. Do you judge by a person's appearance and manner whether what he or she says will be of interest to you?
13. Do you turn your attention elsewhere when you believe a speaker will not have anything interesting to say to you?
14. Do you have to ask the speaker to repeat because you cannot remember what was said?
15. If you feel that it takes too much time and effort to understand something, do you try to avoid hearing it?

You should have answered "Yes" to the first ten questions and "No" to the last five. Even if you had a perfect score, the following suggestions may still help you improve your listening skills.

Prepare Physically for Effective Listening

Listening is a combination of physical and mental activities. The mental part of listening is more complex, but we must also remember and deal with the physical part. We cannot listen to what we cannot hear. Our listening ability improves when we watch the speaker, especially the speaker's lips. The sense of sight helps the sense of hearing.

Here are some suggestions to follow in physically preparing yourself to listen effectively:

1. If you have trouble hearing, have a doctor test your hearing and suggest any necessary corrective measures. (A reputable hearing-aid distributor may test your hearing without charge.)

2. Try to sit or stand in a place with no distracting sights or sounds.
3. Keep your eyes on the speaker from start to finish.
4. Choose a comfortable, well-ventilated, and well-lit place if possible; physical discomforts can distract you.
5. Be prepared: keep a small pad and pencil with you. Business people often need to jot down notes on personal and business conversations as well as on formal speeches and lectures.

Prepare Mentally for Effective Listening

Effective listening is not an accident. It results from (among other things) mental preparation. For example, effective listeners have developed a wide vocabulary, which equips them to understand what they read and hear. The vocabulary learned in high school and college is not enough. Listeners must also master the special vocabulary of the field in which they work.

Every field has its special vocabulary. On entering a new field, set out at once to learn its special terms. Ask people to recommend books on the field, and write down and look up every unfamiliar word that you encounter, whether in reading or in conversation. Until the vocabulary is mastered, problems are sure to result. If a secretary asks an office clerk, for example, to bring a *ream* of typewriting paper, the clerk may return from the storeroom empty-handed because all the packages are labeled "500 Sheets" rather than "One Ream." When possible, it is best to ask the speaker to explain unfamiliar words.

The same policy applies when the speaker uses a familiar word without making clear which of several possible meanings is intended. Since the English language has many words with multiple meanings, the listener often faces this problem. In an office, for example, someone may ask a secretary to *duplicate* a letter. The secretary may not know whether to use carbon paper, a photocopier, or a fluid or stencil duplicator. A simple question will remove the secretary's doubt: "Would you like five photocopies?"

Listen With a Positive Attitude

To be a good listener, you must want to hear what the speaker has to say. It can be difficult to want to hear a speaker when you expect the speaker's views to contradict your own. But you cannot know for certain what someone is going to say until you hear it. You may know the speaker's views without ever having heard the reasons for those views, but it is irrational to pass judgment without hearing the speaker's arguments. Even if the speaker's views and your own are opposed, you must respect the speaker's right to have a point of view. Moreover, listening carefully may help you to organize a better argument against an opposing view.

Usually it is easy to find reasons for adopting a good listening attitude. The main purpose of a lecture or a class discussion is to learn; if students want to learn, they will also want to listen. The stenographer wants to listen when taking dictation in order to record accurately all that is said. The supervisor who wants to have a productive staff wants to hear about the workers' problems and needs. The employee who wants to do a good job and earn a promotion wants to hear all of the supervisor's instructions. Even when reasons for listening are less apparent, the good listener tries to find something of interest in the speaker's message and tries to sustain this interest until the speaker has finished.

Finally, a good listener does not judge what a speaker has to say solely on the basis of personal characteristics such as mannerisms, voice, speech patterns, and appearance. The good listener will notice all these details and take them into account but will focus mainly on the words and ideas.

Develop Techniques of Concentration

Concentration involves more than wrinkling your brow or gritting your teeth. Concentration requires a great deal of effort and the learning of certain techniques. Skilled keyboarders have learned rapid keystroking, keeping their eyes on the copy and maintaining correct posture. Skilled swimmers have learned arm and leg coordination and proper breathing techniques. Similarly, skilled listeners have learned techniques of concentration.

As mentioned earlier, we can comprehend words at least twice as quickly as most people speak. To some people, this extra time is a hindrance, because they waste it by allowing their thoughts to wander from the subject. On the other hand, active listeners use this free time to concentrate on the speaker's words; therefore, they can better understand what is being said. Specifically, the effective listener can use this free time to:

1. Identify the speaker's ideas and their relationships.
2. Summarize the main points.
3. Evaluate the correctness or validity of the message.
4. Take notes.

IDENTIFY IDEAS AND THEIR RELATIONSHIPS. As you begin to grasp the speaker's ideas, look for the relationships between them. Which idea is most important? Do the other ideas support the most important one? Is the speaker leading up to something? Can you anticipate what the speaker is going to say next? Is the speaker giving you cues that show the relationships between the speaker's ideas?

Consider the speech excerpt below.

Two major costs in operating a modern business are absenteeism and tardiness. For instance, if an office with 1000 employees averages 50 absences a month and the average daily rate of pay is $50, the company loses $2500 a month, or $30,000 a year. Such a loss takes a big bite out of company profits.

Note that the first sentence, the italicized words, is the main idea. The word *major* is a cue to the first sentence's importance. The speaker also uses the words *for instance* as a cue to indicate that what follows will support the main idea. Speakers use many other verbal cues: "first," "second," and "third"; "another important consideration"; "on the other hand"; "the most important thing"; "in summary"; and so on. Speakers also use many nonverbal cues: pauses; changes in volume or tone of voice; gestures such as pounding the table and shaking the head. All these cues help the listener to identify the speaker's ideas and see the interrelationships of these ideas.

SUMMARIZE. When you listen, rephrase the speaker's ideas in your own mind. Try to put the speaker's ideas into the simplest, clearest, and most direct words possible. This process should reduce the speaker's message to its most basic terms and help you to understand and remember what you hear. The following example shows what you might be thinking while the speaker is talking.

What the Speaker Is Saying	What You Are Saying to Yourself
I have read many books on selling. There are books that bring up every possible selling situation and give you ways and means to meet those situations—several hundred of them perhaps. But when you are in the presence of a prospect, you cannot recall any of them. However, you *can* remember this formula: ask yourself the simple question, "Just what does this prospect *want*?" If you cannot find out any other way, ask the person. It is often that simple. Too many salespeople think they must do *all* the talking. Avoid it. Listen at least half the time and ask questions. It is only in this way you can uncover unsatisfied wants.[4]	You can't memorize ways of meeting every selling situation presented in books. You should find out what the prospect wants. Ask, if necessary. You don't need to do all the talking—listen half the time, and ask questions.

[4] William Phillips Sandford and Willard Hayes Yeager, *Effective Business Speech,* McGraw-Hill Book Company, New York, 1960, p. 176.

EVALUATE CORRECTNESS AND VALIDITY. At some point, as you summarize the speaker's message and see the structure of the speaker's ideas, you will probably find yourself beginning to agree or disagree with the speaker. Try to trace your agreement or disagreement to the speaker's reasoned arguments. Do the speaker's arguments really lead to the speaker's conclusions? Is the speaker trying to convince you with reason or to persuade you by pleading, coaxing, or insisting? Make sure that you are not in favor of the speaker's views strictly because they were presented with humor, enthusiasm, or charm. In the same way, make sure that you are not against a speaker's views because you dislike the speaker's personal characteristics.

TAKE NOTES. Taking notes is, of course, an excellent way of keeping information for future reference. But notes are more than just aids to memory. They are also tools that help the listener concentrate on the speaker's message. Since the listener cannot write everything, he or she must decide what to include and what to omit. As the listener is making such decisions, the process of summarizing begins. Furthermore, a skilled notetaker uses such devices as underscoring, indenting, and making arrows and brackets to show the relative importance of the ideas expressed by the speaker. Thus the structure of the speaker's message becomes visible on paper.

Here are some suggestions for efficient notetaking:

1. Have available enough paper and an extra pen or pencil.
2. Listen for cues as to what is most important, and number each important idea.
3. Abbreviate whenever possible. Use "1," not "first"; "e.g." instead of "for example"; and so on. Even if you write in shorthand, do not write everything the speaker says. Use key words.
4. Use underscores, indentions, arrows, and brackets to highlight your notes. For example, underscore all main ideas, indent supporting ideas, and put brackets around examples.
5. Read your notes promptly after the speaker has concluded. Add any necessary explanation while the thoughts are fresh in your mind.
6. Label, date, and organize notes so that you can identify them later without any problem.
7. Compare notes with another person who may have listened at the same time.

MAKE GOOD LISTENING TECHNIQUES A HABIT

Effective listening, like effective reading or typing, is a skill, and skills require practice. Take every opportunity to practice the listening techniques you have just read. Opportunities come more often than you probably think. When a public figure gives a speech or a sports figure grants an interview, you can listen to a live or taped broadcast or telecast. You should, of course, take notes. Then the next morning you can compare your notes with reports in the newspaper. You may also have discussions with a friend on some topic of mutual interest; take notes and then compare your summaries.

COMMUNICATION PROJECTS

Practical Application

A. Read again the questions on page 22 to determine your listening strengths and weaknesses. Write a reason for each answer to each question.

B. Your instructor will read a selection to you. Listen very carefully, but *do not take notes*. After the reading, your instructor will ask you to answer questions about the message in the selection.

C. A good listener is able to distinguish facts from opinions. On a separate sheet of paper, indicate which of the following statements are opinions and which are facts.

1. The talk I heard on nuclear warfare was biased.
2. John was told his car was worth only $750.
3. If you park on the street after midnight, you will be given a parking citation.
4. Men are required to wear neckties and jackets to work.
5. The price of gasoline is high.
6. I paid $1.25 a gallon for gasoline.
7. Your choice of printer for your computer was a wise one.
8. Your wristwatch battery should last at least a year.
9. Marian dresses very smartly.
10. They told me that they enjoyed their vacation.

D. Your instructor will read a set of directions to you. Listen to them very carefully, but *do not take any notes*. Then follow the directions given.

E. List 20 words that cause you to feel strong emotions, such as *poverty, happiness, politics, crime*. Be prepared to discuss the following questions:

1. Why do certain words affect people's emotions?
2. Why do words of this type have different shades of meaning for different people?

Editing Practice

Speaking Contextually. Some of the following sentences contain words that are out of context. Correct each sentence that contains a contextually incorrect word. Write *OK* for each correct sentence.

1. Skill in keyboarding is a very important fact in operating a computer.
2. If this program is to be successful, we need the corporation of everyone.
3. The defendant is to be arranged in court next week.
4. Mr. Robbins accused the company of infringing on his patent rights.
5. Discrimination of confidential information is prohibited.

Case Problem

The Careless Clerk.   Ed Bradley was a reservation clerk for Southern Airlines. One afternoon he answered the telephone in his usual way by asking, "May I help you?" Ms. Lily De Sica introduced herself and told him that she wanted to make a reservation on a flight to Atlanta, Georgia, that would get her there in time for a 6 p.m. dinner meeting with an important client. Ed checked the flight bookings for the date and time requested and found that the only space available was on a flight leaving at 7 a.m. the same day. There was a 2:10 p.m. flight, arriving in Atlanta at 4:15 p.m., but all seats had been booked. Ms. De Sica had to attend a meeting that morning and could not leave before noon.

Ed said he would put Ms. De Sica's name on the waiting list for the 2:10 flight and would notify her if there were any cancellations. He told Ms. De Sica that there was a good chance of getting a seat on the 2:10 flight, since her name would be the first one on the waiting list. Ms. De Sica thought this arrangement would be fine, gave Ed the necessary information about contacting her, and hung up. Just as soon as Ed hung up, the customer standing in front of him started asking for information regarding other flights, and Ed neglected to record Ms. De Sica's name on the proper waiting list.

When Ms. De Sica had not received word about her reservation by the day before the flight, she asked her secretary to check with the airline. The clerk who answered the telephone checked the waiting list but, of course, did not find Ms. De Sica's name among the ten listed. With so many names already on the waiting list, chances were poor that a seat could be found for Ms. De Sica. Her secretary passed along the news. Ms. De Sica was furious. She telephoned the general manager of the airline and lodged a complaint.

1. Was Ms. De Sica justified in her complaint? Why or why not?
2. What should the general manager say to Ms. De Sica in order to smooth out the situation?
3. What advice should the general manager give Ed Bradley?

THE READING PROCESS

Skillful reading is essential for anyone working in the business world. Typists must be able to read copy accurately and quickly. Secretaries must be able to proofread letters and to read instructions. Executives must be able to absorb the contents of the innumerable letters, reports, periodicals, and books that cross their desks each day. Accountants must be able to read and check one set of figures against another and to make certain that each group of figures is posted under the correct heading. Supervisors and managers must be able to read production reports, forms, memorandums, schedules, evaluations, and requisitions.

ASSESSING READING SKILL

Although everyone in business must be able to read, employees earn their livings, not for reading, but for taking action based on what they read. The action taken may involve sending a requested product or catalog, writing a reply to a question or request, forwarding a message to the appropriate department, correcting an error, filing a document according to subject, and so on. The faster the employee can read, the more work the employee may be able to handle. Because reading speed affects how much work the employee can do, it helps determine the employee's value to the employer. Reading speed, then, is one important measure of reading skill.

However, speed counts little if the reader does not understand what is being read. Reading well requires much more than moving your eyes rapidly over words on paper. The reader must comprehend the ideas that the words represent. Therefore, reading comprehension is a second important measure of reading skill.

Do you fully comprehend the material that you read? As a student, have you had to spend every evening and weekend completing reading assignments that other students complete in an hour or two a day? If so, then this should be cause for concern, but not for embarrassment or despair. With study and practice, you *can* improve both reading speed and reading comprehension.

Many people have benefited from reading-improvement courses offered by schools, business organizations, and private institutes. The results are often well worth the time and the money. If you are interested in enrolling in one of these reading programs, ask your instructor for advice. In the meantime, however, you can do several things on your own to improve your reading skill.

A READING-IMPROVEMENT PROGRAM

Read and follow the four-step program for improving reading skill that follows on the remaining pages of this section.

Check Physical Factors

Poor vision and eye discomfort can hamper reading proficiency. You must be able to read comfortably, without difficulty or strain. In any case, you should have your eyes checked regularly by an eye specialist, particularly if you wear glasses, have blurred vision or smarting eyes, or need to hold copy either very close to your eyes or at arm's length.

Lighting conditions affect the ease with which you read. Natural light is best, of course, and indirect light is the best artificial light to read by. The light should fall on the copy, not on your eyes, and there should be no glaring or shiny spots before you.

In addition, your physical comfort will affect your ability to concentrate and read. You should sit comfortably in a well-ventilated room kept at a moderate temperature. The room should be free of distracting sights and sounds.

Whether or not you wear glasses, you should practice good eye hygiene. Here are some suggestions:

1. Rest your eyes every half hour or so, either by looking into the distance or by closing them for a few minutes.
2. Exercise your eyes, especially when you are doing close work and your eyes begin feeling tired. One good exercise for strengthening the eye muscles is to rotate the eyeballs slowly without moving your head. Try to see far to the right; then to the left; then up; and, finally, down.
3. Avoid reading when you are in bright sunlight.
4. Have eye injuries or sties attended to immediately by a physician.

Adjust Reading Rate to Material and Purpose

You should adjust your reading speed to the material you are reading and to your purpose for reading it.

READING FOR PLEASURE. When you are reading novels, magazine articles, newspaper items, and the like, you do not need to absorb every detail or remember many specific facts. Therefore, you should be able to read quite rapidly, at a rate of around 400 words a minute.

READING FOR SPECIFIC DATA. When you are looking for a specific name, date, or other item of information, you should be able, by skimming a page, to locate the item without reading every word. When you wish to determine the principal ideas in reading matter, perhaps in order to decide whether or not to read it, skim each page and stop only to read significant phrases.

READING FOR RETENTION OR ANALYSIS. This kind of reading includes textbook reading or other study reading requiring either the memorization of facts or a thorough understanding of the meaning so that you can interpret, explain, or apply it to other situations. Reading for retention or analysis calls for active participation by the reader and may require a slower reading rate. Active participation in reading is discussed on page 41.

CHECKING AND COPYING. This kind of reading includes proofreading typewritten or printed copy, checking invoices, copying material for computer input, and so on. Checking one copy against another or one column of figures against another calls for great concentration, because an error of one digit, one letter, or one syllable can change the entire meaning and the accuracy of a document. Such reading must be done carefully and with concentration and attention to meaning, as well as to correctness. Just one undetected error may be very costly. Unless the following were read for meaning, the error would go undiscovered.

> **Your payment is due January 25 to avoid any surcharge. (January 15 is the date that should be indicated.)**

Increase Reading Speed

Reading-improvement programs cannot enable you to read complicated material as fast as you read light novels or articles. However, you can improve your speed of both types of reading by following these suggestions to help you read all kinds of material faster.

ADD TO YOUR VOCABULARY. Enlarging your vocabulary will help you to read faster and understand better. You will not have to stop to look up unknown words so often or spend so much time interpreting words that have several possible meanings.

READ IN THOUGHT UNITS. Since all words are not of equal importance, read in thought units rather than word by word. Develop your visual span of a thought unit by forcing your eyes to take in more words at each pause. With fewer pauses on each line of print, you naturally read faster. For example, read the following lines:

1. unyqpr
2. table magazine television driver
3. Read in thought units.

Certainly you had no difficulty reading each of these lines, but reading each line should have taken progressively less time. In the first line, you had to read each letter individually; in the second, you read each word separately; but in the third, your eyes could take in and read the whole sentence with one glance.

You should be able to read a line in a newspaper column with only one or two eye pauses and to read a book-width line with not more than four or five pauses. Read the following sentence, and notice the difference in speed when you read word by word and when you read in thought units.

Word by Word

Good / readers / are / more / likely / to / understand / and / remember / what / they / read / if / they / actively / participate / in / what / they / are / reading.

Phrases

Good readers / are more likely / to understand and remember / what they read / if they actively participate / in what they are reading.

KEEP YOUR EYES MOVING FROM LEFT TO RIGHT.   Do not allow yourself to go back and read a phrase a second time. These backward movements of the eyes, called *regressions,* slow the reader and are often habit-forming. Force yourself to concentrate and to get the meaning of a phrase the first time. To do so demands practice, discipline, and the elimination of all distractions that might interfere with your reading.

AVOID VOCALIZATION.   Don't spell or pronounce the words you are reading, not even silently. Such vocalization limits you to reading only as fast as you can read aloud.

READ ONLY WORD BEGINNINGS.   Many words can be identified by reading only the beginnings. For example, you can easily identify the complete words from these first syllables: *remem-, sepa-, funda-, catal-, educa-.* You can tell from the rest of the sentence whether the exact ending of each word should be *remembering* or *remembrance; separate, separately,* or *separation;* and so on. For example: *Did he remem-(remember) to sepa-(separate) the old catal-(catalogs) from the new catal-(catalogs)?*

PRACTICE RAPID READING.   By exercising your willpower and by continually practicing rapid reading, you are certain to increase your reading speed. Reading will improve with proper practice.

Improve Reading Comprehension

Even more important than reading speed to the business worker are comprehension (understanding) and retention (remembering). Many

(*Continued on page 41.*)

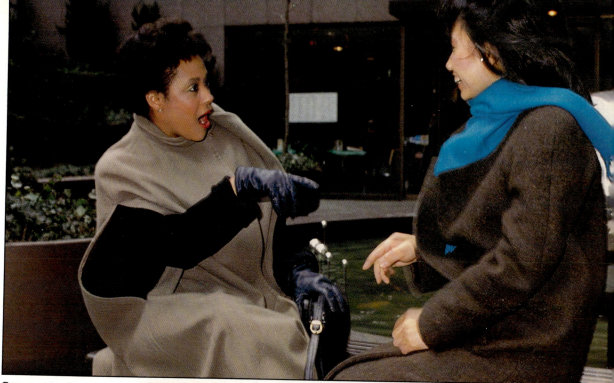

Communication is
the verbal and non-
verbal exchange of
messages.

Messages can be
sent by writing or
speaking.

Teleconferencing allows people in different locations and time zones to confer electronically. Communication occurs through the transmission of text, audio, and video data.

of the suggestions made for increasing reading *speed* will also contribute to greater *comprehension*. Some additional aids follow.

SCAN OR PREVIEW THE MATERIAL.
Before beginning a careful reading, look over the material, noting main headings and subheadings, looking at illustrations, and reading captions and numbered passages. This preliminary survey should not take much time, but it will help you to determine your own purpose in reading and will also let you see at once the importance that the author attached to different parts of the material. Then, after completing a careful reading of the whole piece, you will have read the most important points twice. This will reinforce your memory of the material.

PARTICIPATE ACTIVELY IN YOUR READING.
Reading is, of course, the *receiving* of written communications. We also speak of *absorbing* the content of written materials. But this does not mean that reading is like being a mailbox or a sponge. Reading is an active process. Your mind must *work* both to get information from what you read and to understand that information. In other words, the reader must *extract* the content, like a miner digging for precious stones. This means studying the illustrations, reading the footnotes, and considering the author's examples. The author offers all of these as aids to the understanding of the author's ideas. Skipping these aids may make it more difficult for you to understand the text and may force you to spend more time in the long run extracting the knowledge that you need.

TAKE NOTES.
If you own the book or magazine you are reading, you may wish to underline or otherwise mark key words or phrases. You may also want to make marginal notes. If the publication is not yours, you may take notes in a notebook that you can refer to later.

How do you select the essential material for notetaking? By recording main ideas and related ideas. Never take verbatim notes, even if you know shorthand.

How do you find the main ideas? Usually, writers convey only one idea per paragraph. Often this main idea is in the first sentence, but sometimes it may be in the last sentence. Occasionally there may be two central ideas expressed in a key phrase or sentence within the paragraph. If you have difficulty finding a central idea, you may need to read the paragraph carefully two or three times. In addition to the central idea, you should also note facts, examples, and other ideas that explain, support, and develop the main idea.

REREAD AND REVIEW.
How often you reread or review material will depend on its difficulty and on the use you plan to make of the information it contains. Often a quick skimming or rereading of your notes will be adequate for review if the first reading was done carefully.

If you follow the suggestions made in this section and immediately begin a definite plan for reading improvement, you will find that not only will you be able to read more in the same amount of time, but also you will get more from what you read.

COMMUNICATION PROJECTS

Practical Application

A. To test your reading speed, have someone time you with a stopwatch (or a watch with a second hand) as you read the following selection.

Microcomputers are low-cost, powerful systems that contain hardware components almost identical to display word processors. They differ from display word processors in not being "dedicated" solely to word processing. Often the size of the microcomputer is the only distinguishing characteristic of appearance. Display word processors usually are larger than microcomputers.

The development in the late 1970s of sophisticated word processing software for the microcomputer led to the widespread use of these microcomputers in the office. Word processing software programs make it possible for documents and other forms of written communication to be prepared on microcomputers. Many of the software programs available for microcomputers provide the ease of operation that often is associated only with dedicated word processing systems. Microcomputers with word processing capability now provide large and small business organizations with a low-cost office productivity tool. Today, clerical, professional, and executive personnel use microcomputers with word processing capability to create documents quickly, easily, and accurately. Many professional workers create their documents at the keyboard and later turn them over to clerical support personnel for formatting and printing.

Mini and mainframe computer systems are bigger and more powerful than word processors and microcomputers. Data processing activities, such as payroll preparation and maintenance of personnel and inventory records, are examples of the information that is handled on these systems. As with microcomputers, word processing applications are handled through the use of specially designed word processing software programs.

Word processing represents a challenge for the worker who enters the business world. It provides an opportunity to learn new skills, use existing skills, and explore new careers.

The word processing office has been called the office of the future. The future is now![1] (234 words)

How long did it take you to read the selection? Use the following chart to compute your reading speed. Because the selection is 234 words long, your speed is 234 words a minute if you took 1 minute, 117 words a minute if you took 2 minutes, and so on.

15 seconds	936 wpm
30 seconds	468 wpm
1 minute	234 wpm
1½ minutes	176 wpm
2 minutes	117 wpm
2½ minutes	98 wpm
3 minutes	78 wpm
3½ minutes	68 wpm
4 minutes	58 wpm

B. One excellent reading habit that will help you improve speed is to read only the beginnings of familiar words rather than the entire words. Test your ability to do this by reading as rapidly as possible the following paragraph, in which the endings of some familiar words have been omitted.

The right atti__ makes all the diff__ in the out__ expres__ of your pers__: atti__ toward your work, tow__ your emp__, tow__ life in gen__. You reveal your atti__ tow__ people in the way you resp__ to sugg__. You can reject them in a self-right__, almost indig__ manner. Or you can adopt an in-diff__, "don't care" atti__. These are both neg__ resp__. The pos__ resp__ is to accept sugg__ and crit__ thought__ and graciously. Then you can act upon them acc__ to your best judg__, with resul__ self-impr__.

C. Secretaries, word processing operators, clerical workers, copy editors, and advertising copywriters are just some business workers who must proofread carefully. Proper proofreading calls for the reading of each word not only for spelling but also for its meaning within the sentence in which it is used. Proofread the following letter, and on a separate sheet of paper make a list of all the errors. Then rewrite the letter so that it is free from error.

In accordance with our telephone conservation, we are sent-ing you corected specifacations. Note that instalation of a two-way comunication systems is now required. Also, the thermastat is to be re-located to the upstair hall. Please send us your revise bid, propperly typed on your company stationary, no latter then Oct. 1.

---

[1] Based on Bettie Hampton Ellis, *Word Processing: Concepts and Applications,* 2d ed., Gregg Division, McGraw-Hill Book Company, New York, 1986, p. 18.

D. Copying amounts of money, form numbers, dates, and other figures often results in errors because of reading carelessness. Compare the original list (A) with the copied list (B) to determine if any items have been copied incorrectly.

List A		List B
1.	789836B	789863B
2.	4328765	4328765
3.	$2786.54	27866.54
4.	9833V39	9833V39
5.	LT817745	LT187745
6.	u897V229	U897v229
7.	Wjkti	wkjti
8.	July 23, 1987	July 23, 1978
9.	23 gross @$32	32 gross @23
10.	S768R3456J789	S768R3546J789

Editing Practice

Preparing a Digest of a Letter.　Secretaries and administrative assistants often read incoming letters for their employers. When a manager is very busy or on a business trip, he or she may ask the secretary or administrative assistant to prepare a short digest (summary) of each letter. Using phrases instead of complete sentences, write a digest of the following letter.

Dear Mr. Stacy:

Thank you for arranging to visit our Woodland plant on October 16 to give us some suggestions for improving the work flow in both our accounting office and the manufacturing plant.

Unfortunately, it will be necessary for me to be out of town on October 16 on a business trip. I will be returning on October 20 and would like to suggest some alternative dates for your visit. Will you telephone me before the sixteenth to let me know if either October 24 or November 2 would be convenient for you? In the event that neither date is satisfactory, please suggest an alternative date.

I would appreciate your bringing with you the pamphlet on telephone systems that you told me about at lunch last week.

Very sincerely yours,
Margaret Stern

Case Problem

The Talkative Visitor. Sally Bentham is receptionist and switch-board operator at the Kaplan Furniture Company. One afternoon Albert Diaz, who had an appointment to discuss a new product with Sally's boss, arrived at the office. However, because Sally's boss was in conference and would not be available for about ten minutes, Sally asked Mr. Diaz to be seated until her boss was free. For a minute or two, Mr. Diaz thumbed through one of the magazines lying on the table in the reception room. Then he started talking to Sally, who was not occupied at the switchboard at that moment. Soon, however, the board lit up, but Mr. Diaz continued talking to Sally. The flashing lights indicated that the callers were getting impatient because of the delay, but Sally did not know how to get Mr. Diaz to stop talking to her so that she could attend to her duties.

1. What could Sally say to Mr. Diaz so that he would not be offended when she interrupted him?
2. Suppose Mr. Diaz continued talking. What should Sally do?

CHAPTER
THREE
DEVELOPING
PROOFREADING
AND
EDITING SKILLS

6

THE PROOFREADING PROCESS

Proofreading is examining a document to find errors that should be corrected. Sometimes, proofreading is a verification process, such as checking a letter typed from a handwritten rough draft. There is no document for comparison, however, when proofreading your own work. In either case, you should look for errors in capitalization, content, format, grammar, number usage, punctuation, spelling, typing, and word division.

To be a good proofreader, you must be familiar with each area mentioned and rely on reference sources when in doubt. You may, for example, see the word *accomodation*. You are unsure about the spelling. After checking a dictionary, you change it to *accommodation*.

The proofreading process should begin in the early stages of document preparation and continue through each step, including the final copy. In other words, before keyboarding from shorthand notes, a handwritten draft, or a typewritten draft, check the document for errors. When using a word processor, proofread the document on the screen. Also, proofread the final copy to make sure that it is typed or printed correctly.

RESPONSIBILITY FOR QUALITY

Business writers are responsible for the quality of their communications. Correct communications are important because of the impressions they make on the receiver. Frequently a letter is the first contact someone has with your organization. A correct letter projects a quality image. A letter with errors projects a careless or disinterested image. Likewise, a memo written to your superior can convey a quality or careless message about your performance.

Office personnel sometimes overlook the proofreading process, because they think someone else will do it. A typist may think that the document originator will proofread each communication. The document originator may think that the typist will find and correct all errors before submitting the document for signing. The final responsibility definitely rests with the person signing the document. Ideally, proofreading is a team effort. Both the typist and the document originator should proofread each document.

IMPORTANCE OF PROOFREADING

Uncorrected errors can create a bad impression. They can also cost your company money and cause problems. Consider these two examples:

Suppose, in a handwritten draft, you quoted a price of $32,453 for a new computer. When the final copy was keyboarded and mailed to the customer, the price was wrongly listed as $23,453. If not detected, this simple transposition could cost your company $9000. Correcting the error after the customer received the quotation could cause hard feelings but would have to be done.

Suppose, on a travel itinerary, the airplane departure time was erroneously listed as 10:50 instead of the correct time of 10:05. This simple transposition would mean missing the plane.

In each example, efficient proofreading would have caught the error. Executives encourage the detection and correction of errors to prevent problems. Approach proofreading in a systematic way.

STEPS IN PROOFREADING

There are five major steps in proofreading:

1. Quickly scan for obvious errors such as format errors. Is the date included in letters and memos? Are all headings treated the same way in a report?
2. Read for content to make sure no words were omitted or repeated.
3. Read for capitalization, grammar, number usage, punctuation, spelling, typing, and word division errors.
4. As a separate step, check all numbers and technical terms.
5. After the proofreading process has been completed and the marked changes or corrections made, verify that these changes or corrections were correctly made and that no new errors were introduced.

PROOFREADERS' MARKS

Proofreaders' marks are a quick, simple way to indicate changes or corrections. Study the proofreaders' marks in the accompanying chart. You will need these in proofreading business communications.

DEVELOPING PROOFREADING AND EDITING SKILLS

CAPITALIZATION	Capitalize a letter	texas
	Lowercase a letter	This
	Make all capitals	Cobol
	Lowercase a word	PROGRAM
	Use initial capital only	PROGRAM

CHANGES AND TRANSPOSITIONS	Change a word	price is only $10.98 $12.99
	Change a letter	deductable
	Stet (do not make the change)	price is only $10.98 are
	Spell out	2 cars on Washburn Rd.
	Move as shown	on May 1 write him
	Transpose letters or words	hte time the of meeting

DELETIONS	Delete a letter and close up	strooke or strooke
	Delete a word	wrote two two checks
	Delete punctuation	report was up-to-date
	Delete one space*	good # day /#
	Delete space	see ing

INSERTIONS	Insert a word or letter	in office buildng the
	Insert a comma	may leave early . . .
	Insert a period	Dr Maria Rodriguez
	Insert an apostrophe	all the boys hats
	Insert quotation marks	Move on she said.
	Insert hyphens	up to date report
	Insert a dash	They were surprised even shocked!
	Insert parentheses	pay fifty dollars ($50)
	Insert one space	may leave #
	Insert two spaces*	1. The new machine 2#

* Use marginal notes for clarification.

FORMAT SYMBOLS: BOLDFACE AND UNDERSCORE	Print boldface	Bulletin
	Do not make boldface	Bulletin
	Underscore	Title
	Do not underscore	Title

FORMAT SYMBOLS: CENTERING	Center line horizontally	] TITLE [

FORMAT SYMBOLS: PAGE AND PARAGRAPH	Begin a new page	. . . order was delivered today by common carrier. We have all the . . .
	Begin a new paragraph	. . . order was delivered today by common carrier. We have all the . . .
	Do not begin new paragraph (run in)	. . . order was delivered today by common carrier. No ¶ We have all the materials . . .
	Indent five spaces	5 We have the raw materials in our warehouse. Production will . . .

FORMAT SYMBOLS: SPACING	Single-space	ss [XXXXXXXXXX XXXXXXXXXX
	Double-space	ds [XXXXXXXXXX XXXXXXXXXX
	Triple-space	ts [XXXXXXXXXX XXXXXXXXXX

COMMUNICATION PROJECTS

Practical Application

A. Write *Yes* if the names are the same. Write *No* if they are different.

1. Maria Lopez Diago   Marie Lopez Diago
2. Anthony M. Martinas   Antony M. Martinas

3.	Mr. Steven Brown	Mr. Steven Brown
4.	Ms. Roberta Villas	Mrs. Roberta Villas
5.	Raquel M. Delgado	Raquel N. Delgado
6.	Danielle Benito	Danielle Benito
7.	Elizabeth King	Elizabeth King
8.	Dr. Alicia Fuquay	Mrs. Alicia Fuquay
9.	H. Oscar Baxter	H. Oscar Baxter
10.	Mr. Joseph A. Carr	Mr. Joseph A. Carr

B. Write *Yes* if the items are the same. Write *No* if they are different.

1.	238-45-3928	238-45-3928
2.	803-458-2789	803-548-2789
3.	9:38 p.m.	9:38 p.m.
4.	1,975 pounds	1,975 pounds
5.	June 12, 1987	June 21, 1987
6.	1980–1986	1980–1986
7.	$11,238.56	11,238.56
8.	328 cases	328 cases
9.	212-885-6643	212-885-6643
10.	143,326,881	14,326,881

C. On a separate sheet of paper, write each sentence, making the indicated changes.

1. For more efficient mail service, use the correct Zip CODE.

2. Luis finished the report, and gave it to maria.

3. Have you seen the plans for the New Office Building?

4. Ship the perishible goods the fastest way.

5. He borrowed the van for 2 days.

6. Ralph, please call me as soon the as shippment arrives.

7. The invoice were mailed December 9 and the watch.

8. Miguels Cafeteria opens each morning ta 6:30.

9. Sandra Sartina sold more real es tate last month than any other sales sales representative.

10. Mr. and Mrs. Ben Ortega wrote Wilderness Adventures, a book based on experiences.

Editing Practice

Choosing the Right Word. Make a list of words used incorrectly in the following paragraph. Beside each one, write the word that should have been used.

When we began the project at the Dallas sight, she gave us sum advise. She said that extreme temperatures would effect our computers. We new she was write. Before preceding, we decided to check farther. Sense May, this delay has been quiet costly.

Case Problem

Who's Responsible? In the last few weeks, your assistant has written several memorandums and letters that had errors. When you mentioned the errors, your assistant said that most readers would not notice grammar, punctuation, and spelling errors. The assistant also said that the typist (who works exclusively for your assistant) was responsible for the errors. How should you deal with this situation?

THE EDITING PROCESS

Editing is revising a document to improve it. Obviously, proofreading (see Section 6) is a part of editing. In fact, it is hard to tell exactly where proofreading stops and editing begins.

Editing skill is important for anyone involved with written communication. The purpose of editing is to make the document as effective as possible. This includes detecting and correcting errors and improving a document by seeking the answers to these questions:

1. Is it clear?
2. Is it complete?
3. Is it concise?
4. Is it consistent?
5. Is it correct?
6. Is it courteous?

If the answer to any of these questions is *No,* the communication should be revised.

THE SIX Cs OF EDITING

Is It Clear?

Business communications are written to get action—not to entertain or increase the vocabulary of the reader. Good business writers use simple words and proper English. They also avoid trite language.

Trite language is using words and phrases that have lost their effectiveness because of overuse. A participial closing in a letter is a good example: "Expecting to hear from you soon, I remain . . ." Another example is "business" language: "Enclosed herewith, please find my check."

Is It Complete?

A complete message includes all necessary details. Because the writer is so familiar with the message, omitted details are not always obvious. They are, however, obvious to the reader. Imagine receiving a party invitation that gives only the hour, place, and kind of party. The message is incomplete because the date was omitted. A lot of extra communication is then required to clarify the situation.

Is It Concise?

Unnecessary words, phrases, clauses, sentences, and paragraphs are a barrier to effective communication. Needless repetition of words decreases the effectiveness of your message. The reader is forced to read a lot in order to get a little information.

Is It Consistent?

Business messages should be consistent in fact, treatment, and sequence. A message is consistent in fact if it does not contradict itself, an established fact, or a source document.

Treating similar items the same way achieves consistency in treatment. For example, when listing both men's and women's names, use courtesy titles for all or none of the names. Failing to indent one paragraph in a letter when all others are indented is an error in treatment.

Consistency of sequence (alphabetical, chronological, or numerical) improves content flow. Alphabetical sequence is often used to avoid conveying unintentional bias when mentioning two or more people.

Is It Correct?

Accuracy in content, typing, and mechanics (capitalization, grammar, spelling, punctuation, etc.) makes the message more effective. Proofreading for these kinds of errors is definitely a part of the editing process.

Is It Courteous?

Courtesy in a business communication means that it is eye-pleasing, reader-centered, and positive. Here are some suggestions:

Create an eye-pleasing communication by using several short paragraphs instead of one long one. Using a table format or a list (when appropriate) instead of the traditional paragraph format looks better and makes reading easier.

To make a communication more reader-centered, use "you tone" instead of "I tone." Another method is personalizing by inserting the reader's name in the message body.

Achieve a positive communication by avoiding negative words like these: *can't, don't, error, mistake, no,* and *not.* Use tactful language that preserves reader integrity. Also, use active rather than passive voice when making positive statements.

WORD PROCESSING AND EDITING

Advances in office technology have caused renewed emphasis on editing. Even though word processors and computers with word processing software have made editing easier, this automated equipment is only as good as the person operating it.

Automated equipment has simplified editing through machine functions that allow text manipulation. Small or large amounts of text can be inserted, deleted, or moved from one point in the document to another.

PROOFREADERS' MARKS FOR EDITING

Revision	Edited Draft
Identify block	and the catalog will be mailed.
Insert identified block	Your order will be mailed.
Delete identified block	Your order and the catalog will mailed
Move identified block*	Your order and the catalog will be shipped. The invoice will be mailed.
Query identified block*	Ed will retire at the age of 96. (Are the numbers transposed? Verify age.)
Query identified block*	Make my reservation for June 31 (June has only 30 days. Verify date.)
Query conflicting blocks*	Call me Monday morning at 8 p.m. (Morning or p.m.? Verify time.)

*Use marginal notes for clarification.

These symbols are used to indicate text manipulation functions and to query the accuracy of the copy.

The hard-copy material to be manipulated can be identified by marking the beginning and the end of the segment with a vertical line and labeling the block with a letter of the alphabet. Use marginal notes as needed for clarification as shown on page 54.

Another use of block identification is to mark a hard-copy text segment that should be checked for accuracy before the final document is printed or typed. Identified blocks are marked with a query (question mark) in the margin.

Machine functions also make it necessary for identical changes (usually called *global changes*) to be entered only once. Suppose, for example, the name *Lynn Catolster* was used five times in a document. After keyboarding, you became aware of the correct spelling, *Lyn Catolster*. Using the global function, you would have to make the correction only once; the other four changes would be made automatically. A marginal note can indicate a global change.

COMMUNICATION PROJECTS

Practical Application

A. Are the following sentences clear? Rewrite these sentences, changing difficult words to easier words, correcting substandard English, and eliminating trite wording.

1. The configuration of furniture and equipment is important to the worker.
2. As per your request, we are enclosing herewith our fall catalog.
3. Martha should of gone to the meeting.
4. Expecting your check soon, I remain . . .
5. Our college offers matriculation by mail.

B. Are the following items complete? What detail is missing from each one?

1. Send an application form to Ms. Dorothy L. Denita, Post Office Box 8215, Atlanta, 30306.
2. Please ship some black fine-line magic markers ($10 per dozen) to Office Supply, Inc., 332 Chapman Highway, Knoxville, TN 37916. Charge the order (plus shipping and tax) to my account.
3. The budget committee will meet Friday, May 5, in the conference room.

C. Is each sentence concise? Rewrite each sentence, omitting all unnecessary words.

1. Connect up the printer to the computer.
2. Don't miss out on the meeting.
3. Rafael will work during the time of my absence.

4. My check written for the amount of $312.52 is enclosed.
5. My résumé is enclosed herewith.

D. Rewrite each sentence, making it consistent.

1. The consultant will be here April 1, June 1, and May 1.
2. Gonzales, Banard, and Ruiz asked for the same vacation week.
3. These checks were not in our statement: 614, 618, 620, and 619.
4. Mr. Alfred Grey, Mr. Patrick Torres, and Ellen Wilson applied.
5. Two books were added to the company library: Office Technology and THE OFFICE ENVIRONMENT.

E. Rewrite each item, making it correct.

1. Each applicant sent sent a résumé.
2. He wrote the all applicants.
3. Attitude and ability are improtant.
4. A list of temporary employees were sent to the personal manager.
5. She will be transferred to dallas.

F. Rewrite these sentences, making them more courteous. Delete unnecessary words to achieve a positive "you tone."

1. I want to take this opportunity to express my congratulations on your promotion.
2. Please do not hesitate to call if you have questions.

Personalize the message by adding the name *Alma* within these sentences. Remember to use a comma before and after the name.

3. Without your help, I could not have finished on time.
4. Your raise is effective today.

Change the sentence to active voice.

5. A letter of commendation will be received by you.

Editing Practice

Editing Corrections. Rewrite the following paragraph, making the indicated changes. Assume that B. A. Schlagenhauf is a woman.

B. A. Schlagenhauf after January 1 will be temporarily transferred to San Diego. His expertise is needed there more than it is here because of a plant expansion. This assignment should last six to eight months. Until the transfer, she will spend three days each week in San Diego and two days here.

Case Problem

Training the Staff.   As office manager, you arrange monthly meetings to upgrade the skills of your office personnel. For the next six months, you have decided to work on improving written communications. Here are some problems you have noticed:

1. Many customers call for clarification after receiving letters written by your staff.
2. Necessary details are frequently omitted.
3. Memos, letters, and reports are much too long.
4. Letter styles and punctuation styles are often mixed or used incorrectly. Similar items are treated differently.
5. Spelling, grammar, and punctuation rules are neglected. Sometimes misinformation is given.
6. Many communications lack tact and are hard to read.

Outline the instructional program by selecting a title and choosing topics and subtopics for each month. Include the writing problems mentioned and any others that are closely related.

CHAPTER
FOUR

EXPANDING
ENGLISH
LANGUAGE SKILLS

CR XL 1

RELOC

SHIFT

AN OVERVIEW OF LANGUAGE STRUCTURE

Imagine taking a newly arrived foreign-exchange student to his first baseball game. Although your friend understands basic English, would you expect him to comprehend terms such as *shortstop, double play, inning,* and *safe at home?* Of course not! Although none of these terms is difficult to understand, each will seem confusing—to a stranger.

Likewise, terms such as *adjective, infinitive,* and *predicate* will sound "foreign" and difficult to a beginner. However, each term is really simple to understand *with a little practice.* Just as understanding baseball terms helps the spectator discuss or explain the game, understanding some basic grammatical terms will help speakers and writers communicate more effectively. This section sketches a rough outline of English grammar and uses some of its basic terms. The terms are few—but pay close attention so that you will be sure to master the game!

THE PARTS OF SPEECH

All the many thousands of words in our language can be grouped into one of eight categories: nouns, pronouns, verbs, adjectives, adverbs, prepositions, conjunctions, and interjections. These categories are called the "parts of speech." As you will see, each group describes a special *function*—that is, each category tells one way in which words can be used. Let's begin with nouns.

Nouns

The word *noun* is derived from a word meaning "name": A *noun* is the *name* of a person, place, or thing.

Persons: Mary, Jacob, Ms. Reynolds, Dr. Ford, man, woman, supervisor, mother-in-law, candidates, spectators

Places: San Diego, Canada, West Coast, New Zealand, homes, hotel room, schools, offices

Things: Buicks, Anacin, chair, disk drives, X rays, democracy, computers, happiness, house

Pronouns

Pronouns are words that *replace* nouns; for example, *I, you, he, she, it, we, they, me, him, her, us, them, my, your, his, her, our,* and *their.* Because they serve as substitutes, pronouns add variety to our speech and our writing and provide us with shortcuts.

He specifically requested Model 12-A45. (Another way of saying "*Myron* specifically requested Model 12-A45.")

She returned *their* badges to *them* at the end of the day. (Another way of saying "*Thelma* returned *Bob's and Kathy's* badges to *Bob and Kathy* at the end of the day.")

Checkup 1

Identify the nouns and pronouns in the following sentences. On a separate sheet of paper, label each *N* or *P*. (Watch for nouns that have two or more words, such as *bulletin board.*)

1. The manager asked Gloria for her copy of the report.
2. Leon wants permission to attend the seminar with his assistant.
3. They confirmed the special price for sale items.
4. You and I should have submitted our ideas to the committee.
5. "New York is the site that was selected for the convention," she said.
6. Perhaps you and she will also be asked to work on the project on the West Coast.
7. Arnold and Sheila always double-check the invoices before they return them to us.
8. Ms. Weiss asked her secretary to forward the contracts to her hotel when she arrives.

Verbs

Verbs are commonly called "action words," because they give sentences life; they make sentences "move."

Our company *imports* chemicals and *uses* them in various products. (*Imports* and *uses* are verbs.)

Ms. Trask *bought* the entire inventory and *shipped* the goods to Denver. (*Bought* and *shipped* are verbs.)

These chemicals *have been imported* from Germany. (*Have been imported* is a verb that consists of more than one word.)

Harriet *is planning* a special meeting for next Tuesday. (*Is planning* is a verb.)

Not all verbs indicate an obvious action; some merely show a "state of being," such as *am, is, are, was, were, be, been.*

> Of course, I *am* happy about the good news. Helen and Faye *are* also glad. (*Am* and *are* are verbs that show "state of being.")

> John *will be* here by 2 p.m., but Paula *has been* here since noon. (*Will be* and *has been* are verbs. Note that each consists of two words.)

Checkup 2

Identify the verbs in the following sentences.

1. John is happy about his promotion.
2. Nancy was planning a new brochure for these products.
3. Janice hired two new assistants for her department after she promoted Larry and Frances.
4. Mr. Vernon has been in Cincinnati for about two weeks.
5. Mrs. Lewis purchased 12 acres of land near the parkway.
6. She has purchased 12 acres of land near the parkway.

Now supply a verb for the blanks in the following sentences and indicate whether it is an action verb or a being verb. Use a separate sheet of paper.

7. Jason _____ every night for his upcoming tests.
8. Barry _____ disappointed about the news.
9. We _____ the alternatives for many weeks.
10. She _____ her degree requirements in June and _____ her new job the following month.
11. The president _____ the project and _____ us for our work.
12. Marjorie _____ the word processing department.

Adjectives

Adjectives are words that describe nouns and pronouns.

> *hectic* schedule, *interesting* article, *expensive* cars

The adjectives *hectic, interesting,* and *expensive* tell "what kind of."

> her *former* supervisor, *that* report, *those* folders

The adjectives *former, that,* and *those* tell "which one."

> *one* employee, *several* clients, *few* tickets

The adjectives *one, several,* and *few* tell "how many."

> *a* diskette, *an* employee, *the* paperclip

The words *a, an,* and *the* are a special type of adjective called *articles.*

In the above examples, the adjectives describe nouns. When they describe pronouns, adjectives generally follow verbs such as *is, am, are, was, were, be,* and *been.*

She is *unhappy* with the low salary increase. (The adjective *unhappy* describes the pronoun *she.*)

They have been *patient* for several months. (*Patient* modifies or describes the pronoun *they.*)

Adverbs

Adverbs are also modifiers; like adjectives, adverbs *describe.* Adverbs describe adjectives, verbs, or other adverbs.

He was *very* happy to hear about the merger. (The adverb *very* modifies the adjective *happy.*)

They have been *exceptionally* patient for many, many months. (The adverb *exceptionally* modifies the adjective *patient.*)

Jack has *nearly* completed the assignment. (The adverb *nearly* modifies the verb *has completed.*)

The company *almost* exceeded its all-time sales record. (The adverb *almost* modifies the verb *exceeded.*)

This product is selling *much* better than we anticipated. (The adverb *much* modifies the adverb *better.*)

Francis did well on his exam—in fact, he did *very* well. (The adverb *very* modifies the adverb *well.*)

Note that many adverbs end in *ly* and are therefore very easy to identify:

surely	immediately
suddenly	successfully
badly	happily

In fact, these adverbs are formed by adding *ly* to the adjectives *sure, sudden, bad, immediate, successful,* and *happy.* Although most words that end in *ly* are adverbs, not all adverbs end in *ly.* Here are some adverbs that do not end in *ly:*

very	well
soon	here
quite	there
always	then
not	never

Checkup 3

Identify the words in parentheses as either adjectives or adverbs.

1. An (expensive) shipment of merchandise will arrive (here) on Monday or Tuesday.

2. Frank (immediately) rejected the proposal to buy the (new) building.
3. Several (excellent) sales representatives will be here (soon) to interview for this job.
4. Marjorie (tactfully) suggested that we postpone a decision on this (very) important item.
5. A very (experienced) sales manager, Irene, explained some of her (successful) selling techniques.

Now, on a separate sheet of paper, rewrite the following sentences. As you do so, fill in the blanks with either an adjective or an adverb. Be sure to identify each choice.

6. Ms. DeGroat decided to purchase a _____ monitor for her computer.
7. As you can well imagine, Mr. Larue was _____ delighted to hear the news.
8. Mrs. Weymouth generally reviews these reports _____.
9. Jerry prepares _____ reports.
10. Jerry prepares reports _____.

Prepositions

Prepositions serve to connect words and describe relationships among words. Prepositions are always used in phrases, as shown below:

Preposition	Prepositional Phrase
in	in May, in the morning
for	for Juliet, for us
by	by the parking lot, by tomorrow morning
of	of the owners, of my supervisor
from	from Ms. Diaz, from me

Prepositional phrases are, obviously, very commonly used in sentences:

The meeting will be held *in May*.

James will leave *in the morning*.

The carton *for Juliet* arrived.

Leave a message *for us* if the contract is approved.

In addition to the prepositions listed above, there are many other commonly used prepositions, including these:

to	from	after	at
on	with	before	into
out	over	through	onto

Conjunctions

Conjunctions are words that *join*. What do conjunctions join? They may join words, phrases, or clauses. Note how the conjunctions *and, but, or,* and *nor* are used in these sentences.

Gregory *and* Peter have been assigned to this project. (*And* joins two words—the nouns *Gregory* and *Peter*.)

The folders are lying on the desk *or* on the floor. (*Or* joins two prepositional phrases.)

I went to the seminar, *but* Vera went to the trade show. (*But* joins two clauses.)

Frank refused to attend the meeting, *nor* did he want to discuss the problem. (*Nor* joins two clauses.)

Checkup 4

Identify the words in parentheses as either prepositions (P) or conjunctions (C).

1. The letter (from) Mr. Syms explained the reason (for) his cancellation.
2. Irene (and) Carla went (to) the convention (in) Seattle (with) Ms. Fitch (and) Mr. VanHuff.
3. Bob likes the stationery store (on) the corner, (but) Marie prefers the one (on) Connors Street.
4. Andrew did not order more (of) these supplies, (nor) has he ordered anything else (through) our Purchasing Department recently.
5. (With) Ms. Johnson's approval, the sale will begin (on) Wednesday (or) Thursday.
6. We will try to complete the project (before) June; (in) any case, we will begin our work immediately.

Interjections

Interjections are words used alone that show very strong feeling. They are often followed by exclamation marks, as shown in the following examples.

Congratulations! You have now won the annual sales contest for four consecutive years. (Note that the interjection *Congratulations* is treated as an independent sentence.)

Yes! All of us are delighted to accept your invitation.

SUBJECTS AND PREDICATES

In addition to the parts of speech, you should know a few more important terms, including *subject* and *predicate*. A *subject* tells

(1) who is speaking, (2) who is spoken to, or (3) who or what is spoken about. A subject is usually a noun or pronoun.

1. Who is speaking:

    I approved the proposal yesterday. (The word *I* identifies the subject of the sentence, the person speaking.)

    We approved the proposal yesterday. (The word *We* identifies the subject of the sentence, the persons speaking.)

2. Who is spoken to:

    You have been selected to attend the seminar, Andrew. (The subject *You* identifies the person spoken to, *Andrew*.)

    You have been selected to attend the seminar, Andrew and Jane. (The subject *You* identifies the persons spoken to, *Andrew and Jane*.)

3. Who or what is spoken about:

    Marco is the manager of the Customer Relations Department. (Who is spoken about? Answer: *Marco*, the subject of the sentence.)

    He is the manager of the Customer Relations Department. (Who is spoken about? Answer: *He*, the subject of the sentence.)

In the above examples, the person spoken about was referred to by name, *Marco,* which was then substituted with the pronoun *He.* Now note how these sentences can be rephrased without changing their meanings:

The manager of the Customer Relations Department is Marco.

The manager of the Customer Relations Department is he. (The subject of both sentences is *The manager of the Customer Relations Department.*)

Now that we have seen examples of *who* is spoken about, let's see examples of *what* is spoken about:

This insurance policy covers loss by fire and theft. (What is spoken about? Answer: *This insurance policy.*)

It covers loss by fire and theft. (What is spoken about? *It*, a pronoun that substitutes for *This insurance policy. It* is the subject of the sentence.)

Now note that subjects can be compound:

Marco and Anne are the managers of the two departments. (The subject is *Marco and Anne,* the persons spoken about.)

Marco, Anne, and Jacob are the managers of these departments. (The subject is *Marco, Anne, and Jacob*.)

What is the predicate of the sentence? The *predicate* is simply the part of the sentence that tells what the subject is or does, or what is done to the subject.

Marco, Anne, and Jacob *are the managers of these departments.* (The predicate tells what Marco, Anne, and Jacob are.)

Checkup 5

Identify the subjects of the following sentences. For each subject, try to determine whether the subject is (1) the person(s) speaking, (2) the person(s) spoken to, or (3) the person(s) or thing(s) spoken about.

1. This word processor will be installed next week.
2. The cables will be laid by March 30.
3. Jerry Van Heflin will be the keynote speaker.
4. He will be the keynote speaker.
5. The keynote speaker will be Jerry Van Heflin.
6. I agree that the original price was too high.
7. The total package includes two disk drives, a monitor, and the keyboard.
8. Marla and Nancy will distribute all the brochures to the committee members.

CLAUSES AND PHRASES

Words that are grouped together are classified as a *clause* if the group of words includes both a subject and a predicate. A group of related words that does *not* have both a subject and a predicate is called a *phrase*.

Clauses

A clause, as we said above, has both a subject and a predicate. If this group of words can stand alone—that is, the group of words makes a complete sentence—then it is an *independent* clause. If the group of words cannot stand alone, then the clause is called a *dependent* clause.

Review the following sentences. Note that each has a subject and a predicate and that each *can* stand alone. Each, therefore, is an *independent* clause.

Jay Haggerty is a well-known expert in sales promotion. (The subject is *Jay Haggerty*, and the predicate is the rest of the sentence. Because this group of words *can* stand alone, this is an independent clause.)

A new computer store is scheduled to open May 24 in the Scotchwood Mall. (Here, the subject is *A new computer store*. The predicate is the rest of the sentence. Because this group of words *can* stand alone, this is an independent clause.)

Now read the clauses that follow. Each has a subject and predicate, but cannot stand alone. These are dependent clauses.

If Ms. Sakaguchi accepts the nomination (This is a clause; the subject is *Ms. Sakaguchi,* and the predicate is the rest of the clause. But does this group of words make any sense? No. This is a *dependent* clause. Obviously, more information is required for this group of words to make sense.)

When Mr. Cohen returns from jury duty (Again, this is a clause; the subject is *Mr. Cohen,* and the predicate is the rest of the clause. But once again the words make no sense by themselves. This group of words is a dependent clause. As you read this dependent clause, ask yourself this: "What will happen *when Mr. Cohen returns from jury duty?*" Do you see that more information is required?)

Dependent clauses cannot stand alone as sentences; therefore, they must be joined to independent clauses to make sense.

If Ms. Sakaguchi accepts the nomination, she must resign her present position. (*She must resign her present position* is an independent clause. Thus the dependent clause *If Ms. Sakaguchi accepts the nomination* is correctly joined to an independent clause.)

When Mr. Cohen returns from jury duty, he will review all these proposals. (Again, the dependent clause, *When Mr. Cohen returns from jury duty,* is joined to an independent clause.)

Checkup 6

Determine which of the following groups of words are sentences and which are dependent clauses that are incorrectly treated as sentences. For each dependent clause, suggest an independent clause that would complete it.

1. Because Ms. D'Amato will be on vacation that week.
2. Both Michael and Bernard are planning to work on the advertising brochures for these new products.
3. Before we meet to discuss the sales figures for the months of July and August.
4. If we do not touch up the proofs by September 4.
5. When Francine meets with all the sales representatives in her district.

6. Marion Weber works very closely with our advertising agency to develop effective campaigns.

Phrases

Phrases are groups of words that have neither subjects nor predicates. As you study the following three kinds of phrases, note that none has a subject or a predicate.

PREPOSITIONAL PHRASES. Prepositional phrases are phrases such as *for the interns, in the office, among them, at the seminar, with Mr. Framm, between you and me,* and *from Ms. Hellman.* The nouns and pronouns at the ends of prepositional phrases are not subjects; they are objects of the prepositions.

As you read the examples below, note how prepositional phrases can be used (1) as adjectives and (2) as adverbs.

1. As adjectives:

   The woman *with the briefcase* is Marilyn Choo. (Which woman? The prepositional phrase *with the briefcase* describes the noun *woman.* Therefore, because it describes a noun, this prepositional phrase serves as an adjective.)

2. As adverbs:

   Helen has already gone *to the airport.* (Gone where? The prepositional phrase *to the airport* answers the question Where? This prepositional phrase serves as an adverb.)

INFINITIVE PHRASES. An *infinitive* is the *to* form of a verb: *to drive, to study, to analyze, to review, to compute, to keyboard, to be, to have, to do,* and so on. An infinitive phrase includes the infinitive and any other words that are related to it.

Infinitive phrases may be used (1) as nouns, (2) as adjectives, and, less frequently, (3) as adverbs.

1. As nouns:

   To develop unique educational programs is the objective of our company. (The complete infinitive phrase is *To develop unique educational programs;* it is the subject of the verb *is.*)

2. As adjectives:

   Andrea McGinn is the manager *to ask about employment opportunities.* (Here the infinitive phrase *to ask about employment opportunities* modifies the noun *manager* and therefore serves as an adjective.)

3. As adverbs:

   James returned *to pick up his briefcase.* (Returned why? Here the infinitive phrase answers the question Why? The infinitive phrase *to pick up his briefcase* therefore serves as an adverb.)

VERB PHRASES. In a verb phrase, two or more verbs work together as one verb. In all such cases, the main verb is the last verb in the phrase; all other verbs are helping (or auxiliary) verbs.

> Gregory *will complete* this sales review by Friday. (*Will complete* is a verb phrase. The main verb is *complete; will* is a helping verb.)

> By Friday the sales review *will have been completed.* (The main verb is *completed,* the last word in the verb phrase. *Will have been* is a helping verb.)

A verb phrase is often interrupted by adverbs, as shown in these examples. Do not be misled in such cases.

> Danielle will *soon* be leaving for her West Coast trip. (The verb phrase *will be leaving* is interrupted by the adverb *soon.*)

> Tara and Sean should *already* have been told of the planned changes. (The verb phrase *should have been told* is interrupted by the adverb *already.*)

Checkup 7

Are the words in parentheses prepositional phrases, infinitive phrases, or verb phrases? On a separate sheet of paper, write *PP, IP,* or *VP* for each group of words.

1. Robert's research report (has been drafted) and (will be submitted) (to the committee) (before next Wednesday).
2. Ms. Holmes wants (to visit our branch offices) when she goes (to the East Coast) (with her assistant, Amy Marsh).
3. (During the past week) Karen (has been calling) all overdue accounts (to stress the importance of promptness).
4. (To become a regional manager), you (must have had) at least five years' experience (with our company).

5. Mr. Annucci plans (to leave promptly) (at 9:30 a.m. tomorrow) (with Mr. Loomis).
6. Yes, we (have been receiving) many telephone calls (for Ms. Steuben) (in the last few days).
7. Several exhibits (have been scheduled) (in the auditorium) (for all our customers).
8. (In March or April) Ms. Gooden (will offer) a special discount (to all employees).
9. (To test the validity of the theory), Dorothy (has budgeted) extra money (in her research expenses).

COMMUNICATION PROJECTS

Practical Application

A. Name the part of speech for each word in parentheses in the following sentences. On a separate sheet of paper, write *noun, verb, adjective,* and so on. For each phrase in parentheses, identify the phrase by writing *VP* (verb phrase), *IP* (infinitive phrase), or *PP* (prepositional phrase).

1. The Purchasing Department (has negotiated) a (new) contract (with a leading car rental company).
2. (Employees) will be able (to rent or to lease cars at a discount).
3. The (discount) applies (for both business and personal use).
4. Ms. Francesco (and) Mr. Franklin have (already) submitted outlines for their speeches (on Wednesday).
5. A special offer (will be made) (to all employees).
6. Lisa (and) her brother Raymond (have opened) a computer store (in the Greenwood Building).
7. (Congratulations!) We wish (you) success (with) your upcoming conference.
8. Bertha (and) Raymond (have been named) (to the committee), according (to) our supervisor.
9. Janice (has) a copy (of) the report, (but) (she) is out of town (today).
10. (To set realistic goals) is important (for) a manager, (and) we always stress (realistic) objectives.
11. Henry (usually) arrives at 8:30 a.m., so (he) should be (here) soon.
12. "All the brochures (will be shipped) on Friday," (said) Nancy, "(but) they will not be sent (by) truck."
13. John and Thomas (prefer) the (new) procedure, but (they) claim (it) is very time-consuming.
14. Dr. Chung (generally) stays at the same (hotel) whenever (she) is (in New York).
15. (Anthony) and (Jessica) have (already) received confirmations of (their) reservations (from) the airline (and) from their (hotel).

B. Identify the following clauses as dependent or independent. On a separate sheet of paper, write *D* or *I*.

1. As soon as we receive all the information from the insurance company.
2. Before Mrs. Westerly left for her trip to our Boulder, Colorado, office.
3. Mr. O'Flynn always reviews the travel expenses of all our sales representatives.
4. The ExCo Corporation is well known for its support of local civic organizations.
5. Which all of us hope is true.
6. One of the most important ways we have to prevent accidents on the job.
7. Ms. Lucchesi has already approved all these expense vouchers.
8. While we were waiting for the messenger to deliver the cartons.
9. Usually on Monday mornings when Mr. Rodriguez is here.
10. Although Ms. Karpovich has already received her refund.
11. John will reimburse Mr. LaFleur for the full cost.
12. Babbitt Chemicals has provided us with excellent service and fair prices for many, many years.
13. Martin Gavin or Maria Vasquez, both of whom are in the Personnel Department.
14. When Ms. Banks approves these estimates, we will notify the Arrow Hotel.
15. In my opinion, Jay Kowalski will probably be named the regional manager for the West Coast.

Editing Practice

Editing for Vocabulary Errors. Correct any vocabulary errors in the following excerpt from a business letter.

As Ms. Atkinson already mentioned, we plan to formerly announce our acquisition on February 12. At that time, we will announce our purchase of the sight for our new building, which will become our company's principle residents.

The Word Processing Supervisor. The following excerpt is from a report submitted to you by one of your employees. Correct any errors that you find.

The Vernon Studio has been in busness for many years and has supplied us with sevral award-winning photoes for advertizing and sails promotion use. Among their best photoes were the ones we used in our childrens' clothing ads last year.

Case Problem

An Embarrassing Moment.   Jeanette Nolan, a sales representative for Nationwide Foods Inc., meets Jack Lambert at an out-of-town foods-industry convention. Jack is a new customer who represents a large retail chain. Problem: Jeanette has met Jack twice before but doesn't remember his name! While she is talking with Jack, her boss, Francine Collins, approaches. Obviously, Jeanette must introduce Jack Lambert to Francine Collins, but she still cannot remember his name.

1.   What should Jeanette do?
2.   What, if anything, might Jack have done to avoid the problem?
3.   What could Jeanette have done to remember Jack's name?

THE SENTENCE

We use sentences as our basic units of thought as we read and write and speak. Our ability to use sentences effectively, therefore, determines our ability to communicate.

Review this section carefully in an effort to master this important topic.

WHAT IS A SENTENCE?

Remember this definition: *A sentence is a group of words that expresses a complete thought.* Note especially the word *complete.* Writing incomplete sentences—called "fragments"—is a common but glaring error, one that you will be sure to avoid by studying the following Memory Hook.

No Sense/No Sentence—this is a simple way to distinguish between a complete sentence and a fragment.

Emile wants to attend the conference because the theme of the meeting is microcomputers. (This is a complete thought. This group of words makes sense. This *is* a sentence. Now note how some writers would have split off part of this sentence and created a fragment.)

Emile wants to attend the conference. Because the theme of the meeting is microcomputers. (The first group of words is a sentence. The words *Because the theme of the meeting is microcomputers* do not make sense by themselves. The word *because* leads us to expect more. What happened *because the theme of the meeting is microcomputers?*)

When we receive Ms. Hayworth's approval, we will mail the contracts to Mr. Clark. (This is a complete thought. This group of words makes sense. This is a sentence.)

When we receive Ms. Hayworth's approval. We will mail the contacts to Mr. Clark. (The words *When we receive Ms. Hayworth's approval* do not make sense by themselves; the word *when* leads us to expect more. This is not a sentence. What will happen *when we receive Ms. Hayworth's approval?* The second group of words is a sentence.)

In the examples above, the words *because* and *when* lead us to expect more. Each begins a clause that cannot stand alone. Note that the following words, like *because* and *when,* often begin dependent clauses (clauses that cannot stand alone):

after	provided that
although	since
as	so that
as if	than
as soon as	that
as though	unless
because	until
before	when
even if	whenever
for	where
how	wherever
if	whether
in case	while
in order that	why

SUBJECTS AND PREDICATES

Every sentence has both a subject and a predicate. The subject of a sentence is that part that names (1) the person or persons speaking, (2) the person or persons spoken to, or (3) the person(s) or thing(s) spoken about.

1. *I* requested additional information. (*I* is the complete subject of the sentence, the person who is speaking.)

   We requested additional information. (*We* is the complete subject of the sentence, the persons speaking.)

2. *You* should order a copy. (*You* is the complete subject of the sentence, the person spoken to.)

   Order a copy. (Here the subject is still *you*, but this is an imperative sentence—it is a request or an order. In such sentences, we are usually directly addressing the person spoken to; therefore, it is clearly understood that the subject is *you*.)

   You should order a copy. (Here, more than one person is spoken to. The complete subject is again *you*, but here *you* is plural, the persons spoken to.)

3. *He* is going to the seminar. *They* are going to the seminar. (*He* and *They* are the subjects. *He* is the person spoken about; *They* are the persons spoken about.)

   That book belongs to Henry. *Those books* belong to Kristen. (*That book* and *Those books* are the subjects. *That book* is the thing spoken about; *Those books* are the things spoken about.)

Every time you identify the subject correctly, you simplify your work in identifying the predicate. Reason: The predicate tells what the subject does, what is done to the subject, or what state of being the subject is in.

Checkup 1

Are the following groups of words sentences, or are they fragments? Identify each; then rewrite each fragment to make it a complete sentence.

1. If Mr. Bartoli decides to attend the conference.
2. Each of the microcomputers in our main office.
3. Jason and Edwin have already reviewed all the inventory reports.
4. Because both approvals are required for all checks over $5000.

5. Ms. DeCosta has accepted the lowest bid for this service contract.
6. Although we expected our vice president to reject our suggestion.
7. Laura or Raymond is going to be named regional manager of our East Coast office.
8. When Nora returns from her time-management seminar in New York City.

SIMPLE AND COMPOUND SUBJECTS

The *simple subject* is the main word in the complete subject—the core of the subject.

> The *manager* of these clerks is Jack DeLorenzo. (The complete subject is *The manager of these clerks*. The main word in this complete subject is *manager*, which is the simple subject.)

> Two former *partners* in the Wendell & Crofts Advertising Agency are scheduled to give the keynote address. (The complete subject of this sentence is *Two former partners in the Wendell & Crofts Advertising Agency*. Within this complete subject, the simple subject is *partners*.)

By knowing that the simple subjects in the above sentences are *manager* and *partners,* you will not incorrectly say "clerks *are*" or "Agency *is*." Because the subject of the first example is *manager,* not *clerks,* the correct verb must be *is*. Because the subject of the second example is *partners,* not *Agency,* the correct verb must be *are*. As you can see, therefore, only by knowing how to find the simple subject will you be sure to make subjects and verbs agree.

Compound subjects are two or more equal subjects joined by a conjunction such as *and, but, or* or *nor*.

> The *drivers and loaders* in our company have indicated that they will indeed strike if their demands are not met. (The complete subject is *The drivers and loaders in our company*. The main words in this complete subject are *drivers* and *loaders,* which are joined by the conjunction *and*. The compound subject is *drivers and loaders*.)

> A *cruise* to Bermuda or a one-week *vacation* in Florida is going to be the first prize. (The complete subject is *A cruise to Bermuda or a one-week vacation in Florida*. Can you identify the main words in this complete subject? The main words are *cruise* and *vacation,* which are joined by the conjunction *or*. The compound subject is *cruise or vacation*.)

NORMAL ORDER: SUBJECT, THEN PREDICATE

The normal order of a sentence is subject first, then predicate.

Our managing editor hired extra proofreaders to meet the critical press deadlines. (The complete subject is *Our managing editor.* Because the complete subject precedes the complete predicate, this sentence is in *normal* order.)

To meet the critical press deadlines, our managing editor hired extra editors and proofreaders. (The words are the same, but the order is different. Now part of the predicate precedes the subject. This sentence, therefore, is *not* in normal order. This is in *inverted* order.)

Note that most questions are phrased in inverted order, not normal order.

Does Amy know the estimated cost of this brochure? (Why is this question in inverted order? Because the subject is *Amy,* and part of the predicate—the word *Does*—precedes the subject. Normal order: *Amy does know the estimated cost of this brochure.*)

Now let's see why it is important to be able to distinguish between normal order and inverted order. What, if anything, is wrong with this sentence?

Where's the blank disks that Mark left for us?

Many people almost automatically start sentences with *Where's, There's* and *Here's,* even when these words are incorrect. Normal order quickly points out the error:

The blank disks that Mark left for us *is* where? (Simply put, "The disks . . . is where?" *Disks is* is incorrect, of course; we must say "Disks are.")

Not only in questions but also in sentences is it important to spot inverted order. Note this sentence:

On the shelf in my office is the revised insurance policies you need. (In normal order, this sentence reads: "The revised insurance policies you need *is* on the shelf in my office." Of course, *policies is* is incorrect, and this error is masked by the inverted order.)

Checkup 2

Practice identifying subjects and predicates. On a separate sheet of paper, write the simple subject or the compound subject for each sentence. Be sure to change inverted sentences to normal order first!

1. Has Scot written to the Internal Revenue Service for answers to these questions?

2. Two printing companies and a travel agency have shown interest in buying this property.
3. Iowa or Minnesota may be selected as a site for our new branch office.
4. The résumés that we received from all applicants were exceptionally interesting.
5. One woman in the first session that we conducted asked about the availability of franchises in her city.
6. The inexpensiveness of the equipment was cited as the major factor in its overnight success.
7. A two-week trip and a cash prize will be awarded to the winner of the sales contest for August.
8. Margaret or Jeremy should be selected "Employee of the Month," in my opinion.

COMMUNICATION PROJECTS

Practical Application

A. Read each of the following carefully. Then, on a separate sheet of paper, (1) change any inverted sentence to normal order, (2) write the complete subject, and (3) underline the simple or compound subject.

1. In August or perhaps in September, Mr. Mulcahy and Ms. Liebowitz will begin reviewing salaries of all sales representatives.
2. Are Karen and Michael the only supervisors who were invited to the managers' meeting?
3. On her desk were the three contract folders.
4. When she returned to Tucson, Dr. Sansone opened a new office.
5. Dr. Sansone opened a new office when she returned to Tucson.
6. Although the cost was high, Travis and Andrew decided to purchase the new MultiCom microcomputer.
7. Our only franchise on the West Coast is located in Los Angeles.
8. Five diskettes and a new utility program were given free to promote sales.
9. The only territory in the country to meet its sales goals was the Chicago office.
10. Do Nancy and Allison prefer leaving from Newark Airport?
11. When raises are officially approved, each manager should inform his or her employees within 30 days.
12. In Marsha's office are the two cartons of files on the Burke property.
13. Will Andrea, Jacob, or Alexander be available to help us complete this project?

14. Any employee on the floor of our plant must wear protective goggles at all times.
15. On Monday or Tuesday evening Dorothy will finish writing the new advertising brochures.

B. On a separate sheet of paper, (1) identify each complete sentence below or (2) add the words needed to change a fragment to a complete sentence. Then (3) indicate the normal order of any inverted sentence and (4) identify the complete subject and the simple or compound subject for each sentence.

1. Medical and dental benefits are clearly explained in this booklet.
2. In our Denver office we often conduct tours for local schools.
3. Ms. Friedman or Ms. Ling is responsible for industrial products.
4. Although our bid was the lowest one submitted to the City Planning Department.
5. A seminar on time-management principles will be offered on three consecutive days beginning next Monday.
6. Will one of the new products be displayed at our booth?
7. In an effort to save time on this project, we hired part-time help.
8. The book that we ordered is now out of stock.
9. What is your opinion?
10. In this booklet medical and dental benefits are clearly explained.
11. Whenever Mrs. Conover travels to New York City.
12. Where are the backup disks for this project?
13. Since this plant was purchased by Hamilton Metals in 1985.
14. Will you please give these photo proofs to Marion as you pass her office?
15. In the envelope on the credenza in my office are the checks for Mr. Schwartz.

Editing Practice

Proofreading for Errors. Can you find any errors in the following excerpt from an informal business note?

> Here's the samples you requested last Monday. If there's any more brochures left in the stockroom, I'll be glad to send them to you too.

As a Matter of Fact . . . . Proofreading requires us to look not only for errors in grammar, spelling, punctuation, and so on, but also for inconsistencies and errors in facts. Read and correct the following excerpt from a business memo.

On September 31 we mailed Mr. Benson a check for $200, but we omitted the 8 percent sales tax on this total as well as the shipping charge of $10. Please send Mr. Benson a check for $18 to cover the additional cost of the tax on $200 and the shipping expense.

Case Problem

Introducing People. At his first annual Christmas party with Software Solutions Inc., Ted Reynolds is about to introduce his wife Colleen to Helen Acosta, vice president of marketing for the company.

1. How should Ted introduce them to each other?
2. To prepare for social introductions, what reference book might have been helpful for Ted?

10

VERBS

Among the most serious as well as the most common errors we make as we speak and write are verb errors. Yet forming most verbs correctly is very easy, because most verbs follow one simple pattern, as you will see in this section. The verbs that do not follow this regular pattern are the ones that cause problems; these irregular verbs are discussed in depth in this section also.

VERBS AND THEIR PRINCIPAL PARTS

A *verb* is a word that describes an action.

Mary *signed* the contract.

They *landed* at 4:15 p.m.

I *spoke* to the group this morning.

Ms. Zak *is writing* the draft now.

Mr. Carlin *will be running* on the track during lunchtime.

The verbs *signed, landed, spoke, is writing,* and *will be running* all describe an *action.*

In addition to describing an action, a verb can describe a condition or a state of being.

Jerry *seems* to enjoy his new job.

I *am* the production manager.

Joseph *is* now out of town.

She and Peter *were* absent.

Mr. Levesque *sounds* tired.

Ms. Faulken *will be* here later.

The verbs *seems, am, is, were, sounds,* and *will be* do not describe actions here, yet each is a verb.

Practice your ability to identify verbs correctly—the first step in using verbs correctly.

Checkup 1

Identify the verbs in the following sentences.

1. Sheila asked Mr. Mendoza to the first session.
2. Only Paula is ready for the meeting this morning.
3. Amy noticed the difference immediately.
4. The Amber Chemical Company wants this property for its new plant.
5. Leo and Tyrone will be at our branch office tomorrow.
6. Helen has accepted the nomination.
7. Jack said that he will leave this afternoon.
8. Vera and Frank were in Florida when we discussed this proposal.

PRINCIPAL PARTS OF REGULAR VERBS

As we speak and write, the verbs we use indicate the time of the action. We form verbs to indicate present time ("I type," "I am typing"), past time ("I typed," "I have typed"), and future time ("I will type," "I will be typing"). Knowing how to form the parts of verbs is necessary if you are to use verbs correctly in all such instances.

Fortunately, most verbs in our language form their principal parts by a very simple pattern. The principal parts are the (1) present tense form, (2) the past tense form, (3) the past participle, and (4) the present participle. From these four forms, all the many variations of a verb are derived.

Present Tense	Past Tense	Past Participle	Present Participle
type	typed	typed	typing
prepare	prepared	prepared	preparing
eliminate	eliminated	eliminated	eliminating
call	called	called	calling
enter	entered	entered	entering
borrow	borrowed	borrowed	borrowing

As you read this table, say to yourself "I type," "I prepare," and so on. Thus you see how the present tense is used. Then notice that the past tense is formed simply by adding *d* to verbs that end in *e*. For verbs that do not end in *e*, add *ed: called, entered, borrowed.*

Also helping to simplify this pattern is the fact that the past participle is the same form as the past tense in all cases. And the present participle is formed by adding *ing* to the present form. (Of course, for verbs ending in *e*, you must drop the *e* before adding *ing: typing, preparing, eliminating.*) Except for a limited list of verbs, all the verbs in our language follow this simple pattern.

MEMORY HOOK	

How can you distinguish between the past tense form *called* and the past participle *called?* Answer: You cannot, except by seeing the word *in context.* Remember: A past tense form *never* has a helper; a past participle *always* has a helping verb.

Bette *called* us at 9 a.m. (Here, *called* is a past tense form; it has no helping verb.)

George came to tell us to attend the meeting, but Bette *had* already *called* us at 9 a.m. (Here, *called* is a past participle—the main verb in the phrase *had called.*)

Checkup 2

On a separate sheet of paper, copy the following chart. Then fill in the missing parts correctly for each entry.

Present Tense	Past Tense	Past Participle	Present Participle
1. keyboard			
2.	elected		
3.		governed	
4.			indicating
5. remember			

Present Tense	Past Tense	Past Participle	Present Participle
6.	responded		
7.		stained	
8.			tempting
9. trust			
10.	used		

VERB PHRASES

A *verb phrase* consists of two or more verbs joined together to function *as one verb*. In all cases, the main verb in the phrase is *always* the last verb. The other verbs are helping verbs. Read these examples carefully.

> can *type*
>
> did *prepare*
>
> will *eliminate*

The main verbs in the above three examples are *type, prepare,* and *eliminate*. The verbs *can, did,* and *will* are helping verbs. Note that *type, prepare,* and *eliminate* are the present tense forms listed in the table at the top of page 81.

> has been *typed*
>
> have *prepared*
>
> will be *eliminated*

The main verbs are *typed, prepared,* and *eliminated,* which are the past participles listed in the third column in the table. The verbs *has been, have,* and *will be* are helping verbs.

> are *typing*
>
> is *preparing*
>
> will be *eliminating*

Again, the last word in each phrase is the main verb: *typing, preparing,* and *eliminating,* which are the present participles listed on the chart. The words *are, is,* and *will be* are helping verbs.

Now note how verb phrases generally are used in sentences. Note, too, how the verb phrase can be interrupted by another word.

> Tomorrow Harry *will be typing* the Anderson report. (The verb phrase is *will be typing,* and the main verb is, of course, the last verb, *typing.*)

> Jessica *has* also *been preparing* her résumé. (The verb phrase *has been preparing* is interrupted by the adverb *also.* The main verb is *preparing.*)

The 20 percent discount for employees *has* already *been eliminated.* (*Eliminated* is the main verb in the phrase *has been eliminated. Already* is an adverb.)

In questions, the verb phrase is often more difficult to identify, because the sentence order, as you know, is inverted.

When *did* Mr. Huntz *return* all these cartons? (The verb phrase is *did return.*)

Have Alice and Beatrice already *been working* on this account? (The verb phrase *have been working* is tricky to identify because of the inverted order.)

Checkup 3

Identify the verb phrases in each of the following sentences. For each phrase, name the main verb.

1. Jonathan will be checking all these invoices tomorrow morning.
2. Anthony can complete this entire project by Friday.
3. The candidate will enter the auditorium from the rear door.
4. Horace has been negotiating merit increases since last Wednesday.
5. Have Alan and Frank already approved these brochures?
6. Arcon Chemicals will probably be borrowing more money from our bank.
7. Jason and Albert have been hoping for this news for many, many months.
8. Does Gregory really want another copy of this diskette?

VERB TENSES

The *tense* of a verb is the form that tells the time of the action.

Present Tense

First, remember that *to call, to walk, to type, to borrow, to enter,* and so on, are called *infinitives,* and these forms without the word *to* are present tense forms:

I call	we call
you call	you call
he	
she }calls	they call
it	

As you see, there are only two present tense forms, *call* and *calls.* Use *call* to agree with *I, you, we,* and *they.* Add *s* for the present tense form to agree with *he, she,* and *it* and with singular nouns.

We *call* every morning. (*Call* with the pronoun *we.*)

He *calls* every morning. Harry *calls* every morning. (*Calls* with the pronoun *he* and the noun *Harry.*)

They *enjoy* sales work. (*Enjoy* with the pronoun *they*.)

She *enjoys* sales work. Gertrude *enjoys* sales work. (*Enjoys* with the pronoun *she* and the noun *Gertrude*.)

The present tense is used to show action that is happening now. It is also used to indicate that something is always true (as in, "the sun *rises* in the east").

Past Tense

The past tense is formed by adding *ed* to the present tense form (or *d* if the present tense form already ends in *e*).

I called	we called
you called	you called
he	
she }called	they called
it	

As you see, there is only one past tense form for a verb. (The only exception is the verb *to be,* which will be discussed later.) The past tense is used to indicate action that has already been completed.

Future Tense

To form the future tense of a verb, use *will* plus the infinitive form without the word *to*.

I will call	we will call
you will call	you will call
he	
she }will call	they will call
it	

This tense, obviously, indicates action that is to take place in the future. In addition to these three tenses, each has a correlated "perfect" tense. As you read the discussion on these three perfect tenses, you will surely note that they are very commonly used in our everyday conversation and everyday writing.

Present Perfect Tense

The *present perfect tense* is used to show that an action began in the past. (The action may still be occurring.) This tense is formed by using the helping verb *has* or *have* with a past participle.

Sheila *has redecorated* the entire lobby area. (Present perfect tense for an action that was begun in the past.)

Quincy and Nathan *have debated* the pros and cons of this issue for years. (Present perfect tense for an action that began in the past and may be still continuing in the present.)

Past Perfect Tense

The *past perfect tense* is used to show which of two past actions occurred first. To form the past perfect tense, use *had* plus the past participle of a verb.

Mike *had mailed* his check before he *received* the notice. (The verbs *had mailed* and *received* show *two* past actions. The past perfect tense *had mailed* tells us that this is the *first* past action. After this action was completed, a second action occurred—Mike *received* something. *Received* is past tense, to show the second of the two actions in the order in which they occurred.)

Future Perfect Tense

The *future perfect tense* shows that an action will be completed by some specific time in the future. The action may have already begun, or it may begin in the future. The important point is that it will *end* by a specific future time. To form the future perfect tense, use the verb *will have* plus the past participle of a verb.

The builder *will have completed* the foundation no later than May 15. (*Will have completed* is a future perfect tense verb describing an action that will end in the future.)

The Progressive Tenses

Closely related to the six tenses just discussed are the *progressive tenses,* which depict actions that are still "in progress."

PRESENT PROGRESSIVE TENSE.   As its name indicates, the *present progressive tense* describes an action that is in progress in the present. To form this tense, use *am, is,* or *are* with a present participle.

I *am using* this software program to do my income tax return. (*Am using* shows action in progress now.)

PAST PROGRESSIVE TENSE.   An action that was in progress in the past is described by using *was* or *were* with a present participle.

We *were reviewing* the sales reports when Ms. Nelson arrived. (*Were reviewing* shows action that was in progress in the past.)

FUTURE PROGRESSIVE TENSE.   An action that *will be* in progress in the future is described by using *will be* with a present participle.

Janet *will be taking* the first part of her CPA examination next Thursday. (Is this action in progress now? No. In the past? Again, no. *Will be taking* shows an action that will be in progress in the future—specifically, in progress "next Thursday.")

Checkup 4

On a separate sheet of paper, use each of the following verbs in a sentence.

1. had retyped
2. are waiting
3. will have paid
4. will be

5. have requested
6. wanted
7. has rejected
8. writes
9. were thinking
10. will be waiting

COMMUNICATION PROJECTS

Practical Application

A. Identify the verb phrases in the following sentences. For the main verb in each phrase, tell where it belongs on the chart of principal parts—under (1) present, (2) past participle, or (3) present participle.

1. Elsa has visited our Chicago office recently.
2. Marjorie has been going to the gymnasium after work every day.
3. Next September 15, Jack will have been working for our firm for twenty-five years.
4. Agnes and Frances will be at the next session, according to Mr. FitzRoy.
5. Larry can finish this assignment on Tuesday or Wednesday.
6. Karen is being transferred to Tulsa in October.
7. Have they already hired a replacement for Sarah?
8. You should ask Bert for assistance on this project.
9. Yes, Dr. Ribelow has prepared her speech already.
10. Andy will prepare a rough draft for your approval.
11. Hilda is now preparing a revised agenda for the committee.
12. Sean has been filing contracts all day.
13. All new equipment will have been ordered by December 30.
14. This agreement should be retyped before the end of the day.
15. You and Shirley are being invited to the banquet at the end of the convention.

B. Show your ability to form the principal parts of regular verbs by completing the following table. Use a separate sheet of paper.

Present Tense	Past Tense	Past Participle	Present Participle
1. instruct			
2.	disapproved		
3.		appraised	
4.	assisted		
5. pack			
6.			ensuring

7.				billing
8.			cited	
9.	arraign			
10.		inquired		
11.				devising
12.			preceded	
13.	lease			
14.		facilitated		
15.				proceeding

Editing Practice

The Right Word. Select the correct word for each of the following sentences.

1. Rosemary suggested that we conduct a nationwide (pole, poll) of soft drink consumers.
2. According to Mr. DePauw, the one-year guarantee is one of the (principle, principal) reasons for the success of this equipment.
3. First Line Software has (its, it's) headquarters in Tampa, Florida.
4. Alexis and Roberta are now planning (they're, their, there) sales presentations.
5. If sales continue to drop, we may (lose, loose) as much as 10 percent of our market share.
6. We have estimated the total cost to be about $9000; in any case, the actual cost cannot (exceed, accede) $10,000.
7. The committee's primary task is to develop a (fare, fair) incentive-compensation system for our employees.
8. Has Mrs. Reeves already (collaborated, corroborated) this discount?
9. Our billing department is now trying to (devise, device) a new collection system.
10. The copywriters have a tough task ahead, but (they're, their, there) confident that the brochure will be completed on schedule.

Case Problem

Working 9 to 5. After completing their week-long training class, six new employees begin working in the Customer Relations Department for Western United, a hotel and restaurant chain with headquarters in Los Angeles. Working hours are from 9 a.m. until 5 p.m., and lunch hour is from noon until 1 p.m.

Although Marsha, one of the new employees, works until 5:30 or so on most nights in order to complete some paperwork, she generally arrives 10 to 15 minutes late each morning. When her supervisor privately reminds her of the importance of arriving on time each day, Marsha feels his comments are inappropriate, especially because she works an extra half hour each evening.

1. Is Marsha justified? Why or why not?
2. Does Marsha's working later each day make up for her few minutes' lateness each morning?
3. Is her supervisor justified in commenting on her lateness?

11

IRREGULAR VERBS

In Section 10 you learned the basics of using verbs. Most verbs follow the regular pattern shown in Section 10 for forming the present tense, the past tense, the past participle, and the present participle. There are 50 or more commonly used irregular verbs, however, that do *not* follow this pattern. These "irregular verbs" are discussed in this section. Study them carefully.

PRINCIPAL PARTS OF IRREGULAR VERBS

Review the table on pages 89–90 in detail. As you do so, notice that some common errors are made when we try to treat an irregular verb as if it followed the "regular" pattern—for example, saying "break, breaked" instead of "break, broke" or saying "ring, ringed" instead of "ring, rang." There is no alternative: We must memorize most of these forms, especially those that are commonly used.

Checkup 1

Correct any error in the following sentences. Write *OK* for any sentence that has no error. Refer to the table on pages 89–90 if you must. (Hint: Remember that a past tense form *never* has a helper and that a past participle or a present participle *always* has a helper!)

1. Of course, Lynn known about the announcement for several weeks.

PRINCIPAL PARTS OF IRREGULAR VERBS

Present Tense	Past Tense	Past Participle	Present Participle
am	was	been	being
bear	bore	borne	bearing
begin	began	begun	beginning
bid (to command)	bade	bidden	bidding
bid (to offer to pay)	bid	bid	bidding
bite	bit	bitten	biting
blow	blew	blown	blowing
break	broke	broken	breaking
bring	brought	brought	bringing
burst	burst	burst	bursting
catch	caught	caught	catching
choose	chose	chosen	choosing
come	came	come	coming
do	did	done	doing
draw	drew	drawn	drawing
drink	drank	drunk	drinking
drive	drove	driven	driving
eat	ate	eaten	eating
fall	fell	fallen	falling
fight	fought	fought	fighting
flee	fled	fled	fleeing
fly	flew	flown	flying
forget	forgot	forgotten	forgetting
freeze	froze	frozen	freezing
get	got	got	getting
give	gave	given	giving
go	went	gone	going
grow	grew	grown	growing
hang (to put to death)	hanged	hanged	hanging
hang (to suspend)	hung	hung	hanging
hide	hid	hidden	hiding
know	knew	known	knowing
lay	laid (*not* layed)	laid (*not* layed)	laying
leave	left	left	leaving
lend	lent	lent	lending
lie	lay	lain	lying
pay	paid (*not* payed)	paid (*not* payed)	paying
read	read	read	reading
ride	rode	ridden	riding
ring	rang	rung	ringing
rise	rose	risen	rising
run	ran	run	running
see	saw	seen	seeing
set	set	set	setting
shake	shook	shaken	shaking
sing	sang	sung	singing

PRINCIPAL PARTS OF IRREGULAR VERBS (CONTINUED)			
Present Tense	Past Tense	Past Participle	Present Participle
sit	sat	sat	sitting
speak	spoke	spoken	speaking
stand	stood	stood	standing
steal	stole	stolen	stealing
strike	struck	struck	striking
take	took	taken	taking
tear	tore	torn	tearing
tell	told	told	telling
throw	threw	thrown	throwing
wear	wore	worn	wearing
write	wrote	written	writing

2. Ms. Schlein has wrote some of the most successful ads for these products.
3. Catherine had began revising the documents before her supervisor asked her to.
4. In an effort to get ahead of schedule, Theresa come in early yesterday and today.
5. Ask Lauren who has took the directory from the library shelves.
6. All the chemicals on the floor had freezed overnight.
7. Has the bell rung yet?
8. Our profits have grew steadily over the past three years.

"BEING" VERBS

The "being" verbs are the forms of the verb *to be*. They show no action. Study first the present tense and the past tense forms.

Present Tense

I am	we are
you are	you are
he	
she }is	they are
it	

As you see, then, there are three present tense forms: *am, is,* and *are.*

Past Tense

I was	we were
you were	you were
he	
she }was	they were
it	

There are two past tense forms, *was* and *were.*

Verb Phrases With Forms of To Be

Verb phrases are formed, as you saw in Section 10, by using helping verbs (1) with the infinitive form *be*, (2) with the past participle form *been*, and (3) with the present participle form *being*.

1. *Be* with a helping verb: *will be, may be, can be, would be, might be,* and so on
2. *Been* with a helping verb: *has been, have been, had been, will have been, could have been, might have been,* and so on
3. *Being* with a helping verb: *am being, is being, are being, was being,* and *were being*

You will do well to memorize these eight "being" verbs: *am, is, are, was, were,* helper plus *be,* helper plus *been,* and helper plus *being.*

Because being verbs are so often used as helping verbs, be careful to distinguish between being verbs that are helpers and being verbs that are main verbs in the phrase.

James *should have been* here by now. (The entire verb phrase is *should have been,* and the main verb is therefore *been.* This verb phrase is a being verb.)

That order *should have been canceled.* (Now the verb phrase is *should have been canceled. Should have been* is now only a helping verb. The main verb is *canceled.* The verb phrase is not a being verb—only the helping verb is a being verb.)

Of course, when a form of *be* is the only verb, it is a being verb:

Mr. Pierce *is* the vice president of marketing. He *was* formerly the director of sales. (Both *is* and *was* are being verbs.)

Distinguish carefully between being verb helpers and being verbs that are main words.

Checkup 2

On a separate sheet of paper, write the verbs and verb phrases in the following sentences. Identify each being verb that is a main verb by writing *B* next to the verb.

1. Evelyn has reordered copies of this booklet.
2. Of course, Mrs. Bancroft has been evaluating the union demands carefully.
3. Vernon was an assistant prosecuting attorney at one time.
4. Both Caroline and Emily have been members of the Budget Committee for two years.
5. Carter McGinn, the supervisor of our plant, is on vacation this week.
6. Agnes and Willa have been promoted to department heads.
7. Our company is well known for its civic contributions.
8. Alan has been planning this celebration for many months.

WERE *INSTEAD OF* WAS

Good writing requires that we sometimes use *were* instead of *was* after *if, as if, as though,* and *wish.* Whenever such statements describe (1) something contrary to fact, (2) something that is simply not true, or (3) something that is highly doubtful or impossible, use *were* instead of *was.* If, on the other hand, the statement *is true* or *could be true* (as often happens after *if*), then do *not* substitute *were* for *was.*

> We wish it *were* possible for us to predict future stock prices, but SEC regulations prohibit us from making such claims. (It is not possible. Therefore, "We wish it *were*"—not *was*—is correct.)

> If I *were* you, I would purchase this stock while it is still selling at 19. (Of course, I am *not* you—thus *were* is correct.)

> If Carla *was* here before us, she probably left the contracts with her assistant. (Carla could indeed have already been here; thus this statement could be true. Do *not* substitute *were* for *was.*)

Checkup 3

On a separate sheet, correct any error in the following sentences. If a sentence has no error, write *OK.*

1. If I were Mr. Pattulski, I would reject the offer from Abrams Printing.
2. At times Charles behaves as if he was the only sales representative in the country!
3. She has said that if she was younger, she would open her own firm.
4. Owen sometimes acts as if he was at a party instead of at the office.
5. If Louis was in the overcrowded auditorium, I certainly did not see him.

LIE, LAY; SIT, SET; RISE, RAISE

Like the being verbs, *lie* and *lay*, *sit* and *set*, and *rise* and *raise* deserve very special attention. In fact, to be able to use these verbs correctly, you must first understand the distinction between transitive and intransitive verbs.

Transitive Verbs

A *transitive verb* is a verb that has an object. To find that object, say the verb and ask "What?" or "Whom?" The answer to that question is the direct object. Follow these examples:

1. Jessica rejected the offer.
   a. Say the verb: *rejected.*

b. Ask "What?" or "Whom?" Rejected *what?* Answer: Rejected *offer.* The object of the verb *rejected* is *offer.*

c. Use the answer to determine whether the verb is transitive. Yes, *rejected* is transitive because it has an object, *offer.*

2. Ms. Wesler invited Nancy to the convention center.

a. Say the verb: *invited.*

b. Ask "What?" or "Whom?" Invited *whom?* Answer: Invited *Nancy.* The object of the verb *invited* is *Nancy.*

c. Transitive? Yes, *invited* is a transitive verb because it has an object, *Nancy.*

MEMORY HOOK	Here is an excellent shortcut to save time in finding transitive verbs. Whenever you see a being verb helper used with a past participle, you definitely have a transitive verb.

The award *should have been given* to Myra Bramley. (Do you have a being verb helper? Do you have a past participle? "Yes" to both questions. Therefore, this verb is transitive. What receives the action? Answer: *award.*)

The meeting *was canceled,* according to William. (Again, we have a "being" verb helper, *was,* and a past participle, *canceled.* Thus we know that the subject, *meeting,* receives the action of the verb. *What* was canceled? Answer: *meeting. Was canceled* is a transitive verb.)

Gloria has been nominated to the Executive Committee. (What is the verb in this sentence? Is it transitive? If so, explain why.)

Intransitive Verbs

Verbs that do not have objects are *intransitive verbs.*

Mr. Rosenblatt *travels* very frequently. (Travels *what?* Travels *whom?* No answer. *Travels* is an intransitive verb.)

Ms. Wolfe *will arrive* around noon, according to this itinerary. (The verb *will arrive* has no object; it is an intransitive verb.)

Checkup 4

Identify the verbs and verb phrases in the following sentences. Then label each *B* for "being," *T* for "transitive," or *I* for "intransitive."

1. A new regional manager had been appointed as of last week.
2. Sandra will be there early, Fred.
3. Our next broadcast will be televised on Thursday, August 18.
4. Jeremy and Paulette are negotiating higher wages.

5. The three consultants arrived nearly two hours late.
6. Several part-time word processing operators were hired by Ms. Finnegan.
7. Has Edward told Albert about the proposed changes?
8. Apparently, both of them have left already.
9. As always, she has been very helpful to us on our crash project.
10. Anthony has been reassigned to the Burrows account.

MEMORY HOOK

Now that you have learned to distinguish between transitive and intransitive verbs, you will have an easier task of using *lie* and *lay*, *sit* and *set*, and *rise* and *raise*. Just use the *i* in *intransitive* to remember that the *i* verbs—*lie*, *sit*, and *rise*—are also intransitive.

intransitive

lie

sit

rise

The other three verbs, *lay*, *set*, and *raise*, are all transitive.

Now be sure to review carefully the principal parts of these irregular verbs.

Present Tense	Past Tense	Past Participle	Present Participle	Infinitive
lie	lay	lain	lying	to lie
lay	laid	laid	laying	to lay
sit	sat	sat	sitting	to sit
set	set	set	setting	to set
rise	rose	risen	rising	to rise
raise	raised	raised	raising	to raise

As you review these principal parts, you probably see quickly that one common trap is confusing the present tense form *lay* with *lay*, the past tense form of *lie*. How can you tell which is which? You can tell by remembering what you have learned about transitive verbs.

Yesterday Mark (lay, laid) the cartons in that storeroom.

After jogging, I usually (lie, lay) down for a short while.

This morning, I (lie, lay) down for only five minutes or so.

Let's analyze these sentences. Does the first verb have an object? Yes, *cartons*. Therefore, a transitive verb is needed. As you just learned, *laid* is the past tense form of *to lay,* so *laid* is correct, because *to lay* is the transitive verb.

In the second sentence, is there an object? No. (*Down* is not an object; it is an adverb.) Here you need a form of the verb *to lie,* so the answer is *lie*—I *lie* down.

In the third sentence, the words *this morning* show that past tense is needed. Whichever verb is correct, does it have a direct object? Answer: No. Thus the correct answer is *lay,* the past tense form of *lie,* an intransitive verb.

As you see, some thinking and analysis are needed when choosing among the forms of *lie* and *lay,* so do not choose hastily.

Now let's apply the same principles to the transitive verbs *set* and *raise* and to the intransitive verbs *sit* and *rise.*

Gary and Lana (sit, set) the materials on the conference room table before they left for lunch. (Is an object needed here? Yes. Which is the transitive verb? Answer: *set.* Set what? Set the *materials.*)

As soon as the water level (rises, raises), this pump will automatically go on. (What is needed, a transitive verb or an intransitive verb? Answer: intransitive, because the verb has no object in this sentence. Which, then, is the intransitive verb? The *i* verb, *rises.*)

Checkup 5

Practice your ability to use the verbs *lie, lay, sit, set, rise,* and *raise.* Write your answers on a separate sheet of paper.

1. While she was on vacation, Beverly had (lain, laid) in the sun too long.
2. Everyone in our department is helping to (rise, raise) money for civic organizations in our area.
3. When he works on special writing projects, Daniel generally (sits, sets) in this office.
4. The new union contract has (risen, raised) our salaries by about 11 percent.
5. According to the terms of the new contract, our salaries have been (risen, raised) by about 11 percent.
6. When you retype this report, please (sit, set) your margins for 15 and 70.
7. Both speakers asked that these platforms be (risen, raised) about 3 inches.
8. Tell the messengers to (sit, set) the display units in the storeroom.
9. Because he was so tired, Al (lay, laid) down in the Medical Department for about an hour this morning.
10. The sales reports that you were looking for had been (lain, laid) carelessly in the stockroom.

COMMUNICATION PROJECTS

Practical Application

A. Identify the verb or the verb phrase in each of the following sentences. Label each choice *T* for "transitive," *I* for "intransitive," or *B* for "being."

1. The reason for the delays is explained in this report.
2. Is Phillip buying a new personal computer?
3. Dorothy and I have been very busy on the Trent & Loomis account.
4. Yes, all the forms have been mailed already, right on schedule.
5. Ms. Owens always sits here during our monthly production meetings.
6. Gerald has written an agenda already.
7. Yes, an agenda has already been written.
8. Both of us are being careful about following the new procedures.
9. Diana is planning the marketing strategy for this new product.
10. Unfortunately, my train has been late all week.
11. Kathleen creates most of our direct-mail brochures.
12. Most of our direct-mail brochures are created by Kathleen.
13. Yes, the messenger should have been here by now.
14. Our stock has been rising daily for the last two months.
15. Those important contracts have been lying on the reception desk all this time!

B. Correct any errors in the following sentences. Write *OK* for any sentence that has no error.

[handwritten: written — Its a past participle + it needs a helper]

1. Lloyd has already wrote to the Securities and Exchange Commission concerning these regulations.
2. The calculator that I was looking for was laying on my credenza.
3. When Mrs. VanPelt arrived, we raised to greet her.
4. At this morning's meeting, Jay laid out a comprehensive plan for our project.
5. Has Arnold ever flew to Canada before?
6. David has risen that same objection at every meeting on procedures.
7. After the flight, I went home to lay down.
8. The builder promised us that the foundation will have been lain no later than July 8.
9. Please lay all those packages on the conference room table.
10. Margaret has lent us $100 to buy the materials that we need.
11. The property lays about 200 yards north of our office.
12. Sherry's salary has been risen twice this year.
13. Since he heard the news, Lawrence has sat there very quietly.

14. This morning I laid in bed longer than usual because I was so tired.
15. If these prices do indeed raise quickly, you and I may make high profits on this stock.

Editing Practice

The Word Processing Supervisor. Check the following sentences for spelling errors. Write *OK* for any sentence that has no error.

1. At this morning's meeting with the manager of the Personel Department, we will discuss some specific problems concerning overtime pay.
2. Several of the comittee members offered suggestions that were exceptionally innovative.
3. We have asked various enployees for ideas to solve this problem.
4. Sid and Richard shared with us there unique plan to increase sales during the slow summer months.
5. Although the new systim was installed only last week, it is now operating at full efficiency.
6. Opening this new store presents us with an excellent oportunity to expand our lines of merchandise.
7. The White Plains store has a wide variety of brand names and offers helpful customer servaces.
8. This morning we recieved the final payment from Glenco Enterprises.
9. Bentley Chemicals is a profitable company, but it's plants are very out of date.
10. High-risk stocks are not apropriate investments for Mr. and Mrs. Nussbaum.

Case Problem

Dress Code. New employees for Bennett, Colby, and Ames Advertising Agency are instructed that they must follow a specific dress code during working hours. Jim Kelsey, who has been working for the agency for two months, requests permission from his supervisor to wear jeans, which are prohibited by the dress code.

1. Should Jim be allowed to wear jeans?
2. What should his supervisor tell Jim?
3. Does a firm have the right to insist that its employees follow a code of business dress? Justify your answer.

territory	territories
company	companies
faculty	faculties

Note that this rule does *not* apply to proper names ending in *y*. For proper names ending in *y*, add *s*.

Kennedy	the Kennedys
Mary	two Marys
Brady	the Bradys
Langley	the Langleys

Checkup 1

Correct any errors in the following sentences. Write *OK* if a sentence has no error.

1. According to the report, one of the newly appointed editor in chiefs is Dr. Edna P. Gallagher.
2. The terms of Mrs. Best's will were that her three son-in-laws must continue to operate her business.
3. Our original plan was to meet the Bradies—Gloria, John, and their two children—at the airport.
4. The extra bulletin boards and miscellaneous supplys are being stored in this closet.
5. Several lenss, including telephoto and wide-angle lenss, will be on sale at discounts up to 25 percent.
6. Most of the communitys in these two countys are popular because taxes are low.
7. The assistant district attornies who were assigned to this case are MaryLou Sampson and Connie Weiner.
8. Both companies have subsidiaries in Dallas and in Seattle.
9. Brad Avery and Karen Avery are interested in buying this property, but the Averies have set a ceiling of $500,000 for both the building and the land.
10. When this park is redecorated, benchs will be added for employees' comfort.

SPECIAL PLURALS

Certain plurals cause problems for writers because these forms follow no "regular" rules. For example, how would you form the plural of the abbreviations *Mr.* and *Mrs.?* When you have reviewed these special forms, you will have no difficulty forming these plurals.

Plurals of Titles With Names

When forming the plural of a title *and* the name used with it, make *either* the title *or* the name plural—*not both*.

Before we continue with this discussion, make sure that you know the plural forms of the commonly used courtesy titles *Mr., Mrs., Ms., Miss,* and *Dr.*

Singular	Plural
Mr.	Messrs.
Mrs.	Mmes.
Ms.	Mses.
Miss	Misses
Dr.	Drs.

Note the following:

1. *Messrs.* is derived from *Messieurs,* the French word for "Misters."
2. Likewise, *Mmes.* is derived from *Mesdames,* the French word for "My ladies," and is used as the plural of *Mrs.*
3. *Ms.* is considered nonsexist because it does not identify a woman's marital status, just as *Mr.* does not point out a man's marital status. *Ms.,* by the way, is not an abbreviation. Its plural form is *Mses.*

Now let's see some examples of forming plurals of names with titles. Both plural forms are correct and mean the same thing.

Singular	Plural Title	Plural Name
Ms. Swift	the Mses. Swift	the Ms. Swifts
Mr. Bern	the Messrs. Bern	the Mr. Berns
Mrs. Ford	the Mmes. Ford	the Mrs. Fords

Plurals With Apostrophes

The apostrophe is rarely used to form plurals. Specifically, to form plurals of lowercase letters and abbreviations, use an apostrophe plus *s*:

For some reason, the *t*'s and *f*'s on this printer are nearly illegible.

Our Receiving Department handles all *c.o.d.*'s for the plant.

For plurals of capital letters, an apostrophe is not required unless adding *s* alone could be confusing; for example, *As* instead of *A's, Is* instead of *I's,* and *Us* instead of *U's* could be confusing. Use an apostrophe, therefore, to form these plurals.

In addition, an apostrophe is *not* required to form plurals in phrases such as *ups and downs, temperature in the 90s,* and *dos and don'ts.*

Plurals With Special Changes

Anyone who speaks English has certainly noticed (and perhaps had difficulty with) such oddly formed plurals as the following:

Singular	Plural
man	men
woman	women
child	children
mouse	mice
goose	geese

Checkup 2

Correct any errors in the following sentences.

1. Evelyn asked us to send these packages to the Misses Smiths.
2. This stock is now selling at 15, but it is expected to reach the high 30's by the end of the year.
3. Because of her illness, she received two Is for her incomplete courses.
4. Yes, the Messrs. Martin are indeed acquiring a controlling interest in that company.
5. Wives and husbands of employees, as well as their childs, are invited to the company picnic.
6. Karen and Mike Spence manage our Lexington, Kentucky, office; the Spence's have recommended widening our channels of distribution.
7. Several of the mans and womans on the committee objected to the suggestion.
8. There are two Anthonies in our department—Anthony Jacobs and Anthony DiMartino.

DICTIONARY "MUSTS"

Despite the many thousands of words that form their plurals according to basic, simple rules, there are some words that require us to consult a dictionary. For example, plurals of words ending in *o*, *f*, and *fe* vary greatly. Study the following plurals carefully.

Plurals of Nouns Ending in O

Singular nouns ending in *o* preceded by a vowel form the plural by adding *s*. Some nouns ending in *o* preceded by a consonant form the plural by adding *s*; others, by adding *es*. Note the following examples.

Final *o* preceded by a vowel, adding *s* for the plural:

studio	studios
folio	folios
cameo	cameos
ratio	ratios

Final *o* preceded by a consonant, adding *s* for the plural:

dynamo	dynamos
zero	zeros
tobacco	tobaccos
memento	mementos

Final *o* preceded by a consonant, adding *es* for the plural:

mosquito	mosquitoes
potato	potatoes
echo	echoes
hero	heroes
veto	vetoes
cargo	cargoes

Note that nouns that relate to music and art and end in *o* form their plurals by adding *s: piano, pianos; alto, altos; oratorio, oratorios; solo, solos;* and so on.

Plurals of Nouns Ending in F or Fe

Plurals of nouns ending in *f* or *fe* are formed in one of two ways: (1) by changing the *f* or *fe* to *v* and then adding *es;* or (2) by simply adding *s.*

Change *f* or *fe* to *v*, then add *es:*

shelf	shelves
life	lives
wife	wives
half	halves
self	selves
knife	knives

Simply add *s:*

plaintiff	plaintiffs
roof	roofs
belief	beliefs
proof	proofs
safe	safes
chief	chiefs

Checkup 3

On a separate sheet of paper, write the correct plural forms of the following nouns.

1. tomato, motto
2. domino, lasso
3. leaf, thief
4. loaf, albino
5. strife, gulf

6. bailiff, handkerchief
7. volcano, concerto
8. radio, trio

Plurals of Foreign Nouns

The plurals of foreign nouns are another category of dictionary "musts." As you will see in the following list, these plurals of words of foreign origin are not formed according to our ordinary English rules.

Singular	Plural
addendum	addenda
alumna	alumnae
alumnus	alumni
analysis	analyses
axis	axes
basis	bases
crisis	crises
criterion	criteria
datum	data
hypothesis	hypotheses
oasis	oases
stimulus	stimuli

In addition to the above, some words of foreign origin have *two* plural forms—the "original" plural form (similar to the ones shown above) and an English plural form (a plural formed by treating the singular as if it were an English word).

Singular	Foreign Plural	English Plural
curriculum	curricula	curriculums
formula	formulae	formulas
index	indices	indexes
medium	media	mediums
memorandum	memoranda	memorandums
nucleus	nuclei	nucleuses
stadium	stadia	stadiums
vertebra	vertebrae	vertebras

Troublesome Forms

The following nouns are *always singular*. Use a singular verb to agree with them.

statistics (science)	molasses
mathematics	civics
economics (science)	news
genetics	aeronautics
aerobics	physics

The following nouns are *always plural*. Use a plural verb to agree with them.

statistics (facts)	scales (for weighing)
credentials	belongings
auspices	trousers
proceeds	winnings
premises	scissors
tidings	thanks
jeans	pants
tweezers	antics
riches	tongs
goods	

The following nouns have only one form, which may be used either as a singular or a plural, depending on the meaning intended.

Chinese	Japanese
deer	sheep
politics	salmon
moose	wheat
odds	vermin
cod	corps

When modified by another number, the following nouns usually have the same form to denote either a singular or a plural number.

three *thousand* forms	four *score* years
five *hundred* applicants	two *dozen* seniors

Checkup 4

On a separate sheet, write the correction for any error in the following sentences.

1. All three economists suggested the same stimuluses to help the American steel industry.
2. The passenger's belongings was brought to the front desk.
3. The proceeds from our raffle were given to a worthwhile charity.
4. Many of the alumni are planning to attend the special celebration honoring Professor Inez Mendoza.
5. Byron always says that genetics are his favorite subject.
6. By Monday we had already received nearly two hundreds orders for this new product.
7. Enclose all cross references in parenthesis.
8. The Denton Corporation has experienced several financial crisis in the past three years, some of them quite serious.

COMMUNICATION PROJECTS

Practical Application

A.   Correct any errors in the following sentences. Write *OK* if a sentence has no error.

1. Are there any recent news about the negotiations?
2. At the back of this book are two main indices—an alphabetical index and a chronological index.
3. We have, of course, already notified the Mrs. Wallaces of the change in plans.
4. Because the goods that the shipper delivered was damaged, we returned the entire shipment to the manufacturer.
5. The cost of the new facilitys is expected to exceed $1 million.
6. Mrs. Newby has announced that her two daughter-in-laws will be partners in her new design studio.
7. The large knifes must, of course, be sharpened periodically to keep these machines performing properly.
8. Among the several hundreds competitors in this industry, none has had greater success than Peterson Plastics Inc.
9. Henry and Donna Walsh obviously enjoy operating their business; nonetheless, the Walshs have indicated a willingness to sell.
10. The tax attornies with whom we spoke had different opinions regarding the status of our claims.
11. We tried to call Mr. Kelly several times, but none of the Kellies answered the telephone.
12. Nancy Petrov gives generously to various church's in this area.
13. Among the communitys actively protesting the legislation is Westbrook.
14. Since 1982 the Marxes have owned a controlling interest in Data Electronics.
15. The foundation commissioned three concertoes for the centennial celebration.
16. Perhaps 25 CPA's have already applied for the position that we advertised just this morning.
17. As you probably know, Burke Equipment is the largest distributor of radioes and televisions on the East Coast.
18. These premises are carefully guarded by security officers.
19. Each district manager is responsible for his or her sales representatives and their territorys.
20. Mr. Harmin said that the old benchs in the cafeteria will be replaced with comfortable chairs.

B.   Correct any errors in the following sentences. Write *OK* for any sentence that has no error. (Note: In Sections 12 through 31, Practical Application B reviews some of the principles presented in earlier sections.)

1. On Ed's desk is the January and February sales sheets that you wanted.
2. We have already spoke with Mr. Johanson about the delays from Ford Chemicals.

3. George been exceptionally busy for the past few weeks, hasn't he?
4. The market price of our corporate bonds has risen almost 15 percent in only three weeks.
5. Of course, I wish that I was able to attend, but I will be in Europe for the entire month of August.
6. As you know, winnings of any kind is taxable, according to IRS regulations.
7. In the conference room was Jeffrey, Mark, and Harriet.
8. A prototype was lain on the table for all of us to inspect.
9. Several woman applied for the transfer.
10. Mrs. Wembley suggested that we sit the projector on the shelf at the back of the room.
11. Ms. Simpson has already paid for all the proofs that we received.
12. That carton has been laying there for two weeks.
13. When the water level raises to this point, the pump automatically goes on.
14. The thermostat is generally set in the low 60's.
15. Most of the 28-millimeter lens's will be on sale Friday and Saturday.

Editing Practice

As a Matter of Fact . . . . In addition to checking for spelling and grammatical errors, writers and typists must also check for inconsistencies and contradictions of facts within copy. Read the following statements to find any inconsistencies. Write *OK* if a statement has no error.

1. Because the Acme Equipment Corporation has such a fine reputation for quality merchandise and excellent service, we recommend Ace Equipment when you are buying machinery.
2. Your total cost will be $100 less a 20 percent discount plus, of course, a sales tax of 5 percent. Thus we will send you an invoice for $94.
3. When Mrs. Reisling pointed out that we had overcharged her, we apologized for the error and told Mr. Reisling we would correct her next statement.
4. Ms. Anne Loomis is the supervisor of Customer Relations. We suggest that you call Anna to discuss this problem with her.
5. Although we are out of stock of model A199-2035, we have plenty of model A199-2035 in stock.

Homonyms, Anyone? Correct any errors in the use of homonyms in the following excerpt.

During our long negotiation with the manufacturer, it's representative excepted our original offer, which we knew was a fare settlement

Case Problem

Time Management. Carla Munoz is a tireless worker: she always arrives early, she never abuses her lunch hour privileges, and she often works late to complete her assignments. Moreover, Carla is well liked and well respected in her department.

At an annual employee-appraisal conference, her supervisor tells Carla that despite all her long hours, Carla barely completes as much work as each of the other members of her department. When her supervisor suggests that Carla attend a three-day time-management seminar that the company is sponsoring, Carla is offended.

1. Is Carla justified?
2. What should Carla do?

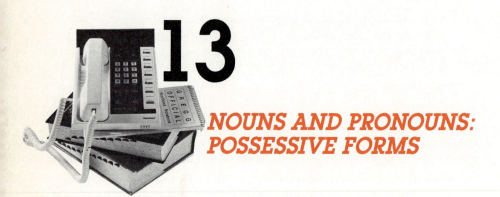

13

NOUNS AND PRONOUNS: POSSESSIVE FORMS

Errors in using possessive forms are among the most common—and the most noticeable—errors made in writing. As you'll see, the error often lies in the use of the apostrophe. Fortunately, there are some very easy ways to master the correct uses of possessive nouns and pronouns. Study this section to ensure that you do.

POSSESSIVE FORMS OF NOUNS

To begin, remember this rule: An apostrophe is *always* used with a noun to show possession. Now let's see some of the specifics of using the apostrophe with nouns.

1. For a noun that does not end in *s*, add an apostrophe plus *s*. This rule applies to *all* nouns, whether they are singular or plural.

    The *man's* briefcase and the *woman's* report were in the conference room.

The *men's* lounge is on this floor; the *women's* lounge is on the top floor.

2. For a plural noun that does end in *s,* add only the apostrophe.

The *managers'* meeting has been rescheduled.

Approximately two *months'* time has been estimated for the entire job.

The *Fords'* newest store is in New Brunswick.

3. a. For a singular noun ending in *s,* add an apostrophe plus *s* if the possessive form is pronounced with an added syllable.

One *witness's* comment was especially effective.

My *boss's* recommendation was obviously helpful.

b. For a singular noun ending in *s,* add only the apostrophe if the possessive form is not pronounced with an additional syllable. Note that this applies mostly to proper names that would sound awkward with the extra syllable.

Jane *Hastings'* promotion will be announced on July 15. (The pronunciation of *Hastings's* would sound awkward.)

MEMORY HOOK	Remember that the possessive word always comes before the object of possession.

the *man's* briefcase (the briefcase of the man, the briefcase belonging to the man)

the *woman's* report (the report of the woman, the report belonging to the woman)

the *Fords'* newest store (the newest store of the Fords)

the *managers'* meeting (the meeting of the managers)

one *witness's* comment (the comment of one witness)

By separating the ownership words from the objects of ownership, you will more easily be able to apply the rules above.

Checkup 1

Correct any errors in the use of possessives in the following sentences. Write your corrections on a separate sheet of paper.

1. John Kileys' investments have risen drastically in the last two months.

2. One actress's personal account of this situation will appear in next Sunday's newspaper.
3. Mr. Gilmore's goal is to operate his fathers business.
4. Helen's latest book discusses womens nutritional needs, and she expects it to become a best-seller.
5. All the applicants résumés are in the file folder on your desk, Ms. Columbo.
6. No, we do not purchase our company cars; all our representatives vehicles are leased.
7. One mans comment was especially negative toward our change in policy.
8. All our supervisor's reservations have been made for them by our Travel Department.

POSSESSIVE FORMS IN SPECIAL CASES

Besides the basic rules of forming the possessives of nouns, there are a few special cases that need your attention. Study the following four discussions.

Compound Nouns

To form the possessive of a compound noun, make the *last word* in the compound possessive. If the last word ends in *s*, add an apostrophe; if the last word in the compound does *not* end in *s*, add an apostrophe plus *s*.

My *brother-in-law's* bid was accepted by the City Planning Department. (Bid belonging to my brother-in-law. *Law* does not end in *s*.)

Henry did not win first prize; *someone else's* entry won highest honors. (The entry belonging to someone else. *Else* does not end in *s*.)

Several *vice presidents'* assistants participated in and contributed to the committee session. (Assistants of several vice presidents. The last word, *presidents*, does end in *s*.)

Joint Ownership? Separate Ownership?

To show joint ownership, add the apostrophe (or the apostrophe plus *s*) to the last part of the compound.

Brandon and Marvin's mother is the one who started this business in 1985. (The mother of Brandon and Marvin. Note the singular noun *mother* and the singular verb *is*.)

Isaac and Virginia's studio is located in Newark. (Studio belonging to Isaac and Virginia.)

To indicate *separate ownership,* add the apostrophe (or the apostrophe plus *s*) to *each* part of the compound.

Brandon's and Marvin's mothers are the ones who started this business in 1985. (Here, we are talking about two different people—in other words, Brandon's mother and Marvin's mother.)

Isaac's and Virginia's studios are located in Newark. (Isaac's studio and Virginia's studio—two studios, each separately owned.)

Before a Gerund

A *gerund* is a verb form that ends in *ing* and is used as a noun. A noun or pronoun used before a gerund must be in the possessive case.

Henry's proofreading was very helpful to us in meeting our schedule. *His* proofreading was very helpful to us. (Possessive *Henry's* or *His*, not *Henry* or *Him*, before the gerund *proofreading*.)

We were unaware of *Wendy's* leaving early. We were unaware of *her* leaving early. (The possessives *Wendy's* and *her* are needed before the gerund *leaving*.)

In Appositives

An *appositive* is a word or a group of words that explains or gives additional information about the word or phrase that comes before the appositive. When a noun that would ordinarily be in the possessive case is followed by an appositive, note that the appositive must then be in the possessive case.

Ms. Kulp, our *supervisor's*, office is on the fifth floor. (Note that *supervisor*, not *Kulp*, is made possessive.)

Checkup 2

Correct any errors in the use of possessives in the following sentences. Write *OK* if a sentence has no error.

1. Don and Sylvia's oldest daughter begins graduate school next semester.
2. Revising the agenda was someone else idea, not Adrian's.
3. As you know, the two vice president's reports are strictly confidential.
4. John was glad to hear about us working overtime to complete the project on schedule.
5. Lou and Anne were engaged last month; Lou's and Anne's wedding is now planned for November 11.
6. Alma and I said that him helping us was instrumental in meeting the deadline.
7. We surely appreciated Alan sending us the check early.
8. Yes, Ella and Bert's jobs are very similar.

POSSESSIVE FORMS OF PERSONAL PRONOUNS

You have seen that possessive forms of nouns *always* have apostrophes. In the following chart, notice that possessive forms of personal pronouns *never* have apostrophes.

Nominative Forms	Possessive Forms	
I	my	mine
you	your	yours
he	his	his
she	her	hers
it	its	its
we	our	ours
you	your	yours
they	their	theirs

Now study the following examples to see the correct uses of these pronoun forms.

Nina asked *her* assistant to redo the report.

The first recommendation is *ours*; the second one is *theirs*.

Please lend me *your* calculator; *mine* is at home.

Note that none of the above personal possessive pronouns has an apostrophe.

POSSESSIVE PRONOUNS IN SPECIAL CASES

The possessive forms discussed above are, unfortunately, easily confused with other similar words, which are compared below.

Its, It's

The possessive pronoun *its* means "belonging to it" or "of it." *Its* is easily confused with the contraction *it's,* which means "it is" (note the apostrophe in *it's*). Only use *it's* when you mean "it is."

This letter-quality printer is expensive and slower, but *its* legibility is superb. (Possessive pronoun *its*.)

Naturally, *it's* exciting to know that the product is so successful. (*It is* exciting . . . .)

Their, There, They're

These three words are indeed pronounced alike. But *their* is the possessive pronoun meaning "belonging to them," and *there* (notice the word *here*) identifies a place. *They're,* obviously, is a contraction; it means "they are."

Ella and Mark said that *they're* eager to begin *their* seminar. (*They are* eager . . . seminar "belonging to them.")

If we leave at 9 a.m., we should arrive *there* before 10. (*There* is an adverb that identifies a place; it answers the question *Where? There.*)

Theirs, There's

The pronoun *theirs* and the contraction *there's* are pronounced the same, but it is easy to recognize quickly that *there's* means "there is" or "there has." *Theirs* means "belonging to them."

The first seat is reserved for Jennifer; these three seats are *theirs*. (Seats "belonging to them.")

There's the diskette we've been looking for! (*There is* the diskette . . . .)

Your, You're

The possessive pronoun *your* means "belonging to you," and the contraction *you're* means "you are."

Leave *your* materials on the desk if *you're* coming back later. (Materials "belonging to you." If *you are* coming back.)

Our, Are

Actually, *our* and *are* should *not* sound alike when they are pronounced correctly. However, some people do pronounce *our* as if it were *are*. Thus the error here is more common in speaking than in writing.

Our plant manager and *our* marketing director *are* planning a special tour for new employees.

Whose, Who's

The possessive pronoun *whose* should not be confused with the contraction *who's*, which means "who is" or "who has."

Do you know *whose* diskette this is? (Diskette "belonging to whom?")

Do you know *who's* in charge of ordering new equipment? (*Who is* in charge . . . .)

Checkup 3

Correct any errors in the following sentences. Write *OK* if a sentence has no error.

1. Whose at the factory this morning, Jerry or Daniel?
2. As Mr. Belov clearly explained, theirs only one problem involved: money.
3. Most of us prefer the orange package because its so much brighter than the other choices.
4. The table near the door is ours; the table near the window is there's.
5. We will distribute the agenda when we know whose planning to speak at the conference.

6. Mr. Sean McGeough and his assistant Timothy will be they're when the convention begins.

7. Although it takes extra effort, of course its certainly worthwhile to request three estimates for such large expenditures.

8. Whenever you're ready to discuss these budgets, please call me.

COMMUNICATION PROJECTS

Practical Application

on test

A. Correct any errors in the following sentences. Write *OK* for any sentence that has no error. *(singular)*

1. Each account executives' suggestion was discussed in great detail.

OK 2. Are you aware that they're both CPAs? *Contraction need*

3. Irene Ellison, whose an excellent copywriter, has developed award-winning brochures for our products.

4. Needless to say, all of us agreed that the womans' original complaint was completely justified. *singular*

5. Although the Bass's have only owned this property since 1985, Bob and Donna Bass have decided to sell. *(need plural — not possess)*

6. Ms. Ford's and Mr. Wilson's boutique is one of the largest in the state.

7. Let me know, please, whether your more interested in receiving monthly income or long-term capital gains.

8. Does Ms. VanCamp know about him offering to complete this project on a free-lance basis?

9. After we compared them carefully, we realized that theirs very little difference between the two models.

10. One of the most profitable departments in our New York store is the childrens' department.

11. Denise's and Margaret's boss's are both veterans.

12. Frankly, we're not sure that its possible to sell these products so cheaply and still make a profit.

OK 13. When Ellen and I heard about the two weeks' delay in the schedule, we were not at all surprised.

14. Most of the members were in complete agreement with him *his* rejecting the union's demands.

15. Despite the fact that the equipment is obviously very expensive, you must realize that it's long-term efficiency offsets it's high initial cost. *possessive needed*

B. Correct any errors in the following sentences. Write *OK* if a sentence has no error.

1. Between you and me, the suggestion that I thought best was your's. *possessive*

2. Everyone who saw her résumé agreed that Ms. Kaplan's credentials ~~is~~ are certainly impressive.
3. Jane ordered about two dozens more pamphlets for our department.
4. To help us compete more effectively, the president ordered that all our list prices be froze immediately.
5. Sandra West and Dorothy West are not related to each other; the West's are always among our top sales representatives in the country.

OK 6. To celebrate their always superior sales, we are giving the Mses. West a special award this year.

OK 7. The actress's role was demanding—very demanding.
8. Yes, he ~~has~~ been our supervisor for more than five years. *Past part, needs helper*
9. Carl retyping the report helped us save a great deal of time.
10. Him retyping the report helped us save a great deal of time.
11. As you might imagine, there are five John Smith's in my company! *needs plural, not possessive*
12. A well-known manufacturer of girl's clothing, Ames and Lowison, is planning to merge with DeWitt Fabrics.
13. All of us are confident that we will complete the entire project in less than four weeks' time. *plural*
14. Leroy ~~seen~~ saw Ms. Wooten this morning at the production meeting. *no helper*
15. I was surprised to find so many messages ~~laying~~ lying on my desk when I returned from lunch.
16. Please check in someone else's office for a blank diskette.
17. We must revise the schedule at tomorrow's status meeting.
18. After the alarm had ~~rang~~ rung, we went to the fire exit. *need past participle*
19. Mario had already ~~went~~ gone to the train station when we called him. *need past participle Verb when helper is present*
20. We studied all the analysis that our regional managers submitted, and most of them were quite helpful. *plural*

Editing Practice

Spelling Alert! Check the following excerpt for spelling errors. How many can you find?

As we explained, we are intrested in learning more about government securitys. According to the materiel we recieved from our broker, a minimum investment of $5000 is requirred. The yield on primary issues is currently aproximately 13.5 percent.

Call an Editor! Read the following excerpt. Then make any corrections necessary.

Marla and I had spoke with Dr. Merriam about training for our word processing operators before Dr. Merriam joined our company. Dr. Merriam and her husband are noted experts in information processing and have wrote many articles on this topic. Copys of some of there articles are enclosed.

Case Problem

The Team Spirit. At 4:30 p.m., Doug Custer gives Janice Taylor a report to type. Doug tells Janice that he will need the report for a meeting with a client at 9:30 the next morning. Janice estimates the report will take about twenty minutes to complete, but she decides to begin typing it when she arrives at 9:00 the next morning.

Although Janice always arrives promptly at 9 a.m., the next morning her train is delayed and she arrives at 9:20—just about the time Doug's client arrives.

1. Is Doug justified in telling Janice that he is disappointed that the report wasn't available?
2. Is Janice justified in saying that it wasn't her fault—after all, how could she know that her train would be late?
3. How could this possibly have been avoided?

14

PRONOUNS: NOMINATIVE AND OBJECTIVE FORMS

When asked to identify the most important skills they seek in job applicants, most business executives list communication skills at the very top of the list. Indeed, when speaking or writing, business workers are communicating their abilities to do their jobs well. To convince *your* coworkers of your ability to communicate well, you must be sure to master the ways in which nominative and objective pronouns are formed—the topic discussed in this section.

CASE FORMS

In the last section, you studied the possessive forms of pronouns. In this section, you will concentrate on the other two case forms of pronouns—the nominative and the objective forms.

Nominative Form	Objective Form
I	me
you	you
he	him
she	her
it	it
we	us
you	you
they	them
who	whom

NOMINATIVE PRONOUNS

Learn these two rules for using nominative pronouns correctly.

Subject of a Verb

When a pronoun is the subject of a verb, the pronoun must be in the nominative case.

I have reviewed the agenda carefully. ("*I* have reviewed," not "*me* have reviewed.")

She and Mr. Scott will speak at the banquet. (*She*, not *her*.)

Who is the supervisor of data processing? (*Who*, a nominative pronoun, is the subject of the verb *is*.)

Complement of a "Being" Verb

As you know, the "being" verbs are *am, is, are, was,* and *were* and *be, being,* and *been* with helping verbs. A pronoun that completes the meaning of a being verb must be in the nominative case.

Perhaps it was (they? them?) who sent us this software. (*Was* is a being verb, and the pronoun that follows it complements the being verb. Therefore, the pronoun must be the nominative *they*.)

It must have been (he? him?) in the car. (The nominative *he* is correct after the being verb *must have been*.)

Exception: For only one being verb, the infinitive *to be,* do not use the nominative case pronoun when *to be* is preceded immediately by a noun or a pronoun.

The customers appeared to be (they? them?). (Is there a noun or a pronoun immediately before the infinitive *to be*? No, there isn't. Therefore, choose the nominative form *they*. The "exception" rule does not apply.)

When she first answered the telephone, Eunice thought Robert to be (I? me?). (Is there a noun or a pronoun immediately before the infinitive *to be*? Yes, *Robert*. Therefore, do not use the nominative case—the answer is *me*. The exception rule does apply.)

<table>
<tr><td>MEMORY HOOK</td><td>To remember the exception rule about the infinitive *to be*, make this connection:</td></tr>
</table>

No subject—*No*minative case

Use the *no* in the word *nominative* to remind you to choose the nominative pronoun when there is *no* subject before *to be*.

Checkup 1

Correct any errors in the use of pronouns in the following sentences. Write *OK* if a sentence has no error.

1. When she heard Clark's voice, Ms. Reynolds thought him to be I.
2. When a caller asks for you by name, you should reply, "This is she."
3. Sam, if you were me, would you send this suggestion to the committee?
4. All of us agree that the winner should be she.
5. Some drivers had suggested that the union delegate should be him.
6. The professional model appears to be he.
7. If I were her, I would review that report very, very carefully.
8. I am convinced that it must be he who is accidentally erasing these tapes.

OBJECTIVE PRONOUNS

Use the objective-case forms *me, us, him, her, them,* and *whom* when they are objects of verbs, prepositions, or infinitives.

Mr. Nelson promoted *her* in July. (*Her* is the object of the verb *promoted*.)

We had already given a copy to *him*, so we bought an extra copy for *her*. (*Him* and *her* are objects of the prepositions *to* and *for*, respectively.)

For *whom* did Elvera order this special printer paper? (*Whom* is the object of the preposition *for*.)

Ms. Weingarten plans to transfer *him* next month. (*Him* is the object of the infinitive *to transfer*.)

Use the objective-case forms for subjects of infinitives:

> Jane wants *him* to travel to Utah in June or July. (*Him* is the subject of the infinitive *to travel*.)

In addition, of course, as you learned in the exception rule on page 117, use the objective-case pronoun following the infinitive *to be* whenever *to be* has a noun or a pronoun immediately before it.

> When she first answered the telephone, Eunice thought Robert to be *me*. (The noun *Robert* precedes the infinitive *to be*; the objective *me* is correct.)

SPECIAL PROBLEMS

In three situations, selecting the correct case form may be confusing. But the following discussion will help you in such situations.

Kevin and I? Kevin and Me?

Compound subjects or compound objects are nouns and pronouns joined by *and* or *or*. When the pronoun is part of a subject, use the nominative case. When the pronoun is part of an object, use the objective case.

Nominative in Subjects	Objective in Objects
Kevin and *I* want . . .	. . . for Kevin and *me*
Ms. Royce or *he* has . . .	. . . asked Ms. Royce and *him*
She and *I* will go . . .	. . . written by *her* and *me*
They and *we* agree . . .	. . . between *them* and *us*

MEMORY HOOK

To simplify choosing the right pronoun in compounds, omit everything in the compound except the pronoun. Then say the sentence aloud, and the correct answer will be obvious.

> Ms. Sinclair and (I? me?) leave for Hong Kong on Monday. (When you omit the words *Ms. Sinclair and*, the answer becomes clear: "*I* leave . . . ," not "*me* leave.")

> Sheila sent carbon copies to Mr. Polski and (I? me?). (Again, omit the words *Mr. Polski and*, and the answer becomes obvious: "sent copies to . . . *me*.")

We Supervisors? Us Supervisors?

When faced with pronoun choice in phrases such as *we supervisors* and *us supervisors*, simply omit the noun following the pronoun and test the sentence with the pronoun choices.

(We? Us?) supervisors met with the union delegates to discuss the issues in detail. (Omit the word *supervisors*, then say "*We* met with . . . " and "*Us* met with . . . " Which pronoun would you choose? The nominative *we*, of course!)

Than I? Than Me?

Another similar pronoun problem arises in sentences such as "Sheila has more vacation time than (I? me?)," and "This problem affects Jason as much as (I? me?)." When the word *than* or *as* is used in such comparisons, it generally represents an incomplete clause. By completing the clause, you will make your choice easy.

Sheila has more vacation time than I (have vacation time). (By completing the clause, you make it obvious that the clause is "*I* have vacation time," not "*me* have . . . ")

This problem affects Jason as much as (this problem affects) me. (The missing words are *this problem affects*, which are deliberately omitted because they are repetitive and because the sentence makes perfect sense without them. But only by completing the clause will you easily be able to make the correct pronoun choice.)

Checkup 2

Correct any errors in the use of pronouns. Write *OK* for any sentence that is correct.

1. The forms were sent to only we three managers.
2. The procedure is to ask Dr. Humphreys or I to approve the expense.
3. The majority of the committee members voted for Helen and he.
4. Do you agree that most of the speakers were not as well prepared as her?
5. Peter is surely a more effective sales representative than me.
6. When she asked we employees our opinions of the new benefits package, we listed the specific changes that we preferred.
7. As you can see, Paul types much more quickly and accurately than I.
8. Only Marsha duPont or him has the authority to approve cash advances over $500.
9. He quickly learned that none of we accountants wants to adopt the confusing new procedures.
10. Between you and me, I know that Catherine O'Malley will be selected regional manager when Mr. Seeley retires.

COMMUNICATION PROJECTS

Practical Application

A. Correct any errors in the following sentences. Write *OK* for any sentence that has no error.

1. Both of us thought the women on the dais to be Gloria and her.
2. We were delighted when Jessica said, "I invited Danielle and he to our conference next April."
3. Apparently, her and Barry have already discussed their bid for this project.
4. Georgianne and Marvin are both CPAs, but Georgianne is definitely more experienced than he.
5. Yesterday the president of our company congratulated we district managers for exceeding our cumulative budgets by more than 35 percent.
6. Last Monday, Larry and me were out of town when the plant inspectors arrived.
7. As we explained, either Mr. Melendez or her will distribute brochures to everyone in the Personnel Department.
8. Yes, please change the hotel reservation for Louis and I.
9. Perhaps it was her in the auditorium yesterday afternoon.
10. When I looked quickly into the conference room, I mistakenly thought your manager to be he.
11. After we interviewed them, Kate and I agreed that Leon shows greater potential than her.
12. Frank, was it Eugene who prepared this annual inventory, or was it her?
13. Either Loren or he scheduled we sales managers for an all-day meeting with Ms. Mancuso next Wednesday.
14. I am not sure, but I think that the vice president of manufacturing is her.
15. We firmly believe that Edna and Hilda are more productive than they.

B. Correct any errors in the following sentences. Write *OK* for any sentence that has no error.

1. When we discovered the wallet, we immediately asked Ms. Elblonk if it was her's.
2. Please check the directory to see whether the Walsh's are still in New Mexico.
3. The blueprints you are looking for are laying on the table in Ms. Walczak's office.
4. Our vice president is planning to take Deborah and I with her on her trip to our Seattle office.

5. Both of Mr. Palmers contracts have been approved, duplicated, and returned to the Legal Department.
6. When there prepared to revise the budget estimates, we will meet to review the figures.
7. If I were she, I would ask Professor Morrison for her approval before beginning her writing.
8. All the proofs that the photographer submitted were black-and-white photoes.
9. Of course, we requested Martin to double-check the Ellises' credit rating before we ship the merchandise to them.
10. There is no question about it: Sherry can handle the project as well as her.
11. Alan had already spoke about the changes in the insurance policies when Helen arrived.
12. Leon been the plant manager in Cleveland for more than 15 years, and our Cleveland plant is our most productive one.
13. Needless to say, each employees' wife or husband is also covered under the terms of the new dental plan.
14. In the supply cabinet is the various sizes you will need.
15. Please try to find out who's contract is up for renewal on May 1.

Editing Practice

Plurals and Possessives. Correct any error in the use of plurals and possessives in the following sentences. Write *OK* if a sentence has no error.

1. The survey evaluated all the departments in each of our warehouses', and as a result, our's received the highest rating.
2. Their entire family—two brothers, their two brothers-in-law, and three nephew's—operate their trucking firm.
3. Our supervisors, as well as the managers to whom they report, agreed fully with the proposal's that we submitted.
4. Their is no doubt that this machinery is expensive, but its worth its price when you consider its effectiveness.
5. Yes, Lucy helping us complete the agenda on time is very much appreciated.
6. Ms. DeNoras assistant, Amy Blackwell, gave Ms. DeNora the analyses she wanted, didn't she?
7. Our employee's won several prizes, but the proceeds is to be donated to charity.
8. One sales representative suggested several stimuluses that could indeed spark business in some regions' that are not doing well.
9. Although we rejected Jayco's offer, of course, we considered it's bid carefully.

10. In our opinion, theirs a distinct possibility that both company's will merge in the near future.

Proofreading Business Documents. The person who keyboarded the following excerpt from a memo didn't proofread the work. Can you find any errors?

In reviewing the insurence policy, we noted that the comissions paid to StateWide are allmost 12 percent higher then last years'. In adition, the proceedures for submitting claims are exceptionally complicated. For these and other reasons, we recomend that we meet with our StateWide agent imediately.

Case Problem

Supervising Others. When Betty Van Der Keller was interviewed for the position of supervisor of the word processing department for her company, she was asked to share her feelings about productive supervision techniques. Betty quickly replied that it is simply a matter of telling employees precisely what is expected of them and pushing them to meet their production goals at all costs.

1. What do you think of Betty's philosophy of supervising others?
2. Do you think that her comments had any effect on the fact that she did *not* get the job?

PRONOUNS: SPECIAL USAGE

This section will complete your mastery of the uses of *who* and *whom*, which were introduced in the preceding unit. In addition, this section will cover the *self*-ending pronouns and some other special usage problems.

WHO *AND* WHOM; WHOEVER *AND* WHOMEVER

The pronouns *who* and *whoever* are nominative forms, and the pronouns *whom* and *whomever* are objective forms. As you have already learned, use the nominative forms as subjects of verbs and as complements of "being" verbs. Use *whom* and *whomever* as you would use other objective forms—that is, as objects of verbs and objects of prepositions.

MEMORY HOOK

You know that *him* is an objective form. Let the *m* in *him* remind you of the *m* in *whom* and in *whomever*, which are also objective forms. In addition, substitute *him* to test whether an objective form is correct.

The consultant (who? whom?) Ms. Naldi recommended is Jay Haggerty. (Make this substitution: "Ms. Naldi recommended *(him)*." Because the objective form *him* is correct, the choice must be *whom*.)

Bertha doesn't know (who? whom?) the committee has selected. (Make the substitution: "the committee has selected *(him)*." The correct choice, therefore, is *whom*.)

We do not know (who? whom?) Mark Trent is. (Make the substitution: "Mark Trent is *(he)*." Because the nominative *he* can be substituted, the correct answer is *who*.)

In Interrogative Sentences

Questions are generally in inverted order. This means the subject comes after the verb. Therefore, change the sentence to normal order before substituting *he* or *him*.

(Who? Whom?) is the consultant Jay Haggerty recommended? (Normal order: "The consultant Jay Haggerty recommended is *(he)*." *Who* is correct because it complements the being verb *is*.)

(Who? Whom?) has the committee selected? (Normal order: "The committee has selected *(him)*." *Whom* is correct because *him* can be substituted.)

Of course, if the question is in normal order, simply substitute *he* or *him*.

In Clauses

When *who* or *whom* (or *whoever* or *whomever*) is used in a clause within a sentence, you must first (1) separate that clause from the rest of the sentence, (2) check that the clause is in normal order, and (3) proceed to substitute *he* or *him*.

1. Separate the clause, which *always* begins with the word *who, whom, whoever,* or *whomever.*

   We are not certain (who? whom?) the employee could have been. (Separate the clause: "(who? whom?) the employee could have been.")

   Share this report with (whoever? whomever?) you worked with on the Klein account. (Separate the clause: "(whoever? whomever?) you worked with on the Klein account.")

2. Change the inverted clause to normal order.

   (who? whom?) the employee could have been (Normal order: "the employee could have been (who? whom?).")

   (whoever? whomever?) you worked with on the Klein account (Normal order: "you worked with (whoever? whomever?) on the Klein account.")

3. Substitute *he* or *him* in each clause.

   the employee could have been *(he)* (Remember that a nominative form must be used to complete a being verb; thus *he* and *who* are correct.)

   you worked with *(him)* on the Klein account (*Him* is correct; it is the object of the preposition *with*. Therefore, *whomever* is the correct choice.)

Note: Interrupters such as *I think, she says, you know,* and *we believe* should simply be omitted when selecting *who* or *whom* in clauses.

   The consultant (who? whom?) I believe we should hire is Alice Galworth. (Separate the clause: "(who? whom?) I believe we should hire." Omit the interrupting words *I believe* and put the clause in normal order: "we should hire *(him)*." *Whom* is correct because *him* can be substituted.)

Checkup 1

Select the correct pronoun in parentheses in each of the following sentences.

1. Perhaps the person (who? whom?) you saw during the press conference was Helene McDonald.
2. Kristen Fasano is one of the people (who? whom?) our supervisor praised for consistently superior work.
3. Eleanor is the copywriter (who? whom?) should be assigned to this campaign.

4. The Ethics Committee can fine (whoever? whomever?) does not observe the regulations.
5. Jim O'Leary, (who? whom?) we consider the best sales trainer in our company, will head up the new department.
6. Does Doris know (who? whom?) the keynote speaker will be?
7. (Whoever? Whomever?) wrote this procedures manual did an excellent job.
8. One of the clients (who? whom?) I met at our luncheon is Ms. Emily Woods.
9. Of course, you should assign this account to (whoever? whomever?) you think will do the most careful follow-up.
10. We asked Peter, (who? whom?) has much experience in tax matters, for his advice.

Now correct any errors in the following sentences.

11. The person who we recommended for the transfer is Gregory Lasky.
12. Do you know whom we should ask for an explanation of this software documentation?
13. Their former supervisor, whom I think now works for the Fields Corporation, established this step-by-step procedure.
14. Please be sure to give this project to whomever you think will be able to meet these tight deadlines.
15. No, I do not know whom Arlene asked for permission to cash this check.
16. Do you know whom I think the company will put in charge of our London office?
17. Do you know who is now in charge of our London office?
18. Who have they assigned to the procedures panel?
19. Please send a swatch to whomever asks for a sample.
20. Please send a swatch to whomever you want.

SELF-ENDING PRONOUNS

The *self*-ending pronouns (*myself, yourself, himself, herself, itself, ourselves, yourselves,* and *themselves*) serve two functions: (1) to emphasize or intensify the use of a noun or another pronoun or (2) to refer to a noun or pronoun that has already been named in a sentence (called "reflexive use").

Intensive Use

Note how *self*-ending pronouns provide emphasis in these statements:

Suzanne *herself* announced the merger. (Much more emphatic than "Suzanne announced the merger.")

We requested Jason *himself* to write the ad copy. (Much more emphatic than "We requested Jason to write the ad copy.")

Reflexive Use

Self-ending pronouns refer to a noun or a pronoun that has already been named elsewhere in the sentence.

The account executives paid *themselves* a compliment. (*Themselves* clearly refers to *account executives*.)

Angela distributed all the copies but forgot to keep one for *herself*. (*Herself* clearly refers to *Angela*.)

Common Errors

A *self*-ending pronoun must have a *clear* antecedent within the sentence. Furthermore, the *self*-ending pronoun must be positioned correctly in the sentence. Note these examples of common errors:

Gordon Moser and *myself* developed the brochure. (To whom does *myself* refer? It has no antecedent in this sentence. Instead, the sentence should be "Gordon Moser and *I* developed . . . .")

When we asked the painter for his advice, he said that he prefers spray painting *himself*. (Obviously, the man does not want to spray paint *himself*! Instead, the sentence should be " . . . he said that he *himself* prefers spray painting." The position of the *self*-ending pronoun must be correct.)

PRONOUNS IN APPOSITIVES

An *appositive* is a word or a group of words used to explain or give more information about a preceding word or phrase. Note the appositives in *italics* in the following sentences.

Julie Radnor, *the principal owner of the company*, issued a statement to the press this morning. Her attorney, *a well-known financial analyst*, commented on Ms. Radnor's statement afterward. (The appositives, the words in italics, help give additional information about "Julie Radnor" and "Her attorney," the words that precede the appositives.

A minor problem arises when choosing pronoun case in appositives such as these:

Two supporters of the proposition, Sidney Fierst and (she? her?), explained their reasons clearly.

We registered the bonds and delivered them to the co-owners, Paul Markham and (she? her?).

In such cases, follow the instructions of the following Memory Hook.

To choose pronouns in the preceding examples, (1) omit the words that the appositive renames, then (2) omit the other words in the compound—that is, *use only the pronoun.*

1. Omit the words that the appositive renames:

    . . . Sidney Fierst and (she? her?) explained their reasons clearly.

    We registered the bonds and delivered them to . . . Paul Markham and (she? her?).

2. Omit the other words in the compound—that is, use only the pronoun:

    . . . (she? her?) explained their reasons clearly. (You would not, of course, say "*her* explained." *She* is the correct pronoun.)

    We registered the bonds and delivered them to . . . (she? her?). (You would not say "delivered them to *she*." The correct pronoun is *her*.)

Checkup 2

Correct any errors in the following sentences. Write *OK* if a sentence has no error.

1. Please find out when our sales managers, Frances Ulster and he, will be leaving for the station.
2. When Elana and myself suggested the idea, we did not realize how time-consuming the project would be.
3. Ms. Frost specifically said that she wants to paint herself.
4. The best idea, I believe, is to assign the project to the most experienced designers, Caryl and she.
5. When they reviewed the estimates, they decided to cancel themselves.
6. Two of our vice presidents, Charles Barcellona and her, will be making a trip to the West Coast on May 15.
7. Among the assistants who contributed to the article were our two new trainees, Clara and he.
8. Be sure to check with our estimators, Andrew and she, to decide whether this price is reasonable.

COMMUNICATION PROJECTS

Practical Application

A. Correct any errors in the following sentences.

1. Only three of us (Ellis, Pat, and me) volunteered to work overtime.

2. If the market price is right, Ralph and myself will definitely sell these securities.
3. Anyone whom presents a discount coupon on Saturdays will receive a gift.
4. You should, of course, invite your managers, Gail and he, to the conference.
5. Donald, Jeanne, and myself will coordinate all the meetings and presentations at the sessions on Monday and Tuesday.
6. Whom in your opinion is the most likely winner of the sales contest?
7. The new editors of the company magazine are Michael and she.
8. Who does Mr. Lippert want us to invite to the grand opening of our Ford Mall store?
9. Ask whomever you think will be the most interesting speaker to open the first session.
10. Whom did you say he is?
11. Either of my partners, Lurene or he, will lend you the equipment while I am out of town.
12. The two candidates for regional manager, Norman and her, will meet with our president this evening.
13. Whomever claimed that this catalog is up to date was certainly wrong.
14. Where are the applicants, Christina and him?
15. Carlotta is the only one in the office whom I believe has the combination to this safe.

B.   Correct any errors in the following sentences. Write *OK* if a sentence has no error.

1. Yesterday Ms. Margolis invited Janet and I to the Washington, D.C., meetings.
2. The attorney who you met at the union meeting is Vanessa Fernandez.
3. Ask Bill if he knows whose responsible for accounts receivable.
4. According to the procedures manual, we must get written approvals from both Mrs. Reynaldo and he.
5. Two assistant district attorneys, Lee Kimoto and he, discussed the case with our attorneys this morning.
6. Murray was asked to join Ms. Weintraub and I when we meet with our clients.
7. Alger Morrison, whom I am sure is a registered agent, will be able to help you with this.
8. Sam, if I were you, I would surely join the company's pension plan and begin making voluntary contributions.
9. The survey clearly showed that our sales representative's consider themselves grossly underpaid.
10. Between Bruce and I, we were able to complete all the invoices before the end of the day.

11. If the personnel manager had asked we engineers, we would have gladly shared our opinions with her.
12. Is Giselle the person whom you think is in charge of purchasing requisitions?
13. Is Giselle the person to whom you sent these requisitions?
14. Neither Brandon nor I have worked on this magazine as long as her.
15. One of the new programmers, Evelyn or him, is to be assigned to this software.
16. Apparently, he been one of the top producers for many, many years.
17. Have you already spoke with Stephen and her?
18. Roland and Edmund's wives are now opening their own businesses.
19. These contracts should not be left lying here on the receptionist's desk.
20. Maurice and I had forgot about the need to get prior approval for such purchases.

Editing Practice

Plurals and Possessives. Correct any error in the use of plurals and possessives in the following sentences. Write *OK* for any sentence that has no error.

1. As soon as your ready to begin reviewing the contracts and estimates, just call us.
2. When we designed these playrooms, the childrens' safety and comfort were our main objectives.
3. Both companys, according to reports, are eager for the merger to be approved.
4. I believe that there ready now to meet with us to discuss the price increases.
5. All of us appreciated him advising us on these financial matters.
6. On July 15 Harry will be eligible for one weeks' vacation.
7. Its obvious, in our opinion, that the advertising budgets are simply too high.
8. All these diskettes are ours; that box of diskettes is their's.
9. One of the editor in chiefs, Barbara McCloskey, convinced the publisher to release the article.
10. The Bradies may indeed be coming, but Mr. Brady hasn't responded to his invitation yet.

Using Your Word Processor. You keyboarded the following on your word processor yesterday but did not proofread it. Please do so now.

Pleas review the enclosed cost estamate for the equipmant we are planning to purchase in Febraury. As you will see, the contract for maintenence is $500 a year, and instalation alone will cost nearly $2000. Let's review this financail data carefully before we proceed.

Case Problem

Improving Business Skills. A company memorandum states that your firm is planning several training seminars for employees who are interested in improving their skills. Among the topics covered in the seminars will be proofreading skills, telephone techniques, and on-the-job interpersonal relations. Your supervisor's approval is required.

1. Could any of these training sessions be helpful to you? If so, which ones?
2. Why, in your opinion, do companies spend the money—and give employees time—for such courses?

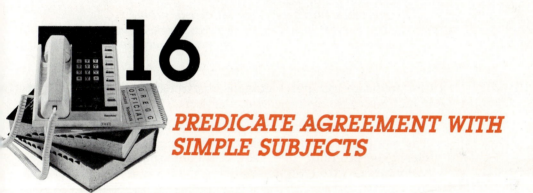

16

PREDICATE AGREEMENT WITH SIMPLE SUBJECTS

Popular songs, television shows, and movies do little to avoid errors such as "he don't" and "I been." As a result, listeners and viewers hear such errors over and over so often that they may start to believe that "he don't" and "I been" are grammatically correct.

Well, they are *not!* Pay special attention to the agreement rules to make sure that you *do* avoid such errors in your speaking and writing.

BASIC AGREEMENT RULE

This is the basic rule of agreement for all sentences: *A predicate must agree with its simple subject in number and in person.* A predicate always includes a verb, of course, and that verb must agree with its subject. In addition, if the predicate includes any pronouns that refer to the simple subject, those pronouns must also agree with the simple subject.

Agreement of Subject and Verb

Note how verbs agree with their subjects in the following sentences.

Mr. Singleton *wants* to review the manual. (The verb *wants* agrees with the subject, *Mr. Singleton*—both are singular.)

Mr. Singleton, our vice president, *wants* to review the manual. (Neither the subject nor the verb has changed. *Wants* agrees with *Mr. Singleton.*)

Two vice presidents *want* to review the manual. (Now the subject is the plural *vice presidents.* Therefore, the plural form *want*—not *wants*—is correct.)

Remember that plural *nouns* usually end in *s* or *es,* but an *s* ending on a *verb* indicates that it is a singular verb.

Singular Noun and Verb	Plural Noun and Verb
the *company wants*	the *companies want*
one *clerk has*	all *clerks have*
Mrs. Simon is	*Mr. and Mrs. Simon are*
a *buyer does*	several *buyers do*

Agreement of Pronoun With Subject

If the predicate includes a pronoun that refers to the subject, that pronoun must also agree with the subject.

The company wants to change *its* image in financial circles. The companies want to change *their* images in financial circles. (The pronoun *its* agrees with *company.* The pronoun *their* agrees with *companies.*)

Mrs. Simon is eager to receive *her* contract. Mr. and Mrs. Simon are eager to receive *their* contracts. (*Her* agrees with *Mrs. Simon.* In the second sentence, *their* agrees with *Mr. and Mrs. Simon.*)

Checkup 1

Choose the correct verbs and pronouns in the following sentences.

1. Generally, the Vernon Corporation (does? do?) not disclose (his? her? its? their?) acquisition plans.
2. All four managers (is? are?) going to bring (his? her? its? their?) analyses with (him, her? it? them?).
3. Helen (wants? want?) to open (his? her? its? their?) third store in the Anderson Mall.
4. The union (has? have?) changed (his? her? its? their?) demands since our last meeting with (his? her? its? their?) delegates.
5. Priscilla always (submits? submit?) all (his? her? its? their?) monthly travel statements on time.

6. Our attorneys said that (he? she? its? they?) will review the new regulations and will give us (his? her? its? their?) opinions by next week.
7. That firm (is? are?) very well respected as a leader in (his? her? its? their?) industry.
8. Mary Burroughs, one of the senior partners, (is? are?) planning to sell (his? her? its? their?) share of the stock before (he? she? it? they?) retires.

AGREEMENT PROBLEMS

The most common problems concerning agreement of subjects and verbs are discussed below. Study them carefully.

Inverted Sentences

Agreement problems most often arise when the subject is difficult to identify, as in sentences with inverted word order—where the verb comes before the subject.

On the counter (is? are?) the appraisals that were done yesterday. (At first glance, the subject and verb may appear to be "counter *is*," but a closer look shows that the subject of this inverted sentence is *appraisals*. The correct verb, therefore, is *are*.)

Sentences or clauses beginning with *there (there is, there are, there has been, there have been)* are in inverted order.

There (is? are?) still several openings. (Until you identify the subject *openings*, you cannot choose the correct verb, *are*.)

Do you know whether there (is? are?) other terminals on this floor? (The simple subject is *terminals*. Therefore, *are* is the correct verb.)

Intervening Phrases and Clauses

Words that separate the subject from its verb may confuse the writer or speaker. Again, the trick is to identify the simple subject.

The reason for the delays (is? are?) that the truckers are on strike. (The subject is the singular noun *reason*. Therefore, the correct verb is *is*. Although the plural word *delays* immediately precedes the verb, *delays* is not the subject of the verb. *Delays* is part of the prepositional phrase *for the delays*.)

The executive vice president, who must approve all expense vouchers signed by our regional managers, (has? have?) cut the travel budgets for all sales personnel. (The subject is *vice president*, not *regional managers*. Therefore, the correct verb is *has*.)

Correct any agreement errors in the following sentences. Write *OK* if a sentence has no error. (Be sure to identify the subject for each sentence.) *turn around + find simple subject*

1. Next to the computer terminals are the manual you will need.
2. When we checked the directory, we found that there is only two stationery stores nearby.
3. Are you sure that there's no more copies in the supply room?
4. The entire building, with all its offices, are to be painted during the summer.
5. The complete manuscript, which consists of more than 600 pages, are to be keyboarded on this computer.
6. On the cabinet in her office is the inventory report from headquarters.
7. There is, as you already know, several excellent applicants from which to choose.
8. Did you know that there's a few damaged machines in the plant?

Pronoun Agreement With Common-Gender Nouns

When the gender of a noun is clearly masculine (*man, father, brother, son*) or feminine (*woman, mother, sister, daughter*), choosing between the pronouns *he* or *she, him* or *her,* and so on, is no problem. Common-gender nouns are those that can be either masculine or feminine, such as *employee, student, teacher, vice president, owner, secretary*, and so on. The traditional rule is to use masculine pronouns to represent common-gender nouns. But many writers now use pronoun combinations such as *he or she, him or her,* and *his or her.*

> Every employee knows *his or her* role in the upcoming conference. (*His or her* agrees with the common-gender noun *employee.*)

> An executive must be sure that *he or she* is fair in promoting employees. (*He or she* agrees with *executive.*)

When such combinations are used too often, they make the message difficult to read. In such instances, consider using plurals to avoid the need for pronoun combinations.

> Executives must be sure that *they* are fair in promoting employees. (*They* agrees with *executives.*)

Indefinite Word Subject

The words *each, either, neither, everyone, everybody, someone, somebody, anyone, anybody, no one, and nobody* are always singular. When they are used as subjects, and when they modify other subjects, their predicates must be singular.

EXPANDING ENGLISH LANGUAGE SKILLS

Each of the printers *has* a 10-foot cable that connects *it* to the computer. (The singulars *has* and *it* agree with the subject *each*.)

Each printer *has* a 10-foot cable that connects *it* to the computer. (Here *each* modifies the subject, *printer*. In all cases, *each* is singular.)

Anyone in your department who *wants* to volunteer *his or her* time should be sure *he or she registers*. (*Wants*, *his or her*, *he or she*, and *registers* all agree with the singular *anyone*.)

Checkup 3

Correct the following sentences. If a sentence has no error, write *OK*. For each sentence, identify the simple subject.

1. Nobody in these two departments have submitted their monthly status report yet.
2. Each of the inventory analysts want to get their own computer terminal.
3. Neither of our two stores carry a full line of Carlisle-brand products.
4. Anyone who wants to attend the company picnic must complete and return his or her form to the Personnel Department.
5. Every executive in this building is permitted to use these facilities if he shows his pass to the guard.
6. Anyone who works in data processing will receive his paycheck on the first day of the month.
7. Neither of the stores we visited have a parking lot for their customers.
8. Every corporate officer in the country is sure to want his executive staff members to attend this conference.

COMMUNICATION PROJECTS

Practical Application

A. Correct any errors in the following sentences, and explain why each is incorrect. Write *OK* for any sentence that has no error.

1. In the Blake catalog is many different kinds of interesting gifts.
2. Yes, the president of our company is establishing a new committee to recommend procedural changes.
3. Don't Jack know how to operate this equipment?
4. Don't you know how to operate this equipment?
5. Every medical doctor in the country have been surveyed to see which option they prefer.

6. To exchange merchandise, each customer must show his or her receipt to the cashier.
7. In the building on Market Street is the offices of a new software publishing company.
8. There's the briefcases that will be on sale next week.
9. Ask each of the secretaries whether he or she is willing to work overtime next week.
10. As you requested, only three copies of the memorandum has been distributed.
11. The primary cause of the strikes have been management's attitude toward the drivers.
12. Of course, the agency is well known for their creative television campaigns.
13. Each secretary in our company have already received their confirmation copy.
14. Everyone who is on our mailing list is going to receive their free copy of this magazine within the next week.
15. Matthew don't know about the change in schedules yet.

B. Correct any errors in the following sentences. If a sentence has no error, write *OK*.

1. Didn't Harold and Jack know that there is more invoices to be checked?
2. Each applicant has been asked to complete the questionnaire and return the form to his or her supervisor.
3. If your still interested in learning more about this equipment, call 555-1780.
4. According to the report that we received from Mr. Norton, these duplicates are their's.
5. Every customer who requests their new credit card will receive them within two weeks.
6. Of course, you must be courteous to whomever asks to exchange merchandise.
7. The survey showed that there is certainly a large market for these new products.
8. Carole been with the company now for more than 10 years.
9. On my desk is all the applications I received this morning.
10. Ms. Paulson, the supervisor of these departments, have rewritten the procedures to conform to the new regulations.
11. According to the new plan, our company will move it's headquarters to Sacramento early next year.
12. Leo and Agnes Farley bought this store in 1984, but the Farley's have decided to sell there business.
13. Each woman in the company was asked for their opinions.
14. Any sales representative who exceeds their sales quota by more than 10 percent will receive a special bonus.

15. The Alcon Company distributes radioes, televisions, and cameras for a Japanese company.
16. At times, Ken acts as if he was the president of the company instead of my assistant!
17. No, she don't want to attend the conference next May, because it conflicts with her vacation plans.
18. All the proceeds is to be donated to a civic organization in this community.
19. Several of the analysis that were submitted have been reviewed by the panel and returned to the managers.
20. Although both cargos were completely destroyed, our insurance will cover our losses.

Editing Practice

Homonyms, Anyone?   Correct any homonym errors in the following sentences. (Look, too, for *pseudohomonyms,* words that sound almost alike.)

On March 15, we will move the Personal Department (accept for Employee Benefits) to the tenth floor, where more space is available to meet it's needs. Then, at a latter date, the Data Processing Department will also be moved to the tenth floor. Both departments will surely find the spacious new accommodations adequate for there needs.

Case Problem

Communicating on the Telephone.   You work for Pro Graphics, a design studio that creates advertising brochures and pamphlets for many advertising agencies in your area. A small company, Pro Graphics has no switchboard operator to screen calls—calls are simply answered by two very busy secretaries.

When the secretaries are away from their desks, employees generally answer the telephone by saying "Hello" or "Hello, this is Jim Barnes." Unless one of the secretaries answers a call, few employees volunteer taking a message from a caller.

1. How would you improve this method of telephone communication for Pro Graphics?
2. Why is it important to have excellent telephone communication skills?

17

PREDICATE AGREEMENT WITH SPECIAL SUBJECTS

Remember the basic agreement rule: *The predicate must agree in number and in person with the simple subject.* As you review some especially troublesome agreement problems, keep this rule in mind.

COLLECTIVE-NOUN SIMPLE SUBJECT

A *collective noun* is one that refers to a group or a collection of persons or things; for example, *class, jury, audience, company,* and *committee.* Because a collective noun may be either singular or plural, its correct number may not be easily recognized. Use the following Memory Hook to help you.

> **MEMORY HOOK**
>
> When the class, jury, and so on, acts *as one group,* treat the collective noun as *singular.* When the constituents of the collective noun act *as individuals,* treat the noun as *plural.*
> In other words, remember:
>
> *One group* is singular.
> *Individuals* are plural.
>
> In a major case, the jury (does? do?) not give (its? their?) verdict quickly. (Is the jury acting *as one group,* or is the jury acting *as individuals*? Answer: As one group. Therefore, treat *jury* as a singular noun: " . . . the jury *does* not give *its* verdict quickly.")
>
> The jury (is? are?) arguing about the charges. (Is the jury acting *as one group,* or is the jury acting as *individuals*? To argue, they obviously would be acting *as individuals.* Treat *jury* as a plural noun: "The jury *are* arguing about the charges."

FOREIGN-NOUN SUBJECT

Nouns of foreign origin do not form their plurals in the "usual" way. Review the list of foreign-origin nouns on page 104. Always be careful to determine first whether the noun is singular or plural before deciding on the correct verb to agree with such nouns.

> The basis for her statements (was? were?) unsound. (*Basis* is singular; therefore, the predicate must be singular. *Was* is correct.)

> The bases for her statements (was? were?) unsound. (*Bases* is plural; therefore, *were* is correct.)

Checkup 1

Correct any errors in the following sentences. Write *OK* if a sentence has no error.

1. The faculty was assigned to its new offices in the recently constructed building.
2. In this report, parentheses is used for references such as page numbers.
3. The stimuli that is being used to spur the economy into action are being hotly debated.
4. Recent crises in the Middle East has caused great concern throughout the country.
5. Yes, the committee are now discussing the suggestions among themselves.
6. The media we prefer for advertising our service is television and radio.
7. If you need more information, the criteria that we use to select the site of each new store is explained in detail in this report.
8. The Honors Class meet once a week.
9. The memoranda, which is on your desk, describes the situation clearly.
10. The jury has reached its decision and will render its verdict soon.

PART, PORTION, OR AMOUNT SUBJECT

Other subjects that may be either singular or plural are those that refer to a part, a portion, or an amount of something. Thus *all, some, half, two-thirds* (or any fraction), and *none* may be either singular or plural. To decide, find the answer to "Part of *what?*" "Portion of *what?*" "Amount of *what?*" In other words, use the complete subject (not the simple subject) for your answer.

> Some of the building (has? have?) been painted. (Building *has.*)

Some of the buildings (has? have?) been painted. (Buildings *have*.)

A NUMBER, THE NUMBER

A number is always plural. *The number* is always singular. (Note that an adjective before *number* has no effect on the choice.)

A number of customers *have* asked about this new policy. (*Have*, because *a number* is always plural.)

The number of customers *is* very surprising. (*The number* is always singular, so *is* is correct.)

MEMORY HOOK	To remember the above principle quickly and accurately, picture the following:

Plural: a

Singular: the

As you see, *plural* is shorter than *singular*, and *a* is shorter than *the*. So use this to remember that *a number* is plural and that *the number* is singular.

Checkup 2

Correct any errors in the following sentences. Write *OK* for any sentence that has no error.

1. The number of new contracts have risen to six.
2. Luckily, none of the shipment were damaged by the fire.
3. Nearly two-thirds of the town was affected by the transit strike.
4. Although the number of registered voters have increased, the actual total votes in each election have not.
5. Our survey shows that a number of employees is becoming concerned over the change in our benefits program.
6. Are you aware that a number of new sales representatives have recently been hired?
7. Some of the machines, Henry told me, was not adequately inspected before shipment.
8. Some of the machine, as you can see, has already begun to rust.
9. None of the advance payment have yet been received, according to our Accounts Receivable Department.
10. All the machines in our Newark factory needs to be checked for safety reasons.

COMMUNICATION PROJECTS

Practical Application

A. Correct any errors in the following sentences. Write *OK* for any sentence that has no error.

1. Our comptroller said that two-thirds of this year's revenue have come from sales of new products.
2. Some of the shipments to Europe has been delayed by the freight strike.
3. The number of back orders in the warehouse are surprisingly low.
4. Most of the managers in the Detroit office prefers the old system.
5. Approximately three-fourths of her time, she says, are spent talking with customers about shipments and invoices.
6. Some of the extra office space in our headquarters are being sublet to a German manufacturing company.
7. Sandra's accurate—and fast—analyses of the chemicals was very helpful to us.
8. According to the laboratory supervisor, the bacteria were harmless.
9. For the duration of the trial, the jury is staying at two hotels in the midtown area.
10. The large number of absences among our administrative staff are responsible for the backlog in billing.
11. Ted's memoranda, which he typed before he left for lunch, is on Ms. Braun's desk.
12. Because a number of people has complained about our discount policy, we are now reviewing it with our Sales Department.
13. The criteria for her evaluation is clearly described in her manual.
14. Half of the area in this warehouse has been converted to office space.
15. Some of the comments we received was highly critical of the merger.

B. Correct any errors in the following sentences. If a sentence has no error, write *OK*.

1. We take special precautions with this equipment because the lifes of so many people are at stake.
2. When we opened these studioes, our rent was almost half what we now pay.
3. You should, of course, consult the Professors Smiths to see what their opinions are.

4. Unfortunately, the beaker has fell and broke, causing terrible fumes.
5. Don't Angelo know how to proofread these invoices before sending them to Accounts Receivable?
6. Why don't you ask Mr. Hammond and she to give you a copy of the report?
7. Crises in the financial community raises the price of gold, as a general rule.
8. On the bulletin board is the notices that we posted concerning the changes in the profit-sharing system.
9. When the number of accidents per year are reduced, the insurance company will lower our premiums.
10. Neither of her assistants have attended the time-management seminar yet.
11. The diskette with all the financial data was laying on the floor!
12. The meeting begun with a review of the sales data for the past two weeks.
13. Although we had took several precautions, we overbid and lost the contract.
14. Beatrice answered clearly, "This is she."
15. Both managers should have asked we dispatchers for our advice.
16. Is Andrea the person who you want to hire?
17. Ms. Pearson did not like us telling anyone about the announcement until it was official.
18. Each employee who is a member of the credit union will receive their statements through interoffice mail.
19. Brett and myself revised the reports because Audrey and Allen were out of town.
20. The editors in chief, Alice and him, have redesigned the entire look of the magazine.

Editing Practice

Using Your Word Processor. You keyboarded the following copy quickly but didn't have time to proofread it. Do so now.

We appreciate your request for information about the HighTop Inn. To answer your questions about convention facilities, we have enclosed our latest brochure.

As you will see in the brochure, the HighTop Inn can accomodate groups with from 20 to 300 people with equal ease—and with the same high-quality service that has made us famous for more than 40 years.

After you have read the brochure, please be sure to call Lynn Bandolo, our Convention Manager, at (800) 555-1234. Ms. Bandolo will be happy to answer any questions that you may have.

Case Problem

The Chatty Receptionist. While an early visitor is waiting for her appointment with the personnel manager, the receptionist on duty and a coworker are busy talking about some of the personality clashes between employees and their disappointment at the small raises each received recently, as well as voicing some specific negative comments about their supervisors.

1. Why is it inappropriate for these two employees to discuss these matters?
2. If you were their supervisor and overheard this discussion, what would you tell these two people?

18

PREDICATE AGREEMENT WITH COMPOUND SUBJECTS

To complete your study of predicate agreement, you will now work on predicate agreement with compound subjects joined by *and, or,* or *nor* and on one other predicate agreement problem: agreement with the relative pronouns *who, that,* and *which.*

SUBJECTS JOINED BY AND

A compound subject joined by *and* is, of course, plural and must take a plural verb.

> Edward *and* Howard *have* the final draft of the report. (The compound subject *Edward and Howard* is plural; the plural verb *have* is correct.)

> A printing company *and* a plastics distributor *are* planning to merge. (The plural form *are* is correct because the compound subject is joined by *and*.)

Two exceptions to this rule are possible:

1. If the two nouns joined by *and* refer to *one* person, then that subject is really singular and takes a singular verb.

   My business partner *and* investment adviser *is* my sister, Mary Beth Williams. (Although the compound subject is joined by *and*, obviously only one person is serving as *business partner* and *investment adviser*. The singular verb *is* is therefore correct.)

   Pie *and* ice cream *is* going to be served for dessert. (*One* dessert, *pie and ice cream*, is intended.)

Note that if two different people or two different desserts were intended, the verbs would then be plural.

   My business partner *and* my investment adviser *are* not in agreement on this issue. (Two different people are intended.)

   Pie *and* ice cream are among the desserts included in the fixed-price lunch. (Here, two different items on the menu are referred to.)

2. If two or more subjects joined by *and* are modified by *each*, *every*, or *many a*, then the predicate is singular.

   ***Each* secretary and assistant *has* been asked to return the completed questionnaire to the Personnel Department by May 15. *Every* supervisor and manager *is* supposed to check the completed questionnaires. *Many a* factory, office, and store throughout the country *is* now following this procedure. (In each sentence, the predicate is singular because the subjects are modified by *each*, *every*, and *many a*.)**

Checkup 1

Correct any agreement error in the following sentences. Write *OK* for any sentence that has no error.

1. Many a computer expert and word processing operator have agreed with this idea.
2. As usual, every sales representative and sales manager are eligible for the incentive-compensation package.
3. Accuracy and speed is emphasized in this keyboarding program.
4. The letter and the envelope have two different addresses.
5. Many an auditor and business owner have complained to the IRS about their feelings on this new policy.
6. Ham and eggs are usually what I order for breakfast.
7. Beth and Marion are on their way to Puerto Rico for the convention.
8. Each partner and associate in the export firms we polled are writing to their representatives to show support for the legislation.

SUBJECTS JOINED BY OR OR NOR

For subjects joined by *or* or *nor*, simply match the predicate to the subject that follows *or* or *nor*.

Our manager *or* her assistants (is? are?) going to discuss (her? their?) ideas at the sales meeting tomorrow. (Matching the predicate to the subject that follows *or*, the correct choices are *are* and *their*.)

The assistants *or* our manager (is? are?) going to discuss (her? their?) ideas at the sales meeting tomorrow. (Now the subject that follows *or* is the singular *manager*. Therefore, the choices are *is* and *her*.)

Neither our manager *nor* her assistants (knows? know?) where Ms. Pauley went. (Which subject follows *nor*? Answer: the plural *assistants*. The choice, therefore, is *know*.)

Either the three Japanese companies *or* ProStar (is? are?) going to discuss (its? their?) plan this afternoon. (The subject that follows *or* is *ProStar*, singular; thus the choices are *is* and *its*.)

Checkup 2

Select the correct words in the following sentences.

1. Either the account executives or Mr. Lehman (like? likes?) to deliver (their? his?) clients' portfolios in special envelopes.
2. Neither Barbara nor the district managers (has? have?) endorsed the suggestion.
3. Dr. Carbonaro or her nurses (is? are?) planning to give us (her? their?) cassettes for transcription by noon.
4. The regional manager or his assistants (is? are?) generally willing to submit (his? their?) itineraries ahead of time.
5. An experienced programmer or word processing operator (has? have?) been sought for this position.
6. Mr. Loomis or her store managers (has? have?) always completed (her? their?) budgets accurately.
7. My brother-in-law or his associates (is? are?) often interested in purchasing such stocks for (his? their?) portfolios.
8. Either her partners or Lucy herself (is? are?) going to coordinate the seminar.

RELATIVE-PRONOUN CLAUSES

The pronouns *who*, *that*, and *which* are called *relative pronouns* because they *relate* to other words (called *antecedents*). The antecedent of the relative pronoun is a noun or a pronoun that is usually immediately before the relative pronoun.

Marla Downey is one of those vice presidents *who* strive for perfection all the time. (The relative pronoun is *who*, and its antecedent is the noun immediately before it, *vice presidents*.)

The Super-Flo pump *that* is on the counter works efficiently and quietly. (If *that* is a relative pronoun, what is its antecedent? Answer: *pump*.)

The discount coupon is good until Friday, *which* is the last day of our sale. (The relative pronoun *which* refers to *Friday*, its antecedent.)

Note that in each sentence the verb in the relative-pronoun clause agrees with the antecedent.

MEMORY HOOK

To choose quickly the correct verb in relative-pronoun clauses, omit the relative pronoun and use the antecedent as the subject of the clause. For example, from the foregoing sentences the omissions would give:

vice presidents . . . strive
pump . . . is
Friday . . . is

Let's look at some other examples:

Elliott prefers one of those monitors that (has? have?) amber readouts on (its? their?) screens. (By omitting the relative pronoun *that*, you have *monitors . . . have . . . their*.)

Kate is one of those designers who (does? do?) (her? their?) best creative work under pressure. (Omit *who* and you have *designers . . . do . . . their*.)

Note: An exception is a clause preceded by *the only one*. Such clauses must take singular predicates.

Shirley is *the only one* of the partners who *has* cast *her* vote against the proposal. (*Has* and *her* are correct.)

Checkup 3

Correct any errors in the following sentences. Write *OK* if a sentence has no error.

1. Lamont is one of those account executives who calls his clients at least once a month.
2. The Owens Company is one of those distributors which has shown an interest in leasing its vans.

EXPANDING ENGLISH LANGUAGE SKILLS

3. All the secretaries prefer using one of those machines which offers letter-quality printing as one of its features.
4. The company will soon close one of the several factories that is now operating at a loss.
5. Matthew is one of those proofreaders who always double-check their copy carefully.
6. Harriet prefers one of those offices that has modern furniture in it.
7. Sandra is one of those trainers who works very closely with her people.
8. Audrey is the only one of the supervisors who wants to revise the procedures drastically.

COMMUNICATION PROJECTS

Practical Application

A. Correct any errors in the following sentences. If a sentence has no error, write *OK*.

1. Every invoice and package that we send customers are carefully checked first.
2. Neither Andrew nor Joanna want to attend the West Coast conference.
3. Tomorrow we should receive all the cartons, which is now more than 10 days late.
4. Each customer and client whom we asked said they enjoy the new convenience.
5. Our sales manager is one of those people who has a positive attitude at all times.
6. Every glass and bottle on the truck were broken in the accident.
7. Many a schedule and launch date for new products was delayed by the strike.
8. Either the security guard or the departmental assistants has access to this storeroom.
9. Your manager or her auditors was notified of the change in regulations.
10. Each editor, proofreader, and designer were invited to a full-day conference on the magazine's future plans.
11. As you probably already know, Mr. Hewitt is one of those engineers who is always late in handling his paperwork.
12. Isopropyl alcohol or methane are generally used in this solvent.
13. Martha said that two small rooms or one large room are enough for our meetings.
14. She firmly believes that the highest-paid editors should be those who are on schedule with all their projects.

15. Neither the diskettes nor the operations manual is on the computer table.

B. Correct any errors in the following sentences. Write *OK* for any sentence that has no error.

1. The committee was arguing for several hours about the pros and cons of the changes.
2. Unfortunately, nearly two-thirds of the goods were damaged during the incident.
3. Two forms of identification or a store credit card are required for cashing checks.
4. A store credit card or two forms of identification are required for cashing checks.
5. Have we received the Kleins response yet?
6. Where's the cable and the dust cover for this computer?
7. According to the rumor, the Messrs. Carsons are planning to sell the entire inventory.
8. The best sales territorys are in the northern part of the state.
9. Steve is the only one of the accountants who understand this procedure.
10. Don't Ingrid prepare in advance for such meetings?
11. Either Lorraine or Tina should have updated this data disk before they filed it.
12. Jason, my supervisor, did as much to win the new account as me.
13. A number of the products we developed has already passed its break-even points.
14. Both sister-in-laws have invested heavily in Janice's new business.
15. After Maria and Evelyn had spoke with Ms. Trask, we understood why Ms. Trask reassigned the project.
16. Nancy and Carole objected to our candidates, but there reasons for objecting were ill-founded.
17. If him and I are selected, we will enjoy working on the committee.
18. All the analysis that we received from our managers made the same point: we must cut costs.
19. In the old storeroom is the files that you'll need to write the background part of this report.
20. As the water level in the tank raises, the pump automatically goes on.

Editing Practice

Plurals and Possessives. Correct any errors in the following sentences. Write *OK* for any sentence that has no error.

1. Mario's superb article on womens' rights appeared in last month's issue.

2. Her credentials for the position of research director for the corporation are excellent.

3. Among the cooking utensils that we import and sell are carving knifes, pots and pans, and baking items.

4. Although all were subpoenaed, only two of the Davis's appeared at the trial.

5. Our company supports the civic activities of several communitys in this part of the state.

6. All c.o.d.'s must be paid for at our receiving desk.

7. Although several of the lens's were damaged, the insurance policy covers their cost.

8. This copier quickly duplicates and collates, but our's works just as well and costs less per copy.

9. No, I was not aware of Ingrid leaving the seminar early.

10. The size and weight of this portable copier are certainly factors in it's favor, but it's price is far too high.

Case Problem

Plan Ahead! Linda Noonan, a new employee in the Customer Relations Department, handles problem calls expertly and answers complaint letters with genuine feeling and understanding. In a short time, she proves that she is a good worker and an asset to your company.

Despite all her pluses, Linda spends far too much time answering customers' letters—and she's aware of it! Linda always begins her responses by writing the full reply in longhand and then rewriting it again and again.

What would you suggest to Linda to help her become more productive?

19

ADJECTIVES

Without adjectives, our speech and our writing would be rather dull and lifeless. Adjectives make nouns and pronouns interesting, vivid, and specific. This section will introduce you to all the many kinds of adjectives and the very few ways that we commonly misuse adjectives. Master adjective use so that *your* speech and writing will also be interesting, vivid, and specific.

IDENTIFYING ADJECTIVES

Any word that modifies or describes a noun or a pronoun is an *adjective*. An adjective usually precedes the noun it modifies. Some of the most commonly used kinds of adjectives are described below.

Articles

The words *a, an,* and *the* are called *articles*. Note how these special adjectives are commonly used:

> *The* first speaker discussed *an* interesting issue; then *a* question-and-answer session followed.

Possessive Adjectives

The possessive adjectives *my, your, his, her, its, our,* and *their* and possessive nouns (*John's, Edna's, Gary's,* and so on) modify nouns.

> *Your* partner reviewed *our* proposal and submitted it to *Frank's* manager.

Limiting Adjectives

Adjectives that tell "how many," "how much," or "in what order" are called *limiting adjectives*.

> The *first ten* sales representatives in the nation will share more than *fifty* prizes. (*First* tells "in what order." *Ten* tells "how many sales representatives." *Fifty* tells "how many prizes.")

> *Each* winner had sold *many* pieces of equipment. (*Each* modifies *winner; many* modifies *pieces*.)

Proper Adjectives

Proper nouns are very often used as proper adjectives:

Noun	Adjective
in *New York*	a *New York* hotel
near *Seattle*	two *Seattle* firms
to *Dallas*	*Dallas* residents

Proper adjectives include words derived from proper nouns, such as *Australian, English,* and *American*.

Compound Adjectives

Two or more words joined to modify one noun or pronoun form a *compound adjective*.

> Otis wanted a *long-term* contract but signed a *two-year* lease instead. (*Long-term* modifies *contract*, and *two-year* modifies *lease*.)

Descriptive Adjectives

The most commonly used adjectives are *descriptive adjectives*—the adjectives that describe or tell "what kind of."

> In a *strong, clear* voice, Andrea rejected the *irresponsible* policies that some firms use to lure *unsuspecting* consumers into buying *overpriced* and sometimes *worthless* products. (*Strong, clear, irresponsible, unsuspecting, overpriced,* and *worthless* are descriptive adjectives.)

Demonstrative Adjectives

The pronouns *this, that, these,* and *those* are also used as adjectives:

As Pronouns	As Adjectives
this is	*this* book
that has been	*that* briefcase
these are	*these* keys
those might be	*those* folders

Note that *these* is the plural of *this;* both *these* and *this* indicate nearness to the speaker. *Those* is the plural of *that,* and *that* and *those* indicate distance from the speaker. Never use the pronoun *them* as a substitute for *these* or *those!*

> Please return *those* folders to Mr. Abernathy. (Not *them* folders.)

> *These* kinds of problems arise often during our busy season. (*These* kinds, not *them* kinds. Note that some writers and speakers incorrectly use "these *kind.*")

Checkup 1

On a separate sheet of paper, identify the adjectives in the following sentences and label each *possessive* (P), *limiting* (L), *proper* (PR), *compound* (C), *descriptive* (D), or *demonstrative* (DM). Disregard articles.

1. The first factory we opened has been a major success for our company.
2. A special class is being established for new employees to learn these important procedures.
3. Two well-known firms bid on this large building, which was formerly owned by Karen's sister.
4. In two weeks her brother will join her company and will work out of the Chicago office.
5. Our one-year forecast is an accurate one, in our opinion.
6. The Los Angeles attorney who represents that company asked my supervisor for additional information on Henderson's contract.

7. One of Kelly's critical accounts is a new client who represents an East Coast broker.
8. These bonds are tax-free investments, according to their new brochure.

COMPARING ADJECTIVES

Descriptive adjectives can be compared. For example, *strong* and *clear* can be compared to show degrees of strength and clarity: *strong, stronger,* and *strongest; clear, clearer,* and *clearest.* These three forms of comparison are called the *positive,* the *comparative,* and the *superlative* degree.

1. The positive degree expresses the quality of *one* person or thing.

    a *strong* position

    a *clear* recording

2. The comparative degree allows us to compare the strength or clarity of *two* persons or things.

    a *stronger* position

    a *clearer* recording

3. The superlative degree enables us to compare the strength or clarity of *three or more* persons or things.

    the *strongest* position

    the *clearest* recording

Now that we know how the three degrees are used, let's see how they are formed.

Forming the Comparative and Superlative Degrees

The comparative degree is formed by adding *er* to the positive or by inserting *more* or *less* before the positive form. The superlative is formed by adding *est* to the positive or by inserting *most* or *least* before the positive form.

Positive	Comparative	Superlative
quick	quicker	quickest
happy	happier	happiest
poor	poorer	poorest
casual	more casual	most casual
	less casual	least casual
decisive	more decisive	most decisive
	less decisive	least decisive

In addition, some very commonly used adjectives form their comparative and superlative degrees by changing the form to another word completely. Memorize these for quick reference.

Positive	Comparative	Superlative
good	better	best
bad	worse	worst
little	less	least
much	more	most
many	more	most

Selecting the Correct Forms

Adjectives of only *one* syllable are compared by adding *er* or *est* to the positive degree. Adjectives of *three* or more syllables add *more* or *less* or *most* or *least*. Adjectives of *two* syllables vary: some add *er* or *est;* others add *more* or *less* or *most* or *least*. However, these two-syllable adjectives are easy to compare because an error would be obvious: *more useful*, not *usefuler; most useful*, nor *usefulest*. Conversely, *happier*, not *more happy; happiest*, not *most happy*.

Avoiding Comparison Errors

MAKING DOUBLE COMPARISONS.   Do not "mix" the different ways in which adjectives can be compared—use only one at a time.

greatest, not *most greatest*

better, not *more better*

COMPARING ABSOLUTE ADJECTIVES.   Adjectives whose qualities cannot be compared are called *absolute adjectives*. For example, a glass of water cannot be *fuller* or *fullest*. *Full* is already tops! Other adjectives that cannot be compared are:

accurate	perpendicular
complete	round
correct	square
dead	supreme
empty	ultimate
immaculate	unanimous
perfect	unique

Although they cannot be compared, the qualities of these adjectives can be approached, as indicated by the following:

more nearly accurate

less nearly complete

most nearly correct

least nearly perfect

You may hear (especially in advertisements) of products that are *most unique*, but *unique* really says it all. Remember that absolute adjectives cannot logically be compared.

Checkup 2

Correct any errors in the use of adjectives in the following sentences. If a sentence has no error, write *OK*.

1. Allen said that we had enough of the solvent, but the container was very empty.
2. Which air conditioner uses the most electricity, Model K123 or Model K987?
3. As you can see, Edward is more happier now that he has been promoted to manager.
4. Which is the largest room, our vice president's office or the conference room?
5. All of us agree that Danielle's suggestion is very unique.
6. The yellow container is obviously fuller than the blue container.
7. These offices are perfect because they are more quiet and more big than our present offices.
8. As compared with Ellen, Raymond is definitely a better sales representative—in fact, Raymond is probably the best sales representative throughout the entire country.

More Than Any Other, More Than Anyone Else

In "more than" comparisons, be sure to include the word *other* or *else* if the person or thing is being compared with *other* members of the same group.

> Brett is *more* productive *than any other* manager in my company. (Brett *is* a manager "in my company." Without the word *other*, this sentence would indicate that Brett is *not* a manager "in my company.")

> Susan is *more* ambitious *than anyone else* in the Finance Department. (With the word *else*, the sentence clearly says that Susan *is* a member of the Finance Department. Without the word *else*, the sentence would indicate that Susan is *not* part of the Finance Department but is being compared with people who are in this department.)

Repeated Modifier

In the following examples, repeating the modifiers *a* (or *an*), *the*, or *my* indicates that *two* different people are intended.

> The accountant and *the* attorney (was? were?) formerly with the Treasury Department. (Repeating *the* shows that *two* people, an accountant and an attorney, are referred to. Thus *were* is correct.)

> The accountant and attorney (was? were?) formerly with the Treasury Department. (One person who is an accountant and attorney is referred to. *Was* is correct.)

For Added Polish

The following short discussions will help you make correct choices when referring to two or more than two persons or things.

EACH OTHER, ONE ANOTHER. Use *each other* when referring to two in number; use *one another* when referring to three or more.

Emily and Fred work very creatively with *each other*. (Two people.)

Several account executives commented to *one another* about the recent changes. (Three or more account executives.)

EITHER, NEITHER; ANY, ANY ONE, NO ONE, NOT ANY, NONE. Use *either* or *neither* when referring to one of *two* persons or things. When referring to *three or more*, use *any, any one, no one, not any,* or *none*.

Either of the stock traders will be able to answer your questions. (There are only two stock traders. Therefore, *either* is correct.)

Any one of the agents in our headquarters office will send you the information. (There are more than two agents; *any one* is correct.)

COMPOUND ADJECTIVES

Hyphenate most compound adjectives that appear before a noun:

first-quality merchandise	*air-conditioned* rooms
no-fault insurance	an *up-to-date* manual
tax-free bonds	*fund-raising* committees
100-mile track	a *three-year* contract

When they appear after the noun, compound adjectives such as *air-conditioned* and *tax-free* retain the hyphen. Most other compounds do not. Use a dictionary to help you decide.

Before the Noun	After the Noun
a *well-known* study	a study that is *well known*
a *coast-to-coast* telecast	a telecast from *coast to coast*
tax-free bonds	bonds that are *tax-free*
air-conditioned rooms	rooms that are *air-conditioned*

Longtime use has made the following compounds so familiar that they are no longer written with hyphens:

a *life insurance* policy	*real estate* services
high school teachers	*social security* benefits

Checkup 3

Apply the rules just presented by correcting the following sentences. Write *OK* for any sentence that has no error.

1. Elmer is a three time winner of the company's annual sales award.
2. Lana's recommendation is better than any recommendation that we have received so far.

3. Mr. Jefferson's court appointed attorney will probably be named this afternoon.
4. A Jackson portable tool is guaranteed to last longer than any power tool on the market.
5. My supervisor, Shelley Weinstein, handles more rush orders than anyone in our department.
6. Jessica scheduled a 15 minute question and answer session after each presentation.
7. Marketing research has shown that word of mouth advertising is our best form of sales promotion.
8. My tax consultant and investment adviser is Hazel Bender.
9. Ask Maureen or Adele—any one of them should have a sample.
10. When Patricia and Diana have more experience, they will work with one another very, very well.

COMMUNICATION PROJECTS

Practical Application

A. Correct any errors in the following sentences. Write *OK* for any sentence that has no error.

1. Passengers may purchase gifts at the duty free shops here in the airport.
2. Every committee member will give a ten minute overview of his or her findings.
3. For security reasons, door to door soliciting is prohibited throughout the building.
4. Although the price is substantially higher, this model is no more better than that one.
5. Most of them cables are inappropriate for computer equipment.
6. This particular model has a heavy duty motor that was especially designed for professional use.
7. Unless otherwise specified, each machine is equipped with a 120-volt, 10-ampere motor.
8. Of our branch offices across the country, the St. Louis branch ships more orders than any office.
9. We evaluated both personal computers carefully, and we decided to order the one that was least expensive.
10. Because they cooperated with one another so well, Beatrice and Benedict were able to complete their project two weeks ahead of schedule.
11. In only two years the new president of our company has broadened our export operations more than any president of this company.

12. Olga and Myrna have been with Wesco Pharmaceuticals for several years, but I believe that Myrna has been here longest.
13. No, these kind of damages are not covered under the warranty.
14. Our three project managers always work closely with one another to meet their schedules.
15. The room has no windows, but it is well-ventilated.

B. Correct any errors in the following sentences. Write *OK* for any sentence that has no error.

1. There has been several interesting jobs posted on the bulletin board lately.
2. Because of his seniority, Jesse receives a higher commission on net sales than anyone in our company.
3. The Wilson Furniture Company reported revenues of $1 million last year—their best year ever.
4. Whom has Mona selected to help her work on the committee, Brian or her?
5. Ms. VanCleef wants we assistants to develop good work habits.
6. As of Monday afternoon, we had received several dozens responses to the classified ad.
7. Has Katherine or Peggy flew to Arizona before?
8. Although I am not sure, the person who left this package could indeed have been her.
9. One managers' recommendation was to replace the forklift trucks every three years.
10. Several of the analysis that were submitted were rather startling, in our opinion.
11. Please find out who's purchase order this is.
12. Scot and me both enjoy working with the advertising agency on special promotions.
13. After you have met with Mr. Kamen and she, prepare a summary report of your discussion.
14. Deborah said that the Ellis's were invited to the conference.
15. Next month we will begin lying our plans for next year's catalog.
16. Two designers, Mr. Lorca and her, have been assigned to the annual report.
17. Of course, Marcella and myself are convinced that we will complete the brochures well ahead of the deadline.
18. The candidate who Denise likes best of all is Gary Abrams.
19. Joan been working in the Personnel Department ever since she was graduated from college.
20. If the Messrs. Kennedys are available, please confirm both the date and the time.

Editing Practice

Plurals and Possessives.   Correct any errors in the use of plurals and possessives. Write *OK* for any sentence that has no error.

1. My editor in chief's comment was, "Send a copy to the Legal Department for approval."
2. Gail's and Jane's newest boutique will be opened on July 1 at the Westfield Mall.
3. Because Rose and Lia Norton are well-known consultants in this field, the Norton's are certainly worth their high fee.
4. Mr. Bellantoni does not think its worthwhile to spend so much on a machine of limited use.
5. Lisa and I enjoyed Terry working with us to write the report.
6. As soon as you receive there tickets, please send them to the district managers.
7. My supervisors' husband is a well-respected builder in this community.
8. The striker's finally voted to accept the contract offer the company had originally presented.
9. Sharon managing the office has helped us to save time and to work much more efficiently.
10. If the Smith's accept the offer, our company will then become the largest distributor of automobile accessories in the state.

Using Your Word Processor.   Proofread the following excerpt from a printout.

> **A three day seminar about planning and implementing strategy has been scheduled for June 13 through June 15. All manager's in our Chicago office is invited to attend this practical, action oriented program.**

Case Problem

A Need for Help.   Marilyn Jessups and Rona Barton work in the billing department of a small stock brokerage firm. To prepare for the monthly settlement date for payments, Marilyn must send out reminders or personally call clients who have not yet sent in their payments.

Because Marilyn was out ill for a few days, she has a large backlog, yet she *must* complete all the mailing and calls for settlement by the end of today. Rona is not very busy; moreover, their supervisor, Tanya Fordyce, is out on vacation.

1. Should Marilyn ask Rona for help?
2. If so, what specifically should Marilyn tell Rona?

20

ADVERBS

Like adjectives, adverbs modify or describe. You will see several similarities between adverbs and adjectives as you read this section, including some common confusions in their use.

IDENTIFYING ADVERBS

An *adverb* is a word that modifies an adjective, a verb, or another adverb. Adverbs answer questions such as "Why?" "When?" "Where?" "How?" "How much?" "To what extent?" Many adverbs are formed very simply by adding *ly* to an adjective.

Adjective	Adverb
clear	clearly
hasty	hastily
perfect	perfectly
adequate	adequately
immediate	immediately

In fact, most words that end in *ly* are adverbs, but not all adverbs end in *ly,* as the following adverbs show:

also	never	soon
always	now	then
hard	often	there
here	quite	too
much	right	very

Note how adverbs are used in the following sentences.

Ms. Anderson arrived *late*. (Arrived when? Answer: *late*. The adverb *late* modifies the verb *arrived*.)

That is a *very* good computer. (*How* good? *Very* good. The adverb *very* modifies the adjective *good*.)

She worked *quite* well under the pressure of the tight deadlines. (*How* well? *Quite* well. The adverb *quite* modifies another adverb, *well*.)

COMPARING ADVERBS

Adverbs of one syllable are compared by adding *er* or *est* to the positive form:

fast, faster, fastest
late, later, latest
soon, sooner, soonest

Adverbs ending in *ly* are compared by using *more* or *most* (or *less* or *least*):

quickly, more quickly, most quickly
quickly, less quickly, least quickly

confidently, more confidently, most confidently
confidently, less confidently, least confidently

casually, more casually, most casually
casually, less casually, least casually

Certain adverbs form their comparative and superlative degrees by completely changing their forms:

well, better, best
badly, worse, worst
much, more, most

CONJUNCTIVE ADVERBS

Conjunctive adverbs, as their name clearly tells, are adverbs that serve as conjunctions—words that *join.* These adverbs are also known as "transitional words."

accordingly	nevertheless
consequently	otherwise
furthermore	then
however	therefore
likewise	thus
moreover	yet

These adverbs join two *independent* clauses, as shown in the following sentences:

Fixed investments such as bonds pay a higher interest rate; *moreover,* the investor receives regular payments of principal plus interest.

Our sales through June 30 are about 20 percent under budget; *however,* we expect to have a strong second half.

Note, again, that each sentence consists of two *independent* clauses joined by a conjunctive adverb.

ADVERBIAL CLAUSES

Subordinating conjunctions introduce *dependent* clauses that serve as adverbs modifying an adjective, verb, or adverb in the main clause. Some commonly used subordinating conjunctions are:

after	if
although	since
as	unless
because	until
before	when
for	while

Note the following examples of adverbial clauses introduced by subordinating conjunctions:

Vera will travel to Boston *when the seminar date is confirmed.* (The adverbial clause *when the seminar date is confirmed* modifies the verb *will travel* in the main clause.)

Our new personal computer will be successful *if we market it properly.* (The adverbial clause *if we market it properly* modifies the adjective *successful.*)

Checkup 1

Identify the italicized words in the following sentences by labeling each *simple adverb* (SA), *conjunctive adverb* (CA), or *subordinating conjunction* (SC).

1. The deadline for our bid on the project is next Friday; our manager, *therefore,* has approved our working overtime.
2. *If* you would like more information on this exciting new product, call this toll-free number.
3. The new equipment works *quietly* and *efficiently;* it does not, *moreover,* require much maintenance.
4. Priscilla has been *very* busy *since* she opened her own law office.
5. *Since* she opened her own law office, Priscilla has been *very* busy.
6. We will review our progress on this project *when* Mr. Nielsen returns from the West Coast.
7. *When* Raymond arrived *here,* he *immediately* called his broker.
8. Jack *always* works *diligently* on the end-of-year inventory, and he *usually* completes the entire report *early.*
9. *Because* Veronica was busy, she stayed *here late* on Monday and Tuesday.
10. The client *specifically* indicated that she wanted spacious rooms; *accordingly,* our architects designed *very* large quarters.

PITFALLS

In speaking and writing, many people violate five principles of adverb use. These principles are neither tricky nor difficult, so you will be sure to avoid these pitfalls if you study them.

1. Position of the Adverb

Place an adverb as close as possible to the word that it modifies. Sometimes the meaning of a sentence can be changed by the position of the adverb.

> Only Miss Berenson has a computer terminal in her office. (No one else has one.)

> Miss Berenson has only a computer terminal in her office. (She has nothing else in her office, only a computer terminal.)

> Miss Berenson has a computer terminal only in her office. (She has one nowhere else but in her office.)

2. Double Negative

Adverbs that have negative meanings (*scarcely, hardly, only, never,* and *but*) should not be used with other negatives.

> Sean *has scarcely* any money left in his advertising budget. (**Not:** Sean *hasn't scarcely* . . . .)

> From the back of the room, Pamela *could hardly* hear the speaker. (**Not:** Pamela *couldn't hardly* . . . .)

> Alicia *couldn't help suggesting* an alternative plan. (**Not:** Alicia *couldn't help but suggest* . . . .)

3. Never or Not?

Never and *not* are both adverbs, and both have negative meanings. *Not* expresses simple negation, but never means "not *ever*" (note the word *ever*). Use *never* only when an appropriately long time is intended.

> Charlotte has *not* called me yet this week. (*Never* would be incorrect because the meaning "*not ever* . . . this week" would be wrong.)

> I have *never* been to Australia. (*Never,* meaning "not ever," is correct in this sentence.)

4. Where for That

The subordinating conjunction *that* (not the conjunctive adverb *where*) should be used in expressions such as the following:

> I read in a magazine *that* the Diamond Battery Company has been sold. (**Not:** I read in a magazine *where* . . . .)

> We saw in the newspaper *that* the mayor has endorsed Mrs. Simmons for governor. (**Not:** We saw in the newspaper *where* . . . .)

5. Badly or Worst Way for Very Much

Too often, we hear people say *badly* or *in the worst way* when they really mean *very much*. Study these illustrations:

> Janice said that she wanted a vacation *very much*. (**Not:** "wanted a vacation *badly*" or "wanted a vacation *in the worst way*.")

ADJECTIVE AND ADVERB CONFUSIONS

Several adjective-adverb pairs cause special problems for writers and speakers. In the following pairs, the adjective is listed first.

Bad, Badly

Bad is an adjective; *badly* is an adverb.

> John works *badly* under pressure. (Works how? *Badly*. The adverb *badly* modifies the action verb *works*.)

The problem in selecting between *bad* and *badly* arises following no-action verbs:

> Margaret felt (bad? badly?) when she heard about the merger. (Here, *felt* is a linking verb, not an action verb. The answer here will not modify the verb *felt* but the noun *Margaret*. Thus an adjective is required because an adverb cannot modify a noun. Margaret felt *bad*.)

The "being" verbs *am, is, are, was, were, be, been,* and *being* are all no-action, or "linking," verbs. In addition to these being verbs, verbs of sense such as *feel, appear, seem, look, sound, taste,* and *smell* can be used as no-action verbs. Remember that adjectives, not adverbs, must follow linking verbs.

> Ms. Jeffreys was (angry? angrily?) when she heard about the delay. (The being verb *was* links the subject *Ms. Jeffreys* to the adjective *angry*. The verb *was* shows no action.)

> Ms. Jeffreys appeared (angry? angrily?) when she heard about the delay. (Like *was*, the linking verb *appeared* shows no action; thus the adjective *angry* is correct.)

> The strikers were (patient? patiently?). (Because the verb *were* indicates no action, the adjective *patient* is correct.)

> The strikers seemed (patient? patiently?). (Like the no-action verb *were, seemed* links the noun *strikers* to the adjective *patient*; thus *patient* modifies *strikers*.)

Beware: Some of these verbs can also be used as action verbs. Judge each sentence carefully.

> Dr. Giordano felt carefully for a possible fracture. (Here, *felt* is an action verb; thus the adverb *carefully* modifies the verb *felt*.)

Real, Really; Sure, Surely

Real and *sure* are adjectives. Use the *ly* endings to remind you that *really* and *surely* are adverbs. In the following examples, note that you can substitute the adverb *very* or *certainly* whenever *really* or *surely* is correct.

> Wilma and Leo were (real? really?) delighted to hear that they were promoted. ("*Very* delighted" makes sense. The adverb *really* is correct.)

> Paula (sure? surely?) was smart to purchase this stock when it was half its present price. ("*Certainly* was" makes sense. The adverb *surely* is correct.)

Good, Well

Good is an adjective, and *well* is an adverb. The adjective *good* can modify nouns and pronouns; the adverb *well* can modify adjectives and verbs.

> Vanessa generally prepares *good* reports. (The adjective *good* modifies the noun *reports*.)

> Vanessa generally prepares reports *well*. (The adverb *well* modifies the verb *prepares*. Prepares reports how? Prepares *well*.)

Exception: *Well* can also be an adjective, *but only when referring to personal health.*

> Because Agatha did not feel *well*, she left the office at 3:30. (Here, *well* is an adjective referring to a person's health.)

Remember the term *well-being* and you'll be sure to recall that *well* is an adjective only when it refers to health.

Some, Somewhat

Some is an adjective; *somewhat* is an adverb. To use *somewhat* correctly, test to be sure that you can substitute the word *a little bit*.

> As we predicted, Ms. Feingold was (some? somewhat?) critical of the new organization plan. (Does "a little bit critical" make sense? Yes—thus *somewhat* is correct.)

> As we predicted, Ms. Feingold had (some? somewhat?) criticisms of the new organization plan. (Does "a little bit criticisms" make sense? No—thus the adjective *some* is correct.)

Most, Almost

Most is an adjective, the superlative of *much* or *many,* as in *much, more, most. Almost* is an adverb meaning "not quite" or "very nearly."

> (Most? Almost?) supervisors have already submitted their recommendations. (Because "very nearly supervisors" makes

no sense, *almost* cannot be correct. "*Most* supervisors" is correct.)

Jaclyn brought (most? almost?) enough copies for everyone on the committee. ("Very nearly enough copies" *does* make sense. *Almost* is correct.)

Checkup 2

Correct any errors in the following sentences. Write *OK* if a sentence has no errors.

1. Olivia was some surprised by the news about the transfer.
2. Most of us in the financial community found the reports real distressing.
3. After almost two years, the productivity plan has worked out very well.
4. Of course, she was sure justified in her request for equal pay.
5. Because you don't feel good, James, we suggest that you stay at home tomorrow.
6. Amy appeared angrily at the idea of closing the plant.
7. Because of the recent problems, we were somewhat hesitant to discuss this sensitive issue.
8. This discounted price is a real good bargain.
9. Needless to say, she and I felt badly when we heard that Ms. Jordan was retiring.
10. Because she was rushed, Olga sketched the drawing badly.

COMMUNICATION PROJECTS

Practical Application

A. Correct any adverb errors in the following sentences. Write *OK* if a sentence has no error.

1. All of us were glad when we read in the newspaper where the proposed tax legislation had been defeated.
2. Although this luncheon special does smell deliciously, I really am not very hungry right now.
3. Fred and I only know about the planned merger; no one else knows about it yet.
4. In our opinion, holding our present retail prices should sure work very well during the upcoming holiday season.
5. Because Tim has been late so frequent, Ms. Gardiner has spoken with him about the importance of arriving on time.
6. No, Jack, Mr. Tyler never told me that the package arrived early this morning.
7. We immediately noticed that Louis had fallen and that he needed help in the worst way.

8. Laura appeared very confident as she presented each of her staff with the special merit award.
9. As you know, our sales decreased some during the months of July and August.
10. Did you notice that this soft drink tastes very bitterly?
11. We are so close to the harbor that we can clear hear the tug boats from our offices.
12. Needless to say, we felt very badly when we heard that Ms. Jensen was moving to another branch office.
13. Follow these guidelines, Dolores, to make sure that you prepare your speech good.
14. The report that Glenn and Francine submitted hasn't scarcely one fresh suggestion for tackling this problem.
15. "We have," John said, "a real good chance of winning the contract."
16. According to Judy, Ms. Campbell wants to win the award in the worst way.
17. Yes, I do believe that his suggestion will work out very good.
18. Gregory never received the package from our Los Angeles office, although the carton was mailed more than a week ago.
19. As we expected, all the brokers are real concerned about the possible change in the commission schedule.
20. The credit for writing the brochure so good must go to Marion.

B.   Correct any errors in the following sentences. Write *OK* if a sentence has no error.

1. Gloria's estimates were due last Monday, but because she was so busy, Gloria never completed them.
2. According to Peter's supervisor, Peter works most as well as Carl.
3. Last year, Elaine had three assistants in her department; since the budget cutbacks, however, she hasn't but one assistant.
4. Here is all the swatches that you asked for, Ms. Hammond.
5. Of course, Barry and myself will be happy to help if you get really busy.
6. As you can well imagine, the Smiths' were really happy to learn that the interest on their investments is tax-free.
7. Gwen sent Jeffrey to the Medical Department because he wasn't feeling very good.
8. Neither the two managers nor the four assistants, in our opinion, has the time to devote to this extra paperwork.
9. Because Joanne been dedicating all her time to the upcoming convention, she has hired part-time help.
10. Elmer and Donna will help you process all them invoices if you fall behind, Martin.
11. Where's the keys to the storeroom and the supply closet?

12. Sabina has been doing very good since she was transferred to the Sales Department.
13. Be sure to focus careful so that you get a crisp, sharp picture.
14. Carla sure does a superb job of handling customer complaints.
15. Are these kind of diskettes available through our Purchasing Department?
16. Perhaps the two best writers in our office are Janet and him.
17. Of course, if Dana and me are selected to attend the convention, we will be really delighted.
18. There's about three or four applicants for the position we advertised in Sunday's classified ads.
19. The surrounding communitys use our auditorium and other facilities from time to time.
20. Only the Walsh's have requested specific changes in the standard contract.

Editing Practice

Proofreading for Accuracy. Proofreading accurately requires more than spelling and grammar expertise—it requires accuracy in *every* detail. Check the following excerpt carefully. Does it have any errors?

The following discount schedule will become effective on September 31:

On Purchases Over	Discount
$ 500	0.5%
1,000	0.75%
1,500	1.0%
2,000	1.25%
5,000	1.5%
10,000	1.75%
20,000	20.%

Using Your Word Processor. You are proofreading the following draft of a memorandum that you wrote. Before you print a copy, are there any errors that must be corrected?

The Office Trianing Center has recieved an overwhelming response to our recent proposal to add a basic programming course to our list of after-work course offerings. Begining on January 15, therefore, we will offer a variety of new programming courses; please see the enclosed catalog for a complete listing and time schedule.

If you are interested in these new programming courses (or any other courses, for that matter), please complete the registration form and send it to the Training Center as soon as possible. Registration for each course will be limited to the first 20 aplicants.

Case Problem

Introducing Yourself. During your first week on a new job, you are asked to attend a luncheon in one of the company dining rooms. When you arrive, you find that there are about 20 other employees in the room, all clustered in small groups and actively engaged in conversation. You know none of the employees.

1. What do you think you should do?
2. If you were in charge, what might you do to make it easier for a newcomer in such a situation?

21

PREPOSITIONS

Prepositions such as *for, of,* and *to* are used so often that we generally pay no attention to them. In order to avoid some common preposition errors, however, we must pay attention to the few rules presented in this section.

IDENTIFYING PREPOSITIONS

A *preposition* is a connecting word. It is always connected to a noun or a pronoun, and the preposition combined with that noun or pronoun makes up a *prepositional phrase*. Note the following commonly used prepositions and some sample prepositional phrases.

Prepositions			Prepositional Phrases
about	but*	off	*off* the shelf
above	by	on	*above* the typewriter
after	except	over	*after* our meeting
among	for	to	*to* the new airport
at	from	under	*from* Gary and Mona
before	in	up	*before* your first session
below	into	upon	*into* the auditorium
beside	like	until	*like* that book
between	of	with	*with* my partner

But is a preposition only when it means "except." In other cases, *but* is a conjunction.

The noun or pronoun that follows the preposition in the phrase is the *object* of the preposition. The phrase may include modifiers, for example, *new* in *to the new airport* modifies *airport,* which is the object of the preposition *to.* Also, the phrase may have compound objects, as in *from Gary and Mona.*

Because prepositional phrases often interrupt the subject and the verb in a sentence, your ability to make subjects and verbs agree will sometimes depend on your ability to identify prepositional phrases. Note the following examples.

The word processing operators *in this department* are reviewing these procedures carefully. (The prepositional phrase *in this department* separates the subject *operators* from the verb *are.* A careless speaker, therefore, may incorrectly say "department *is,*" which is wrong, of course.)

One executive *on both committees* has agreed to serve as the liaison. (The prepositional phrase *on both committees* separates the subject *executive* from the verb *has agreed.*)

Checkup 1

Identify the prepositions and the prepositional phrases in the following sentences.

1. The primary reason for the delay is that Ms. Petrovski is on vacation.
2. Most of the invoices that Laura placed on my desk have been checked and sent to our supervisor.
3. Only one of the women indicated that she was dissatisfied with our suggestion.
4. Because Mr. Sanders was in a rush, Larry drove him to the station.
5. On my desk are the folders that you will need.
6. Between you and me, I do not believe that investing in that stock was a smart idea.
7. Samantha went into the conference room, I think, with her assistant.
8. The final decision on this project will be discussed among the managers.

WORDS REQUIRING SPECIFIC PREPOSITIONS

Through years of use, certain expressions are now considered "correct," even though there may be no rule or logical reason to make them correct. Such usage, called "idiomatic usage," governs many expressions in our language. The use of certain prepositions with certain words is idiomatic—that is, long-accepted use has made it correct to use these prepositions, as in the following examples:

abhorrence *of*
abhorrent *to*
abide *by a decision*
abide *with* a person
abound *in* or *with*
accompanied *by* (attended by a person)
accompanied *with* (attended by something)
acquit *of*
adapted *to* (adjusted to)
adapted *for* (made over for)
adapted *from* a work
affinity *between*
agree *to* a proposal
agree *with* someone
agreeable *to* (*with* is permissible)
angry *at* a thing or condition
angry *with* a person
attend *to* (listen)
attend *upon* (wait on)
beneficial *to*
bestow *upon*
buy *from*
compare *to* the mirror image (assert a likeness)
compare *with* the reverse side (analyze for similarities or differences)
compliance *with*
comply *with*
confer *on* or *upon* (give to)
confer *with* (talk to)
confide *in* (place confidence in)
confide *to* (entrust to)
conform *to* (be in conformity *to* or *with*)
consist *in* (exist in)
consist *of* (be made up of)
convenient *for* (suitable for, easy for)
convenient *to* (near)
conversant *with*
correspond *to* or *with* (match; agree with)

correspond *with* (exchange letters)
credit *for*
deal *in* goods or services
deal *with* someone
depend or dependent *on* (but independent *of*)
derogatory *to*
different *from* (not *than* or *to*)
disappointed *in* or *with*
discrepancy *between* two things
discrepancy *in* one thing
dispense *with*
employ *for* a purpose
employed *at* a stipulated salary
employed *in, on,* or *upon* a work or business
enter *into* (become a party to)
enter *into* or *upon* (start)
enter *in* a record
enter *at* a given point
exception *to* a statement
familiarize *with*
foreign *to* (preferred to *from*)
identical *with*
independent *of* (not *from*)
inferior or superior *to*
need *of* or *for*
part *from* (take leave of)
part *with* (relinquish)
plan or planning *to* (not *on*)
profit *by*
in regard *to*
with regard *to*
as regards
retroactive *to* (not *from*)
speak *to* (tell something to a person)
speak *with* (discuss with)
wait *for* a person, a train, an event
wait *on* a customer, a guest

The idiomatic expressions that are used (and misused) most often are given special attention below. Be sure to learn to use these expressions correctly.

Agree With, Agree To

Use *agree with* when the object of the preposition is a person or idea; use *agree to* when the object is not a person or idea.

> Does Blake *agree with* Amanda concerning the need to increase our discount to wholesalers? (Because the object of the preposition is a person, the preposition *with* is correct.)

> Yes, Blake *agrees to* the proposal to increase our discount to wholesalers. (Here, the object of the preposition is *proposal*; because the object is not a person or idea, *agree to* is correct.)

Angry With, Angry At

Use *angry with* when the object of the preposition is a person; use *angry at* when the object is not a person.

> Glenn appeared to be *angry with* Jacob because of the delay in shipment. (*With* is correct because its object is a person, *Jacob.*)

> Glenn appeared to be *angry at* the delay in shipment. (Now the object of the preposition is not a person; thus *angry at* is correct.)

Part From, Part With

Part from means "to take leave of"; *part with* means "to relinquish," "to give up."
Part from is generally used when the object of the preposition is a person.
Part with is generally used when the object is not a person.

> As soon as we *part from* Ms. Morrison at the computer center, we will return to the office. (*Part from* a person.)

> Although we certainly appreciate the timesaving advancements of the new equipment, we hate to *part with* our familiar old machines. (*Part with*, meaning "to relinquish," "to give up.")

Discrepancy In, Discrepancy Between

Use *discrepancy in* when the object of the preposition is singular; use *discrepancy between* when the object specifically denotes *two* in number.

> I checked this chart carefully, and I found no *discrepancy in* it, Ms. Williams. (Note that *one* chart is mentioned.)

> Compare these two graphs carefully; then let your supervisor know if you find any *discrepancy between* the two. (Note that *two* graphs are mentioned.)

In Regard To, With Regard To, As Regards

All three terms are equally correct, but be sure to note that only the word *regard* (not *regards*) can be used in the phrases *in regard to* and *with regard to*.

Jerome has already consulted Mr. Johanson (in? with? as?) regard to the changes in schedule. (Either *in* or *with* is correct.)

(In? With? As?) regards the changes in schedule, please be sure to consult Mr. Johanson. (Only *as* is correct—*as regards*.)

Different From, Identical With, Plan To, Retroactive To

Memorize the correct prepositions that go with these phrases so that you will use them properly.

different *from* (not different *than*)

identical *with* (not identical *to*)

plan *to* (not plan *on*)

retroactive *to* (not retroactive *from*)

Checkup 2

Correct any errors in the following sentences. Write *OK* for any sentence that has no error.

1. When she discovered that the cartons had been carelessly handled, Ms. Cutter was angry at the messenger.
2. Rosemary obviously plans on opening her own store when she raises enough money to do so.
3. Of course, I was disappointed to find several discrepancies in the appendix to the report.
4. We have already spoken with our assistants in regards to the need to check each new account form carefully.
5. Sharon said that the most difficult aspect of leaving our company was parting from all her good friends.
6. Ronald slowly explained how the first machine is different than the second one.
7. Sue and I proofread both analyses; fortunately, we found no discrepancy in the two of them.
8. No, I frankly do not agree with Louis concerning the need to cut our advertising budget.
9. According to the union delegate, the contract will surely be retroactive from January 15.
10. Although this year's model looks different, it is really identical to last year's machine.

PITFALLS

When to use *between* and when to use *among* are among the preposition choices that trap many writers and speakers. Other pitfalls concern adding unnecessary prepositions and omitting prepositions that *are* necessary. Study the following to avoid the most common preposition pitfalls.

Between, Among

Use *between* when referring to *two* persons, places, or things, and use *among* when referring to three or more.

> The account forms were divided *between* Marjorie and Horace. (Between two people.)

> The remaining brochures were divided *among* our three branch offices. (Among three offices.)

Between may also be used to express a relationship of one thing to each of several other things on a one-to-one-basis.

> A separate agreement was signed *between* the parent company and each of the franchises.

Beside, Besides

Beside means "by the side of"; *besides* means "in addition to."

> Yes, the person seated *beside* Ms. VanBuren is Harold Boonton, our guest speaker. ("By the side of" Ms. VanBuren.)

> Do you know who is scheduled to speak *besides* Mr. Boonton? ("In addition to" Mr. Boonton.)

Inside, Outside

Do not use the preposition *of* after *inside* or *outside*. When referring to time, use *within*, not *inside of*.

> The conference room door is the first door *inside* the main entrance. (Not *inside of*.)

> We expect to have our forecasts completed *within* the week. (Not *inside of*.)

All, Both

Use *of* after *all* or *both* only when *all* or *both* refers to a pronoun. Omit *of* if either word refers to a noun.

> All the contracts were signed by Ms. Loomis. (*Of* is not needed.)

> All of them were signed by Ms. Loomis. (*Of* is required here.)

At, To; In, Into

At and *in* denote position; *to* and *into* signify motion.

> Bertha arrived *at* the airport and immediately went *to* the ticket counter. (*At* for position; *to* for motion.)

> They went *into* the hotel and set up the display *in* the main ballroom. (*Into* for motion; *in* for position.)

Note: When either *at* or *in* refers to a place, use *in* for larger places and *at* for smaller places.

> Edgar lives *in* Orange County and works *at* the local community college. (*In Orange County*, the larger place; *at the local community college*, the smaller place.)

Behind, *Not* In Back Of

Use *behind*, not *in back of. In front of*, however, is correct.

> Until the messenger arrives, place these cartons *behind*, not *in front of*, the file cabinets.

From, Off

From is generally used with persons; *off* is used with things. (*Off* is used with persons only when something on the person is physically being lifted away.) Never use *of* or *from* after *off*.

> Get some extra copies of this pamphlet *from* Barbara. (Not *off Barbara*.)

> After a few minutes, take the cold compresses *off* your arm. (Something is physically being lifted away.)

> Let's take these packages *off* the computer table. (Not *off of* the computer table.)

Where, *Not* Where . . . At *or* Where . . . To

Adding *at* or *to* to *where* is an illiteracy.

> No, I do not know *where* Dr. Franzetti is. (Not *is at*.)

> *Where* did John go? (Not *go to*.)

Help, *Not* Help From

Do not use the word *from* after *help*.

> Although we wanted to leave early, we could not *help* asking Mr. Bartholomew some questions. (Not *help from asking*.)

Opposite, *Not* Opposite To

Do not use the word *to* after *opposite*.

> The Marlings Building is directly *opposite* the Jennings Academy. (Not *opposite to*.)

Like, *Not* Like For

Omit the word *for* after *like*.

> We told Ms. Adams that we would *like* her to give the keynote speech at the banquet. (Not *like for*.)

Checkup 3

Correct any preposition errors in the following sentences. Write *OK* for any sentence that has no error.

EXPANDING ENGLISH LANGUAGE SKILLS

1. I'm sure that Harry knows where the blank diskettes are at, doesn't he?
2. In our opinion, Marlena cannot help from winning the sales contest this month.
3. Please call his office to find out where Jerome has gone to.
4. I believe that the new computer store is opposite the bus station.
5. Perhaps we should go in the auditorium to test these audiovisuals.
6. We may attend these classes at no charge if we attend outside of working hours.
7. The entire award of $10,000 was shared between Fred, Roseanne, and Vincent.
8. When we arrived at the hotel, we immediately pulled in the garage.
9. Is the man seated besides Andrew the new vice president of finance?
10. Let's leave all of these booklets in the van.

COMMUNICATION PROJECTS

Practical Application

A. Correct any errors in the following sentences. Write *OK* for any sentence that has no error.

1. Do you know yet what Mr. Fitch plans to do in regards to the changes in the contract?
2. We now know that the directions for the entire assignment were inside of the office.
3. Beside all the department heads, you should send a courtesy carbon copy to the regional managers.
4. Have you asked Nancy where Roberta went to?
5. Tell all the guests to park their cars in back of the building.
6. Leo and Agnes will take all this equipment off of the conference room table.
7. Lila's recommendations were virtually identical to the recommendations we received from our branch office managers.
8. Of course, we would very much like for Mrs. Russo to be our guest at the dinner.
9. Ms. Kumar plans on working next Saturday to prepare her speech for the convention.
10. Unfortunately, Mr. Smyth, your name was taken off of our mailing list in error.
11. Of course, T. J. was angry at his manager until he realized the reason for the transfer.
12. Maria carefully proofread the entire report to ensure that there was no discrepancy in it.

13. The restaurant that you mentioned is opposite to the library on Willow Avenue.
14. Helen dislikes parting from the special pieces in her collection.
15. Who besides Jim will be transferred to the new office?
16. Most of us could not help from wondering why the advertising budget was cut so drastically.
17. If we ship the cartons Tuesday, you should receive them inside of two weeks.
18. As all the invoices are received, they are divided among the three clerks in this department for processing.
19. With regards to the possibility of our voting for a strike, we have been asked to make no comments to the press.
20. In terms of strength, this new plastic is no different than this metal.

B. Correct any errors in the following sentences. Write *OK* for any sentence that has no error.

1. A number of complaints about this new model has been received by our product manager.
2. Yes, Edna generally works longer hours than me.
3. George, do you know whose in charge of the Purchasing Department?
4. Albert, who you met at the luncheon last Thursday, has been named head of the Sales Department.
5. Each of our many branch offices have their own studio.
6. Don't Phyllis want to attend the first session on Monday morning?
7. Don't Bernice and Phil want you and I to help them with their report?
8. Among the stores that we manage are The Computer Wizard in the Raymond Street Mall.
9. I think that you should order more of them sizes, because they're very popular.
10. Do these specifications conform with the standards in this brochure?
11. The manager of these two departments are revising these old-fashioned procedures.
12. If you were the head of this department, who would you select to be your assistant?
13. Have you already asked the Benson's whether they plan to vacation in Hawaii again this year?
14. In your opinion, who is the best sales representative in our company, Denise or he?
15. Margaret always does a real good job on the inventory reports.
16. Perhaps the reason Albert doesn't feel good is that he has poor eating habits.
17. Janet thinks that Louis proofreads much more accurately than her.

18. Every executive in the country will surely improve their management skills by reading this informative new book.
19. Vera, our supervisor, said that you and me will receive a good raise because of our superlative work all year long.
20. No, I certainly was not angry at Mark for his blunt remarks on the status of the project.

Editing Practice

Using Business Vocabulary. From the list below, select the word that best completes each of the blanks. On a separate piece of paper, write the corresponding letter of the correct word for each sentence.

a.	comptroller	f.	irreparable
b.	cumulative	g.	miscellaneous
c.	enumerate	h.	monopolize
d.	hesitant	i.	negligible
e.	inexhaustible	j.	unscrupulous

1. At this morning's meeting we discussed _____ topics.
2. The insurance adjustor agreed that the damage is _____, and therefore she will authorize payment of our claim.
3. Michelle appeared somewhat _____ to discuss the plans to reorganize our departments.
4. Fortunately, the amount of smoke damage to the supplies in the storeroom was _____.
5. The committee should not allow any one person to _____ the discussion.
6. To make this agenda clearer, you should _____ the topics in list form.
7. The first monthly column lists January sales; each succeeding column lists _____ sales for the preceding month.
8. Mr. Mobley, the _____ of our company, completed the requirements for an M.B.A. degree in June.
9. She wrote a best-selling exposé of excessive profiteering by _____ companies during the oil shortage.
10. Our supply of this metal is virtually _____, but mining it is very expensive.

Writing Sentences. Each of the following words is a "must" for your vocabulary and your spelling lists. Do you know the meaning of each word? Can you spell each one correctly?
  Write a sentence using each word.

1.	accommodate	6.	guarantee
2.	campaign	7.	necessary
3.	dissatisfied	8.	omission
4.	equivalent	9.	potential
5.	exorbitant	10.	questionnaire

Case Problem

Corporate Ethics.   All companies have rules prohibiting the use of company supplies and company equipment for employees' personal use. One day Elaine O'Toole, the supervisor of the mail room for Ross Chemicals, finds a batch of personal letters written by an employee, Ted Harris, on company stationery, mixed in with his business mail. Elaine doesn't know whether Ted's action was deliberate or accidental.

1. What should Elaine do about this situation? Explain your answer.
2. What should Elaine say to Ted?

22

CONJUNCTIONS

A *conjunction* is a word that is used to *connect* words, phrases, or clauses within a sentence.

> The printer *and* the monitor are included in this low, low price. (In this sentence, the conjunction *and* joins the words *printer* and *monitor*.)

> You may get a copy in my office *or* from the library. (The conjunction *or* joins two phrases, *in my office* and *from the library*.)

> Wanda wants to buy this computer, *but* she is waiting for a sale. (The conjunction *but* joins the two main clauses.)

Writing varied sentences and punctuating them correctly become much simpler once you have mastered the uses of conjunctions. This section presents three different kinds of conjunctions and then discusses the most common pitfalls in using conjunctions. Finally, this section considers parallel structure, an important topic that is closely related to conjunction use.

CLASSIFICATION OF CONJUNCTIONS

Three conjunction types are discussed below: *coordinating*, *correlative*, and *subordinating conjunctions*. As you will see, coordinating and correlative conjunctions connect two or more items of equal rank. Subordinating conjunctions, however, connect a subordinate clause to a main clause.

Coordinating Conjunctions

The four coordinating conjunctions—*and*, *but*, *or*, and *nor*—are very commonly used. Note that they connect only *like* elements of grammar: two or more words, two or more phrases, or two or more clauses.

Lunch *and* dinner are included in the total price. (The conjunction *and* connects two words, *lunch* and *dinner*.)

Breakfast, lunch, *and* dinner are included in the total price. (Here the conjunction *and* joins *three* words.)

Karen has been on the telephone *or* in meetings most of the day. (The conjunction *or* joins two prepositional phrases, *on the telephone* and *in meetings*.)

Edward planned to leave for New Orleans next Friday, *but* he couldn't get airline reservations. (The conjunction *but* connects two independent, or main, clauses.)

Correlative Conjunctions

Correlative conjunctions are *pairs* of conjunctions that are regularly used together to connect like elements. (Note, again, that both coordinating and correlative conjunctions connect *like* elements only.) The most commonly used correlative conjunctions are:

both . . . and
either . . . or
neither . . . nor
not only . . . but also
whether . . . or

Like coordinating conjunctions, these correlatives connect words, phrases, or clauses.

Not only Bob *but also* Fay will attend the luncheon next Wednesday. (Here the correlatives *not only . . . but also* connect two words, *Bob* and *Fay*.)

Henry has been working on his project *not only* in the office *but also* at home. (Two phrases, *in the office* and *at home*, are joined.)

Not only does Daniel intend to win the sales contest, *but* he *also* plans to break the old record. (Here two clauses are connected.)

Subordinating Conjunctions

Subordinating conjunctions join clauses of *un*equal rank. A subordinating conjunction introduces a subordinate (or dependent) clause and connects it to a main (or independent) clause.

> *Although* we lowered the list price, sales still dropped significantly. (*Although* is a subordinating conjunction, and it introduces the subordinate clause *although we lowered the list price.* Further, *although* connects this subordinate clause to the main clause.)

> Ask Ms. DiPinto for a registration form *if* you plan to sign up for this course. (The subordinating conjunction *if* introduces the subordinate clause *if you plan to sign up for this course* and connects this clause to the main clause.)

Study the following list of commonly used subordinating conjunctions so that you will be able to identify subordinate clauses.

after	before	provided that	when
although	even if	since	whenever
as	for	so that	where
as if	how	than	wherever
as soon as	if	that	whether
as though	in case that	unless	while
because	in order that	until	why

Checkup 1

Identify the conjunctions in the following sentences. Label each "coordinating," "correlative," or "subordinating."

1. Barry will discuss these new procedures as soon as he returns from his business trip.
2. While Ms. Bernardo was on vacation, her promotion was approved by the president of the company.
3. Have you already sent in both the completed registration form and your check?
4. Our supervisor and the manager of the Purchasing Department carefully reviewed the entire order.
5. Order today if you would like to receive this tremendous discount offer.
6. You will save an additional 10 percent by enclosing your payment now, unless you prefer to be billed at a later date.
7. Frances, do you know whether Alvin or Larry has called this client yet?
8. Yes, I'm sure that Larry called him already.
9. Please ask either Marvin or Thelma to go with you to the conference.
10. You may pay 12 monthly installments, or you may save $100 by paying before January 30.

PITFALLS

The following discussion focuses on the major conjunction pitfalls—mainly (1) choosing a conjunction that does not accurately convey the meaning intended and (2) choosing a preposition when a conjunction is needed.

But or And?

The conjunction *but* provides a contrast while *and* simply joins two elements. Use *but* when a contrast is intended.

> The difference in price between the two models is minimal, *but* only one model is energy-efficient. (*But* for contrast.)

Who, Which, or That?

Use *who* to refer to persons and *which* to refer to objects. Never say or write *and who* or *and which*.

> Send a carbon copy to Mr. Reasons, *who* is the new director of marketing. (*Who* refers to a person.)

> We were instructed to send all recommendations to the Finance Committee, *which* is responsible for all pricing decisions. (*Which* refers to an object.)

That may be used to refer to persons, objects, or animals.

> The speaker *that* you heard is Edwin Tobin, a well-known business lecturer. (*That* refers to a person. Note that *whom* could also have been used, of course.)

> One seminar *that* you will find interesting is Time Management. (Here, *that* refers to an object.)

> A racehorse *that* Martha bought has been insured for more than $1,000,000. (*That* refers to an animal.)

Since or Because, *Not Being That*

There is no such conjunction as *being that*. Use *since* or *because* instead.

> *Because* we did not have all the important data, we decided to postpone our committee meeting. (*Because*, not *Being that*.)

"The Reason Is That"; Pretend That"

Do not say or write "the reason is *because*" and "pretend *like*." Instead, say "the reason is *that*" and "pretend *that*."

> The reason for the sudden strike, according to informed sources, is *that* the company has threatened to lay off 1000 workers. (Not *reason . . . is because*.) Of course, we cannot pretend *that* sales are healthy. (Not *pretend like*.)

Unless, *Not Without or Except*

Without and *except* are prepositions, and a preposition always introduces a prepositional phrase. (*Remember:* A prepositional phrase consists of a preposition plus its noun or pronoun object and any modifiers.) Yet many writers and speakers incorrectly use these prepositions as substitutes for the subordinating conjunction *unless.*

> You cannot return this application *without* Ms. Ford's approval. (This is correct. *Without Ms. Ford's approval* is a prepositional phrase: *approval* is the object of the preposition *without,* and *Ms. Ford's* is a modifier.)

> You cannot return this application *unless* Ms. Ford approves it. (Again, this is correct. The subordinating conjunction *unless* introduces a clause. An error occurs, however, when people incorrectly say or write *without Ms. Ford approves it.* The preposition *without* cannot introduce a clause.)

As, As If, As Though, *Not* Like

Remember that *like* is a preposition ("a car *like* mine") or a verb ("I *like* this model"). It is *not* a conjunction. Therefore, do not use *like* when *as, as if,* or *as though* is intended.

> Sheila seemed *as if* she were angry. (*As if,* not *like.*)

Checkup 2

Correct any errors in the following sentences. Write *OK* for any sentence that has no error.

1. She told Bill not to sit around like he has no work to do.
2. Please make sure that Ms. Pyle doesn't leave without she signs these contracts.
3. Ella's new job is quite time-consuming, and she enjoys it very much.
4. According to the newspaper reports, the main reason for the sudden increase in oil prices is because production has been curtailed by OPEC.
5. Anne recommended several competent artists which have studios nearby.
6. Randy said, "It seems like sales are suddenly improving."
7. No, Jonas, do not send this package to Mr. Martin without you get official authorization from your supervisor.
8. Do not send this package unless you get official authorization.
9. You certainly shouldn't act like you did not contribute to this project, Bernie.
10. Todd, please do not mail this confirmation slip except I ask you to do so.

PARALLEL STRUCTURE

Observing the rules of parallel structure will provide balance to your writing. Note the following examples:

> This laser printer works quietly and quickly. (The conjunction *and* joins two parallel elements—two adverbs, *quietly* and *quickly*.)

> This laser printer works quietly and with speed. (Now the same ideas are expressed but not in parallel form. Here we have an adverb, *quietly*, joined to a prepositional phrase, *with speed*. These two grammatical elements are not alike; they are not parallel.)

Study the following subsections to ensure that you master parallel structure with coordinating and correlative conjunctions.

With Coordinating Conjunctions

Coordinating conjunctions connect *like* elements: an adjective with an adjective, a prepositional phrase with a prepositional phrase, and so on. Therefore, make sure that the elements before and after a coordinating conjunction match.

> These machines are checked carefully and (regularly? with regularity?). (An adverb, *carefully*, appears before the coordinating conjunction *and*; therefore, the adverb *regularly* should follow *and*. Together, *carefully*, and *regularly* achieve parallel structure.)

> Writing the first draft is easy, but (editing? to edit?) it is more difficult. (Which choice matches *writing*? Answer: *editing*. Both *writing* and *editing* are gerunds.)

Checkup 3

Balance the following sentences to make them parallel.

1. Completing this course will help you understand the basics of finance and applying these basics to your job.
2. The health instructor said, "Eating the proper foods is important, but to exercise is also important."
3. In my opinion, both assistants seem to be personable and have courtesy.
4. You may submit your credit card request by telephone, by mail, or you can come in person.
5. This special new material can be bent, rolled, or is even immersible in water.
6. As you probably know, these machines require monthly maintenance and an overhaul every year.

With Correlative Conjunctions

As you already know, correlative conjunctions are used in pairs. To achieve parallelism with correlative conjunctions, simply make sure that the element that follows the first conjunction is the same as the element that follows the second conjunction.

Mrs. Lauren generally wants *either* her assistant *or* me to check all these inventory reports. (The elements that follow *either . . . or* are a noun *(assistant)* and a pronoun *(me)*. Nouns and pronouns are considered like elements because pronouns are substitutes for nouns. Thus the phrase *either her assistant or me* is parallel.)

The new catalogs are available *not only* in all our stores *but also* through our mail-order department. (Notice the parallelism of two prepositional phrases, one after each of the correlatives.)

Not only did Deborah win the sales contest, *but* she *also* broke the previous record. (*Not only* is followed by an independent clause, and *but also* is followed by an independent clause. The sentence is parallel. Do not be misled by the inverted order of the first clause.)

Checkup 4

Balance the elements joined by correlative conjunctions so that they are parallel.

1. In an effort to save fuel, we are trying to either form car pools or to use public transportation.
2. The final report will be signed either by Mr. Jordan or his assistant.
3. Among the activities I like best are both canoeing and to ski.
4. Maude neither agreed with Jeremy nor Clark.
5. Higher discounts are generally either given to our best customers or to our employees.
6. This book is both well written and has colorful illustrations.

COMMUNICATION PROJECTS

Practical Application

A.   Correct any errors in the following sentences. Write *OK* for any sentence that has no error.

1. Store policy states that refunds are not allowed without a receipt.
2. Store policy states that refunds are not allowed unless the customer has a receipt.

3. Our manager neither feels that overtime nor part-time help will quickly ease the backlog.
4. Theresa seems to give away free samples of merchandise like they cost the company nothing.
5. Late payments are neither allowed for our large customers nor for our small customers.
6. The reason she arrived late is because the airport was closed during the snowstorm.
7. After a very long discussion, they not only agreed on the final list prices but also on the discount to distributors.
8. The small model sells very well, and the larger model is probably the better value.
9. The man which you heard is the manager of our New York store.
10. Because you looked like you were tired, we decided not to bother you.
11. Please do not mail this check without Clara signs it first.
12. Please do not mail this check except Clara signs it first.
13. The committee members seem objective and to be impartial.
14. Your duties will include screening applicants and to interview candidates.
15. Being that Mr. York was out of town, we postponed the meeting until Thursday.
16. The deadline is only a few hours away, and we will be able to complete the report on schedule.
17. As I suspected, the reason total sales increased in the fourth quarter was because each regional office sponsored a sales contest.
18. You must test applicants for their skills in typing, filing, and to take dictation.
19. When you are at the podium, pretend like you are talking to a few close friends.
20. Please do not throw out these tapes except I ask you to do so.

B. Correct any errors in the following sentences. Write *OK* for any sentence that has no error.

1. A large number of applicants, according to Rory, was interviewed during the last two days.
2. Mr. Reynoldo claims that the Blanton's are very eager to sell their property.
3. We are looking for one of those printers that sells for under $1000.
4. Last week Mr. Carruthers invited Cora and I to visit his company's annual art exhibit.
5. All the forms on the desk in her office was received only this morning.
6. No, Leonard, we have no brochures and not any postcards.

7. Yes, there's been a few problems with the new payment system, but we are confident that the new system will work out well.

8. Irma does not plan on ordering any new printers until she tests them for compatibility with our computers.

9. Have you received any more information in regards to the changes in our medical and dental coverage?

10. "When talking with your clients," our sales manager suggested, "pretend like our products are the only ones on the market."

11. We decided to purchase all our equipment from Conti Computers Inc. being that CCI has such a great reputation for knowledge and service.

12. Have you read in our company newsletter where we may open a branch office in Dayton next month?

13. Sam, don't Norma know about the 4 o'clock deadline for placing classified ads?

14. Giselle left a message with Dr. Ashford's service this morning, but Dr. Ashford never called back.

15. If you and me complete this entire report today, we will send it to the Duplicating Department immediately.

16. Jeanne neither completed the forms correctly nor mailed them to us on time.

17. We received many, many excellent suggestions; Kenneth's recommendation, however, was the most unique.

18. On the bulletin board in the main hallway is the announcements in regard to the upcoming sales contests.

19. If your looking for value, quality, and durability, we honestly believe that the Eton computer should be your choice.

20. Are the Ellis's still in San Francisco, or have they returned to Dallas?

Editing Practice

Using Your Word Processor. Proofread "on-screen" the following excerpt from a memorandum that you wrote. Must any errors be corrected before you print out a copy of this memo?

Begining March 15, account executives must sign each new-account form before sending the form to the Sales Department. Each account executive should proofread the form carefully to make sure that the client's name and address (as well as the details of the transaction, of course) are correct in every detail.

Remember that an error in the new-account form can delay shipments of merchandise to your client and cause errors in billing, both of which will contribute to poor customer relations. Lets strive to get it right the first time!

Plurals and Possessives. Correct any errors in the following sentences. Write *OK* for any sentence that has no error.

1. Among the people who were not able to attend were the Ross's, because they have been in Europe since April 11.
2. One of the foremost childrens' clothing stores is Kids' Stuff, a nationwide chain whose headquarters is in New York City.
3. According to the will, his three brothers and his sister-in-laws will share the money equally.
4. Most of the designs that we reviewed showed creativity and flair; however, the one that all the committee members preferred was her's.
5. Retype this column of numbers, making sure that the zeroes and the decimals align properly.
6. I believe that some of the ratioes given in this table are incorrect; please proofread them carefully.
7. Alvin and Mike's new apartment is only about ten minutes away.
8. Tonights' guest speakers, the Messrs. Klein, will surely entertain the audience.
9. My inventory report may have an error, because it does not agree with your's.
10. No, I was not aware of Dean leaving early, but apparently our supervisor gave him permission to do so.

Case Problem

Quantity and Quality. Joan Griffiths is preparing the first performance appraisal of one of her new assistants, Grace Pembroke. In Joan's opinion, Grace has many obvious assets, including a high degree of job knowledge and excellent productivity. One serious flaw in Grace's performance is that virtually every letter and memo she prepares has one or more spelling errors—and Grace's job description includes heavy writing responsibilities.

When Joan tried discussing this with Grace, Grace showed that she was aware of her poor spelling and simply accepted it as her "weakness." Confident that she was indeed performing well in all other areas, Grace seemed to deliberately take her spelling errors lightly.

1. If you were Joan, what would you tell Grace?
2. Why is it important for Grace to improve her spelling?

CHAPTER
FIVE

APPLYING THE MECHANICS OF STYLE

23

PERIODS, QUESTION MARKS, AND EXCLAMATION POINTS

Punctuation marks do for writing what pauses, changes in pitch, and gesturing do for speaking: They provide the necessary road signs to help readers and listeners understand our messages correctly. The three marks discussed in this section are used to end sentences. In addition, they have some other uses, which are also discussed in this section.

PERIODS

It's important to learn when to use periods and when *not* to use periods, as well as to avoid some common pitfalls in using them.

When to Use Periods

Use periods (1) to end declarative or imperative sentences, (2) to end requests that are phrased as questions simply for the sake of courtesy, and (3) to end indirect questions.

AFTER DECLARATIVE AND IMPERATIVE SENTENCES. Declarative sentences make statements, and imperative sentences order someone to act.

> You should proofread these contracts carefully. (Declarative sentence.)

> Proofread these contracts carefully. (Imperative sentence.)

AFTER REQUESTS PHRASED AS QUESTIONS. In an effort to soften commands and orders, speakers and writers often phrase such orders as questions. Because such statements are not really questions, use periods to end these sentences.

> Will you please send us your check immediately. (Not a question—no answer is required.)

> May we have the complete order shipped by the fastest method. (A polite way of saying, "Send the order as fast as possible." Not really a question.)

Will you be able to deliver the entire order by Friday? (This requires a "Yes" or "No" answer. This is a question and requires a question mark.)

AFTER INDIRECT QUESTIONS. An *indirect question* is a question restated as a declarative sentence.

Pat, have you already sent a confirmation copy to Ms. Samuels? (A question.)

She asked me whether I had already sent a confirmation copy to Ms. Samuels. (Restated as a declarative sentence, this sentence requires a period.)

Checkup 1

Which of the following sentences should end with periods and with question marks?

1. May we leave at 3:30 today
2. Karen asked Ms. Shipley whether she plans to cancel the order
3. May I have your complete payment by next Monday, March 15
4. Sharon, may I use this data diskette
5. Edna asked permission to leave at 3:30 today
6. Will you be able to send the remainder of the merchandise before the end of the month
7. Submit your suggestions to your supervisor before December 30
8. Did he say the deadline is December 30

When Not to Use Periods

Do *not* use periods in the following instances.

AFTER SENTENCES ENDING IN ABBREVIATIONS. Do *not* use two periods for sentences that end with abbreviations that take periods. Only one period is required.

As you know, the reception will begin at 8 p.m. (Not *8 p.m..*)

AFTER HEADINGS OR TITLES OR AFTER ROMAN NUMERALS. Headings that are set on separate lines (for examples, see the headings in this textbook) should not be followed by periods. Also, roman numerals used with names or titles should not be followed by periods.

Peter Mendez III has been appointed assistant corporate counsel. (Not *Peter Mendez III. has been . . . .*)

AFTER NUMBERS OR LETTERS IN PARENTHESES. Do not use periods after numbers or letters that are enclosed in parentheses.

Their portfolio consists mainly of (1) government bonds, (2) corporate bonds, and (3) municipal bonds.

When numbers or letters are not in parentheses and are displayed on separate lines, use a period after each.

Their portfolio consists mainly of:

1. Government bonds.
2. Corporate bonds.
3. Municipal bonds.

Note: In the above example, each item in the list grammatically completes the introductory statement and, therefore, ends with a period. If each item did not grammatically complete the introductory statement, no period would be needed.

Their portfolio includes the following:

1. Government bonds
2. Corporate bonds
3. Municipal bonds

Of course, if each item in a list is a complete sentence or a long phrase, use a period.

AFTER EVEN AMOUNTS OF DOLLARS. Except in tables (when it is important to align numbers), do not use periods or unnecessary zeros in even dollar amounts.

We appreciate your sending us your $75 deposit so quickly. (Not *$75.* and not *$75.00*)

Checkup 2

Find any errors in the following sentences. Write *OK* for any sentence that has no error.

1. For a limited time only, you can renew your subscription for two years for only $125. a year.
2. The new contract will be signed tomorrow at the headquarters of Long Island Computers, Inc..
3. Have you heard that former Mayor David W. Wiseman III. has been elected to our board?
4. The enclosed materials include (1) a booklet describing the medical benefits program, (2) an application form, and (3) a postage-paid envelope.
5. By renewing your subscription now, you can save $39.00 over the newsstand price.
6. The survey polled the following employees:
   a. Commission sales representatives
   b. Executives
   c. Clerical personnel

Pitfalls

Using a period at the end of an *in*complete thought is called the "period fault." Using a comma when a period is needed is called the "comma-for-period fault." Both are discussed below.

THE PERIOD FAULT.   An *in*complete thought is not a sentence and therefore cannot stand alone. Generally, joining the incomplete thought to a main clause will solve the problem.

> The company is not planning to expand its sales force. Because it expects customer demand to drop drastically next year. (The second group of words cannot stand alone. This dependent clause should be joined to the preceding independent clause as shown in the following example.)

> The company is not planning to expand its sales force, because it expects customer demand to drop drastically next year. (Now the dependent clause does not stand alone but is joined correctly to an independent clause.)

THE COMMA-FOR-PERIOD FAULT.   A comma should *not* be used to join two independent sentences. A period is needed.

> Sandra will answer these questions at our meeting next Monday, she will also discuss some changes in order processing. (A period should follow *Monday*, separating these two independent sentences.)

> Our new catalog is enclosed, an up-to-date price list will be sent to you within the next two weeks. (Again, these two independent sentences should be separated by a period.)

Checkup 3

Are there any period faults or comma-for-period faults in the following sentences? Make any necessary corrections. Write *OK* for any sentence that has no error.

1. As we discussed at our recent meeting on marketing strategies. We must direct our advertising to the top manufacturing companies in the South.
2. Although the budget money had been completely exhausted. He recommended that additional funds be allocated if necessary to complete the project.
3. Adelaide is now exploring certain investment opportunities, she is especially interested in tax-exempt bonds.
4. Dr. Lo invited the entire staff to the luncheon next Tuesday, she will announce some promotions then.
5. Orders for disk drives and monitors will be filled at the end of the month, our warehouse is currently out of stock.
6. The negotiations ended abruptly Friday afternoon. When the union delegate walked out of the meeting.

7. Maude and Claire placed the checks in Ms. MacGrail's safe. Because the checks were cashier's checks.
8. We have gained nearly 25 percent more of the market for computer magazines. Since we launched our sales promotion campaign two years ago.

QUESTION MARKS

Use question marks after direct questions and in series of questions.

After Direct Questions

Direct questions always end with question marks.

Have you completed your monthly inventory report?

Mr. Andrews, have you received your airline tickets yet?

Should we stamp these cartons "Fragile"?

Betty asked, "Where is the original copy of this purchase order?"

Sentences that begin as statements but end as questions are considered questions. Use question marks at the end of such sentences.

Maureen shipped all the merchandise to the Main Street store, didn't she? (The question at the end of the statement—*didn't she?*—requires a question mark at the end of the sentence.)

James is planning to take the proofreading course after work, isn't he? (Again, the question following the statement makes this an interrogative sentence. Use a question mark at the end of the sentence.)

In Series of Questions

When a sentence contains a series of questions, the series may be joined by conjunctions and commas (like other series) and end with one question mark. On the other hand, each question may be separated from the main sentence and may have its own question mark. Note the following pairs.

Have you already sent this confidential report to the president, the executive vice president, and the treasurer? (The items in the series are joined by commas and the conjunction *and.* The sentence ends with a question mark.)

Have you already sent this confidential report to the president? the executive vice president? the treasurer? (Each item in the series is separated from the main sentence, and each ends with its own question mark. Note that a lowercase letter begins each item to show that it is connected to the main sentence.)

14. Colleen is going to Middletown next week, isn't she.
15. Gregory wants to know whether the cartons have arrived from our warehouse?

B. Correct any errors in the following sentences. Write *OK* for any sentence that has no error.

1. Are you certain that she said to send all these cartons c.o.d.
2. Nancy appreciated us helping her with her annual inventory report.
3. Mr. Johanssen, our assistant manager, asked whether these computers are also on sale?
4. There's only two or three billing clerks scheduled to work overtime tonight.
5. With the 10 percent discount, this computer will sell for only $950.00.
6. Please ask the Purchasing Department to send the extra cartons to Thelma and I.
7. Proofreading all these figures was more hard than we expected it to be.
8. To make sure that we will be able to meet the tight deadlines, we divided all the invoices between Marie, Jason, and me.
9. Sometimes John acts like he were the president of this company instead of its assistant regional manager.
10. Andrew, do not release these checks without your supervisor approves them.
11. We discontinued the sale. When we depleted our inventory.
12. You should sign up for this course now, only fifteen people will be accepted.
13. We predict that this advertisement will be more effective than any advertisement we ever placed.
14. Usually Joanne don't like to take an early lunch hour.
15. Jessica is confident that she and her staff will exceed their sales goals, her group is only about $100,000 short of its budget.
16. As you can see, each customers' account is carefully checked before a monthly invoice is mailed.
17. If you require more of these pamphlets, additional copys are available from our warehouse.
18. Must all these specification sheets be approved by the president? the comptroller? the chief engineer?
19. Janice or Margaret are going to open the office next Saturday.
20. Only one of the supervisors were against the idea of reducing our total production for the next month.

Editing Practice

Are We in Agreement?   Correct any agreement errors in the following sentences.

1. As you know, every customer has the right to see his credit history.
2. On the shelf in Ms. Simmons' office is the latest reports on industrial pollution.
3. The use of preservatives in children's food is the subject of the analysis.
4. All tax records before 1980 has been discarded, according to Mr. Reilly.
5. The number of customers who asked for more information on the new credit accounts are surprisingly high.
6. The newspaper article said that some of the area have already been purchased by a major land developer.
7. James, here is the slide projector and the remote-control device that you requested.
8. Every executive in the country will improve their productivity by reading this helpful study.
9. Pauline said that either Louis or Raymond have been assigned to the newsroom.
10. Dependability and initiative is important for advancement to executive positions.

Spelling Alert!   Correct any misspelled words in the following excerpt.

> As a valued longtime customer of Fromm's Furniture Shop, you are invited to a specail one-day sale of quality merchandise. Among the items that will be reduced as much as 35 percent are sofas, recliners, dining room sets, and many other peices of furniture, all from name-brand manufacturers.
>
> Remember the date and the time: Saturday, Febuary 10, from 9 a.m. until 9 p.m.

Case Problem

Retaining Goodwill.   Louisa Gerard, a supervisor in the business office of Fromm's Furniture Shop, found carbon copies of letters to a customer written by Errol Denton, a new employee. Among the comments that Louisa especially noted were (1) "Of course, Ms. Greenberg, no one can prove that scratches on furniture are caused by us." (2) "We cannot accept responsibility for surface stains and scratches once the merchandise has been delivered to the customer."

1. What do you think of these statements?
2. If you were Louisa, what, if anything, would you say to Errol?

24

SEMICOLONS, COLONS, AND DASHES

In the preceding section you saw how periods, question marks, and exclamation points are used to *end* sentences. Now you will learn three marks of punctuation that are used *within* sentences— semicolons, colons, and dashes. Each has its own specific function, as you will see in this section.

SEMICOLONS

Semicolons are intended to make the reader pause; by providing "timing cues," they guide the reader in understanding the message clearly. Semicolons are used (1) as indication of the omission of a conjunction, (2) before an introductory word that begins the second clause in a sentence, and (3) before explanatory or enumerating words.

As Indication of Omission of a Conjunction

A compound sentence has two or more independent clauses, which are usually connected by commas and a conjunction.

> The Office Training Center offers a variety of courses for personal enjoyment and professional development, and we encourage our employees to take advantage of these offerings. (This is a compound sentence; it has two independent clauses connected by a comma and the conjunction *and.*)

The conjunction and comma in a compound sentence such as the one above may be omitted, and a semicolon may be used to replace them.

> The Office Training Center offers a variety of courses for personal enjoyment and professional development; we encourage our employees to take advantage of these offerings. (Here, a semicolon joins the two independent clauses, replacing the comma and the conjunction.)

Before a Second Clause Starting With an Introductory Word

In some compound sentences, the second clause starts with an introductory word such as:

accordingly	however
again	indeed
also	moreover
besides	nevertheless
consequently	otherwise
furthermore	therefore

In such sentences, the semicolon provides the necessary pause between the independent clauses, and the introductory word tells the specific relationship between the two clauses, making the meaning clearer.

> To save energy, turn off all lights before you leave the office; however, please do leave on lights in hallways and stairways. (The semicolon separates the two independent clauses, and the introductory word *however* signals the reader to contrast the two clauses.)

> This corporate bond offers a 10 percent after-tax return; consequently, we are increasing our total investment. (Again, the semicolon separates the two independent clauses and tells the reader to pause. The introductory word *consequently* establishes a specific relationship between the two clauses; it shows that the second statement is a result of the first statement.)

Note that the introductory word is not always the *first* word in the second clause.

> To save energy, turn off all lights before you leave the office; please do leave on lights in hallways and stairways, *however*.

> This corporate bond offers a 10 percent after-tax return; we are, *consequently*, increasing our total investment.

Before Explanatory or Enumerating Words

Use a semicolon before terms such as *for example*, *for instance*, and *that is* when they introduce an independent clause, an enumeration, or an explanation that is incidental to the meaning of the rest of the sentence.

> Marge is expanding our newspaper advertising; for example, she now advertises our products in all the major dailies in the state. (*For example* introduces an independent clause.)

> Jack is now looking at several possible ways to cut expenses; for instance, leasing rather than buying delivery

vans, using less expensive cartons and packing materials, and buying in larger quantities. (*For instance* introduces an enumeration.)

Make any necessary corrections in the following sentences. Write *OK* for any sentence that has no error.

1. Our department will be closed for inventory next week, nevertheless, our manager and her assistant will be at work.
2. In the summer, we manufacture our winter line, in the winter, we manufacture our summer apparel.
3. The new policy states that we must request at least three estimates for such projects, accordingly, we have asked three suppliers to bid on this job.
4. No chemicals of any kind are included in our products; our company has always prohibited their use.
5. Dr. Harley's presentation was interesting and informative, indeed, the local newspapers called it "fascinating"!
6. Ms. White has decided to open another factory, the new one may be located in Boston.
7. Rachel will be promoted to manager next month, we expect, therefore, to see many changes in procedures in the future.
8. We canceled the order because we have not been happy with the service from Empire Printers, besides, we already have an oversupply of brochures and pamphlets.

COLONS

Colons make readers pause and take note of what follows.

Colons Before Listed Items

When expressions such as *the following, as follows, this, these,* and *thus* are used to introduce a list of items, they are often followed by colons. The list itself may follow on the same line as the colon, or it may be typed on a new line.

At our committee meeting next Wednesday, we will discuss these topics: (1) marketing strategies for next year, (2) the advertising budget, and (3) expansion of our warehouse facilities.

At our committee meeting next Wednesday, we will discuss these topics:

1. Marketing strategies for next year
2. The advertising budget
3. Expansion of our warehouse facilities

Sometimes the words *the following, as follows,* and so on, do not directly lead into the list; for example, an "interrupting" sentence appears between the lead-in sentence and the list. In such cases, a period, not a colon, should be used. Follow these examples.

Note that the schedules have been changed as follows. A revised completion date is listed next to each product. (A period, not a colon, is used after *as follows* because the actual list does not follow directly. A sentence separates the lead-in *as follows* and the actual list.)

The following techniques will help you to use your time more effectively. Read them carefully; then read the examples of how to apply each technique. (Again, the first sentence does not directly lead into the listing, so the sentence ends in a period, not a colon.)

Colons Instead of Semicolons

You already have learned that semicolons are used before expressions such as *for example* and *that is* when these expressions introduce independent clauses, enumerations, and explanations that are incidental to the rest of the sentence. However, when the explanation or enumeration is anticipated, a colon is used instead of a semicolon.

Glen cited two good reasons for postponing our decision: namely, the cost of oil is now dropping rapidly, and our lease expires at the end of June.

Colons to Emphasize

Writers most often use colons to emphasize or to point up important thoughts or words.

Karen quickly pointed out the most important factor: cost. (The colon provides special emphasis to "the most important factor.")

Remember: Beginning Monday, no employee will be permitted to enter the laboratory without his or her identification badge. (More emphatic than "Please try to remember that beginning Monday. . . .")

Capitalizing After Colons

Capitalize the first word following a colon if (1) it begins a complete sentence requiring special emphasis or (2) it begins a sentence stating a formal rule.

The salary adjustment applies to only two groups of employees: hourly employees and commission employees. (Not a sentence; the first word is not capitalized.)

Peter cited one good reason for approving the idea: It will save money. (Complete sentence; the first word is capitalized because the sentence requires special emphasis.)

The first step is the most important: Create an outline for your report. (Complete sentence; the first word is capitalized because the sentence states a formal rule.)

Checkup 2

Correct any errors in colon use in the following sentences. Write *OK* for any sentence that has no error.

1. The changes in benefits affect these areas, medical insurance, dental coverage, and maternity leave.
2. Two exciting speakers will be on hand: Don't miss this opportunity. One speaker is Irene Copley; the other is Frank Trudeau.
3. We finally discovered why the messenger had not arrived: He went to the wrong address.
4. Marie gave these reasons for increasing the order quantity. Each reason is explained in her memo.
5. Only two people in our department were invited to the board meeting: My supervisor and Jeff Shannon.
6. Raymond repeated the deadline for all to hear. March 15.

DASHES

Dashes share some of the features of semicolons and of colons: All three stop the reader—but dashes do so more forcefully. Compare, for example, the different impact in each of the following examples. Notice how the dash provides greater impact than either the semicolon or the colon.

Your advertising dollar will bring you the greatest return if you buy time on OKTV; this is the television network that statistics prove is tuned in by most viewers in this area. (A good sentence, but not a forceful one.)

For the best return on your advertising dollar, do this: Buy time on OKTV, the television network that statistics prove is tuned in by most viewers in this area. (This is a better sentence, a more forceful one.)

Your advertising dollar will bring you the greatest return if you buy time on OKTV—the television network that statistics prove is tuned in by most viewers in this area. (The dash snaps off the main thought and thereby adds power to the rest of the message. This is the most forceful sentence.)

The semicolon provides the needed pause between clauses, but the colon provides more than a pause: It promises that something important will follow. The dash goes even further by drawing special attention to what follows the dash. Therefore, the dash makes the third example the strongest of the three. These three punctuation marks allow the writer to guide the reader through the message. At the same time, they allow the writer to provide variety and interest to the message.

Forceful Summarizing, Forceful Repetition

When you are writing, you will sometimes summarize the main points of your message to make sure that your readers remember these key points. Besides summarizing, you will often deliberately repeat a key point to make a stronger impression on your readers. (The same is true when you are speaking, of course.) When you are summarizing or repeating, use a dash to separate the summary or the repetition from the rest of the sentence.

> Challenging games, helpful business programs, educational software—all are available at the CompuCenter nearest you. (The dash provides forceful summarizing.)

> Remember to get all your computer needs from CompuCenter—CompuCenter, the store with you and your computer needs in mind. (Forceful repetition. Here, the writer deliberately repeats the most important part of the message—the store name.)

Dashes With Afterthoughts

To add variety to their writing, to arouse the reader's curiosity, to soften a statement that might otherwise offend, to provide special emphasis—for all these reasons, good writers *plan* their afterthoughts.

> Our Labor Day sale will be sure to save you money—and offer you some exciting *un*advertised specials! (To provide variety in writing style and to arouse the reader's curiosity.)

> Of course, we wish that we could send you all the free samples that you requested—but company policy limits the number of swatches that we may send. (To soften a refusal.)

> This catalog is sent only to our credit card customers—no one else receives one! (To reemphasize a statement.)

Checkup 3

Add dashes where needed. Write *OK* for any sentence that has no error.

1. Fine restaurants, department stores, art galleries these are among the many places where you will enjoy using your new SuperCard.
2. To see our new Long Life carpets in person, just visit any of our convenient locations or better yet, just call to enjoy the comfort of our shop-at-home service!

3. Our company is unable to take advantage of your discount offer at least, for now.
4. Complete and mail the enclosed card for your free sample but don't delay.
5. Our convention plans seem to be taking shape but more about this later.
6. The complete set of cassettes, the cassette player, the instruction booklet all are yours if you order before May 30.

Punctuating Words Set Off by Dashes

AT THE END OF A SENTENCE. To set off words at the end of a sentence, only one dash is needed. The dash is placed before the words to be set off; a period, question mark, or exclamation point then ends the sentence.

> **This computer package has several features not found in other brands at this low price—512K, dual disk drive, letter-quality printer. (The dash precedes the words to be set off; then a period ends this declarative sentence.)**

Note that no punctuation is used with the dash unless an abbreviation or quotation precedes the dash. No punctuation ever follows the dash.

> **The company we selected is Abrams Supplies Ltd.—Ms. Fordyce approved. (The period before the dash belongs with the abbreviation.)**

WITHIN A SENTENCE. To set off words within a sentence, two dashes are needed. Again, no punctuation is used with the first dash unless an abbreviation or quotation precedes the dash. The second dash may have a question mark or an exclamation point *before* it, but only if the words set off require a question mark or an exclamation point.

> **Our new Director of Personnel—what is his name?—will head the committee meeting. (The dashes set off a question; thus a question mark precedes only the second dash. Note that the sentence ends with a period.)**

> **Janice Glynn won—for the second consecutive year!—the company's Outstanding Achievement Award. (The words set off by dashes require an exclamation point. Note that the sentence ends with a period.)**

> **Many sales representatives in our district—Dan Conklin, Marvin Stork, and Beatrice Webber are among them—have suggested that the incentive compensation plan should be changed. (No period before the second dash.)**

Note in the above examples that commas are used within dashes in the "usual" way.

Correct any punctuation errors in the following sentences. Write *OK* for any sentence that has no error.

1. Send these contracts by Express Mail to Ms. Gunther—she's still in San Francisco, isn't she—before she leaves for Houston.
2. The meeting on Monday will begin precisely at 9 a.m.—but I suggest that you arrive no later than 8:45.
3. It will probably be Lee & Crowell—do you agree—who will win the contract.
4. Service, dependability, fair prices,—these are the reasons for dealing with O'Connell Automotives.
5. When she won last year's award—there was a $5000 cash prize.—she traveled to Europe for four weeks.
6. Friendly people, reasonable prices, expert skiing facilities— these are some of the reasons the Sunview Motel is the most popular meeting place in the Catskills.

COMMUNICATION PROJECTS

Practical Application

A. Correct any errors. Write *OK* for any sentence that has no error.

1. In long-term international trade transactions, these are the three major problem areas for exporters;(1) losses, (2) delayed payments, and (3) political risks.
2. Here is the new policy: accept no personal checks for purchases under $25.
3. The nurse in our Memphis office is Sharon Vernon; the nurse in our New York office is Paul Jakway.
4. Many of the employees polled were in favor of the four-day workweek; however, the majority favored keeping our present system.
5. Hardware from Milan, statues from Florence, foods from Naples,—these were among the items imported this week.
6. The rule is clear: smoking is prohibited in this area of the building.
7. The following changes in the benefits plan will become effective January 1: Note that employees will not pay extra for the additional coverage.
8. The brochures were due from the printer on June 12, however, the recent strike delayed the delivery.
9. Our newest model is temporarily out of stock—all other models are in inventory.—but we will have more no later than Friday.
10. Three credit cards—Visa, MasterCard, and American Express—are accepted by this store.

11. Fay Allen is a very interesting speaker,—interesting and very informative too.
12. Subscribe today to make sure that you hear the latest news on: interest rates, the bond market, stock picks, and much more.
13. The Training Center—have you ever visited it—has all the most up-to-date equipment.
14. The original contract was signed on November 11, however, it was later amended.
15. The original contract was signed on November 11, it was, however, later amended.
16. Remember: no employee may enter the restricted area without a safety helmet.
17. At first the bank offered a very high interest rate—wasn't it over 15 percent—before we negotiated better terms.
18. The Jensen Company has a virtual monopoly on these lower-price printers; the Pembroke Company has a virtual monopoly on the higher-price printers.
19. Unfortunately, tickets are no longer available for the May 3 performance, more tickets may soon become available, however, due to cancellations.
20. When we heard the report, both Francine and I had the same reaction, no comment!

B. Correct any errors in the following sentences. Write *OK* for any sentence that has no error.

1. The final copy of the report will be ready, according to Ms. Stanley, within one weeks' time.
2. Do you know whether the person who you spoke with is Mr. Pendergast, the head of the department?
3. Within the next six months or so, there should be opportunities for May and I to transfer to the Atlanta office.
4. Ms. D'Ambrosio, here is the revised copies that you requested this morning.
5. Karen said that we'll get a taxi whenever your ready to leave for the airport.
6. Any employee who wants to apply for a job listed on the bulletin board should leave their name with Mr. Weston in the Personnel Department.
7. As you probably know, Mr. Fernandez is one of those accountants who insists on meticulous proofreading.
8. Most of the word processing operators' in this department prefer this new equipment.
9. She reminded us not to mail them checks until Mrs. Hadley has approved each one.
10. Beside her small apartment building in Sacramento, Denise owns a home in San Francisco.
11. It was obvious that Gail couldn't hardly wait to return home after her three-week tour of our branch offices.

12. Did Dominick say that he plans on beginning his draft of the report over this weekend?
13. Yes, Evelyn already seen Mr. Matthews about the revisions in the advertising copy.
14. Why don't James or Hilda head the committee meeting in Sylvia's absence?
15. We returned all the damaged merchandise to the manufacturer, the rest of the cartons were sent to our warehouse.
16. There's still extra catalogs in the supply room if you should need them, Marjorie.
17. We do not accept credit cards for purchases under $10. Because it is not profitable for us to do so.
18. The estimate, in our opinion, was certainly reasonable, in fact, it was only 5 percent over the price we paid two years ago.
19. We will lease cars from O'Connell Automotive—the cost is only $175 a vehicle.—as soon as we get official approval from our corporate headquarters.
20. Eric will sure be happier in his new position.

Editing Practice

Using Business Vocabulary. On a separate sheet of paper, fill in the missing words with the correct word from those listed below.

a.	allocated	e.	fragile	i.	persuasive
b.	efficiency	f.	grievance	j.	resources
c.	eliminate	g.	itemize		
d.	foreign	h.	permissible		

1. Together, the union delegates and management's representatives established a (?) committee to hear employees' complaints.
2. All cartons with breakable merchandise must be marked (?).
3. According to IRS regulations, it is not (?) to deduct commutation expenses.
4. Because we do not have the (?) to complete this huge assignment in such a short time, we hired a firm to do so.
5. Be sure to (?) the costs on each estimate before you submit the estimate to the Purchasing Department.
6. Our manager is now exploring opportunities to expand our (?) trade.
7. Everyone who works with Mr. Aliano knows just how (?) he can be!
8. The total expense dollars were carefully (?) by the committee.
9. To process orders faster, we are now studying ways to (?) unnecessary, time-consuming steps in the handling of telephone and mail orders.
10. Clearly, the analysis shows that the new machinery will increase our overall (?).

A business writer should easily be able to supply a synonym for each of the italicized words below. Write your synonyms on a separate sheet of paper.

1. The president is *aware,* of course, of our marketing strategies.
2. Louise was *truthful* in describing the problems we are now facing.
3. A business worker cannot *shirk* his or her responsibilities.
4. Allen was indeed *generous* in sharing the credit with his staff.
5. Mr. Sylvester has had *intermittent* problems in getting his new store open to the public.
6. Several of these suggestions will *mitigate* the present strain between management and labor.

Case Problem

Addressing Your Managers. Alvin Mance was recently hired as a trainee in the firm of Dawkins, Zuckerman, and D'Amico. There is an obvious air of informality in the office; most employees, for example, call David Dawkins, the president, by his first name. Alvin has been calling him "Mr. Dawkins."

1. Should Alvin call the president by his first name, or should he continue to call him "Mr. Dawkins"?
2. Generally speaking, do you think that employees should call their coworkers by their first names? Under what circumstances should a courtesy title such as *Ms., Mr.,* and so on, be used?

25

COMMAS

Effective speakers know precisely when to pause so that their listeners are, first, able to *grasp,* and then *connect,* thought after thought after thought. Similarly, effective writers use commas to separate elements within sentences, showing readers where to pause and how the elements are connected.

Because there are many different ways in which writers connect thoughts, there are many different ways in which commas are used. A thorough discussion of commas, therefore, requires three complete sections—this section and the following two sections. As you can see, then, using commas correctly will be especially important to you in your business writing.

IN COMPOUND SENTENCES

Note in the following sentences how commas are used with the conjunctions *and, but, or,* and *nor* to join two independent clauses.

> Jeanine started working on the draft about two weeks ago, and she completed it just yesterday afternoon. (The comma and the conjunction *and* join two independent clauses.)

> The company originally planned to build a warehouse on the property, but it subsequently decided to sell the land instead. (The comma and the conjunction *but* join two independent clauses.)

> Claude will probably travel to Maine for the computer conference, or he will visit our district office in Scranton. (The comma and *or* connect two independent clauses.)

> Marcia does not want to be transferred to the Boston office, nor does she want to stay in the Training Department. (The comma and *nor* connect two independent clauses.)

Reread the above sentences, noting that each clause can stand alone as an independent sentence. But note that when the second clause does not contain a subject, that clause is no longer *independent*—it cannot stand alone. No comma is needed in such cases.

> Jeanine started working on the draft about two weeks ago and completed it just yesterday afternoon. (Note that the subject *she* has been omitted from the second clause in the original sentence.)

> The company originally planned to build a warehouse on the property but subsequently decided to sell the land instead. (The subject *it* has been omitted from the second clause of the original sentence.)

> Claude will probably travel to Maine for the computer conference or will visit our district office in Scranton. (The subject *he* has been omitted from the second clause in the original sentence.)

The exceptions to the use of commas in compound sentences are discussed below.

No Comma Between Very Short Clauses

When the independent clauses are very short, the comma is usually omitted. Read the following examples aloud; as you do so, note that each sentence sounds "natural" without a pause before the conjunction.

> Shirley wrote the draft and Leon retyped it. (The two independent clauses are short; no comma is needed.)

> Mr. Hershey went to Detroit and Ed went with him. (Again, two short independent clauses do not require a comma.)

Semicolons to Avoid Possible Misreadings

If either clause of a compound sentence already contains a comma (or more than one comma), a misreading may be likely. If so, use a semicolon, not a comma, to separate the two clauses.

> The goal of the week-long seminar is to improve our skills in writing business letters, memos, and informal reports; and formal reports, too, will be covered if time permits. (The semicolon provides a stronger break and prevents this possible misreading: *informal reports, and formal reports . . . .*)

When the two independent clauses in a compound sentence are very long, the brief pause of a comma may not be strong enough. A semicolon may be required. (Better yet, write such lengthy clauses as independent sentences.)

> The findings of our research chemists clearly point to the possible effectiveness of polyvinyl chloride (PVC) as a replacement for the more expensive materials we are now using; and we fully support the need to fund further research to explore the uses of PVC for our entire line of products.

Checkup 1

Correct these sentences. Write *OK* for any sentence that has no error.

1. Harris wants to go, but Elsa does not.
2. Keith recommended Yvette, Ivan, and Samantha, and Everett recommended two of his staff members.
3. Nancy does not want to continue using Acme Printing for our brochures nor does she suggest that we order any more letterhead from Acme.
4. The accident was reported to the insurance company late yesterday but the chemicals have already been cleaned up.
5. Wendy will chair the new committee, but will not be able to attend the first meeting.
6. I received the press proofs this morning, and have checked all of them already.
7. We should revise these estimates, or we should request up-to-date bids.
8. The meeting began promptly this morning but ended late.

IN SERIES

A *series* consists of three or more items in a sequence. As you will see in the following examples, the items may be words, phrases, or clauses. Remember: If a series has four items, there are three commas; five items, four commas; and so on.

The Office Training Center offers courses in shorthand, keyboarding, word processing, and business writing. (A series of words. Note that a comma is used *before* the conjunction.)

The cartons were stacked in the aisles, on desktops, and on shelves. (A series of three phrases: *in the aisles, on desktops, on shelves.*)

Jeffrey will be moving to our Honolulu office, Anne will take his place at headquarters, and Rhonda will become Anne's assistant. (A series of three independent clauses.)

When Etc. Ends a Series

Etc. means "and so forth." Never write *and etc.* because that would mean "*and and* so forth"!

When *etc.* ends a series, use a comma before and after it (unless *etc.* ends the sentence).

According to the agenda, we will discuss sales, expenses, advertising, *etc.* (A comma before *etc.* No comma after it because it ends the sentence.)

We will discuss sales, expenses, advertising, *etc.*, according to the agenda. (A comma before *and* after *etc.*)

Semicolons Instead of Commas in Series

When the items in series are long clauses or if the items already contain commas, use a semicolon to provide a stronger break between the items.

We should like you to do the following: arrange our goods into shipping units; transport them to the place where they are to be consumed; store them there if storage is necessary; and obtain a signed receipt showing the time of delivery and the condition of the goods. (You can see that a long pause is needed between the items.)

During our vacation trip last year, we stopped at the following places: Oil City, Pennsylvania; Ann Arbor, Michigan; Gary, Indiana; Kansas City, Missouri; and Santa Fe, New Mexico. (A semicolon to separate the parts of the series holds the reader long enough for him or her to grasp the meaning immediately.)

When Not to Use Commas

Do not use commas in the following situations.

AT THE END OF A SERIES. Do not use a comma after the last item in a series (that is, the item following the conjunction) unless the sentence structure requires a comma. Only the items before the conjunction are separated by commas.

> Ben, Lisa, and Carl will coordinate the training sessions for new employees. (No comma after *Carl*, the last item in the series.)

> Ben, Lisa, and Carl, who are supervisors in our headquarters office, will coordinate the training sessions. (The comma after *Carl* is required because of the sentence structure here.)

WITH REPEATED CONJUNCTIONS. When the conjunction is repeated between items in the series, no commas are needed.

> She will probably assign the project to Pamela or Joe or Burt. (Because the conjunction *or* is repeated between items in the series, no commas are needed.)

IN CERTAIN COMPANY NAMES. Company names should be written exactly like the official name. Some companies write their names *without* a comma before *and;* others, *with* a comma. In all cases, no comma is used before an ampersand (&).

> Smith, Evans, and Warner won the contest. (Follows the official company name precisely.)

> D'Amato, Ford & Wilkens is an excellent consulting firm. (Never use a comma before an ampersand: &.)

Checkup 2

Correct any errors in the following sentences. Write *OK* for any sentence that has no error.

1. At the end of the convention, we will have time for fishing, swimming, sailing, and etc.
2. The firm with the lowest estimate for the building is Loomis, Kresky, & Diaz.
3. Appliances, furniture, computer programs, etc. will be on sale next week at all our stores.
4. Alinda will order all the supplies, James will print and mail the agendas and Barbara will handle registration.
5. You may pay for your purchases by check, cash, or money order or if you prefer, we will bill you later.
6. Please tell Jack, Andrea and Bettejean to submit their reports by Friday and ask them to send copies to Ms. DeLeo.
7. Excellence Press prints all our brochures, pamphlets, and direct-

mail advertising, catalogs, however, are printed by the Boston Printing Company.

8. This computer will be equally useful in school, at home or in the office.

FOLLOWING INTRODUCTORY WORDS, PHRASES, AND CLAUSES

Commas follow introductory words, phrases, and clauses to provide a needed pause and thereby prevent possible misreading or confusion.

Introductory Words

Commas follow introductory words at the beginning of the sentences or clauses. Among the most commonly used introductory words are:

consequently	naturally
finally	no
first	now
however	obviously
meanwhile	originally
moreover	therefore
namely	yes

Naturally, we were disappointed with the results of the survey. (The introductory word *naturally* is at the beginning of the sentence. A comma follows the word.)

The survey showed that our product was the least favorable in consumers' opinions; naturally, we were disappointed. (Here, the word *naturally* introduces the second clause in the sentence. Again, it is followed by a comma.)

We received the survey results this morning; we were, naturally, keenly disappointed. (In this example, the introductory word interrupts the second clause. Note that a comma is used before *and* after *naturally.*)

Introductory Phrases

Commas are often needed after infinitive phrases, participial phrases, and prepositional phrases.

AFTER INFINITIVE PHRASES. An infinitive phrase that begins a sentence or a clause is followed by a comma (unless the phrase is the subject of the sentence or clause).

To read quickly, you must concentrate more intently. (The infinitive phrase *to read quickly* introduces the sentence. It modifies the subject *you.*)

To read quickly is your goal in this course. (Here, the infinitive phrase is the subject of the sentence.)

AFTER PARTICIPIAL PHRASES. A participial phrase is always followed by a comma.

> Suspecting that the strike was imminent, Ms. Hawthorne increased her order of supplies. (Use a comma after the participial phrase.)

> Injured by the blast, Mr. Herbas was taken to the Medical Department. (Comma after a participial phrase.)

Do not confuse participial phrases with gerund phrases. A gerund phrase at the beginning of a sentence is always a subject. A participial phrase is always an adjective.

> Controlling costs carefully is every manager's responsibility. (*Controlling* is a gerund. The gerund phrase *Controlling costs carefully* is the subject of the sentence.)

> Controlling costs carefully, Marla was able to make the store profitable in a very short time. (Here, *Controlling* is a participle—an adjective that modifies the subject, *Marla.*)

AFTER PREPOSITIONAL PHRASES. Use commas after long prepositional phrases and prepositional phrases that contain verbs.

> For the new sales promotion campaign for these products, we are planning to advertise on radio and television all year long. (Long prepositional phrase.)

> In creating her award-winning photograph, Sandra spent many hours on location. (Note the gerund *creating* in the prepositional phrase.)

Do not use a comma if the prepositional phrase is short or if it flows directly into the main thought of the sentence.

> By tomorrow afternoon we will have this entire matter settled. (The prepositional phrase *By tomorrow afternoon* is short and flows directly into the sentence.)

Introductory Clauses

A comma is needed after a subordinate clause that precedes a main clause. Note how the comma provides a necessary pause in the following example.

> When Mr. Madison returned, we met with the attorneys and discussed the terms of the contract. (Comma after a subordinate clause that precedes the main clause.)

To apply this comma rule, you must of course be able to identify the words and phrases that commonly begin introductory clauses. To remember the following list better, try using each word or phrase to introduce a clause.

after	even if	provided	when
although	for	since	whenever
as	how	so that	where
as if	if	then	whereas
as soon as	inasmuch as	though	wherever
as though	in case	till	whether
because	in order that	unless	while
before	otherwise		

Checkup 3

Correct any comma errors. Write *OK* for any sentence that has no error.

1. At 9 a.m. tomorrow and again at 11 a.m. next Thursday Mrs. Naldi will discuss the corporation's five-year plan.
2. Although we certainly have plenty of time to complete the assignment we should begin right away.
3. Proofreading the computer printouts, took Tom and Connie all morning.
4. Proofreading the computer printouts, Tom and Connie worked carefully all morning long.
5. We should be able to leave Dallas Friday afternoon; therefore we should arrive home by 9 p.m.
6. Unless Sherri disapproves of our plan we will be able to begin next Monday.
7. To compute the compounded interest use the enclosed chart.
8. If you prefer you can pay the total in ten monthly installments.
9. To succeed in this business, requires persistence, determination, and drive.
10. Mr. Felix finally gave his consent to the incentive-compensation plan; he approved moreover an additional bonus for the top sales representatives.

COMMUNICATION PROJECTS

Practical Application

A. Correct the following sentences. Write *OK* for any sentence that has no error.

1. The supervisors of the Word Processing Department, the Billing Department and the Accounting Department have reviewed these new procedures.
2. Tomorrow, we will screen the candidates who have applied for this position.
3. Star International manufactures and distributes appliances, electronic games and gadgets, automotive equipment, and etc.

4. While Ms. Johanssen is on jury duty, her assistant will approve all vouchers and invoices.
5. Waiting patiently, she sat in the reception area for nearly an hour.
6. To submit accurate figures on these reports, is important because we will then send the statistics to the IRS.
7. The awards were as follows: Ed Randall, $500; Martha Grice, $750; and John Aliano, $1000.
8. The building was originally scheduled to be completed by June 14; delays, however, have pushed that date to August 3.
9. As soon as we get "official" approval, we will call to let you know.
10. This booklet will describe the advantages of fixed-income investments such as corporate bonds, municipal bonds, and government bonds.
11. When Dr. Levine finishes her presentation, she will make the announcement.
12. One of the finest law firms in the country is Quicker, Gregus, & Michaels.
13. She will ship the entire order by truck, or send it airfreight.
14. A bank check, certified check, or cashier's check is acceptable.
15. Did she say that a bank check or a certified check or a cashier's check is acceptable?

B.   Correct any errors in the following sentences. Write *OK* for any sentence that has no error.

1. See the following books for more information: Each book will surely be helpful.
2. Store these and all similar chemicals in a safe place, that is, you should keep them out of the reach of children.
3. Heat, electricity, water, and etc., are included in these utility estimates.
4. Agnes and Mark, have already completed several of these effective training sessions.
5. The office manager asked us whether we found the new equipment easy to use?
6. You can save $30 by subscribing now for two full years or you can save $45 by subscribing for three years.
7. The SuperSpeed copier is not inexpensive nor is it easy to service.
8. The training film covers all the major topics in detail and is bright and lively however it is far too long to be effective.
9. Ted and her are very interested in buying a new scanner for the Word Processing Center.
10. The assignment is tough, but there's plenty of time to complete it on schedule.
11. Current interest rates are high, and are still climbing.

12. Whenever you and Jennifer have time call me to discuss the Wilson account.
13. The preliminary sites are Detroit, Boston and Philadelphia.
14. His wifes' new store is in the Chapel Hill area, isn't it?
15. If you and him decide to attend, just call the Travel Department to make your reservations.
16. Obviously, you will need more graphs, charts, illustrations etc.
17. She said she will set up a consulting company before the end of the year; moreover, she plans to open offices both in Austin and in Houston.
18. One of the committee members were opposed to spending so much on this project.
19. Why don't Mr. DeMille like the package design for this product?
20. Several attorneys' have already reviewed the contracts and have agreed that we are perfectly within our rights.

Editing Practice

A Matter of Agreement.   Correct any agreement errors in the following sentences. Write *OK* for any sentence that has no error.

1. The number of requests for information about IRAs have been overwhelming.
2. Elvera don't have her airline confirmation yet.
3. Where is the last three forms we must send to the Records Retention Department?
4. Most of the orders for this letter-quality printer has been filled already.
5. There seems to be several qualified candidates for the position you advertised.
6. Only one of the supervisors has fully implemented the new system.
7. Where's Leonard and Vernon holding their weekly production meeting?
8. Every employee in the warehouse and the regional offices has the opportunity to increase their medical and dental insurance coverage for a nominal fee.
9. Generally, either Ms. O'Toole or Mr. Frohm approve each radio or television ad personally before broadcasting.
10. Erica is one of those designers who do their best work under pressure.

Using Your Word Processor.   Before you left the office yesterday, you saved on a diskette the following draft of a memorandum you are preparing. Edit it now, before you print out copies. Can you find any errors?

Car-leasing rates from the top three agencies in our area varied very slightly. As the enclosed chart shows, the rates for compareable six-cylinder cars ranged from $23.95 a day (from Able Cars and Vans) to $25.95 a day (from Dependable Auto Rental).

We recomend that we use Able for all our rental needs not only because Able offers the lowest daily rate but also because Able permits us to return rented cars to any of their locations. The other agencies specify that cars must be returned to the same place from which they were rented; otherwise, the low rates quoted do not apply.

Case Problem

Telephone Technique.   Criticize the following telephone conversation. Then rewrite it to avoid the types of errors you criticized.

Person answering:	Hello.
Caller:	Who is this?
Person answering:	Who do you want?
Caller:	I was trying to get the credit department.
Person answering:	This is the credit department.
Caller:	Is George Becker there?
Person answering:	Yes, he is.
Caller:	May I speak with him, please?

26

COMMAS (CONTINUED)

As we speak, we use pauses to separate words that are not essential to the clarity of the message. When we write, we utilize commas to separate nonessential words from the rest of the sentence. If the words *are* essential to the clarity of the message, we do not need pauses and therefore do not use commas. Learning these basic uses of commas is as important to writing skill as knowing when to pause is to speaking skill.

SUBORDINATE CLAUSE FOLLOWING MAIN CLAUSE

We have already seen that a subordinate clause preceding a main clause is always followed by a comma.

> As we agreed in our last committee meeting, we will review the commission rates for full-time and part-time sales representatives. (Comma after subordinate clause preceding a main clause.)

> After he has had an opportunity to review them, Mark will meet with us to discuss these contracts. (Comma after subordinate clause preceding a main clause.)

But when the subordinate clause *follows* the main clause, use a comma only if the subordinate clause offers *non*essential information—information not needed to complete the meaning. As you read the following examples, note how the subordinate clauses differ.

> We will review the commission rates for full-time and part-time sales representatives, as we agreed in our last committee meeting. (The words *as we agreed in our last committee meeting* are certainly not critical to understanding the meaning of the sentence. They merely provide extra information. A comma thus separates nonessential words.)

> Mark will meet with us to discuss these contracts after he has had an opportunity to review them. (No comma here because the words *after he has had an opportunity to review them* are important to the meaning of the sentence. They do *not* provide additional information; they provide *essential* information. They tell precisely *when* "Mark will meet with us.")

When writing such sentences, you will of course know the meaning you intend and will have an easier job of deciding whether a comma is needed or not.

INTERRUPTING, PARENTHETIC, AND EXPLANATORY ELEMENTS

Interrupting Elements

Interrupting elements do not provide essential information. Use commas to set off interrupters.

> The importance of this government contract, naturally, has been explained to everyone on our staff. (Commas set off the interrupting word *naturally*.)

> Our director, consequently, has assigned the entire staff to work on the proposal. (Again, commas set off the interrupter *consequently*.)

Parenthetic Elements

As we speak and write, we add words, phrases, and clauses within sentences to emphasize a contrast, express an opinion, soften a harsh statement, qualify or amend the meaning, and so on.

> Any change in these regulations, as I see it, must be approved by the finance committee. (The parenthetic expression *as I see it* is not essential to the meaning of the sentence and is set off by commas.)

> The building, but not the store on the main level, will be leased to another company. (The parenthetic statement separated by commas emphasizes the contrast.)

Explanatory Elements

Additional information that is not essential to the meaning of the sentence is set off by commas. To determine this, read the sentence without the additional information to be sure it makes sense.

> Our supervisor, knowing that the order was marked "priority," assigned it to Lawrence and me. (Read this sentence aloud. As you do so, note how you would pause at the beginning and at the end of the participial phrase *knowing that the order was marked "priority."* Use commas to set off such explanatory elements.)

> Mrs. Brady, who developed this procedure, is a senior vice president. (The clause *who developed this procedure* is set off by commas. Again, read this aloud to note how you would pause before and after the explanatory element.)

Note, however, that clauses that *are* essential are not set off by commas.

> Our firm has four senior vice presidents. The senior vice president who developed this procedure is Mrs. Brady. (In this sentence, the clause *who developed this procedure* does not provide *extra* information; it specifies *one* of the "four senior vice presidents." Note that in reading this sentence aloud, you would *not* pause before and after the clause.)

Checkup 1

Are commas used correctly in the following sentences? Make any necessary corrections. Write *OK* for any sentence that has no error.

1. The person, whom you should ask for help, is Irene Whitcomb.
2. Anne waiting for the call from our West Coast office did not go out for lunch.
3. One possible alternative as we discussed yesterday is to delay this shipment until Trent & Fitch has paid its bills.
4. Mr. Rudolf, who is a CPA, explained why such expenses are not deductible.

5. The manager, who is in charge of keeping those geographical listings up to date, is Abner Fulkerson.
6. The interest received but not the principal returned is subject to taxation.
7. The only person on our staff, who is a CPA, is Arnold Rudolf.
8. Schedule the meeting for next Friday, if Eric and Jack will be in town.
9. An effective alternative Larry and I think will be to postpone the production of these items until after the summer rush.
10. The New Orleans warehouse, but not the store, will be sold by the end of the year.

APPOSITIVES AND RELATED CONSTRUCTIONS

The use of commas with appositives, degrees and titles, calendar dates, and state names is discussed below.

Appositives

An appositive is a word or a group of words that gives more information about a preceding word or phase. When an appositive is not essential to the message, it is set off by commas.

The director of marketing services, Allen B. Fine, will review our budgets next Friday. (The appositive, *Allen B. Fine*, offers additional information and is set off by commas.)

The president of our company, a well-known college professor, is an expert in corporate finance.

When the appositive is very closely connected with the noun that precedes it, no commas are used to separate the appositive. One-word appositives frequently do not take commas.

Her husband Richard is also an attorney for March, Patton & Wells. (The appositive *Richard* is very closely connected to the noun preceding it; therefore, no commas are needed.)

The year 1995 will mark the 100th anniversary of our firm. (Here, *1995* is essential to the meaning of the sentence. It is not set off by commas.)

Degrees, Titles, and Other Explanatory Terms

Several commonly used abbreviations offer additional information about the names that precede them. For example, *M.D.* following a person's name tells that he or she is a doctor of medicine, and *Inc.* following a company name tells that the firm has been incorporated.

Abbreviations such as *M.D.*, *Ph.D.*, and *D.D.S.* are always set off by commas.

Bradford W. Kelly, M.D., is the head of our company's medical department.

Alice O. Bruno, Ph.D., is the director of research and development for the Chemical Division of Allied Products.

The abbreviations *Inc.* and *Ltd.* may or may not be set off with commas, depending on the preference of each individual company. Always follow the style shown on a company's letterhead.

Send checks to Owens & Rusk, Inc., at its Memphis office. (*Owens & Rusk, Inc.,* is the official company name.)

Ms. MacGrath works for Time Inc. in New York. (*Time Inc.* is the official company name.)

Like *Inc.* and *Ltd.,* the abbreviations *Jr.* and *Sr.* may or may not be set off with commas. Follow the preference of each individual when writing *Jr.* and *Sr.* or roman numerals after a person's name.

William D. Achison Jr. has been named to the Board of Directors. (Mr. Achison prefers no commas setting off *Jr.*)

Henry Dawson, III, is a senior partner of Reynolds, Wimby, and Feld. (Mr. Dawson prefers commas setting off *III* following his name.)

Note that when commas are used to set off abbreviations such as *M.D., Inc.,* or *Jr.,* they are used in pairs. Do not use a single comma to set off such abbreviations.

Calendar Dates

In month-day-year dates, the year is set off with two commas. In month-year dates, the commas are generally omitted because they are not needed.

On February 9, 1986, we purchased the land for this office building.

In February 1986 we purchased this land.

State Names

Two commas set off the name of a state when it follows the name of a city.

A new district office will be opened in Spokane, Washington, next April.

Checkup 2

Are there any comma errors in the following sentences? Make any necessary corrections. Write *OK* for any sentence that has no error.

1. One of our outstanding staff engineers, Dr. Freda B. Jamison, was recently interviewed in several national magazines.
2. Nehemiah Edwards, one of our sales representatives, has lived in Boise Idaho for many years.

3. Next week James W. Preston, Jr. will be officially named to the board of directors.
4. Did you see that the stock for Bond & Ward, Inc. has risen to $50 a share?
5. Two of their designers, Ed Phelps and Joan Gross are now working on some preliminary sketches.
6. On December 31, 1995 our lease will expire.
7. One of our divisions Simco Chemicals has been very active in the field of pollution control.
8. Our next meeting will be in Topeka, Kansas on April 19.
9. Send the original art to Ames & Blackstone, Inc. as soon as possible.
10. Her sister Phyllis is considering opening her own consulting firm here in Akron.

THAT *AND* WHICH

Clauses that are not necessary to the meaning of a sentence should be introduced by *which* and, of course, set off by commas. Clauses that are necessary to the meaning of a sentence are introduced by *that*. They are not set off by commas.

Only the inventory that is damaged will be sold at a 50 percent discount. (No commas separating a "that" clause.)

The damaged inventory, which includes radios and stereos, will be sold at a 50 percent discount. (The "which" clause gives additional information and is correctly set off by commas.)

PITFALLS

Here are two more comma pitfalls that trap many writers: (1) using a comma to separate a subject from its predicate and (2) using a comma to separate a verb or an infinitive from its object or complement.

Comma Separating Subject From Predicate

Never separate a subject from its predicate by a single comma.

All price increases, must be approved by the executive vice president. (Wrong. No comma should separate the subject from its verb.)

All price increases, according to the president of the company, must be approved by the executive vice president. (Correct. Now *two* commas separate a phrase that gives additional information.)

Comma Separating Verb From Object

Never separate a verb from its object with a single comma. Likewise, never separate an infinitive from its complement with a single comma.

Since 1985 Carol has been, one of the company's most prolific researchers. (Wrong. A single comma should never separate a verb from its object.)

All of us were delighted to hear, that the merger is now "official." (Wrong. One comma should never separate an infinitive from its complement.)

Checkup 3

Find and correct any errors in the following sentences. Write *OK* for any sentence that has no error.

1. Our Nashville outlet which is one of the largest in the South is our company's most profitable revenue division.
2. A nationwide survey showed, that consumers prefer natural foods with no preservatives.
3. Any item, that is on sale, will be further reduced during this one-day-only special event.
4. The enclosed catalog which also includes an order form is yours at no extra charge for opening an account with us.
5. Several employees in our Oklahoma City office, are being considered for the new opening in our headquarters office.
6. The customer must pay the shipping charges, which amount to $57.

COMMUNICATION PROJECTS

Practical Application

A. Correct any errors in the following sentences. Write *OK* for any sentence that has no error.

1. Marco has been in charge of advertising for Kimball & Mahoney, Inc. for nearly ten years.
2. Quantity discounts however are limited to orders of $500 or more.
3. Sam will forward the check to you, as soon as it arrives.
4. Linda Parker who is the director of the Data Processing Department will explain these reports at the first session tomorrow morning.
5. Since March 16, 1985, Judie McCabe has been the manager of our Lansing, Michigan office.
6. The parts, that we ordered today, will be shipped within the week.
7. Our goal is to add to, not detract from the advantages we now enjoy in the marketplace.
8. One of the reasons for the increase in costs is, the higher price of medical insurance.

9. Lynette McNally, Ph.D. has been named Director of Research for the corporation.
10. The estimates, which were prepared by Mr. Kylish, were very helpful to us in budgeting next year's expenses.
11. One of Claudine's most interesting articles, will be printed in our employee newspaper.
12. On November 4, 1984 we signed a contract giving us exclusive distribution rights to these products.
13. Her sister Claire, is also a chemical engineer, isn't she?
14. Is it true that Charles Barcellona, the manager of our Honolulu office won the Outstanding Employee Award?
15. Please return to Paul Ewing, any correspondence that you have on this project.
16. Inflation, which has been curbed during the last few years, is no longer in the headlines every day.
17. The announcement, that the plant will be closed from July 10 through July 16, was greeted with applause.
18. One of the reasons that Mr. Henshaw disapproved, is that television advertising is so costly.
19. Did Ms. Heffner say that she would be in Newark, Delaware on May 2, or did she say in Newark, New Jersey?
20. Julie was happy to hear, that her raise was retroactive to June 1.

B. Correct any errors in the following sentences. Write *OK* for any sentence that has no error.

1. After her presentation we spoke with Ms. Durkin about her interesting topic.
2. The plan is, to completely renovate the men's lounge and the women's lounge before September 1.
3. On the showroom floor was high-speed printers, color monitors, modems, etc.
4. If the Jones's wish, they could complete the renovation in less than two months.
5. Between you and I, Jack, I am positive that the new product line will prove very successful.
6. Is Allen Seidel one of the consultants who we met at the recent word processing convention?
7. There is, as you know, only two or three people on our staff who can handle this assignment.
8. Beginning April 15, each client will receive their monthly statements on the 15th of the month.
9. Don't Allison know that Dr. Chu left for Madison, Wisconsin, yesterday?
10. No one was surprised to hear that Harry is doing very good in his new position with Myers & Bowers.

11. Deborah asked us to set up a meeting for next Wednesday to discuss these estimates?
12. By noon today, Ms. Cushman had already went to the Mayor's office for the committee meeting.
13. Neither of the two vice president's is free to meet with us next Friday, August 4.
14. When Keith, Dennis, and her arrive, we will go to the auditorium to see the training films.
15. It appears like we will easily exceed our sales goals for this year.
16. The cartons that are laying on the floor in the supply room are to be delivered to the Records Retention Department.
17. Here's the revised specifications for the new model.
18. Stephanie has nearly finished her report on the security system, hasn't she.
19. Either Donald or Shirley are supposed to be working late tonight.
20. Eleanor and Fred's father was one of the original partners in this firm.

Editing Practice

Homonyms.   Read the following excerpt carefully, paying special attention to homonyms. Make any necessary corrections.

You're May 4 order will be shipped to you no later than May 19. As you requested, the entire cost of this order ($576.89) plus the cost of shipping ($29.75) will be charged to your account.

Because your order totaled more than $500, you will find a special discount coupon enclosed. This coupon entitles you to a $25 discount on any future order of $100 or more.

Thank you for buying from Jackson & Roth. Its our pleasure to serve you.

Plurals and Possessives.   Correct any errors in the use of plurals and possessives in the following sentences. Write *OK* for any sentence that has no error.

1. The Harnett Corporation has manufactured childrens furniture for more than three generations.
2. A special sale on ladies' clothing will begin next Monday, September 6.
3. Janet and Suzanne opened there new restaurant in the Midtown Mall.
4. As you know, Mr. Truscott disapproves of us leaving early.
5. The Harrisons' partners have agreed to sell their shares to the Harrisons for a total of $2 million.

6. All the sales representatives' will receive their bonus checks by March 1.
7. Ms. Arness claims that their are plenty of appliances in inventory for the upcoming sale.
8. We expect to complete the entire report within three weeks time.
9. Are you sure about David requesting a transfer?
10. I do not know whose attaché case this is, but I am positive that it is not her's.

Case Problem

Correcting the Boss.   Lenore Wilkins and her supervisor, Camille Ferrara, are meeting with an important client. During the meeting, Camille incorrectly tells the client that his order will be shipped on May 3. Lenore, however, knows that as of this morning the date was delayed to May 10.

Should Lenore correct Camille? What should Lenore say?

COMMAS (CONCLUDED)

Our discussion of the many uses of the comma is completed in this third section on comma use. Study these last few applications so that you will be able to use the comma expertly in your writing.

WITH MODIFYING ADJECTIVES

When two or more adjectives separately modify a noun, use a comma to separate the adjectives. To test whether the two adjectives *separately* modify the noun, use the word *and* between the adjectives, as shown below.

Adele gave an interesting, informative speech. (Comma between the adjectives *interesting* and *informative*. Note that the word *and* can be used between them: a speech that is interesting *and* informative.)

Jill and Gary are the most creative, most experienced, most versatile designers on our staff. (Commas between the adjectives that *separately* modify the noun *designers:* most creative *and* most experienced *and* most versatile.)

Note that no comma follows the last adjective—that is, no comma separates the last adjective from the noun.

We discussed conservative financial investments with our adviser. (You would *not* say "investments that are conservative *and* financial." Here, the adjective *financial* modifies *investments,* of course. But the adjective *conservative* modifies the unit *financial investments.* In other words, "financial investments that are conservative.")

Her new nonfiction book has earned Agnes over $100,000 in less than one year. (Using the word *and* between the adjectives *Her new nonfiction* makes no sense. These adjectives do *not* separately modify the noun *book.*)

Checkup 1

Insert commas as needed between adjectives in the following sentences. Test, of course, by using the word *and* between adjectives. Write *OK* for any sentence not requiring a comma or commas.

1. Thomas is considered a brilliant reliable ambitious investment analyst.
2. We attended several lengthy staff meetings yesterday and this morning.
3. The latest marketing research reports are available in Mr. Luciano's office.
4. The new machine produces sharp clean copies.
5. Jonas & Westerly manufactures lightweight thermal blankets.
6. The Sunview Motel offers neat spacious rooms at reasonable prices.

FOR OMISSIONS, WITH REPEATED EXPRESSIONS, AND IN DIRECT ADDRESS

The comma is also used to save time and words, to emphasize an important thought, and to set off names and terms in direct address. These are the uses discussed in this section.

Omissions

Sometimes writers can use the comma to avoid repeating words that have already been stated in the sentence. The comma makes the reader pause long enough to mentally supply the omitted words. Note these examples:

Production meetings are held once a week; inventory meetings, once a month. (The words *are held* are not repeated in the second clause. The comma indicates this omission and slows the reader long enough to supply the missing words.)

Starting on June 15, Mr. Hart will be in charge of the Bennett account; Ms. Dirkins, the Hastings & Ames account; Ms. Ellison, the Barker Chemical account; and Mr. Donnelly, the Henderson Trucking account. (Rather than repeat the words *will be in charge of* three times, the writer uses a comma after each name to tell the reader to pause long enough to supply these words.)

Repeated Expressions

Repetition is one of the most effective ways to emphasize an important point. Repetitions, of course, must be planned if they are to be effective, and the repeated words must be separated by a comma.

The manual says, "Never, never accept credit charges for amounts under $25." (Note the comma that separates the repetition *Never, never.*)

Direct Address

In writing, when we address people directly, we set off their names (or similar terms) with commas.

As you requested, Mrs. Greene, we are sending you two copies of our latest catalog.

Thank you, friend, for supporting our charitable organization.

Checkup 2

Do the following sentences correctly illustrate use of commas for omissions, for planned repetition, and for direct address? Make any needed corrections. Write *OK* for any sentence that has no error.

1. Ms. Lockard we sincerely appreciate your helping us.
2. Helen has been working very very hard to complete her assignment on schedule.
3. The Detroit office is scheduled to be audited on August 3; the Milwaukee office August 10; and the Indianapolis office August 17.
4. Ms. Corelli came out of retirement to help us in a few rare rare instances.
5. The reports confirmed that Brett & Hastings had contributed $10,000 to the Senator's campaign; Able Industries, $15,000; and Northern Commerce, $20,000.
6. We sincerely appreciate your helping us Ms. Lockard.
7. Frank's comments were correct absolutely correct.
8. Her original patent was filed in 1979; her second in 1984.

IN NUMBERS AND BETWEEN UNRELATED NUMBERS

Use a comma to separate ten thousands, hundred thousands, millions, and so on, in numbers of five or more digits. This function of the comma prevents misreading of numbers.

> Our company payroll exceeded $1,500,000 last year and is estimated to be $1,800,000 this year.

> We sold 7158 model T47 calculators last month.

When unrelated numbers are written together, a comma should separate them.

> As of December 31, 750 employees had signed up for the optional insurance plan. (The comma slows down the reader and makes each number distinct.)

PITFALLS

Now that you know all the important uses of the comma, be sure to master the last principles for *not* using a comma.

In Numbers

Never use commas in the following numbers, regardless of the number of digits: years, page numbers, house and telephone numbers, ZIP Code numbers, serial numbers, and decimals.

in 1985	1191 Hunter Avenue	Dallas, Texas 75201
page 1318	(201) 555-2184	RD 14315789
		12.75325

In Weights, Capacities, Measurements

Never use a comma to separate the parts of *one* weight, *one* capacity, or *one* measurement.

> The broadcast lasted exactly 1 hour 25 minutes 15 seconds. (No commas to separate the parts of *one* time measurement.)

Checkup 3

Did the writers of the following sentences fall into any of the comma pitfalls described above? Correct any errors. Write *OK* for any sentence that has no error.

1. By 1988 500 employees will have received their college degrees through our firm's tuition-assistance program.
2. Surprisingly, the question-and-answer period lasted 2 hours 45 minutes.
3. The discussion on pages 1,445 and 1,446 explains the procedures for getting government aid.
4. In 1982 she moved her store to 1,870 Rockland Street.

5. As you will see on Invoice 17-19853, 14 items were shipped, not 15.
6. My copy of Policy 80,876 is in my safe-deposit box.
7. The display cabinet is precisely 9 feet, 7 inches high.
8. Her deposit, which totaled $1700, will be refunded to her if the item is out of stock.

COMMUNICATION PROJECTS

Practical Application

A. Correct any errors in comma use in the following sentences. Write *OK* for any sentence that has no error.

1. See the enclosed booklet for the latest, government tax regulations.
2. Dr. Loiseaux is an energetic entertaining speaker who is frequently invited to be the keynote speaker at national meetings.
3. As of 1986 114 of our franchise operations were owned and managed by individuals.
4. No, that isn't Mr. Kane. Mr. Kane is a tall slim friendly-looking man.
5. If you prefer paying the entire balance at the end of each month Ms. Keller we will send you monthly statements.
6. Sign and date the copies all four copies.
7. You must purchase the strongest toughest materials to protect this merchandise during shipping.
8. We enjoy this motel because it has such warm modern spacious rooms.
9. The carton was heavier than we thought; it weighed 25 pounds, 10 ounces.
10. The budget was originally set at $9000; actual expenses, however, totaled $11000.
11. I approved a merit increase for Anne for $2,000; for Jacob, $1,900; and for Dina, $2250.
12. As always, Gail gave a good presentation a very good presentation.
13. Brian listened in his calm unemotional way and then settled the argument.
14. Thank you Mr. Jung for opening an account with our firm.
15. As we told you Martha we prefer having all new clients sign this account form.

B. Correct any errors in these sentences. Write *OK* for any sentence that has no error.

1. Any employee, who has not yet received this packet of materials, should contact the Benefits Department.

2. Mr. Wilson sent the check to us on Friday afternoon, we credited his account.
3. Patrick, Ed, and Jean, have reviewed all these forms and approved them.
4. As you predicted Morris ABC Chemicals has merged with Fitch Plastics.
5. Ms. Jansen said that we should bring order forms, catalogs, brochures, and etc.
6. When she returned from San Antonio Ms. Hill signed the contracts for the building construction.
7. The month before Mr. Reynolds retired from our company after 25 years with the firm.
8. By 1994 1000 cars a month will be sold by this dealership alone.
9. Remember Richard that you are scheduled to meet with the tax advisers at 10:15.
10. She still plans to use space ads and television spots, doesn't she.
11. Have copies been sent to Mr. Chironis? Ms. Zuckerman? Dr. Campbell?
12. Call me, if you need more information.
13. One of the new account representatives, asked some especially insightful questions.
14. Maria generally handles all purchase orders, she deals with all our suppliers.
15. All the managers, who work for our company, are eligible for this new training program.

Editing Practice

The Word Processing Supervisor. The president of your company is sending a personal letter to all 750 technicians and engineers employed by the company to thank them for a special achievement. Read the following excerpt from the president's letter. Does it contain any errors? Make any necessary corrections.

Many of you have already seen the article in the August issue of *Consumer World* magazine naming our television number one in each of the ten categories tested. Never before has any appliance been rated first in all ten test categories. Needless to say, I am exceptionally proud of this accomplishment, and I congratulate all our sale representatives, service technicians, and engineers for achieving this singular honor.

Precisely how did we accomplish this goal? Through expert communication. Our sales representatives and our service technicians accurately communicate to our engineers the wants and needs of our customers. And our engineers, in turn, are designing our products not only with the customer in mind but also with the service technician in mind. The result: a better product, an easier-to-service product.

Case Problem

The Mumbling Dictator.   Jean Walker recently has been hired as a secretary in the law firm of Beatty and Barnes. Mrs. Barnes does most of her dictating to a recording machine, and Jean transcribes the dictation as soon as possible. Although Mrs. Barnes's voice is loud enough, Jean has difficulty understanding her; many of her words are garbled. Jean suspects that Mrs. Barnes dictates with a hard candy in her mouth, but she is not really sure.

1.   How should Jean handle this situation?
2.   If you were Mrs. Barnes, would you object to Jean's criticizing your dictation technique?

28

QUOTATION MARKS, PARENTHESES, AND APOSTROPHES

Quotation marks serve primarily to tell the reader the exact words that someone used. But quotation marks also serve other important uses. Parentheses share some (but not all) of the uses of commas and dashes. Apostrophes have one common use besides indicating ownership.

Study the uses of these three marks of punctuation—the last three punctuation marks you will study in this text.

QUOTATION MARKS

The common uses of quotation marks are described below.

For Direct Quotations

To indicate the *exact* words that someone has written or spoken, use quotation marks. In the following examples, note how commas, colons, and periods are used together with quotation marks.

Ms. Daley said, "We invested in high-grade corporate bonds." (A comma precedes the direct quotation.)

"We invested in high-grade corporate bonds," Ms. Daley said. (A comma ends the quotation, separating it from the explanatory words that follow the quotation.)

"We invested," Ms. Daley said, "in high-grade corporate bonds." (Note how *two* commas are used to separate the interruption. The quotation marks still enclose the speaker's *exact* words.)

Ms. Daley said: "We invested in high-grade corporate bonds. One reason is that a certain portion of the interest is exempt from taxation. Another reason is that the bonds are yielding more than other comparable investments." (Use a colon before a long quotation, including a quotation that includes more than one sentence.)

"We invested in high-grade corporate bonds," Ms. Daley said. "One reason is . . . ." (Again, note that the interrupting expression is separated by a comma and a period from the exact words of the speaker.)

Remember that *indirect* quotations are not enclosed in quotation marks. Indirect quotations are often introduced by the word *that*.

She said that we invested in corporate bonds. (This is an *indirect* quotation.)

For Quotations Within Quotations

Use single quotation marks for words quoted within other quoted words.

Derek asked, "Did she say '16 days' or '60 days'?" (Note the position of the question mark *inside* the double quotation mark [because the question mark belongs to the entire sentence] but *outside* the single quotation mark.)

"We disagree, of course, that their offer was 'reasonable,'" said Claire. (A final comma is placed inside both the single and the double quotation marks.)

Claire said, "We disagree, of course, that their offer was 'reasonable.'" (A period that ends a quotation is also placed inside both the single and the double quotation marks.)

For Definitions, Special Expressions, Unfamiliar Terms, Translations, and Slang

Use quotation marks to enclose definitions and special expressions following *known as, marked,* and *signed*.

In the following table, the abbreviation *YTM* means "yields to maturity." (Quotation marks for definitions.)

Bonds known as "bearer bonds" are not registered in any way; they are anonymous. (Quotation marks for expressions following *called, known as,* etc.)

Note that words introduced by *so-called* do not require quotation marks since *so-called* itself provides them with sufficient emphasis.

Likewise, use quotation marks for unfamiliar terms and for translations.

The above illustration shows a "flat," which is used in photo-offset printing. (Quotation marks for unfamiliar terms.)

Par avion is simply the French term for "airmail." (Quotation marks for translations.)

Slang may be deliberately used to add punch to a message, to attract attention, or to make a point. (Of course, such uses should be limited.) Use quotation marks to enclose a slang expression, a funny comment, or a grammatical error.

There are only two selling days left in the month, but Al Kelly says the sales contest "ain't over yet!" (Quotation marks for grammatical error.)

We are all very eager to hear Pat's "brief remarks." (Quotation marks for a humorous expression.)

Checkup 1

Are quotation marks used correctly in the following sentences? Add quotation marks as needed and correct any errors. Write *OK* for any sentence that has no error.

1. "The new catalog will be distributed to customers by April 11" said Victor.
2. "The new catalog said Victor will be distributed to customers by April 11."
3. "Judy has the original contract replied Howard but she has taken it with her to the Legal Department."
4. Howard replied "Judy has the original contract, but she has taken it with her to the Legal Department.
5. Their so-called "panel of experts" knew very, very little about word processing!
6. We marked all the cartons Fragile, of course.
7. Gordon said, "Mark all the cartons Fragile."
8. In printing jargon, a *widow* is simply a "short last line of a paragraph".
9. Next week I will make my "debut" as sales manager.
10. The check was signed Samuel Clairmont, but the teller double-checked it with the signature on file.

For Titles of Articles, Etc.

Use quotation marks for the titles of articles, poems, lectures, chapters of books, essays, sermons; and for mottoes and slogans.

> She wrote "How to Invest Money Wisely," which appeared in last month's issue of Intelligent Investing. (Quotation marks for article title.)

In the preceding example, note that while the article title is in quotation marks, the title of the magazine is underscored. In addition, book titles are underscored, as well as the titles of newspapers, booklets, long poems, plays, operas, and movies.

> His new book, Coping With Financial Success, was favorably reviewed in The New York Times. (Underscores for book title and for name of newspaper.)

> See Chapter 4, "Computing Yields," in this book, Municipal Bonds, for a chart that will be helpful. (Quotation marks for chapter title; underscores for book title.)

Note that underscoring in typewritten or handwritten copy is equivalent to *italics* in printed copy. Note, too, that while chapter titles are enclosed in quotation marks, other book parts are not. Words such as *preface, index, introduction,* and *appendix* are not enclosed in quotation marks. They are capitalized only when they refer to other parts within a book.

> Read the Introduction before you start Chapter 1, "Milestones."

Punctuation at the End of Quotations

For a summary of how to use periods, commas, colons, semicolons, question marks, and exclamation points with quotation marks, study the following.

1. Periods and commas are *always* placed within the closing quotation mark.

   > "All travel expenses," according to the memorandum, "must be carefully documented."

2. Colons and semicolons are always placed *outside* the closing quotation mark.

   > She disagrees that these stocks are "blue chips": American Metals, Inc.; Paige Industries; Clemson Rubber Company; and Verona Plastics.

   > Mr. DuPont, too, believes that the construction estimates we received are "flagrantly excessive"; however, he has little hope of getting lower estimates from other bidders.

3. Question marks and exclamation points may be placed either inside or outside the closing quotation mark. Follow these rules to decide.

a. If the quoted words make up a question, then the question mark belongs with those quoted words. Place the question mark *inside* the closing quotation mark.

Mrs. Early asked, "Do you think that next year's sales budget is too high?" (Only the quoted words make up the question; thus the question mark belongs with the quoted words—*inside* the closing quotation mark.)

Treat exclamations the same way.

Mr. Wynn said, "I don't believe these prices!" (Only the words in quotations make up the exclamation; thus the exclamation point belongs with those words—*inside* the closing quotation mark.)

b. If the quoted words do *not* make up a question (that is, if the quotation is *part of* a question), then the question mark belongs to the entire sentence. Place the question mark *outside* the closing quotation mark.

Do you agree with Mr. DuPont that these construction estimates are "flagrantly excessive"? (The entire sentence is a question; the quotation is only *part of* the question. The question mark belongs *outside* the closing quotation mark.)

Treat exclamations the same way.

Imagine calling these stocks "blue chips"! (The entire sentence is an exclamation; the quoted words are only *part of* the exclamation. The exclamation point belongs *outside* the closing quotation mark.)

Checkup 2

Correct any errors in the use of quotation marks. Write *OK* for any sentence that has no error.

1. Jerry said that the costs were "ridiculously overstated;" moreover, he said that he would prove his charges.
2. Did Mr. Anselm specifically say "25 percent off the retail price?"
3. During her speech, she quoted a few lines from Robert Frost's well-known poem "The Road Not Taken".
4. "Waste not, want not" is an appropriate slogan for our cost-cutting campaign.

5. The index to John's book, *Planning for Your Retirement,* is thorough and comprehensive.
6. She included these people in her list of "top performers:" Bernard Quinn, Dorothy Fishlock, and Duane Barrett.
7. As he entered the conference room, we shouted, "Surprise"!
8. Do you know that Ms. Perry considers these sales statistics "abysmally low"?

PARENTHESES

As we already noted, commas, dashes, and parentheses share certain common uses. However, they are not interchangeable. Just as words that have similar meanings still have subtle distinctions, so, too, do commas, dashes, and parentheses have distinctions. The careful business writer is aware of these distinctions. Study the use of parentheses discussed below.

For Words That Give Additional Information

Commas, dashes, and parentheses may be used to set off words that give additional information. The words set off by commas may be omitted, but they generally add something to the main thought. The words set off by dashes are often given additional emphasis by the dashes. But the words set off by parentheses are clearly de-emphasized; they may be omitted.

Adam Fonda, our chief financial officer, explained the new system. (The words set off by commas may be omitted, but they do add something to the main thought.)

Last year, four representatives in our region—including Anne Morrow, a new representative—won the Million Dollar Sales Award. (The words set off by dashes may be omitted; however, the writer deliberately uses dashes to draw attention to these words.)

In the past year, we lost only one account (Benson Plastics, which had small billings for the past three years). (The words in parentheses are extraneous; they contribute little to the main thought.)

For References

Parentheses are very useful for enclosing references and directions.

The Bibliography (see page 539) includes an up-to-date listing of magazines and periodicals that may be of interest.

Add water slowly to the powder (be sure that the room is well ventilated), and stir carefully.

Punctuation With Words in Parentheses

Parentheses may be used to enclose words within a sentence, or they may be used to enclose an entire independent sentence.

PARENTHESES WITHIN A SENTENCE.   No punctuation mark goes *before* the opening parenthesis within a sentence. Whatever punctuation would normally be used at this point is placed *after* the closing parenthesis.

> When we meet next Thursday (at the weekly planning meeting), we will discuss the new salary schedules. (The comma that is needed after the clause *When we meet next Thursday* is placed *after* the *closing* parenthesis, not *before* the *opening* parenthesis.)

> Ms. Drury suggested that we keep the list price low (under $5), and Mr. Richards assured her that we could easily do so. (The comma needed to separate the two independent clauses is placed *after* the *closing* parenthesis, not *before* the *opening* parenthesis.)

> Kilgore Electronics estimated a total unit cost of $1.26 (see the itemized statement enclosed); however, this applies only to manufacturing 100,000 units or more. (The semicolon is placed *after* the *closing* parenthesis.)

Note that these rules do not affect any punctuation needed *within* the parentheses. Study the following examples:

> As soon as we decide where we will hold our next product information meeting (probably Chicago, Illinois, or Washington, D.C.), we must immediately reserve 100 rooms for our sales representatives.

> Let's visit their main office (is it on the East Coast?) and give them a formal presentation on our services.

If an independent clause in parentheses within a sentence is a question or exclamation, the question mark or exclamation mark is included within the parentheses. If the independent clause is a declaration, however, no period is used within the parentheses. Note, too, that when parentheses are included within a sentence, the first word in parentheses is not capitalized (unless, of course, the first word is a proper noun) even if the words in parentheses are an independent clause.

> Be sure to ask Bob Trout (he's in charge of our word processing center) to review this report.

PARENTHESES FOR COMPLETE SENTENCES.   When the words enclosed in parentheses are entirely independent (that is, they are not part of another sentence), the first word in parentheses is capitalized and normal end punctuation is used before the closing parenthesis.

> As you requested, we have amortized these costs over a 5-year period. (Please see Appendix A, page 105.)

At this special price, our supply won't last long. Thus we urge you to send in your order form now. (Can you afford *not* to?)

Are parentheses used correctly in the following sentences? Correct any errors.

1. According to the specifications (see the diagram on page 176,) fireproof insulation is required around the perimeter of the room.
2. Abercrombie Industries, (formerly known as "Abercrombie Travel Services"), is expanding at a very rapid pace.
3. This printer can be quickly connected to your computer terminal (see the directions on page 18;) the only tools required are a screwdriver and a pair of pliers.
4. Do you know whether Mr. Dudley would prefer this model (the price is the same?),
5. Ms. Phelps insists that all these invoices (every one of them!) be processed by the end of the day.
6. If S&D merges with Renco Electronics (We think they will do so.), the newly formed company will be the largest manufacturer in the state.
7. In next month's issue we will use our old basic product ad, (see the attached sample) and in the following month we will use the new ad.
8. The plan is to introduce the product at a special low price (say, $19.95); then, in three or four months, we can test the feasibility of raising the price.

APOSTROPHES

As you already know, the primary use of the apostrophe is to form possessives of nouns (*John's* office, several *managers'* recommendations, etc.). A second common use of the apostrophe is to form contractions, which are shortened forms of one or more words.

Contraction	Full Form
I'm	I am
you're, we're, they're	you are, we are, they are
she's, he's, it's	she is, she has; he is, he has; it is, it has
I've, you've, we've, they've	I have, you have, we have, they have
I'd, you'd, he'd, she'd, we'd, they'd	I had, I would; you had, you would; he had, he would; she had, she would; we had, we would; they had, they would

I'll, you'll, he'll, she'll, we'll, they'll	I will, you will, he will, she will, we will, they will
there's, where's	there is, there has; where is, where has
won't, don't, doesn't, didn't, couldn't, wouldn't	will not, do not, does not, did not, could not, would not

One last use of the apostrophe is to show that the first two figures have been omitted from year dates, such as *'84* and *'85* as shortened forms of *1984* and *1985*.

COMMUNICATION PROJECTS

Practical Application

A. Correct any errors in the use of quotation marks, parentheses, or apostrophes in the following sentences. Write *OK* for any sentence that has no error.

1. Dont Hugh and MaryJo know that the price changes are effective May 30?
2. As our attorney explained, *nolo contendere* is a legal term that means "no contest".
3. When asked if we would receive bonuses for this past year, Ms. Hammond responded, "Definitely"!
4. The new billing system (its already operational) will save us time and will help us serve our customers better.
5. Jennifer asked, "Will this dental policy also cover my husband and my family"?
6. "Perhaps" said Mrs. Vreeland, we should include a clause that gives us the right to renew this lease."
7. We discussed the rental agreement with Randi (shes our real estate expert) to see whether she considers the terms favorable.
8. Nearly 90 percent of our employees have signed up for the additional coverage. (Our survey had shown that the majority of them were very interested in expanding their life insurance).
9. "We decided to ask the Finance Committee to review these budget changes," said Ms. McCrory, "naturally, we felt that the members would be interested in the reallocation of funds."
10. Since 1979 Seidel Alarm Systems has advertised its well-known motto: Safety With Confidence.
11. Mr. D'Amico said "that we should review the list to be sure that only active credit card users are included."
12. We will place signs in all the windows (each sign will read "Special Sale"!) and will advertise in the local papers.
13. As the commercial ends, the announcer will say, "Hurry— supplies are limited"!

14. Harriet Shane, the financial adviser on WNEW 1120 on your dial will interview several Wall Street brokers tomorrow at 9 a.m.

15. Stephen said, "Their so-called experts could not even read the schematic diagrams"!

16. Please take all these specification sheets to Ms. Tyler (is she still on the second floor) before you leave for lunch, James.

17. One client asked whether all the bonds in the portfolio were rated "AAA."

18. No, I believe that they havent submitted their monthly summary forms yet.

19. Carefully mark each package of diskettes "Handle With Care".

20. When she completed her master's degree, (she graduated in the class of '84) Evelyn began working in our Legal Department.

B. Correct any errors in the following sentences. Write *OK* for any sentence that has no error.

1. A brief explanation of the new system is included (see pages 10 through 15.).

2. Please refer to the "Appendix" for further statistics on this issue.

3. I believe that it was Peggys idea to develop a less expensive model.

4. Bart suggested that, the unused portion of the advertising budget be added to the travel and entertainment budget.

5. Remember this rule, "No employee is permitted to enter the power plant without his or her identification badge."

6. The list price is approximately $500.00, but this desktop copier will be on sale next month.

7. Mr. Hawks said, "Because Kenneth been with our firm for more than ten years, we will certainly miss him when he moves to the East Coast."

8. Ellen's article on job-hunting tips, Planning Your Career Moves, will soon be reprinted in several magazines.

9. The seminar will cover (1.) time-management techniques, (2.) interpersonal relations, and (3.) decision making.

10. "The manufacturing cost is almost $10 a unit," said Anthony, "consequently, our selling price must be at least $50 a unit."

11. The Appendix lists several excellent sources for more information (see page 1,265).

12. In our storeroom is a carton of purchase order forms and an unopened package of floppy disks.

13. As a safety measure, technicians check the cables, wires, switches, and etc., on a regular basis.

14. He asked, "What is a non sequitur?" She replied, "A non sequitur is a 'statement that does not follow.'"

15. "According to bank policy," said Ms. Handel, "A teller must verify the signature for any check over $500."
16. Esther moved here in 1986 (she had been the manager of our office in Davenport, Iowa,).
17. If you read the book *Success Without Stress,* pay special attention to Chapter 5, "The Importance of Communication Skills".
18. If you need more information on the policy for merit increases, call Donna Gregus (extension 4750.).
19. Martin don't really believe that we will lose the account.
20. Only one of the managers are here to approve these purchase orders.

Editing Practice

The Editing Desk.   Correct any verb errors in the following sentences. Write *OK* for any sentence that has no error.

1. Marion said that she been to Puerto Rico twice within the past year.
2. Although a number of applicants were interviewed today, we have not yet hired anyone for the position of manager of data processing.
3. Don't Mr. Edgar want to keep a duplicate copy of all invoices that we receive?
4. More than a million dollars was raised for the new firehouse.
5. "The increasing number of careers open to women is encouraging," said Dr. Benedict.
6. Has Beatrice already went to the seminar at the Advertising Club?
7. The teller found checks and cash laying on the floor.
8. Have Carla and Jerome wrote their reports yet?
9. Where is the new catalog and the price list that we received this morning?
10. Surprisingly, the number of people who requested free samples were very, very low.

Case Problem

Solving Problems by Discussion.   The small-group discussion technique is often used to solve problems. Shared ideas and experiences of a group often provide better solutions to problems than the limited ideas and experiences of an individual. Here is the way this technique works: (1) Divide the group into small sections of four, five, or six. (2) Make certain everyone in each group is acquainted. (3) Elect a chairperson and a recorder for each group. The recorder will take notes and will later report the major points of the discussion to the entire class. (4) Make certain that everyone understands the problem to be discussed. (5) Be sure that everyone enters into the discussion.

Here is the problem: What are the most important subjects (besides those "majored in") for business students? Why?

CAPITALIZATION

The rules of capitalization help the writer make words distinctive, to emphasize words, and to show that certain words are of special importance. Some of the rules for capitalization cause writers no problems because they are very well known, long-established rules. These rules are reviewed briefly in this section. Other capitalization rules do cause problems; these pitfalls are fully discussed in this section, as well.

FIRST WORDS

Always capitalize the first word of:

1. A sentence or a group of words used as a sentence.

    The lease expires at the end of this year. (Complete sentence.)

    Yes, *this* year. (Group of words used as a sentence.)

2. Each line of poetry.

    I advocate a semi-revolution
    The trouble with a total revolution
    (Ask any reputable Rosicrucian)
    Is that it brings the same class up on top.
    —Robert Frost

3. Each item in an outline.

    The committee recommended that:
    1. We double the budget for the project.
    2. We notify all our customers of the temporary changes.
    3. We assign full-time personnel to handle the project.

4. A sentence in a direct quotation.

   The attorney specifically said, "Be sure to get permission from the copyright holder to reprint this excerpt."

5. A complete sentence after a colon when that sentence is a formal rule or needs special emphasis.

   Her long-standing rule is this: There is no "sure thing" when it comes to investments. (Rule.)

   Time-management experts always stress this point: Spend your time on high-priority tasks only. (For emphasis.)

   Also capitalize the first word after a colon when the material that follows consists of two or more sentences:

   She discussed fully the two main reasons for increasing prices: First, the truckers' strike has substantially increased shipping costs. Second, the cost of importing the raw materials has doubled in the past ten months.

6. A salutation.

   My dear Mr. Rothke:

7. A complimentary closing.

   Sincerely yours,

MAIN WORDS

Always capitalize the main words of headings and titles of publications. The words that are *not* capitalized are articles, conjunctions, and short prepositions (that is, prepositions of three or fewer letters), unless they are the first word or the last word in the heading or title.

   In this morning's edition of *The New York Times,* under the headline "The Need for Financial Constraint and Strict Monetary Policy," Myra Sikorsky complimented the House for its budget cuts. (*The* is capitalized both in the name of the newspaper and in the title of the article because it is the first word. The preposition *for* and the conjunction *and* are not capitalized in the article title.)

   In "The Company I Work For," a humorous look at corporate culture, Peter Arkman discusses his career with Merlin Inc. (Here, *for* is capitalized because it is the last word in the title.)

Hyphenated titles follow the same rules:

   Read "Once-in-a-Lifetime Investment Opportunities for Novices and Experts" in this month's issue of *Money and You.*

Make any needed corrections in the following sentences. Write *OK* for any sentence that has no error.

1. Do you consider "very respectfully yours" too formal a closing for my letters to Sandra Wykoski?
2. How much will the entire project cost? no more than $5000.
3. Remember: always keep receipts of all expenses.
4. An interesting and helpful article, in my opinion, is "Income-tax Problems And How To Avoid Them."
5. Frankly, there is really only one good reason for changing from metal to plastic: Plastic is less expensive!
6. We are now reviewing our needs for the following hardware:
   1. hard-disk drives
   2. laser printers
   3. modems
7. Are we still interested in the project? only if the price is right.
8. He is now writing "Tips For Men And Women In Business" for *Business And Industry* magazine.

NAMES OF PERSONS

Names of people are capitalized, of course. The problems surrounding the capitalization of names concern the use of prefixes such as the following:

O'. *O'Brien, O'Toole, O'Malley.* The prefix *O'* is followed by a capital letter and no spacing.

Mc, Mac. *McMillan, Macmillan, MacMillan.* The prefix *Mc* is followed by a capital letter and no spacing. The prefix *Mac* may or may not be followed by a capital.

D', Da, De, Di. *D'Amato, d'Amato; Da Puzzo, daPuzzo, DeLorenzo, De Lorenzo, deLorenzo; DiFabio, Di Fabio, diFabio.* Spell each name precisely as the person spells it.

Van, Von. *Van Fossen, van Fossen; van Hoffman; Von Huffman; von der Lieth, Von der Lieth, Von Der Lieth.* Follow the capitalization, spelling, and spacing used by each person.

In all cases, be sure to write each person's name precisely the way he or she writes it—this refers not only to capitalization but also to spelling of and spacing in names. However, note that even prefixes that begin with lowercase letters are capitalized when the surname is used without the first name.

We spoke with Jane la Follette last Thursday evening. (She writes her name *la*.)

I think that La Follette's suggestion is a good one. (When her first name is not used, capitalize *la* to avoid misreading.)

NAMES OF PLACES

Capitalize names of geographical localities, streets, parks, rivers, buildings, and so on, such as *South America, Main Street, Bryant Park, Delaware River, Medical Arts Building.*

Capitalize the word *city* only when it is a part of the corporate name of a city: *Dodge City,* but the *city of Boston.*

Capitalize the word *state* only when it follows the name of a state: *Kansas State,* but the *state of Kansas.*

Capitalize the word *the* in names of places only when *the* is part of the official name: *The Hague,* but *the Maritime Provinces.*

Capitalize *north, south, east,* and *west* whenever they refer to specific sections of the country and, of course, when they are part of proper names. They are not capitalized when they refer merely to direction.

> We need a warehouse in the West in order to solve our present shipping problems and lower our shipping costs. (Specific part of the country.)

> She filmed the commercial in South Dakota. (*South* is part of a proper name.)

> Fortunately, the airport is only 15 miles east of our office. (Here, *east* simply indicates direction.)

NAMES OF THINGS

Capital letters identify official names of companies, departments, divisions, associations, committees, bureaus, buildings, schools, course titles, clubs, government bodies, historical events and documents, and so on.

> Several employees are taking Typing at County Business School. (*Typing* is the official course title; *County Business School* is the official school name.)

> Several employees are taking a typing course at a nearby business school. (No capitals.)

> Ms. Dimitrios is a consultant for the Hamilton Investment Company, which has offices here in the Fairchild Building. (Capitalize the official name of the company and the building.)

> She is a consultant for an investment company in this building. (No capitals.)

> She now works for the Engineering Department, which is in the Ryerson Building. (Official department name; official building name.)

Capitalize the names of the days of the week, the months of the year, religious days and holidays, and imaginative names of eras and periods: *Tuesday, Wednesday; March, June; Easter, Passover; the Roaring Twenties, the Middle Ages.* Do not capitalize the seasons of the year: *summer, fall, winter, spring.*

PROPER ADJECTIVES

Capitalize proper adjectives, which are adjectives formed from proper nouns; for example, *American, Canadian, Puerto Rican,* and so on. (Note that certain adjectives [*venetian* blind, *india* ink, *turkish* towel, and *panama* hat, for example] are no longer capitalized, because through many years of use they have lost their identification as proper adjectives. Consult a dictionary when in doubt.)

Checkup 2

Are capitals used correctly in the following sentences? Correct any errors. Write *OK* for any sentence that has no error.

1. Elise D'Amato wrote a satirical article called "It's Un-american To Be Poor."
2. Ship all this merchandise to our Dodge city store by the 15th, please, phil.
3. My friend de la Vega owns and operates the Sunview motel in the Catskill mountains.
4. Miriam's speech, "Women In Business: a Guide For Today's Executives," is both amusing and informative.
5. According to the Mayor, the national education association is exploring the possibility of buying the Herald building.
6. Our last fourth of july sale was a smashing success, von hoffman tells me.
7. Read "Doing Business In Japan—an Up-to-date Approach."
8. In Winter we manufacture our Summer fashions and vice versa.

PITFALLS

The following discussion presents some useful solutions to some of the typical problems writers face in using capitals correctly.

Short Forms

Writers often substitute one word for the complete name of a person, place, or thing. Such substitutions are usually lowercased when they are intended to indicate a specific person, place, or thing. Some short forms are capitalized if they are personal titles of high rank, organizational names, or governmental bodies.

> The most recent biography of the Admiral is entitled *Nimitz in the Pacific.* (Here, *Admiral* is a personal title of a specific person.)

APPLYING THE MECHANICS OF STYLE

She has written a biography about an admiral who was famous in World War II. (Because *admiral* does not refer to a particular person, it is not capitalized.)

When the engineers had completed inspecting the Lincoln Tunnel, they concluded that the tunnel was completely safe. (Lowercase *tunnel*, because it is a common noun.)

The words *company, department, association, school, college*, and so on, are not usually capitalized when they stand alone, even though they may substitute for the official name of a specific organization.

Her company is considering a merger with Fitch & Sellers.

We visited the college when we were in Los Angeles recently.

Ms. Helms is now interviewing two candidates for secretarial positions in our department.

The terms *government* and *federal government* are not capitalized. *Federal* is capitalized of course, when it is part of an official name, such as *Federal Communications Commission*.

Personal and Official Titles

Always capitalize a title written before a name.

Among the directors are Colonel Brown, former Senator Elias, and Professor Goodrich.

A title written after a name or without a name is capitalized when (1) it is a very high national or international title or (2) it is part of an address.

Kurt Waldheim, the Secretary General of the United Nations, is scheduled to speak on tonight's broadcast. (Always capitalize this internationally known title.)

In yesterday's column, she discussed the President's economic policies. (*President*—referring to the President of the United States—is always capitalized.)

Erica Godfrey, president of Godfrey Electronics, announced the acquisition of a major European manufacturing company today. (Do not capitalize *president* in such situations.)

Ms. Erica Godfrey, President
Godfrey Electronics, Inc.
1500 College Avenue
Racine, Wisconsin 53403
(Capitalize a title that is part of an address.)

When joined to titles, *ex-* and *-elect* are not capitalized. Also, *former* and *late* are not capitalized.

Among the dignitaries invited to the dinner was former Mayor Haley.

The late President Johnson is the subject of this short documentary film.

Governor-elect Helms said that she would make our transportation system one of her top priorities.

Next semester, ex-Senator Seeley will teach a course on political science.

Commercial Products

Distinguish carefully between a proper noun that is part of the official name of a product and a common noun that names the *general* class of the product. For example, you would write *Arch Saver shoes,* not *Arch Saver Shoes,* because the official brand name is *Arch Saver.* Note the following:

Kleenex tissues	Xerox machine
General Electric appliances	Goodrich tires

Checkup 3

Correct any errors in the use of capitalization in the following sentences. Write OK for any sentence that has no error.

1. The head of the sales department, which is now located on the tenth floor, is Marion Webber.
2. The old warehouse will be closed, and the warehouse North of Atlanta will take over all operations.
3. Barton Electronics will announce the appointment of a new President by this afternoon.
4. Throughout the country we lease as many as 10,000 General Motors Cars.
5. Yes, the federal Bureau of Investigation does have a regional office nearby.
6. When your Supervisor returns, Homer, please ask her to meet with us in the Auditorium.
7. Send the original copy to the Manufacturing Division at our headquarters office, of course.
8. William Eli, President of Universal Cameras, will retire at the end of the year.
9. Please make two Xerox Copies of this agenda.
10. Which Agency currently has the Folgers Coffee account?

COMMUNICATION PROJECTS

Practical Application

A. Correct any capitalization errors in the following sentences. Write *OK* for any sentence that has no error.

1. Our Company now has exclusive distribution rights to these products anywhere on the East Coast.
2. The Senator is expected to seek reelection, according to Washington sources.
3. Marla Mendez, President of Kline & Mendez Inc., purchased the property last week.
4. She suggests that we use "cordially" or "cordially yours" for less formal closings.
5. "Stocks And Bonds: an Investor's Guide" is the title of her recent article.
6. Our Flight leaves from O'Hare Airport at 4:45.
7. To entertain our clients, we went to the Metropolitan Opera House and then to Lincoln center.
8. Before she was named Manager of the Chicago regional office, Melita was a supervisor in one of our District offices.
9. All stores will be closed, of course, on New Year's day.
10. For years the policy has been the same: always get approval on purchases over $500.
11. Most of our stores are in the south, but our headquarters is in the State of Maine.
12. Our largest manufacturing plant lies about 20 miles South of Sioux Falls.
13. For two weeks we will call on clients in the States of Iowa, Kansas, Nebraska, and Illinois.
14. Rae Ann has been traveling back and forth to the west coast for several months now.
15. Because of the success of our Fall fashions, we have exceeded our revenue goals for the year.

B. Correct any errors in the following sentences. Write *OK* for any sentence that has no error.

1. Martin, the assistant supervisor, sometimes acts like he was the president of the company!
2. The entire shipment, according to the dispatcher, will be delivered inside of two weeks.
3. Please be sure that all these invoices, statements and vouchers are processed before the end of the day.
4. This machine is nearly fifteen years old, but it still works as good as our newer equipment.
5. Do you know whether there is a Federal Government Agency that helps small businesses?
6. Yes, the official name of the agency is the U.S. Small Business Administration.
7. The maps that you're looking for are in back of those cabinets.
8. Don't Maureen know that the production costs for this project are already $50,000 over estimated costs?

9. When she saw the design, Caryl could not help but tell the committee why the design was inappropriate.
10. Where's the inventory report and the sales chart for the monthly meeting?
11. Is that woman sitting besides Maryanne the new regional vice president?
12. Betty, do you know where Diana and Donna are at?
13. No, I do not know where they went to, Harold.
14. Send all complaints like this one directly to the Legal Department immediately.
15. My manager quickly asked, "What is your opinion of these financial analyses, Howard"?
16. One of the new sales representatives who you met at this morning's orientation is Wilma's brother.
17. Elvera Fasano, former president of the Retail Jewelers Association, has been named to the Governor's committee.
18. The only one of the regional managers who was aware of the merger, was Andrew Abbate.
19. Each managers assistant will also be invited to the banquet on the last evening of the convention.
20. Because Cynthia has been working with our Denver staff for the last two weeks her assistant publisher has been handling these negotiations.

Editing Practice

Using Your Word Processor.   Edit the following sentences to correct any errors they may contain. Write *OK* for any sentence that has no error.

1. Being that we did not pay the bill within ten days, we cannot deduct the 2 percent discount.
2. Please do not leave for lunch without you get someone to replace you.
3. Jack, do you know where Myron went to?
4. One of the reporters asked her several questions in regards to the proposed government legislation.
5. All the extra paperwork will be divided between the three shift supervisors, Mike, Carolyn, and Elaine.
6. According to the announcement, the increases are retroactive from last January.
7. Did you realize that the price on this invoice is different from the price listed in the catalog?
8. We read in the company newspaper where Elliot has been made manager of our California office.
9. Todd couldn't hardly wait to leave for Puerto Rico.
10. As you can well imagine, Ms. Madison was real angry when she heard that the contract had been canceled.

Using Business Vocabulary. On a separate sheet of paper, fill in the missing words with the correct word from those listed below.

a.	approximate	f.	freight
b.	bankruptcy	g.	irrelevant
c.	chronological	h.	mandatory
d.	exhaustive	i.	negotiate
e.	extension	j.	valuable

1. Stocks, bonds, and all other (?) securities must be locked in a fireproof vault overnight.
2. At tomorrow's meeting we will try to (?) a 5-year loan at 12 percent interest per year.
3. All us jurors considered Mr. Martin's testimony (?) to the case.
4. Because Norton Industries has been unprofitable for three years, (?) proceedings will begin early next month.
5. Please take all these invoices and arrange them in (?) order, beginning with January invoices.
6. The (?) cost for the entire project is $10,000.
7. According to the contract, the shipper pays the (?) charges.
8. Because they could not meet the payment deadline, we have agreed to a 30-day (?) for the total balance.
9. The Research Department has conducted an (?) survey to discover our customers' preferences.
10. Wearing safety equipment is (?) in the laboratory because of toxic fumes.

Case Problem

Making It Clear and Simple. You have been asked to revise and simplify a memorandum that contains the following paragraph. Rewrite the paragraph in everyday, clear language.

Subsequent to April 10, Mr. Lawrence terminated his contract with this organization after completing a considerable amount of years of continuous and exemplary service. Apropos to his decision to sever relations, Mr. Lawrence stated that he had procured an infinitely superior contract that was the quintessence of betterment. We must employ perseverance in endeavoring to replace this lost contract with one of comparable caliber.

30

ABBREVIATIONS

Abbreviations provide writers with shortcuts, and shortcuts are certainly appropriate *at times*. As a business writer, you must know when abbreviations are acceptable—and when they are *not*. In addition, you must know the correct forms of abbreviations.

PERSONAL NAMES

Study the following rules for using abbreviations before and after personal names.

Before Personal Names

Most of the titles used before personal names are abbreviations.

Singular	Plural
Mr.	Messrs. (from the French, *messieurs*)
Mrs.	Mmes. or Mesdames
Ms.	Mses.
Miss	Misses
Dr.	Drs.

Other titles used before personal names are spelled out whether the full name or only the last name is given: *Governor* McCord, *Superintendent* d'Ambrosio, *Senator* Gomez, the *Honorable* Jane W. Cleary, the *Reverend* Arthur Franks Jr., *General* Holmes, and so on.

After Personal Names

ACADEMIC DEGREES AND SIMILAR ABBREVIATIONS. Abbreviations of academic degrees, religious orders, and similar abbreviations generally have internal periods: *M.D., D.D.S., Ph.D., B.S., Ed.D.; S.J., D.D.* Check your dictionary whenever you are not sure of the abbreviation.

When such abbreviations follow a person's name, use a comma before the abbreviation. Do *not* use *Mr., Ms., Mrs., Miss,* or *Dr.* before the person's name.

Henry Clancy, Esq. *or* **Mr. Henry Clancy** (Not: *Mr.* Henry **Clancy,** *Esq.*)

Jane T. Prentiss, M.D. *or* Dr. Jane T. Prentiss (Not: *Dr.* Jane T. Prentiss, *M.D.*)

Price S. Raymond, Ph.D. *or* Dr. Price S. Raymond (Not: *Dr.* Price S. Raymond, *Ph.D.*)

Other titles before the person's name may sometimes be appropriate:

Reverend Peter Goode, S.J.

Professor Alicia P. Stevens, Litt.D.

Note that in a sentence, any such abbreviation following a name must be set off with *two* commas, unless the abbreviation ends the sentence.

Jane T. Prentiss, M.D., is the subject of today's "Woman in the News" column.

JR. AND SR. Omit the comma before *Jr.* and *Sr.* when either follows a person's name (unless the person specifically uses a comma, as some people still do).

Mr. Sloan P. Jacobi Jr.

Dr. A. Phillip Charlton, Sr. (Dr. Charlton *does* use a comma before *Sr.*)

Do not use *Jr.* and *Sr.* with a person's last name only.

Initials

Initials are abbreviations of names; in some cases, the initials *are* names because they do not really "stand for" anything. Write an initial with a period and a space after it (always following, however, a person's individual preference).

Does J. C. plan to appeal the decision?

Get approval from T. J. Fordyce before we leave today.

Note: Reference initials written at the end of memos and letters are usually written with no periods and no spaces. See Sections 40 and 42 for examples.

Checkup 1

Are abbreviations used correctly in the following sentences? Correct any errors. Write *OK* for any sentence that has no error.

1. We wrote to Elmer J. W. Hawkins Jr., just as Ms. Weinstein told us to, but Mr. Hawkins Jr. has not responded yet.
2. According to the agenda, Sen. Glynn will speak at the banquet Saturday evening.
3. The property has been owned by the Messrs. Fleming since the 1970s.

4. Dr. Lucretia T. Harter, M.D., will be named director of the institute within the next few weeks.
5. His assistant specifically said that Mister Cipriano had already left for the railroad station.
6. I read in the news that Ms. Jessica W. Taft, Ph.D., has resigned her university position.

COMPANIES AND ORGANIZATIONS

Always write the name of a company or an organization precisely as its *official* name is written:

LaSalle & Erskine Inc.

Olsten and Jonas, Inc.

Fun 'n' Games Stores Incorporated

Black Star Construction Company

Quick Contracting Co.

Landry Bros.

Harrison Brothers

The Loomis/Nettleton/Roth Group

Inc. and Ltd.

As with *Jr.* and *Sr.,* omit the comma before *Inc.* and *Ltd.* in company names. Again, however, always follow the *official* name.

Karen works for Time Inc. in New York City.

Write to Garden Cameras, Inc., for more information. (Note *two* commas to set off *Inc.*)

All-Capital Abbreviations

Many names of organizations, associations, government agencies, and so on, are abbreviated in all-capital letters with no periods or spaces between the letters:

AAA	American Automobile Association
AFL-CIO	American Federation of Labor and Congress of Industrial Organizations
AT&T	American Telephone and Telegraph
FBI	Federal Bureau of Investigation
IRS	Internal Revenue Service
NASA	National Aeronautics and Space Administration
NEA	National Education Association
UAW	United Auto Workers
USDA	United States Department of Agriculture

In addition, the call letters of broadcasting stations are always written in all-capital letters without periods.

WPAT-FM   WNBC-TV   KCBT

When *United States* is abbreviated (before the name of a government agency, for example), periods are used.

the U.S. Office of Education

BUSINESS ABBREVIATIONS

Besides their use with personal names and in the names of companies and organizations, abbreviations are used in many other instances in business correspondence.

Address Abbreviations

STREET NAMES. On envelopes, space restrictions sometimes make the use of *St.* and *Ave.* necessary. In letters, however (and on envelopes whenever possible), avoid abbreviating the words *Street, Avenue,* and so on. When abbreviations such as *NW, SW,* and *NE* appear after street names, use a comma to separate the street name from the abbreviation. (Note that the abbreviations *NW, SW,* and so on, should be spelled out in other cases.)

121 West Fifth Street

89 Parsons Boulevard

317 Cortelyou Avenue, NW

POST OFFICE BOX NUMBERS. The words *Post Office* may be abbreviated or not with box numbers. In fact, the words *Post Office* may be omitted.

Post Office Box 605 *or* **P.O. Box 605** *or* **Box 605**

CITY NAMES. Except for the abbreviation *St.* in city names such as *St. Louis* and *St. Paul,* do not abbreviate city names.

STATE NAMES. In inside addresses, use either (1) the two-letter abbreviations of state names or (2) the full spelled-out name. The U.S. Postal Service prefers the two-letter state abbreviations on envelopes. In both cases, always use a ZIP code.

Dr. Francine P. Dana
1301 Westerly Avenue
St. Louis, MO 63121
or **St. Louis, Missouri 63121**

When state names are used elsewhere (that is, not on envelopes or in inside addresses), spell them out or, if abbreviations are appropriate, use the "traditional" state abbreviations such as "Mo." or "Minn."

Do not be surprised to see mail with computer-printed labels in all-capital letters with *no* punctuation and nearly everything abbreviated.

> DR F P DANA
> ST LOUIS HOSP
> 2500 CLARK ST
> ST LOUIS MO 63121-1234

Units of Measure

GENERAL USE. In routine correspondence, units of measure are spelled out: *yards, pounds, kilograms, degrees, meters, gallons,* and so on. Use figures with units of measure.

Each swatch is about 3 inches by 4 inches.

We will need at least eight 1-gallon containers.

The sample that we tested contained about 3 grams of zinc.

TECHNICAL USE. In technical work and on invoices, units of length, weight, capacity, area, volume, temperature, and time are usually abbreviated. Among the commonly used terms are these:

yd	yard, yards	g	gram, grams
in	inch, inches	kg	kilogram, kilograms
oz	ounce, ounces	m	meter, meters
pt	pint, pints	mm	millimeter, millimeters
gal	gallon, gallons	km	kilometer, kilometers
ft	foot, feet	L	liter, liters
lb	pound, pounds	cm	centimeter, centimeters

Expressions of Time

Write *a.m.* and *p.m.* in lowercase letters with no spacing. Always use figures with these abbreviations, and do not use *o'clock* with *a.m.* or *p.m.* Remember: *a.m.* means "before noon" and *p.m.* means "after noon."

The meeting will be at 10:15 a.m. on Thursday. (**Not:** 10:15 o'clock a.m.)

Days and Months

The days of the week and the months of the year should be abbreviated only when space forces the writer to do so (as in tables and lists). In such cases, use the following abbreviations. Note that *June* and *July* are not usually abbreviated.

Days of the Week	Months of the Year
Sun., Mon., Tues. (or Tue.), Wed., Thurs. (or Thu.), Fri., Sat.	Jan., Feb., Mar., Apr., May, June (or Jun.), July (or Jul.), Aug., Sept., Oct., Nov., Dec.

No.

The abbreviation *No.* is used only before a figure: *License No. 465-75E, Patent No. 769,878,* and so on. Note that it is spelled out when it is the first word in a sentence and that it may be omitted after words such as *Room, Invoice,* and *Check.*

Have you found copies of the following purchase orders: Nos. 125-76, 125-89, and 126-13? When you do, bring them to Room 29-15.

Number 5632 is the only outstanding check, Ms. Gleason.

The symbol # may be used on forms or in technical copy.

Miscellaneous Abbreviations

Besides the abbreviations discussed so far, there are many, many more that are used in business, including these few:

ASAP	as soon as possible
asst.	assistant
CBT	computer-based training
CEO	chief executive officer
ETA	estimated time of arrival
OTC	over the counter
PE	price-earnings (ratio)
reg.	registered
YTM	yield to maturity

Check a reference book for a complete list of terms and their acceptable abbreviations.

Checkup 2

Are abbreviations used correctly in these sentences? Correct any errors. Write *OK* for any sentence that has no error.

1. Ms. Wolfe, who is an aeronautical engineer, works in Houston for N.A.S.A.
2. According to the revised agenda, the second session will begin promptly at 10:15 AM.
3. Because of a conflict in schedule, we will meet on Wed., Aug. 3, instead.
4. The chip is about 2 inches long, which is equal to slightly more than 5 CM.
5. She is now completing her master's degree at a college in St. Cloud, MN, where she works for KIBO radio.
6. We will probably need 2 gal more of this chemical.
7. After she speaks in N.Y., Caren will travel to N.J. and to R.I.
8. Since he retired and moved to Mt. Pleasant, Mr. Klimkowski's health has improved.

COMMUNICATION PROJECTS

Practical Application

A. Correct any errors in abbreviation use in the following sentences. Write *OK* for any sentence that has no error.

1. Fay, who has been in charge of our Saint Louis office since 1984, will now take over all our offices in the state of MO.
2. One of our research chemists, Dr. Joy Jackson, Ph.D., holds Patent No. 987,789.
3. A reporter for W.A.B.C. interviewed two VPs of our firm.
4. Most of Annemarie's territory is in the NW part of the state, isn't it?
5. A university instructor, Prof. Dean serves as a consultant to our committee.
6. To save gas, just add 16 oz of Magic Oil to every 15 gal of gasoline.
7. No. 456-654 is the only file that is missing.
8. Ms. Hines requested that we hold the meeting next Mon. a.m.
9. Our guest speaker for the charity drive will be the Rev. Freeman J. Williams Jr.
10. Perhaps we should send copies of these I.R.S. forms to Mister DePaul.
11. This U.S.D.A. booklet offers helpful tips on nutrition.
12. Station WZXY-FM has almost 30 percent of the morning "drive time" audience.
13. Our only office in Florida at this time is in the Ft. Myers area.
14. Check the files for License Number 393-576, please, Alfred.
15. We signed the original lease on Feb. 10, 1982.
16. Packages weighing over 25 lb will be shipped at book rate.
17. Jason now works for T.W.A. in LA, doesn't he?
18. Sherri reserved Room 2914 for the conference next Tuesday.
19. Louisa T. Clarkson, M.D. is the head of the Medical Dept.
20. Please call Sen. Greene's office this morning to confirm our appointment.

B. Correct any errors in the following sentences. Write *OK* for any sentence that has no error.

1. Traffic circles in England are called roundabouts.
2. Yes, either Christina or Joe are going to supervise the completion of the project.
3. Mr. Martin replied, "perhaps the solution is to revise the sales territories in these states".
4. Naturally, we're confident that our Fall fashions will sell very, very well.
5. On her desk is the sales report for the first quarter and the performance evaluation for each staff member.

6. As a result of our campaign, we raised more than $5000 for U.N.I.C.E.F.
7. Don't Angela need these graphs and charts for her presentation tomorrow morning?
8. When you finish, please call Ms. Blakes assistant to change our meeting to Friday afternoon.
9. Do you know where Sean has gone to, Frank?
10. We don't have time to check these cartons now, so just let them lay there until this afternoon.
11. Whom has been named to head the Finance Committee?
12. All these terminals are connected to our mainframe computers in our N.Y. office.
13. Jim was included because he is such a hard-working dependable experienced copywriter.
14. Our current inventory will last only until June or July, you should plan, therefore, to reorder in time for the summer rush.
15. ARC Plastics sent a deposit in September, the rest of the payment is due in November.
16. Send all these cartons to the warehouse on Third Ave. unless Mr. Conroy instructs you to do otherwise.
17. One comp. on the West Coast has estimated the total cost to be under $10,000.
18. The original invoice was for $2000, our current balance is only about $450.
19. All of us agreed that my supervisors suggestion would probably help us fill all the backorders quickly.
20. Although Marisa is out of town for two weeks. We have been able to complete the inventory reports and submit them to headquarters as usual.

Editing Practice

Plurals and Possessives. Rewrite any sentences that contain errors. Write *OK* for any sentence that has no error.

1. Do you know whose going to be assigned to handle the Brancusi account?
2. Mike keeping a chronological file is an excellent idea.
3. Obviously, their are still some problems to be resolved.
4. Miss Burke's asking for a transfer surprised all of us.
5. The Paulsons home will be put up for sale as soon as the mortgage for their new home is approved.
6. Gale and Ellen's jobs are very different, even though they are both sales representatives.
7. The first two suggestions are mine; the rest of the suggestions are theirs.
8. Mrs. Chang commented on you helping others to complete their projects.

9. The doctor's lounge, which is now being redecorated, is on the second floor of the hospital.
10. In about three weeks time, we should know just how well this new product will sell.

Spelling Alert! Correct any spelling errors in the following sentences. Write *OK* if a sentence has no error.

1. The decision to make the salary increases retractive to May has been changed.
2. The attornies both agreed that we should bring suit against the Exeter Corporation.
3. The newspaper reports were clearly eroneous; there is no truth to the story.
4. We are now equiping each store with its own computerized inventory-control system to help reduce out-of-stocks.
5. Our supervisor coroborated Michele's statement concerning the sale of the Chicago property.
6. In our opinion, the value of the building and the property is overated by as much as 30 percent.
7. All of us agree that Mr. Bennett exagerated the damage that had been caused by the flooding.
8. In carefully controled experiments, we proved that our product removes stains better than any other product on the market.
9. Because Phyllis is an intelligent, compatent accountant, I'm sure that she will enjoy a successful career here at Dunn Iron and Steel Company.
10. The pronounciation of *Messrs.* is "mes-ərz."

Case Problem

A Ticklish Situation. Mr. Noble is one of the best customers of the Paterson Electrical Supply Company. On March 15, he sent payment for an invoice dated March 1, with terms of 2/10, n/30. Mr. Noble deducted the cash discount, to which he was not entitled. When the credit manager at the Paterson Electrical Supply Company called the matter to his attention, Mr. Noble indicated that he always makes payment within the discount period but that someone in his office slipped up and forgot to mail this month's payment on time.

1. What should the credit manager for the Paterson Electrical Supply Company do about this situation?
2. Suppose Mr. Noble made a habit of deducting the cash discount whenever he paid after the expiration of the discount period. What might you, as credit manager, write Mr. Noble in your letter refusing to accept the deduction?

31

NUMBERS

Numbers are obviously *very* commonly used in business to express sums of money, order quantities, discounts, time, measurements, percentages, addresses, dates, sales statistics, computer programs, and more. Just as obviously, their importance is often critical to clear, accurate communication. Errors in number use can cause more than simple confusion; they can be expensive, time-consuming, and exceptionally disruptive. Be sure to master the following principles of number usage, and be sure to proofread numbers carefully whenever you write business messages.

USING WORDS TO EXPRESS NUMBERS

Why is it important to know when to express numbers in figures and when to express them in words? One reason is that long-established use dictates certain rules. Another reason is that figures and words have different effects on the reader. Figures, for example, tend to emphasize a number, while words tend to de-emphasize a number: *$100* is more emphatic than *a hundred dollars*. Thus we use figures when the number is a significant statistic or deserves special emphasis, while we use words for numbers in a formal message and for numbers that are not significant and need no special attention.

The business writer must know the general rules for expressing numbers in words and for expressing them in figures and must be able to manipulate the rules when it is necessary to achieve a greater degree of formality or to provide greater emphasis. First let's see when the writer should use words to express numbers. Then we will see when the writer should use figures to express numbers.

At the Beginning of a Sentence

Use a spelled-out word, not a figure, at the beginning of a sentence. If writing the word is awkward, then rewrite the sentence so that the number does not occur first.

Ninety-two percent of the employees whom we surveyed said that they prefer the new plan. (Not: *92 percent . . . .*)

Of the employees whom we surveyed, 92 percent said that they prefer the new plan. (Better than *Ninety-two percent . . . .*)

Numbers From One Through Ten

In business correspondence, numbers from *one* through *ten* are generally spelled out.

Last week, nine people in our department were out of the office.

Ms. Lordi began as an account executive ten years ago.

Their store was formerly on Fifth Avenue. (Note that numbered streets from *first* through *tenth* are also spelled out.)

Fractions

Fractions are expressed in words in general business correspondence.

About one-fifth of our customers account for nearly four-fifths of our business.

Only one-third of our sales representatives have been with our firm for more than three years.

However, a mixed number (a whole number plus a fraction) is expressed in figures.

Our new warehouse is at the center of 7½ acres of a beautiful hilly region.

Indefinite Numbers

Spell out indefinite numbers and amounts, as shown in these phrases:

a few million dollars

hundreds of requests

several thousand employees

Ages and Anniversaries

Ages are spelled out—unless, of course, they are significant statistics.

Our supervisor will be twenty-six years old tomorrow.

She is in her early thirties.

Angela Russo, 27, has been appointed director of marketing. (A significant statistic.)

When ordinal numbers (*1st, 2d, 3d, 4th,* and so on) are used for ages and anniversaries, they are generally spelled out.

his twenty-first birthday

our seventeenth anniversary

But when more than two words are needed to spell the number, or when special emphasis is desired, express the numbers in figures.

our company's 125th anniversary (Not *one hundred and twenty-fifth.*)

A 10th Anniversary Sale! (For emphasis.)

Centuries and Decades

Centuries are generally expressed in words.

the nineteen hundreds (But for emphasis, the *1900s.*)

the twentieth century

eighteenth-century fashions

Decades, however, may be expressed in several ways.

the nineteen-nineties *or* the 1990s *or* the nineties *or* the '90s

Checkup 1

Correct any errors in number use in the following sentences. Rewrite the sentences if necessary. Write *OK* for any sentence that has no error.

1. The completed report, which should be about 8 pages long, will be duplicated and distributed tomorrow.
2. John Dill Inc. bought this property in the late 1970's, when it cost less than $100,000.
3. Last year, less than 1/3 of our budget was spent on advertising.
4. 47 percent of the customers whom we surveyed valued quality over discounts, according to this summary report.
5. Employees between the ages of 19 and 35 will pay only $10 a month for dental insurance; employees over 35 will pay slightly higher premiums.
6. Our Denville district office is responsible for three and a half times more revenue than our next highest producer.
7. 16 applicants had already applied for the job as of this morning.
8. James, do you think that we should reprint a few 1000 more of these order forms?

USING FIGURES TO EXPRESS NUMBERS
For Numbers Higher Than Ten

As you know, numbers from *one* through *ten* are spelled out. Numbers higher than *ten* are expressed in figures.

We now have 12 tellers in this branch.

She gave each of us a copy of the 18-page report.

However, express related numbers in the same way. If any of the numbers are above 10, express all the numbers in figures.

In Conference Room B we will need 4 tables, 24 chairs, and 2 easel stands. (Because one of the related numbers is above 10, all are expressed in figures.)

Note: Figures are more emphatic than words because figures stand out clearly (especially when they are surrounded by words). Therefore, when greater emphasis is required for a number from *one* to *ten*, use a figure to express that number. For example:

only 5 minutes (More emphatic than *five minutes.*)

a 3-year loan (More emphatic than a *three-year loan.*)

For Sums of Money

Sums of money are written in figures.

This invoice totals $119.79.

We have already exceeded the budget, which was $500. (Not *$500.00.* The extra zeros are unnecessary.)

We spent between $4000 and $5000. The unit cost is estimated to be 55 cents. (Not *$0.55.* Use the symbol ¢ in tables and in technical copy.)

Note that words *and* figures are often used to express amounts of a million or more.

$9 million or 9 million dollars

$12.5 million or 12.5 million dollars

Be sure to repeat the word *million* in expressions such as this:

between $2 million and $3 million (Not *between $2 and $3 million.*)

Also be sure to treat related numbers in the same way.

between $500,000 and $1,000,000 (Not *between $500,000 and $1 million.*)

Remember that indefinite amounts are spelled out:

We spent a few hundred dollars.

They bought about a thousand dollars' worth of merchandise.

In Addresses

Use figures for house numbers except for *One.* For street numbers, spell out the numbers from *first* through *tenth.* Use figures for all other street numbers.

Our main office is located at One Wall Street. (Spell out *One* when it is a house number.)

The bookstore that was at 121 West 12 Street has now been moved to 94 West 14 Street.

When the house number and the street number are not separated by *East, West,* or a similar word, use the ordinals *st, d,* and *th* with the street number.

2131 96th Street (The ordinal *96th* helps to prevent possible confusion.)

ZIP Code numbers are, of course, always given in figures.

New York, New York 10020 (Note that no comma precedes the ZIP Code number.)

New York, NY 10020-1221 (New nine-digit ZIP Code number.)

Checkup 2

Correct the following sentences. Write *OK* for any sentence that has no error.

1. Please note that the term of the loan is 2 years, not 4 years, as had originally been requested.
2. Commercial paper is an unsecured note that has a maximum maturity of two hundred and seventy days.
3. Only twelve people in this department are vested, according to this Personnel Department report.
4. All these securities must be delivered by messenger to Ms. Sara Kenyon, 190 12 Avenue, by 2 p.m. today.
5. The potential market for this product, according to our preliminary estimates, is between $4 and $5 million.
6. The catalog gives a list price of $200.00, but I believe we can get a 15 percent discount through the Purchasing Department.
7. If you subscribe now, you will pay only 75 cents instead of the much higher newsstand price.
8. We now have eight terminals connected to our mainframes, our Denver office has nine terminals connected, and our New York office has 13 terminals connected.

With Units of Measure and Percentages

Use figures with units of measure and with percentages, as shown below:

Each office is 10 feet by 12 feet.

This television screen measures 19 inches diagonally.

Each vial contains exactly 5 cubic centimeters of the serum.

For the special sale, we have reduced our prices an average of 12 percent from the manufacturer's suggested list price.

Note: Use the symbol % only in tables and forms. In other cases, spell out *percent*.

With Decimals

Decimal numbers are always expressed in figures:

Mix this powder with water in a ratio of 4.5 parts powder to 1 part water. (A ratio may also be expressed as follows: 4.5:1 ratio of powder to water.)

When no number appears before the decimal, add a zero to help the reader understand the number quickly.

A very slight increase—0.5 percent—was reported for the month of March. (Without the zero, the reader might read "5 percent.")

With a.m. and p.m.

As you already learned, always use figures with *a.m.* and *p.m.*

at 9 a.m.

between 11:45 a.m. and 12:30 p.m.

With O'Clock

With the word *o'clock,* either figures or words may be used. For greater emphasis and less formality, use figures. For more formality but less emphasis, use words.

You are cordially invited to join us at eight o'clock on Friday, the first of June, to celebrate the one hundredth anniversary of the founding of Marsh Enterprises. (*Eight o'clock* is more formal than *8 o'clock*.)

All district managers and regional managers are invited to meet the members of the Executive Committee at a dinner at 8 o'clock, on Thursday, March 15, in our fiftieth-floor dining room.

In Dates

Use figures to express the day of the month and the year in dates:

March 19, 1982 (Not March *19th*, 1982.)

April 29, 1983 (Not April *29th*, 1983.)

When the day is written before the month, use an ordinal figure or spell out the ordinal number.

the 4th of June *or* the fourth of June

the 21st of April *or* the twenty-first of April

Note: The ordinal figures are *1st, 2d, 3d, 4th,* and so on.

With Consecutive Numbers

Consecutive numbers should be separated by a comma when both numbers are in figures or when both are in words.

In 1981, 121 employees were promoted.

Of the eight, three were delayed by traffic.

But if one word is in figures and the other is in words, no comma is needed.

On May 12 two executives retired from Piedmont Industries Inc.

When one of the numbers is part of a compound modifier, write the first number in words and the second number in figures (unless the second number would be a significantly shorter word). Do *not* separate the numbers with a comma.

two 9-page booklets (But 200 nine-page booklets.)

fifty $10 bills (But 100 ten-dollar bills.)

Checkup 3

Correct any errors in the following sentences. Write *OK* for any sentence that has no error.

1. The maturity date for this bond is July 1st, 1995.
2. Mrs. DeGordon will be late tomorrow, so let's schedule the meeting for two o'clock in the afternoon.
3. On March 15 76 stockholders will meet with the president in the auditorium.
4. For best results, mix five and a half parts of TruGlo liquid to two parts water.
5. The coupon rate of this municipal bond is 6.5 percent.
6. The annual shareholders' meeting has been scheduled for the fifth of June.
7. Your session will begin at 11:30 a.m. and will end by 12:45 p.m.
8. This room is small (it measures only ten feet by twelve feet), but it will serve well as a storeroom.

COMMUNICATION PROJECTS

Practical Application

A. Correct any errors in number use in the following sentences. Write *OK* for any sentence that has no error.

1. According to the agreement, the monthly interest charge will be one and a half percent over the prime rate.
2. Before the end of the year, our headquarters will be moved to the new building on 3rd Avenue.

3. During the first quarter, our net operating profit was 12.5% higher than for the same period last year.
4. Mr. McChesney approved overtime for the 7 people working on the Ballantine & Cutter account.
5. The first day of the word processing convention is the 6 of June, isn't it?
6. The federal government has allocated a total of $400,000,000 to the mass-transit improvement program.
7. The unit cost for printing these brochures is $0.19 in quantities of 10,000 but only $0.16 for 25,000 or more.
8. Each lifelike reproduction stands 18 inches high and weighs about 10 pounds.
9. Next year Mr. Gorton, now 64, plans to retire as CEO.
10. According to this computer printout, we have given away about two thousand five hundred samples so far this month.
11. The sixty-seven cars that are now in our fleet will be replaced within the next six months or so.
12. We have three estimates for the cost of repaving six and a half acres of the parking lot.
13. The difference between the estimated cost and the actual cost was minimal (only .7 percent).
14. Please pick up 250 twenty-two-cent stamps at the post office today.
15. As many as 2/3 of our employees have indicated an interest in our evening training courses.
16. Ms. Prescott said, "We expect to begin the 1990s as a billion-dollar corporation thanks to the success of all 4 of our divisions."
17. The new auditorium will accommodate a few 1000 people, according to the company newspaper.
18. If you order now, you may pay four monthly installments of $25.00 each.
19. We must follow the agenda strictly, so please be sure to start your session at 11:15 a.m. and to end it no later than 12:30 p.m.
20. We have forecast an increase of 12.5 percent in gross sales and 14.5 percent in net income.

B. Correct any errors in the following sentences. Write *OK* for any sentence that has no error.

1. Do you subscribe to "Business Week"?
2. For the past several years, Ms. DiFrancesco's commissions have averaged $15,000.00.
3. The governor has appointed one of our executive vice presidents to the new panel on corporate taxes.
4. Between you and I, Jack, I doubt that this line of products will compete effectively.

5. Edwin's older sister Dr. Rona Vincent works for our Chemical Division in San Diego.

6. Next Tuesday morning we will meet with Gregory X. Smith, President of MicroToys Inc.

7. Because the cost of printing these full-color brochures is so expensive. We decided to spend the money on other forms of sales promotion.

8. We plan, for example, to run two page ads in major magazines.

9. The bonds that we discussed are rated "AAA"; therefore they are very safe investments.

10. The new procedure for getting approvals for cost overruns are detailed in this operations manual.

11. The deadline for the March issue is January 5, for the April issue February 4.

12. The recent rail strike caused a two week delay in shipping the lumber from our mills in the Northwest.

13. Anthony, don't your supervisor want you to attend the convention next month?

14. Its major subsidiary, the AmCo Supply company, is responsible for nearly 60 percent of the parent corporation's profits.

15. When Kathryn returns from Switzerland on June 15 we will discuss our new export agreement.

16. It may be too late Carl to run this ad in the July issue.

17. If your planning to sell this product for less than $10, you should explore less expensive packaging.

18. Jane Cresskill is the only one of the regional managers who like the idea of merging both plants into one large plant.

19. Nancy and I reviewed the production schedules for the next two months but we were not able to find any easy way to push up the product-completion date.

20. Send this draft to the district managers; ask each to respond by April 15th.

Editing Practice

Using Your Word Processor. Proofread the following excerpt "on-screen." Correct any errors.

Please send me 100 copies of your pamphlet, *Principals of Time Management,* which was advertised in the November issue of *Effective Management.* I have enclosed a check for fifty dollars to cover the cost of these pamphlets, including the mailing cost.

I should like to have the pamphlets by Febuary 21, when we will conduct a workshop for supervisors. Therefore, I would be happy to pay any extra charge for shipping the pamphlets to me by that date.

Case Problem

The Difficult Caller. Manuel Ortiz, assistant to Richard Gibson of the Lakeland Insurance Company, receives a telephone call for Mr. Gibson from Patricia Harrow, a customer who is a representative of a business machine firm. Gibson often purchases equipment from Mrs. Harrow.

Manuel tells Mrs. Harrow that Gibson is out of the office for the day. Mrs. Harrow insists on telling Manuel her troubles. She is irate because the Lakeland Insurance Company purchased three new adding machines from a competing firm. She wonders why, since she is both a policyholder of and a supplier for the company, she was not given the opportunity to make the sale. She even threatens to cancel her insurance.

1. What should Manuel say to Mrs. Harrow?
2. What should Mr. Gibson do about the situation when he returns?

CHAPTER
SIX

USING WORDS
EFFECTIVELY

32

USING THE DICTIONARY AND OTHER REFERENCE MATERIALS

Words are the devices we use to communicate messages orally and in writing. Like artists, who create pictures by using paints, writers and speakers create pictures by using words. The greater the facility artists have in using their tools, the better are their pictures. The greater the facility the communicators have in using *their* tools—words—the more effective will be their communications. Therefore, the greater the number of words in a communicator's vocabulary, the clearer the picture the person can present.

The English language offers an immense choice of words. For every occasion, English has a word to communicate the right meaning in a way that will be clearly understood. The most convenient place to find a needed word quickly is in your own memory. If you do not know the needed word, however, three quick reference books are at your disposal: a dictionary, a thesaurus, and a dictionary of synonyms. Using these books not only will solve the immediate problem of finding the right word for a single occasion but also will stock your vocabulary for future occasions. With practice in using these three reference books, you need never settle for less than the precise word.

THE DICTIONARY

The most useful and most often *used* reference for those in search of the right word is the dictionary. Learning to use the dictionary is part of learning to use the language. Every successful writer, secretary, editor, proofreader, executive, and student keeps a dictionary within reach and is adept at using it.

The choice of a dictionary is important. A standard abridged (concise) dictionary serves most of the needs of ordinary office and school use. Pocket-sized dictionaries, however, contain too few words, give less information about each word, and lack the supplements that make a good dictionary a broad reference book.[1]

---

[1] The dictionary used as the source for this discussion and throughout this text (except where noted) is *Webster's Ninth New Collegiate Dictionary*, Merriam-Webster, Inc., Springfield, Mass., 1985.

For our purposes we will divide dictionary information into two kinds: "Word Information" and "Other References."

Word Information

The primary use of the dictionary is, of course, to obtain information about specific words—their spellings, definitions, synonyms, and whatever other information may be available to help the communicator. As an example of the extensive information provided by a good dictionary, read the entry for the word *business* as it appears in the dictionary (see below).

SPELLING. First the dictionary entry tells how the word *business* is spelled. Many people face a problem at this point because they do not know which letters stand for which specific sounds. Section 34, "Mastering Spelling Techniques," provides the hearing and seeing skills needed for finding words in the dictionary. Here are some other guideposts for good spelling:

Be sure that you see the letters in their correct order; for example, *niece*, not *neice*.

Be sure that you have not inserted letters that are not there, as *athaletic* instead of *athletic*.

Be sure that you have included all the letters that are in the word; for example, *embarrass*, not *embarass*.

Be sure that the word is not some other word that is spelled somewhat like the one you are seeking. *Read the definition.* Suppose you are writing this sentence: "Mr. Chin sent me a *(complementary/complimentary)* copy of his book." You need to verify the spelling of *compl?mentary*. In the dictionary you will find *complementary*, followed by the definition *"serving to fill out or*

busi·ness \'biz-nəs, -nəz\ *n, often attrib* (14c) **1** *archaic* : purposeful activity : BUSYNESS **2 a** : ROLE, FUNCTION ⟨how the human mind went about its ∼ of learning —H. A. Overstreet⟩ **b** : an immediate task or objective : MISSION ⟨what is your ∼ here at this hour⟩ **c** : a particular field of endeavor ⟨the best in the ∼⟩ **3 a** : a usu. commercial or mercantile activity engaged in as a means of livelihood : TRADE, LINE ⟨in the ∼ of supplying emergency services to industry⟩ **b** : a commercial or sometimes an industrial enterprise ⟨sold his ∼ and retired⟩; *also* : such enterprises ⟨∼ seldom acts as a unit⟩ **c** : usu. economic dealings : PATRONAGE ⟨ready to take his ∼ elsewhere unless service improved⟩ **4** : AFFAIR, MATTER ⟨a strange ∼⟩ **5** : movement or action (as lighting a cigarette) by an actor intended esp. to establish atmosphere, reveal character, or explain a situation — called also *stage business* **6 a** : personal concern ⟨none of your ∼⟩ **b** : RIGHT ⟨you have no ∼ hitting her⟩ **7 a** : serious activity requiring time and effort and usu. the avoidance of distractions ⟨immediately got down to ∼⟩ **b** : maximum effort **8 a** : a damaging assault **b** : a hard time : REBUKE, TONGUE-LASHING **c** : DOUBLE CROSS
syn BUSINESS, COMMERCE, TRADE, INDUSTRY, TRAFFIC mean activity concerned with the supplying and distribution of commodities. BUSINESS may be an inclusive term but specifically designates the activities of those engaged in the purchase or sale of commodities or in related financial transactions; COMMERCE and TRADE imply the exchange and transportation of commodities; INDUSTRY applies to the producing of commodities, esp. by manufacturing or processing, usu. on a large scale; TRAFFIC applies to the operation and functioning of public carriers of goods and persons. *syn* see in addition WORK

This dictionary entry provides extensive information about the word *business*. (By permission. From *Webster's Ninth New Collegiate Dictionary* © 1985 by Merriam-Webster Inc., publisher of the ®Merriam-Webster Dictionaries.

complete." This definition is not the meaning you want. But look under *complimentary* and you will find "given free as courtesy or favor." Now you know that the word you seek is *complimentary*.

Many words have more than one spelling. The dictionary shows spellings that are equally correct by joining them by *or*. For example, the dictionary entry for *traveler* reads "traveler *or* traveller." This indicates that both spellings are standard and both are commonly used. When one spelling is less commonly used, the dictionary joins them by *also:* "lovable *also* loveable" shows that both spellings are used, but the second less commonly so.

Pay particular attention to compound words to determine whether they are written as one word *(shortcut)*, two words *(sales check)*, or a hyphenated word *(left-handedness)*.

Be sure to include any accent marks that are part of a word. For example, *résumé* is a noun that means "a summary"; but *resume* is a verb that means "to assume or take again."

HYPHENATION.   Sometimes a word must be divided at the end of a line of writing. Unless the word is divided at a certain place or places, the reader may be confused and will be delayed. Here is an example of this kind of problem:

Please return this signed statement promptly if you want a refund.

Dictionary entries use centered periods to indicate the correct places for hyphenating words: *busi · ness; col · lege; ap · pre · ci · ate,* but *ap · pre · cia · tive.*

CAPITALIZATION.   The dictionary shows if a word is to be capitalized when it is not the first word of a sentence. For example, the word *south* is usually not capitalized, but when it refers to a specific region, it *is* capitalized.

PRONUNCIATION AND DIVISION INTO SYLLABLES.   Immediately after the regular spelling of a word, the dictionary shows the word's phonetic spelling. This indicates how the word, when spoken, should be broken into syllables and which syllable or syllables should be accented. If phonetic symbols are new to you, refer to the section of the dictionary that explains them. (Many dictionaries show a convenient phonetic guide on every page or on every other page.)

The dictionary shows that the pronunciation of *business* is *biz-nəs.* The hyphen indicates syllable breaks. (*Webster's New Collegiate Dictionary* and some other dictionaries show major and minor stresses by placing an accent mark *before* the stressed syllable or syllables. In this text we place an apostrophe *after* a syllable to show that the syllable is stressed, and we show only major, not minor, stresses.)

WORD ORIGIN. A word's origin, also called its "etymology" or "derivation," is interesting and informative and often fixes the word's meaning in memory. The origin of the word *radar,* for example, is shown as "*ra*dio *d*etecting *a*nd *r*anging." This will help us remember the word's correct meaning and spelling. Words that are formed, like *radar,* from the initial letters of a compound term are called "acronyms." When you know their etymologies, acronyms are easy to remember.

DEFINITION. A good dictionary lists all of a word's definitions, usually in the order in which they developed. Often the dictionary gives examples of the word's use in more than one sense. For example, see page 275, where the entry for *business* shows several examples of the word's use.

INFLECTIONAL FORMS AND DERIVATIVES. The dictionary shows the irregular plural of nouns, the past tense and participial forms of irregular verbs, and the comparative and superlative forms of irregular adjectives and adverbs. After the definition of the noun *contract,* for example, are its derivative noun *contractibility* and its derivative adjective *contractible.* And the entry for the irregular verb *sell* gives its past, *sold,* and its present participle, *selling.*

SYNONYMS. For many entries the dictionary also lists synonyms (words that have almost the same meanings as the entry). The entry for *invent,* shown below, lists three synonyms. Note that although they have what the dictionary calls a *"shared meaning element,"* each synonym has its own distinct shades of meaning. Columbus did not *invent* America, but he did *discover* it. The Wrights did not *discover* the airplane, but they did *invent* it.

ILLUSTRATIONS. A good dictionary often uses illustrations to make a word's meaning clear. Illustrations are especially helpful in understanding definitions of terms that denote complex physical forms and objects. The meanings of some of these terms, in fact, are difficult to grasp from words alone but become clear at once after looking at an illustration. Can you visualize a *sousaphone* without the aid of an

> **in·vent** \in-'vent\ *vt* [ME *inventen,* fr. L *inventus,* pp. of *invenire* to come upon, find, fr. *in-* + *venire* to come — more at COME] (15c) **1** *archaic* : FIND, DISCOVER **2** : to think up or imagine : FABRICATE **3** : to produce (as something useful) for the first time through the use of the imagination or of ingenious thinking and experiment — **in·ven·tor** \-'vent-ər\ *n* — **in·ven·tress** \-'ven-trəs\ *n*
> **syn** INVENT, CREATE, DISCOVER mean to bring something new into existence. INVENT implies fabricating something useful usu. as a result of ingenious thinking or experiment; CREATE implies an evoking of life out of nothing or producing a thing for the sake of its existence rather than its function or use; DISCOVER presupposes preexistence of something and implies a finding rather than a making.

The last six lines of this entry offer synonyms for *invent* and explain the differences in meaning among them. (By permission. From *Webster's Ninth New Collegiate Dictionary* © 1985 by Merriam-Webster Inc., publisher of the ® Merriam-Webster Dictionaries.)

illustration? a *dray?* a *blockhouse?* After looking at the illustrations in a good dictionary, you will have no difficulty understanding these terms.

Other Information

A good dictionary provides much more than just word information. For instance, a good abridged dictionary contains a guide to the organization and use of the dictionary, explanatory notes about the kinds of information contained at each entry, a key to phonetic symbols, a guide to correct punctuation, a list of abbreviations used in the word entries, and more. Here are some of the extra aids you may find helpful.

SIGNS AND SYMBOLS.   This section comprises signs and symbols frequently used in such fields as astronomy, biology, business, chemistry, data processing, mathematics, medicine, philately, physics, and weather.

BIOGRAPHICAL NAMES.   The names of famous people, each with the proper spelling and pronunciation, are listed under this heading. Such biographical data as dates of birth and death, nationality, and occupation are also given. This section may be used, for example, to check the pronunciation of names to be used in a speech or to identify unknown names encountered in reading or conversation.

GEOGRAPHICAL NAMES.   This section provides information about places—name, pronunciation, location, population, and so on. This section, therefore, can be helpful when checking the spelling of places to which correspondence is to be addressed.

HANDBOOK OF STYLE.   This very useful section contains rules on punctuation, italicization, capitalization, and plurals; sample footnotes; forms of address; and style in business correspondence.

THE THESAURUS

If you know a word, the dictionary will give you its meaning. The thesaurus works the other way around: if you know the general idea that you wish to express, the thesaurus will give you a choice of specific words to express that meaning. Thus the thesaurus offers a selection of different expressions, all related to the same idea. Look up the general idea, and you can choose the expression that is most appropriate.

Roget's International Thesaurus and *Webster's Collegiate Thesaurus,* two popular references, are arranged differently. *Roget's* has two sections: the main section and the index to the main section. For example, to find a synonym for the adjective *creative,* look up *creative* in the alphabetic index. There you will find these three entries, each followed by a key number: *productive 164.9, originative*

166.23, and *inventive 533.18*. The key numbers refer to numbered paragraphs in the main section. Thus, if *inventive* is closest to the idea you wish to convey, turn to entry number 533 in the main section and find paragraph 18 for a listing of synonyms.

Like a dictionary, *Webster's Collegiate Thesaurus* has only one list of entries that are arranged in alphabetic order. To find synonyms for *creative*, just turn to the entry *creative*. Within this entry the capital letters for the word *INVENTIVE* indicate that more information can be found at that entry, which is also in alphabetic order.

Whichever thesaurus you select, be certain to learn how to use it properly. The thesaurus will be especially helpful when you wish to (1) find the most suitable word for a given idea, (2) avoid overusing a word by finding a suitable synonym, (3) find the most specific word, or (4) replace an abstract term.

To Find the Most Suitable Word

Suppose you are a writer of advertising copy and you wish to write an advertisement about the new fall clothing styles. One aspect you wish to emphasize is their smartness. Using your thesaurus, you find *smart* may be expressed as *chic, fashionable, dapper, well-groomed, dressed up,* and *dressy,* among a number of other words and expressions.

To Avoid Overusing a Word

Suppose you have written a paper for another class you are taking and you have used the word *great* over and over. The index of your thesaurus refers you to such other adjectives as *considerable, eminent, important,* and *excellent.* After checking the additional lists of words to which you were referred, you now have a multitude of other words to use instead of so frequently repeating *great.*

To Find the Most Specific Word

Often you may know a general word for a particular object or idea, but the word you know is not the specific word you would like to use. For example, you may be discussing the possibility of taking a *trial* vote, but that is not the specific word you want to use. You look up

---

creative *adj syn* INVENTIVE, demiurgic, deviceful, ingenious, innovational, innovative, innovatory, original, originative
rel causal, institutive, occasional; Promethean
ant uncreative

---

inventive *adj* adept or prolific at producing new things and ideas <had a very *inventive* turn of mind> <he was an *inventive* genius>
syn creative, demiurgic, deviceful, ingenious, innovational, innovative, innovatory, original, originative
rel fertile, fruitful, productive, teeming; causative, constructive, formative
con sterile, uncreative, unproductive
ant uninventive

By permission. From *Webster's Collegiate Thesaurus* © 1976 by Merriam-Webster Inc., publisher of the ®Merriam-Webster Dictionaries.

the word *vote* in your thesaurus, and among the many choices shown is the expression *straw vote*, which is precisely the expression you are seeking.

To Replace an Abstract Term

Imagine that you are writing a memorandum and that you wish to replace the word *precipitous* in the phrase *"a precipitous decision."* Among the substitutes you would find in your thesaurus are *hasty, abrupt, hurried,* and *sudden.*

A thesaurus such as *Roget's International Thesaurus* or *Webster's Collegiate Thesaurus* is a writer's tool that will increase in value as you become more adept in its use. With a good thesaurus on your reference shelf, you will not have to reach far for the flavor, color, and fresh images that will make you an effective writer.

THE DICTIONARY OF SYNONYMS

A single example will show the value of a dictionary of synonyms. *Roget's International Thesaurus* lists approximately a hundred types of hats. If you need only to be reminded of the exact name of a familiar type of hat (for example, *fedora*), then the thesaurus ends your search. But what if you don't know the difference between a fedora, a beret, a bowler, a busby, a derby, a homburg, a shako, a snood, and a toque? Then you have to return to the dictionary and look up each of these words until you find the definition that matches the description given you ("a felt hat with a lengthwise crease in the top"). Clearly, this will take time.

A dictionary of synonyms not only *lists* words of similar meaning (as does a thesaurus) and *defines* words of similar meaning (as does a dictionary), but also lists synonyms and gives brief definitions, pointing out what distinguishes one synonym from another—all in one place. This saves many long searches through the dictionary.

COMMUNICATION PROJECTS ▬▬▬▬▬▬▬▬▬▬

Practical Application

A.   Using a thesaurus, list five words that can be used to express each of the following ideas:

1.   A pleasant vacation
2.   An interesting book
3.   A good dinner
4.   A well-qualified secretary
5.   A pretty scene

B.   For a speech she was preparing, Rita referred to the following people. Using a dictionary, indicate the pronunciation of each name and give some identifying information about the person.

1. Cellini
2. Faneuil
3. Lehman
4. Stokowski
5. Zeuxis

C.   In the same speech, Rita referred to the following places. Using your dictionary, indicate the pronunciation of these places and where they are located.

1. Kuala Lumpur
2. Gloucester
3. Dubrovnik
4. Leman Lake
5. Sault Sainte Marie

D.   The following words should be part of your vocabulary. For each, write the correct pronunciation and the most common definition. Then use each word in a sentence.

1. excise	6. franchise
2. lien	7. mortgage
3. bankruptcy	8. accrual
4. ecology	9. incumbent
5. depreciation	10. cartel

E.   The writer of the following sentences confused two similar words. Replace the incorrect word with the correct one. Define both the correct and the incorrect one.

1. We located a good factory cite in Ohio.
2. The secretary gave the clerk some good advise.
3. Ms. Dunn was formally employed by our company.
4. The supervisor notified all personal about the early closing.
5. Ms. Ramirez designed the new corporate stationary.

F.   In each of the following pairs, which is the preferred spelling?

1. canceled, cancelled
2. saleable, salable
3. centre, center
4. envelope, envelop (noun)
5. installment, instalment
6. judgement, judgment
7. sizeable, sizable
8. advisor, adviser
9. acknowledgement, acknowledgment
10. theatre, theater

Editing Practice

Hidden Pairs.   From each group of words below, two can be matched because they are similar in meaning. Find each pair. Write the letters that indicate the pairs.

Example: (a) practice (b) proscribe (c) placate (d) preempt (e) annoy

Answer: c and e

1. (a) wield (b) procure (c) wither (d) obfuscate (e) obtain
2. (a) circumstance (b) sanitation (c) cenotaph (d) situation (e) accident
3. (a) dispense (b) depreciate (c) spend (d) disburse (e) disperse
4. (a) devalue (b) keep (c) locate (d) retain (e) indicate
5. (a) unlawful (b) illegible (c) ineligible (d) unreadable (e) uncouth
6. (a) deny (b) alleviate (c) ease (d) solder (e) obfuscate
7. (a) wretched (b) rotated (c) obsolete (d) antiquated (e) meticulous
8. (a) new (b) original (c) despicable (d) deplorable (e) showy
9. (a) fireplace (b) decrease (c) scarcity (d) dearth (e) bravery
10. (a) pay (b) prescribe (c) replace (d) prejudge (e) remunerate

Case Problem

Tactful Words. The office manager of the Lind Company found, when she examined letters written by Ralph Lee, that Ralph was not very tactful when he wrote to customers of the company. He frequently used expressions like *your error, you claim,* and *you failed.* In discussing this problem with Ralph, the office manager learned that Ralph did not understand that these expressions were negative and could result in the loss of goodwill—or even customer business. "After all," said Ralph, "when customers are at fault, why shouldn't we tell them so?" How should the office manager answer Ralph?

33

IMPROVING VOCABULARY POWER

Words not only communicate ideas, they also stir the emotions, either favorably or unfavorably. Words can lift spirits, inspire action, or soothe injured feelings. If chosen without care, words can bewilder, depress, and even enrage. This fact is all too clear to anyone who has ever had to say, with downcast eyes, "I'm sorry—I did not mean it that way."

The words that you use in writing and speaking can earn you the respect and admiration of those with whom you communicate, or they can mark you as unimaginative—and even uneducated. Often, the words you use can brand you as insensitive. As an effective communicator, you must acquire precision in word usage, which means you must know many words, you must use the right word at the right time, you must be concerned with correctness in the words you use, you must avoid overusing words, and you must be able to predict how listeners or readers will interpret the words you use. Therefore, one of the first steps you must take to become an effective communicator is to follow the guides presented in this section.

THE CORRECT WORD

Careful speakers and writers know the difference between correct usage and illiterate usage. This difference is not merely a matter of what some authority somewhere declares to be correct. Illiterate usage is illiterate because it does not make sense. Consider the word *irregardless*. We can break it into three parts to reveal its confused meaning : *ir regard less*. When attached to the end of a word, *-less* means "without." *Hopeless* means "without hope"; *regardless* means "without regard." Attached to the beginning of a word, *ir-* means "not" or "without." *Irrelevant* means "without relevance." *Irregardless,* then, means "without without regard." It makes no more sense than *irhopeless* does. Although your listeners or readers may understand what you mean, the illiteracy will tell something about you.

Irregardless, like some other illiteracies, probably came about as the result of combining parts of two correct expressions, *regardless* and *irrespective of.* Another cause of illiteracies is mispronunciation. If *relevant* is mispronounced, for example, we may hear the mysterious word *revelant.* Does it mean "revealing"? Does it have anything to do with revels? While the listener ponders this, the speaker may say many intelligent things that the listener will not hear.

Other illiteracies arising from mispronunciation are *irrepair'able* for *irrep'arable, renumeration* for *remuneration* (although *enumeration* is correct), *hunderd* for *hundred, strinth* for *strength, compare'-able* for *com'parable.*

Mistrust and avoid any words that you cannot find in the dictionary.

HOMONYMS

Words that look or sound alike—but have different meanings—are known as *homonyms.* Choosing the incorrect word (although it may sound or even look correct) is one of the most frequently committed errors of word usage.

For example, the tenants of a large apartment house receive a letter urging that "All the *residence* should protest the increased tax rate." This important message might be ignored simply because the writer cannot distinguish people, *residents,* from a place, *residence.* Another letter writer may request a ream of *stationary,* much to the amusement of the *stationer* supplying it.

Below are some homonyms that every business writer should know.

aisle, isle	loan, lone
allowed, aloud	mail, male
altar, alter	medal, meddle
ascent, assent	miner, minor
assistance, assistants	overdo, overdue
attendance, attendants	pain, pane
bail, bale	passed, past
brake, break	patience, patients
canvas, canvass	peace, piece
cereal, serial	presence, presents
cite, site, sight	principal, principle
coarse, course	raise, raze
complement, compliment	rap, wrap
correspondence, correspondents	residence, residents
dependence, dependents	right, write
desert, dessert	sole, soul
dual, duel	some, sum
foreword, forward	stake, steak
forth, fourth	stationary, stationery
grate, great	strait, straight
hear, here	their, there, they're
instance, instants	threw, through
intense, intents	to, too, two
lean, lien	wait, weight
leased, least	waive, wave
lesser, lessor	weak, week

Pseudohomonyms

Pseudohomonyms are words that sound somewhat alike but have different meanings. They are called "pseudo" because, when pronounced correctly, these words do *not* sound exactly alike. For example, the statement "Smith, Jones, and Hill earned $300, $500, and $800, respectfully," is incorrect. The communicator has confused the word *respectfully* (meaning "courteously") with *respectively* (meaning "in the order given"). The pseudohomonyms that give the most trouble are listed here.

accept, except	adapt, adopt
access, excess	addition, edition

adverse, averse
advice, advise
affect, effect
allusion, illusion
appraise, apprise
carton, cartoon
cooperation, corporation
dairy, diary
deceased, diseased
decent, descent, dissent
deference, difference
detract, distract
device, devise
disburse, disperse
disprove, disapprove
elicit, illicit
eligible, illegible
emigrate, immigrate

eminent, imminent
expand, expend
extant, extent
facilitate, felicitate
fiscal, physical
formally, formerly
ingenious, ingenuous
later, latter
liable, libel
our, are
persecute, prosecute
personal, personnel
precede, proceed
reality, realty
recent, resent
respectfully, respectively
statue, statute
suit, suite

Spelling

If you were a business executive, would you hire an engineer whose résumé listed a degree in *compewter* science? You would look even less kindly on an applicant who wrote to request a position as a *fial* clerk. Poor spelling would make you doubt that these people could do the jobs that they sought. Poor spelling makes a terrible first impression, because everyone has access to a dictionary. The poor speller has few excuses.

Business executives complain more about employees' poor spelling than about any other single shortcoming in the use of language. In the world of business, improving your spelling improves your prospects. You can improve your spelling by giving careful attention to the similarities and differences between homonyms or pseudohomonyms and to the suggestions in Section 34 at the end of this chapter. The most important step to improved spelling, however, is developing the dictionary habit.

WORDS SUITED TO THE AUDIENCE

In a speech to a social club, a computer specialist would lose the attention of the audience if, in discussing how a computer could be useful to everyone, he or she used such technical terms as *backups, checkdisk,* and *batch file.* But if the speaker used nontechnical terms, such as *made copies of, asked the computer how much space has been used and how much remains,* and *a file composed of a number of directions,* the speaker could better hold the attention of the audience. Using a strange vocabulary with an audience is as big a mistake as speaking in a foreign language to an audience unfamiliar with that language. Real communication takes place only when a speaker chooses words geared to the interest and knowledge of that audience.

WORDS WITH DIFFERENT SHADES OF MEANING

English offers many ways to describe the same basic facts with altogether different implications. A solitary person, for example, might be called a *wallflower,* a *sneak,* or a *rugged individualist*. The wrong choice of terms can distort the speaker's or writer's intentions and perhaps even offend someone.

Only an unskilled writer or speaker would use the word *cheap* to mean *inexpensive*. Certainly no salesperson would make that mistake. *Cheap* means "worthless or shoddy"; *inexpensive* refers only to cost, not to quality. Sometimes an *inexpensive* suit is a bargain; a *cheap* suit never is.

A competent host would never introduce an honored guest as "notorious for his gifts to charity." *Notorious* means "unfavorably known." *Famous* may be either favorable or unfavorable. *Infamous* does not mean "unknown" but "having a reputation of the worst kind."

Whenever in doubt about a word's meaning, check the dictionary before proceeding. If there is no time to look up the unknown word, then phrase your idea in a way that avoids the unknown and potentially damaging term.

WORDS TO AVOID

Building a successful business or a successful career requires building goodwill. Because words play a vital part in the creation of goodwill, a skilled communicator chooses words and phrases that the listener and reader can appreciate. In general, this means choosing positive rather than negative terms, presenting information directly and without repetition, and using fresh and current expressions rather than old, stale ones. The information below will help you avoid words that will hamper your efforts to create goodwill.

Avoid Negative Words

Which of the following paragraphs is more likely to retain customer goodwill?

> You omitted stating the quantity and the colors of the slacks you ordered. We cannot ship with such incomplete order information.

> The size 36 slacks you ordered will be on their way to you just as soon as you tell us how many pairs you want and in what colors—tan, gray, navy, or maroon.

Although the second paragraph is the obvious selection, note that both paragraphs try to say the same thing. The second paragraph is positively worded and avoids such unpleasant expressions as "you omitted" and "cannot ship with such incomplete information." Negative words are almost sure to evoke a negative response. The customer reading these may cancel the order.

Words create negative responses when the reader feels blamed or accused. Most expert business writers consider *failed*, *careless*, *delay*, and *inexcusable* negative words, regardless of how the words are used, and recommend avoiding these words. Actually, such words are unpleasant primarily when they are accompanied by *you* ("you failed") or *your* ("your delay"). "Your oversight," "your error," "your claim" signal the reader to react negatively; but "our oversight," "our error"—though not necessarily wise choices of words—carry a different impression entirely.

The following words can sound only negative when used with *you* or *your* and thus cannot promote good business relationships.

blunder	defective	inability	regret
claim	delay	inadequate	trouble
complaint	dissatisfaction	inferior	unfavorable
criticism	error	mistake	unfortunate
damage	failure	neglected	unsatisfactory

Avoid Unnecessary Words

Words that are repetitious are a waste of the reader's or listener's time. Such words clutter the message and can distract, delay understanding, and reduce emotional impact. The italicized words in the following expressions are unnecessary and should be omitted.

adequate *enough*	connect *up*
as yet	continue *on*
at above	*and* etc.
up above	*as to* whether
both alike	*past* experience
new beginner	*free* gratis
cooperate *together*	inside *of*
same identical	my *personal* opinion
lose *out*	rarely (seldom) *ever*
meet *up* with	repeat *back* or *again*
modern methods *of today*	refer *back*
over *with*	*true* facts
customary practice	—

Avoid Out-of-Date Words

Words that are out of date suggest that the speaker or the writer is behind the times. Imagine the reaction to a sign that said "ESCHEW SMOKING"! In certain uses, the words below have a similar effect.

advise or state (for *say*, *tell*)
beg
duly
esteemed
herewith (except in legal work)
kindly (for *please*)

party (for *person*, except in legal work)
same ("and we will send you same")
trust (for *hope, know, believe*)
via

Avoid Overused Words

Replacing overused words with more exact and colorful terms can change a dull communication into a bright and compelling one. The adjective *good* is overused and weak: a *good* maneuver, a *good* negotiator, a *good* speech, a *good* employee. Instead, for greater interest, say: an *adroit, clever,* or *nimble* maneuver; a *patient, forceful,* or *wily* negotiator; a *thought-provoking, informative,* or *engrossing* speech; a *loyal, diligent,* or *industrious* employee.

Adjectives such as *awful, bad, fine,* and *great* are also overused. Often these adjectives have no more meaning than a grunt or a moan. The following sentences show how meaningless these words can be.

1. Friction among staff members can result in a *bad* situation.
2. The meeting last Thursday was *great*, and the resolution passed was *great* too.
3. We have an *awful* backlog of orders.
4. The company gave a *fine* luncheon for him when he retired.

While these vague, dull terms deaden the sentences, the choices below impart life and zest.

Sentence 1: *difficult, painful,* or *troublesome* situation

Sentence 2: *important, productive,* or *memorable* meeting; *constructive, salient,* or *eloquent* resolution

Sentence 3: *enormous, gigantic,* or *overwhelming* backlog

Sentence 4: *delightful, fitting,* or *splendid* luncheon

By substituting more precise adjectives for the imprecise and overworked *great, awful, bad,* and *fine,* you will create full, more distinct descriptions. Words, like people, become less effective when overworked. Examine your own speech and writing to discover the words that you overwork.

Avoid Overused Expressions

To be *brutally frank*, if a *goodly number* of clichés are *part and parcel* of your *manner of speaking*, then it is *crystal clear* that your English is a *far cry* from *passing with flying colors* the *acid test of top-notch, A-number-1 King's English according to Hoyle*. How can so many words say so little! Most of those words are parts of overworked expressions that long ago lost their strength. In other words, if you rely on such clichés, your English is weak.

Clichés say much about you. The use of clichés exposes a lack of imagination—the tendency to repeat the familiar, even when the familiar is not worth repeating, rather than to think of new and forceful expressions. Clichés waste time, obscure ideas, and bore readers and listeners. Your imagination is sure to provide better expressions once you resolve to avoid clichés.

Some commonly overused words and expressions, together with suggested substitutions for them, are listed below.

For	Substitute
along the lines of	like
asset	advantage, gain, possession, resource
at all times	always
by the name of	named
deal	agreement, arrangement, transaction
each and every	each *or* every
face up to	face
factor	event, occurrence, part
field	branch, department, domain, point, question, range, realm, region, scene, scope, sphere, subject, theme
fix	adjust, arrange, attach, bind, mend, confirm, define, establish, limit, place, prepare, repair,
inasmuch as	since, as
input	comment, information, recommendation
in the near future	soon (or state the exact time)
line	business, merchandise, goods, stock
matter	situation, question, subject, point (or mention what is specifically referred to)
our Mr. Smith	our representative, Mr. Smith
proposition	proposal, undertaking, offer, plan, affair, recommendation, idea
say	exclaim, declare, utter, articulate, express, assert, relate, remark, mention
reaction	opinion, attitude, impression
recent communication	letter of (give exact date)
run	manage, direct, operate

WHAT TO STRIVE FOR

Avoiding hackneyed words and expressions is like giving away worn-out clothes: now you must find something to replace them. There are reference books to help you in the search for variety in expression, but you cannot expect to find ready-made words and phrases to express every new idea. Achieving variety in word usage demands creativity. To develop creativity, you need to understand, study, and apply the following suggestions.

Become Word-Conscious

When you hear or see an unknown word, you feel curious—you feel the urge to know what it means. Curiosity is your natural ally in building an effective vocabulary, so use it to your advantage. Remember the word (or write it down) until you can get to a dictionary. Becoming word-conscious means satisfying your curiosity every time you encounter a new word. To do otherwise is to choose ignorance.

Once you become word-conscious, you will be amazed to discover how many new and interesting words will come to you each day. You will hear new words in class, on the job, on radio and television, and in the movies and the theater. You will see new words in newspapers, magazines, textbooks, novels, advertisements, and even on package labels.

Keeping a notebook of new words will speed your progress. Keep a record of words and their definitions and review them from time to time. If you hear a new word, be sure to note its pronunciation. If you read a new word, be sure to note its spelling. New slang expressions are worth noting too. You should always label them as slang, however, and realize that they are inappropriate in most business situations.

Learn to Use Word Tools

A good vocabulary is a vast and complex structure that must be built piece by piece. Your own inborn curiosity will give you the necessary energy to build your vocabulary, but you will also need the right tools: a dictionary, a thesaurus, and a dictionary of synonyms. Besides making the construction easier, these tools will ensure that your vocabulary will be strong and lasting.

Select Suitable Synonyms

Choosing suitable synonyms is the most direct means of achieving variety. A synonym, as you know, is a word that has the same or nearly the same meaning as another word; for example, *new, novel, modern, original,* and *fresh* are synonyms. Although synonyms have the same basic meaning, each synonym has a different shade of meaning. To select the synonym that best expresses a specific idea, you must go beyond the basic idea and learn the distinctions.

Instead of using the overworked word *bad,* for example, you might look in the dictionary and find these synonyms: *evil, ill, wicked,* and *naughty.* These synonyms cannot be used interchangeably. The dictionary entry is instructive: Murderers are worse than *naughty,* and mischievous children at their worst do not deserve to be called *evil.* But both *naughty* and *evil* are more vivid than saying "The murderer is very bad," or "The children aren't too bad." By using each of the synonyms for *bad* in appropriate cases, you introduce variety and color.

Sometimes a dictionary will refer you to another entry for synonyms. For example, when looking for synonyms under the adjective *exact,* you will read "see *correct.*" There, under the entry for *correct,* are listed the synonyms *correct, accurate, exact, precise, nice,* and *right.* If no synonyms are listed for the word you seek and there is no reference to another entry, you can create a phrase to achieve variety. Under the word *explore,* for example, the dictionary lists no synonyms, but look at its definition: "to search through or into; to examine minutely; to penetrate into; to make or conduct a systematic search." Thus, instead of using *explore,* you can make a phrase to fit: "*search* the area *thoroughly,*" "*examine* the records *minutely,*" "*systematically search* the files."

An excellent source of synonyms, of course, is the thesaurus. With the help of the thesaurus you can avoid trite expressions and develop variety in word usage. For instance, suppose you are preparing a report in which you claim "Capable office workers are few and far between." You wish to avoid the expression *few and far between,* partly because it is trite and partly because it does not exactly express the thought you would like to convey.

The dictionary will provide limited assistance here. The word *few* is defined as "not many; consisting of or amounting to a small number." The thesaurus, on the other hand, gives many additional similar words and phrases; for example, *sparseness, handful, meager, small number, hardly any, scarcely any, scant, rare,* and *minority.* So you might say, "Capable office workers are in scant supply."

Use Appropriate Antonyms

An *antonym* is a word that means *exactly* the opposite of another word. For example, *light* is an antonym of *dark.* Antonyms may also be "created" by using such prefixes as *il-, in-, ir-, non-,* and *un-* before a word. For instance, *legible* becomes *illegible; credible, incredible; trustworthy, untrustworthy; expensive, inexpensive; delivery, nondelivery; responsible, irresponsible;* and so on.

Facility in the use of antonyms opens broad possibilities to the communicator. While *additional* reading sounds like an added burden, *unrequired* reading sounds as if it might even be fun. It is sad when the dead are *forgotten*, but sadder still when they are *un-mourned*.

Choose Picture-Making Words

Picture-making words make readers or listeners "see" what is being described—often with themselves in the picture. A necktie with an *intricate pattern* is difficult to visualize, but a *gold and crimson paisley* calls an image to mind. Notice that more specific words are better at picture-making. Since the thesaurus is the best aid in the search for specific terms, it is a treasure house of picture-making words as well. Let's say that you start with a vague description like a *big, hairy dog*. The thesaurus can supply more specific terms for *big* and *hairy dog* like *hulking* and *St. Bernard*. You can complete the picture by visualizing it more fully and then describing what you see: a *hulking St. Bernard leaving a trail of coarse, white hairs on the carpet*.

Advertising copywriters must make each word count since each word is costly to the client. The copywriter's language is sometimes extravagant, but it always makes pictures. A shirt has *windowpane* checks; an evening gown has *spaghetti* straps; a scarf comes in *crayon-bright* colors; a coat has a *face-framing* collar. Notice the colorful words in the following advertisements:

This compact car will still be sipping its first drink when the gas-guzzlers are lining up for a third round.

Our down comforter will keep you toe-curling cozy all winter.

Our new acoustical ceiling soaks up excess noise.

Using picture-making words will improve your messages, whether spoken or written, but it requires much work and practice to develop this skill. You can develop it, however, if you force yourself to visualize a complete picture of what you want to describe, and then consult the thesaurus until you find the most specific descriptive terms that apply. First comes the idea, then the full picture, and finally the right words. If you see this process through, you will be able to hold the attention of your readers and listeners in school, business, and private life.

Practice Using New Words

A new word really becomes a part of your vocabulary only when you first write it or speak it correctly. As soon as you are certain that you understand the meaning and shades of meaning of a new word, use it in business and social conversation or correspondence. Each new word makes possible greater variety and precision in word usage, both of which increase your power to express and advance your views. As a result, practice with new words gives you the excitement of exerting your new word power.

COMMUNICATION PROJECTS

Practical Application

A. Which words in the following sentences are used incorrectly? Write the incorrectly used word and next to it the word you would use in its place.

1. Their prices acceded the usual market price.
2. Please canvas the staff about their vacation plans.
3. Mr. Kimball is adverse to reducing the normal workweek.
4. The teller could not gain excess to the vault.
5. Which addition of the book did you use?

B. In each of the following sentences, select the word in parentheses that correctly completes the thought intended.

1. The mayor's calming speech (disbursed, dispersed) the crowd.
2. As one of the signers of the contract, he is not (a disinterested, an uninterested) party to the negotiations.
3. Being trapped in the elevator for four hours had no (affect, effect) on her mood.
4. All the (fiscal, physical) assets of the company are to be sold at auction.
5. He was appointed (council, counsel) in the company's legal section.
6. The work was done without the (assistance, assistants) of the accountants.
7. Ms. Gregory was asked to prepare a (bibliographical, biographical) description for her employer to use in introducing the speaker to the audience.
8. He waited (awhile, a while) before calling his secretary.
9. This account is long (passed, past) due.
10. The typesetter made a (sleight, slight) change in the style of type.

C. Recast each of the following negative sentences in positive terms.

1. Not until today did your letter reach us, too late for our special offer, which ended last week.
2. There is no excuse for misunderstanding my clear instructions, even if you were interrupted while I was talking.
3. Since you failed to state whether you want legal- or letter-size, we cannot send the filing cabinets that you ordered.
4. I will not be in the office on Tuesday, so I will be unable to help you then.
5. Do not use a transistor radio battery with this calculator because the circuitry cannot withstand such high voltage.

D. Substitute more precise words for the overworked words in the following phrases.

1. fix the vending machine
2. a good meeting
3. a fine program
4. fix the letter
5. a good presentation
6. a fine supervisor
7. a good secretary
8. fix the broken space bar
9. a fine building
10. fix this error

E. Find original replacements for the clichés italicized below.

1. a worker who never *leaves you in the lurch*
2. must stop *passing the buck*
3. get it done *somehow or other*
4. *ironing out the bugs in* our procedure
5. thought about *calling it quits*
6. he *gets on his high horse*
7. she *racked her brains*
8. he *sets no store by*
9. she *made short work of it*
10. likes to *toot her own horn*

F. Write an antonym for each of the following words.

1. ethical
2. implausible
3. exorbitant
4. penalize
5. sensitive
6. fascinating
7. trivial
8. synthetic
9. accept
10. encourage

Editing Practice

Picture-Making Words. Rewrite these sentences, substituting exact, picture-making words for the italicized words.

1. The high waves *hit* the side of the ship.
2. They felt *good* sitting on the rug in front of the fireplace.
3. When he lit the cigar despite their objections, they all *looked* at him through the smoke.
4. When the bus finally arrived, they were all *very cold*.
5. His anger was *noticeable* just beneath the surface.

Case Problem

The Uninformed Employees. The Gonzales Manufacturing Company makes cardboard boxes, as well as other paper products. The vice president in charge of production, Ron Wallen, saw a demonstration of a new machine that folds boxes more efficiently than the one now owned by the company. While this new machine would not reduce labor, it would do a better job of folding. Mr. Wallen decided to order the new machine on a trial basis. When the machine was delivered to the room where it would be used, it was not unpacked because the manufacturer's representative could not set it up until the following week. Of course, most of the employees noticed the box and could see from the markings on the crate that it was a new folding machine. Soon rumors began to spread that this new machine would replace many of the employees and that they had better start looking for new positions.

Within one week after the machine arrived, Tom Carol, the head supervisor, came to Ron Wallen and told him of the discontent arising in the department, all because of lack of information about the new machine. Tom emphasized that the employees had many reasonable questions about the machine and the effect it would have on their work.

1. Who should handle this problem—Tom Carol or Ron Wallen?
2. What can he tell the employees in order to allay their fears?
3. What should have been done to prevent this problem from occurring?

34

MASTERING SPELLING TECHNIQUES

A poor speller may ask: "So long as the reader understands the meaning of my message, why does it matter if a word is misspelled?" One might reply, "So long as you are clothed, why does it matter if your clothes are dirty or if you are wearing a purple tie with a bright orange shirt?" The answer should be obvious. The misspelled word, the dirty clothing, and the poor choice of colors all convey an impression to the observer that says that this person does not care, is not knowledgeable, or is lazy. All of these create negative feelings that will result in negative reactions. Furthermore, the reader must waste time deciphering the mystery that pretends to be a word since the writer did not take time to consult the dictionary. The reader must bear a burden that belongs to the writer, and naturally the reader feels annoyed.

Poor spelling makes both you and your company look inept. Consequently, your employer may be reluctant to let you represent the company in dealing with customers. As a result, your opportunities for advancement will be limited. Therefore, you should make every effort possible to overcome any spelling difficulties you may have. A good start in this direction is to study and apply the principles presented in this section.

GUIDES TO CORRECT SPELLING

Although there are many variations in the spelling of English words, some spelling principles always hold true. Every writer must know and be able to apply these principles—the basic guides to correct spelling.

Final Y

Many common nouns end in *y: company, industry, entry, territory, warranty, vacancy, attorney, survey, monkey.* The spelling of the plurals of these common nouns depends on whether the *y* is preceded by a consonant or a vowel. If preceded by a consonant, the *y* is changed to *i* and *es* is added: *company, companies; industry, industries; entry, entries; territory, territories; warranty, warranties; vacancy, vacancies.* If preceded by a vowel, only *s* is added: *attorney, attorneys; survey, surveys; monkey, monkeys.*

Ei and Ie Words

Among the most frequently misspelled words are these: *believe, belief, deceive, deceit, perceive, conceive, conceit, receive, receipt, relieve,* and *relief.* The word *Alice* is a clue to their correct spelling. In *Alice* we see the combinations *li* and *ce.* These combinations can help you remember that the correct spelling after *l* is *ie (believe);* after *c, ei (receive).*

Endings Ful, Ous, Ally, Ily

To spell the endings *ful, ous, ally,* and *ily* correctly, a writer needs to remember that:

The suffix *ful* has only one *l: careful, skillful, gainful, peaceful.*

An adjective ending with the sound "us" is spelled *ous: previous, various, miscellaneous, gratuitous.*

The ending *ally* has two *l's: financially, originally, incidentally, fundamentally.*

The ending *ily* has one *l: necessarily, craftily, hastily, busily.*

(Continued on page 301.)

Proofreading usually involves comparing a final document against an original rough draft.

Complex statistical or technical material can be more easily proofread when one person reads the original aloud while the other checks the final document.

Reference sources
can be consulted
when you are unsure
of spellings or
meanings.

Doubling a Final Consonant

Knowing when to double and when not to double a final consonant is easy for the person who can determine the sound. The only rule needed is this: If the last syllable of the base word is accented, if the vowel sound in the last syllable is *short,* and if the suffix to be added begins with a vowel, double the final consonant.

compel	compelled, compelling
equip	equipped, equipping
occur	occurred, occurrence, occurring
omit	omitted, omitting
prefer	preferred, preferring
regret	regretted, regretting

In each of the following words, the accent is on the *first* syllable; therefore, in the preferred spelling, the final consonant is *not* doubled.

benefit	benefited, benefiting
cancel	canceled, canceling (*but* cancellation)
differ	differed, differing
equal	equaled, equaling
marvel	marveled, marveling, marvelous
travel	traveled, traveler, traveling

Words of One Syllable

If you can hear the difference between long and short vowel sounds, you can tell whether or not to double the final consonant of a one-syllable word. If the vowel sound is long, do *not* double; if the vowel sound is short, double the final consonant.

hope	hoping *(long vowel)*	hop	hopping *(short vowel)*
plane	planing *(long)*	plan	planning *(short)*
pine	pining *(long)*	pin	pinning *(short)*
cause	causing		
seize	seizing		
lose	losing		

Checkup 1

On a separate sheet of paper, correct any misspelled words in the following sentences. Write *OK* for any sentence that has no error.

1. The warrantys on our computer disk drive and printer have expired.
2. The company supply cabinet was fuly equipt.
3. They cancelled their order this morning.
4. We are hopeing to see you at the convention.
5. Are you planing to attend the convention?
6. Mr. Abbott referred us to the necessarily cautious attorneys.
7. The accident occured yesterday morning.
8. There are a number of miscellanous items on the list.

DICTIONARY ALERTS

Everyone needs to use a dictionary, even the best of spellers. However, no one has time to look up every word encountered. Therefore, one skill you should acquire is to learn how to recognize the types of words that are most likely to be misspelled—spelling pitfalls. These pitfalls alert careful spellers to the need to consult the dictionary.

The most common spelling pitfalls are presented here so that you, too, will be alert to the tricky combinations that send even excellent spellers to the dictionary. *Remember:* Use the dictionary whenever in doubt, but especially if the word in question contains one of these prefixes or suffixes.

Word Beginnings

Words beginning with the prefixes *per, pur* and *ser, sur* present a spelling obstacle because they sound alike. If you are not absolutely certain of the correct spelling of any given word, check a dictionary. Study the following words:

perimeter	purloin	serpent	surmount
perplex	purpose	servant	surplus
persist	pursuit	service	surtax

Word Endings

The following groups of word endings are tricky because they have similar sounds or because they may be pronounced carelessly. The spellings of these endings, however, differ. Do not try to guess at spellings of words with the following ending sounds.

"UNT," "UNS." If these endings were always clearly enunciated as *ant, ance, ent, ence,* they would present no problem. However, because they are so often sounded "unt" and "uns" and because there are so many words with these endings, they are spelling danger spots. They must be spelled by eye, not by ear. Some common words having these endings are the following:

accountant	maintenance	incompetent	existence
defendant	perseverance	dependent	independence
descendant	remittance	permanent	interference
tenant	resistance	silent	violence

"UHBLE," "UHBILITY." The sound "uhble," which might be spelled *able* or *ible,* is another trap. The alert writer consults a dictionary in order to avoid misspelling this ending. Some common "uhble" and "uhbility" words are the following:

enjoyable	availability	collectible	flexibility
payable	capability	deductible	plausibility
receivable	mailability	reversible	possibility
returnable	probability	ineligible	visibility

"SHUN," "SHUS." Words ending in "shun" might be spelled *tion, sion,* or even *cian, tian, sian, cion,* or *xion.* The ending "shus" might

be *cious*, *tious*, or *xious*. Learn the spelling of the words listed here, but at the same time, remember never to trust a "shun" or a "shus" ending.

audition	dietitian	conscious	complexion
collision	anxious	suspicious	conscientious
connection	suspension	technician	pretentious
ignition	suspicion	statistician	propitious

"SHUL," "SHENT." The ending that sounds like "shul" is sometimes spelled *cial* and sometimes *tial*. A "shent" ending might be *cient* or *tient*. Look at the following words and learn how they are spelled, but never take chances on the spelling of any word ending in "shul" or "shent."

artificial	essential	omniscient	impatient
beneficial	partial	deficient	proficient
judicial	substantial	efficient	quotient

"IZE," "KUL." The ending "ize" might be spelled *ize*, *ise*, or even *yze* *(analyze)*. A "kul" ending could be *cal* or *cle*. An expert writer, therefore, consults a dictionary for words with these endings. Study the following "ize" and "kul" words:

apologize	advertise	identical	obstacle
criticize	enterprise	mechanical	particle
realize	improvise	statistical	spectacle
temporize	merchandise	technical	vehicle

AR, ARY, ER, ERY, OR, ORY. *Stationary* and *stationery* end with the same sound, but they are spelled differently. Words that end in *ar*, *ary*, *er*, *ery*, *or*, or *ory* should be recognized as spelling hazards; you should always verify each spelling. Memorize the spellings of the following words:

calendar	advertiser	debtor
customary	adviser	inventory
grammar	customer	realtor
temporary	carpenter	advisory

"SEED." Although only a few words have "seed" endings, they are frequently written incorrectly because the ending has three different spellings. When studying the following list of "seed" words, memorize these facts: (1) The *only* word ending in *sede* is *supersede*, and (2) the *only* words ending in *ceed* are *exceed*, *proceed*, and *succeed*. All other "seed" words, then, must be spelled *cede*.

sede	ceed	cede	
supersede	exceed	accede	precede
	proceed	cede	recede
	(*but* procedure)	concede	secede
	succeed	intercede	

On a separate sheet of paper, correct any misspelled words in the following sentences. Write *OK* for any sentence that has no error.

1. Henry pursisted in going to Rochester this morning.
2. Ms. Albert's secretary was incompetunt.
3. Three bills proved to be uncollectable.
4. We are fortunate to have such a conscientious staff.
5. The company plan is very benefitial for our employees.
6. The merchandise arrived this morning.
7. Little particals of dirt prevented the typewriter keys from functioning.
8. Our grammer facility exceded our spelling ability.

YOUR SPELLING VOCABULARY

Business writers cannot take the time to verify the spelling of every word. They must, therefore, take the time to learn the correct spellings of the words used most often in their communications. Knowing how to spell troublesome words requires more than memorization. You must analyze each word and fix in your mind its peculiarities, as illustrated by the analyses of the following twenty words.

accommodate (two *c*'s, two *m*'s)
aggressive (two *g*'s, two *s*'s)
believe *(ie)*
chief *(ie)*
convenient (ven, ient)
definite *(ni)*
develop (no final *e*)
embarrass (two *r*'s, two *s*'s)
forty, fortieth (only *four* words without *u*)
ninth (only *nine* word without *e*)
occasion (two *c*'s, one *s*)
occurred (two *c*'s, two *r*'s)
precede *(cede)*
privilege *(vile)*
proceed *(ceed)*
receive *(ei)*
recommend (one *c*, two *m*'s)
repetition *(pe)*
separate *(par)*
until (only one *l*)

COMMUNICATION PROJECTS

Practical Application

A. Without using a dictionary, write the correct forms of the words enclosed in parentheses. Then check your answers in a dictionary.

1. When did they develop a storage and (retrieve) system for our files?
2. According to the warranty, the company is responsible for the (maintain) of the typewriter.
3. It was (presume) of the customer to take the discount.
4. We are (scrap) the ineffective procedures.
5. Your account should be (pay) by the first of each month.
6. Your (defer)-payment plan is of much value to us.
7. These contracts are (original), not duplicates.
8. It would be (waste) to dispose of the contents too (hasty).
9. That was a most (moment) decision to make.
10. It proved to be (advantage) to both of us.

B. Make any spelling corrections needed in these sentences. Write *OK* for any sentence that has no error.

1. You are to be congradulated on your success.
2. The contract was signed in Febuary.
3. What were the procedes of this sale?
4. Sales are steadaly increasing.
5. Adjacent offices would be convient.
6. The Hotel Alpine has modern accomodations.
7. The error placed us in an embarassing position.
8. Make a list of the uncollectable accounts.
9. Their payment included only interest, no principle.
10. Please type the city and state on seperate lines.
11. Ms. Polensky agreed that there is no noticable difference in quality.
12. Our firm needs some compitent secretaries.
13. We have a large advertizing budget.
14. These new proceedures should save a great deal of time.
15. The new plan benefitted everyone in the organization.

C. On a separate sheet of paper, write the misspelled words in the following letter. Next to each misspelled word, write the correctly spelled word.

Dear Ms. Renchik:

We would like to take this occassion to reccommend our new Charge Plus account to you. This new account gives you many priviledges, all of which you recieve with this convient method of charging all your perchases. You will find inclosed a broshure describing Charge Plus.

If you have any questions, please notefy us so that we can clearify any misunderstandings.

Very truely yours,

Editing Practice

Why Be Trite? Rewrite these sentences, using lively and different words for the trite italicized expressions.

1. Our new office supervisor is a *tower of strength*.
2. She advanced in the company by *the sweat of her brow*.
3. Despite heavy use, the old typewriter is *none the worse for wear*.
4. The idea came to him *like a bolt from the blue*.
5. *In this day and age,* mastery of English is essential for a business career.

Proofreading a Memo. Even though memos go to coworkers rather than to customers, the messages should be correctly written. Correct any spelling errors in the following memo.

Since we hired six new sales representatives last March, our sales have increased dramaticalley. As a result, we are now having difficultys in producing all the products that are now back-ordered, and we are faceing the problem of not being abel to meet all the commitmants we made to customers.

We must, therefore, act quickly to change this potentialy harmfull situation. If we cannot fill customers' orders as promised, we must then explore such possibilitys as refunding deposits and curteously cancelling orders, asking customers whether they would acept late deliverys, hireing part-time or full-time production help, and subcontracting the manufacture of some of our componants. Of course, there are other alternatives too.

Let's meet to discuss these and other possible actions on Wednesday, November 12, at 2 p.m. in our conferance room.

Using Business Vocabulary. On a separate sheet, write the letter and the correct word from the following list to complete the sentences.

a.	delinquent	f.	personnel
b.	emphasized	g.	principal
c.	estimated	h.	principle
d.	mutually	i.	retrieval
e.	personal	j.	visualize

1. Have you compared the actual costs to the (?) costs?
2. Mr. Turner suggests that we turn over all (?) accounts to a collection agency.
3. Ms. Hall (?) the need to make the laboratory safe for all employees.
4. The slides helped us to (?) the procedures that Daniel was describing.
5. We have a sophisticated (?) system for storing all our files.
6. Granting them exclusive rights to market our products will, we hope, prove to be (?) beneficial.
7. Mr. Scanlon wrote a (?) note to Ms. Bowen to congratulate her on her promotion.

USING WORDS EFFECTIVELY

8. The president stressed that the safety of all employees was her (?) concern.
9. The (?) in our department are well-trained, experienced salespeople.
10. Although we stand little to gain from the lawsuit, Mr. Heller feels it is a matter of (?).

Case Problem

Leading a Discussion.   Lily Andrews was chairperson of the banquet committee for the Business Club at Sayer Secretarial School. The committee was meeting to plan the annual graduation dance, and Fred Ade made a suggestion to get a name band to play for the dance. Lily did not think the suggestion was feasible, since a name band would cost more than they would take in through ticket sales. However, Lily, as chairperson, did not want to oppose any suggestions made by members of the committee. She hoped someone in the group would say something in opposition to the suggestion, but no one said anything except that it was a good idea.

1. What is the function of a group leader?
2. Should Lily let the group go ahead with the suggestion even though it will certainly be a failure?
3. What can Lily say to get the committee to see the misdirection of the suggestion without appearing as though she is trying to force her own opinion on the group?

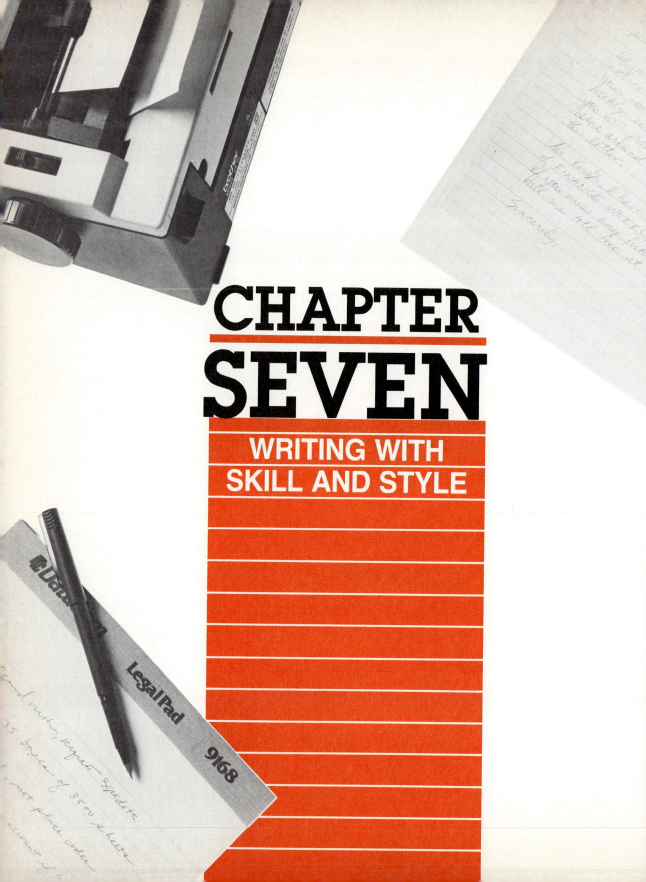

CHAPTER
SEVEN
WRITING WITH SKILL AND STYLE

35

PLANNING YOUR WRITING EFFECTIVELY

Businesses should plan for every contingency. Whether interest rates rise or fall, whether inflation worsens or eases, whether times bring boom or recession, businesses must be ready. The success of any business operation depends in large measure on planning and organizational skill.

Written communications are a major business activity. The vast and eager market for word processing products shows the importance that businesses place on written communications. But recognizing this importance may not prepare you for the following statistic: Business correspondents write every year the equivalent of 300 letters for every person in the United States. This figure does not include the millions of direct-mail advertising pieces and interoffice memorandums and reports produced every year.

Like other business operations, written communications require careful planning and organization. In order to contribute to the success of your company, you will need the planning and organizational skills required by all business operations. Dashing off a letter can lead to serious mistakes in business. The purpose of this section is to equip you with the planning and organizational skills that good business writing requires.

THE MECHANICS OF PLANNING

Writing business communications is a serious and difficult job. In order to write a successful business communication, the writer must first think through the task at hand: *why* is the communication being written, *what* information is to be conveyed, and *how* can the message be made most effective? Only then can the writer hope to produce a clear, convincing message.

Determining Your Purpose

Every forceful business letter has a guiding purpose. Everything in the letter, from the salutation to the complimentary close, is done to achieve that purpose. Usually the purpose is simple: to persuade a supplier to extend further credit; to refuse a customer's request without causing offense; to order supplies; to promote goodwill; to sell a product. As you face each writing project, you would do well to begin by writing down the purpose of the letter or memo. You might make notations like the following:

Answer inquiry about room rates at the hotel.

Request prices for stereo tape deck and speakers.

Accept an invitation to speak at a Rotary Club dinner.

Get credit information about Allen's Sports Car Repair Company.

Refuse Alexander & Associates extra credit as requested.

Assembling the Information

After you define the purpose of your letter, your next step is to gather all the information necessary to achieve that purpose. Failure to do the proper research before writing a letter will force you to write another letter answering questions about the information you left out of the first letter. Although follow-up letters are sometimes unavoidable, usually the first letter should get the job done.

Suppose, for example, that you are asked to write a routine letter requesting a rush price quote on paper for the company's high-speed printer. You are told that the company will need 120,000 sheets of 16-pound paper in the next month. Knowing that 500 sheets make up a ream, you do a quick calculation and fire off this letter:

Please quote us your best price for 240 reams of 16-pound paper.

Two days later you receive a letter from the paper supplier asking several questions: Does your printer, like most high-speed printers, feed long, continuous forms of paper to the platen? If so, are the forms packaged as rolls, or as folded and perforated sheets? How is the paper advanced—by friction-feed or pin-feed? Does your printer use 8½- x 11-inch sheets, or 14½- x 11-inch sheets? Do you want plain white paper or the more popular green-bar format? Do you really want the paper supplied in reams, or would the usual current packaging of 3500-sheet continuous forms be acceptable? And what method of payment will you use?

Obviously, you should have assembled all the pertinent information before writing the letter, as in the following notes. (The numbers in parentheses are discussed in the next section.)

Remind rush; request expedite (6)
Need 35 boxes of 3500 sheets (2)
14½ x 11 inch green-bar format (2)
16-lb economy bond (2)
Request bid, not place order (1)

Pin-feed, fanfold (2)
Company to open account if bid acceptable (3)
Prefer charge paper to account unless credit review would
delay delivery (4)
Deliver loading dock on Wisner Avenue side of building (5)

Orderly Presentation

Your notes now cover all the necessary information. You have jotted
them down, however, without regard to the best order for presenting
the information in your letter.

The final step in assembling the information is to number your
notes in the most logical order. (The numbers in parentheses after
the items listed in the preceding discussion illustrate how to present
these topics. Note that all the paper specifications are grouped in
item 2.) Now you have assembled the facts for a successful letter.

The Social Framework—The Letter as Visit

You now know *why* you are writing and *what* you must say, but
something essential to a good letter is missing. It is the same thing
that is missing from the following visit.

> Edward Moran walks into Lamont Office Supply and sees the
> proprietor, Ellen Lamont. He walks straight toward her and
> says, "Sixteen number 2 pencils, 1 electric pencil sharpener,
> 12 boxes paperclips, 14 yellow legal pads."
>
> Ms. Lamont replies, "One hundred fifty-four dollars and
> ninety-five cents."
>
> Mr. Moran hands Ms. Lamont a check. Ms. Lamont hands Mr.
> Moran a package.
>
> Exit Mr. Moran.

Why is this scene so strange and unreal? Neither Edward nor
Ellen acts as one human being does on meeting or visiting another.
They both ignore the inescapable social framework of their business
transaction.

Business letters that include only the necessary facts are lacking in
the same way as the strange visit described above. Just like a visit, a
good letter must contain the following social elements:

1. Greeting: "Good morning, Ms. Lamont."
2. Statement of purpose: "I stopped by because my office is almost
   out of supplies."
3. Business of the occasion: Edward specifies what he needs.
4. Leave-taking: "Good-bye, Ms. Lamont, and thank you for helping me so promptly."

This procedure is the outline for a personal visit. It could also be
the outline for a visit by mail.

GREETING. The salutation is the greeting of a letter. If the letter is written to an individual, the salutation should be *Dear Mr. Ford* or *Dear Mrs. Liles,* not the cold *Dear Sir* or *Dear Madam.*

PURPOSE OF THE VISIT. When making a personal visit, you follow the greeting with a statement of the purpose of the call. Similarly, after the salutation, the opening paragraph of a letter tells the reader what will be discussed in the letter. Here are three examples of opening paragraphs that state the purpose of the call:

> We are comparing the advantages of leasing and purchasing outright the construction equipment that we use in our major projects. Please send us financial and tax information about your leasing program.

> Because a recent burglary has made us security-conscious, we would like information about your locks, alarms, and electronic surveillance systems.

> We are delighted that your August 4 letter expressed interest in our company's debentures, and we have enclosed both a prospectus and some general information about our operations.

BUSINESS OF THE CALL. This is the "meat" of your call. If, for instance, you were writing that letter ordering paper for a high-speed printer, here is where you would make the orderly presentation of the facts that the supplier will need.

LEAVE-TAKING. Sometimes a letter has another paragraph that becomes a part of the leave-taking. Consider the following examples:

> Your sales of our products have been outstanding, and we look forward to filling many more of your orders this year.

> We have come to rely on the excellent sales that result from buying advertising time on your station.

> Thank you for giving us an opportunity to explain our policy on discounts and back orders.

If you add another paragraph, there are two pitfalls to avoid. First, never use a participial closing, an *ing* expression, such as *Wishing you the best of luck in your new venture, we are* . . . or *Looking forward to seeing you at the conference, I am* . . . . Instead, simply write, *We wish you the best of luck in your new venture.* Or, *I am looking forward to seeing you at the conference.* Second, never offer thanks in advance. To do so would be presumptuous. Express gratitude for a favor or a service when you can acknowledge it, not before.

In all letters, the complimentary closing completes the leave-taking and affords the writer a last chance to set the tone of the communication. The choice ranges from the cold *Very truly yours* to the warm *Cordially.* An incongruous closing can be confusing, as shown in the following examples:

> **This is to inform you that we are seeking an eviction order to remove you from the offices in our building.**
>
> > **Cordially yours,**

> **We are delighted that you have accepted our invitation to appear at the benefit dinner to be held in your honor.**
>
> > **Very truly yours,**

BEYOND THE MECHANICS

A mastery of the mechanics of planning, although necessary for effective business writing, takes us only so far. If we stopped there, our letters would have limited influence on our readers. Planning must go beyond the mechanics if we are to influence our readers in ways more subtle than extending normal courtesies, stating the facts of our business, and presenting arguments. Courtesies, facts, and reasoned arguments are not the only ways in which a letter can guide the reader's judgment. Every letter carries with it a certain atmosphere. The techniques that follow will show you how to create an atmosphere in which your message will appear at its best.

Atmosphere Effect

All of us have had the experience of meeting someone and immediately responding with a judgment like "I'll bet he's smart" or, on the other hand, "Oh, what a bore!" If asked the reasons for our judgment, we probably couldn't offer any. We know only that something about that person registered an impression and we cannot reason it away. For want of a better term, we might call it the "atmosphere effect."

Let's see if we can make impressions, or atmosphere effect, work for us in our business writing, so that our readers will think, "I'd like to do business (or I like doing business) with this company."

FIRST IMPRESSION. The reader's first impression on opening a letter might be "a quality firm," "a very ordinary company," or even "a shoddy operation." To create a desirable atmosphere effect, the stationery must be of good quality, the letterhead design attractive, the typing imprint uniform, the right-hand margin even, and the corrections not discernible. Automated equipment has eliminated corrections on the final copy.

FURTHER ACQUAINTANCE. After registering the first impression created by your letter, the reader looks for confirmation. Correct and polished grammar, spelling, punctuation, word usage—all these are needed to solidify the "quality firm" first impression. Avoid using clichés like *attached hereto, the writer,* and *under separate cover;* otherwise, the atmosphere effect of your letter would be that of a stale, unprogressive business operation.

PARAGRAPH LENGTH. Paragraph length is a key factor in creating a good first impression. The length of paragraphs in a letter is so important to atmosphere effect that it merits special treatment (Section 38).

As you plan your letter, remember that reading can be *hard work.* You do not want your reader to open your letter, see a densely packed page, and think "What a job to wade through this!"

Facilitating Action

We often tend to follow the course of least resistance. We do immediately the tasks that are easy and put off those that will take time and effort. Recognition of this human tendency suggests ways of increasing the chances of getting quick and favorable responses to your letters and memorandums.

REPLY COPY. A reply copy is a duplicate that is sent with the original letter. This device is effective when the reader can reply by writing answers in the margin of the copy. The reason for its effectiveness is that the reader is relieved of the chore of planning and composing a reply.

For example, suppose you are president of a statewide photography association and are writing to give one of your colleagues a choice of dates for the annual meeting and to ask for recommendations for a speaker for that meeting. If you send a reply copy, your colleague can answer your letter by writing in the margin *January 21* and *Dr. Crouch, Professor of Graphic Arts Technology at City College.* What do you think are the odds that you will get a quick answer?

When you assemble information for a letter that will be accompanied by a reply copy, one of your notes should be *Call attention to reply copy.* When you are composing that letter, be sure that you convey to the reader the no-work-involved idea. For example, say something like this:

> **Just jot your comments in the margin of the enclosed copy and return it to me.**

ENCLOSED CARD OR RETURN SLIP. Another method of bringing about a prompt and favorable response is to enclose a card or return slip with the letter. Suppose your firm, The Sports Center, is planning a new campaign for customers. Your job is to write the promotional copy that will go to thousands of people on a newly obtained mailing list. Management has decided to offer each potential new customer a free copy of the company's latest discount catalog. An addressed return card will be enclosed, postage-paid.

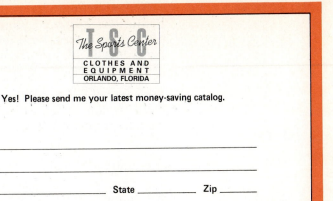

Positive words such as *yes* and *money-saving* help to make this return card an effective way to stimulate action.

The psychological motivation for your letter will be financial gain—making money by saving money—and the spur to action will be a final paragraph such as this:

> **You will start to save money just as soon as you fill out and return the enclosed card. No postage is necessary.**

ATTACHED PERFORATED FORM. Still another means of facilitating action is to use a perforated return form that can be detached from the letter. This method can be just as effective as a separately enclosed slip and is much easier to prepare and mail.

When you write this type of letter, be sure to include a paragraph that calls attention to the form. For instance:

> **To renew your subscription—and to receive a bonus of six free issues!—fill in the form at the bottom of this page, tear it off, and mail it *today*.**

WATCH THAT *IF!* Our readers almost always have a choice of what to say in response to our messages. When reminded of the choice, however, people are more likely to decide against a new proposal. The writer, therefore, should never remind readers that they have a choice. Always assume that the readers will act favorably. Your confidence will help make the case for your proposal.

If is the word that indicates a choice; and *if* is the word to watch. Perhaps we can best illustrate this bit of psychology by rewording the last two examples.

> **If you would like to receive the latest edition of our money-saving catalog, just fill out and return the enclosed card. No postage is necessary.**

If you wish to renew your subscription—and win the bonus of six free issues!—fill in the form at the bottom of this page, tear it off, and mail it *today*.

The *if* in either of these examples suggests to your readers that they might *not* like to receive or wish to renew—and the chances are that they will go along with the *not*. Be aware that the *if* in each of these paragraphs is the word that risks losing the order.

Rereading Your Letters

Many employees never climb from the bottom of the salary heap because they do not add extra polish to the work they do. There is no future for people whose philosophy is "That's good enough."

A business writer's extra polish is the final check of each communication. After you finish your letter-writing stint for the day, reread the letters as if they were addressed *to* you, not sent *by* you. From this fresh and different viewpoint, you should be able to spot any errors you have made, either in language or in psychology. And although additional time and effort are involved, your intelligence tells you that only by spending that time can you produce a top-notch job.

COMMUNICATION PROJECTS

Practical Application

A. Assume that you are inviting Lorraine Smathers, a local certified public accountant, to speak to your campus business club's dinner meeting. Her meal is complimentary. Work with a classmate to plan the letter. First, list the items the letter should cover. Then number them in the order they should appear in the letter. Use your imagination to supply needed details such as time and place.

B. As the owner of Mountain Summer Camp, you are answering a letter that asks about your summer camping programs. You have made the following notes. Now, number them in the order they should appear in the letter.

a. All sessions are coeducational.
b. Camp for sixth and seventh graders—June 16–30.
c. As you can see from the enclosed brochure, many activities are provided for our campers in the beautiful mountains of Virginia.
d. Please complete and return an application for each prospective camper.
e. Enclosed are five application blanks.
f. Camp for junior high band students—July 16–30.
g. Camp for fourth and fifth graders—June 1–15.
h. You may make copies of the application blanks if you need more.

i.   Thank you for asking about the camping programs at Mountain Summer Camp.
j.   Camp for eighth, ninth, and tenth graders—July 1–15.
k.   We offer four 2-week sessions.
l.   Call or write us if you need additional information.
m.   Select the appropriate session on the basis of the camper's grade level for next fall.

C.   Using the notes you have just arranged in Application B, write the letter.

D.   List three business writing situations that could effectively use a reply copy.

E.   Choose one of the business situations from Application D and write a letter that could use a reply copy.

Editing Practice

Trimming Extra Words.   Rewrite the sentences below, eliminating all redundancies. Write *OK* for any sentence that has no error.

1.   The usual and customary practice is payment within ten days.
2.   After Peter made the remark, he repeated it again.
3.   Both of his assumptions were incorrect and wrong.
4.   You will get a refund of your money back if you are not satisfied.
5.   Please bring a pad, a pencil, a notebook, a ruler, and etc.
6.   Andy's watch quit running and stopped when he dived into the pool.
7.   The engineers agreed on the necessary action.
8.   To receive a free complimentary ticket to the concert, you must agree to help clean the auditorium.
9.   Call me tomorrow morning at 10 a.m.
10.   A new air-conditioning unit will be expensive and will cost a lot.

Case Problem

Keeping Confidences.   As an assistant in the manager's office, you hear much information that is confidential. The branch manager recently resigned, and the office "chatterbox" is trying desperately to find out from you the name of the new branch manager. You know who the replacement is.

The chatterbox has tried such tactics as these:

"As important as you are, I'm sure you know who the new branch manager will be."

"The previous assistant would have known what was going on. Doesn't the manager trust you?"

"If you tell me, I promise not to tell anyone else."

"If you tell me, I'll give you the latest office scoop."

Should you reveal the new branch manager's name? How could revealing the name hurt or help you in the organization?

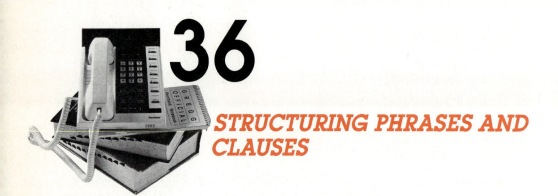

36

STRUCTURING PHRASES AND CLAUSES

In the writing of every message, words must be grouped with care; otherwise, the reader will be confused. Small differences in the grouping or placement of words can make huge differences in meaning. Consider the following example:

> **Calling the meeting to order, the new toothpaste drew the praise of the marketing director.**

> **When the meeting was called to order, the new toothpaste drew the praise of the marketing director.**

While we can understand how a new kind of toothpaste might please the marketing director, even in this age of technological miracles we can't expect toothpaste to call a meeting to order. In order to avoid the confusion and embarrassment that accompany such a ridiculous statement, the writer must learn to keep together words whose meanings belong together.

A combination of words that properly belong together is called a *thought unit*. When the writer correctly places the words of a thought unit, the reader can understand the meaning quickly and easily. When the writer incorrectly places the words of a thought unit, however, the reader may get a completely mistaken idea of the writer's meaning. Sometimes the mistaken idea is laughable, but in business such mistakes are more likely to cause serious problems, as in the example below.

> **If our new Road Snuggler tires don't satisfy you, just fill out the enclosed warranty forms and send them back to us— we'll pay the postage.**

The difference between the cost of mailing the warranty forms and the cost of mailing the tires would be considerable. Does the pronoun *them* stand for the papers or the tires? Let's hope that the writer's employer won't mind paying the postage for both.

The first step in developing your writing skill is to learn to structure phrases and clauses in a way that makes your meaning unmistakable. This section will show you how.

WORDS IN THOUGHT UNITS

Sometimes a confusing, laughable, or simply false meaning is conveyed because a single word is not connected with its proper thought unit. The following advertisement is an example of a misplaced adjective.

Gnarled women's walking sticks for sale at unbeatable prices.

Placement of the words seems to indicate that *gnarled women's* is a thought unit. But what woman wants to be described as *gnarled?* Women who answered this ad would be more likely to hit the salesclerk with a walking stick than to buy one. The correct thought unit is *gnarled walking sticks.* Therefore, the copywriter should have written the ad as shown below.

Women's gnarled walking sticks are on sale at unbeatable prices.

Misplaced adverbs, too, can lead to confusion:

The idea for changing our sales emphasis came to me after I had opened the meeting suddenly.

The thought unit *opened suddenly* is incorrect. The *idea came suddenly,* and so the sentence should read as follows:

The idea for changing our sales emphasis suddenly came to me after I had opened the meeting.

PHRASES IN THOUGHT UNITS

Incorrectly placed phrases, as well as incorrectly placed words, can change the meaning of a message completely. Expert writers edit their work carefully to see that they have placed phrases correctly. An expert writer would reject the following sentence:

These repairs can be performed by anyone who has studied the technical manual in fifteen minutes.

Surely no technical manual could be studied in fifteen minutes, but someone who had spent weeks studying a technical manual might be able to perform a minor repair in fifteen minutes. The sentence, then, should read:

> These repairs can be performed in fifteen minutes by anyone who has studied the technical manual.

Now read the following classified advertisement and see the confusion that results from an incorrectly placed thought unit.

> **For rent:** Three-room apartment for working couple with balcony only.

This ad might bring to the real estate office only those couples who already have a balcony. But how many couples can there be who have a balcony but don't have an apartment? The ad should say:

> **For rent:** Three-room apartment with balcony for working couple only.

Two misplaced phrases can be even worse than one. Imagine receiving a direct-mail advertisement that contained the following sentence:

> Our glazed ceramic tiles are guaranteed to please you and your family without qualification in your bathroom.

The correct thought units are *tiles in your bathroom* and *guaranteed without qualification*. The following revision would be more likely to sell you the tiles:

> Our glazed ceramic tiles in your bathroom are guaranteed without qualification to please you and your family.

CLAUSES IN THOUGHT UNITS

Misplacing a car is a bigger mistake than misplacing a bicycle. We shouldn't be surprised, then, to learn that a misplaced clause can have even more devastating consequences than a misplaced word or phrase. How would the public react if the president of your company made this announcement?

> Our goal as a new company is to get the public to try our products until we become better known.

The sentence sounds as if once your company *is* better known, no one will want to try your products. Moving the *until* clause clears up the matter.

> Until we become better known, our goal as a new company is to get the public to try our products.

Because clauses pose a special hazard since they often are used to explain people's motives. Consider the following statement:

> Ms. Carr hardly noticed the flowers that were sent by her husband because she was concentrating so intensely on the labor contract she was negotiating.

Imagine the loving note that Mr. Carr must have sent with the flowers: "Thank you so much for concentrating intensely on the labor contract. I will always remember this as one of the most touching moments in our life together."

Unless Mr. Carr is a member of management of the labor union, he could hardly be expected to send his wife either the note or the flowers as described above. More likely the following sentence better describes the situation:

> Because she was concentrating so intensely on the labor contract she was negotiating, Ms. Carr hardly noticed the flowers that were sent by her husband.

Now Ms. Carr's reason for taking little notice of the flowers is easy to understand.

AMBIGUOUS WHICH CLAUSES

The word *which* is a pronoun that refers to another word in the sentence. If the word referred to is unclear, confusion will result. A mark of the expert writer is the ability to place a *which* clause with the word modified, explained, or amplified.

Here is an example of one misuse of a *which* clause—simple misplacement.

> We have a prospectus on gold bullion, which we send free of charge on request.

Placing *which* immediately after *gold bullion* alters the meaning of the sentence. Will the *gold* be sent without charge? The writer of the sentence above actually intended to say that the *prospectus* would be sent. Accordingly, the *which* clause should have been placed as follows:

> We have a prospectus, which we will send free of charge on request, that deals with gold bullion.

While clear and a definite improvement, the rewritten sentence would gain force and polish if the *which* clause were removed in favor of the version below:

> On request, we will send you our prospectus on gold bullion.

Another misuse of a *which* clause will be familiar to all. Although it is perfectly acceptable for *which* to refer to a broad idea rather than to a single noun, the writer must take extra care to see that the reference is clear. Pronoun reference in the sentence below is ambiguous:

> **Further resistance to the board's decision will only jeopardize your position, which neither of us wants.**

The problem here is that the *which* clause may refer either to the broad idea *will only jeopardize your position* or to the single noun *position*. Although most of us can guess the meaning intended, incorrect interpretations come more easily. *Which* seems at first to belong to the thought unit *your position*. If neither of the persons referred to wants the position, why should either one care whether the position is jeopardized? A clearer statement of the sentence's intended meaning would be as follows:

> **Further resistance to the board's decision will only jeopardize your position, and we do not want to jeopardize your position.**

Here is an example of a *which* clause making clear reference to a broad idea:

> **He predicted that the discussion would become heated, which is precisely what happened.**

Used with care, *which* clauses perform valuable service. In the sentence below, the *which* clause achieves a degree of clarity that would be difficult to equal in as few words.

> **Read clause 5, which contains the productivity standards under the new contract.**

WHO DID WHAT?

In business communications, as in any other kind of communication, it is essential that the writer make it absolutely clear *who* has done or will do a specific thing. Sometimes, however, the writer confuses the thought by having the wrong person or thing connected with an action, so the meaning intended is not conveyed to the reader. Such a violation of the thought-unit principle can cause doubt or uncertainty as to *who* did *what*.

> **If not satisfied, we will return your money.**

Consider the thought unit *If not satisfied, we*. The meaning here is that *we* are the ones who might not be satisfied. If a customer returned the goods and asked for a full refund, the manufacturer could refuse on the grounds that the manufacturer was well satisfied with the customer's money. The correct meaning is immediately apparent to the reader when the sentence is revised.

> **If you are not satisfied, we will return your money.**

Occasionally, if the who-did-what principle is violated, the sentence becomes ridiculous, for an object, not a person, seems to be performing an action.

Entering the room, the projector was seen teetering on the edge of the table.

The thought unit *entering the room, the projector* pictures the projector as entering the room. This kind of phrasing shows a serious lack of communication know-how. In this revision, a person performs the action:

Entering the room, Mr. Formanov saw the projector teetering on the edge of the table.

Here is another illustration of this type of error:

After climbing to the top of the tower, the whole city lay spread before us.

What does the thought unit *after climbing to the top of the tower, the whole city* mean? How could a city climb to the top of the tower? Revised, the sentence would read:

After climbing to the top of the tower, we saw the whole city spread before us.

A who-did-what violation, sometimes called a *dangler,* does not necessarily occur at the beginning of a sentence. For example, note the error in the following sentence:

Mr. Paine saw the expected caller glancing up from his desk.

As written, the thought unit is *caller glancing up from his desk.* Was the caller at his own desk, and did he glance up from that desk? Was the caller glancing up from Mr. Paine's desk; and if so, what physical contortions were necessary to perform the act? Most likely, it was Mr. Paine who glanced up from his own desk. In order to eliminate the confusion, the sentence should be written like this:

Glancing up from his desk, Mr. Paine saw the expected caller.

INDEFINITE, CONFUSING PRONOUN REFERENCES

Each pronoun borrows its meaning from a noun. When the writer fails to make clear which noun a pronoun refers to, the pronoun loses its meaning or assumes an incorrect and unintended meaning. One vague or mistaken pronoun reference can garble an entire message. The careful writer checks each pronoun used in order to make certain that its reference is clear.

Confusing He or She

When you use either the pronoun *he* or the pronoun *she,* you must make certain that the antecedent is clear. If more than one man or more than one woman is mentioned in the sentence, the writer should take special care in placing the pronoun as near as possible to the person referred to. The following sentence leaves the reader wondering "Who returned from the conference?"

> Mr. Mulloy sent Tom to hand-deliver the bid immediately after he returned from the engineering conference.

Does the *he* in this sentence refer to Tom, or to Mr. Mulloy? If the reference is to Mr. Mulloy, then the sentence should be revised as follows:

> Immediately after he returned from the engineering conference, Mr. Mulloy sent Tom to hand-deliver the bid.

If, on the other hand, Tom is the one who attended the conference, then the sentence should read:

> Immediately after Tom returned from the engineering conference, Mr. Mulloy sent him to hand-deliver the bid.

Indefinite It

Using the pronoun *it* to refer to something that is not immediately clear is a common offense.

> I will place the football in punt position, and when I nod my head, kick it.

Kick what? This indefinite *it* could result in a painful injury, wouldn't you say? The indefinite *it* must be replaced by the noun to which it should refer. The revised sentence reads:

> I will place the football in punt position, and when I nod my head, kick the ball.

Inept writers tend to use the pronoun *it* as a catchall word, even if there is no antecedent to which the *it* can refer.

> It is the positive sales approach that is the effective element in these letters.

In this example the *it* reference is vague and serves only to make the sentence wordy. Consider how much more effective the sentence would be if it were written like this:

> The positive sales approach is the effective element in these letters.

Other Indefinite Pronoun References

Speakers who are uncertain of their sources frequently use the careless "they say" as a reference. Writers who use the same vague reference are considered amateurish; in written communication, references must be definite and exact. For example, read the following sentence:

They say that sales will decrease during the next six months.

Who is meant by *they* in this sentence? A lack of definiteness earmarks a poorly trained writer. A precise writer would present the information this way:

Market News **reports that sales will decrease during the next six months.**

Another type of indefinite reference that is puzzling and annoying to a reader is illustrated in this sentence:

Although I dictated all morning on Tuesday, my secretary typed only two of them.

The slipshod *two of them* is vagueness carried to an extreme. Two of what? stories? letters? reports? news releases? A clear and explicit thought could be communicated by writing:

Although I dictated all morning on Tuesday, my secretary typed only two of the letters.

CORRECTING THE THIS AND THUS FAULTS

A common writing fault is the use of *this* or *thus* to refer to an entire preceding thought. This lack of precision sometimes forces a reader to read a sentence several times to comprehend the writer's meaning. This inexact use of *this* and *thus* can spoil an otherwise fine writing performance.

Employees can't find parking spaces. This has existed since we hired 50 new employees.

To what does the *this* refer? *This* refers to the *shortage of parking spaces.* Stating the point specifically makes the meaning clear.

Employees can't find parking spaces. This shortage of parking spaces has existed since we hired 50 new employees.

Now read the following sentence, which is another example of unclear word reference.

Ms. Kent has passed the CPA examination, thus proving that she is a competent accountant.

Thus, as used here, is ambiguous. The thought could have been expressed more clearly and more directly as follows:

The fact that Ms. Kent passed the CPA examination is proof that she is a competent accountant.

COMMUNICATION PROJECTS

Practical Application

A.   Rewrite each sentence, making sure all thought units are clear.

1.   Casey took the computer out of the box, which everyone had been waiting to see.
2.   After finishing the report, the clock struck three.
3.   Because of numerous dents and scratches, Angela got an estimate from the auto body shop.
4.   Pin-striped men's suits are selling well this year.
5.   Hold the two pieces in place with your fingers and glue them together.
6.   Being very hard to tune, Bradley sold his guitar.
7.   After revising the last paragraph, the sales letter got a good response.
8.   Sitting close to the window, the skyscrapers were clearly visible.
9.   People often buy things with credit cards that they don't need.
10.   The new computers, with little or no training, can be operated by good keyboarders.
11.   After deboning, customers are usually willing to pay more for flounder.
12.   Your rental agreement says that you may not have animals or children unless caged.
13.   After doing much planning, the budget finally balanced.
14.   The mixer truck was wrecked by a substitute driver only half full of cement.
15.   We have a picture of the historical mansion which we will send you free.
16.   Our special this week is a six-legged lady's lounge chair.
17.   When walking through the office, the printer noise was distracting to the visitors.
18.   Covered with proofreader's marks, Ms. Kantor sent the draft back for corrections.
19.   After traveling all day, our hotel was still miles away.
20.   To remove paint without scraping, you should plan on a two-hour soak in solvent.

B.   These sentences have confusing pronoun references. Rewrite them, making the specified corrections.

1.   Alex called Tony when he was in Waco last week. (Alex was in Waco.)
2.   Lynn and Judy researched the topic, but she did the actual writing of the report. (Judy wrote the report.)
3.   Dan told Charlie that his explanation was not clear. (Dan's explanation was not clear.)

4. They feel that more research should be done on the new arthritis treatment. (*They* refers to Dr. Anne McCurry and Dr. Ben Lawson.)
5. Although we interviewed 30 applicants, we hired only 3 of them. (*Them* refers to engineers.)
6. It is a positive attitude that can make the difference between success and failure. (Remove the *It*.)
7. The computer terminal is on my desk. Don't move it for any reason. (*It* refers to the computer terminal.)
8. It may be a good idea to redecorate the office. (Remove the *It*.)
9. The representative showed us a printer for $3500 and one for $5200. I think we should buy it. (*It* refers to the more expensive one.)
10. Tom asked Steven to pay the invoice as soon as he received it. (Tom had received the invoice.)

C. Rewrite each sentence, correcting the *this* or *thus* references.

1. The meeting adjourned without our taking any action or making any decisions thus causing us to be dissatisfied.
2. When we transferred the files, several folders were misplaced. This was not Dexter's fault.
3. When the power was unexpectedly interrupted, several computer files were damaged. This will cause us to work late.
4. Many of our best inspectors have missed two days of work because of a virus. This has affected our quality control.
5. Mildred ignored the rumors thus proving that she had strong character.

Editing Practice

Pronoun Practice. Correct the pronoun errors in the following sentences. Write *OK* for any sentence that has no error.

1. Its not clear which letter arrived first.
2. Alan, Ted, and him wrote memos asking for the same vacation week.
3. They are planning to ride with us to the convention.
4. Who's request should be granted?
5. Will you give your recommendations to William or I?
6. What one of the secretaries was transferred?
7. Whom is going to the meeting in Houston next week?
8. The article was written by she last summer.
9. The prize money will be divided between you and I.
10. Durability and appearance are it's strong points.
11. Both lawyers are proud of there success.
12. There's a strong possibility that we may expand our operations to Texas.

Using Your Word Processor. Correct the typographical errors in the following sentences.

1. After the meeting, all the managers wemt to the cafeteria for lunch.
2. The discussion at the cafeteria helped us understand how the group reallly felt about the new procedures.
3. Almost everyone wanted to accept the the new procedures.
4. Most of the procedures were designed to improve efficiency adn safety.
5. Efficiency and safety definitely important.

Case Problem

The Missing Cups. Gene and Linda were responsible for the morning refreshments at a company-sponsored seminar. They had decided to serve fruit juices, coffee, and pastries. When the participants came to be served, Gene and Linda noticed that there were cups for cold beverages but no cups for hot beverages.

They began to debate who was to blame for the problem. Gene said it was Linda's fault, and Linda said it was Gene's fault. Then, they thought it may have been the caterer's fault. What should they have done?

37

WRITING EFFECTIVE SENTENCES

A good business communication flows smoothly. Unaware of sentences, clauses, and phrases, the reader moves with the continuous flow of ideas. Nothing interrupts the reader's concentration—no awkward phrases, vague references, or imbalanced constructions.

Because a good letter moves so easily for the reader, the reader may feel that the letter flowed as easily from the mind of the writer. But in reality, the letter as it first occurred to the writer was probably much the same as a first draft of anyone's writing—full of awkward phrases, vague references, choppy sentences, and imbalanced constructions. The writer took the time, however, to look and listen for problems in the rough draft, and then applied the writing techniques learned in this book to eliminate the problems.

Becoming an effective business writer takes time and practice. It is a cumulative skill. In other words, you cannot forget what you learned in the previous sections. You must combine that knowledge with what you are learning now and what you will learn in later sections.

WORD USAGE

Words combine to make sentences, and sentences combine to make paragraphs. You cannot write a good paragraph without using the right words. Here are some suggestions for improving written communications.

1. Use positive words.
2. Use planned repetition of words to emphasize important points.
3. Identify and revise combinations of words that produce harsh or awkward sounds.

Positive Words

Positive words are pleasant to hear and to read. They are words that create a receptive, pleasant impression in the mind of a reader. Consequently, the skilled writer deliberately uses words that produce this desirable psychological effect. The words in the first list cause a positive response, and the words in the second list cause a negative response.

Positive Words

advancement	courage	happy	success
cheerful	easy	profit	welcome
agreeable	capable	enjoy	pleasure
fun	integrity	warmth	eager

Negative Words

failure	problem	complaint	cannot
no	difficult	loss	sad
anxious	incapable	apologize	dishonest
blame	sorry	damage	wrong

Negative sentences should be reworded to make them more positive.

Negative: We did not experience a loss this quarter.

Positive: We have a profit this quarter.

Planned Repetition of Words

Although careless repetition of words shows a lack of imagination, *planned* repetition can sometimes achieve striking emphasis of an important idea. Repeating the words *too* and *easy* in the following examples helps to emphasize each point.

She studied too little too late to pass the test.

He did the easy things the easy way, and he was easy to replace.

A major goal of any advertisement is to make readers remember the name and purpose of the product. Sometimes this goal is accomplished by simple repetition of the name. Clever writers manage to vary the order of the repeated words to prevent monotony. Consider the clever and purposeful transposition of the words below.

VITATABS will add muscles to your body, and VITATABS will add body to your muscles.

The Sound of Words

Excessive repetition of sounds can make tongue twisters that detract from the message. Even when reading silently, the reader cannot ignore sentences like:

Frank found five fine foreign cars in Finland.

Sound repetition can cause problems other than being tongue twisters. Although easy to say, the following sentence is hardly a pleasure to hear:

Steer your weary, dreary body to O'Leary's Health Spa.

Avoid unpleasant sounds, and do not attempt to write business letters that sound musical or poetic. The letter, like everything else in business, has a job to do. For the greatest effect, concentrate on that job.

PROPER SUBORDINATION OF IDEAS

Proper subordination of ideas depends on the ability to determine the difference between an important idea and a lesser idea. The important thought is expressed as a main clause, and the lesser idea is properly written as a subordinate clause. The principle can be remembered as follows: "Main idea—main clause; subordinate idea—subordinate clause." Consider the following sentence:

I had just started to write up our bids when your revised specifications arrived.

Which idea is more important, the fact that *I had just started to write up our bids* or the fact that *your revised specifications arrived?* The arrival of the revised specifications is the more important idea; therefore, it should be expressed as the main clause. The sentence should read:

Your revised specifications arrived just as I had started to write up our bids.

Coordination Versus Subordination

When a sentence contains two ideas of equal importance, divide the sentence into two main clauses. For example, consider the following:

The work is difficult, but the rewards are great.

On the other hand, writing power is diluted when the writer fails to see that the thoughts belong, not in two main clauses, but in a main clause and a subordinate clause.

There were other candidates, and Ruth received the promotion.

This sentence places equal stress on what the writer considers to be two main ideas. The emphasis should properly be placed on Ruth's receiving the promotion, even though there was competition. For force, as well as for clarity, the sentence should be written:

Although there were other candidates, Ruth received the promotion.

Interrupting Expressions

Unwittingly, some writers destroy the forcefulness of proper subordination by writing the lesser idea as an interrupting expression. For instance, read this sentence:

You are, considering the risks involved in such an investment, very fortunate.

The main thought, *you are very fortunate,* is interrupted by the lesser idea, *considering the risks involved.* This interference with the flow of the main thought is so distracting that the force of the statement is completely lost. Properly written, the sentence reads:

Considering the risks involved in such an investment, you are very fortunate.

Correcting the So and And So Faults

Whenever you read a sentence that uses *so* or *and so* to introduce a clause, you can improve the sentence greatly by substituting a more meaningful conjunction. Notice how weak the connection is between the two clauses in the following sentence:

Barbara has worked here for only one month, so we are unable to tell you much about her.

The first clause gives the reason for the second clause. *Because* is a better choice for joining clauses that give causes and results. The following sentence is stronger, clearer, and more polished than the version above.

We are unable to tell you much about Barbara because she has worked here for only one month.

And so is not a two-word conjunction. It is two conjunctions used to form some vague connection between two clauses. Consider the following sentence:

Mr. Donovan is a talented artist, and so we recommend that you hire him.

The first clause is the reason for the second. The relationship is easier to detect in the following revision:

Because Mr. Donovan is a talented artist, we recommend that you hire him.

ACTIVE VERSUS PASSIVE VOICE

Voice is that property of a transitive verb that shows whether the subject acts or is acted upon. Any verb phrase composed of a past participle with a "being" verb helper is in the passive voice: *will be shipped, has been sent, was done, is frozen.* In the active voice, the subject is the doer of an action; in the passive voice, the subject is acted upon.

Gibson sent us a message. (Active voice.)

A message was sent to us by Gibson. (Passive voice.)

The active voice expresses thoughts in a stronger, livelier way than does the passive voice. Compare these two sentences:

Your order will be shipped on Monday, July 8. (Passive voice.)

We will ship your order on Monday, July 8. (Active voice.)

Both sentences state the same information, but the active voice sentence is more direct. In the following pair of sentences, note that the sentence using the active voice makes a stronger selling point than does the weak, passive sentence.

Last year our machines were sold to 75 out of every 100 business firms in Detroit. (Passive voice.)

Last year, we sold our machines to 75 out of every 100 business firms in Detroit. (Active voice.)

The passive voice has its uses in business writing, usually to soften the impact of negative news. In the following sentences, note how the sentence using the passive voice is the more diplomatic of the two.

You did not fill in the quantity you wish to buy, so we cannot ship your order. (Active voice.)

Your order will be shipped when the quantity is filled in. (Passive voice.)

BALANCING TECHNIQUES

Parallel structure is a must for similar parts of a sentence. A noun should be parallel with a noun (or a pronoun), an adjective with an adjective, and a phrase with a phrase. For example, look at this sentence.

The new printers are quiet, efficient, and require little maintenance.

Lack of parallel structure causes the sentence to lose momentum. The writer erroneously coordinated two adjectives and a clause. The revision below is strong to the end.

The new printers are quiet, efficient, and maintenance-free.

Coordinating the three adjectives makes the sentence grammatically parallel and effective.

In the paragraphs that follow, you will study techniques of balancing comparisons, modifiers, verbs, prepositions, conjunctions, and clauses. Studying these paragraphs will help you write with greater force and consistency.

Balancing Comparisons

Comparisons are balanced only if they are complete. They can be complete only if they include all the necessary words. The omission of one necessary word can throw a comparison out of balance.

Recent studies show that women spend more money on eating in restaurants than men.

As written, the sentence could mean that women spend more money on eating in restaurants than they spend on men. The comparison lacks balance, as well as sense, because an essential word is omitted. One word, properly placed, can make the meaning of the sentence clear.

Recent studies show that women spend more money on eating in restaurants than men spend.

Or the sentence could be rearranged.

Recent studies show that women spend more money than men do on eating in restaurants.

Here is another imbalanced comparison:

Ms. Wall's position in the organization is more than a trainee.

This sentence lacks sense because essential words are omitted. This revision improves the clarity.

Ms. Wall's position in the organization is more than that of a trainee.

An imbalanced comparison like the one that follows provides a chance for skillful revision.

Dan can program just as well, if not better, than George.

Disregarding the words set off by commas, the sentence reads as follows: "Dan can program just as well than George." Of course, no one would say "as well than." The first revision below is acceptable, but the second one is a much better sentence.

Dan can program just as well as, if not better than, George.

Dan can program just as well as George, if not better.

Balancing Modifiers

Omission of single-word modifiers can destroy balance in several ways. Such an omission can produce, for example, this illogical message:

We need a welder and plant nurse.

Failure to write "*a* plant nurse" makes "a welder and plant nurse" the same person. Dim, indeed, is the prospect of hiring a person who can serve in the dual capacity of welder and plant nurse.

Modifiers should be repeated when necessary. What is wrong with this sentence?

The supervisor requested a secretary, mail clerk, and administrative assistant.

Because the modifier is not repeated with each member of the series, *a* is understood as the modifier for all three parts of the series. But "a administrative assistant" would never be acceptable writing. For balance, the series should read, "a secretary, a mail clerk, and an administrative assistant."

Do you see why the next sentence is out of balance?

Mr. Gonzalez speaks often of his parents, wife, and children.

The modifier *his* is the correct modifier for all three members of the series and is technically correct; however, a writer with a "feel" for language would repeat the modifier *his* to achieve a fullness and roundness of tone. The following revision sounds much better:

Mr. Gonzalez speaks often of his parents, his wife, and his children.

Balancing Verbs

Structural balance demands that whenever the parts of verbs in compound constructions are not exactly alike in form, no verb part should be omitted. The following sentence breaks this rule:

John always has, and always will, do a good job.

Omitting the past participle *done* with the auxiliary *has* causes the meaning to be "John always has do and always will do a good job." The verbs in this compound construction are not exactly alike in form; therefore, no verb part should be omitted. The sentence should be revised.

John always has done and always will do a good job.

The following sentence shows the same kind of error:

Your check was received yesterday and the machines shipped by express.

The omission of the auxiliary verb after *machines* structures the sentence like this: "Your check was received yesterday, and the machines was shipped by express." The plural noun *machines* requires a plural verb; therefore, the sentence must read:

Your check was received yesterday, and the machines were shipped by express.

Balancing Prepositions

The omission of a preposition can also throw a sentence off-balance. Some words must be followed by specific prepositions. When two prepositional constructions have the same object, you must use, in each construction, the preposition that is idiomatically correct. Failure to supply the correct preposition results in a mismatch.

Word processing operators should have knowledge and experience with their equipment.

In this illustration *knowledge* and *experience* form a compound, both parts of which are modified by the prepositional phrase *with their equipment*. *With* is the preposition used with both *knowledge* and *experience*. It is incorrect to say "knowledge with their equipment." The correct preposition to use with *knowledge* is *of*. To be balanced, the sentence should read:

Word processing operators should have knowledge of and experience with their equipment.

Balancing Conjunctions

In speech, subordinating conjunctions, particularly *that* and *when,* can often be omitted without causing any confusion. In writing, however, such omissions may destroy the balance of the thought units of a sentence and thus confuse the reader. Read the following example aloud:

Marc often talks about the time he had neither money nor position.

If this were an oral communication, the speaker could make the meaning clear by pausing slightly after the word *time*. The reader, however, might see the thought unit as *Mark often talks about the time he had,* with the result that the words following *had* would not make sense. The reader would have to reread the sentence to get the meaning. In business communications, you want the reader to get the message the first time it is read. The sentence should be written as follows:

Marc often talks about the time when he had neither money nor position.

The following sentence may also be misread:

We investigated and found the furniture was shipped on June 2.

The reader may see *We investigated and found the furniture* as one thought unit. The subordinating conjunction *that* adds clarity and comprehension.

We investigated and found that the furniture was shipped on June 2.

In informal writing, subordinating conjunctions may be omitted if their omission will not confuse the reader.

We do have the stationery you requested.

Balancing Clauses

Another mark of writing distinction is to avoid incomplete (elliptical) clauses whenever failure to write the complete clause would confuse the reader. In the sentence "You are a faster typist than I," the meaning "than I am" is clear. But listen to this:

Did Mr. Martin pay the bill or his accountant?

This sentence could be interpreted as follows: "Did Mr. Martin pay the bill, or did he pay his accountant?" It could also be interpreted this way: "Did Mr. Martin pay his bill, or did his accountant pay the bill?" The following sentence clarifies the intended meaning:

Did Mr. Martin pay the bill, or did his accountant pay it?

COMMUNICATION PROJECTS

Practical Application

A. The sentences below repeat like sounds too often. Rewrite the sentences to make them less distracting to the reader.

1. The lawyer summarized some of his comments.
2. Of course, she took a course in economics.
3. Miss Bertram missed Miss Carr's call.
4. The board became bored by noon.
5. We sold the pair of pear trees.

B. Rewrite each sentence by using positive words.

1. I failed to finish the report this morning, but I will finish it by 5 p.m.
2. I am sorry that I can't meet with you until 10:30 on Monday.
3. Please call us if you have any trouble with our product.
4. Installation instructions should not be difficult to understand.
5. Cashiers should not be dishonest.

C. Rewrite these compound sentences, subordinating the less important ideas.

1. The copier was broken, and we could not distribute the report that was typed yesterday.
2. My plane was late, and I missed my first appointment.
3. You did a superb job on the project, and you will get a raise.
4. The sales figures were not accurate, and we underestimated our profit.
5. You are the most qualified applicant, and we are going to hire you.

D. Rewrite each sentence, correcting the *so* and *and so* faults.

1. The manager was concerned about the rising cost of raw materials, so he raised the price of his product.
2. We bought word processing units for our secretaries, and so we have agreed to reimburse them for taking a word processing course at City College.
3. My flight to Dallas was canceled, so I spent an extra night in New York.
4. Jim has been transferred, so he will be moving next month.
5. The shipment was damaged in transit, and so I refused to accept it.

E. Rewrite each sentence in accordance with the directions given in parentheses.

1. Gary was praised by Mrs. Bonney when his design was accepted by the board. (Change to the active voice.)
2. We cannot accept your credit application because of your short employment history. (Change to the passive voice.)
3. Training seminars are enjoyed by Carol and the other managers. (Change to the active voice.)
4. The new procedures were outlined by Mr. Sokolovsky, and the details were filled in by Mr. Conte. (Change to the active voice.)
5. They prohibit smoking in the conference room. (Change to the passive voice.)

F. Rewrite each sentence, correcting the balancing problems.

1. Our service is better, not equal, to theirs.

2. Did Steve call the client or his assistant? (Who called the client?)
3. I have, and will continue to try, to contact her.
4. The latest survey shows that women own more stock than men.
5. Furniture movers damaged an end table, lamp, and radio.
6. Sarah reminded me about the time she had neither money nor employment.
7. I have much respect and confidence in Ms. Nelson's decisions.
8. Management wants to hire a programmer and plumber.
9. We need temporary personnel to keyboard documents, to proofread correspondence, and answering the phone.
10. Both advertising promotions were as good, if not better than, ones we have previously used.

Editing Practice

Choosing the Right Word. On a separate sheet, write the word that correctly completes each sentence.

1. The board of directors plans to (adapt, adopt) its first policy manual.
2. Most employees can (access, excess) the computer files by telephone.
3. Jolene gave me some good (advice, advise) when I graduated from college.
4. Please order some letterhead (stationary, stationery).
5. Much planning (preceded, proceeded) the warehouse expansion.
6. Rafael (lead, led) the trainees in sales last quarter.
7. The report (cited, sighted) several studies supporting our position.
8. Brendan, (formally, formerly) a director, chairs the board.
9. The customers are completely satisfied with (their, there) purchases.
10. Sam is more qualified (than, then) Max.

Case Problem

Keeping Track. Elizabeth is always kidding Jean about her "lists." Before beginning work each day, Jean makes a list of things she must do that day. Then, she numbers the tasks in the order that they should be completed. She also has a list of tasks to be done tomorrow and a list to be done this week.

Elizabeth says that such lists are a waste of time. However, Jean has noticed that Elizabeth often misses deadlines and sometimes forgets an important assignment from her supervisor.

Whose work style is better? Why?

38

WRITING EFFECTIVE PARAGRAPHS

Writing effective paragraphs requires writing good sentences and combining them to get the message across to the reader. Even though sentences may be grammatically correct, they may not contribute positively to the paragraphs they compose.

In a paragraph, sentences should be joined so that the series of thoughts expressed supports a single, more general, main idea. If sentence structure is faulty or if paragraph organization is poor, the whole communication will fail.

ONE MESSAGE, ONE IDEA, ONE THOUGHT

Each business communication should have one message. Each paragraph in the message should have one main idea. Each sentence in a paragraph should have one main thought, and that thought should support the main idea of the paragraph.

MESSAGE CONTROL

Business communications, such as letters and memorandums, should be limited to one main message. Two or more main messages within a communication can cause confusion or can cause one message to seem more or less important than another message.

A message should have a definite purpose, or it should not be written. If a business writer sends numerous, insignificant communications, readers routinely receiving them will soon categorize all mail from that writer as unimportant. This categorization will cause an isolated "important" communication not to get the attention it deserves.

PARAGRAPH CONTROL

Achieving paragraph control requires the writer to focus on one main idea. All sentences in the paragraph should help support the main idea.

The first sentence of a paragraph should be written with the paragraph's idea in mind. The writer must know where the paragraph is going before attempting to guide the reader there. The writer who does not know what conclusion the paragraph is to have should stop writing and start thinking.

Paragraph Length

In general, a paragraph should not be longer than six to eight lines. If the development of one thought requires more than six to eight lines, the writer should carry that thought over to another paragraph. Readers seem to need a visual break (paragraphs) but not a continuity break (interruption in message content).

Transitional Devices

The polished communication carries the reader along by interest in its message, by the rhythm and momentum of its words, and by the seamless transitions between paragraphs. Skillful use of transitional words and phrases can move the reader through the communication—from one idea to another—without a continuity break that can detract from the message.

Writers can ensure this continuity by using appropriate transitional words or expressions. Here is a partial list of such expressions.

accordingly	however
after all	in addition
again	likewise
also	meanwhile
at the same time	moreover
besides	nevertheless
consequently	notwithstanding
equally important	on the contrary
for this purpose	on the other hand
further	similarly
furthermore	still
hence	therefore

Let's look at an overlong paragraph that would benefit both from transitional expressions and from being broken into shorter segments.

We are sorry that you did not enjoy our Modern Magellan Nature Tour of the Amazon in Brazil last month. We feel that our literature gave you an accurate impression of what to expect. Our literature states, "Modern Magellan Nature Tours are not for the faint of heart. Our naturalist-guides take you to the most remote and primitive areas remaining on earth. You'll see all the natural wonders that the area of your choice has to offer. You'll look down from the peaks, look up at the waterfalls, and see eye to eye with birds and beasts." This does not say explicitly that you are going to wake up and find a 30-foot anaconda in your tent. But everyone knows the anaconda is a snake native to the Amazon. You must admit that faint of heart is exactly what you were when you discovered the snake curled around your cot. Of the 42 members of your tour group, only one other complained. He felt the tour lacked excitement. We are now trying to arrange something more stimulating for him. I am afraid that we must refuse your request. We cannot arrange another tour for you or refund your money paid for the first tour. We clearly stated this no-refund policy in our brochures.

There are various editing possibilities for this paragraph, but one revision might go like this:

We are sorry that you did not enjoy our Modern Magellan Nature Tour of the Amazon in Brazil last month. We do feel, however, that our literature gave you an accurate impression of what to expect. Our literature states, "Modern Magellan Nature Tours are not for the faint of heart. Our naturalist-guides take you to the most remote and primitive areas remaining on earth. You'll see all the natural wonders that the area of your choice has to offer. You'll look down from the peaks, look up at the waterfalls, and see eye to eye with birds and beasts."

Although this does not say explicitly that you are going to wake up and find a 30-foot anaconda in your tent, the anaconda is an animal native to the Amazon. Of the 42 members of your tour group, one person said that he felt the tour lacked excitement. We are now trying to arrange something more stimulating for him.

I regret that we must refuse your request: We can neither arrange another tour for you nor refund your money paid for the first tour. As we indicated in our brochures, the price of the tour cannot be refunded.

Paragraphing Decisions

Paragraphing decisions can create an attractive, uncluttered format that can make business communications easier to read and understand. Here are some simple paragraphing suggestions that can improve a communication's appearance and readability.

Obviously, content must determine paragraphing decisions. However, when it is practical, adjust paragraph length to fit the guidelines below. These are guidelines, *not* hard-and-fast rules.

1. Keep the first paragraph short, usually two to five lines.
2. Have middle paragraphs average four to eight lines, and make them longer than the first and last paragraphs.
3. Keep the last paragraph short, usually two to five lines.
4. Vary paragraph length.
5. Use several short paragraphs instead of one tremendously long paragraph to create an uncluttered appearance.
6. Combine several short paragraphs to correct a choppy appearance.

7. Avoid a heavy appearance (all paragraphs too long).
8. Avoid a top-heavy appearance (beginning paragraphs too long).
9. Avoid a bottom-heavy appearance (ending paragraphs too long).
10. Use an "odd" number of paragraphs. Three paragraphs look better than two, and five paragraphs look better than four.

SENTENCE CONTROL

Long sentences tend to be harder to understand than shorter ones. Yet, shorter sentences can often seem choppy and boring. What is the solution to the sentence-length problem? Variety.

Variety in Length

Most sentences should range in length from 10 to 20 words. This range is a guide. To provide variety, some sentences will have fewer than 10 words; others will have more than 20 words.

Extremely long sentences seem to bury the main thought. Beyond a certain length, sentences seem to grow weaker with each added word. This unnecessary length frustrates most readers. Lengthy sentences may be grammatically correct, but often they are wordy. Look at the following example:

> Thank you for informing us in your letter of May 30 that you have still not received the illustrated *Home Repair Manual* that we shipped to you by parcel post on or about last May 1, but there's no need for you to worry, because we are going to start inquiries with the post office and perhaps file an insurance claim, meanwhile sending you another copy of this truly spectacular handbook on the techniques of successful home repairs.

The reader has to swallow far too many words merely to learn that another copy of the desired book will be sent. The writer was correct, of course, to point out that the post office is to blame for the delay. The writer could have expressed that thought better, however, in a separate sentence. Study the following revision:

> Thank you for letting us know that your copy of the *Home Repair Manual* has not reached you. We are mailing you a new copy at once and asking the post office to make certain that this one reaches you soon.

On the other hand, a succession of short sentences weakens writing, because the reader is jerked along from thought to thought.

> We received your letter. It arrived this morning and was most welcome. All the sales representatives read it; they liked your suggestions. Your letters are always friendly. We enjoy hearing from you.

An expert would never write such a stop-and-go communication. Instead, the expert would smooth out the bumps like this:

Your letter arrived this morning, and all the sales representatives liked your suggestions. Your letters are always so friendly that we enjoy hearing from you.

In some situations, the planned use of short sentences can be very effective. Short sentences are useful to bring out a series of important facts, to emphasize a point, and to break up a series of longer sentences.

The Shutter Machine camera is made especially for quick-moving action photography. Its motorized film-advancer prepares you for your next shot a fraction of a second after you press the shutter. You just focus and shoot! Its easy-open back permits you to insert a new cartridge faster than you can in any other camera. You can reload in 15 seconds! Best of all, the Shutter Machine is equipped with a computerized flash that works on a rechargeable battery. You have a built-in flash! See your dealer for complete details.

Variety in Structure

Communications that lack variety lack interest. One sure way to produce a dull communication is to use only simple sentences. Equally dull is a communication with all compound sentences or one with all complex sentences. Study the following paragraph:

Your new Maxi Motors Diesel Transport Truck costs more and offers more features. The diesel engine is durable, and you will enjoy its trouble-free operation. The engine uses less fuel while idling, and it uses less fuel on the road. Diesel trucks stand up to years of wear and have high resale value. You chose the right truck, and the years will prove it.

Too many compound sentences and too many *ands* make the above paragraph dull. See what an improvement structural variety makes in the following version.

Your new Maxi Motors Diesel Transport Truck costs more, but it offers more features too. Because the diesel is durable, you will enjoy years of trouble-free operation. You will use less fuel both when idling and when on the move. Furthermore, because diesel trucks stand up to years of wear, they have high resale value. The years will prove that you chose the right truck.

COMMUNICATION PROJECTS

Practical Application

A. Edit the following paragraph, making sure that each sentence has one main thought and that each sentence supports the main idea of the paragraph. If the paragraph contains more than one main idea, break it into two or more paragraphs.

> The operator's body should be erect; he or she should sit well back in the chair and lean forward slightly from the waist. Feet should be placed firmly on the floor. The body should be about a handspan from the front of the keyboard. Sitting too close to the machine can cause bottom-row errors, just as sitting too far away can cause top-row errors. Likewise, sitting too far to the left or right causes errors of the opposite hand. Keyboarding speed increases only through practice.

B. The following paragraph uses short, monotonous simple sentences. Rewrite the paragraph, varying the sentence structure. Some sentences will be combined.

> There will be a seminar Monday, April 5. It will be sponsored by our company. The seminar topic will be "Letter-Writing Techniques." All executives are encouraged to attend.

C. Paragraphs should have one main idea. Each paragraph below has one sentence that does not relate to that main idea of the paragraph it is in. However, it does relate to the main idea of another paragraph. Rewrite the letter, putting the sentences in the *right* paragraph.

> Dear Mr. Grant:
> Thank you for requesting information about Ocean Front Family Campground. Baby-sitting services are available ($3 per hour) through the local teen club.
> Free activities include morning aerobic workouts, afternoon water games, and nightly cartoons. Jeep safaris, island tours, and fishing expeditions—all reasonably priced—are offered daily.
> You may select various optional services, which are available at very low rates. Cable television, water connections, and electrical hookups are the most popular selections. Each Saturday night, the camp recreation director arranges free entertainment such as puppet shows, folk singing, and short plays.
> The enclosed brochure lists our rates. Our grounds, arranged to provide privacy, can comfortably accommodate tents, camping vehicles, and mobile homes. Please phone us soon to make sure that you get the reservations you want.
> Sincerely yours,

D. Rewrite each incorrect sentence. Write *OK* for any sentence that has no error.

1. Where was the cases shipped?
2. Ms. Daniels and myself wrote the report last Friday.

3. Before being considered, each applicant must send their résumé.
4. The committee on human relations meet tomorrow at 7 p.m.
5. The customer spoke abruptly to Grace and I.

Editing Practice

One Word or Two?   Some words can be written together or separately depending on the context of the sentence. In the following paragraphs, words have been incorrectly written together or incorrectly written separately. Rewrite the paragraphs, correcting the errors.

Thankyou for telling us about your experience with our products. Eventhough we have strict quality control procedures, some defective products maybe getting by our inspectors.

Of course, comments like yours help us improve. We have all ready initiated actions that maybe helpful. Inasmuchas we respect your opinion, we plan to try your suggestions for awhile and monitor the results.

Your special order is already and will be shipped some time later today. We sincerely appreciate your business.

Case Problem

Performance Appraisal.   As district sales manager, you supervise five sales representatives and a secretary. Nancy, the secretary, was hired three months ago. You and the sales reps are out of the office for the majority of the workweek.

Last week, you began getting complaints about Nancy. She often tells the sales reps that she does not have time to do their work. One rep said that she is abrupt in dealing with visitors, callers, and the representatives. Nancy complains about her job, her work schedule, and her salary.

The work that she completes is usually good. However, she does not like the reps to make suggestions for improvement. The reps have experienced difficulty in reaching Nancy by phone. Sometimes she is away from her desk for an "extended" coffee break. Most of the time, however, the line is busy while she makes personal calls.

What do you think the problems are in this case?

CHAPTER
EIGHT

WRITING
BUSINESS MEMOS

39

MEMO USES AND TYPES

Memorandums represent more than 50 percent of written communications in businesses today. Memos, as they are often called, are written to someone within your own organization. Letters, on the other hand, are written to persons outside your organization. Memos can be used within a department, between departments, and between company branches at different geographic locations.

IMPORTANCE OF MEMOS

Memos can be as complex and as important as the communications sent outside your organization. Two employees, for example, in different departments of the same company must agree on a position before either of them can write to one of the company's customers or suppliers. Unless they reach agreement themselves before communicating with an outsider, the employees may unknowingly make conflicting statements. Such poor internal communication is certain to confuse the outsider and to embarrass the employees.

When the matter is important or complicated, employees within a company will want to put it in writing. This is what makes a memo as much an essential part of business life as the business letter is.

ADVANTAGES OF MEMOS

Memorandums have become increasingly popular because the need for improved internal communication is more evident. Businesses are larger and more diversified. Branches or divisions of a company are often located in different states or in other countries. The efforts of many people must be coordinated. For many reasons, memos seem the logical way to exchange messages.

```
                        MEMORANDUM


          Date:     December 22, 19--

          To:       Paul Epstein, Transportation Supervisor

          From:     Deborah Carpella, Comptroller

          Subject:  Mileage Reimbursement


          Effective today, employees using their own cars for approved travel
          will be reimbursed at a rate of 22 cents per mile.  This increase is
          due to the rising cost of operating a vehicle.

          Please make this increase known to those who regularly use their
          cars.  I would appreciate your posting the attached copy of this memo
          on the bulletin board in the company garage.

                                      DC


          cbc
          Enclosure
          cc Lawrence Tolleson
```

This memo is entirely typewritten. Headings with initial capitals only are used to facilitate typing.

3. The addressee happens to have the same name as another employee, or a very similar name, so that the writer must make clear which of the two people is intended to receive the memo.

TO: Edwin Willis, Assistant Chief Engineer (Edward Willis is the production manager.)

In large companies, it may be helpful to include address information in the *TO* line of an interoffice memo. For example:

TO: Carl Pappas, Room 3301, Benefits Office

TO: Annette Kane, Laboratory 3, Research Department

If the memo is going to more than a few people, the writer should consider typing "Distribution Below" on the *TO* line and placing the list of recipients at the end of the memo under the heading *Distribution*. Placing the distribution list at the bottom gives the memo a more balanced appearance and spares the readers the chore of reading the long list of names until after they have read the heart of the memo—its message.

```
                    MEMORANDUM

DATE:      October 4, 19--

TO:        Branch Managers--Distribution Below

FROM:      Grant Forsythe, General Manager

SUBJECT:   Meeting for Branch Managers


The Employee Relations Department has announced improvements in the
employee benefits plan.

A meeting to explain our new benefits package will be held on Monday,
October 10, at 10 a.m. in the conference room adjoining my office.

Please read the enclosed comprehensive booklet about the package and
bring it with you to the meeting.

                         GF


dk
Enclosure


Distribution:

Michael Baxter
Amy Dillingham
Jon Henderson
Andrew Poplin
Madge Wray
```

This typed memo shows how a distribution list is typed. Note the *TO* heading.
These guide words are typed in all-capital letters.

The FROM Line

It is usual for the writer of a memo not to use a courtesy title before
his or her own name. If required, the writer may include a job title,
department affiliation, room number, and telephone extension.

**FROM: Edith Welch, Researcher, Investment Department,
Room 2403, Ext. 988**

The DATE Line

In both letters and memos, the date should be written in full rather
than abbreviated or given in figures only.

DATE: December 19, 19— (*or* 19 December 19—)

The day-month-year style is used in military correspondence.

The SUBJECT Line

The writer should state the subject of a memo clearly and briefly. Only in exceptional cases—such as technical matters—should the subject of the memo require more than a single line. The example below says all that is necessary; the rest should be left to the body of the memo.

SUBJECT: Request for Additional Terminal

The Body

The memo, unlike the business letter, includes no salutation. Instead, the writer leaves two blank lines beneath the subject line, then goes directly to the text. The body is single-spaced (but if the message is unusually short, it may be double-spaced). The block paragraph style is usual, but paragraphs may be indented. Many companies decide these matters according to a style of their own; thus new employees should ask if there is a "house" style for memos.

The Signature

The writer's initials are typed on the second to fourth line below the message. (Typing or signing the full name is unnecessary because the full name appears after *FROM*.) Most writers also *sign* their initials on each memo (either next to the name on the *FROM* line or near the initials at the bottom of the memo).

Below the signature the typist includes his or her own initials and any notations (for example, enclosure notations and carbon copy notations) that may be needed. Thus the end of the memo may look like this:

JBW

cb
cc Adele Blake

For more details, see a comprehensive reference manual.

TONE OF THE MEMO

The tone of a memo depends largely on the position of, and the writer's relation to, the person to whom the memo is addressed. In some ways, the choice of tone is easier in business settings than in many social settings: Relationships are often clear between two persons on different levels within the corporation. In general, the writer of a business memo chooses a more formal tone when addressing top management than when writing to an equal or a subordinate, unless the writer knows that the addressee prefers an informal tone.

Even within clear corporate structures, of course, there will be times when the writer is not certain what tone to use in a memo. The best course in these cases is to choose a middle way—neither too formal nor too deferential. Avoid using contractions like *you'll* and *here's,* but do not resort to elevated, artificial, or stilted language either. Stick to business. For example:

> Here is the report on last month's production, with the changes that you requested yesterday. The figures on Model 26 are now broken down to show the number of completed units that have received the modifications recommended by the Customer Service Department. In addition, all tables now have an added line showing production for the same period last year.

Subject matter also helps to determine the choice of tone for a memo. A memo announcing the schedule of the company's softball team would obviously have a lighter tone than a memo justifying costs that ran over budget. The more serious the topic, the more serious the tone.

ORGANIZATION OF THE MEMO

The form and the tone of a memo are only means to help the writer convey his or her message. The memorandum's organization is another means to the same end. A memorandum tries to "sell" its readers a point of view. This holds true whether the writer wishes to convince a superior of the need for new office equipment or to convince someone under the writer's supervision of the need to maintain high work standards. The memo is more likely to achieve its goal if it is brief and to the point without seeming brusque or incomplete. A memo is usually even more sparing in its use of words than a good letter.

The organization of a memorandum should be simple and clear. There is no need for more than these three elements: (1) a statement of purpose, (2) a message, and (3) a statement of future action to be taken. An example of a simple memo is shown on page 362.

Statement of Purpose

The subject line tells the reader what the memorandum is about but does not usually state the writer's reason for writing. Often the writer can make the purpose clear simply by referring to an earlier memo (whether written or received) or to a previous meeting or telephone conversation. Here are some examples of how a writer can state the purpose of a memo.

> At the last meeting of the Media Research staff, I was assigned to investigate and report on the comparative costs of print and broadcast advertisements in the northern part of the state. Here is a summary of what I found.

> I received the attached letter just this morning. I think you will agree that it shows the need for a speedy change in our procedures for taking telephone orders.

INTEROFFICE MEMORANDUM

To: Susan C. Restaino

Dept.: Advertising and Display

Subject: July Newspaper Advertisements

From: James Peterson

Dept.: Carpets and Rugs

Date: May 10, 19--

Purpose	Our semiannual carpet and rug sale is planned for July 15 through 22, and we will need to run ads in the local newspapers to announce it.
Message	I would like to meet with you to discuss copy preparation and photography and to provide you with samples and suggestions.
Future Action	Would you let me know when it is convenient for you to meet to plan these ads?

Jim

JP

mbc

This brief memo contains the three organizational elements—purpose, message, and future action.

> As the new board of directors requested at the June 12 meeting, I am sending you a summary of the company's present provision for Individual Retirement Accounts.

Message

After the statement of purpose, the writer should go directly to the main points of the message. The object is to help the reader grasp the main points as easily and clearly as possible.

> Tenants can conserve electricity by cutting down lighting in passageways and halls and by instructing employees to turn off lights at the end of the workday.

> A new form has been designed to simplify taking telephone orders. A copy is attached.

Statement of Future Action

The memorandum should usually end with a statement of future action to be taken or with a request for further instructions, as illustrated in the following examples:

> I will send further details about the reasons for this recommendation if you wish, including a full explanation of the financial analysis provided by the research staff.

41

BUSINESS LETTER

Think about the people you h
hours. Were any two people
people say precisely the same

Chances are that except for u
cers, fire fighters, and restaura
have seen recently were dresse
son was different (either *slight*
others. Also, the *content* of the
son was probably different. In
differed from that of the other

These two style factors—*ap*
used to describe a business lett
did the letter *say?* The appea
letter make up that letter's *styl*
and the content of his or her co
style.

The style of a business lette
success as a person's style con
ously, then, if your business le
must first learn how to control
letter, both of which will be di

THE FIRST IMPRE

Imagine receiving a letter from
firm. Further, imagine that th
letter looks even worse. The le
wrinkled, and it appears to hav
As a busy executive, how much
workday to read the contents of

Letters that do not make a go
serious attention from busy prof
ing a good impression is to use

---

you saw a memo on blue p
was from the manager. O
attention. The color used
could announce good new
something that needs imr
fire escape is broken); an
(Our audit will be Friday

A Word of Caution. If the
become commonplace and the
priately and sparingly.

COMMUNICATION PROJECTS

Practical Application

A.   Answer these questions.

1.   How can you increase m
2.   What are some special for
     be used with memos?
3.   Why should you be cauti
     memo writing?
4.   Is it correct to use courtesy
     a trend to omit courtesy
5.   When are distribution list
6.   What are the three basic

B.   On a separate sheet, desi
have printed as a snap-out set.
the finished product as possib

1.   Choose your business.
2.   Use your creativity to choo
     tion) that will be printed
3.   Include the form title "Inte
     ings.

C.   After six months' full-tim
for tuition reimbursement for e
local colleges. Employees mu
they enroll. Jim Arizo, person
to write a memorandum requ
the course, the credit hours, th
cost, and how successful comp
company.

You want to take Office Au
College. The course begins t
meets each Monday for twelv

Please notify me of your decision as soon as possible so that
I can start either to carry out this plan or to develop a new
one.

SPECIAL TECHNIQUES FOR MEMOS

Memos, just like letters, can be effective or ineffective, depending
on how they are written. Here are some suggestions for increasing
memo effectiveness.

Writing for Greatest Effectiveness

1.   Cover only one major topic in each memo. When memos cover
     too many topics, a main thought may go unnoticed or may not
     receive the attention due it.
2.   Consistently use a simple familiar heading that includes, but is
     not limited to, information such as *DATE, TO, FROM,* and
     SUBJECT. People getting messages from you regularly will
     know exactly where to look for specific information. Of course, if
     your company uses printed memo forms, the heading has al-
     ready been standardized.
3.   Choose a brief but appropriate subject line. Subject lines should
     identify the topic—not give all the details.
4.   Present the key idea first. The idea presented at the beginning
     will usually receive the most emphasis.
5.   In most instances, use a personal, pleasant, and somewhat infor-
     mal tone. You will know most of your receivers because they are
     in your organization. Special situations, however, such as writ-
     ing to your superiors or reprimanding an employee, may require
     a more formal treatment.
6.   Strive to make memos clear, complete, concise, consistent, cor-
     rect, and courteous.

Even though written primarily to people that you know, memos
still should accomplish the purpose you had when you wrote them.
Taking too many shortcuts can decrease effectiveness.

Special Formatting and Mechanical Aids

Formatting techniques and mechanical aids can "catch the reader's
eye" and thereby encourage further reading. Some suggestions follow.

1.   Use enumerations to list important items.

     Please do the following things before tomorrow morning:

     1. Make 12 copies of the sales report and the expense re-
         port.
     2. Collate and staple the reports and put a copy in each
         manager's folder.
     3. Call the managers and remind them of the meeting.

2. Use columns with h... easier.

Below are the inve:

Numbe

Y-3346
Z-4384
M-8729

3. Use solid capitals a... tail.

Tomorrow at 8:30 a... cuss our

NE

Please arrange for
attend . . .

4. Use underlining an... memo.

Our new vacation ...

Employees—Six M...
Employees who ha...
less will receive on...
month of employm...

Employees—Seven...
Employees who ha...
ven months will re...
tion for each mont...

Employees—One t...
Employees who ha...
years will receive f...

5. Use bullets to empl...

Here are some thir...
meeting:
• Sales incentives ...
• Stock purchases ...
• Employee develo...

6. If you are using a w...
tures, use boldface ...

Invest in our **U.S.** ...
This investment of ...

7. Use color coding to ...
sages from a certain...

CHAF

NII

**WRIT
BUSINESS**

Business Letter Parts

Letter *format* refers to the placement of letter parts on the page. Before we discuss various formats, therefore, let's review letter parts. All the letter parts are illustrated on page 374. (Note that *optional* parts are labeled; all other parts listed are *always* included in business letters.)

1. LETTERHEAD. The term *letterhead* can refer to either (1) the printed information at the top of business stationery or (2) the actual sheet of paper itself.

The printed information always includes the company's name, full address, and phone number. In addition, the letterhead may include other information—for example, the company's slogan, a listing of its divisions, or the company's logo (a symbol that identifies the company). See page 371 for illustrations of letterheads.

When the letterhead is typed rather than printed, the information should be attractively arranged, starting 1 inch from the top of the page (line 7). Word processing equipment simplifies keyboarding a letterhead such as the following:

> **General Data Services**
> **200 North Harrow Avenue**
> **Whitewater, Wisconsin 53190**
> **(414) 555-7500**

2. DATE LINE. The first item typed below the letterhead is the date of the letter.

3. INSIDE ADDRESS. The inside address repeats the information that is typed on the envelope; for example:

> **Ms. Vera Ann Tewksburry**
> **General Manager**
> **Ames Printing Company**
> **85 East Perth Road**
> **Conway, AR 72032**

Thus the inside address includes the name of the person to whom the letter is addressed, the person's title, and his or her company's name and full address.

4. ATTENTION LINE (OPTIONAL). The attention line is an optional letter part. When it is used, the attention line follows the inside address, but the inside address then does not include a *person's* name, only the *company's* name.

The attention line is used by writers who want to stress that the letter is technically intended for the *company,* not the *person*—thus the omission of the person's name in the inside address. A general salutation such as *Ladies and Gentlemen:* is used to show that the company is being addressed. See the letter on page 374 for an example of an attention line.

Well-designed letterheads help readers form positive first impressions.

5. SALUTATION. The salutation, which is the letter equivalent of saying "Hello," immediately precedes the body of the letter. Unless the letter is written to someone known very well and is rather informal, the salutation includes a courtesy title such as *Mr.* or *Ms.* If the letter is intended to be less formal and more friendly, then the salutation will address the writer by first name.

Dear Ms. Hammond: Dear Sir or Madam:
Dear Andrew: Ladies and Gentlemen:

Note the colon in each of the above examples. Traditionally, the salutation ends with a colon. However, *in the block letter format,* some writers opt to drop both the colon after the salutation *and* the comma after the complimentary closing (see below). They reason that the vigorous, aggressive block format does not require the traditional punctuation marks after the salutation and the complimentary closing.

6. SUBJECT LINE (OPTIONAL). Another optional part is the subject line, which is used to identify quickly the topic of the letter. When a subject line is used, it immediately follows the salutation. See the letters on pages 374 and 375.

7. BODY. The body, the main part of the letter, is typed single-spaced with an extra line of space between paragraphs.

8. COMPLIMENTARY CLOSING. The "Good-bye" of the letter, the complimentary closing is an ending such as the following:

Cordially,   Cordially yours,
Sincerely,   Sincerely yours,

9. COMPANY SIGNATURE (OPTIONAL). Some writers (and companies) prefer using a company signature; others do not. When it is used, the company signature appears below the complimentary closing. See the letter on page 374.

10. WRITER'S IDENTIFICATION. This consists of the writer's name and title.

11. REFERENCE INITIALS. This refers to the *typist's* reference initials—a way of identifying who typed the letter.

12. ENCLOSURE REMINDER (OPTIONAL). When something is sent along with the letter, the word *Enclosure* (or *Enclosures*) is typed beneath the reference initials.

13. COPY NOTATIONS (OPTIONAL). When a copy of the letter is to be sent to a third party, the writer may indicate this fact by writing, for example, *cc Sonia Edwards* below the reference initials (or below the enclosure notation, if one was used). The abbreviation *cc* means "carbon copy," but it can also be used for photocopies.

14. POSTSCRIPT. The postscript *belongs* to the body of the letter but is positioned at the *end* of the letter—deliberately or as an afterthought. Because it is part of the body of the letter, it is typed as the paragraphs in the body of the letter are typed.

Business Letter Formats

Now that we have reviewed the parts of business letters, let's look at the various acceptable formats for letters. As you proceed, note that the *sequence* of the letter parts (including the optional parts) does not vary from one letter format to another. The differences in formats primarily concern whether a particular part is indented or not.

BLOCK FORMAT. In the *block* letter format, all letter parts begin at the left margin. Because there are no indentions, the block style is easy to set up and is therefore very popular. See page 374 for an example of a letter in block format.

MODIFIED BLOCK FORMAT. Long popular, the *modified block* format (as its name hints) has certain changes in the basic block style— namely, the date line, the complimentary closing, and the signer's identification line are indented so that they start at the center of the page. See page 375 for an example.

MODIFIED BLOCK FORMAT—WITH INDENTED PARAGRAPHS. One variation of the "standard" modified block format is to indent the paragraphs five spaces rather than start them at the left margin. See page 376 for an example.

SIMPLIFIED FORMAT. In an effort to simplify letter writing, the Administrative Management Society (AMS) developed what it calls the "*simplified* letter style." Illustrated on page 377, the simplified letter:

1. Begins each part at the left margin (except *un*numbered lists, which are indented five spaces).
2. Omits the salutation and the complimentary closing. As a substitute for the salutation, the first paragraph always includes the addressee's name.
3. Has an all-capital subject line.
4. Has an all-capital writer's identification line, which includes *both* the writer's name *and* the writer's title all on one line.

Other Letter Formats

In addition to the formats just discussed, you will also find the personal-business and the social-business letter formats useful.

Printed
Letterhead

ELGIN
CONSTRUCTION COMPANY INC.

75 Oakwood Terrace Elgin, Illinois 60120 (312) 555-1550

Date Line

December 8, 19--

Inside
Address

Pompano Gardens Inn
500 Courtside Way
Pompano Beach, FL 33061

Attention
Line

ATTENTION: MS. COLLEEN GREGUS

Salutation

Ladies and Gentlemen:

Subject
Line

Subject: Accommodations for Annual Conference

We would very much like to explore the possibility of holding next
year's National Sales Conference at the Pompano Gardens Inn. Our
meeting is scheduled to begin on Sunday, June 16, and end on Saturday,
June 22. We will require single rooms for a minimum of 325 employees
and guests for the entire week.

Our needs for meeting rooms are described in the enclosed tentative
agenda for our week-long conference. The times of the meetings,
breaks, and meals are specified in this agenda, as well as the
approximate number of attendees for each session.

Body of
Letter

Will you please provide us with brochures and pamphlets describing
your room accommodations, dining facilities, and sports and
recreational facilities? Also, please suggest menus for the scheduled
lunches and dinners that are listed on the enclosed agendas and
estimate the approximate cost per person for both the rooms and the
meals.

After we have had an opportunity to review your brochures and
estimates, I would like to visit Pompano Gardens Inns so that I may
have the pleasure of <u>seeing</u> your highly talked-about resort.

Complimentary
Closing

Sincerely yours,

Company
Signature

ELGIN CONSTRUCTION COMPANY INC.

(Mrs.) Doris P. Weingart

Writer's
Identification

Doris P. Weingart
National Sales Manager

Reference
Initials

acd

Enclosure
Notation

Enclosure
cc Tyrone Pernell

Copy Notation

The **block format** is considered very modern and streamlined. In the block format every part begins at the left margin, so it is easy to type. The vertical sequence of the illustrated letter parts does not vary.

ELGIN
CONSTRUCTION COMPANY INC.

75 Oakwood Terrace Elgin, Illinois 60120 (312) 555-1550

December 8, 19-- ↓5

Ms. Colleen Gregus
Convention Manager
Pompano Gardens Inn
500 Courtside Way
Pompano Beach, FL 33061 ↓2

Dear Ms. Gregus: ↓2

SUBJECT: ACCOMMODATIONS FOR ANNUAL CONFERENCE ↓2

We would very much like to explore the possibility of holding next
year's National Sales Conference at the Pompano Gardens Inn. Our
meeting is scheduled to begin on Sunday, June 16, and end on Saturday,
June 22. We will require single rooms for a minimum of 325 employees
and guests for the entire week. ↓2

Our needs for meeting rooms are described in the enclosed tentative
agenda for our week-long conference. The times of the meetings,
breaks, and meals are specified in this agenda, as well as the
approximate number of attendees for each session. ↓2

Will you please provide us with brochures and pamphlets describing
your room accommodations, dining facilities, and sports and
recreational facilities? Also, please suggest menus for the scheduled
lunches and dinners that are listed on the enclosed agendas and
estimate the approximate cost per person for both the rooms and the
meals. ↓2

After we have had an opportunity to review your brochures and
estimates, I would like to visit Pompano Gardens Inns so that I may
have the pleasure of <u>seeing</u> your highly talked-about resort. ↓2

Sincerely yours, ↓4

(Mrs.) Doris P. Weingart

Doris P. Weingart
National Sales Manager ↓2

acd
Enclosure
cc Tyrone Pernell

The modified block format. A subject line may be typed in all-capital letters centered below the salutation, as shown here, or in capital and lowercase letters typed at the left margin, as illustrated in the block letter on page 374.

375

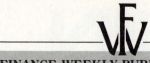

FINANCE WEEKLY PUBLICATIONS, INC.

One Wall Street   A Global Industries Company
New York, New York 10005   (212) 555-2000

November 28, 19--↓5

Mr. Jerome P. Kirsch
840 Woodland Avenue
Fall River, MA 02720↓2

Dear Mr. Kirsch:↓2

    Thank you for calling to tell us that you have not
been receiving your issues of FINANCE WEEKLY since you
moved to your new home. We have corrected our oversight
so that normal service can now resume.↓2

    As you suspected, your address-change notice had not
been processed. Of course, your new address has now been
included in our weekly subscriber mailing list. In fact,
you will probably receive the first December issue around
the same time you receive this letter.↓2

    Mr. Kirsch, I have enclosed the two issues of FINANCE
WEEKLY that you missed. If you miss any future issues,
please call me toll-free at 1 (800) 555-1212.↓2

               Sincerely,↓4

               (Ms.) Marcia Alcott

               Marcia Alcott
               Circulation Manager↓2

jpc
Enclosures↓2

    PS: To apologize for our being late with two issues
of FINANCE WEEKLY, I am sending you the new FINANCE WEEKLY
ALMANAC as soon as it is available. I hope that you will
enjoy using this popular reference book, which sells for
$9.95 at newsstands nationwide.

The **modified block format with indented paragraphs** has an "executive look." Note that the post-script is formatted like the paragraphs—that is, indented five spaces.

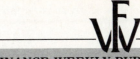

FINANCE WEEKLY PUBLICATIONS, INC.

One Wall Street　　　　　　　A Global Industries Company
New York, New York 10005　　　　　　　(212) 555-2000

November 28, 19-- ↓5

Mr. Jerome P. Kirsch
840 Woodland Avenue
Fall River, MA 02720 ↓2

SUBSCRIPTION DELAY ↓2

Thank you, Mr. Kirsch, for calling to tell us that you
have not been receiving your issues of FINANCE WEEKLY
since you moved to your new home. We have corrected our
oversight so that normal service can now resume. ↓2

As you suspected, your address-change notice had not been
processed. Of course, your new address has now been
included in our weekly subscriber mailing list. In fact,
you will probably receive the first December issue around
the same time you receive this letter. ↓2

Mr. Kirsch, I have enclosed the two issues of FINANCE
WEEKLY that you missed. If you should miss any future
issues, please call me toll-free at (800) 555-1212. ↓5

(Ms.) Marcia Alcott

MARCIA ALCOTT - CIRCULATION MANAGER ↓2

jpc
Enclosures ↓2

PS. To apologize for our being late with two issues of
FINANCE WEEKLY, I am sending you the new FINANCE WEEKLY
ALMANAC as soon as it is available. I hope that you will
enjoy using this popular reference book, which sells for
$9.95 at newsstands nationwide.

The **simplified format** has every letter part beginning at the left margin. It does *not* have a salutation or a complimentary closing; instead, it always has an all-capital subject line and an all-capital writer's identification line. Note, too, the use of the addressee's name in the beginning of the first paragraph.

PERSONAL-BUSINESS LETTER FORMAT. Personal-business letters are generally not typed on letterhead stationery. Instead of a letter-head, a three-line *return address* is typed at the top of the page, as follows:

1195 Brooks Terrace
Nashville, TN 37203
November 12, 19—

As you see, the return address includes the writer's full address and the date, but the writer's name is not included (it will be typed at the end of the letter). See page 379 for an example of the personal-business letter format.

SOCIAL-BUSINESS LETTER FORMAT. A special format is sometimes preferred for letters written to business associates when the subject is more social than business. For samples of this format, see Section 46, "Writing Social-Business Messages."

Formatting Guidelines

LETTERS. Whichever letter style a writer selects, the letter must be keyboarded and formatted properly. The margins must be adequate, the spacing between parts should adhere to certain standards, and so on.

The letters illustrated on pages 375 to 377 have notations that show the number of lines of space generally left between letter parts. Use these notations to guide you in the vertical spacing of letter parts.

Generally, try to achieve a line length of 5 inches. When a letter is short (under 75 words) or long (over 225 words), you may want to vary the line length and make other changes that will help you prepare an attractive, balanced letter. In such cases, you may find the following guidelines helpful:

Words in Body	Line Length*	Date Typed On	From Date to Inside Address	Space for Signature
Under 75	40P/60E	Line 15	5–8 lines	3–6 lines
75–225	50P/60E	Line 15	5 lines	3 lines
Over 225	60P/70E	Lines 12–15	4–5 lines	2–3 lines

*P for "pica"; *E* for "elite."

ENVELOPES. To prepare standard business envelopes (called "No. 10 envelopes"), follow these guidelines:

1. Begin typing the mailing address on line 14, about 4 inches from the left edge.
2. Use a block style and single spacing.
3. Always be sure to include the ZIP Code. Also, leave only 1 space between the state and the ZIP Code.

See page 380 for an illustration of a properly typed envelope.

```
                              119 Sumter Avenue
                              Fanwood, NJ 07023
                              August 2, 19--↓3


Kuji Industries of America
120 Highland Parkway
Riverside, CA 92504↓2

Attention:  Service Department↓2

Ladies and Gentlemen:↓2

In April I purchased your Kuji "1600" daisywheel printer
and, at the suggestion of the Kuji dealer, a tractor-feed
attachment.  According to the Kuji dealer, the tractor-
feed attachment would "pay for itself" because it would
allow me to use continuous-form paper and print page after
page automatically, without monitoring the printer.  I had
to admit that it certainly sounded well worth the $125
price tag.↓2

Imagine my disappointment when my Kuji printer regularly
miscued in vertical spacing from one line to another!  Two
or three times on every page, the printer "returns" less
than a full line of space, causing copy to be overprinted
and, of course, messy and illegible.  Please see the
enclosed sample.↓2

An authorized Kuji service center has installed a new
motor that is supposed to solve the problem, but the
linespacing problem persists.  Despite its higher price, I
bought the Kuji printer because Kuji has a reputation for
dependability.  Will you please prove to me that this
reputation is well deserved by telling me how I may get my
printer serviced and working properly?↓2

Please call me at (201) 555-2184 or write to me at the
above address. ↓2

                         Sincerely,↓4

                         Harold P. Cornwall

                         Harold P. Cornwall↓2



Enclosure
```

This **personal-business letter** uses a modified block format. The return address at the top of the page includes the writer's full address and the date; the writer's name is included in the writer's identification at the end of the letter.

The **envelope** information should parallel the inside address of its letter. If the letter has an attention line, then the envelope should have an attention line. This envelope was prepared for the letter on page 374.

If you are not using standard-size stationery or envelopes, or if you need specific formatting instructions, refer to a typing manual or business writing handbook.

THE LASTING IMPRESSION: CONTENT

As important as it is to make a good first impression, it is even more important to make a positive *lasting* impression. With your business letters, the lasting impression will be made by the content of your messages, by the combined effect of the *words* you use.

Your words will determine whether your reader considers you out of date, verbose, and pompous instead of modern, businesslike, and down to earth. Your words will convince your reader that you are the best person to do business with—or the worst.

Pay attention to the following techniques for ensuring that your words will support the most positive image of you and your company.

Use Modern Expressions

Expressions, like fashions, change. Few people today would choose the cumbersome, confining clothes worn a few generations ago. In letter writing, fashions change too. Some expressions are just as old-fashioned as celluloid collars and high-buttoned shoes, but many people continue to use them in business letters. Make sure that you know the expressions that are out of date so that you can avoid them; but also make sure that you know and use modern expressions in your letters.

Use	Do Not Use
say, tell, let us know	advise, inform
now, at present	at this time, at the present time, at the present writing
as, because, since	due to the fact that, because of the fact that
regarding, concerning	in re
if, in case	in the event that
please	kindly
for	in the amount of
according to	in accordance with

Eliminate Redundancy

Redundancy in writing or in speech results from using words that are unnecessarily repetitious; for instance, using *free gratis* for *gratis*. Since *gratis* means "free," *free gratis* means "free free." The following list includes some common redundancies that should be avoided.

Use	Do Not Use	Use	Do Not Use
about	*at* about	enter	enter *into*
above	*up* above	etc.	*and* etc.
alike	*both* alike	experience	*past* experience
beginner	*new* beginner	identical	*same* identical
check	check *into*	otherwise	*as* otherwise
connect	connect *up*	repeat	repeat *again*
continue	continue *on*	same	*exact* same
converted	*converted over*	together	*both* together
cooperate	cooperate *together*		

Use Plain, Simple Words

Even some people who would never *say* "I have amended and rectified the errors" sometimes *write* such fancy prose. Of course, a simple "I have corrected the errors" says it all!

The goal of a business letter is to convey a message efficiently and politely, not to show off the writer's vocabulary. Don't use a fancy word, a long word, or an impressive-sounding word when an *everyday* word will communicate your meaning just as well.

For example, saying "We are appreciative of your felicitations" certainly sounds fancy, but is it better or clearer than simply saying "We appreciate your best wishes"? Also, imagine writing "The store and all its appurtenances were sold" instead of "The store and its furnishings were sold."

Similar to using too fancy words is using jargon inappropriately. *Jargon* is technical language that is common in a certain profession or trade—but foreign *outside* that trade. For example, if someone in the movie industry were talking with a colleague about a *trailer* (a new-movie preview that is used at the end of a feature film), that person would certainly be communicating appropriately. But using the word *trailer* with someone who is *not* in the movie industry would probably cause confusion.

Moral: Keep it *simple*.

Be Concise

Imagine that you're having an extremely busy day when you receive a letter that begins with this paragraph:

> In reviewing your proposal—in response to which we have arrived at a decision—we considered everything fully and completely. We looked at the financial aspects of the proposal, at the practical aspects of the proposal, and at the managerial aspects of the proposal. We don't just jump into things. It's not our way. To the best of our knowledge, ability, and belief, we overlooked nothing before reaching our decision, which is final, irrevocable, and nonnegotiable. I'm afraid that we have decided that the proposal is unworkable under present economic conditions, circumstances, regulations, and restrictions.

Would you be eager to continue reading? Definitely not. If the writer had considered your time and your needs, perhaps the letter would have come to the point sooner, as in this revision:

> Thank you for sharing your proposal with us. We explored every aspect of the proposal—financial, practical, and managerial. Despite its positive features, we concluded that your proposal would not succeed in the current economic climate.

Get to the point and do it quickly (without being abrupt, curt, or rude, of course). Cut out irrelevant words, sentences, or paragraphs. You will save your time and your reader's, and you will improve your letter.

Be Specific

Clear writing is a reflection of clear thinking and is therefore *specific*. Note how the following statements are unclear, how they mislead the reader.

> Marilyn gave Anne the key to the supply room, but *she* is out of town now. (To whom does *she* refer—to Marilyn? to Anne?)

> Ms. Van Buren wants the paper shipped to the Smith Street warehouse and the other box to the main office, but she doesn't want *it* shipped until next Monday. (What does *it* refer to?)

The effective business writer knows the value of being specific.

> Marilyn gave Anne the key to the supply room, but *Anne* is out of town now.

Ms. Van Buren wants the paper shipped to the Smith Street warehouse and the other box to the main office, but she doesn't want *the paper* shipped until next Monday.

Don't keep the reader guessing: Be specific.

Be Coherent

Help the reader to see specifically *how* your thoughts are interrelated by using "connecting words" such as the following to tie your ideas together:

because	of course
since	as a result
naturally	on the other hand
however	nevertheless
thus	therefore
for example	as a matter of fact

For example, read the following sentences without the italicized words to appreciate how *nevertheless* and *because* contribute to the coherence of these sentences.

The Executive Committee is very enthusiastic about the proposal. *Nevertheless,* we must wait until next month *because* only then will all the members be here to vote.

Be Complete

In an effort to be concise, some writers become "word shy" and become *too* concise—abrupt, really. As a result, they omit essential information. For example:

Dear Ms. O'Shea:

We would like to order 10 more rotary pumps—the same kind we ordered last time.

Thank you.

Although the writer may know all the specifics—the purchase order number, the date of the original order, the catalog number, the price, and so on—the reader may *not* have this information right at hand and may have to spend time checking files to find information that the writer should have included.

Be sure that your messages are complete:

Dear Ms. O'Shea:

Please send us 10 of the same rotary pumps you shipped to us on April 12 (Invoice 755-123)—that is, 10 all-cast-iron rotary gear pumps for $\frac{1}{8}$-inch pipe (Lexite Catalog No. A970-5588).

In April we paid $32.11 for each pump. The enclosed purchase order, therefore, is for $321.10 plus shipping charges. Please let me know if there is any change in this price.

As usual, Ms. O'Shea, please ship this order to us by Parcel Post.

Sincerely,

COMMUNICATION PROJECTS

Practical Application

A. Using the simplified letter style, write a letter to your instructor stating whether you think the simplified style is appropriate for all business letters. Include your reasons why or why not.

B. Using the letter style you prefer, write a letter to your instructor explaining how the style selected is superior to the other styles discussed in this section.

C. Modernize the following expressions.

1. In re your letter of 27th last, . . .
2. At the present writing we have still not received . . .
3. Please be advised that your payment is overdue.
4. Your order of December 3 is being processed, and we will ship same to you within the week.
5. Due to the fact that your check in the amount of $135.99 has been returned because of insufficient funds, . . .

D. Find and eliminate any redundancies in the following sentences.

1. Past experience shows that most businesses use the same practices.
2. Danforth & Company is using the same identical display.
3. Unless the whole staff cooperates together, we won't finish the report in time.
4. The requirements of the two forms are both alike.
5. The heating system has been converted over from gas to solar power.

E. Make the following sentences clearer and more forceful by using simple words.

1. From the expression on the president's face, we knew that he was engaged in deep ratiocination.
2. The general manager discommended the proposal.
3. She was the cynosure of the board meeting.
4. His dark blue suit was in every way comme il faut.
5. He attempts to get his way by hectoring his opponent.

Editing Practice

Updating Vocabulary. Rewrite these excerpts from business letters, eliminating all outmoded words and expressions.

1. I would like to make an appointment at your earliest convenience.
2. Hoping to see you soon, I remain,

   Sincerely yours,
3. Kindly advise us of your decision soon.
4. At the present writing, we are developing a new model.
5. Due to the fact that our profits are falling, we are trying to lower costs.
6. Thank you in advance for your help.
7. We have received your order for a rheostat and are shipping it at the present time.
8. Enclosed please find our remittance.
9. In the event that you have an accident, this policy will cover your liability.
10. Finances were not part of the vice president's purview.

Using Your Word Processor.   Are there any spelling errors in this paragraph?

> Because we specialize in the needs of attornies, our building is uniquely equipped to serve lawyers. Each suite already has a large room furnished with shelves and tables—ideal for a legal liberry. In addition, there are rooms suitable for large and small conferences, and, of course, several private offices.

Case Problem

Carbon Copies.   In some firms it is a practice to make a carbon copy of a reply to a routine letter on the back of the letter being answered. Suggest some possible advantages and disadvantages of this procedure.

42

WRITING REQUESTS

Some of the most routine business tasks involve requests of some kind—for example, asking for appointments, reserving conference rooms, obtaining price lists and catalogs, asking for copies of reports and studies, seeking technical information about products and services, and asking favors. In getting a favorable response to these and many other routine requests that business workers perform daily, writing an effective request letter or memorandum is the key.

Although requests are truly routine (that is, they are common), they are not to be treated routinely. And extraordinary requests require extraordinary planning and writing skills! However, whether the request is simply for a copy of a catalog that the reader should be glad to send or for a busy, important executive to go out of her way to speak at your conference, follow these guidelines in writing requests:

Be complete.
Be precise.
Be reasonable.
Be courteous.

BE COMPLETE

When writing a request, always ask yourself, "What can I provide the reader to make sure that he or she has *all* the information needed to grant the request?" Also, "Will any more information be helpful for some reason?" Consider the following situations:

You are requesting materials for a speech that you're planning to give. Tell the reader the purpose of your request. He or she might have additional materials to share with you or might grant the request solely to get publicity for his or her company.

You are assuming the reader will remember facts from your last letter or your last conversation. Don't assume! Repeat the model or type, the catalog number, the price, the preferred shipping method, and so on.

You are ordering extra stock so as to qualify for a quantity discount. Be sure to mention the discount you expect.

You are having something shipped to an address other than the one in your letterhead. Tell the reader where the materials are to be shipped. Don't assume the reader knows because he or she has handled your requests before; the order may be delegated to someone else this time.

Put yourself in the reader's place to better understand how the reader might feel and what more he or she might want to know. Note, for example, how the requests on pages 387 and 388 successfully answer "Who? "What?" "Why?" When?" and "Where?"

In your effort to be complete, however, do not fall prey to the temptation to give the reader an overdetailed description of needless information. Decide whether it will help the reader to know that you

INTEROFFICE MEMORANDUM

To: Charles Hiller, Office Manager

From: Dorothy Monroe, Mailroom Supervisor

Subject: Need for Another Postage Meter

Date: January 23, 19--

Our use of postage has increased more than twofold in the last six months. The volume of outgoing first-class letters has risen from an average of 390 a day to almost 1000. The increase in second-class mailings has been almost as great. In the same period, postal rates have gone up 18 percent. It is no wonder that our postage meter seems to run out of postage every day.

Simply putting more postage in the meter would help but would not solve the problem. It is company policy never to leave the mailing of a completed first-class letter until the next day. Since most outgoing first-class letters reach the mailroom between 3 and 5 p.m., there are only two hours available for processing approximately 800 letters. Using a single meter, we simply do not have enough time to place postage on every item.

The result, I am afraid, has been late delivery of some company mail. During the past week, we have received three complaints about this from outside the company and two complaints from within.

I am sure that you will agree that another meter is needed. I have obtained a purchase order and filled it out for your signature, and I would be grateful if you would authorize the purchase as soon as possible. I will send a member of my staff to get the second meter as soon as I receive authorization.

DM

Whether a request is routine or is complicated, it should be complete. It should also be precise, reasonable, and courteous.

THE**G**RILLO**A**GENCY

13 East Taylor Road   White Plains, New York 10604   (914) 555-9300

September 13, 19--

Ms. Frances P. O'Flaherty
Training Director
National Insurance Institute
500 Independence Way
Cleveland, OH 44015

Dear Ms. O'Flaherty:

I read with interest in Insurance Today about your new
training booklet, "The 100 Most-Asked Questions About
Casualty Insurance." This booklet sounds as if it will be
especially suited for training our new personnel.

Ms. O'Flaherty, will you please send us 30 copies of this
booklet? I have enclosed a check for $27 to cover the
cost of the booklets and shipping.

Because we are planning to use these booklets on January
14 for a training session, we will be glad to pay any
additional costs for airmail or parcel post shipping to
ensure that we receive the materials in time. In this
case, please bill me for any additional costs.

                              Sincerely yours,

                              Anthony Grillo

                              Anthony Grillo
                              President

jt
Enclosure

A request letter should answer the questions "Who?" "What?" "Why?" "When?" and "Where?"

are planning to give a speech. If it *will* help, include this fact in your request; if it is likely to be useless information, omit it. Likewise, decide whether you must include the model or type, the catalog number, and so on. If all this information is already included in the enclosed purchase order, then there may be no need to repeat it in the letter too.

BE PRECISE

More than once, newspapers have reported stories of the wrong convicts being released because the approved release form listed the *wrong convict number!* Although an error in your written requests may not have such strong repercussions, the error may be very embarrassing, troublesome, costly, and time-consuming.

Learn to be a good proofreader. Don't delegate the entire responsibility to others. Share the proofreading of your request letters and memos with your secretary or your assistant. Look for ways to ensure accuracy such as reading to each other statistics in the letter against statistics in the original invoice, etc. List statistics in a table (rather than in sentences) if the table format makes the information easier to comprehend. See page 390 for an example of a letter that illustrates how to be precise.

BE REASONABLE

Even people who are usually reasonable will sometimes make *un*reasonable requests when faced with job pressures or when they do not fully understand that what they are asking is exceptionally difficult or time-consuming or complicated.

Whatever the reasons, be sure to avoid making unreasonable requests. Consider what you are asking *from the reader's perspective*. Are you asking too much of someone's time? Are you taking advantage of a colleague's influence? Are you asking for a character reference from someone who hardly knows you? Can you reasonably expect this person to expend such effort on your request? Consider these factors *beforehand*.

BE COURTEOUS

Courtesy is a must in business communications. Whether you are requesting something that is legally or morally due to you, something that you have paid (or will pay) for, something that is yours and should be returned, or something that the reader should be delighted to send to you—in every case, you should be courteous in writing your request. Just as you deserve common courtesy, you must show common courtesy.

WESTWOOD ART STUDIO
One Sun Valley Road
Baltimore, Maryland 21211
(301) 555-7575

August 14, 19--

Merlin Graphic Arts Supply Inc.
901 Brenton Drive
Princess Anne, MD 21853

Attention: Order Department

Ladies and Gentlemen:

Please ship the following materials to us airfreight and bill our
account.

Quantity	Item (Catalog No.)	Unit Price	Total ↓2
12	Nonskid rulers, 18" (138255)	$ 5.00	$ 60.00
1	Leroy Lettering Set (211501)	313.00	313.00
1 doz.	Ebony drawing pencils (07824)	3.00	3.00
5 gal	Best-Test Rubber Cement (119590)	19.90	99.50
			$475.50

We would appreciate receiving the entire order within two weeks.
Please charge the total to our account (No. 47/344).

Sincerely,

Beatrice Keller

Beatrice Keller
Office Manager

dbc

Listing information in a table format often helps the writer to communicate precisely.

Although few people intentionally write discourteous requests, in their rush to complete a job, to place an order, to mail a letter, and so on, people *do* write impolite requests. For example, read this request for a free catalog that was advertised in a trade journal:

> Send me the free catalog of artists' supplies that you advertised in *Graphic Arts World*. Send it to the address in the letterhead.

The reader *did* advertise free catalogs, obviously in the hope of promoting certain products and attracting new customers. But does this mean that the reader of the request letter does not deserve common courtesy? Of course not! The writer would have shown more thoughtfulness, more respect for the reader, by writing the request along these lines:

> I read with interest in *Graphic Arts World* that your artists' supply catalog is available free to professionals in the graphic arts industry. My colleagues here at the Westwood Arts Studio and I would appreciate receiving a copy. Will you please mail one copy to me at the Westwood Studio address on the letterhead?
>
> We are especially interested in a catalog of drawing tables, storage cabinets, and so on, because we will soon be opening a second studio. Are these supplies listed in a separate catalog? If so, we would appreciate receiving a copy of that catalog too.
>
> Your company has enjoyed a fine reputation in the graphic arts industry for many years. All of us are therefore eager to see your new catalog!

The writer might have reaped additional benefits from this revised, more courteous request. The reader will gladly send not only the catalog advertised but another catalog that lists artists' furnishings, because the writer took the time to state specific needs and did so *courteously*.

When writing a request, write the request that *you* would like to receive if you were the reader.

COMMUNICATION PROJECTS

Practical Application

A.   Write a letter to Whitesmith's Business Supply, 1199 Memorial Boulevard, Des Plaines, Illinois 46043, to order a desk. Before writing the letter, jot down answers to each of the following questions:

Why are you writing?

What kind of desk are you ordering?

How do you want to pay for and receive the desk?

When do you want the desk?

Where do you want the desk delivered?

B. Find in magazines or newspapers two advertisements that invite you to write for additional information about products and services. Write a letter to each company to ask for a catalog, sample, brochure, or other descriptive information.

C. Write a letter notifying your favorite magazine that you have changed your address and would like to have your subscription transferred to the new address.

D. Write a letter to the Superintendent of Documents, U.S. Government Printing Office, Washington, DC 20402, asking for a list of publications about an occupation that interests you.

E. An advertisement for Rhenish Business Machines has interested you in a new high-speed copier. Write the company asking for the names and addresses of Rhenish dealers in your area.

F. At a meeting of the Consumer Awareness Club, someone proposes subscribing to the periodical *Consumer Reports,* published by Consumers Union, Mount Vernon, New York 10962. One club member has heard that a group of people can subscribe to the magazine and the *Annual Buying Guide* at reduced cost. You volunteer to request information from Consumers Union about group subscriptions. Write the request letter on behalf of the club.

G. A valuable oil painting was given to you as a gift. One morning you notice a crack in the painting. Write the Fine Arts Museum requesting its booklet *Care and Preservation of Oil Paintings*.

H. How many ways can you express "please" and "thank you" without using the actual words? Consider yourself *good* if you find five ways; *excellent* if you find eight; *expert* if you find ten.

Editing Practice

Using Your Word Processor. Edit and rewrite the following paragraph, correcting all errors.

> Please send me the compleat two-volume set of *Marketing and Distribution.* I understand that for the price of $39.95 I will also receive a one-year subscription to *American Business Today,* along with a callendar for business executives. Please refrane, however, from placing my name on any mailing lists.

Rewrite Desk. Improve the following first lines from request letters.

1. You are hereby informed that your warranty has expired. Please read the company service regulations herewith before requesting any maintenance hereafter.

2. Here is the booklet.
3. We have not received your scheduled payment and want it now.
4. Your letter of October 9 fails to make clear which model you own.
5. We could surely use the advice of a management consulting firm like yours.

Case Problem

Positively Friendly.   Positive statements are more likely to win goodwill and to promote business than are negative ones. Rewrite these statements to make them sound more friendly.

1. Nothing is more frustrating than a customer who fails to understand the instructions that go with your blender. There isn't much we can do to fix the blender now.
2. I'm sorry, but you can't very well expect us to replace damaged merchandise when you are responsible for dropping the typewriter.

43

ANSWERING REQUESTS

If writing requests is a common business task, then answering requests is obviously equally common. Each request letter and memorandum illustrated in Section 42 deserves a response from the reader. Common courtesy demands a reply.

Common courtesy also demands that the response be written *promptly.* Whether the response is an easy-to-write positive reply or a more difficult rejection, the reader should not be kept in suspense. Also, the writer should try to *help* the reader as much as possible, even if the request must be refused.

Writing a response—whether the reply is positive or negative—presents an opportunity to promote goodwill and to make a sale. Thus the response should be *sales-minded.* In addition, the response (like the request) should be *specific* and *complete.*

As you can see, then, answering requests requires the writer to:

Be prompt.
Be helpful.
Be sales-minded.
Be specific.
Be complete.
Be positive.

Let's take a closer look at each of these six rules for answering requests.

BE PROMPT

Many companies have policies requiring their employees to respond to letters within 48 hours—some, within 24 hours. Why? Because the companies realize that being prompt in replying is simply good business.

Even when an inquiry cannot be answered in detail, common business courtesy demands that a reply (at least an acknowledgment of the request) be sent *promptly*. For example:

> Dear Mr. Mendez:
>
> Your recent request for a price quotation for four 5000-watt alternators (Rayco No. 4700) is being handled by Nancy Klein. Rayco, the manufacturer, now has these alternators on back order. Ms. Klein is checking with Rayco to determine how soon these alternators will be available and what the price change (if any) will be.
>
> Ms. Klein expects to have this information for you by October 15. In any case, she will write to you before then to give you an update on your request.
>
> Sincerely yours,

This prompt response (1) acknowledges the request, (2) tells the potential customer specifically who is taking care of his request, and (3) tells him when he can expect an answer. (The writer in this situation would send a carbon copy to Ms. Klein and place another copy in a tickler file—a reminder file—for October 15.)

Because promptness is both a courtesy and a sign of good business, your reader will always be impressed by your promptness. Therefore, take advantage of situations in which your promptness will be a plus. Note how one writer capitalized on a quick response:

> When I received your request in this morning's mail, I checked immediately to make sure that we could reserve the conference rooms you requested for your March 19 meeting. I am pleased to tell you that we can confirm the availability of . . . .

Modern business writers use word processors to help them save time in answering requests promptly—especially when replies must be written in large volumes. As you will see in Section 47, word processing equipment permits writers to develop individually personalized letters in a fraction of the time it would take to do so *without* such equipment.

Another shortcut that allows writers to achieve promptness when faced with large volumes of responses is to *print* a card or letter. The card or letter may have blanks that the writer can quickly fill in, or it may simply give a printed message with no blanks. Despite their lack of personalization, printed responses allow a company to respond to hundreds or thousands of requests *promptly*. Imagine, for example, the number of responses a nationally famous magazine would need to send as a result of advertising a half-price subscription offer! Without printed "Dear Subscriber:" responses, such as the one on page 396, prompt replies would be impossible. Printed responses certainly do serve a purpose.

BE HELPFUL

A customer or a potential customer who asks for information expects to receive assistance, whether the customer is asking in person, on the telephone, or in writing. Not only does the customer expect assistance, but management also *wants* its employees to offer their assistance to customers, suppliers, and coworkers.

When responding to a request, try to understand why the person is asking for help and remember why your company wants you to help. Remember, too, that you are the expert. Whether or not you can grant the request, consider whether there is something additional you can do to help the person. Do you know of a store where the person can find the product he or she needs? Do you know of a company that makes the product he or she is looking for? Do you know of a book that covers the very topic the person wants to research? Do you know of a service organization that can help the person?

Note how the writer of the following letter did more than fill the request—the writer anticipated Ms. Kroll's interest in a closely related product. Good salesmanship? Good business? *Both!*

Dear Ms. Kroll:

It's good to know that you are considering ImageMaker, our telephone facsimile transmitting system. One of our most popular items, the ImageMaker will enable you to send any graphic design 24 by 24 inches or smaller to any office in the world equipped with an ImageMaker and a telephone. The ImageMaker should be particularly valuable to you and your partner-architects in other cities. Now you won't have to wait days to react to one another's latest sketches.

(Continued on page 401.)

FINANCE WEEKLY PUBLICATIONS, INC.

One Wall Street   A Global Industries Company
New York, New York 10005   (212) 555-2000

Dear Subscriber:

THANK YOU...

for renewing your subscription to FINANCE WEEKLY. We received your
payment, and we have credited your account.

In the coming year, we know that you will continue to enjoy all the
feature stories and the up-to-the-minute reporting on important
financial news--the kind of information for which you rely on FINANCE
WEEKLY.

We encourage you to take a moment to complete the "From the Reader"
card that is included in every issue. By quickly checking the
features you most like, you can help ensure that future issues of
FINANCE WEEKLY will continue to serve your interests and meet your
needs.

Sincerely,

(Ms.) Marcia Alcott

Marcia Alcott
Circulation Manager

lmg

This printed letter helps a publisher acknowledge all its subscription renewals *promptly*.

Notes are helpful in planning and organizing a written communication.

Before you mail a letter, ask yourself whether it will make a favorable impression on the receiver.

Boilerplate text and form letters make preparing a larger mailing more efficient.

A wonderful complement to ImageMaker is our reducing, high-resolution photocopier, the ImageReducer. With no discernible loss in precision, the ImageReducer will reduce graphic designs as large as 48 by 48 inches to 24 by 24 inches—small enough to transmit using the ImageMaker. The combination of ImageMaker and ImageReducer will save not only the transit time of mailing or of shipping by airfreight but also the cost.

We very much appreciate your interest in our products and would be happy to demonstrate them for you soon.

Sincerely,

Although it is rather easy to be helpful when you are granting the request, you can also be helpful in many situations when you cannot grant the request, as the writer of the following letter proves:

Dear Mr. Gooden:

I wish that we were able to fill your recent order for the 15-millimeter, f/2.8 Caxton underwater lens. Although we generally carry this superb lens, we are currently out of stock, and Caxton will not be shipping more until September or October.

Because you mentioned that you wanted the lens for your upcoming scuba diving trip, I called another supplier to find this lens. Good news: The F Stop, a photography specialty store, has just what you want. You may call the F Stop toll-free at (800) 555-1800.

Good luck! And please be sure to try us again *next time.*

Sincerely,

This letter has certainly won a friend for the writer's company—just by being helpful.

BE SALES-MINDED

Whenever you respond to a request letter, you should look for possible ways to make a sale. After all, whether you work in the Sales Department or not, your company depends on sales to make a profit and to pay your salary.

But the "hard sell" approach is rarely effective; you will not make much progress by bluntly saying "Buy this product!" Yet you *can* help sell your company's products or services. Two ways that you can help were already discussed—by responding promptly to requests and by being helpful. Both will make your readers appreciate the quality customer service your company provides and convince them to deal with *your* firm.

In addition to these indirect sales techniques, there are other more direct ways to help sell your company's products and services when responding to requests. For example, if you are sending a potential customer a catalog, include *both* an order blank *and* an addressed envelope to make it easy to place an order. If a customer complains about having had to wait a long time to receive a previous order, spend a few minutes to write an apology and an explanation—better yet, tell the customer to write directly to *you* next time so that you may personally help track down the order. Such "extras" are really techniques for selling.

Can you uncover the indirect selling methods the writer of this letter used?

Dear Mr. D'Aguilera:

Thank you for asking about the service contract for Walton's Model-X radial-arm saw. We are pleased to share some information with you.

Mr. D'Aguilera, the enclosed booklet includes a list of all the specific items that are covered by our service contract. In fact, it also lists (in equally large print) the few items that are *not* covered in the contract, so that there will be no "surprises" if something should happen to the product; you will know exactly what is covered. The Walton management insists that we stand behind all our products and that we inform our customers precisely *how* we stand behind our products. By doing so, we avoid the unfortunate experience that you described in your letter.

May I make a suggestion? Because service is such an important factor in your buying decision, I recommend that you ask your local Walton dealers how they rate the service of two or three of the brand names that they sell. (A list of dealers in your area is enclosed.) Further, I invite you to visit Charles Hammond of Hammond & Sons in Woodmere, which I believe is just a few miles from you. Mr. Hammond has operated an authorized Walton service center for more than 20 years. Not only will visiting Charles be informative, but this also will give you a chance to meet the person who would service any Walton product that you own.

Of course, please review the enclosed booklet. Then let me know of any way that we can be helpful. You may call me toll-free at (800) 555-9250 whenever you have any questions for us. We would be delighted to be of service.

Sincerely,

Throughout the letter the writer stresses what is most important to the reader—*service*. The writer:

1. Provides a booklet that gives all the details of Walton's service contract.
2. Subtly *challenges* the reader to visit the Walton service center nearest his home (a "see for yourself" test).

3. Adds a personal touch by providing him with the name of the local service center manager.
4. Gives the reader a toll-free number, and asks him to call if he has any questions.

As you respond to requests, look for ways in which you can help sell your company's products or services.

BE SPECIFIC

The need to *be specific* is a general rule; it applies, of course, to *any* letter or memorandum, whether the message is a request, a response to someone's request, or any other type of communication.

When acknowledging receipt of money, for example, cite the exact amount:

> We appreciate receiving your check for $125 in payment of Invoice 17290.

When discussing dates, times, airline flight numbers, or other specific statistics, cite them clearly.

> I am very pleased to accept your invitation to speak on July 10 at the annual Photographers' Club Conference, which will be held July 9–11 at the Chancellor Inn in Chicago. The topic, "Copyright Protection for Photographers," is one of special interest to me.

> As I mentioned in our conversation earlier today, I will arrive at O'Hare at 2:30 p.m. on Monday, July 8, on Northwest Orient flight 741 . . . .

When you receive something of value, acknowledge its receipt, including any specific information that is appropriate. Remember that your letter will become part of the reader's files—proof that you received the important papers.

> Your manuscript for "How to Keep Records for Your At-Home Business" (pages 1–52 plus illustrations) arrived this morning, while Ms. Voorhees is away on a business trip.

When acknowledging receipt of an order, include the date of the order and the purchase number. Although the reader already knows this information, it is repeated because the letter will be filed for future reference. In addition, mention how the materials will be shipped, when the reader can expect to receive the merchandise, and so on.

> We are delighted that you are taking advantage of our annual stock-reduction sale. Your Order 575, dated June 20, will be shipped by United Parcel this afternoon. As you requested, the merchandise will be delivered to your Houston Street store.

BE COMPLETE

Again, the need to *be complete* is a general rule. Although many writers *try* to be complete, important information is often omitted because of carelessness.

One way to make sure that your responses are complete is to underline the specific points in the request letter. Another way is to note in the margin each answer to a specific point in the request letter. The underlined points or the marginal notes serve as excellent outlines in writing the reply. For example, when Marion Lemaster received the letter of inquiry illustrated on page 405, she made marginal notes to make sure that her response, illustrated on page 406, would be *complete*.

One technique that fosters completeness is listing major points item by item. In this follow-up letter, which confirms the various points agreed upon during a telephone conversation, the writer enumerates five specific items that were covered in the conversation:

> Dear Clarence:
>
> I am writing to confirm our telephone conversation of this afternoon regarding the first Estes Stores Celebrity Amateur Golf Tournament. We reached agreement on the following points:
>
> 1. Susan McDowell will handle liaison with the charities that will benefit from the tournament's proceeds.
> 2. You will be responsible for recruiting celebrities to play in the tournament alongside local amateurs.
> 3. I will coordinate plans with both the Amateur Golfers' Group and the Stebbing Golf Club.
> 4. The tentative date for the tournament is June 23, 19—.
> 5. A Coordinators' Committee will be formed of Estes Stores' management, with full charge of financial arrangements for the tournament.
>
> Please let me know if you see the need for further arrangements of any kind. Thanks for your help in organizing this important public-service event.
>
> Cordially,

BE POSITIVE

The need to *be positive* is especially important when handling problem requests. Saying "no" to people who have applied for credit, who do not qualify for discounts, whose warranties have expired, who have asked for confidential information, who have requested contributions that must be turned down—these situations require extra tact and diplomacy from the writer. Remember: Whatever the cause of the problem, the writer's goal is to keep the reader's goodwill.

1783 Lincoln Boulevard
Westwood, Virginia 23205
April 2, 19--

Ms. Marion Lemaster
Sales Manager
Electrostatic Cleaner Company
896 Kingston Avenue
Chicago, Illinois 60613

Dear Ms. Lemaster:

I am very much interested in the Electrostatic electronic
air cleaner that was advertised in the March issue of Home
Products. There are some questions I would like answered
about your air cleaner to help me decide whether yours is
the make that best suits my needs.

1. Under what principle does your air cleaner work? *agglomerate*

2. Where does the unit have to be mounted? *Vertical, horizontal, underneath*

3. How often does the collecting cell have to be *18 mos.*
   washed?

I should appreciate your answering these questions in time
for me to make a decision by May 10.

Very truly yours,

James A. Daughtrey

James A. Daughtrey

Jotting comments in the margin of a request letter helps the recipient to be thorough in responding.

Perhaps the most positive aspect of such refusals is to hold out hope for the future.

Perhaps next year we will be able to . . .

When our needs expand, we may . . .

Of course, we will keep your application on file so that . . .

Once again, remember to put yourself in your reader's place. When you read your reply *from your reader's perspective,* you will seek creative ways to be positive.

COMMUNICATION PROJECTS

Practical Application

A.   Steven Crowell, 23 Saltway Drive, Saltway, Florida 33596, requested from your company, Allword Publishing Inc., a copy of your new magazine, *Microwave Chef.* Demand has exceeded expectations, and the first issue has sold out. Write an appropriate response to Mr. Crowell.

B.   Patricia Thompson, Sales Manager for Bermuda Beauty Lawn Products, 1132 South Market Avenue, Claremore, Minnesota 54335, has received an order from the Howard House and Garden Shop, 853 Wallace Street, Dearfield, Illinois 62705. The order, dated March 1, is large and is the first received from Howard House and Garden. Terri Sturz, the manager of Howard, wants to know the terms of payment and how and when the merchandise will be shipped. Write Ms. Thompson's reply to Ms. Sturz.

C.   Alice O'Toole, Director of Public Relations for Smithton Typewriter Manufacturers, 332 Phillips Avenue, Manchester, New Hampshire 03110, has telephoned Gerald Maurice, Chief Advertising Consultant for New England Best Business Consulting, 212 Crofts Street, Peterborough, New Hampshire 03484, and asked him to make a presentation on "Advertising in the Electronic Age" at the convention of the New England Advertising League. The presentation is to take place on June 24 at the Merrick Hotel in Cambridge, Massachusetts 02138, starting at 4:30 p.m. Mr. Maurice is to make a 40-minute presentation and then participate in a 20-minute discussion period. The meeting will be held in the Peerless Ballroom and will be followed by dinner from 5:30 to 7 p.m. Mr. Maurice is invited to the dinner as a guest of the Advertising League. Write the letter that Ms. O'Toole should send to Mr. Maurice to confirm all the details of his participation in the convention.

D.   Suppose that Mrs. Andrea Childs, 2224 Humbolt Street, Akron, Ohio 44313, owner of an Infinite Video Computer Game

System, made by Infinite Video, 833 West San Pedro, Mountain View, California 94041, has sent a defective unit to the factory for repair. Unfortunately, there is a shortage of a usually abundant silicon integrated circuit, or "chip," needed to repair the game system. Integrated circuits have been ordered from Japan but are not expected for two weeks. Write a letter explaining the delay and telling Mrs. Childs when to expect the return of her repaired unit.

E.　The Association of Women for Charity has asked you to speak at its monthly meeting on January 15. The topic is to be "Organizing the Office." Since you received the invitation only on January 8, however, you do not feel that enough time remains for you to prepare a good speech. Write a note of refusal to the chairperson, Mrs. Blanche Ludlum, 8788 North Filmore, Blacksburg, Virginia 24060.

F.　You are a new employee in the sales office of a manufacturer of motion picture projectors, screens, and accompanying audio equipment. Your predecessor has been fired, leaving behind a stack of half-finished correspondence. How would you revise the following draft of a letter left in the out-basket?

Mr. Geoffrey Boole
1100 Davona Drive
Indianapolis, Indiana 46226

Dear Sir:

Your order for a Zapamattic movie outfit has reached us. As manufacturers, we do not deal directly with the buying public. Therefore, we cannot fill your order as requested. Contact Hagen Camera Retailers, 668 Northpoint Street, Indianapolis, Indiana 46221. Let us know how you make out.

Yours truly,

Editing Practice

Updating Correspondence.　Rewrite these excerpts from letters, replacing any dated expressions.

1. The information in your application has been duly noted.
2. We wish to extend our thanks to you for taking the time to complete the questionnaire.
3. I have before me your letter of October 10.
4. Up to the present writing, we have not received your payment for last month.
5. We will be sending the service manuals to you under separate cover.
6. I am enclosing an invoice in the amount of $210.98.
7. In the event you will be unable to accept the offer, please advise.
8. I am sending herewith the annual report for last year.

Case Problem

Right Meeting—Wrong Report.   Mark Maxwell works in the sales department of the Rapier Razor Company. His supervisor asked him to attend an important meeting of the advertising department staff to explain how the two departments can work together more effectively to increase sales in the year ahead. Mark misunderstood the subject he was to discuss and, instead, prepared a talk on the function of the sales department. Listening to the introduction, Mark realized that he had misunderstood the topic.

1.   What should Mark do when he is called upon?
    a.   Give the report he prepared.
    b.   Admit his mistake and ask that the meeting be rescheduled if necessary.
    c.   Blame his supervisor for giving him the wrong information.
    d.   Bluff his way, hoping that no one will notice.
2.   How could this situation have been prevented?

44

WRITING CLAIM AND ADJUSTMENT LETTERS

Whether a business is a multinational conglomerate or a small family store, it will have customers who claim that they received fewer items than they ordered; damaged goods; the incorrect size, color, or model; unsatisfactory merchandise; and so on. Each customer's letter must be answered, of course, and each situation must be studied. (After all, the business must determine first whether the claim has any merit and then how the merchandise was damaged or why the wrong item was shipped so that the same mistake will not happen again.) In many cases an *adjustment* will be made—the customer will receive a full or a partial credit, will be allowed to exchange the merchandise, or will be granted a refund.

Not only will a business *receive* claim letters, but it will also *write* claim letters to its suppliers. The ability to write convincing claim letters and negotiate satisfactory adjustments is a strong business asset. It is essential, therefore, that an effective business communicator be able to write claim and adjustment letters.

WRITING CLAIM LETTERS

The person who writes a claim letter *believes,* of course, that he or she has been wronged. Indeed, the claim *is* justified if the writer:

1. Ordered Model R-75 but received Model R-57.
2. Requested 150 copies but only 100 were shipped.
3. Specified brand X but received brand Z.
4. Enclosed full payment but was billed anyway.

Sometimes, however, the writer *intended* to order brand X but forgot to specify this particular brand. Or neglected to proofread the order letter or purchase order and did not correct the "100" copies to "150." Or wrote the check for full payment but did not enclose it. The first step in making a claim, therefore, is to get the facts—*before* you write your claim.

Get the Facts

Before you make a claim, try to find out what happened and why. If part of the order is missing, is there a packing slip that clearly says the rest of the order will be shipped separately? Check your original order to be sure that the "missing" merchandise *was* ordered.

If merchandise was damaged, should you write your claim to the supplier, or should you write it to the shipping company? You will be embarrassed if you write a strong letter to the supplier and later discover that the shipping company was at fault—or worse, the Shipping Department in your own company.

If the wrong merchandise was delivered, check the original order first. Then try to find out if, perhaps, anyone telephoned a change in the order before you write your claim letter.

When you write a claim letter, you should be relying on facts as the basis of your claim. Until you have sufficient facts, do not write the letter. When you do have all the facts, use them to describe the claim completely and accurately.

Describe the Claim Completely and Accurately

It is especially important to be complete and accurate when writing claim letters because the writer is making an accusation. Both to make a convincing argument *and* to be fair to the reader, you should present all the facts and you should do so accurately.

Read, for example, the following letter. As you do so, note how the writer cites all the necessary details—size, quantities, times, descriptions, and so on.

Dear Mr. Bonner:

We have received your invoice for twenty-five 100-pound bags of polypropylene resins of injection-molding grade. When we placed this order 17 days ago, we stressed the need for speedy delivery of the resins and were promised delivery within 10 days. Your invoice for 25 bags arrived on the tenth day, but we received none of the resins until the fifteenth day, when we received only 5 bags.

We would appreciate your checking your records to make sure that all the resins have been shipped. If so, please check with the shipping company at once. Our customer desperately needs the items to be made from these resins and is understandably upset that we have not delivered them as promised. We are counting on you to help us make up for lost time.

Please let us know the minute you find out what has happened to this vital shipment of resins. We will hold your invoice until we receive all 25 bags of resins. Then, of course, we will be happy to send payment.

Sincerely yours,

Not only does the writer tell the reader *everything* that happened concerning the materials that were ordered but does so in chronological order. By giving complete information and delivering it accurately, the writer makes an honest, believable claim.

Let's look at another example of a claim letter that is both complete and accurate.

Dear Ms. Higgins:

I was distressed to receive your notice of March 1 indicating that you have canceled my automobile insurance policy No. AZ1843687 for failure to pay the premium of $350 due on January 15.

On January 4, I mailed Check 186 for $350. On January 17, the check, endorsed by your company and stamped "Paid," was returned to me. I reported this information to you on the back of a notice of cancellation mailed to me January 30. Since I received no further word from you, I assumed that the matter had been straightened out satisfactorily.

I am enclosing a photocopy of the front and back of my canceled check. Would you please send me a notice of the reinstatement of my insurance.

Very truly yours,

The letter gives *all* the details—completely and accurately—so that the insurance company can quickly correct its error. Note, however, that even though the above letter is filled with facts, it does not accuse, threaten, or demand.

Avoid Accusations, Threats, and Demands

The goal of the claim letter is to get the missing merchandise, to correct the billing error, to return the damaged goods—in other words, to get results, *not* to blame someone, to threaten, or to demand. For example, assume that the above letter to the insurance company was not answered in a reasonable time. What would you do? Write a threatening letter? Demand that the company send you a formal apology? These are reactions, not *solutions*. Writing a letter saying "You know very well that I paid my premium" or "You failed to reply" or "I will sue you" would be a waste of time.

Instead, writing a reasonable letter, this time addressed to the president of the agency that handles your insurance, would probably get results:

> Dear Ms. McDonald:
>
> I am enclosing a photocopy of a letter I wrote to the main office on March 5. My letter has not yet been acknowledged, and I am concerned about whether my automobile insurance is in force.
>
> I should very much appreciate your looking into this matter for me and providing written notification regarding the status of my automobile insurance.
>
> > Very sincerely yours,

Without threatening, demanding, or accusing, the letter will get results. After all, if *you* were the president of the agency, would you overlook this letter? The president would obviously understand that the next step is legal action.

Suggest Reasonable Solutions

The opposite of accusing, demanding, or threatening is to suggest reasonable solutions. Remember: Except in rare circumstances, you are dealing with honest business people who have made a mistake *and realize it*. By suggesting reasonable solutions, you strengthen your chance of getting a just settlement quickly. For example, if you placed an order and received only part of it, one solution might be to indicate that you will accept the missing portion if it arrives by a specific date, as shown by the following statement:

> We shall be happy to accept the 6 lamps if they reach us before February 5, the first day of our Anniversary Sale.

Or suppose that you were overbilled $50 on an order. In this case, you might say:

> Our records indicate that we were billed $250 for the merchandise on our Purchase Order 3290, dated July 7. The figure should have been $200. Therefore, please credit our account for $50 and send us a credit memorandum for this amount.

It is usually best to suggest the kind of solution that you consider acceptable. If you received defective merchandise, for example, you might request replacement of the merchandise, cancellation of the order, a credit of the amount to your account, or substitution of a similar item that meets your needs. By suggesting a solution, you will let the company know what kind of action you want taken. When your suggestion is reasonable, there is a good chance that the company will follow it.

As you see, then, to make the best claim for your case, you should:

Be sure of the facts.
Describe the claim completely and accurately.
Avoid accusations, threats, and demands.
Suggest reasonable solutions.

EVALUATING CLAIMS AND MAKING ADJUSTMENTS

To evaluate a claim, determine a fair adjustment, and finally approve the adjustment require business experience; company authority; familiarity with company policy, industry standards, and consumer laws; and good common sense. You are essentially playing the role of judge, but since you have a vested interest in the case, being impartial is even more difficult. Yet an equitable adjustment requires you to be reasonable, fair, honest, and impartial in making your decision.

Making the right decision, therefore, is a difficult task. The sources of evidence that you must weigh are the company, the claimant (the person making the claim), the transaction, and, in some cases, the law. Let's look at each source to see how it influences or affects the final decision.

The Company

Your company, like most other companies, is ethical in its dealings. (You would not want to be associated with a company that is not.) Ask yourself the following questions to determine the extent of your company's responsibility in causing the claim. Do you know, without a doubt, that the company is not at fault? Could anyone in the company have made a misleading statement? Could the advertising be misinterpreted? Could your records be at fault? Is it possible that someone in the company made a mistake? If such questioning reveals an element of blame on the part of the company, you, the adjuster, will probably decide to honor the claim, at least in part.

The Claimant

To help you evaluate the claimant's share in causing the claim, ask questions like these: Could the claimant be mistaken? Is the claim, if true, the kind that a reasonable person would make? Has the claimant provided all the information you need to check the claim and fix responsibility for it? Does the claimant have a record of fair dealings with your company? Even if you find that the claimant *is* wrong beyond any doubt, does good business sense tell you that perhaps the claim should be honored anyway?

The Transaction

The answers to the following questions will help you arrive at an equitable decision about the transaction. Did your company carry out all its obligations—both explicit and implied—to the customer? Has your company made any claims with reference to this product such as, "Double your money back if you are not absolutely satisfied"? Were any misleading statements made to the customer by your sales personnel? Is there evidence of faulty materials or workmanship in the product? Were the instructions for use of the product clear and complete? If you find a defect either in the product or in the handling of the transaction, you should decide in favor of the claimant. This is just one more application of the almost universal business rule of trying to please the customer.

Sometimes you will have to seek further information before you can answer the above questions. You may need to question some of your coworkers or to write the claimant before you have all the facts at your disposal. The following letter is an example of an inquiry addressed to the claimant.

Dear Mrs. Slezak:

Thank you for your October 17 letter reporting a malfunction of your Ralston 299 air filter. We are sorry that you are having problems with the filter, a product that is usually quite reliable.

We have looked in vain for a copy of your warranty agreement, which should be on file here. The period of the warranty is normally six months. If you could send us the number from the top right corner of your receipt, we could date the purchase. If you do not have the receipt, then please give us the name of the dealer from whom you made the purchase and the approximate date of purchase.

As soon as we receive the information, we will be happy to make an adjustment.

Sincerely yours,

When you receive the necessary information, you will be able to make an equitable decision on the claim.

The Law

In some cases, there may be laws that will affect your decision. Laws intended to protect consumers, for example, allow a consumer to cancel certain contracts within three days "without penalty or obligation." State or local laws may apply in special situations in your industry.

In any case, you should realize that there *are* potential legal problems in some situations. Although you now know that you should not threaten when making a claim, many writers *will* threaten you with legal action in their first claim letters just because they believe that making such threats will get results. Does your company have a policy that requires all employees to notify the Legal Department *every* time there is a possibility of a lawsuit? Whether it has such a policy or not, you *should* notify someone in authority (perhaps your supervisor *and* the Legal Department) whenever a lawsuit is even remotely possible.

WRITING ADJUSTMENT LETTERS

After probing all the sources of evidence and reviewing all the facts in a claim, you may determine that (1) the claim is indeed allowable, (2) the claim is only partially allowable, or (3) the claim is *not* allowable. Now comes the task of using your writing skill to achieve your goal.

An Allowable Claim

Mistakes occur in *every* business. What separates a well-run business from a poorly run business is not simply a matter of *whether* the company makes mistakes but *how it handles* its mistakes.

Question: What do you do when the error is yours? Answer: Admit that it was your fault, without quibbling or trying to avoid responsibility. Note the following letter:

Dear Dr. Fowler:

Thank you for your December 9 letter reporting a problem with your new barometer.

From your description of the problem, we believe that your aneroid barometer was mistakenly calibrated for use as an altimeter. We manufacture altimeters and aneroid barometers using the same mechanism—only the calibrations are different. Somehow our normally efficient production staff and inspectors must have placed the wrong model number and name plate on the mechanism that you received. We are reviewing our procedures in an effort to prevent this kind of mistake from happening again.

We are very sorry for our mistake, and we have shipped you a new barometer by airfreight. We hope our error did not spoil any of your weather forecasts. If we can be of further assistance to you, Dr. Fowler, please don't hesitate to write or call.

Sincerely yours,

The writer obviously admits the error without quibbling and certainly strives to keep the customer's goodwill. In an effort to maintain goodwill, in fact, some companies will even grant doubtful claims if the costs are not exorbitant. In this way they develop excellent reputations among their customers and gain new business.

A Partially Allowable Claim

Allowing a claim is rather easy. Slightly more difficult is reaching a compromise with a claimant. For instance, if the transaction involves a heavy piece of equipment worth $10,000, the manufacturer will probably be reluctant to exchange the equipment and pay for double shipping charges besides. Yet that may be what the claimant asks for.

Suppose, for example, that a recent purchaser of a commercial automatic film processor wants to exchange the processor. The customer states that the processor is no good because the developed film comes out wet instead of dry. You feel certain that the problem is caused by failure of the small fan under the drying hood. Replacement of the fan will take one of your service technicians ten minutes and cost you only $25. Exchanging the entire processor, which weighs 200 pounds and is valued at $9000, will be expensive because of shipping costs. Moreover, the customer will have to wait at least three weeks for arrival of a new processor. You decide to seek a compromise adjustment.

How much of an adjustment a company makes in a case like this depends on company policy. You believe that the customer will be satisfied with the processor after the fan is replaced. You are also willing to offer the customer a $50 discount toward the purchase price as compensation for the inconvenience caused by the failure of the fan. Your letter describing this proposed adjustment might read as follows:

Dear Ms. Hammond:

We very much regret the news that your new SuperSpool Rapid Film Processor is not working properly. The problem sounds to us as if the fan under the drying hood is at fault. Although we thoroughly test each processor before it leaves our plant, the machines are sometimes damaged by rough handling in transit.

Exchanging your processor for a new one would require subjecting another unit to the hazards of shipping. In addition, you would be without a processor for at least three weeks. We seriously question the wisdom of exchanging the entire unit when only one small component is the cause of all the trouble.

We realize that the fan's failure has inconvenienced you, Ms. Hammond, and we want you to be satisfied with our products and our service. We believe that the following adjustment would serve you well. We can send a service technician to your plant with a new drying fan. Replacement of the defective fan should take only 10 minutes, and you can test the processor immediately to make sure that everything is working properly. In addition, we have included a $50 discount certificate.

If this adjustment is satisfactory, please call our service center at 555-2243 to make an appointment at your convenience. We will make sure that someone answers your call promptly.

We are also confident that your SuperSpool Rapid Film Processor will provide good service for years to come.

Sincerely yours,

The writer is trying to reach a fair settlement with the customer. Nonetheless, Ms. Hammond may reply by asking to be compensated for all the film wasted as a result of the fan's failure.

A Nonallowable Claim

Although it may strive to satisfy its customers and may have the easiest claim policy in its industry, a business will be faced with situations in which claims simply cannot be allowed. One customer, for example, may try to return a perfectly good lamp that he ordered simply because he no longer wants that style. Another customer may wrongly insist that she ordered merchandise *before* a price increase. If the business granted such claims once, of course, it would set a dangerous precedent. Besides, it would be poor business to do so. Whatever the reason, the company is faced with the uncomfortable (but necessary) task of saying "no" to a customer.

Assume, for example, that you are employed by Acme Distribution Company, a computer products wholesaler. Last month you featured a special offer on the complete Epic Model KL computer system. In your mailer to dealers, you specifically stated that you are discounting your current inventory of the KL model by 30 percent "to make room for new inventory." Many dealers took advantage of the superb discount offer. You specifically stated in the mailer that this was a "clearance sale" and that no returns would be permitted. (Acme Distribution, by the way, has one of the most liberal returns policies in the industry.)

Melissa Teele, manager of the TriBoro Computer Center, purchased 50 of the Epic KL systems, sold 20, and then asked permission to return the remaining 30 systems. Because TriBoro is a good customer, in the past you have "bent the rules" to allow Ms. Teele special return privileges for unsold merchandise. However, you simply cannot accept the 30 Model KL systems. You must write to Ms. Teele to tell her "no," but you must also try to retain her goodwill—and her future business. To do so, perhaps you would send the following letter:

Dear Ms. Teele:

Thank you for complimenting us on our special offers on the top brand names in computers. We at Acme pride ourselves on being the number-one computer distributor in the state, and we sincerely appreciate having the opportunity to do business with the number-one computer *store* in the state, TriBoro Computer Center.

As you know, Ms. Teele, no other distributor has offered such a drastic discount on Epic computers as our recent 30 percent discount. We did so, frankly, because we were forced to make room for new inventory, and to do so, we simply had to clear out our stock at the time of the special sale. That's why we specifically stated that the sale was on a no-return basis. I'm sure that you, too, have been faced with similar situations.

As much as we would like to help you, we really cannot accept a return of 30 Epic KL systems. For one reason, we now have on order *more than 500 of the new Epic XP system.* As you can imagine, these 500 systems will take up much warehouse space as well as inventory dollars. At the same time, we are also increasing our inventory of other major brands so that we can continue to deliver to dealers like TriBoro *all* computer merchandise in the minimum amount of time. By serving you better, of course, we help you to serve *your* customers better.

May I make a suggestion? A few days ago Nick Ruck of Computer World (in the Warren Mall) was eager to get more Epic Model KL systems. Perhaps you can make an arrangement to sell your stock to Mr. Ruck. Of course, if I should hear of any other dealers who are looking for Epic KLs, I will be sure to call you.

By the way, let me give you some "advance notice" of a special sale we are planning for next month. We will be offering the popular Apex disk drive for only $125 and the Apex modem for only $195!

Sincerely yours,

Although the reply is obviously "no," the letter:

1. Has a positive tone throughout.
2. Acknowledges Ms. Teele's claim courteously.
3. Explains specifically why the claim cannot be granted and cites reasons.
4. Suggests a possible solution for clearing her excess stock.
5. Maintains the customer's goodwill by giving her advance notice of an upcoming sale and by showing appreciation for her business.

COMMUNICATION PROJECTS

Practical Application

A. The City-Wide Newspaper Delivery Service, 322 Oxford Street, Detroit, Michigan 48226, has billed you for a month's delivery of both daily and Sunday newspapers. You ordered only the daily newspaper, however, and that is all you received. The delivery service has charged you $7.20 for 24 issues of the daily newspaper and $3.40 for 4 issues of the Sunday newspaper. For an adjustment to your bill, write to Ms. Sylvia Ferrer, the customer service representative for the City-Wide Newspaper Delivery Service.

B.   Sylvia Ferrer receives your letter seeking an adjustment to your monthly bill (see A above). Her records confirm your claim that you ordered and received only daily newspapers. Compose the adjustment letter that Ms. Ferrer should send in response to your claim.

C.   Review the letter of adjustment addressed to Ms. Hammond (page 417) concerning the problem film processor. Assume that Ms. Hammond is not satisfied with your offer to replace the fan and to send a $50 discount. Instead, Ms. Hammond agrees to accept replacement of the fan, but she also wants full compensation for all film wasted as a result of the defective fan. You decide to write Ms. Hammond offering to send a claims adjuster to her photography business to examine the wasted film and determine its value. But you also decide not to commit yourself at this point to pay for all film wasted. Write the letter.

D.   After visiting Ms. Hammond's photography business (see C above), your adjuster tells you that five 100-foot rolls of 12-inch-wide film were ruined because the fan failed. Since the film is valued at $.50 per foot, the cost of the film wasted is $250. Your adjuster says that the fan is definitely the immediate cause of the wastage. The adjuster adds, however, that Ms. Hammond should have stopped running the processor and called for service after the first roll or two of film were ruined. Decide how much compensation Ms. Hammond is entitled to, and write a letter to her either accepting or denying her claim to compensation for all 500 feet of wasted film.

E.   Write a letter for William Steiner, the manager of Le Crepuscule, a French restaurant located at 665 Darien Street, Omaha, Nebraska 68108. Today Mr. Steiner has received a new, heavy-duty commercial food processor, but his chef shows him that it does not slice foods as precisely as advertised. Write the manufacturer, Whirling Wonder Kitchen Aids, One Bluegrass Way, Lexington, Kentucky 40506, requesting replacement of the food processor.

F.   You work in the Claims and Adjustments Department of Whirling Wonder Kitchen Aids. You receive a letter from the manager of Le Crepuscule (see E above) requesting replacement of a food processor that is not slicing evenly. You know from experience that uneven slices usually result from a damaged slicing disk. Write Mr. Steiner, the manager of Le Crepuscule. First, ask whether the food processor performs correctly with other attachments, such as the two-bladed knife and the shredding disk. Explain that if the machine does correctly dice, chop, grate, grind, and shred, the problem is definitely the damaged slicing disk. Offer to replace the slicing disk at no cost if this is the problem.

Editing Practice

Applied Psychology. Rewrite the following sentences so that each promotes goodwill.

1. There is no chance that we will be able to deliver your order on time because a number of smarter consumers placed their orders before you.
2. Since you were careless and failed to sign your Check 210, we are returning it.
3. You must be too lazy to open your mail, because we have already written you once about this matter.
4. Your October 3 letter fails to explain satisfactorily your delay in paying.
5. Your failure to reply has made the problem even worse.
6. We will repair the chair that you claim was damaged in transit.
7. You are the only person who ever found our football helmets unsatisfactory.
8. You neglected to indicate the number on our invoice.
9. You complained that Order 977 did not arrive on time.
10. You made a mistake of $27 on our March 15 invoice.

Case Problem

Attending to Customers. Charles Winthrop is a sales representative in the men's furnishings department of Lambert's Department Store. Early on Saturday morning his supervisor came by and said, "Charles, see if you can get your new merchandise marked and put on the shelves as quickly as possible. It's going to be a busy day, and I have several special things for you to do." While Charles was rushing to complete the job, a customer, Mr. Casey, entered the department. Even though Charles was the only available sales representative, he continued marking the merchandise and let the customer wait. Just as Charles finished his marking and went to wait on the customer, Mr. Casey walked out.

1. Was Charles justified in ignoring Mr. Casey in order to finish marking the new merchandise? Why or why not?
2. What should Charles have said to Mr. Casey as soon as he saw him?

45

WRITING PUBLIC RELATIONS LETTERS

Public relations is the business of influencing the public's feeling or attitude toward a company or an organization. Business and industry spend many millions of dollars a year on magazine and newspaper advertisements, radio and TV commercials, billboard signs, cards, posters, and letters intended, not to sell a specific product, but to promote good public relations. Favorable public relations means that the public has a positive opinion of the company or organization; unfavorable public relations, a negative opinion.

Major corporations have public relations departments that specialize in creating favorable images of their firms and minimizing the negative impact when their firms get "bad press." You may not work in the public relations department; however, as an employee, you will certainly affect your company's public image.

Question: When will you have an opportunity to influence public opinion about your company? Answer: Whenever you communicate with the public as a representative of your company—when you talk with or write to anyone outside the company, you have an opportunity to affect the public's attitude toward your firm. Your communication skills, therefore, can contribute to your firm's favorable public image, as you will see in this section.

SPECIAL PUBLIC RELATIONS OPPORTUNITIES

You have seen signs that say, for example, "Working Hard to Keep You and Your Family Safe . . . FENTON FIRE ALARMS." This sign is not designed specifically to sell Fenton's Model 121-E fire alarm, nor to sell Fenton's line of products, but to promote the Fenton Company *in general*. The ad is designed to convince you that the Fenton Company has *you* in mind. Why? So that when you *do* shop for a fire alarm, you will (subconsciously or otherwise) select Fenton— a name you can trust.

The PR specialist looks for opportunities to show the company in the best possible light. When an employee receives a commendation from her community for her civic work, the company might send a press release to various newspapers to share this good news with the public. The good civic work of one of its employees helps the firm to look good too. On the other hand, the PR specialist tries to minimize anything the public could possibly interpret in a negative way. For instance, if a store is expanding, the noise and dust of the construction work may irritate passersby. The PR specialist may place several sidewalk signs, such as the one illustrated here, in key locations for passersby to see. Reason: To politely explain (and apologize for) the temporary mess and show that the store shares its neighbors' concerns about the noise and dust.

Unfavorable public opinion can ruin a firm. If a newspaper report states or implies that the Jordan Meat Company has been labeling nonbeef products "100 percent beef," public opinion of that company will almost surely drop—even if the report is later proved false. Consumers who remember the negative report may start buying another brand if they doubt the integrity of the company.

Knowing the benefits of good public relations, all businesses strive to create—and to keep—a favorable image of their organizations in the eyes of the public. An oil company may televise a short film showing the public that the company strives to protect the environment wherever it drills for oil. A well-known, reputable person narrates the film to lend it additional credibility. At no time does the narrator say "Buy your oil and gas from _____." Instead, the narrator points out all the good things the company is doing for the public.

Here are some specific situations in which public relations specialists seek to influence public opinion.

1. A commuter railroad is operating at a deficit. Although fares have increased 200 percent in the past five years, the company

To help build a favorable image of Clark's among its neighbors and its customers, the store places signs at key locations for passersby to see.

is still losing money and must ask for another increase. Of course, the railroad is sensitive to the opinions of its customers; it needs their understanding and their support. The PR department of the railroad may place advertisements in newspapers, may purchase radio time, may issue circulars to riders, and may write letters to leading citizens in order to explain why the railroad has found it necessary to seek authority to raise fares.

2. A private water main on the grounds of a manufacturing plant bursts, submerging a low stretch of a nearby public road in two feet of water. The company provides a detour road on its own grounds, posts large signs with directions to drivers and apologies to the community, and employs someone to direct traffic until repairs are complete. In addition, the company publishes apologetic letters in the local newspapers, explaining how the accident happened and what steps are being taken to prevent a recurrence.

3. The manager of the local airport writes to homeowners who live near the landing field to apologize for the noise created by the jet engines and to assure these people that improvements will be made soon.

4. A large public school system plans to use modular scheduling in all its schools starting next fall. A news release is issued to newspapers, and a letter is written to parents and to various civic organizations to inform the public of this new development.

5. A growing university has changed its name from Bowdark Teachers College to Bowdark University of Arts and Sciences. The university's PR department writes a special letter to the alumni of the institution in order to inform them of the school's new name.

6. A newspaper reports that several accidents have been caused by defective XYZ-77 tires. The XYZ Corporation prepares a news release helping customers to identify the specific tires in question and outlining how they may then be checked or replaced. In addition, XYZ writes to its retailers and to all customers who have bought its "77" model tire.

The public relations specialist tries to win friends and customers when faced with the opportunity to:

Promote a new business.
Invite someone to open a charge account.
Announce a special privilege or service to preferred customers.
Offer special incentives to charge customers to stimulate their use of their credit cards.
Welcome new residents (new *potential customers*) to the community.
Congratulate someone for an achievement.
Invite someone to a lecture, art show, demonstration, or film.

Remind a customer about an upcoming holiday.
Thank someone for his or her business.

Let's take a closer look at some of these special PR opportunities.

Promoting a New Business

To promote a new business, the first step toward establishing good public opinion is to announce the grand opening—for example, in a letter such as this:

MAY WE INTRODUCE YOU TO—

Colleen Fielder

manager of Chalon Hills' newest and most unusual specialty shop for women:

TRÈS CHIC BOUTIQUE

located in El Camino Real Shopping Square, Devonshire Road and Pillar Drive. Perhaps you already know Colleen. She grew up in the city and attended Southeastern University, where she majored in Fashion Arts and Business Administration.

Many of the new fashions you will find at TRÈS CHIC BOUTIQUE were designed by Colleen herself. Her staff will be on hand at all times to ensure that you always get the proper fitting and the styling that most becomes you. You'll also find a large selection of ready-made fashions in the latest styles to suit every occasion.

Do drop by to say hello to Colleen at TRÈS CHIC BOUTIQUE. She will be glad to see her old friends and to meet new ones at Chalon Hills' loveliest new shopping spot.

Cordially yours,

This letter alone, however, is only one step in a PR campaign. To effectively promote this grand opening requires newspaper ads, spot announcements on local radio stations, circulars, and press releases, all focused on the general theme and tone of this letter. Together, these messages make up a PR campaign that will surely reach the residents in the Très Chic Boutique area.

Then, to continue the campaign, the Très Chic Boutique would send a thank-you letter to each person who visited the store. Note how this follow-up letter continues to build on the image of the Très Chic Boutique as a unique store for women's fashions.

Dear _____:

Thank you for visiting TRÈS CHIC BOUTIQUE this week. We are pleased to welcome you as a new customer, and we are delighted that you gave us an opportunity to show you some of the newest designs in women's wear.

Whatever your needs in women's wear, be assured that your choices from TRÈS CHIC will always be of superior quality.

Careful attention by an efficient, courteous staff ensures you of clothes that fit you perfectly. Whatever your needs—a resort dress, a business suit, or an exclusive gown for a special occasion—we are prepared to cater to your every fashion wish.

Stop by frequently and browse. You will see new selections each time you visit, for only by moving our stock quickly can we keep one step ahead of the fashion market.

Cordially,

To continue the momentum, soon after its grand opening the Très Chic Boutique might send out an announcement of something special—perhaps a fashion show. The opening paragraph of the announcement might start like this:

In response to popular demand, TRÈS CHIC BOUTIQUE is pleased to announce a daily fashion showing of its latest creations. While dining at the Larkspur Restaurant in Chalon Hills, between 12 and 2 p.m., watch the lovely models who will circulate throughout the dining room, showing the newest TRÈS CHIC fashions.

Through these PR communications, the Très Chic Boutique capitalizes on every opportunity to put its name before potential customers in a favorable light.

Encouraging Charge Account Use

Because so many sales today are charge account sales, public relations is often employed to increase credit card use. The end result of increased credit card use is, of course, *sales*.

One obvious step toward increasing credit card use is to invite cash customers to open a charge account. The invitation letter will include, of course, an application form. From time to time, the store may have employees hand out applications as customers enter.

Another way to increase credit card use through public relations letters is to create a special occasion "for charge card customers only." Because charge customers buy more than cash customers and return to the store again and again, it is to the store's advantage to develop a sale exclusively for charge customers. Note the following letter:

Dear Mrs. Ferrara:

You are invited to a special courtesy shopping day at Bender's next Friday, April 7. As a valued charge customer, you will enjoy double privileges. In the splendor of the Tropical Promenade on the fourth floor, you will sip complimentary refreshments while you see a preview of the latest Milan fashions. You will also be entitled to make purchases in every department at special bonus savings not advertised to the public.

The fashions to be modeled will not be placed on our selling floors until April 22. We want you, a valued charge customer of Bender's, to have first choice. Your Bender Charge Card is your ticket to this spectacular shopping event. Tell your friends about this exclusive event if you must—but please come alone. This special show and sale is just for YOU from your friends at Bender's.

Cordially yours,

A well-run business knows not only its most frequent charge customers but also its least frequent charge customers. Yet another way to encourage charge account purchasing, therefore, is to aim a special letter at credit card holders who seldom use their cards. One clever writer developed this unique, intriguing letter for inactive charge card holders:

Dear Customer:

You've	
Earned	
50¢	Is it worth 50 cents a line to you to read this
$1.00	letter?
1.50	We'll gladly pay you that amount—but only if you
2.00	read the entire letter.
2.50	Now, we reason this way: You really are a valued
3.00	customer. But lately you haven't been in even to say
3.50	"Hello." We would like you to come back; we would
4.00	like to see you often; we would like you to reopen
4.50	your account. We think that it is better for us to
5.00	have a longtime customer like you on our books
5.50	than a new customer whom we don't know. And
6.00	since it would cost us at least $12 to open a *new* ac-
6.50	count, we would rather pass this amount to you.
7.00	So we say, "Here is a $12 credit on the house."
7.50	Come in and select anything you wish from our ex-
8.00	tensive stock of nationally advertised clothing and
8.50	shoes for the entire family. Invest in that household
9.00	appliance—food processor, microwave oven—you
9.50	have been dreaming about. Or do your gift shopping
10.00	early for such items as diamonds, watches, stereos,
10.50	and glassware.
11.00	The enclosed credit, worth $12, is your down pay-
11.50	ment.
$12.00	Why not come in tomorrow?

Cordially yours,

Handling Other Special Opportunities

The sharp businessperson has an eye for opportunities to improve public relations—and takes advantage of those opportunities. For example, a clothing store manager with a list of names of newborns might take the opportunity to congratulate the proud parents with this letter:

Dear Mark:

You're a mighty discerning young man to have chosen the parents you did, and that's why I'm writing this letter to you instead of them. Congratulations!

Here's your first pair of long pants. A little early, perhaps, but I want you to get used to coming to Hayden's for all your clothing needs. Your dad has been a friend of ours for some time now. We like to think he is well satisfied with his purchases, and we hope you'll bring him in to see us often.

Tell you what: If you'll come in with your dad one year from now (I'll remind you), I'll have a present for you that you can really use.

Sincerely,

Note how the following letter stimulates holiday sales:

Dear Dad:

Mind if we slip a small string around that middle finger of your left hand?

Not that we think you're absentminded. Far from it. But just in case the press of business has made you suffer a temporary lapse of memory, we thought it would be helpful to remind you that May 12 is Mother's Day. You hadn't forgotten? Good.

We know you'll also remember that Peterson's is the store where Mother would purchase her own gift if she were doing the shopping. We have all those lovely things that women appreciate—jewelry, boudoir sets, manicure sets, leather-crafted desk sets, luxurious handbags, elegant luggage.

Drop in this week for a chat with our Mrs. Mendez. From years of experience, Mrs. Mendez knows the gifts that women cherish forever. She can help you choose the perfect gift for this occasion.

Cordially yours,

For examples of how to *create* special occasions, see the letters illustrated on pages 429 and 430.

EVERYDAY PUBLIC RELATIONS OPPORTUNITIES

Unless your job is in the Public Relations Department, you may not have all the "special" PR opportunities that have been discussed so far. But the techniques you learned will be useful, because you *will* have everyday opportunities to improve public relations for your company.

Whenever you reply to routine requests, for example, you will have opportunities to build your company's image. In Section 43,

the sports shop

101 East Adams
Chicago, Illinois 60603
(312) 555-1234

January 2, 19--

Ms. Francine Byrd
21 Victor Street
Mankato, MN 56001

Dear Ms. Byrd:

Let's talk about golf. Yes, I know that there's snow on the ground
and not a leaf on the trees. The fairways aren't fair, and the
temperature is unmerciful.

But January is golden weather at The Sports Shop. The floor is abloom
with the most fantastic selection of golf balls, clubs, bags, shoes,
carts, jackets, caps--everything you can imagine. Come stand under
our palm tree and see our fresh white rows of golf balls, the
roll-a-way Bermuda Rug putting green, the warm, gleaming woods, and
the sunny golf fashions. Once the golfers in your family get their
hands on these, can spring be far behind?

To make The Sports Shop even warmer, we've slashed prices by 25
percent. Why not come down and get a little bit of spring right now,
at our fabulous Spring-in-January sale.

Sincerely yours,

Conway Isaacson

Conway Isaacson
Manager

The Sports Shop *creates* a special occasion—a "Spring-in-January" sale!

DePAUL FINANCE COMPANY
(201) 555-9580 Route 22 Mountainside, New Jersey 07092

June 12, 19--

Mrs. J. P. Crane
120 Raritan Road
Scotch Plains, NJ 07076

Dear Mrs. Crane:

Congratulations--your Chevrolet sedan is all yours as of today. The
enclosed canceled note is evidence that you've made all the payments.

You don't owe us any more payments, but we feel we owe you this one
last statement--a statement of how pleased we are with you as a
customer. You made every payment right on time. We hope you'll call
on us again whenever you need financing.

The enclosed certificate entitles you to preferred credit privileges
at the lowest available rates. Just present this certificate to any
of our branch offices for fast service on loans of any kind. As long
as we have money to lend, we'll be pleased to help you.

Cordially yours,

Karen Ann LoPresti

Mrs. Karen Anne LoPresti
Vice President

ge

The writer makes an opportunity to contact a former customer and thank her for her patronage—and, at the same time, reminds her that she has credit privileges with DePaul Finance Company the next time she is thinking of making a purchase that will require financing.

"Answering Requests," you read the following paragraph in a routine reply:

> Mr. D'Aguilera, the enclosed booklet includes a list of all the specific items that are covered by our service contract. In fact, it also lists (in equally large print) the few items that are *not* covered in the contract, so that there will be no "surprises" if something should happen to the product; you will know exactly what is covered. The Walton management insists that we stand behind all our products and that we inform our customers precisely *how* we stand behind our products. By doing so, we avoid the unfortunate experience that you described in your letter.

Note that the writer does not *sell a product* here; the writer *sells the company*. In other words, the writer employs good public relations techniques in replying to a routine request for information.

Assume that you are working for a Florida hotel that specializes in convention meetings. You might have the opportunity to write a letter such as this to a valued customer:

> Dear Mr. Klein:
>
> All of us here appreciate your thinking of the Pompano Gardens Inn as *the* place to hold your annual sales conventions. Thank you for the compliment!
>
> For several years now, you have used our facilities to host your special dinners, to demonstrate products to customers, to train your new representatives, and to lodge your employees and guests whenever they are in our area. We do, indeed, make special efforts to make all your meetings successful, because your appreciation of our efforts always shows.
>
> Mr. Klein, we sincerely enjoy serving you, your employees, and your customers. Thank you for doing business with us.
>
> Cordially yours,

As you see, then, public relations is part of every letter you write for your company. When you write your letters, even *routine* letters, look for ways to incorporate the good public relations techniques discussed in this section.

COMMUNICATION PROJECTS

Practical Application

A. Suppose that you are a college graduate with five years of business experience either as (1) a secretary in an attorney's office, (2) a travel agent in a large agency, or (3) a tax accountant in a public accounting firm.

You decide to set up your own (1) public stenographer's office, (2) travel agency, or (3) tax accounting business. You choose to begin promoting your new business by writing a letter and sending it to 100 businesses in the community. You wish to emphasize both your business experience and your excellent college education. Write a letter that includes all the details that will improve your chances of succeeding in your own new business.

B.   Develop a letter that encourages charge customers of a retail store to use their charge accounts. Use your ingenuity in making the letter different from others you have seen.

C.   You are the manager of Trendy's Department Store. Trendy's has always provided charge cards without charging any fee other than interest. Extremely high interest rates and tight credit force you to introduce a $10 annual fee for charge cards in order to cover Trendy's own increased borrowing costs. Write a letter explaining this new store policy tactfully. *Remember:* Your customers have for years been accustomed to paying no fee, and you are imposing the fee through no fault of the customers.

D.   You work for Newlook Decorators, an interior decorating firm that is introducing a new line of furniture and decorations this spring. A special preview showing of the new line is planned for charge customers, including family and friends, at the Newlook showroom, 657 Woodside Avenue, March 21, from six until nine in the evening. You are assigned to write a letter of invitation. Admission will be by ticket only, and you are enclosing a ticket with each invitation. The general public will not see the new line until March 28. Write a letter that makes the most of this occasion.

E.   You are manager of Rexroth's Hardware Store, an established firm on the outskirts of a large city. Traditionally, your customers have come from the city. New towns and neighborhoods are springing up beyond city limits, however, and you are looking for a way to develop business with the residents of these new areas. You decide to write a letter, enclosing a discount coupon worth $5, that invites each resident of the new areas to visit your store. Write an appealing invitation addressed to new residents.

Editing Practice

Editing to Improve Writing Techniques. Edit the following sentences to improve any poor writing techniques.

1.   Arriving at 10 a.m., I told Tim that he should allow more travel time in order to avoid being late again.
2.   Did you learn why the charge customers returned their monthly statement?
3.   Ellen borrowed the stapler which was on my desk.
4.   Judy said she couldn't find any stamps for the letters after looking in the desk drawers.

5. You may use either of these four calculators to help with the bookkeeping.
6. In order to prepare the invoice, all the figures will be needed by you.
7. Within two days after I sent my complaint to Ms. Carruthers, a reply was received from her.
8. There is no future for the business communicator who is careless or indifferent to the techniques of writing.
9. The mail would lie in the out-basket for hours and sometimes days.
10. Our engineers have made many improvements in design, and so we shall be able to produce a better product.
11. The committee must complete the research, assembling of facts, and writing the report.
12. In his writing, Ed consistently used unnecessarily big words, thus making his communications ineffective.
13. Perry always has and always will be late for meetings.
14. Sylvia is one of the best if not the best secretaries in the office.
15. He felt the facts should determine his reply.

Plurals and Possessives. Indicate the correct plural or possessive forms of the words enclosed in parentheses.

1. The Wood Building has only (attorney) offices on the first 20 floors.
2. (Marie and Laura) telephone, which they share, is on Marie's desk.
3. All the (secretary) in this company speak Spanish fluently.
4. The two (general manager) reports were in agreement.
5. My (boss) desk is always cleared at the end of the day.
6. Each employee received a box of (handkerchief) at Christmas.
7. All the (analysis) that have been submitted support this recommendation.
8. Each choir member sang two (solo).
9. The (President-elect) room was provided as a courtesy by the hotel.
10. For good investments, buy stock in public (utility).
11. (Children) excess energy often gets them into trouble.
12. Dr. Knowles is a man (who) experience is highly regarded.
13. All notices of employment opportunities in the department are posted on (it) bulletin board.
14. Many (chintz) are used for making curtains.
15. The (Lynch) are not remodeling their downtown store.

Case Problem

Making Statistics Meaningful. As an employee of the public relations department, Nora Nadel is responsible for taking visitors through the company plant and for telling them facts and figures about the company. Here is part of the talk she uses on her tours: "Five years ago, we had only 127 production workers. Today, we have 1270. Five years ago, we produced 19,550 timers each year. Today, the workers produce 247,000 timers annually. Five years ago, we were losing $1000 a week. This year, our profits will be about $250,000." These facts are an important part of Nora's presentation, but they are difficult for visitors to grasp because of the way in which Nora presents them.

Can you present the facts in such a way that visitors will grasp them more readily?

46

WRITING SOCIAL-BUSINESS MESSAGES

When you buy a new car or a new home, start a new business, get a promotion, or get married, you expect your lifelong friends and your closest relatives to congratulate you—to show somehow that they share the joy of the occasion. On the other hand, if you suffer the loss of a parent, you expect those same friends and all your other close relatives to show their sympathy for your loss of a loved one. Common courtesy and tradition demand that people communicate their congratulations or their sorrow in these instances.

In business, likewise, common courtesy and tradition demand that business workers congratulate one another on special occasions, send letters of condolence when a business associate suffers the loss of a loved one, reply properly to a formal invitation, write a thank-you note for a special favor or gift, and so on. Just as you would appreciate hearing from your coworkers and business associates in these situations, you should let them hear from you whenever appropriate.

Writing *social-business communications,* as they are called, is considered difficult only by those people who have had little experience writing such messages. By reading this chapter, studying the sample letters, and practicing the exercises provided, you will prepare yourself to tackle all your social-business correspondence and develop your messages expertly.

SOCIAL-BUSINESS LETTER FORMAT

As you learned in Section 41, the *format* of a letter refers to the arrangement of letter parts on the page.

On Company Letterhead

For a social-business letter typed on company letterhead, use the social-business letter format illustrated on page 436. As you see, this social-business letter format has all letter parts in the "usual" position *except the inside address,* which is placed last, positioned at the bottom of the page. In addition to this format change, the social-business letter has a change in the "usual" punctuation pattern for business letters: The salutation ends with a comma rather a colon. (Reference initials, copy notations, and so on, are not included.)

Some companies provide *monarch* letterhead or *baronial* letterhead for social-business and other letters. (Monarch stationery measures 7¼ by 10½ inches; baronial, 5½ by 8½ inches.) Many people consider these sizes especially fitting for executive correspondence.

In either case, if you are using monarch or baronial letterhead, follow the same format described for standard-size stationery. (Note that for baronial stationery, a shorter line length—say, 4 inches—must be used.) See page 437 for an illustration of a social-business letter typed on monarch stationery.

On Plain Stationery

When a social-business letter is typed on plain stationery, follow the same format as for personal-business letters, but use a comma after the salutation. See the letters illustrated on pages 438 and 439.

CONGRATULATIONS LETTERS

Special honors and special events provide ideal PR opportunities. They present you with an appropriate occasion to say "Congratulations!" Your reader will appreciate your thoughtfulness, and you will certainly score points in your favor and your company's. Remember: Everyone wants to be respected and admired, and a congratulatory message shows your respect and admiration for someone's accomplishment or recognition.

For Promotions

Suppose you read in a trade magazine that Laura Tipton, a woman who worked in your bank a few years ago, was promoted to vice president for Willow Grove Bank & Trust Company. During the

Prepared in block
stationery. Note t
tion.

three years that you worked together, you and she were friendly. Since she left, you have seen her at various banking industry meetings and conventions, the two of you have served together on a banking industry committee, and you have had lunch with her from time to time. Should you send her a note congratulating her on her promotion? Of course!

Your note might follow this example:

Dear Laura,

How delighted I was to read in *The Banking Journal* that you were recently promoted to Vice President of Willow Grove Bank & Trust. Congratulations!

Having had the pleasure of working with you, I know very well that you worked hard for and fully earned that promotion. I also know that there isn't a nicer person in the entire banking industry. For both reasons, I'm truly happy for you.

Needless to say, Laura, I wish you success in your new position. I know that I'll be hearing more good news about you *soon*.

                    Sincerely,

The message is clear: You really *are* pleased by Laura's good fortune. You are sure to make her happy—and solidify a business friendship.

The degree of friendliness or informality of your congratulatory note will depend on the specific relationship you have with the reader. For two more examples of similar congratulatory notes (one more formal and the other more friendly), see the letters illustrated on pages 437 and 438.

Congratulatory letters are also written to employees of the same company. In fact, it is virtually *mandatory* for executives to acknowledge promotions of employees in the company. The following letter is obviously written to a valued employee:

Dear Preston,

Congratulations to you on your promotion to District Manager. You certainly are "the right person for the right job."

Nancy Kelly has been talking about promoting you to this position since she became Marketing Manager six months ago. All of us in management are equally convinced that you will be able to continue to turn in the high sales volume that the Southern District is well known for.

In any case, Preston, I certainly am happy to welcome you to the sales management team for our Consumer Division, and I wish you success in your new position.

                    Sincerely,

Prepared i
(1) the insi
a colon. T

For Anniversaries

A coworker's anniversary also calls for a written congratulations. Note the friendliness and informality—and the sincerity—of this letter:

Dear Paul,

Congratulations on your tenth year with Wolfson Products Inc. I remember your first day with the company, when Andy Graves introduced you to me and my staff. When Andy retired one year later, I *knew* that you were the right person to replace him—and you've continued to prove that for the last nine years.

Paul, I think you know just how pleased I've been to have the opportunity to work with you for ten years. Thanks to your manufacturing expertise and management leadership, the Production Department is the best in the industry. My staff and I appreciate your fine work. You certainly help make things easier for the rest of us!

Cordially yours,

For Retirements

The retirement of a coworker or of a business associate also deserves recognition. Retirement letters also deserve extra care; unless you are sure that the person *welcomes* retiring, you must be sensitive in writing the note.

Dear Freida,

What will Reynolds Publishing be like without you? Our authors, our suppliers, and of course all our coworkers have come to depend on that smiling face, that cheerful voice, and that friendly attitude whenever we approach the Graphic Arts Department. It seemed as if you were always there to help a lost visitor, to reroute a messenger, and to answer the phone when no one else was around. I know that you *were* always there to help me.

Thank you, Freida, for all you did to help me since the first day I joined the company. All my best wishes to you in your retirement. I hope that you will enjoy many, many years of health and happiness with your family and your numerous friends. I hope, too, that you will visit us from time to time.

Sincerely,

For Individual Honors

When a business friend or associate has been named, appointed, or elected to a special position, show your congratulations with a message such as the one illustrated on page 438.

For Company Recognition

A congratulatory letter to another company or organization is appropriate when, for example, the firm receives a special civic award, builds a new headquarters office, or (as illustrated on page 439) acknowledges a special milestone—in this case, the 100th anniversary of a family-owned company.

THANK-YOU LETTERS

During our daily interaction with people, we always have many opportunities to say "thank you." A special occasion, however, requires a *written* thank-you—for example, when we receive a gift, hospitality, or special courtesy from a business associate.

For Gifts

Business executives may receive gifts from suppliers and vendors. When they do, courtesy demands that they write a thank-you note to the giver.

Dear Warren,

Thank you for your thoughtfulness in sending me such a beautifully bound edition of *The History of the Theater*. You certainly selected a book of very special interest to me, as you very well know. Since I received your package late Friday afternoon, I have done little else but read, read, read. Admittedly, I spent lots of time on the pictures too!

Warren, my sincere appreciation to you for your kindness. You may be sure that I will enjoy this book again and again and again.

Cordially yours,

Some companies have policies prohibiting employees from accepting such gifts under any circumstances. If your firm has such a policy, you will of course adhere to it. Your thank-you letter, then, will obviously require a different approach.

Dear Warren,

Thank you for your thoughtfulness in sending me such a beautifully bound edition of *The History of the Theater*. You certainly selected a book of very special interest to me, as you very well know.

I wish, Warren, that company policy permitted me to keep this thoughtful gift, but we have a specific policy that prohibits my doing so. Therefore, when I have completed reading the book, I will give it to the company library with this inscription: "Donated to the Owens-Mandel Library by Ridgefield Printers Inc."

My sincere appreciation to you for your kindness. You may be sure that I will borrow this book from the library *often;* when I do, I will remember your thoughtfulness.

Cordially yours,

For Hospitality

A business associate's hospitality is not to be taken for granted. Even if the person is also an employee of your company, he or she still deserves a thank-you letter for special hospitality.

Dear Mrs. Erickson,

Thank you for the many courtesies extended to me on my recent visit to Mill Valley. My stay was certainly much more pleasant because of your thoughtfulness in arranging for my comfort.

The high spot of the entire visit was the evening spent in your beautiful home. You and Mr. Erickson are most gracious hosts. The food was excellent; the conversation, stimulating; the people, delightful. The time passed so quickly that I was embarrassed to find that I had stayed so long—so engrossed and comfortable was I in being part of such good company.

I have mailed you a small package as a little token of my appreciation for the many kindnesses shown me. I shall not soon forget my visit to Mill Valley.

Sincerely yours,

For Courtesies

When you receive a letter congratulating you for a promotion, an honor, a special recognition, or an achievement, you should acknowledge the letter with a thank-you. For example:

Dear Roger,

You were very thoughtful to write me about my recent promotion. One of the most satisfying things about being promoted is that one often gets such pleasant letters from the nicest people! I already like my new job very much, and I know that I will enjoy it even more after I have really become accustomed to this completely different work.

Thank you, Roger, for all your good wishes and your thoughtfulness. About that offer to be of assistance—I may be calling on you sooner than you expect, so be prepared!

Sincerely,

For Recommendations

Many businesses flourish almost solely on the basis of the recommendations of clients, friends, suppliers, and other business associates. When someone recommends you or your firm, he or she is doing you a special favor—a favor that certainly deserves a thank-you letter.

Dear Mr. Martinez,

This morning we visited Mr. Bruce Stargell of Stargell's Sports Center Inc. Mr. Stargell mentioned your recommendation when he placed an order for display and storage equipment for his chain of new stores that he will open this fall.

We thank you, Mr. Martinez, for recommending us to Mr. Stargell. We appreciate the order immensely, but not one bit more than we appreciate your confidence in us. You have paid us the highest form of compliment. Please accept our thanks for this favor. I assure you, we will repay your kindness at the earliest opportunity, which we hope will be soon.

Cordially yours,

The Sales Executives' Club

requests the pleasure of your company
at a formal showing
of its new film
"Selling the American Dream"
Tuesday, the tenth of May
at eight o'clock
Cavalier Room of the Century Hotel

R.S.V.P.

A printed formal invitation.

Mr. and Mrs. Delbert Anderson
request the pleasure of
Mr. and Mrs. Peter De Merrit's company
at a dinner party
on Saturday, the Fourth of July
at eight o'clock
5208 Lupin Drive

R.S.V.P.   Telephone 555-7116

A handwritten formal invitation.

CONDOLENCE LETTERS

When business associates and friends suffer tragedies or misfortunes, common courtesy requires you to communicate your sympathy with a condolence letter. (Depending on your specific relationship, you may send a printed sympathy card.)

Condolence letters are difficult to write simply because it *is* difficult to console and comfort someone who has recently suffered a tragic loss. For the same reason, however, they are always very much appreciated. You may type a condolence letter, but if you really wish to give your letter a personal touch, write it in longhand.

> Dear Carl,
>
> The news of your brother's untimely death yesterday has stunned and saddened me. I know that you have suffered a great loss. Please accept my sincere sympathy.
>
> When my mother died last year, a friend sent me a copy of Dylan Thomas's poem "And Death Shall Have No Dominion." I found the poem a source of consolation again and again. I hope the poem will serve you as well as it did me. My heart goes out to you and your family in your time of grief.
>
> Sincerely yours,

FORMAL INVITATIONS AND REPLIES

From time to time, business people receive formal invitations to such events as an open house, a special reception to honor a distinguished person, a special anniversary, or a formal social gathering. Such invitations are usually engraved or printed and are written in the third person.

The illustrations on pages 444–446 show the formal printed invi-

> Ms. Audrey Brennan
> accepts with pleasure
> the kind invitation of
> The Sales Executives' Club
> for Tuesday, the tenth of May

A handwritten reply accepting an invitation.

Mr. and Mrs. Peter De Merrit
regret that a previous engagement
prevents their accepting
Mr. and Mrs. Anderson's
kind invitation
for the Fourth of July

A handwritten reply refusing an invitation.

tation, the formal handwritten invitation, the handwritten accept-ance, and the handwritten refusal. An acceptance or a refusal is occasionally typewritten; however, this practice is not recom-mended. Handwritten invitations and replies are written on personal stationery or special note-size stationery. Plain white notepaper may also be used.

COMMUNICATION PROJECTS

Practical Application

A.   You are president of a medium-sized company, Starbuckle Dec-orative Metals. When informed that one of the company's oldest employees, bookkeeper Carl Wickford, is retiring after thirty years with Starbuckle, you genuinely want to thank him for such long service. You decide to write a letter thanking Mr. Wickford for his years with the company and to enclose a check for $200. Write the letter.

B.   Marianne Mullinix was a classmate of yours in college. You read in the newspapers that Marianne, after only three years at Destry Investing, has been chosen Outstanding Financial Analyst. Marianne's reward is twofold: a promotion to assistant director of financial analysis and an expense-paid tour of the Orient. Write a letter of congratulation to Marianne on her achievements.

C.   You have just returned from a business trip to Louisville, Kentucky. During your three-day stay in Louisville, you were the house guest of Barbara and Peter Lembo, longtime friends of your family. Barbara even met you at the airport and insisted on personally driving you to your business appointments, rather than having you experience the difficulty of getting around a strange city in a rented car. (Taxi drivers were on strike during the time you were in Louisville.) Write a note of thanks to the Lembos, who live at 87 Mark Twain Drive, Louisville, Kentucky 40204. Today you ordered a gift to be sent them as a small token of your appreciation.

D.   You have just learned of the illness and death of Mrs. Frederick Olson, the wife of one of your company's suppliers who has become a friend of yours. In addition to Mr. Olson, Mrs. Olson (Helga) leaves a married daughter (Anne) and three young grandchildren, Tom, Alex, and Inga. Write a letter of condolence to Frederick Olson, Director of Marketing for Ludlow Manufacturing, 668 West Ludlow, St. Louis, Missouri 63399.

Editing Practice

Editing for Redundancies.   Eliminate all unnecessary repetitions in the sentences below.

1.   We are planning to revert back to personal contact as our main sales strategy.
2.   The expense accounts submitted by Lois and Maury are both alike.
3.   The report was supplied free, gratis.
4.   By the time I arrived, the inspection was over with.
5.   The manager refused to repeat his remarks again for the employees who arrived late.
6.   The desk will fit just inside of the entrance.
7.   Past experience shows that Fred is habitually late.
8.   Clean your typing element daily, as otherwise you will not get sharp copy.

Case Problem

Listening for Essential Ideas.   Your instructor will read an article to you. Listen carefully; then summarize the article in as few words as possible.

47

USING FORM LETTERS AND BOILERPLATE

You have learned that writing quality business communications takes much time and effort. Because time and effort cost money, many companies look for acceptable ways to reduce the amount spent. One very good way to reduce writing costs is to use form letters. *Form letters* are letters in which the same message is sent to many addressees. Sometimes details of the message, called *variables,* change from letter to letter. Sometimes form letters are composed by combining various prewritten paragraphs, called *boilerplate,* into a particular communication.

ADVANTAGES OF USING FORM LETTERS

Here are the major advantages of using form letters.

1. Using form letters saves time in planning, dictating, and transcribing.
2. Executives can respond more quickly to routine writing situations. This means that the receiver gets an answer sooner.
3. The content quality will be better. Much time and thought can go into writing the form letters.
4. Fewer errors will result, because the spelling, punctuation, and grammar have to be approved only once.
5. When prepared on automated equipment, form letters and paragraphs do not have to be rekeyboarded. They are simply selected and printed.

DISADVANTAGES OF USING FORM LETTERS

As with most good ideas, there are some disadvantages. Here are three:

1. Some of the "personal touch" can be lost in mass-producing letters. Attempts should be made to make letters more personal. You could, for example, include the person's name within a sentence. "I look forward to seeing you, Mr. Ashton, Friday, at 2 p.m."

2. If readers find out that they have received a form letter, they may feel somewhat disappointed. A manager, for example, wrote you a congratulatory message when your son finished college. You felt good about the letter until your coworker showed you one exactly like it. His daughter finished college. The purpose of the letter was goodwill, and the goodwill was lost.
3. Using form letters and boilerplate can be abused. Some business writers try to use them when they are inappropriate or do not quite fit the writing situation.

TYPES OF FORM LETTERS

Executives often find that they are repeatedly writing the same content in response to frequently occurring—almost identical—writing situations. When this happens, they should invest some time and effort in developing general responses that can be used and reused. These general responses fall into three main categories.

Form letters
Form letters with variables
Form letters with boilerplate paragraphs

Form Letters

Form letters are used to respond to identical situations. The letter shown on page 450 would be used to respond to any general inquiries about fall bus tours. The entire body of the letter remains the same; the date, inside address, and salutation are the only changes. These letter parts are highlighted in the example.

Form Letters With Variables

Form letters with variables are used when similar, but not identical, responses are needed. In addition to the date, inside address, and salutation, other details are changed throughout the body of the letter. These changes are called *variables*. On page 451, the letter on the left shows the form letter with the variables highlighted. The letter on the right is in finished form, with specific information added for the variables.

To simplify requests for form letters and form letters with variables, printed request forms are used. The example shown on page 452 requests Form Letter B, which uses variables. List the variables in the order in which they should appear in the letter.

Form Letters With Boilerplate Paragraphs

For similar writing situations that occur frequently but vary in content, experienced business communicators use form or boilerplate paragraphs. Paragraphs are written that cover most of the repetitive writing situations. Each paragraph has a number. Instead of dictating each letter, the executive gives the transcriber the date, inside address, salutation, and a list of paragraphs (by number). Sample boilerplate and a letter are shown on page 453.

Current Date

Name
Address
City, State ZIP Code

Salutation

Thank you for asking about our fall bus tours through the New
England states. Our "Fall Color Tours," as
our most popular excursions.

Enclosed is our brochure that lists the
tours. The pictures will give you an idea o
views and the historical sites that you will

Please complete and return the enclosed
as possible. Space is limited, and the tour

You owe yourself a luxurious trip. We
details. All you have to do is have a good

Sincerely,

TERRIFIC

Betty Wea
Manager

??
Enclosure

"TERRIFIC TOURS, INC."

Post Office Box 2310   Atlanta, Georgia 30301 (404) 555-8124

May 21, 19--

Mrs. Melody Larson
3628 Oakwood Road
Atlanta, GA 30306

Dear Mrs. Larson:

Thank you for asking about our fall bus tours through the New
England states. Our "Fall Color Tours," as we call them, are some of
our most popular excursions.

Enclosed is our brochure that lists the dates and costs of the
tours. The pictures will give you an idea of some of the breathtaking
views and the historical sites that you will enjoy.

Please complete and return the enclosed reservation form as soon
as possible. Space is limited, and the tours are filling fast.

You owe yourself a luxurious trip. We take care of all the
details. All you have to do is have a good time!

Sincerely,

TERRIFIC TOURS, INC.

(Ms.) Betty Weaver

Betty Weaver
Manager

dk
Enclosure

This is Form Letter A of Terrific Tours, Inc. The body of the letter remains the same; only the highlighted date line, inside address, salutation, and reference initials change.

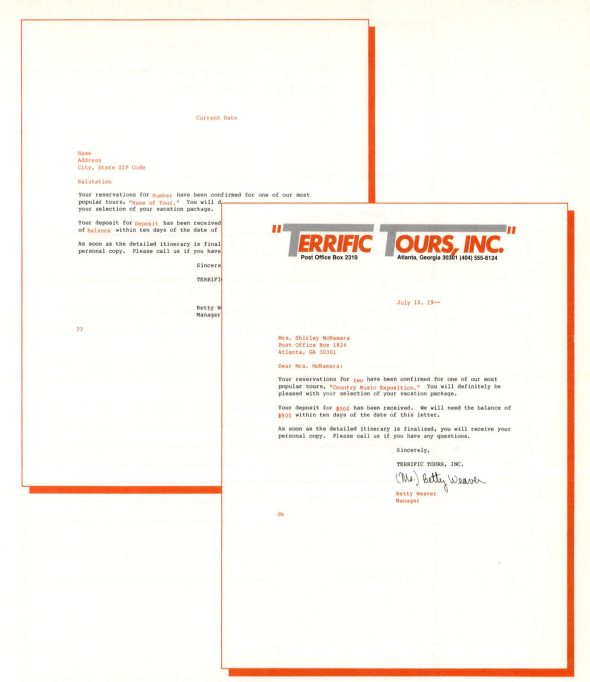

Current Date

Name
Address
City, State ZIP Code

Salutation

Your reservations for Number have been confirmed for one of our most
popular tours, "Name of Tour." You will d
your selection of your vacation package.

Your deposit for Deposit has been received
of Balance within ten days of the date of

As soon as the detailed itinerary is final
personal copy. Please call us if you have

Sincere

TERRIFIC

Betty W
Manager

??

"TERRIFIC TOURS, INC."
Post Office Box 2310   Atlanta, Georgia 30301 (404) 555-8124

July 10, 19--

Mrs. Shirley McNamara
Post Office Box 1824
Atlanta, GA 30301

Dear Mrs. McNamara:

Your reservations for two have been confirmed for one of our most
popular tours, "Country Music Exposition." You will definitely be
pleased with your selection of your vacation package.

Your deposit for $500 has been received. We will need the balance of
$900 within ten days of the date of this letter.

As soon as the detailed itinerary is finalized, you will receive your
personal copy. Please call us if you have any questions.

Sincerely,

TERRIFIC TOURS, INC.

(Ms.) Betty Weaver

Betty Weaver
Manager

dk

Form Letter B of Terrific Tours, Inc., has variables in the *body* of the letter. The
highlighted items are those that change from letter to letter.

CHAPTER
TEN
PREPARING REPORTS AND SPECIAL COMMUNICATIONS

48

WRITING MEMORANDUM REPORTS

In the business world, a report is probably the primary method for providing information. This information is intended to help executives, supervisors, managers, department heads, and others to perform their duties. Likewise, many of these people also write reports to supply others with essential information. Therefore, anyone who wishes to succeed in today's business world must be able to prepare reports.

A report may be given orally, but usually it is written. Any important information should be in written form so that there is some record that may be useful sometime in the future. "Put it in writing" is the basic principle behind most reports.

The values of a written report, compared with an oral one, are obvious. An oral report may be misunderstood. Much of an oral report may be quickly forgotten, especially statistical data. Even a forceful oral report will grow weaker with each passing day, whereas a written report can be referred to again and again. With each reading, the reader reinforces the message conveyed in the report. Moreover, a precise and permanent record exists in the report itself.

One way to classify reports is according to the length of the report—*informal* (shorter reports) and *formal* (longer) reports. Because formal reports usually require extensive research, documentation, investigation, and analysis, the style of the presentation is usually different from the style used for a short report. You will learn how to prepare a formal report in Section 49. But first you will learn how to prepare an informal report, the type you will probably prepare most often, at least in the early years of your career.

STYLE OF INFORMAL REPORTS

In Chapter 8, you learned how to use a memorandum as a means of corresponding with other employees within an organization. The same memorandum form is used for writing informal reports, hence the name *memorandum report*.

The memorandum report begins with the same information that was included in the memorandum you learned to use for interoffice correspondence:

To:
From:
Date:
Subject:

Whether you use this exact form or adapt it will depend upon the circumstances under which you are working at the time you are preparing the report. *How* you use the above outline will depend on a number of variables.

To

The way you address the person to whom the report is going depends primarily upon the degree of formality or informality of your office atmosphere. For instance, if everybody addresses the boss by his or her first name and the boss approves, and if the report is of a personal nature, you might write:

To: Al Powers

But suppose you know that the report will be read by other persons besides the boss or that the report will be filed for future reference. Then it would be better to write:

To: Mr. Albert Powers

From

The *From* line should match the tone of the *To* line. For example, the first two lines of a very informal memorandum report written only for the personal information of the boss would appear as:

To: Al Powers
From: Jan Packer

For a report that is not for the exclusive information of the boss or that is to be filed for future reference, a different *From* line would be used. You should keep in mind that all readers are likely to know the boss, but they may not know who you are. Therefore, you might write:

To: Mr. Albert Powers
From: Janice Packer, Administrative Assistant

Subject

The *Subject* line should be a comprehensive, yet clear and precise, statement that will prepare a reader for rapid assimilation of the information given in the report. Composing a good subject line, therefore, requires a high degree of skill. Let's look at some illustrations. Here is a subject line for a credit manager's report to the vice president in charge of credit.

Subject: Credit

Of course, such a subject line would be meaningless to the vice president. One could not tell what the report is really about without reading the report itself. The following line, however, would orient the reader immediately.

Subject: Credit Applications Handled During March 19—

Suppose that you are a personnel director and receive a report with a subject line like this one:

Subject: Employee Absenteeism

Possibly you have forgotten that you asked for a report on some phase of employee absenteeism. If that is the case, the above subject line will not refresh your memory or prepare you to quickly grasp the facts presented in the report. Wouldn't the following subject line be more helpful?

Subject: Causes of Employee Absenteeism, January 19—

Date

Because conditions change so rapidly that facts presented on one date may not be valid at a later date, every report should contain the date on which it was written. And how frustrating to search for a report in the files, a report that could prove very valuable if only you knew when it was written!

Wherever dates are given in the body of a report, those dates must be specific. Instead of writing, "Last Friday, we sent . . . ," you would write, "On Friday, May 10, 19—, we sent . . . ."

Adapting the Memo Form

Although the memo form we have been using is the one most frequently used, there are variations that may sometimes be more appropriate. For example:

Carla Mendoza
March 31, 19—
Causes of Employee Absenteeism, January 19—

This adaptation shows that Carla Mendoza wrote the report and gives the date; but it states the subject as a heading, or title. The assumption is that this report would go only to the person requesting the report and, therefore, requires no additional name. However, if an addressee's name is necessary, the body of the report could start like this:

Mrs. Alvarez: The causes of employee absenteeism in January 19— are as follows:

File Copies

Whenever you write an informal report, even if you think it is not important, be sure to make a copy for your own files. Anything important enough to put in writing is important enough to be retained.

You may never need to refer to your file copy, but you cannot be certain that you or someone else in the company will not need some of the information contained in the report sometime in the future. The best precautionary measure against lost or misaddressed reports is to have in your files a folder marked "Reports," which contains a copy of every report you write.

PLANNING AND WRITING INFORMAL REPORTS

Many people, including some correspondents, think that writing involves merely sitting down and dashing off a few words. This is a false notion that largely accounts for the fact that good business writers are scarce and therefore very much in demand.

Actually, a top-notch writing effort of any kind represents hard work and is the result of much thought, careful planning, and excellent training. For the know-how that will enable you to write informal reports of the very best quality, you need to study, think about, and apply the following principles.

Be Clear, Complete, Correct, and Concise

As you know, writing that is *concise* is not writing that is incomplete. To be concise, you must say everything that needs to be said, but you must say it in the fewest possible words.

You are also well aware that your writing must be clear and complete. You would not write a "fuzzy" sentence like this:

Ms. Olsen told Mrs. Wertz about the overtime situation in the mail room, and she said she would have the report on her desk in a few days.

Instead, you would write a clear, complete, specific message, such as this one:

Ms. Olsen reported to Mrs. Wertz that she would have the report on mail room overtime on Mrs. Wertz's desk on Wednesday, May 18, 19—.

All reports must be correct in every detail. Perhaps we should use the stronger term *accurate*, because any information important enough to be reported must be more than substantially correct; it must be completely accurate. For example, if you are asked to report the number of free-sample requests that come in on a given day, you'd better be sure that you give an exact, not an approximate, count.

Wording

The wording of reports differs from that of letters. A letter is designed to do more than convey a message, for its accompanying purpose is to win new customers or clients for the company and to retain old ones. Therefore, the tone of a letter is warm and friendly. A report, on the other hand, is a straightforward, factual presentation— and it should be worded as such.

As an illustration, read the following opening paragraph of a letter answering a request for information about your company's free tuition program for employees.

> **In response to your April 10 request, we are pleased to tell you that we do provide free tuition for employees taking work-related courses in local schools under the following circumstances: (Then you would itemize and explain the circumstances under which your company pays the tuition for its employees.)**

Now, note how the wording changes when the same information is given in a report:

> **Employees taking work-related courses in local schools will be reimbursed for tuition when the following requirements have been met:**
>
> **1. The course has been approved in advance by the employee's supervisor.**
> **2. The employee earns a grade of "B" or better.**
> **3. The employee has been with this company for one year or more.**

FORMS OF PRESENTATION

How brief or how detailed should your informal report be? Should you give the requested information in a single paragraph? Should you present the information in outline form? For the most effective presentation, should you tabulate the information?

Because you are preparing the report, no one but you can answer these questions. Only you are close enough to the situation to know why the report was requested, to be able to project the probable uses of the information, and so on. To be able to make a wise decision about the form your report should take, though, you must know the types of presentations and the purposes that each best serves.

Paragraph Form

The paragraph form is used for the presentation of a simple fact. For example, if your boss has requested that you report how many hours of overtime were paid the previous month—and you are certain that the only statistic your boss wants is the total number of hours—you might write the following in a memo-style report:

> **In the month of March 19—, the total number of hours of overtime in the Accounting Department was 12 hours.**

Or, if you would like to give a little extra information, you might add to the above statement:

There are 30 employees in the department, and 5 employees (16 percent) accounted for the 12 hours of overtime.

Outline Form

If, however, you know that your boss has a personal interest in the staff, you might correctly believe that you should list the names of the persons who worked overtime. You could present all the information necessary in outline form, as follows:

Information regarding overtime in the Accounting Department during March 19— is as follows:

1. Total employees in department: 30
2. Total hours of overtime: 12
3. Employees working overtime: 5 (16 percent)

    James Miles, 2 hours
    Doris Tyson, 2 hours
    Kenneth Ulrich, 1 hour
    Ina West, 3 hours
    Robert Williams, 4 hours

Note how the outline form is used to highlight the suggestions in the memo shown on page 463.

Table Form

In some cases, the most effective way to present information is in table form. The advantage of a tabulated presentation is that the reader can more easily see the total situation at a glance without wading through a great many words. Obviously, the decision to tabulate should be influenced by the amount and the kind of information to be included and also by the writer's projection regarding the uses to which the information is likely to be put. In table form, the previously discussed overtime report would look like this:

ACCOUNTING DEPARTMENT OVERTIME
MONTH OF MARCH 19—

Employee	Overtime Hours	Reason
Miles, James	2	To complete January billing
Tyson, Doris	2	To prepare expense statement
Ulrich, Kenneth	1	To complete checking cost estimates
West, Ina	3	To prepare cost analysis
Williams, Robert	4	To analyze travel expenses

Total employees: 30
Overtime hours: 12
Total employees working overtime: 5
Percent: 16

INTEROFFICE MEMORANDUM

To: Ms. May Chan   From: Armand Ortiz

Subject: Increasing Credit Card Use   Date: July 1, 19--

Our firm has issued 3152 credit cards to customers during the past two years. However, a survey made recently by our credit department indicates that only 35 percent of these credit card holders have made purchases exceeding $100 during this same two-year period. The average charge is $85.

A national study recently made by the American Credit Association revealed that the average purchase by credit card holders is $225. This figure would seem to indicate that we are not getting the maximum benefits from the credit cards we issue and that we should be able to increase our volume of credit business by encouraging greater use of credit cards by our customers.

I am, therefore, recommending that we undertake a campaign to encourage customers who hold credit cards to make greater use of their cards. The initial steps of this campaign should include the following:

1. Preparing folders encouraging new customers to apply for credit cards. An application form should be a part of this folder, which would be available not only in the credit office but also at numerous locations within the store.

2. Placing full-page advertisements in both the morning and the evening newspapers, explaining how customers can more widely use their credit cards and not get into economic difficulties by overcharging.

3. Buying television time for spot announcements with a theme similar to that of the newspaper advertisements.

I would suggest that representatives from both the credit and the marketing departments form a committee to plan the strategies of this program not later than the end of this month.

I will be happy to discuss any aspects of these suggestions with you at your convenience.

AO

as

Ideas for increasing efficiency, productivity, or profitability are often welcomed. Note how the subject line in this unsolicited report appeals to the reader's interest.

UNSOLICITED REPORTS

An unsolicited report is, quite simply, one that you make on your own initiative rather than one you are asked to prepare. In business, any idea that you might have for increasing efficiency, productivity, or profit making will usually be welcome. And more than likely you will want to put your idea in writing so that you can present it in the most complete, logical, and generally effective manner. See the unsolicited report shown on page 463.

How do you go about preparing and submitting an unsolicited report? Before you begin to write, consider these details.

To

You will want to direct your suggestion or idea to the person who has the authority to put it into effect. Usually this person will be your boss; but even if it happens to be someone else, courtesy and protocol demand that the suggestion be routed *through* your boss *to* that other person. For example:

> To: Ms. Marika Gilbert (your boss)
> Mrs. Margaret Henry (the "authority" person)

Subject

In any report, the subject line should tell the reader what the report is about. In an unsolicited report, though, you should slant the wording of the subject so that it will appeal to the reader's particular interest. For example, if you know that your boss is particularly interested in increasing customer use of credit cards, your subject line might read:

> Subject: Suggestions for Increasing Credit Card Use

COMMUNICATION PROJECTS

Practical Application

A. Your supervisor, Ms. Marley Hopkins, is considering the purchase of a home computer so that she can perform some of her office responsibilities at home during the evenings and weekends. She asks you to check the prices of various home computers available in your community in terms of number of disk drives and memory. Ms. Hopkins has specified what she needs, so you will investigate only models that meet her specifications. You obtain the following information: (1) *Homeworker,* monochrome display $1900 and color display $2122; *Homecompute,* monochrome display $2100 and color display $2400; *Speedster,* monochrome display $1600 and color display $1900; and *Comp Pute,* monochrome display $2600 and color display $3000. All carry 1-year warranties, and service contracts are available after the expiration of the warranty. Both the *Homeworker*

(Continued on page 469.)

Telecommunication messages, being expensive, are usually written concisely.

Almost all businesspeople in offices and stores have some contact with the public, either in person or on the telephone.

Although oral communication is important to everyone in business, some positions require a high degree of skill. A salesperson, for example, depends on oral communication to make a living.

and the *Homecompute* are available at Computerworld and each comes with a carrying case. The *Speedster* is available at Charles Computer Sales, and the company will extend its warranty for 6 additional months if you have not required service during the first year. The *Comp Pute* is available at Comp Pute, Inc., which will give a free spreadsheet program with each purchase. Organize this information into a concise, easy-to-read memorandum and submit it to Ms. Hopkins.

B. Select two stocks or bonds that are listed in your local newspaper's stock market report. From the information provided in the newspaper, write an informal report about the status of these securities during the past five days. Address the report to your instructor.

C. Prepare a tabulation report, similar to the one on page 462, for the following information:

> Sources of Employees Hired During the Year 19—: The state employment service referred 36 candidates; 16 were hired. Local college placement offices referred 27 candidates; 19 were hired. Private placement services referred 41 candidates; 17 were hired. Newspaper advertising resulted in 53 candidates; 10 were hired. Unsolicited applicants included 6 candidates; 1 was hired. Notices in employee service magazines resulted in 12 candidates; 7 were hired.

D. From *one* of the following areas—accounting, secretarial services, marketing, management, or economics—indicate three subject lines that would be likely for short reports. For example, a possible subject for a short report in the marketing area might be "Sources of New Clients."

Editing Practice

Using Your Word Processor. Can you find any spelling or homonym errors in the following excerpts from a circulation department report?

> Newsstand sales plus subscription sales acceded 1.5 million copies in the month of December. Clearly, the principle reason for this sharp increase is that our radio and television advertising in November and December was well planned. In fact, we expect our February addition to reach 1.6 million copies; sales should than level off in March and April and (as usual) decrease over the summer months.

Case Problem

To Ask or Not to Ask Questions. One of the most important things new employees must learn is when to ask for help and when to use their own judgment in trying to solve a problem. People who solve their own problems are appreciated only when their work is correct. On the other hand, new employees who make mistakes because they are afraid or hesitant to ask questions may very well find themselves in serious trouble. What would you do in the following situations?

1. Peggy's boss asks her to make six copies of a report. On the list of those who are to receive a report is "Ms. Lincoln." There are two Ms. Lincolns in the company—one is the supervisor of the word processing center and the other is the office supervisor. Because the report concerns the purchase of new typewriters, Peggy decides that the supervisor of the word processing center is the one who should receive the report. Without asking the boss, Peggy sends the report to the supervisor of the word processing center.

2. Carl has just started work as an order editor and finds on his desk an order for an item that he has not heard of. He knows that recently many items were declared out of stock, and he assumes that this is one of them; therefore, he notes this information on the order.
   a. Do you agree with Carl's action?
   b. Should he have checked further?
   c. What could be the consequences of his action?

49

WRITING FORMAL REPORTS

How do formal reports differ from the memorandum reports that you learned to write in the previous section? Formal business reports, in addition to being longer than the informal memorandum report, are usually concerned with more complex problems or questions necessitating investigation, analysis, research, and documentation. Some typical formal report subjects might be an analysis of the methods of marketing a company's products; a feasibility study to determine whether to change a method of operating a particular aspect of a business, such as a study to determine whether to install a system of computer accounting and billing; or an experiment to determine how to improve the quality control of a product.

The writing of a formal business report may require weeks or even months of extensive research and reading related to the topic of the report, and the completed report could contain anywhere from several pages to more than a hundred pages. Regardless of its length, a formal report must be expertly written, because often the report is the basis upon which a company decides whether or not to spend many thousands of dollars.

Who generally does the actual writing of a report? Not everyone is capable of writing an effective formal report. Even though an executive or an engineer or other technician may actually conduct the research that may be the basis for the report, often a secretary or an administrative assistant will be closely involved in the actual preparation of the report itself. Your skill in this direction is an important way of increasing your value to your employer.

Some companies conduct a considerable amount of research and write many reports concerning these research projects. Such companies often employ specialists (sometimes called "technical writers") whose sole function is to take the material assembled by the researcher and put it into report form. If the researcher writes the report, the technical writer assists the researcher in preparing the report. Technical writers are, of course, in top salary brackets because of their expertise, which is in short supply.

You have a head start in learning how to write longer formal reports because you have already learned how to write informal reports. This knowledge will serve as an excellent background for learning how to write the more complex formal report.

PREPARING TO WRITE FORMAL REPORTS

Not all reports look alike. There are some variations in the style and form used for preparing formal reports. These variations are usually determined by the nature of the subject being investigated. A technical report, such as one that specifies the requirements for manufacturing computer components, may be organized in outline form with very little text. Similarly, the reports of chemists, engineers, and other scientists are likely to include many tables, charts, and graphs, with a relatively small amount of written interpretation. On the other hand, many business reports are mainly narrative, possibly with some tabular material. Despite this variation in the style and form of reports, most formal reports include these main sections:

Introduction
Summary
Body
Conclusions and recommendations
Supplementary material

Before commencing the actual writing of the formal report, the writer-investigator must first determine the purpose and the scope of the report. To make this determination, the investigator must gather reliable facts, assemble and analyze those facts, draw conclusions from the factual analysis, and, finally, make recommendations that are reasonable in view of company needs.

Defining Purpose and Scope

Why is the report being written? The answer to this question should appear in the introductory section of the report. For example, in a study to determine whether a company should disband its word processing center (and let each department handle its own communication needs), the purpose of the report might be stated as follows:

1. To determine current methods of preparing communications.
2. To determine the efficiency of these methods.
3. To determine the feasibility of returning responsibility for correspondence and report writing activities to individual departments.

A report writer must avoid selecting a topic that is too large in scope to be handled effectively. The experienced report writer, therefore, clearly defines the scope of the problem and sets boundaries that keep the research within reason. For example, think how difficult it would be to do research involving "Telephone Techniques of Office Workers." This topic is much too broad in scope to be treated in one report, if it could be treated at all. The topic needs to be limited to a more specific group. A revision that would be more practical might read "Telephone Techniques of Secretaries of the Roberti Manufacturing Company."

Gathering Information

"No report is stronger than the facts behind it." Computer specialists, in speaking of the preparation of reports by machine, emphasize this statement vividly with their term *GIGO* (pronounced *guy-go*), standing for "garbage-in, garbage-out." The value of any report depends on the quality of the material going into its production. If "garbage" goes in, "garbage" is bound to come out. With reliable facts behind it, a reliable report can be written; with questionable data, only a questionable report can result.

In gathering information and documenting it, writers should be familiar with the authoritative references in their fields. There are, of course, many general references that everyone needs. Such standard sources as the *Reader's Guide to Periodical Literature, The Business Periodicals Index, Facts on File, The World Almanac,* and *The New York Times Annual Index* are invaluable helps to nearly any writer.

In each field of business, such as accounting, marketing, or office administration, there are basic references as well as current periodicals that should be reviewed frequently by report writers. Naturally, anyone doing research must first learn how to find and use books, periodicals, card catalogs, data bases, and various indexes. Section 59 suggests additional basic references and specialized references. In addition, it suggests ways to use the library for research activities.

When data is to be obtained in other ways, such as through the use of questionnaires or personal interviews, other research techniques must be mastered.

WORKING BIBLIOGRAPHY.   In consulting the various reference works pertinent to the subject, the writer should make up a list of the books, periodicals, reports, and other sources to be used as references in the report. This preliminary list of sources is called the *working bibliography*. If the writer makes each entry of the working bibliography on a separate card (5 by 3 or 6 by 4 inches), the cards will make it easier to assemble the final bibliography of sources actually used. The writer will also find the bibliography cards useful when footnoting material in the report.

A book card for a working bibliography should contain all the following information:

Author's full name (last name first)
Title (and edition, if there is more than one)
Name and location of publisher
Date of publication (latest copyright date)

In addition, it is helpful to include for the writer's own use the library's call number for the reference. The following illustration shows a bibliography card that has been prepared for a book reference.

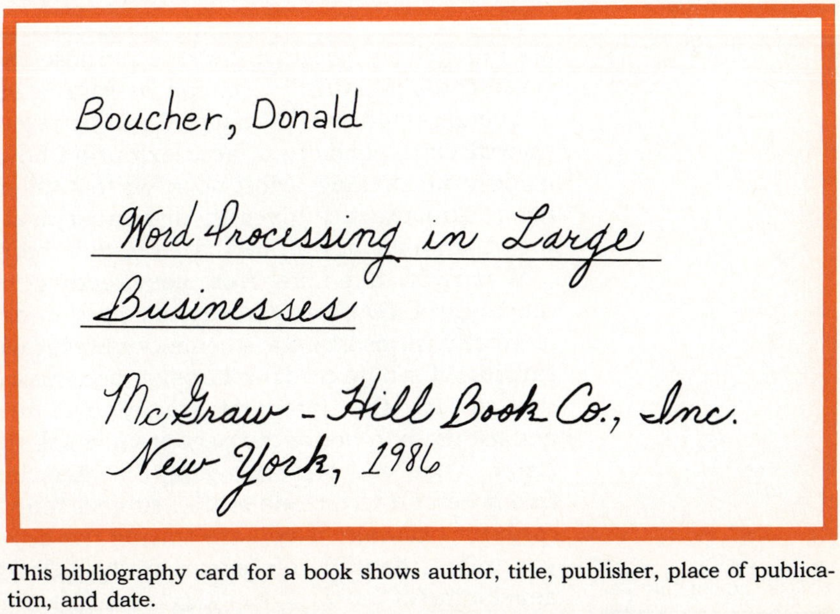

Boucher, Donald

Word Processing in Large
Businesses

McGraw - Hill Book Co., Inc.
New York, 1986

This bibliography card for a book shows author, title, publisher, place of publication, and date.

Singe, Kioshi
"Minicomputers and Word Processing"

The Journal of Office Competency,
April 1989,   pp. 72-76
Vol. 8, No. 4

Be sure that a bibliography card for an article includes the date, volume and issue number, and page numbers as well as author, article title, and periodical title.

When consulting a magazine, newspaper, or other periodical, the writer prepares a bibliography card like the one above. This card should show the full name of the author, the title of the article (in quotation marks), the name of the publication (and location, if a newspaper), the date, volume, and number of the publication, and the page numbers.

NOTETAKING.   The writer also uses cards for taking notes. Cards are much more practical for this purpose than sheets of paper because cards are sturdy and can be sorted and re-sorted easily.

The ease with which material can be organized and a report can be written depends to a large extent on how well notes have been made from reading. Most good writers take more notes than they need. This practice gives them a great deal of information, which they can "boil down" to the essentials before writing the report.

When you take notes from your reading, be sure to identify each source carefully. Always use a new card for each new source or topic. Normally, summary statements or phrases with page references are sufficient for note cards. Whenever you use a quotation, however, be sure to copy the statement exactly, enclose it in quotation marks, and list the number of the page from which the quotation was taken. Later, when you are organizing the material for writing, you may find it helpful to include a brief subject reference at the top of each card; for example, if you are tracing the development of a product, you might identify references by "year," "developer," or "site of development."

ORGANIZING THE REPORT

After all the material related to the topic has been collected and studied, the writer can begin to organize the report. At this time, the note cards should be revised, sorted by topic, and tentatively organized into a logical sequence for the report.

Outline

Using organized note cards as a guide, the writer next makes an outline to serve as the structure, or framework, of the report. The outline should be kept as simple as possible. While determining the outline, the writer should keep in mind the kinds of topic headings the report requires. If outline entries are carefully thought out, many of them can be used as topic headings in the final report. The writer should keep in mind the following points in making the outline:

The purpose of the report is to convey information efficiently.
A good report structure gives the reader a sense of movement; one thought naturally leads into another.
The outline is a time-saver when the writer starts writing.
The outline should be arranged to present material in logical units and in logical sequence.

Headings

Most books, articles, and business reports utilize headings to indicate the organization of the material. Headings of equivalent weight should be styled alike. For example, the main divisions of an article, a report, or a chapter in a book may be centered, and the subdivisions of each main heading may be typed as paragraph headings. When there are more than two divisions, however, the following arrangement of headings should be used:

CENTERED FIRST-ORDER HEADING

Side Second-Order Heading

Run-In Third-Order Heading. Text follows on the same line . . . .

If the report writer is consistent in the use of headings, the reader will better understand the report's organization and content. Consistency should be observed in the form as well as in the style of the headings. In general, a topic form is preferred to a sentence form. For example, "How to Write Reports" is preferable to "This Is How to Write Reports."

WRITING THE REPORT

There are considerable differences between the informal writing style of business letters and memorandums and the writing style commonly found in formal reports. These differences will be pointed out in the following discussion.

Writing Style

Long business reports are important documents upon which management bases many of its high-level decisions. Consequently, such reports tend to be written in a serious, formal style, usually in the third person. The impersonal style helps the writer avoid interjecting a personal tone which might weaken a report by making it seem merely a statement of one person's opinions and beliefs, instead of a sound evaluation of the data gathered for the report. Of course, usually only one person, the writer, is evaluating the facts, but the more the writer can de-emphasize the *I* and cite facts to back the evaluation, the more objective and more persuasive the report will sound.

A poor report writer presenting a report on letter-writing practices might make these statements:

It seems to *me* that the modified block style of letter takes too much time to type.

Personally, I would *prefer* to use the simplified letter for all company correspondence.

Even though most of the other departments prefer mixed punctuation, *I* have a strong *preference* for open punctuation, which *I* feel we should adopt.

Even though the facts may provide a sound basis for the evaluations given in the examples above, these sentences do not seem objective because the writer has used so many personal references. In addition, the writer has not shown *how* judgments are drawn from the data gathered.

On the other hand, the good report writer knows that merely stating a judgment will not persuade anyone to accept it, no matter how soundly based on fact and reason the judgment may be. Therefore, the expert writer uses an impersonal style and relates all evaluations to the facts found in the study. This writer carefully avoids any expressions that may imply that the evaluations are based on personal opinions instead of sound reasons and facts. Instead of the sentences given above, the expert writer would write the following:

The evidence revealed by this survey indicates that the modified block style of letter takes 15 percent more typing time than the simplified style.

Use of the simplified letter style would be appropriate for the Thompson Insurance Company because the style has the modern look of simplicity and is also faster and easier to type.

Three of the five departments studied use mixed punctuation; however, adoption of open punctuation would have the following advantages: (Explanation of these advantages would follow.)

The same impersonal writing style illustrated above should characterize every section of the report. Remember that making it possible for the reader to reason from the facts presented is an important factor in the success of any business report.

Title Page

The title page usually includes the complete title of the report, the name and title of the author, the name and title of the person for whom the report is prepared, and the date the report is submitted. Each of these items should be attractively arranged on the page. A typical title page is illustrated on page 478.

Table of Contents

This section is prepared after the report has been completed. One commonly accepted form is illustrated below.

CONTENTS

Introduction

The introduction section of a long report is designed to tell the reader why the report was written, how the data was gathered, and what the report does or does not do.

Suppose that Marvin Polski, president of the Alliance Insurance Company, has assigned Ruth Kaplan, the director of administrative services, the job of investigating the feasibility of establishing a central word processing unit, in order to improve the company's correspondence function and also to cut costs. In such a report, Ms. Kaplan would include in the introduction the *purpose* and *scope* of the report, as well as a description of the *procedures* followed to collect and analyze the data presented in the report.

PURPOSE AND SCOPE. First, the writer should state why the report was written. Next, the writer should clearly list the basic objectives of the report:

This report was prepared at the request of Mr. Polski, president of the Alliance Insurance Company. The purposes of the report are:

1. To determine what practices are used in preparing communications in each department of the company.

THE FEASIBILITY OF ESTABLISHING
A WORD PROCESSING CENTER
AT
ALLIANCE INSURANCE COMPANY

Prepared by

Ruth Kaplan
Director of Administrative Services

Submitted to

Marvin Polski
President

June 10, 19--

This title page shows the complete title of the report, the name and title of the author, the name and title of the person for whom the report is prepared, and the date the report is submitted.

2. To determine what equipment is used in preparing communications in each department of the company.
3. To determine the costs involved in preparing communications.
4. To determine whether the establishment of a word processing center would improve company communications and/or decrease the cost of producing company communications.

In addition, a brief statement of the scope of the investigation may be included in this section.

This investigation is limited to the communication practices in the home office of the Alliance Insurance Company in Longmeadow, Massachusetts.

PROCEDURES. The introductory section of the report should describe the methods that were used to collect and analyze the data. Here is an example:

To collect valid information for this report, all supervisors responsible for correspondence in each department and all technical writers were interviewed. The questionnaire shown in Appendix C of this report was sent in advance and was completed by each supervisor and technical writer. The questionnaires were reviewed carefully and were analyzed during the final interview conducted by Ms. Alvarez. Major manufacturers of word processing equipment were contacted, and each manufacturer presented a demonstration of its equipment. In addition, current periodicals were consulted so that the results of this company survey could be compared with recommended practices for handling communications in other companies.

Summary

For the busy executive, the summary is placed early in the report (following the introduction). This section contains the most significant information in capsule form, which is helpful to the reader who cannot take time to read the entire report. When time permits, the reader can complete the reading of the report. The length of the summary may range from one paragraph to four or five pages, depending on the material that has been gathered. The following example is the opening paragraph of the summary of the feasibility study to determine whether a word processing center should be established at the Alliance Insurance Company:

SUMMARY
This study recommends that a word processing center be established at the home office of the Alliance Insurance Company and shows that such a center would improve correspondence practices and decrease correspondence costs.

The specific data gathered during this investigation resulted in the following conclusions that led to the above recommendation:

1. More time than is necessary is expended in both the dictation and the transcription processes.
2. There is a great variation in letter styles used throughout the company.
3. Correspondence often is not answered for as many as two to three days after it is received.
4. Many letters that are individually written could well be form letters.

Body

The body is the actual report. In this section the writer tells what was done, how it was done, and what the writer found. Writing this section should present no great difficulties if the writer follows a carefully prepared outline and has good notes. The writer should stick to accurate, verifiable facts and present them in a clear, concise manner. The suggestions given in Chapter 7 for forceful, clear writing apply to the writing of reports.

Conclusions and Recommendations

This section can easily be the most important one in any report, for it is here that the real results of the report appear. The writer's conclusions tell the busy executive, on the basis of the most reliable data available, "Here is what the report shows."

Personal observations should be reduced to a minimum—conclusions should be drawn from the facts only. In the light of the conclusions and from experience with the company, the writer can make recommendations. (*Note:* As a guide to making worthwhile recommendations, the writer should glance back at the listed purposes of the report. As a rule, there could well be at least one recommendation for each stated purpose.)

By referring to the purposes stated in the introduction of the report on the feasibility of establishing a word processing center at the Alliance Insurance Company, the writer might include the following conclusions and recommendations:

CONCLUSIONS AND RECOMMENDATIONS
From an analysis of the data gathered in this study, the following conclusions are drawn:

1. Current dictation and transcription practices waste time.
2. Almost half the letters that are individually written could be form letters or could make use of form paragraphs.
3. Little use is made of available dictation equipment.

4. Most of those who dictate do not know how to dictate properly.
5. Secretaries are rarely permitted to compose letters.
6. Fewer than half the secretaries have easy access to word processing equipment.
7. A variety of letter styles is used, depending upon each dictator's preference.

With these conclusions in mind, the following action is recommended:

1. Establish a word processing center, using a dedicated word processing system.
2. Make dictation equipment available to each dictator.
3. Provide each dictator with instruction in how to dictate properly and how to use dictation equipment properly.
4. Adopt the simplified letter as the standard letter style to be used throughout the company.
5. Keep comparative communication costs as a basis for determining whether word processing centers should be established in the various branch offices of the company.

Supplementary Information

Supplementary information, which is given after the conclusions and recommendations, provides substantiating data for the report. One or both of the parts discussed below may be included.

APPENDIX. The appendix consists mainly of supporting information to back up the material in the body of the report. Long tables, charts, photographs, questionnaires, letters, and drawings are usually placed in this section. By including such material at the end of the report, the body of the report is freed from the kind of detail that makes reading difficult.

BIBLIOGRAPHY. This section is an alphabetic listing of all the references used in the report. Bibliographical entries are listed in alphabetic order by author. Forms for book and periodical entries are shown below.

Books

Braun, Harold F., Communication Procedures, Westly Book Company, New York, 19—.
Schrag, A. F., How to Dictate, McGraw-Hill Book Company, New York, 19—.

Periodicals

Greene, Arnold, "Word Processing Centers," The Office Worker, Vol. XV, No. 6, 19—, pp. 89–100.
Zane, Anthony, "Cutting Communication Cost," The Executive, Vol. IV, No. 3, 19—, pp. 34–38.

Letter of Transmittal

A short letter of transmittal shown below, composed after the report has been completed, accompanies the report. It is written in the form of a memorandum and usually contains such information as:

A reference to the person who authorized the report.
A brief statement of the general purpose of the report.
Appropriate statements of appreciation or acknowledgment.

Progress Reports

As indicated earlier, it sometimes takes months to complete an investigation and prepare the finished product, the written report. When such is the case, it is a good idea to keep the person who requested the investigation informed as to the progress being made. How many such progress reports will be called for depends upon how much time elapses following the original request.

 ALLIANCE INSURANCE COMPANY

INTEROFFICE MEMORANDUM

To: Mr. Marvin Polski, President

From: Ruth Kaplan, Director of Administrative Services

Date: June 10, 19--

Subject: Attached Report on the Feasibility of
         Establishing a Word Processing Center

On April 30, 19--, you authorized a feasibility study concerning the establishment of a word processing center. This study is now completed. The results of the study, together with my conclusions and recommendations, are contained in the attached report.

The results are significant, and I hope that they will be of value to you. Much credit should be given to Carmen Alvarez, my assistant, who conducted several of the surveys and helped a great deal with the organization and writing of this report.

If you wish, I shall be glad to discuss the report with you at your convenience.

                            RK

ca
Enclosure

When a formal report is intended for a person within the organization, the letter of transmittal is prepared in the form of a memo.

A progress report generally is made in memorandum form. Suppose that you were requested on April 30 to make an investigation of the feasibility of establishing a word processing center at the Alliance Insurance Company home office. On May 15, you might prepare the following memorandum:

As you know, you asked me on April 30 to investigate the feasibility of establishing a word processing center. As of today, I have completed all the preliminary investigation and am ready to analyze the data I have gathered. I am in the process also of investigating word processing equipment available from the leading manufacturers. I expect to complete all my investigation and analysis by May 30 and to have the completed report on or before June 10.

MECHANICS OF REPORT WRITING

An immaculate physical appearance, expert placement, and careful attention to the mechanics of English, spelling, and punctuation emphasize the importance of the finished report. For this reason, mechanics, as well as organization and writing style, are important in preparing the report.

Of course, all the mechanics of English, spelling, and punctuation discussed in earlier chapters apply to report writing. Some suggestions for setting up a report are also necessary, and they are presented in the following paragraphs.

1. Use common sense and show variety in paragraphing; take care to avoid too many long and too many short paragraphs. Keep in mind that the topic sentence, telling what the paragraph is about, very frequently appears first. Also, the closing sentence is often used to summarize the meaning of the paragraph.

2. Be generous in using headings. Take care to leave plenty of white space around major headings, tables, and other display materials. Be sure that all headings of the same value within a section are parallel in wording. For example:

Nonparallel	Parallel
Writing the Introduction	Writing the Introduction
The Body	Writing the Body
How to Write the Closing	Writing the Closing

3. Use footnotes to give credit when the ideas of others are used, either verbatim or modified. A footnote may be placed at the bottom of the page carrying the footnoted item, or all the footnotes may be listed at the end of the report. Footnotes should always be numbered consecutively, whether they appear at the bottom of each footnoted page or are grouped at the end of the report. The information usually given in a footnote includes the

footnote number, author, book or periodical title, publisher, place and date of publication, and page numbers. Since footnote styles may vary, it is advisable to consult the company's reference manual or a standard reference manual.

4. Select carefully any tables, charts, diagrams, photographs, drawings, and other illustrated materials used to supplement the writing. To promote better understanding of the contents, choose the items that contribute most to the report. Try to eliminate any items that are not pertinent.

5. Bind the report attractively. Many types of binding, from the single staple to an elaborate sewn binding, can be used. Reports that are subject to frequent, rigorous use should be placed inside a special hardback report folder for protection. Do not rely on a paper clip to bind the report; the chances of losing part of the report are very high.

6. Observe these rules of good manuscript form:
   a. Type all reports on standard 8½- by 11-inch paper. Legal-size paper will not fit standard office files.
   b. Use double spacing except for long quotations (usually three or more lines), for which single spacing is preferred. Of course, type on only one side of the sheet. Consult a standard style manual for other spacing details.
   c. Leave ample margins. Commonly accepted margins are these:
      Left margin: 1½ inches to allow for side binding.
      Other margins: 1 inch.
      First page only: When it contains the title, allow a 2-inch top margin.
   d. Always prepare at least one carbon copy.
   e. Traditionally, the first page is not numbered when it contains the title. All other pages, beginning with 2, should be numbered in the upper-right corner.
   f. Follow this pattern for any material presented in outline form:
      I.
         A.
            1.
               a.
                  (1)
                     (a)

COMMUNICATION PROJECTS

Practical Application

A. In memorandum report form, write a report for your instructor that describes the function of each of the following parts of a report:

1. Title page
2. Table of contents
3. Introduction
4. Summary
5. Body
6. Conclusions and recommendations
7. Supplementary material

B. Write a progress report for your employer, Kenneth Wilson, using the following information:

1. Nature of the study: dictation habits of executives at ABC Company.
2. Assigned March 31; due May 1; progress report April 16.
3. Completed so far: interviews with 20 executives, the total number of executives in the company; visits and interviews with three distributors of dictating equipment.
4. Remaining research: library research, analysis of data gathered, determination of conclusions and recommendations. Add any additional items you think should be included.

C. Prepare a questionnaire that might be suitable for gathering data for a report on "The Study Habits of College Students." The class will discuss the validity and wording of the questions submitted by the class members.

D. You have been asked by your supervisor, Brian Kent, to attend a meeting on employee turnover and to write a report as a result of what you learn from the meeting. From the notes you took, prepare a report, supplying other data that you think might be appropriate. Here are your notes:

1. Annual turnover rate: manufacturing employees, 20%; office, 15%.
2. Reasons given for leaving the company (in order of frequency): Manufacturing—working conditions undesirable, higher salary in another company, friction with supervisors, no opportunity for advancement. Office—better salary, no opportunity for further advancement, working conditions disliked, friction with managers, difficulty of commuting, inadequate employee benefits.
3. Recommended actions: Improve facilities by (1) redecorating offices and installing air conditioning and (2) replacing old furniture and equipment with modern and efficient articles; encourage frequent departmental meetings that will give employees an opportunity to express their opinions; institute training program for supervisors; initiate a salary survey of similar businesses; study promotion policies; obtain services of a management consultant to make recommendations concerning employee bene-

fits; consider the possibility of designating a personnel relations counselor to handle grievances.

4. Department managers are to consider the turnover problem with reference to their experiences with employees under their supervision, are to be prepared to discuss the problem further, and are to make recommendations at a special meeting to be held on August 18. Prior to this meeting, by August 3, managers should submit a memorandum on morale in their departments.

5. In the discussion, it was brought out that there seems to be an atmosphere of unrest and that morale is generally low. It was also pointed out that the commuting problem may be eased shortly, when the proposed new bus route (direct from the Riverside area) goes into effect.

Editing Practice

Editing for Writing Power.   Edit and rewrite these sentences for the purpose of improving writing power.

1. Ms. Andrews is the new administrative assistant, and she is very proficient in computer operation.
2. We specialize in quality; but price, too, receives careful consideration.
3. Come to Kaye's, and there you will find many sale items.
4. Desiring to avert a strike, a discussion of fringe benefits was held.
5. Not having been able, through the various agencies at his disposal, to obtain any information about loans; and as he did not know the procedures for making such loans, the new manager decided we must deal on a cash basis.
6. One of our new products was discontinued, when all plans for our television advertising campaign had to be dropped.
7. We liked your report. It was complete. We hope to be able to implement many of your suggestions.
8. Although wanting to visit the plant, but he couldn't spare the time away from the office, Jim's plans were indefinite.
9. The report to the executives about the new billing system that was started recently for the Toledo branch, was very long and complicated so then the credit manager had to call a special meeting to explain it.
10. The report on sight possibilities hear in Davenport was presented by the reality agents.

Case Problem

The Avid Conversationalist.   Mark Rosenthal, the mail clerk at Zee's Inc., is supposed to complete his daily delivery of mail by 10:45 a.m. and then return to the mail room in time to process the outgoing mail for a 12:15 p.m. pickup. However, when Mark gets to the sales department, Tom Rouse usually engages him in a lengthy, one-sided conversation. As a result, in several instances Mark has not completed processing all the outgoing mail on time. Today Mark is late starting his deliveries, and Tom tries to engage him in another lengthy conversation.

1. What can Mark say to Tom without offending him?
2. What should Mark do if Tom persists in talking?

50

WRITING MINUTES, NEWS RELEASES, AND TELECOMMUNICATIONS

In addition to short memorandum reports and long formal business reports, there are two other types of reports used in business that you should know how to prepare. One of these communications is a report of what occurred at a meeting, called "minutes" of the meeting. Minutes actually summarize everything that happens at a meeting.

Another type of special report is called a "news release," which is used to report newsworthy events to newspapers. It is hoped that the newspapers to whom such a report is sent will prepare an article for publication, using the news release as a basis for this article. Knowing how to prepare these special reports is another way of making yourself valuable to your employer.

Still another special type of communication used by many businesses comes under the category of telecommunications. Telecommunication messages are transmitted electronically. Some companies have their own telecommunications facilities, but most companies buy these services. A form is often used to compose the message (a telegram, a cablegram, a radiogram, or a telex), and the message is written in as few words as possible. Since one of the factors involved in the cost of telecommunications is the number of words in the message, you must develop the skill of conveying a clear and complete message with a minimum number of words.

First, let us consider minutes, which you are likely to prepare more frequently than news releases.

MINUTES OF MEETINGS

Every organization, business or social, has meetings and must keep a record of what happens at these meetings. These records of the proceedings of meetings are called *minutes*. The minutes serve as a permanent record of the decisions reached and the actions that are to be taken, as well as inform those who were not at the meeting of what took place. Nearly every business employee, at one time or another, may serve as secretary to a group or committee and thus will be responsible for keeping an accurate set of minutes.

Recording the Minutes

The accurate recording of the proceedings of all meetings is an important function, for the minutes usually serve as the only historical record of a meeting.

There is probably no one best way to record what happens at a meeting. The secretary of the meeting must be the judge of what is unimportant (and hence not worth recording). If an agenda of the meeting has been prepared beforehand, the secretary should receive a copy. The agenda lists briefly the business to be transacted and acts as a guide to the person who presides at the meeting. The agenda also helps the secretary check to be sure that all scheduled items are accounted for in the minutes. Much of the success of good notetaking revolves around the personal efficiency of the secretary. However, any secretary preparing to record the proceedings of a meeting should find the following general guides helpful:

1. Record the time and place of the meeting.
2. List the persons attending and those absent. In a small group, actual names can be given; in a large group, however, it is usually sufficient either to state the number of people present, such as "Forty-five members were present," or to list the names of the absentees only.
3. In the opening section of the minutes, mention the fact that the minutes for the previous meeting were read and approved, amended, or not approved.
4. Develop the art of recording the important points in the discussion of each item on the agenda. Why? Sufficient supporting facts are required so that those who were present can recall the discussion from reading the minutes and those who were not present can be informed. Papers read during the meeting are often attached to the final typewritten minutes, because it is usually not possible for the secretary to record verbatim all such information.
5. Record verbatim all resolutions and motions, as well as the

names of the persons who introduced and seconded the motions. If there is difficulty in getting such information when the motion is first made, the secretary should request that the motion be repeated or even put in writing so that the exact motion is recorded.

6. Type the minutes first in draft form so that they can be edited before being prepared in final form. Sometimes, too, the secretary may want to get another person's approval before issuing the minutes in final form. The secretary signs the minutes, thus certifying their accuracy. Sometimes the presiding officer countersigns them.

7. Normally, make one copy of the minutes and file it in the folder, notebook, or binder used for this purpose. Usually minutes are duplicated and sent to each person present at the meeting or to designated officers who would be interested in the business of the meeting.

Format of Minutes

Various formats are used for the minutes of a meeting. The main purpose, however, is to make sure that all the essential information appears in a neat, well-arranged form. Some organizations prefer to emphasize the main points on the agenda by using a standardized format.

The minutes on page 490 illustrate an acceptable format. Notice the standard pattern and the topical headings that are used for all meetings of this group and the way in which the motions and discussion are concisely summarized.

Other groups use a more traditional format in which the proceedings of the meeting are written in rather complete detail. The example on page 491 illustrates this style.

NEWS RELEASES

Publicity, advertising, public relations, goodwill—all these terms denote the effort of a business to get its name, its reputation, and its product before the public. In fact, large companies—even schools and colleges—today employ a public relations staff, whose job is to attract favorable public attention to their organizations.

An important means of getting the planned publicity of business into the hands of the public is the news release. Whenever a business plans an event that it considers newsworthy or capable of enhancing its public image, its public relations personnel prepare and submit a news release to various news outlets for publication or broadcasting. Such a news announcement may concern the appointment of a new company president after a meeting of the board of directors; it may tell of a large local expansion in a company's plant, which will increase the work force and have a great impact on the economy of the

ASSOCIATION OF BEST COMPANY EMPLOYEES

MINUTES OF MEETING OF MAY 12, 19--

TIME, PLACE, ATTENDANCE	The monthly meeting of the Association of Best Company Employees was held in the Blue Room at 5:30 p.m. The president, Jan Dixon, presided. All members and officers were present.
MINUTES	The minutes of the last meeting, April 10, 19--, were read and approved.
OFFICERS' REPORTS	Treasurer: The treasurer reported receipts of $650, disbursements of $150, and a balance of $967 as of April 1, 19--. Tony Valenti moved the acceptance of the report. Anne Terry seconded the motion. Motion carried.
COMMITTEE REPORTS	Chairperson William Ferris presented the report of the nominating committee. The nominees are:

	President:	Meg Andrews
	Vice President:	James Brown
	Secretary:	Antonio Valdez
	Treasurer:	Garth Kimberly

Rosa Sanchez moved that nominations be closed and that a unanimous ballot be cast for the slate of officers presented by the committee. The motion was seconded by Yamen Abdulah. Motion carried.

UNFINISHED BUSINESS	Plans for the Annual Retirement Dinner to be held June 30 were discussed. Tory's Inn and Edwin's were suggested for this event. The president will report to the group at the next meeting about these restaurants.
NEW BUSINESS	The president reported that the Board of Directors is considering a policy change regarding tuition reimbursement for college courses taken. The change would involve getting approval for each course in advance. The feeling of the group was to recommend to the board that the words "unless prior approval is not feasible" be added to this change in policy.
ADJOURNMENT	The meeting adjourned at 6:15 p.m.

Respectfully submitted,

Ivy Lewis

Ivy Lewis

This two-column format for minutes uses topical headings.

```
                    MINUTES OF THE MEETING

                           of the

                     Board of Directors

                    Mercantile Sales, Inc.
                       April 10, 19--

Presiding:  Sandra Michel

Present:    Dale Thompson
            Marta Maez
            Jo Ann Keith
            Frank Ericson
            Hideko Chang

Absent:     Samuel Smyth


The meeting was called to order at 11 a.m. by Ms. Michel.
The principal topics for discussion concerned recommended
changes in two company policies, one related to donations
to charitable organizations and the other related to
reimbursing employees for tuition for college courses.

With reference to donations to charitable organizations,
Ms. Keith proposed that all donations be limited to a
maximum of $300.  After some discussion, the Board agreed
and voted unanimously to add this limit to the present
policies concerning charitable donations.

Mr. Ericson proposed that tuition reimbursement should be
made only if the employee has received prior approval of
the course submitted for tuition reimbursement.  The
present policy does not require that approval be given in
advance.  Mr. Chang was opposed to the change and
suggested that this proposal be tabled until the next
meeting.  In the meantime, employee opinion regarding the
change should be sought.  The board voted to table the
proposal until the May meeting and asked Mr. Chang to
consult with the Executive Board of the Associated
Employees regarding pros and cons of this change.  The
meeting adjourned at 12:30 p.m.

                        Respectfully submitted,

                        Kenneth Dorsey

                        Kenneth Dorsey, Secretary
```

The proceedings of the meeting are written in complete detail in this format for minutes.

community; it may publicize the introduction of a new line or new product; it may concern the awarding of some honor (perhaps for long, faithful service) to a member of the organization; and so on. Any item that will interest the public and create goodwill for the organization is an appropriate subject for a news release.

Any news story sent by a company must, of course, be approved for publication. In large companies, the director of public relations would have this responsibility. In small companies, individual department heads might handle their own news and distribute it in keeping with company policy, or releases might be issued from the office of the president or of one particular executive.

In order to be published and thereby serve its purpose, the release must be newsworthy; that is, the contents of the release must be of sufficient interest to the public to justify being published. Naturally, the writing style of the news release, as well as the form in which it appears, will have a strong effect on the newspaper editor who decides whether or not the news is published.

Form of the News Release

With hundreds of releases coming to their desks each week, newspaper editors will select for publication the items that require the least amount of rewriting, everything else being equal. Therefore, the news release must give complete, accurate information in a "news style" of writing that presents the facts in a clear and interesting way.

Many organizations use a special form for issuing news releases. These forms are arranged so that editors can get to the heart of the story without wasting time. Like a letterhead, a news release form usually contains the name and address of the company or organization and the name, address, and telephone number of the person responsible for issuing the release to the public.

1. The news release is double-spaced and has generous margins for possible changes by the newspaper editor.
2. The writer includes a tentative headline in all-capital letters to identify the story. An editor, of course, will change this title to fit the style and space requirements of the publication.
3. The news release indicates the time when a story may be published. In the example, note the prominence of the phrase *For Immediate Release*. A release may be sent to newspapers before an event occurs so that news will reach the public at almost the same time the event takes place. For example, if a company plans to announce a million-dollar gift to a local hospital at a banquet on Saturday, June 25, the release might read *For release after 6 p.m., Saturday, June 25*.
4. In a long release, subheads may be inserted between parts of the release to relieve the reading monotony and to guide the editor who wants to scan the story.

News Release
Emanuel Gomez
Director of Public Relations

1678 State Street
Boston, Massachusetts 02102
(617) 555-3405

Ralph Greene
Manager
Boston News Bureau
(606) 555-7500

For Immediate Release   May 30, 19--

GLORIA ATWATER NAMED PERSONNEL DIRECTOR

OF LORIMER NATIONAL BANK

Boston, May 30, 19--. Gloria Atwater has been named

personnel director of Lorimer National Bank in Boston by

its president, Mark Rider.

Ms. Atwater succeeds Arno Polczy, who retired from the

bank on April 15 after serving for 30 years.

The new personnel director joined the Lorimer National

Bank in Covington a year ago as a training director.

Before that, she was a business education teacher and

guidance counselor at Lexington High School. Ms. Atwater

is a graduate of the University of Massachusetts and a

member of the Boston Chamber of Commerce.

-xxx-

A news release must give complete, accurate information in a "news style" of writing. Note that this company has a special preprinted form for its news releases.

5. If there is more than one page to the release, the word *MORE* in parentheses is added at the end of the first and each intermediate page. At the end of the last page of the release, the symbol -×××-, ###, o0o, or -30- (adapted from the telegrapher's abbreviation *30,* which means "the end") is typed to indicate the end of the release.

Writing the News Release

However good the form of a written communication, it is the words that determine whether it will be read and used. In writing a news release—just as in writing letters, memorandums, and reports—certain guides will help the writer develop an effective writing style and will improve the chances of getting the release printed. Especially important is the arrangement of paragraphs in the news release.

The opening paragraph of a news release should summarize the entire story and should present the most newsworthy information first. In this opening section, the writer should give the *who, what, why, how, when,* and *where* of the news story in such a form that this paragraph can stand by itself. If, for example, an announcement is to be made of the appointment of Sandra Michel as personnel director of the Lorimer Bank, a poor lead paragraph might read:

Mark Rider, president of the Lorimer Bank in Boston, announced today the appointment of Ms. Sandra Michel as personnel director.

Mark Rider is not the person the article is about; therefore, the lead paragraph should read:

Sandra Michel has been named personnel director of the Lorimer Bank in Boston by its president, Mark Rider.

Each succeeding paragraph should supply background facts in the order of decreasing importance. In this way, editors who need to shorten the release because of space limitations can easily "kill" the story from the bottom up. For example, notice that the first two paragraphs in the news release illustrated on page 493 make a complete news story by themselves. The remainder of the copy provides additional details.

TELECOMMUNICATIONS

Telecommunications are messages transmitted electronically. They are used when speed is required. In addition, this type of message is often superior to a letter because people associate telecommunications with important and urgent messages. Therefore, they are likely to give more attention to a telecommunication than they would to a letter.

Some types of telecommunication include the telegram (for domestic use), the telex (for overseas use), and the mailgram, a combined service of Western Union and the United States Postal Service. The two aspects of telecommunications that distinguish them from other types of written communications are (1) they are composed on a special form and (2) the style of writing the message differs from that used in letters. Each of these aspects is explained and illustrated below.

Brevity in telecommunications is important because the cost of sending a message is based on the number of words. Therefore, any redundancy in the messages should be avoided, so long as the message is still clear.

It is permissible to compose a telecommunication without using complete sentences and to dispense with some typical courtesies of the business letter. Notice these differences in the paragraph from a business letter and a telegram, in which the telegram expresses in 11 words the essentials of what the letter says in 85 words.

Letter	Telegram
We would like to have you check our letter of May 1 and the accompanying purchase invoice, Number A751C. We requested that you deliver the furniture to our store to reach us by August 1. However, we have planned a summer sale that is to begin on June 15 and would like to advertise this furniture if we can be certain that it will be in stock when we announce the sale. Please let us know promptly if delivery can be made by May 30.	Confirm immediately if order A751C can be delivered by May 30.

For telecommunications, details regarding the sending of the message, the word count, and the charge for each word vary according to the type of service used and the company providing the service. To send a telegram, for example, you can call Western Union and dictate the message and name and address of the person who is to receive the communication. Western Union will send your message by teleprinter to the branch office nearest the recipient, and the branch office will deliver it. The cost of sending a telegram can be charged to your telephone number.

Many large companies with branches, divisions, or subsidiaries in many locations facilitate communication by installing telecommunications equipment. With teleprinters in each location, a communication system can be set up that cuts the cost and time involved in sending messages. Western Union provides two such services, Telex and TWX (teletypewriter exchange service).

COMMUNICATION PROJECTS

Practical Application

A. The EPA (Environmental Protection Association) held its first organizational meeting on your campus last evening. Margot Hayden was elected president, and you were elected secretary-treasurer. The faculty sponsor is Professor Sidney Allen, chairperson of the science department. The group plans to meet bimonthly on the first and third Wednesday of each month. Its aims are to publicize instances of local pollution and toxic waste dumping, to investigate possible conservation measures in the community, and to recommend publicity to make the college community more conservation-oriented. Write a news release about the organization—its officers, aims, plans—for your local newspaper. Supply any additional facts that you feel are needed.

B. Write the minutes for the second meeting of the EPA (see Application A). Assume that various projects were proposed at the meeting—a recycling drive for newspapers and metals, bikeways throughout the city, field trips to local industrial plants to see how they handle waste products, a film entitled *The Water We Drink*, and a poster contest for high school students. Also, add any other worthwhile activities that you would recommend. Supply all the specifics, such as motions passed or defeated, and so on.

C. Your boss, George Theopolus, vice president of Zeta Paper Manufacturing Company of Portland, Oregon, requests that you write a news release for the *Portland Sentinel* announcing the retirement of the company president, Philip Alvarez, at the end of this year. The newspaper may make the announcement immediately since the board of directors has already regretfully accepted Mr. Alvarez's notice of retirement. Alvarez has been with the company for 25 years, serving as president for the last 10 years. He started his career with the company as a shop supervisor and then became factory manager within 2 years. Alvarez became a vice president shortly thereafter and remained in that position until 10 years ago, when the board of directors elected him president. Following his retirement, Mr. Alvarez will serve as chairman of the board of directors. Alvarez lives in Seacrest with his wife. They have two married sons and one married daughter, all of whom live in Portland. Alvarez is a graduate in accounting from Youngstown College, where he was class president during his senior year. Alvarez has served on the

Portland Chamber of Commerce for 5 years, is a member of both Rotary and Kiwanis, and has headed the City Beautification Committee for the last three years. Using an acceptable format, write a news release. Supply any information that should be included.

D. Assume that you are the secretary of the Staunton Employees' Association, charged with the responsibility for taking minutes at all meetings and distributing copies to each member. From the following information, prepare in a concise format the minutes of the latest meeting:

1. The meeting, held in Room 5A, Tyler Building, was called to order by President Karl Swensen at 5:30 p.m., March 15, 19—.
2. Correction in minutes of preceding meeting (February 15) approved: Ina Singer, not Rita Singer, was appointed chairperson of the Welfare Committee.
3. Karen Bjorn reviewed employee suggestions for January. Awards of $100 each for two accepted suggestions were approved. Bjorn to make arrangements for presenting the awards at the spring banquet.
4. Revised written procedure for handling employee suggestions presented by Jack Carlson. Accepted with editorial revision to be made by appropriate committee.
5. Meeting adjourned at 6:15 p.m., with the understanding that the next meeting would be a dinner meeting at Jackson's Restaurant, April 21, to begin at 6:30 p.m.
6. The following members were absent: Holden, Reardon, Witmer.

E. Your employer, Theresa Riendeau, will speak at the June 15 meeting of the Women Executives Club at the Hotel Washington in Kansas City. She has asked you to wire the hotel for reservations for June 14, 15, and 16 and to request a two-room suite with bath. (While in Kansas City, Ms. Riendeau will be interviewing candidates for positions as sales representative for your company.)

1. Find out the fastest telegraphic service available in your community, the rate, and the base word count.
2. Staying within the base word count, compose the message, asking for confirmation of the reservation. Also ask for information regarding the availability of a videocassette recorder, a monitor, an overhead projector and a screen to be used during Ms. Riendeau's presentation.

F. Revise the following telecommunications so that none exceeds 15 words. Aim for brevity, clarity, and completeness.

1. We are shipping by airfreight today the 4 parts you ordered for our copier #34AC, except for part #YC14, which will be shipped to you next Thursday, also by airfreight.

2. Proposed contract for reconstruction of fire-damaged Plant A125 received. Must also have target dates for completion of each section of contract. Wire dates in time for our board meeting Friday morning.
3. Phillip Goetz expects to arrive in Boston on Wemas Flight 15 on Friday morning. Please arrange to pick him up at the airport and brief him on Tracy-Phelps contract en route to board meeting.
4. Our Purchase Order 7683 for four mahogany desks and matching executive chairs has not arrived, and our inventory is depleted. If the order has not yet been shipped, arrange shipment for six of each by fastest method.
5. The computer printout of the March sales forecast was lost and never reached us. Please airmail two copies immediately.

Editing Practice

Supply the Missing Words. Indicate a word or words that you think would make sense if inserted in the blank space within each sentence.

1. If this pamphlet does not give you the . . . you desire, please write us again.
2. Thank you for being so . . . in filling our order.
3. We are happy to tell you that your . . . has been established at the Okidata Hotel.
4. We hope that we shall have the pleasure of serving you whenever you have . . . to use our repair service.
5. Once you know the . . . of a credit card, you will never shop without your card.
6. Please sign the original copy and return it to us in the enclosed envelope, retaining the . . . for your files.
7. We understand that you will probably . . . to purchase as much as $3000 worth of merchandise monthly on your account.
8. We hope that your clerical staff will . . . some means of checking purchases made by persons of the same name but of different addresses.
9. We have taken steps to see that there is no . . . of this error.
10. We hope that our business dealings will be . . . pleasant and profitable.
11. The report . . . the data that had been gathered by the newly appointed committee.
12. The new inventory system was . . . just before the Christmas rush began.
13. An office worker's . . . is judged not only by the volume of work completed but also by the accuracy of the work.
14. All the payroll . . . were noted on the check stub.
15. Government . . . are available to many different groups.

Case Problem

To Bluff or Not to Bluff. During an interview for a position as assistant office manager, Leonard Kaiser is asked to express his feelings about word processing. Unfortunately, Leonard knows very little about word processing.

1. Should Leonard bluff his way through or admit that he knows very little about word processing?
2. What should he say that will not make him look bad during this interview?
3. What risks does he take if he should bluff?

CHAPTER
ELEVEN

DEVELOPING ORAL COMMUNICATION SKILL

51

THE ORAL COMMUNICATION PROCESS

As you enter the reception area of the Webster Building, you are greeted by the warm smile and friendly voice of the receptionist asking, "May I be of assistance to you?" You reply, "I have a ten o'clock appointment with Mrs. Alvarez." The receptionist tells you, "Mrs. Alvarez's office is on the twentieth floor, Suite 2059. May I please have your name so that I may telephone Mrs. Alvarez to let her know that you are on your way up to see her?" The receptionist then directs you to an express elevator that stops on the twentieth floor. You are already favorably impressed with the Webster Company, based on this first encounter with one of its employees.

As you step from the elevator on the twentieth floor and enter the tastefully furnished office of the Webster Company, you notice a number of employees busily engaged in a variety of activities. A young man approaches you. "Good morning, (your name); I'm Josh Brown, Mrs. Alvarez's administrative assistant. She will be with you just as soon as she completes a long-distance telephone call that came in while you were on your way up. Please make yourself comfortable here, and I would be happy to bring you a cup of coffee or tea."

As you glance around the busy office, you notice several employees quietly engaged in telephone conversations. In a corner of a partitioned section, someone is explaining and demonstrating how to operate a new duplicating machine. In a glass-enclosed conference area, a small group is gathered around a table listening to an explanation of some figures on a flip chart. A young executive in another office is using a dictation machine. You notice on a nearby bulletin board an announcement of a sales training conference; another announcement indicates that there will be a meeting of the Office Employees' Association next Monday morning.

Your communication instructor was right—oral communication *does* play an important role in the daily activities of every office employee! Then, as you are shown into Mrs. Alvarez's office, you realize how fortunate you are to have had some training in oral communication. Why do you consider yourself so fortunate? Well, you are in Mrs. Alvarez's office to be interviewed for a position that you very much want. You are about to make your training in oral communication work for you.

THE IMPORTANCE OF ORAL COMMUNICATION IN BUSINESS

Even before you began to work in the business world, you were convinced of the importance of oral communication in all business activities. This conviction will grow stronger each day. From the receptionist who greeted you in the lobby to the president on the top floor, information is continually being transmitted orally from one employee to another, from employees to customers and vendors on the outside, and from these and other outsiders to employees of the firm. The success enjoyed by any business organization depends, to a very large degree, upon the success of its members in making themselves understood and in persuading others to accept their ideas.

Though written communication is important in transacting business, oral communication is used more often and by more people. Some business positions require the use of oral communication almost exclusively, and the people who fill these jobs are hired on the strength of their ability to speak well. The sales representative, the office receptionist, the switchboard operator, the person who handles customer service or complaints—all these people must be highly skilled in oral communication. The office or factory supervisor, the public accountant, the personnel manager, the bank teller, the business executive, and the secretary are only a few of the other workers who make extensive use of oral communication in carrying out the responsibilities of their positions.

If you aspire to a position of leadership in business, your ability to speak forcefully, persuasively, and convincingly will play a vital role in helping you achieve your goal. At meetings and conferences, speakers will include all levels of employees, top management people, and outside consultants. On many occasions, you will do much of the talking. You will seek to solve grievances of employees; you will conduct meetings and small group discussions; you will give talks to employees, to the public, and to business and professional groups. In your daily contacts with supervisors and coworkers, you will use oral communication for reporting, instructing, reprimanding, giving information, and asking for information. This power to communicate orally is important to every business leader.

DEVELOPING ORAL COMMUNICATION SKILLS

THE ROLE OF ORAL COMMUNICATION
IN BUSINESS

Oral communication is used by business employees in a variety of ways and in a variety of settings. Among the ways business employees depend upon oral communication are:

To sell goods and services. All salespeople, whether they are selling goods or services, rely on their oral communication ability to help them make sales. Whether it is an insurance agent who canvasses you at home or the retail salesperson who asks, "Would you like a tie to go with that shirt?" both use their oral communication abilities to sell. Even the airline ticket agent uses oral communication to assist you in arranging your proposed business or vacation trip.

To give instruction to an individual or a group. The teacher, whether performing in a school situation or in special business or industrial classes on the job, is dependent on oral communication; the sales manager who conducts special training classes for sales representatives must be an effective oral communicator; even the computer programmer who must instruct a new assistant relies heavily on oral communication.

To explain or report to supervisors, subordinates, and those on the same level. The sales manager may report orally to the vice president in charge of sales; the supervisor in the office interprets a new company policy for employees; an employee explains a grievance to the supervisor; the general manager's secretary tells the file clerk to pull all correspondence with a particular company.

To give information to customers and potential customers. A customer calls a department store for information about the sizes, colors, and prices of vinyl tile; another customer telephones for advice about the best method of cleaning recently purchased rugs.

To give formal speeches before groups. The president of a company is asked to give a speech before the members of the Rotary Club; an accountant is asked to talk to a college class in advanced accounting; the secretary to the president of a large manufacturing firm is asked to address a group of college students on "The Advantages of Becoming a Secretary."

To participate in social-business conversation. The office manager telephones the secretary of Kiwanis to cancel a reservation for the luncheon meeting tomorrow; a sales representative congratulates two former associates who have gone into partnership.

To interview employees and prospective employees. The personnel manager and the section supervisor interview applicants for an accounting position; the supervisor discusses an employee's merit rating at the end of the probationary period.

To acquire information necessary to conduct the everyday affairs of business. The credit manager of a department store calls the local credit bureau to determine the credit rating of a new customer; the mail clerk telephones the post office to find out which class of mail to use for a special mailing the company is planning; the accountant visits the Internal Revenue Service office to discuss methods of figuring depreciation on equipment; a secretary telephones a travel agency to get information about hotel accommodations in Seattle.

To purchase goods and services. A homeowner asks a department store salesperson many questions about a rug she would like to buy; the purchasing agent telephones a local stationer to order a filing cabinet; the manager of a truck fleet inquires about a truck-leasing plan.

To provide service for customers and potential customers. The credit manager explains to a customer the procedure for opening a charge account; the section manager in the bedding department tells a customer why bedding can't be returned for exchange or refund.

To participate in meetings. A sales manager conducts a meeting of the Sales Executives Club; a secretary contributes ideas for the convention of the National Secretaries Association to the members of the planning committee.

To participate in informal discussion with fellow employees. The receptionist takes up a collection to buy a gift for a co-worker who is in the hospital; the mail room supervisor organizes a committee to plan the office Christmas party; the sales promotion manager gets all the employees in the office together for lunch.

These are just a few examples of oral communication activities that may be observed every day in business—activities that rely for their success almost wholly upon effective oral communication.

FORMS OF ORAL COMMUNICATION IN BUSINESS

Oral communication in business is found in many different forms. Some forms are used more frequently than others. Among the most commonly used methods of oral communication are the following:

Face-to-face conversation—interviews, sales, social-business situations, informal discussions between supervisors and employees.

Telephone conversation—with another office, with customers, with suppliers.

Conversation via interoffice communication devices—between executive and secretary-receptionist, between sales representative on selling floor and clerk in stockroom.

Dictation and recording—dictating a letter to a secretary, using a dictating machine for dictating letters, recording meetings electronically.

Radio and television appearances—giving interviews or reporting information.

Formal speeches—debates; panels; addresses to employees, the public, customers, or professional groups.

Leadership of, or participation in, group discussions or meetings—leading employee group discussions, participating in stockholders' meetings and in meetings of business and professional organizations.

Instruction—teaching training classes for sales representatives and retail store employees.

Each of these methods of communication requires a slightly different technique. The difference may be in the amount and kind of prior preparation, the manner in which the voice is projected, or the style in which the speaker makes the presentation. For example, speaking over the telephone requires a knowledge of how far the telephone mouthpiece should be held from the lips and how much the speaker's voice should be projected. A radio or telephone presentation may be read from copy and, therefore, requires a knowledge of how to read without giving the impression that you *are* reading. Leading a meeting requires a knowledge of parliamentary procedure. Teaching a class requires that the teacher know how to ask questions properly. Participating in a panel or in a group discussion requires the ability to think quickly and to put thoughts into understandable language without hesitation.

EFFECTIVE BUSINESS RELATIONSHIPS THROUGH ORAL COMMUNICATION

Regardless of what position you hold in business, the effectiveness of your oral communication with people both inside and outside the company will have an important influence on your personal success in business. Furthermore, your verbal contacts can influence the success of the company that employs you. When employees get along with one another—with those on the same job level as well as with those on levels above or below them—they are likely to be more productive employees. Moreover, satisfactory interpersonal relationships among employees also contribute to better relationships with those outside their company. The result of effective public relations is almost certain to be increased business.

In business, how does oral communication help develop the most desirable atmosphere for effective employee relationships? By establishing an environment that provides for a free flow of information and ideas between management and employees. When employees have frequent and easy means to discuss and express their ideas and concerns, morale is likely to be high. And when morale is high, work efficiency is greater. Personal conferences with employees, committee meetings, group conferences, and informational speeches that provide for question-and-answer sessions are some of the primary situations in which oral communication contributes to improved relations among employees and between management and employees.

How does oral communication contribute to effective public relations? By ensuring that every spoken communication with a customer is a positive experience. Although business spends considerable time and money to plan and create carefully worded letters and advertising copy to keep customers and to win new ones, often the oral contacts are overlooked. Successful businesses do not neglect the importance of oral communication and, therefore, train their employees in areas such as public speaking, correct telephone techniques, and group discussion leading. The manner in which a customer is treated on the telephone or in person is just as important in developing goodwill as is the written communication—sometimes even more important. *All* employees—salespersons, secretaries, receptionists, accountants—create a public image of the company they represent by the manner in which they speak to customers and potential customers. A curt or rude employee can cause a business to lose many sales—and even to lose customers of long standing. Every employee a customer comes in contact with *is* the company. Therefore, the telephone conversation or the face-to-face conversation must, through the words and tone used by the employee, make these customers feel that their interests are important and that the company wants them to be satisfied.

A PROGRAM TO IMPROVE YOUR ORAL COMMUNICATION

At the beginning of this section, you became aware of how oral communication helped you to develop an initial impression of the company you visited. The receptionist who greeted you the moment you entered the building certainly contributed to your positive impression. Also, during your visit, you observed how a variety of oral activities played an important role in the performance of many employees' daily tasks. Finally, as you were about to participate in a job interview, you became even more appreciative of the need for effective oral communication.

The manner in which you use your oral communication skills on the job can either help or hinder you in performing your everyday activities and advancing to higher positions. The remaining sections of this chapter provide you with the opportunity to learn techniques for improving your oral communication skills when dealing with both coworkers and the public.

COMMUNICATION PROJECTS

Practical Application

A.   For each of the following business positions, indicate the oral communication activities that you think would be typical in that position:

1.   Accountant
2.   Retail salesclerk
3.   Secretary
4.   Personnel interviewer
5.   Receptionist

B.   Be prepared to discuss each of the following topics:

1.   The Importance of Communication Skills for Success in College
2.   The Importance of Communication Skills for Success in Business
3.   How Ineffective Communication Leads to Problems

C.   Be prepared to take the affirmative or negative side in a debate on this topic: *Resolved: That beginning business employees do not need effective communication skills as much as more experienced business employees.*

D.   Under three headings—Home, School, Business—list as many oral communication activities as you can.

E.   Practice reading aloud the following instructions for talking on the telephone so that you do not sound as though you are reading the material or have memorized it.

Clear enunciation is extremely important if you wish to be understood by the listener. Each word and each syllable must be pronounced distinctly. Your voice should be well modulated, and you should move your lips, tongue, and jaw freely. Hold the mouthpiece about an inch from your mouth, speaking directly into the transmitter. Keep your mouth free of gum, candy, and other objects that could affect your pronunciation or cause you to slur your words. Often, you can tell if your words are being heard clearly by the number of times the listener asks you to repeat what you have said.

F.   Without using any gestures or diagrams, give oral directions for the following situations:

1.   How to walk to the nearest shopping area from your school.
2.   How to get to the administration office of your school from the classroom in which your communication class meets.
3.   How to fold a letter for insertion in a No. 10 envelope.

G.   Orally describe an object without telling the class what the object is. If you have described the object clearly, the class should be able to identify it from your description.

Editing Practice

Spelling and Vocabulary.   Some of the following sentences contain spelling errors; some test vocabulary; some are correct. Correct each incorrect sentence. Write *OK* for any sentence that has no error.

1.   How will the change effect your work?
2.   What plans does your company have for disposel of waste?
3.   Which proceedures apply to this job?
4.   We will have a sale to celabrate our anniversary.
5.   What was the occasion for the closing of the office?
6.   The new equiptment arrived this morning.
7.   Have you recieved the specifications yet?
8.   The new president was formally introduced to the employees today.
9.   I adviced the accountant regarding the handling of that item.
10.   On what sight will the new factory be erected?

Editing for Context.   Rewrite any sentence containing words that do not fit the context. Write *OK* for any sentence that has no error.

1.   The need for foreclosing compiled us to consult with our attorney.
2.   Did you receive all the items on the manifest?
3.   His actions did not ward our taking any steps at this time.
4.   Their quite concerned about the number of errors.
5.   Sign the affidavit where indicated.
6.   I applied for the job at the personal office.
7.   All the employees will benefit tremulously from the changes.
8.   The error demented our confidence in his ability.
9.   We addended to a set of rules established by the board.
10.   To countenance serious problems, drastic budget cuts must be made.

Case Problem

The Rude Caller? Mr. May's secretary answered the ringing telephone, and the voice on the other end asked to speak to Mr. May. The secretary responded by asking, "May I ask who is calling?" The voice at the other end curtly said, "No, you may not," and hung up. "How rude," thought the secretary, with a perplexed expression on her face.

1. Who was the rude one, the secretary or the caller? Why?
2. What should the secretary have asked in order to get the information desired? Why is this a more desirable way of handling the caller?

52

PREPARING FOR ORAL COMMUNICATION

Let's eavesdrop on two executives who are discussing the candidates for a promotion to an important and well-paying position. Perhaps you are one of the candidates they are considering for this position.

"Both Rita and Carmen have similar qualifications and experience, so how can we decide which one to select for this position?"

"Well, we must remember that one of the most important aspects of this position is the ability to conduct meetings to train sales representatives, as well as to handle meetings with buyers and customers."

"Yes, that's probably the most important aspect of this job. Furthermore, a great deal of business is conducted over the telephone. Also, we shouldn't overlook the monthly community consumers' meeting, where the person in this position must give a formal presentation and lead the group discussion that follows the presentation."

"It is very obvious that the person we select must have outstanding oral skills, particularly in the areas of making formal presentations and leading group discussion. Do you feel that both candidates are equally qualified in these areas of oral communcation?"

"Rita has demonstrated that she can do a superior job in making presentations and in talking on the telephone. Remember how well she led that group discussion at the personnel meeting last month?"

"She certainly is a very effective speaker and group discussion leader; she uses language well; and she impresses people very favorably with her appearance. On the other hand, Carmen is extremely weak in her oral communication skills. There is no doubt in my mind that we should select Rita for this position."

Would you agree with the selection made by these executives? In terms of the job qualifications and the qualifications of the two candidates, you would have to agree with them. It is unfortunate that so many candidates for good positions eliminate themselves from consideration for promotion because they are weak in their oral communication skills. In most business positions, oral communication probably is used more frequently than written communication. Furthermore, obtaining a good position and succeeding in it depend very heavily upon persuasive oral skills. That is why it is so important that you become aware of the two major factors that determine a person's effectiveness in communicating orally—physical appearance and speech qualities. These two aspects will be discussed in Sections 52 and 53, while the application of these skills will be discussed in the remaining sections of this chapter.

APPEARANCE

Except for situations involving the use of the telephone or dictating machines, the speaker is visible to the listener and creates an impression that often influences the degree of acceptability of his or her words upon that listener. This first impression is based primarily on such factors as posture, the use of the speaker's hands, eye contact that the speaker makes with the listener, body and head movement, and the speaker's overall personal appearance—dress, grooming, and so on.

A speaker's physical appearance often sets the stage for the acceptance or nonacceptance of the speaker's words. A speaker who makes a good physical impression quickly gains the interest of listeners. (A speaker must have something interesting and worthwhile to say—and must say it in an effective manner—to hold the attention of the listeners for any length of time.) The first barrier to effective oral communication will be overcome if the speaker has good posture, is dressed appropriately, is well groomed, and knows how to make each listener feel that the listener is being spoken to directly.

Posture

Many speakers make the serious mistake of underestimating the importance of good posture to overall good physical appearance. Regardless of how short or tall you may be, you should always stand up to your full height. You'll find that good posture will help you develop better breath control. Good posture will also make you appear more confident and give your audience the impression that you know what you are talking about and that your message is really important. Of course, no speaker should appear stiff or pompous and all-knowing. Instead, you should develop a natural posture, constantly reminding yourself to stand erect, with shoulders back and stomach in. Such posture helps improve your voice quality and gives you the appearance of authority.

Hands

While you are speaking, do not distract your audience by pulling at your clothing, putting your hands to your face or hair, or toying with something you are holding. Listeners will automatically direct their attention to your physical maneuvers and will soon lose track of what you are saying to them. If you are standing, it is probably best to place your arms and hands in a relaxed position at your sides (rather than behind your back or folded in front of you). From time to time, make natural gestures. If there is a lectern in front of you, you may wish to place your hands on either side of it. However, remember *never* to lean on the lectern!

When you are talking from a sitting position, you will be heard better if you sit slightly forward in your chair. You may rest your arms and hands in your lap, on the arms of the chair in which you are sitting, or partially on the edge of the table or desk in front of you. However, never use the desk or table as a place to rest your head and elbows. A lazy-looking speaker encourages apathy on the part of the audience.

Facial Expressions

A speaker's facial expression influences the listeners' impressions. A relaxed, pleasant, interested expression will create a better atmosphere for communicating, of course, than a wrinkled brow and turned-down mouth. As you look in a mirror from time to time, see whether you can capture your personality as others see it. Are your facial muscles relaxed? Is your smile natural, pleasant, and genuine? What characteristics in your facial expression are appealing to those around you? See if you can develop animation and show enthusiasm in your facial expression. Above all, you must look alert and interested if you want to impress your listeners.

Eye Contact

One of the best ways to appear interested is to look at your audience, whether that audience is composed of just one person or of more than a hundred. Everyone likes to feel directly addressed by the speaker. Therefore, your eyes should never leave your audience for any extended period of time; it's hard for your listeners to stay interested when you are looking constantly at your notes, the wall, the ceiling, or out the window. When talking to one or two persons, look squarely into the faces of your listeners (without, of course, staring them down) unless you are directing their attention to an object such as a chart. When speaking to a large audience, move your eyes over the entire audience; look into the faces of your listeners and not over the tops of their heads.

Body Movement

Body movement also contributes a great deal to the physical effect created by a speaker. The effective speaker never paces back and forth, because excessive movement will distract an audience. It is permissible to move your body from the hips in order to turn from side to side or to move your body in a forward motion to add emphasis to a remark. Of course, if you are using a chart or other illustrative material, you must move from time to time to the visual device. However, when speaking, you should try to face the audience as much as possible and to stay in one place as long as you can.

Grooming and Dress

Personal appearance—grooming, cleanliness, and attire—is also an important factor in effective communication. How a speaker looks and dresses expresses personality just as much as speech and conduct do. There are so many factors involved in personal appearance that not all of them can be considered here in depth. If you are interested in better oral communications, you should be aware that you communicate best when you appear your best. Good appearance breeds confidence. Appearing clean, being dressed neatly and conservatively, avoiding extremes in personal grooming and clothing styles, and selecting attire and accessories that are tasteful and in harmony with one another and with your personality are some of the factors of personal appearance that you should consider. A speaker who ignores any one of these suggestions cannot hope to be very persuasive as an oral communicator.

SPEECH QUALITIES

Although a speaker's physical appearance creates the first impression on the audience, the quality of speech may have an even greater influence on the audience. The quality of speech is determined by the following factors:

Force or volume of voice
Pitch or level of voice
Tone
Rate or tempo of speech
Enunciation
Pronunciation

The force of a speaker's voice and the pitch and the tempo of speech depend, to a great extent, on the speaker's breath control. The volume of air that is taken into the lungs and breath control help determine how much force a speaker's voice will have; both factors also affect the voice pitch. The rate of speaking will be determined by how frequently a speaker must breathe more air into the lungs. The speaker should talk only when breathing air out—never when taking air into the lungs. Good posture can help a speaker breathe in the maximum amount of air and can help to control the amount of air expended.

Force (Volume)

In order for oral communication to be effective, the message must be heard and heard clearly. Sufficient volume, therefore, is required; and good breath control is important to achieve sufficient volume. If your voice is too soft and you have trouble being heard, you should practice breathing deeply and controlling your breath with your diaphragm and abdominal muscles, just as a singer does. The large abdominal cavity should be used to store a supply of air that can be released evenly to produce a clear, sustained tone. How much force you must use will, of course, be determined by such factors as how good the acoustics are in the room in which you are speaking, how large your audience is, and whether or not you are using a microphone or other electronic device to amplify your voice.

Pitch (Voice Level)

A speaker's voice will be more audible if it has a pleasing pitch. *Pitch* refers to the level of a sound on a musical scale. Practice can help correct the shrillness of a voice that is pitched too high or the excessive resonance of a voice that is pitched too low. Equally in need of correction is the constant pitch that results in a monotone. An effective speaker varies the pitch. The rising and falling of voice pitch is called *intonation*. Intonation can indicate that a statement is being made, that a question is being asked, or that a speaker is pausing. A drop in pitch indicates finality or determination and is, therefore, used at the end of a declarative sentence. For example, in reading the following sentence you should close with a drop in pitch.

I cannot *possibly* attend the dinner meeting, especially on Monday. (Emphasize the word *possibly*.)

You should raise your pitch when you ask a question or when you wish to express suspense, doubt, or hesitation. Read the following sentences, closing with a rise in pitch.

What *more* can I do? (Emphasize *more.*)

I'm *so* sorry I can't go with you today, but I will *definitely* go next week. (Emphasize the words *so* and *definitely*.)

Gliding the pitch up and down or down and up usually expresses sarcasm or contempt, as in the slang expression, "Oh, yeah?"

The most important aspect of pitch is variation. Variation of pitch not only helps hold the audience's attention but also helps listeners know the exact meaning intended. Important words can be stressed by a rise in pitch. Comparisons can be stressed by using the same pitch for each element; contrasts, on the other hand, can be made by pitching the first element high and the second low.

Notice the different shades of meaning that emerge as you read the following sentences and emphasize the italicized words.

Antony gave her the book. (Antony did, not someone else.)
Antony *gave* her the book. (It was a gift.)
Antony gave *her* the book. (Only she was given the book.)
Antony gave her *the* book. (The particular book or special book.)
Antony gave her the *book*. (He gave her the book, not something else.)

Tone

The tone of your voice often reveals your attitudes and feelings. Naturally, a pleasant and cheerful tone is more desirable because it will have a better effect on your audience. On the telephone, the tone of your voice must substitute for your facial expression. Hence, the observation, "The voice with the smile." In addition, variation in tone, as well as in volume and pitch, can be used to add interest to your speaking voice. The kind of tone you use should be appropriate for the words and ideas you are expressing.

Speaking Rate (Tempo)

The rate at which you speak should be varied, too, to avoid extremes in either direction. You should not speak so rapidly that words are not understood, but neither should you speak so slowly that the audience does not pay close attention to what is being said. You should regulate your rate of speaking so that you are able to enunciate each word clearly so that the listener will hear each word without difficulty. A good speaking rate is 125 words a minute; oral reading rates and radio speaking tend to run slightly faster—about 150 words a minute. To determine what a rate of 125 words a minute sounds like, read aloud the paragraph below in a half minute. Reread the paragraph as many times as necessary until you achieve the desired rate. At the end of a quarter minute, you should be at the diagonal line. Use this line as a guide to either increase or decrease your speaking rate.

A good speaker talks slowly enough to be understood by the listeners and speaks in a pleasant voice, articulating and pronouncing each word correctly and distinctly. To develop a good / speaking voice, you must spend sufficient time practicing the elements of good speech. An effective speaker is a definite asset to business and will usually find more opportunities for advancing in the job. (63 words)

Changing the rate contributes to variety, as well as to clarity. Important words should be spoken slowly; unimportant words or phrases, more rapidly.

Try to speak in thought units so that you can assist the listener in interpreting your words. If the sentence is short, obviously the thought unit will consist of the entire sentence, as in "My office is very pleasant." When there are several thought units within a sentence, then the speaker should pause slightly after each thought group, as in "My office is very pleasant; / but I must agree, / some days are much more hectic than others."

Use pauses to stress major points. By pausing between major points or after important statements, you add variety and emphasis to the points you want the audience to remember.

Enunciation and Pronunciation

Since good enunciation and pronunciation are such important aspects of effective business speaking, they receive separate treatment in Section 53.

COMMUNICATION PROJECTS

Practical Application

A.   Reread the first page of this section. Assume that you are also a candidate for the position discussed. How would you compare your oral communication skills with those of the other two candidates? List your strengths and weaknesses, including such factors as your personality, the first impression you make on others, your personal appearance, your facial expressions, and your mannerisms. Briefly comment on each of these factors. Would you be a likely candidate for this position? Why or why not? Would it be possible for you to overcome any handicaps?

B.   Select three prominent people (in politics, sports, or the arts) who frequently appear before the public in some type of speaking role. List the factors—pro and con—that affect their speaking effectiveness.

C.   Read each of the following sentences three times. Each time, emphasize a different word in the sentence, which will change the meaning of the sentence.

1.   Marty mailed the letter yesterday morning.
2.   I liked London more than any other city I visited on my trip.
3.   Did you see Ethel at the banquet this week?

4. If possible, please arrive earlier on Saturday.
5. I really didn't expect to arrive so late; please forgive me.

D. Read the following sentences silently once or twice. Then, standing in front of the class, read them through from beginning to end. Try to keep your eyes on the audience as much as possible while reading them.

1. John is never late for work, if he can avoid it.
2. I doubt very much that I will be able to attend the office banquet next week.
3. No, in my opinion, the new computer does not perform so efficiently as the old one.
4. What difference does it make whether or not I attend the meeting scheduled for next Tuesday?
5. Do you really think that Fred will be able to complete that complicated assignment on time?

E. Read the following paragraphs silently twice. Then, standing in front of the class, read them aloud, keeping your eyes on the audience as much as possible.

1. To be an effective speaker, you must be aware of your audience at all times, not only in selecting and preparing your topic but also in giving your speech. Audiences respond favorably only to speakers who talk directly to them and who smile occasionally. The speaker who looks at the ceiling, at notes, or into space quickly loses rapport with the audience.
2. Nearly every speech of any length is brightened considerably by touches of humor and by human interest narratives. Of course, such stories should not dominate the speech. Observe the following rules: Use stories and jokes that add interest to the subject or illustrate a particular point. Before telling a joke to an audience, test it on friends to make sure it has a punch line. Make sure that stories and jokes do not offend or embarrass the audience. And time your stories to make sure that they are not too long.
3. When you are talking to an audience, pretend that you are carrying on a face-to-face conversation with just one person. Remember that the audience is just as eager for you to perform well as you are to do so. Don't be upset if you are nervous—even experienced speakers and actors are. Feeling nervous is a result of anxiety about doing a good job, and most authorities feel that a little stage fright provides needed tension.
4. Most people take telephone usage for granted—and this is one of the reasons so many office workers are ineffective telephone communicators. Too many employees assume that a business telephone conversation is the same as a personal telephone call. Actually, the telephone is one of the most important communication media in business, and it must be used with great skill,

especially when talking with outside callers and with superiors in the office.

F. Present a three-minute (approximately) talk to the class on a topic of your choice. Try to make each person in your audience feel as though you are talking individually to that person.

Editing Practice

Synonyms or Antonyms? In each item below, two words are synonyms or antonyms. For each item, identify the pair by letter and indicate whether the words are synonyms or antonyms. Use a dictionary if necessary.

1. (a) excellence (b) disparity (c) slander (d) reference (e) equality
2. (a) chasten (b) start (c) hunt (d) perform (e) discipline
3. (a) sagacity (b) hypocrisy (c) opener (d) glamour (e) candor
4. (a) odd (b) erudite (c) old (d) reconciled (e) estranged
5. (a) affable (b) garrulous (c) gracious (d) precious (e) joyous
6. (a) busy (b) boisterous (c) happy (d) quiet (e) clever
7. (a) phlegmatic (b) stolid (c) involuntary (d) sordid (e) respiratory
8. (a) faultless (b) modest (c) excusing (d) pretentious (e) extraneous
9. (a) concave (b) cadaverous (c) convex (d) solid (e) harrowing
10. (a) demise (b) undershirt (c) death (d) contrive (e) contract

Editor's Alert. Thoroughly examine the following sentences for needed corrections. Make those corrections, rewriting any poorly worded sentences. Write *OK* for any sentence that has no error.

1. The managers desks should be locked before the office is closed.
2. Ther're no reason for you to be absent so frequently.
3. Will you and him be at the banquet tomorrow?
4. Carl ordered 10 reams of letterhead paper at $6 each, making a total of $60.
5. Please continue on as though nothing were said.
6. Complete your questionaire not later than June 2.
7. You should follow-up the requests made in each peice of correspondence.
8. This company has always in the past—and always will—be noted for prompt delivery.
9. The raise was only given to Morgan and I last week.
10. 10 candidates applied for the position advertised on television.

Case Problem

Who's to Blame? Jean Lee and Ted Wayne both type for Mr. Carr. One morning Mr. Carr came to Jean with a typed letter in which there were many errors. He was most irritated because of the careless proofreading and requested that the letter be retyped. Jean noted that the reference initials were "TW."

1. If you were Jean, what would you do about the situation?
2. What suggestions would you make to prevent a similar situation from happening again?

53
ENUNCIATION AND PRONUNCIATION

Edith Polinski, a secretary for the Juarez Electric Appliance Company, handed her supervisor a letter she transcribed from a dictation disk and then returned to her desk to continue with her next task. In a few minutes, her supervisor came rushing out of his office, a frown on his face, obviously disturbed about something.

"Edith, you're gonna havta do this letter over. Ya made a terrible error that wudda cost us a lotta money if I hadna caught it—and, darn it, I was in a hurry to get this letter in the mail."

"What did I do wrong?" asked the distressed Edith.

Her supervisor explained, "See here, where you have 'forty tables for $14,000'? It's supposta be *fourteen* tables for $14,000."

"I'm sorry," apologized Edith, "but that's what you said on the dictation disk, *forty*."

"I cudna said that. Play that part again."

When the disk reached the word in question, it became apparent that Edith's boss so poorly enunciated the *fourteen* that anyone would have mistaken the word for *forty*.

The boss apologized, but regardless of who was at fault, Edith had to take the time—and additional stationery—to revise the letter. However, it was indeed fortunate that the error was caught before the letter was mailed and resulted in a large monetary loss to the company.

One could cite many other instances in business—and even in social situations—where poor enunciation has led to costly delays, unnecessary expense, and the loss of goodwill. That is why it is so important for all business employees, particularly those who have face-to-face or telephone contact with customers and vendors and those who use dictation equipment, to both enunciate and pronounce words clearly and correctly.

ENUNCIATION VERSUS PRONUNCIATION

Although the terms *enunciation* and *pronunciation* are closely related, they do have slightly different meanings. Understanding the difference between the two terms and making a strong effort to eliminate the barriers to effective enunciation and pronunciation will contribute greatly to improved speech.

Enunciation

Enunciation refers to the distinctness or clarity with which you articulate or sound each part of a word. For instance, saying "walkin" for *walking* or "gonna" for *going to* are examples of careless enunciation. Careless enunciation often occurs in *ing* words, such as "willin" for *willing* and "askin" for *asking*. Also, whenever we speak rapidly, most of us have a tendency to run our words together, dropping some of the sounds. Saying "dijago" for *did you go* and "meetcha" for *meet you* are examples. A person who slurs too many words is likely to be misunderstood or not heard at all, particularly over the telephone or on transcribing equipment. It is annoying for both the listener and the speaker if the listener must ask the speaker to repeat something several times. With transcribing equipment, errors may be made if the speaker cannot be reached for verification. Such difficulties can often be avoided if we simply speak more slowly.

Pronunciation

Pronunciation refers either to the sound that the speaker gives to the various letters or combinations of letters that make up a word or to the way in which the speaker accents the word. A person who says "pro*noun*ciation" instead of "pro*nun*ciation" is guilty of a pronunciation error. Should you say "libary" or "library," "com′ · par · able" or "com · par′ · able"? The dictionary indicates that the pronunciations are *library* and *com′ · par · able;* and these are the pronunciations used by careful speakers.

Of course, there are regional differences in pronunciation; and, in addition, a number of words have more than one acceptable pronunciation. In the latter case, the dictionary lists the preferred pronunciation first.

Many difficulties in pronunciation arise because some letters or combinations of letters are pronounced one way in some words and another way in others. For example, the combination *ow* is given a long "o" sound in *know* but an "ow" sound (as in *ouch*) in *now*. Other difficulties in pronunciation arise because a letter may be sounded in some words while in other words the same letter is silent; for example, *k* is sounded in the word *kick,* but it is not sounded in such words as *know* and *knee.* Because of these inconsistencies in our language, it is essential to consult the dictionary whenever you are in doubt about the pronunciation of a word.

Though errors in pronunciation are less likely to cause misunderstandings than errors in enunciation—you would know what was meant if someone said "com · par′ · able" instead of "com′ · par · able"—such errors tend to distract the listener and may even cause the listener to consider the speaker careless or uneducated. The business employee who is eager to succeed does not wish to be marked with either of these labels.

Furthermore, since so many words are written according to the way they sound, you can improve your spelling ability by carefully and correctly pronouncing and enunciating each word you use. Many words are misspelled because letters that should be sounded are overlooked. Those who repeatedly say "goverment" instead of "government" probably overlooked the *n* in this word. Some words, on the other hand, are misspelled because extra sounds are inserted where they do not belong; for example, pronouncing "athaletic" instead of "athletic." In still other instances of mispronunciation, the sequence of letters in the word may be rearranged. How many people do you know who say "ir*rev*elant" when they really mean "ir*rele*vant"? You can easily see how taking sufficient care in pronunciation will help prevent other errors, such as "quite" for *quiet* and "praps" for *perhaps.*

Most business employees have to give and to receive information and instructions over the telephone or in face-to-face conversation. To prevent the costly misunderstandings that are often caused by improper pronunciation and enunciation, you should make every effort to develop and practice intelligible speech.

IMPROVING ENUNCIATION AND PRONUNCIATION

Follow this four-step plan to help you improve your enunciation and pronunciation:

1. Use the dictionary to determine the preferred pronunciation of words about which you are uncertain.
2. Speak slowly enough, and with sufficient care, so that each letter in a word is sounded as it is supposed to be sounded and so that words are not run together.
3. Learn to use your jaw, your lips, and your tongue (the physical organs of speech) properly.
4. Practice frequently the correct enunciation and pronunciation of words that are often mispronounced or poorly enunciated.

You have already learned how to use the dictionary to determine the preferred pronunciation of words, and you have also learned how to control your speaking rate. Now you will learn how to use effectively the speech organs that assist in correct enunciation and pronunciation. Also, you will practice enunciating and pronouncing words that frequently cause difficulty.

Develop a Flexible Jaw

A rigid jaw results in muffled speech. Many sounds need to be vocalized and should, therefore, be made by movement of the mouth. If such sounds are forced through a locked jaw, a jaw that does not move up and down on its hinges, these sounds are certain to be muffled and indistinguishable. Keeping your jaws locked tight, try to pronounce these words—*neither, capable, try*. Can you understand what you are saying? Obviously you cannot, and you could not expect any listener to understand words that are pronounced in this manner.

To be an intelligible speaker, you must move your jaw freely between an open and a closed position. Say each of the vowels and notice the different positions of your jaw as you say *a, e, i ,o, u*. Compare your jaw positions as you say first the sound "ow," as in *how,* and then the sound "oo," as in *room*. When you say "ow," your jaw is dropped. However, when you say "oo," you move your jaw only slightly if at all.

Practice will help give you the free-moving feeling of a flexible jaw. First, stand before a mirror and practice the following words to be certain that your jaw is unlocked.

only	winning	about	seventy-five
try	capable	arrive	nine eight one
fine	evening	idea	reporting

Practicing the phrases below will exercise your jaw and help make it flexible.

going to go	down and out	up and around
around and away	sky high	down, up, and out
I've been	you've been	I've seen

Finally, practice saying these sentences to prove that your jaw is flexible enough so that each word is clearly enunciated and pronounced.

1. Shirley-Ann placed the pencil on the table today.
2. Many men and women have power, prestige, and financial ability.
3. Please telephone (805) 555-8867 this morning.
4. Your flexible jaw will contribute to better speech through clearer enunciation.

COMM

saying these phrases properly, first in isolation and then in an original sentence that you create for each phrase.

give me	did you	going to	do you	got to
being there	want to	kind of	come here	will you
have been	didn't you	don't know	going to go	have to

B.   From one of your textbooks, select a paragraph that you think will be of interest to the class. Read the paragraph aloud to the class, and be careful to enunciate words clearly and to pronounce them correctly. Each member of the class will list every word you enunciate poorly or mispronounce.

C.   You want your secretary to place a number of long-distance telephone calls for you. Dictate the following names and telephone numbers, making certain that the names and numbers are intelligible. Spell the difficult or unusual names; for example, "Irvine (I-r-v-i-n-e) Insurance Company of Nashua (N-a-s-h-u-a), Minnesota. I want to talk with Mrs. Phillips. The number is (612) 555-7814."

Person to Be Called	Company and City	Telephone Number
1. Marvin Rosenberg	Westchester Employment Service Worcester, Massachusetts	(617) 123-9876
2. Personnel Manager	Poughkeepsie Manufacturing Co. 101 Smith Street Poughkeepsie, New York	(914) 455-6389
3. Will speak with anyone	Marcy & Yates Associates Oxnard, California	(805) 488-3770
4. Ms. Carolyn Lehr	Lehr Advertising Agency New York, New York	Don't know the number
5. Dr. Grace Bohlander	Riverside Hospital Albuquerque, New Mexico	(505) 111-8347, Extension 183

D.   You wish to send the following message by telegraph to one of your customers. You will be called on in class to read all the information as you would read it over the telephone to the telegraph office.

To be sent to: Mr. Andrew Rosenthal, Moderne Living, Incorporated, 3452 Cranberry Drive, Trenton, New Jersey 07202.
The message: Returning 40 assorted lampshades. Replace with ten each of models 98, 79, 34, and 72 in beige and eggshell only.
Sender: Your name and address.

E.   As office manager, you find it necessary to order a number of items from a local stationer. Since you need the items in a hurry, you telephone the information to the stationer. Assume that you have dialed the number and that the person at the other end says, "Torrance Stationers; may I help you?" Pick up the conversation from this point, and place the order for the following items:

1. Six boxes of medium-hard carbon paper, No. 880, 8½ by 11½, Stock No. 2-105-19
2. Four boxes 20-lb white continuous-form paper, 8½ by 11, Stock No. 13-1276
3. One dozen No. 2 pencils, Stock No. 54-927

Editing Practice

States, Capitals, Principal Cities.   In each item below, there are two states, capitals, or principal cities that are misspelled. Spell them correctly.

1. Lincoln   Colombus   Cheyanne   Pierre   Jefferson City
2. Racine   Laramie   Pittsburg (Pa.)   Bethlahem   Portsmouth
3. Michigen   Idaho   Arizona   Montanna   New Jersey
4. Honalulu   Albany   Richmond   Charleston   Indiannapelis
5. Seattle   Spokane   Hoboken   Scenectady   Cincinatti
6. Wichita   Clevland   Agusta   Duluth   Butte
7. Olympia   Providence   Topeka   Frankfourt (Ky.)   Helana
8. Minnesota   Colorado   Pensylvania   Virginia   Rhode Island
9. Minnapolis   Juneau   Trenton   Charleston   Jeferson City
10. Brooklyn   Pasedena   Brockton   Levenworth   Lowell

Editors' Alert.   In each of the following sentences, make any changes that will correct or improve the sentence. Carefully check *every* detail.

1. This portable computer is to heavy to move.
2. The number of visitors in attendence was quiet large.
3. We will male the package tomorow, however, we cannot do so until the afternoon.
4. All there employees' are covered by insurance.
5. We did consider the investment a year ago and decided against it at that time but perhaps the situation is different now and you can tell us how the venture would now be profitable for us.
6. I do like filing, to type, and being given dictation.
7. 7 men and women worked from six to 7 p.m. for over-time pay.
8. We do not beleive it feasible to instal the equiptment at present.
9. On May 12 341 items disapeared before they could be loaded on the vans, which we are at a loss to explain.
10. Jamie spoke to Ron about the error he made.

Case Problem

The Helpful Busybody. Carl Gray has been working at the Ulster Accounting Services for only a month, but his boss, Ira Keogh, asked Carl to prepare a special report for him and gave very specific instructions regarding the preparation of the report. Marvin Kelsey, a longtime employee, observed Carl preparing this report and indicated that it was being prepared incorrectly. Said Marvin, "I've been with the company over ten years, and I've prepared many similar reports. You are not doing your report correctly."

1. If you were Carl, how would you handle the situation?
2. Was Marvin entirely at fault in his actions?

54

FACE-TO-FACE AND TELEPHONE COMMUNICATION

High on the list of communication activities of most business employees—if not at the very top of the list—is communicating orally on a face-to-face basis. Business employees talk with colleagues in their own departments, with their supervisors, with top management, and with such service workers as messengers and custodians many times during the working day.

In addition, many employees talk either on the telephone or in face-to-face meetings with individuals outside the company—customers, sales representatives, suppliers, visitors, and various people soliciting or giving information. As a matter of fact, many business employees depend to a great extent on their oral communication skill to earn their living—sales representatives, personnel interviewers, and receptionists are just a few examples. Every business worker who has contact with the public plays an important role in developing and promoting the company image. When the agent of an insurance company speaks to customers, it is not as an individual but as a representative of the company. The same is true of a receptionist, a secretary, or a credit clerk. In one sense, those who speak for the company *are* the company to those people who do business with that firm.

GUIDELINES FOR ONE-TO-ONE COMMUNICATION

The following suggestions should serve as guidelines for communicating effectively on a one-to-one basis, whether communicating face-to-face or over the telephone.

Listen Attentively

The ability to listen attentively is one of the most important skills connected with effective oral communication. Being attentive and showing interest in the other person are just two attributes of the good listener that lead to more effective communication. For example, if you are attacked verbally by an irate customer for something over which you have no control, you can go a long way toward soothing the customer by merely listening attentively. Often, you need not say anything, because what the customer most wants is an attentive and sympathetic listener.

Use the Person's Name

Be certain that you clearly hear the name of the person whom you have met or talked with on the telephone for the first time. Repeat the name right after it is given to you: "I'm happy to meet you, Mr. Colontoni." If you aren't absolutely sure of the person's name, ask that it be repeated; you can say, "I didn't hear your name clearly," or "How do you pronounce (or spell) your name?" Then, after hearing the name, pronounce it aloud in order to fix it in your mind. Whenever appropriate, use the name once or twice during the conversation. "Yes, I understand, Mr. Colontoni." Finally, always be sure that you say the person's name in your good-bye: "Good-bye, Mr. Colontoni; I was happy to talk with you."

Permit Others to Talk

Don't do all the talking. Give the other person a chance to talk, while *you* listen attentively. Watch for signs that the other person wants to say something or is becoming bored and not listening carefully. No matter how interesting you think the conversation is or how well informed or articulate you think you are, you must give your listener a chance to speak. Otherwise, you will not keep your listener's attention and respect.

Encourage Others to Talk

Sometimes the other person seems to prefer listening to talking. Remember, however, that a good conversationalist is one who not only talks well but also encourages the listener to contribute to the conversation. Ask frequent questions to let the other party know that you are interested in listening too. And prove your interest by listening attentively.

Look at the Speaker

Of course, this guideline applies only to face-to-face conversation. A speaker likes to have the listener's complete attention. When you speak, you like to feel that your listeners are focusing on what you are saying and not being distracted by objects or sounds coming from other directions—conversations in another part of the office or something that is happening outside the building, for example. So when you listen, make eye contact with the speaker; look at the person who is talking.

Compliment When Suitable

Many people with whom we come in contact are seeking approval. Compliments are always welcome, so compliment whenever the occasion is suitable. Paying a compliment is especially effective during tense situations. If a valued employee or a customer has a complaint that you cannot justify or remedy, you can put that person in a better frame of mind for a "No" answer by paying a compliment. Compliment the employee for work well done or for loyalty. Compliment the customer for paying promptly or for his or her good taste. In all conversations, be generous with praise when it is timely and when it is deserved. However, never pay a compliment unless you can do so honestly and convincingly. Insincerity is easily detected.

Keep Conversations Concise

Since you should not prolong conversations, you should keep your conversation to the point. If you are asked for opinions, give them quickly and clearly. However, being concise does not mean you must be brusque. Try to sense what the situation calls for and act accordingly. Most people do not want to hear unnecessary details or to listen to prolonged excuses for your inability to do something they have requested. Tell them enough to satisfy them; and if you are in doubt, the best rule to follow is to keep your conversations short.

Establish the Best Atmosphere

It is said that Napoleon had his desk raised so that he could look down on everyone who came to see him. Some executives sit behind a huge desk when they talk to visitors for the same reason. These executives feel that they appear more important, more powerful, and more dominating.

The trend today for good relations with colleagues and customers is to create a conversational atmosphere that is more relaxed. Executives who are effective communicators move from behind their desks and face their visitors without a barrier between them. This type of atmosphere makes possible a better give-and-take situation and, therefore, more effective communication.

RECEIVING THE PUBLIC

Although in most companies the receptionist greets all visitors, many employees also have contact with the public. In small offices and in most retail establishments, this situation applies to every employee. You should, therefore, be familiar with the basic procedures for meeting the public.

Give Prompt Attention to Visitors

Recognize a visitor's presence immediately. Even if you are busy, you can interrupt your work for as long as it takes to smile and say to the new arrival, "I'll be with you in a moment. Won't you sit down?"

Greet Visitors Pleasantly

Greet visitors with a pleasant smile and voice, and show friendliness by using their names in your greeting whenever possible. Add a personal touch to your greeting, such as "Good afternoon, Dr. Ward. It's a pleasure to see you again." Such friendly greetings make callers feel that they are getting special treatment and put them in a better frame of mind to do business with your company.

Be Courteous to All Visitors

Every visitor should receive friendly and courteous treatment, regardless of the purpose of the visit. Even if the visitor is obviously upset about something and acts accordingly, you must overlook any discourtesy and show that you are understanding. It may be that your visitor is annoyed about what he or she feels is "unfair treatment" from your company. There may be some justification for this feeling, so you now have an opportunity to mend a business problem. Even if you can do nothing about the situation, you can listen understandingly to the complaint. Treating an annoyed customer discourteously will only tend to make the situation worse. Usually a person responds well to pleasant treatment, and your courteous attitude will help to calm the visitor and will give your company a chance to make amends.

Apologize for Delays

If an appointment cannot be kept promptly by the person who is to receive the visitor, you should explain the delay ("I'm sorry, Mr. Blake, Miss Evans has been delayed at a meeting with the president"), and you should tell the visitor about how long the wait will be ("Miss Evans should be able to see you about 10:45"). Make the visitor comfortable (a selection of current magazines and today's newspaper should be available, or offer a cup of coffee if it is available). You might ask, "Shall I telephone your office and tell your secretary that you will be delayed a half hour?"

You may have some visitors whose shabby appearance leads you to believe they could not possibly have business of interest to one of the company executives. Don't be too sure! Sometimes the one who scorns that well-groomed look is a VIP—perhaps even the most important stockholder in the company. Everyone is, of course, entitled to your most courteous treatment.

Find Out the Purpose of the Visit

Almost every caller will have an appointment with an executive or other member of the company. For example, a visitor may say to you, "I am Mary O'Neill; I have an appointment with Miss Evans," and you will usher her to the appropriate office or telephone the executive that her visitor has arrived. If you do not know, however, whether the visitor has an appointment, you must ask, "May I help you?" or "Whom do you wish to see?" If the visitor has no appointment, take his or her name, the name of the company he or she represents (if any), and the purpose of the call. Relay this information to the person who you think can be of most help to the caller. After getting permission to show the visitor in, invite the person to follow you to the appropriate office. Then present the visitor like this: "Miss Evans (hostess), this is Ms. Mary O'Neill (visitor)."

Be Discreet and Tactful

Protect both your employer's and the company's interests by being discreet in your comments to visitors. For example, if your employer is late coming to the office in the morning or returning from lunch, it is not necessary to supply all these details to the visitor. Instead of saying, "Mrs. Stein is late getting in this morning," say, "I expect Mrs. Stein about 9:15." If she is late returning from lunch, you might say, "Mrs. Stein had an important luncheon meeting and should return shortly." Avoid making conversation about company business or personnel. If the subject comes up, be noncommittal and change the topic of conversation as quickly as you can. Never engage in negative statements, such as "Hasn't business been poor lately?" or "We have a terrible time getting good secretaries."

Be discreet in giving any opinions solicited by the visitor. The person the visitor will see may have a different opinion from your own. For example, the visitor may want to show you certain products and ask whether you think your company might be interested in buying them. Unless you are responsible for company purchases, however, you should not give an opinion about the company's possible interest in buying the products. Of course, you should not be rude even though you are pressured for comment. Simply say pleasantly, "I am sorry, but I do not purchase our company's supplies."

COMMUNICATING BY TELEPHONE

Communicating by telephone requires techniques that are quite different from those used in one-to-one conversation. Since those engaged in telephone conversations are unable to see one another, they must depend entirely upon their voices to communicate friendliness, interest, and a willingness to be helpful.

Since most people assume they know how to use the telephone properly, when as a matter of fact they do not, many office workers are ineffective telephone communicators. Furthermore, too many employees assume that a business telephone conversation requires the same treatment as a personal telephone call. Actually, the telephone is one of the most important communication media in business, so it must be used with great skill, especially in conversations with callers from the outside and with superiors in the office.

The following suggestions may seem elementary to you. Nevertheless, you should read them carefully and follow them whenever you use the telephone for either personal or business use:

Talk directly into the mouthpiece.

Talk slowly and naturally. Exaggerate your enunciation slightly. Shouting is never necessary.

If a caller must be transferred to someone else in the company, say, "If you will hold on just a moment, I will have your call transferred." Then depress the telephone plunger twice, very slowly, and repeat until the operator returns to the line. Then say, for example, "Will you please transfer this call to Rod Campbell on extension 4103." If your equipment permits you to transfer the call yourself, enter the extension carefully.

If, while talking, you must put down the receiver, place it on a book or magazine rather than drop it on a hard surface. In this way, you will protect the caller's ear from irritating noises.

Place the receiver gently in the cradle when you hang up.

Guidelines for Effective Telephone Communication

Courtesy is the key to effective telephone communication. Greet all callers pleasantly. This pleasantness is achieved by the words you use and the tone of your voice. If you know who the caller is, you might say something like this: "Good morning, Ms. Alvarez," or "Hello, Bill." If you do not know who the caller is, identify yourself first—"Mrs. Rossi speaking" or "Karen White." When answering the telephone for a department, be certain to identify both the department and yourself—"Accounting Department, Ms. Park" or "Word Processing Center, Jerry Asher." A secretary usually answers the employer's telephone like this: "Miss Bertrand's office" or "Miss Bertrand's office, Ms. Gomez speaking."

Your voice should be friendly and your manner courteous, regardless of who is calling. This manner is *especially* important when talking to outside callers. Remember that the impression created by your voice should be that of a friendly smile. Show the caller that you want to be helpful; always listen attentively, and don't interrupt. So that the caller will know you are listening, occasionally acknowledge comments with a "Yes" or with some other simple oral response. Use the caller's name at least once before hanging up, and conclude the call with a remark like "Thank you for calling us, Dr. Goldstein," or "We will look into the matter for you right away, Ms. Koch."

Originating Calls

The telephone company makes the following suggestions for originating calls:

1. Plan the conversation before you call. A little forethought will save both time and money. If your conversation will be an involved one, jot down notes in advance.
2. Place your own calls. Not only is it faster and easier to do so, but it is also more courteous. No busy executive likes to be greeted with "Hold on, Mr. Gomez, I have Mr. Carpenter on the line." Mr. Gomez then has to wait until Mr. Carpenter gets on the line. Since Mr. Gomez is the person being called, it is discourteous to keep him waiting.
3. To avoid delays, identify yourself promptly and state the purpose of your call. For example, say, "This is Janey Archer of Litton and Warren. I would like to speak to the person in charge of adjustments."

Receiving Calls

To ensure efficient use of the telephone when you receive a call, observe the following suggested procedures:

1. Answer promptly and identify yourself immediately. You should answer at the first ring, if possible, and not later than the second ring.
2. Respond to inquiries graciously, take appropriate notes, and verify important details. "Yes, we shall be glad to send you a duplicate copy of last month's statement. You want the December, 19—, statement; is that correct?"
3. At the close of the conversation, take the required action. Be certain that you keep all promises you make to the caller.
4. Allow the caller to hang up first.
5. If you are going to be away from your telephone, let someone know, and indicate how you would like calls handled that are directed to you during your absence.

Answering for Others

Two special suggestions are appropriate when you are answering telephone calls for other people in your firm.

1. If the person called is not available, offer to be of help or to transfer the call to someone who can help.
2. If the caller wishes to speak to only one individual and that person is not available, obtain the caller's name and telephone number and record the caller's message, if any.

Handling Complaints

The true test of your ability to handle telephone calls effectively will be revealed when you must deal with an annoyed customer who has a complaint. You must remember that you represent your company and that little or nothing is to be gained by allowing yourself to become angry. Your task will be made much easier if you follow these suggestions when you are required to handle complaints on the telephone.

1. Listen carefully to the caller's complaint. Take careful notes of all important details.
2. Express interest in and an understanding of the caller's problem. "Yes, I can see why you were annoyed by the mistake in your bill, Mr. Hayakawa, but I am sure we can correct it right away."
3. Tell the caller what action you will take. If you cannot make the adjustment yourself, refer the caller to someone who can. Don't make the caller repeat the entire story to someone else; each time the message must be repeated to another person, the caller becomes angrier.

COMMUNICATION PROJECTS

Practical Application

A.   You are the administrative assistant to Oliver Malcolm, president of Malcolm Electronics Inc. Mr. Malcolm will be holding a very important conference in his office for the next two hours and has told you that he does not want to be disturbed under any circumstances. The following situations occur during the hours Mr. Malcolm does not want to be disturbed. What would you say to each of the people involved in the following situations?

1. The plant manager, Fred Yates, telephones and says that it is urgent that he speak with Mr. Malcolm.
2. Mrs. Malcolm, the president's wife, telephones and asks to speak with her husband.
3. Mr. Graves, an important customer from out of town, arrives an hour early for an appointment he has with Mr. Malcolm.
4. The chairman of the board of directors, Y. C. Potts, telephones and asks to speak with Mr. Malcolm.

B.   The administrative services manager, Marcella Kingston, has requested that you prepare a one-page memorandum on "Improving Telephone Usage." Prepare the memo.

C.   How should a receptionist respond to the following visitors who approach the reception desk and say:

1. "Good morning."
2. "I would like to see Mr. Nakama."

3. "Is there someone who can help me get this stupid error on my bill straightened out?"
4. "I am a sales representative from Lincoln Drapery Cleaners and would like to demonstrate our high-quality service to the person in your company who takes care of drapery cleaning." (The building superintendent is the person responsible.)
5. "I have a nine o'clock appointment with Ms. Rappaport." (Ms. Rappaport has not yet arrived at the office, and it is just 9 a.m. now.)

D.   How would you handle a telephone caller with whom your boss does not wish to talk because this person has an unwarranted complaint that your boss has spoken to him about several times previously?

E.   List the qualities of a good listener.

F.   Suggest three greetings a receptionist might use to find out the purpose of a visit by a customer.

Editing Practice

Editing to Improve Writing Techniques.   Rewrite the following sentences, and correct all evidence of poor writing techniques.

1. The jury reached their decision, and its not a majority vote.
2. The defendant was persistent in his stand.
3. Mary Lou will continue on in the same position.
4. Jack left the office a hour early.
5. The group made the best choice of the two possibilities.
6. The receptionist recognized the caller looking up from the desk.
7. Where did you loose your breif case?
8. Karl told Erik that he would be promoted.
9. Is this stock one that is considered a "Blue Chip?"
10. I know that you can handle this problem as well, if not better, than me.

Case Problem

The Unqualified Employee.   Mary Toyer, head of the sales department, received the following written report from Daniel Friedman, a supervisor.

I cannot recommend Helen Anderson, my secretary, for a salary increase at this time. During her first six months on the job, she tried very hard to do good work, but she soon lost interest. Now my work is taking second place to her long coffee breaks and her personal visits and telephone calls. Yesterday, for example, it took three hours to get three short letters typed.

Accordingly, Mary must talk with Helen about the quality of Helen's work and the reason for her not getting a salary increase. What should Mary say to Helen in the discussion?

55

GROUP DISCUSSIONS

If one were to ask most business executives how many meetings they attend weekly, a typical answer is likely to be "Too many!" Such responses are based on the fact that many executives spend a large part of each working day attending some kind of meeting, either as a participant or as a leader of that meeting. Often, it becomes necessary for these executives to take work home to complete because there is insufficient time during the usual working day. Although group conferences are among the most important ways to exchange ideas and report information within business, the time spent at meetings is complained about by almost everyone. Reducing the time spent at meetings is possible if meetings are organized and conducted more efficiently.

As a responsible business employee, you are likely to have frequent opportunities to participate in a variety of capacities in many types of group conferences. You might be selected as a member of a *standing* (permanent) committee that meets regularly, such as a planning committee, a publicity committee, or a finance committee. You may also be called upon to serve on a committee formed for a particular purpose only, such as a committee appointed to study employee grievances or to plan the company's 25th anniversary celebration. These temporary committees, formed for a special purpose and then disbanded after the purpose has been achieved, are called *ad hoc* (pronounced *ad hock*) committees. You may even be selected as chairperson of one of these committees, with the responsibility of planning and conducting the meetings.

Because meetings consume so much time and talent in the typical business organization, they should be organized and conducted efficiently. The time spent on meetings adds up to many thousands of dollars every year for the typical business organization. In addition to attending meetings during business hours, the business worker often goes to many meetings and serves on a number of committees outside the company—for example, in professional, social, religious, political, and civic groups.

PARTICIPATING IN MEETINGS

Everyone invited to participate in a group discussion has an obligation to contribute his or her best thinking and suggestions. Here is your opportunity to exhibit your interest in the business in which you are employed, as well as your knowledge regarding the work you are doing. Too often, time and money are wasted because so many employees take meetings for granted and do not contribute their maximum efforts to the discussion. They often come to a meeting unprepared, uninterested, and uninspired. The six basic rules for participating effectively in a meeting are:

Prepare for the meeting.
Express opinions tactfully.
Make positive contributions.
Be courteous.
Keep remarks concise and pertinent.
Take notes.

Prepare for the Meeting

The first rule for effective participation in a meeting is to come prepared. Find out in advance all that you can about the topics to be discussed at the meeting. If there is an agenda (see page 540), study each item carefully and learn more about those topics you are not familiar with. For example, if the subject of personnel evaluation is to be discussed, be sure that you know what the current company procedures are for evaluating personnel and the advantages and disadvantages of these procedures. You may wish to refer to books or articles dealing with this topic or to examine company forms that are currently in use. In addition, it is often useful to get the opinions of knowledgeable people who will not be present at the meeting. If there is to be a discussion of a revision of the evaluation form, study the form thoughtfully, try it out, and ask various people who use the form what they like and do not like about it.

Being prepared also means coming to a meeting with a set of well-founded opinions. Opinions that are worth listening to in a business meeting are the ones backed up by facts. People are often opposed to a new idea merely because they don't know enough about it. The old saying "You're down on what you're not up on" applies to participation in a meeting. Make certain that this saying never applies to you.

Express Opinions Tactfully

When someone asks you for your opinion or when you volunteer an opinion, be tactful in expressing yourself. Often, opposing points of view can cause strong disagreement. No matter how strongly you may feel that you are right and that the other person is wrong, your chances of winning that person's support are no better than your tactfulness in presenting your views. For example, don't say, "You're wrong, and here's why." Instead, you might say, "Your point of view certainly has merit, Frank, but I have doubts because . . . " Never tell someone that he or she is wrong—*wrong* is a strong term, and your right to use it requires indisputable evidence. In selling your point of view, the "Yes, but . . . " technique is effective; that is, acknowledge the other person's point of view and show your respect for it. Then present your own ideas. For example, "Yes, I agree that the solution seems simple and that your idea represents one way to approach the problem, but . . . "

In expressing yourself, separate facts from opinions. Label as facts only those statements for which you have solid evidence. Opinions should be signaled by such words as "it seems to me," "as I understand it," or "in my opinion."

Make Positive Contributions

One of the most unwelcome participants in a group meeting is the person who thinks "No." This person's primary mission seems to be that of killing the ideas and proposals that others voice. Such a participant seldom presents a positive idea but is always quick to say of someone else's idea, "That won't work."

Most meetings are held for the purpose of solving problems, and problems cannot be solved in a negative atmosphere. Participants must be willing to approach a problem with the attitude that the only way to solve it is to present as many ideas as possible. No one immediately vetoes an idea someone else has presented; instead, each person tries to see the idea's merits and to enlarge upon the idea's possibilities, no matter how weak it may seem at first. To smother ideas before they are fully aired is not only rude but also extremely disheartening to those who are genuinely trying to reach intelligent decisions.

Be Courteous

The ideal meeting is one in which everyone participates freely. The overaggressive speaker who monopolizes the discussion will discourage the participation of others. Even though you may be more knowledgeable about the topic than anyone else in the group, you should never display your knowledge in an offensive, overbearing manner. You may win the skirmish and lose the battle—the too sure, know-it-all person often does.

More victories have been won in group discussion by modesty and tact than will ever be achieved by overaggressiveness. Don't jump in while others are speaking; wait your turn patiently. Show interest in what others are saying. You will win more friends by listening and taking notes on remarks by others than by interrupting their remarks—regardless of how inane the remarks may seem to you. Acknowledge that others may have as much information as you have or perhaps even more than you have.

Courteous group members do not (1) resort to sarcasm when they disagree with someone, (2) interrupt the person who is talking, (3) fidget, (4) gaze into space, or (5) carry on side conversations with other members of the group while someone else has the floor.

Keep Remarks Concise and Pertinent

Some participants in a meeting take a roundabout route to reach the point they want to make. They ramble endlessly. If you have something to say, get to your point quickly. Meetings become boring and unproductive mainly because some participants insist on relating personal preferences, experiences, and opinions that have little or no bearing on the discussion at hand.

Take Notes

It is a good idea to develop the habit of taking notes at meetings, because the act of taking careful notes (1) keeps you alert, (2) tells speakers that you consider their remarks worth remembering, and (3) provides a valuable reference source both during and after the meeting. Take notes not only on what the speaker is saying but also on what *you* want to say when it is your turn to speak. Jot down your key remarks in advance so that your comments are well organized and complete.

LEADING GROUP DISCUSSIONS

The success or failure of a group meeting is very often determined by the leader of the group. By skillful direction, the leader can turn an ordinary meeting into an extremely profitable experience for each participant. Without good leadership, the most promising meeting can result in a waste of time for everyone concerned. To become a good discussion leader, follow the suggestions outlined here.

Prepare Thoroughly

A successful meeting or conference requires that the leader prepare thoroughly far enough in advance to make all the necessary arrangements and to contend with any problems that may arise. The discussion leader needs to know the time the meeting is to begin, the length of the meeting, and the place in which it is to be held. The leader also needs to know the names of those who are to attend and the objectives that should be accomplished at the meeting. Notification of a meeting of a standing committee usually takes the form of an agenda (a list of the topics to be discussed and the names of the persons who are to lead the discussion). The agenda should be sent as far in advance of the meeting as possible to allow the participants ample time to prepare for their roles in the meeting. For a monthly meeting, the agenda should be sent at least a week ahead of the meeting date. For a weekly meeting, the agenda should be received a day or two before the meeting. The sample agenda on page 540 shows the topics in the order in which they will be discussed. Under new items, those that are most important should be listed first in the event that there is not sufficient time to discuss them all.

Prepare the Meeting Facilities

All the arrangements for the meeting facilities must be planned in advance so that the room, the furniture, and the equipment to be used are available and properly set up in time for the meeting. It is the responsibility of the group leader to see that the job is done properly and on time. Otherwise, there may be an insufficient number of chairs, there may be no ashtrays (or overflowing ashtrays), the room may be poorly ventilated, the audiovisual facilities may not be available, refreshments may not arrive in time for the break, and so on.

In order to make certain that the meeting starts promptly, it is best to check at least forty-five minutes before the meeting that everything in the meeting room is in order. This prior checking, such as making sure that audiovisual equipment is on hand and is in working order, makes it possible to take care of any problems before the meeting begins. If an operator for projection equipment is required, the meeting date should be confirmed the day before the meeting. Also, make certain that the film is available, that there is an electrical outlet, and that the extension cord is long enough. Problems can be more easily resolved if they are discovered sufficiently in advance of the meeting.

Arrive Early

The chairperson of the meeting should be at the meeting place a few minutes early to check the facilities and to set an example for the others. Arriving early also gives the leader a chance to distribute the agenda. (Even though everyone has received an advance copy of the agenda, not everyone will remember to bring it to the meeting.) The leader or the leader's secretary should also bring along a few extra pencils and pads (there will be some participants who will have neither) and extra copies of reports or other papers to be discussed, even though copies may have been distributed in advance.

Establish a Businesslike Atmosphere

The chairperson sets the tone of the meeting. If the leader begins late or is apathetic about getting the proceedings under way, the

```
LORMEAU INSURANCE COMPANY

Meeting of Regional Agents

April 23, 19--, 1:30 p.m.
at Carmel Home Office


AGENDA


1.  Call to order by Chairperson Miyako.

2.  Approval of the minutes of the March meeting.

3.  Approval of and additions to agenda.

4.  Announcements.

5.  Unfinished Business:

    a.  Report of employee welfare committee.

    b.  Continuation of discussion of hiring procedures.

6.  New Business:

    a.  Recommendations for additional office locations.

    b.  Changes in advertising media.

    c.  Proposals for collection procedures.

    d.  Additional items.

7.  Adjournment.

8.  Coffee Hour.
```

An agenda lists the topics to be discussed at a forthcoming meeting. Under "New Business," an agenda usually lists the items in order of importance.

participants are likely to lose whatever enthusiasm they may have had when they entered the room. Generally it is best to start a meeting precisely at the hour for which it is scheduled, even though there probably will be latecomers. If the members of a group realize that the meeting will start without them, they are likely to make an effort to be punctual.

Guide the Discussion

The good leader talks as little as possible and draws out the opinions of the participants. Unfortunately, some people think that *leader* and *talker* are synonymous terms when it comes to running a meeting. The skillful leader brings out each participant's best thinking. The leader's function is not to show how much he or she knows but to steer the discussion in the proper direction. The experienced leader knows that the greater the participation—that is, the more minds at work on a problem—the better the chances are of accomplishing the objective of the meeting.

Encourage Participation

Everyone invited to a meeting should be able to make some contribution to the discussion. However, some people are shy and will not say anything unless they are encouraged to speak. Call on these people in a manner that will offer them encouragement; for example, "Lillian, you have had a lot of experience in advertising. What do you think of Ernest's layout for next week's ad?" or "Ken, we would be interested in having the benefit of your experience in the word processing center. Do you think we need to change the facilities to make for a more conducive environment?"

A leader encourages positive participation by saying something complimentary after a speaker has made a worthwhile contribution; for example, "Thank you, Isaac, for that very timesaving suggestion," or "That's an excellent idea, Ms. Stein. Could you tell us a little more about how you think that plan will function?" Such types of comments are effective when they are obviously sincere. Negative comments, on the other hand, discourage participation and should, therefore, be kept to a minimum and be presented so tactfully that they do not discourage others from making suggestions. "That idea would work beautifully if . . . ."

Discourage Excessive Talkers

In any group there will always be one or two people who want to do all the talking. Certainly they have a right to be heard, but unless they are listed on the agenda as the principal contributors, they should not be permitted to monopolize the discussion. Only a strong leader can prevent a loudmouth from taking over the meeting. The chairperson should be tactful but firm. "That's very interesting, Joe, but I think we ought to hear from Edna," or "Let's get back to you a little later, Irene. I think we would all be interested in having as many points of view as we can get."

Keep the Discussion Pertinent

Meetings sometimes tend to get off the track, and if the chairperson permits the discussion to wander for too long, the principal problems to be resolved at the meeting will be bypassed entirely. All too often, a subject comes up that is of genuine personal interest to all those present at the meeting but has little or no bearing on the main topic. People just naturally like to tell about their personal experiences, likes and dislikes, and amusing anecdotes. These digressions should be permitted now and then because they lighten the discussion; we can't be completely serious all the time. However, when side issues begin to waste valuable time, they must be cut off tactfully by the leader and the discussion must be brought back on track. "That certainly was an interesting experience, Harry, but let's get back to our discussion of the employees' handbook. Damien, what changes do you think are necessary in the section on retirement?" Usually you can keep the discussion on the track without being rude to anyone, but bluntness is sometimes necessary as a last resort. "Jerry, time is getting away from us, and we want to avoid having to call another meeting to settle this problem. Do you have any specific solutions?"

Summarize Periodically

It is neither necessary nor desirable for the chairperson of a group discussion to evaluate everyone's remarks as soon as they are presented. The group leader should always listen attentively but does not need to comment except, perhaps, to stimulate further discussion. "Excellent—that's an interesting point. I gather that you think this plan will be more effective than the one we have been following. Is that a correct assumption?" Above all, the leader does not tear down ideas or argue with participants; doing so will only discourage others in the group from expressing themselves. Since the leader of the meeting is only one member of the group, it is usually poor practice to judge every idea expressed instead of letting other members of the group participate.

From time to time, the chairperson should summarize the major points that have been presented. "We all seem to agree that we should not add more branch stores at the present time. Instead, you feel we should enlarge the existing branches and increase our advertising budget. Is that correct? Well, let's discuss which branches should be enlarged and how we should make use of an increased advertising budget. Nora, do you have any suggestions regarding which branch stores should be enlarged?"

Know How to Conclude

If the chairperson has prepared the agenda carefully and has conducted the meeting efficiently, the meeting should end fairly close to the time scheduled for adjournment. If the discussion seems likely to extend beyond the closing hour and it is important to continue, get the approval of the group; for example, "Ladies and gentlemen, it is

INTEROFFICE MEMORANDUM

To: Mrs. Lola Peterson   From: Karl Seltzer

Subject: Retirement Section of   Date: June 13, 19--
         Employees' Handbook

This memorandum is to remind you that at the meeting
yesterday of the Handbook Revision Committee you
volunteered to conduct a survey of all retired employees
to determine their suggestions for improving the
retirement section of the handbook.

You also indicated you would set up a subcommittee to work
on this revision and would report to the parent body at
its September meeting any suggestions for changes that
result from your survey and the discussion at your
subcommittee meetings.

Thank you, Lola, for agreeing to assist in this most
worthwhile project.

                                              KS

After a meeting, the chairperson should remind each participant of his or her assignment.

five minutes of twelve, and it looks as though we won't get out of here by noon. Shall we continue the discussion, or would you rather schedule another meeting for this afternoon?"

After the meeting, the secretary should write up the minutes and distribute them as soon as possible. Memorandums should be written to those who are assigned special responsibilities at the meeting. Such a memorandum is illustrated above.

Know How to Conduct Formal Meetings

Many groups conduct their meetings on a formal basis, following parliamentary rules. If you are elected to office in such a group, you should read *Robert's Rules of Order*, the standard guide to parliamentary procedure.

COMMUNICATION PROJECTS

Practical Application

A. Evaluate the following statements made by group discussion leaders. If the statement is not an appropriate one, what should have been said?

1. "I don't think that idea would work."
2. "We'd like to hear more about the plan."
3. "What has been your experience with this problem?"

B. Prepare an interoffice memorandum to all supervisors, calling a meeting at which you and they will discuss the orientation program for all new employees. You want the supervisors to evaluate the present program, to talk with new employees hired since January 1 of this year, and to do some research regarding orientation programs used in other local businesses. These aspects will be discussed at the meeting, and the supervisors will draw up a revised program that will be put into effect September 1. Supply any other information you feel would be helpful in preparing for this meeting.

C. Evaluate your ability to conduct a meeting, using as guidelines your previous experience, if any, and the qualities you consider necessary in an effective leader of group discussions.

D. How does one establish a businesslike atmosphere at a meeting?

E. Make a list of the steps you would take to prepare a meeting room for an all-day discussion.

F. Prepare an agenda for an ad hoc committee for which you are to act as chairperson. Select a discussion topic of your own choice. Then develop a list of topics concerned with phases of this subject and assign them to individuals in your class.

G. At a meeting of the Employee Retirement Planning Committee, Marietta Hart was assigned the responsibility of gathering information regarding the facilities for the retirement banquet and dance. Write a follow-up memorandum to Ms. Hart reminding her of the assignment. Supply all the details for the memorandum.

Editing Practice

Applied Psychology. The wording of the following letter excerpts does nothing to cement good human relations. Revise the sentences.

1. You made an error of $25 in totaling our last statement.
2. We fail to understand why you claim that the two vases do not match.
3. We are unable to grant you credit because you are a poor payer.
4. You claim that your check was sent last week, but we have not yet received it.
5. You have put us through a great deal of trouble getting the merchandise to you on the date you requested.

Case Problem

The Poor Chairperson. As chairperson of the social committee, Emily was greatly discouraged after the first meeting. She couldn't understand why so many committee members were late. Hadn't she telephoned all the members that very morning to ask if they could meet at 2 p.m.? She waited until 2:30 before enough members were there to start the meeting. When she asked the group what social activities they wanted to discuss, she got little response. Those ideas suggested did not seem practical to Emily, and she quickly discouraged them. The meeting adjourned at 4 p.m. with nothing decided other than that another meeting would be called soon. What went wrong with Emily's meeting?

56

PREPARING AND DELIVERING A SPEECH

For many business executives, the ability to speak effectively before groups may be an important requirement of their position. How much speech making they are likely to do depends upon many factors: the kind of position they hold, the degree of responsibility that comes with their position, and the effectiveness of their speech making.

The responsible business executive may be expected to represent the company before professional organizations and many different civic, religious, and educational groups. These outside speaking duties are beyond those duties involved in speaking to members of one's own company at employee meetings or in making presentations at board meetings or at stockholders' meetings.

However, even those who are not top executives often are called upon to participate in activities involving speeches before either large or small groups—introducing a speaker, explaining a new company policy to a group of employees, greeting a group of visitors, or presenting an award at a meeting of company employees and their families.

A speech, like a letter, reflects an image of the company that employs the speaker. An effective speech, like an effective letter, should convey a message clearly and convincingly and, at the same time, build an image of goodwill. Since nearly everyone is called upon at one time or another to "say a few words" to an audience, every business employee should be prepared to represent his or her company in a way that will reflect favorably on the company.

In order to deliver an effective speech—whether it is a two-minute introduction, a five-minute commentary, or an hour's presentation—the first step the speaker should take is to plan the speech carefully. Planning involves previewing the speaking assignment, gathering and organizing the material, outlining the speech, and rehearsing the presentation.

PREVIEWING THE SPEAKING ASSIGNMENT

Regardless of whether the speech topic has been selected for the speaker or the topic is the speaker's own choice, every speaker must answer three basic questions before gathering and organizing material: (1) What is the purpose of the speech? (2) To whom is the speech to be given? (3) How much time is allowed for the speech?

What Is the Purpose of the Speech?

Every speech should have a very specific purpose—to *explain* something, such as a new company policy; to *describe* something, such as the features of a new product or the steps in a new procedure; or to *report* on something, such as the results of a market survey. The primary goal of a speech may be to present a point of view, to inspire, to inform, or to win support for a new proposal. Whatever the purpose may be, every speech must be organized to fit its purpose.

Assume that you have been asked to tell the company sales representatives about a sales promotion plan for your new wristwatch computer. If your speech is entitled "Sales Promotion for the Ancet Wristwatch Computer," obviously you are not expected to talk about how the product is made or how much it costs to produce. The purpose of your talk is to tell the sales representatives how the company plans to promote the sale of this product through advertising and any other promotional efforts the company plans to make—and how these sales representatives fit into this promotional program. Your remarks should concentrate on these promotional activities and convince the sales representatives that they will receive sufficient support to help make the selling job more efficient.

To Whom Is the Speech to Be Given?

The effective speaker finds out as much as possible about the audience before gathering material for the speech. If you are to discuss word processing techniques before a group of executives, your emphasis will be quite different from the one you would use in discussing the same topic with a group of secretaries. If your speech is one of several that are to be given, you should inquire about the rest of the program so that you can put your topic in perspective with the others. You should find out as much as you can about the interests, occupations, and age levels of the audience. In addition, it is helpful to know the expected audience size and the general background of the people. The program chairperson can supply this and other useful information. With this help, you can find out what the audience already knows about the subject and what the audience expects to learn from the presentation. With such knowledge at hand, you can avoid repeating facts already known and can give particular emphasis to areas of most interest to the audience.

How Much Time Is Allowed for the Speech?

The speaker must know precisely how much time is allowed for the speech. Obviously, you should not try to crowd into thirty minutes a topic that requires an hour. Therefore, once you know the amount of time you have been allotted, you should plan your speech so it can be adequately presented in this time period.

The clever speaker, when assigned forty-five minutes, takes only thirty-five or forty minutes. This leeway makes certain that the speech will not run overtime, and if there are five or ten minutes left, the time may be used to answer questions from the audience.

If you have been assigned a very broad topic like "Word Processing," you should select the phase of the subject that best fits the audience. For example, your speech may deal with "Improved Dictation Methods" for an audience composed of executives, or it may deal with "How to Proofread Efficiently" for an audience composed of operators who work in word processing centers.

GATHERING AND ORGANIZING DATA

There is no substitute for preparation. Even the most gifted speakers always prepare carefully beforehand, whether they are to speak for only a few minutes or for an hour. If your topic is one that you can prepare for by reading, read as widely as possible. Find a good library that has up-to-date magazines, books, and bulletins on your topic, and get as many points of view as you can. Check and double-check on facts—especially statistical information. Take notes—more than you can possibly use in your speech. Put the notes on cards and start a new card for each new subject or source. Identify on the card the source of your information in case you want to refer to it later.

The advantage of writing notes on cards is that it is easy to discard unwanted material and to arrange and rearrange the remaining material in the best order for the preparation of your speech outline. In fact, if your notes are prepared well, your final arrangement of the cards will represent an outline.

For many topics, valuable and interesting information can be obtained from talking with people who are involved in the subject of your speech. For example, if you are going to speak on "Requirements for Success in Accounting," you might talk with a number of successful accountants to determine what they feel led to their success in the profession. Take notes on your findings, and use this information in preparing your speech. Firsthand information makes any presentation more interesting.

OUTLINING AND ORGANIZING THE SPEECH

After selecting the topic and gathering and organizing the data, the speaker is ready to begin outlining the speech. The following is a guide to preparing an outline:

1. Speech Title—   Time Allotted—
2. Purpose of Speech—
3. Introduction (arouse interest and give purpose)—
4. Body of Speech—Principal ideas to support purpose
   a. Principal idea No. 1
      Supporting information and material
   b. Principal idea No. 2
      Supporting information and material
   c. Principal idea No. 3
      Supporting information and material
5. Conclusion
   a. Summary of principal ideas
   b. Plea for action (if applicable)

The Introduction

The introductory remarks should be brief and should arouse the interest of the audience in the speaker and in the subject. Various methods of introducing the talk may be used; for example:

1. A direct statement of the subject and its importance to each member of the audience.

   The title of my presentation is "The Computer—Friend or Foe?" Each of you has a stake in the computer revolution because your future in the accounting profession will depend upon how well you use the computer in your work.

2. An indirect opening that is of vital interest to the audience, with a statement connecting the subject with this interest.

   Tomorrow, your job may be abolished or changed so drastically that you won't recognize it. Why? Because so many of the things that you are still doing by hand can be done much more efficiently by computer.

3. A striking example or comparison that leads up to the purpose or subject of the speech.

   Recently, a well-known authority in computer development compared the cost of the computer to the cost of an automobile. He stated that, if in the last ten years the cost of automobiles had decreased proportionally to the cost of computers, today a Mercedes would sell for about $1000.

4. A strong quotation relating to the subject of the speech.

    "Computer technology must be understood by every CPA, whether or not that CPA makes firsthand use of the computer," declared T. J. McGuire, chief examiner of the Professional Accountancy Board of Examiners, in the May issue of the *CPA Journal.*

5. Relevant statistics regarding the subject.

    A recent survey revealed that more than 2000 office workers were replaced by some type of machine in 19—.

6. A brief anecdote.

    Last week my secretary handed me a clipping from a local newspaper. It was about experiments that are now being made with a voice-input word processor. The manufacturers hope to perfect it so that the dictator merely dictates into the machine, and the letter comes out all transcribed, ready for mailing. My secretary never once thought about being replaced by such a machine but was worried only about whether it could straighten out the grammar and punctuation that I insist on mangling!

The Body of the Speech

Once audience interest is aroused, you are ready to provide the principal ideas that will support the purpose you have established for your speech. How many ideas you will present and develop will depend wholly upon the amount of time you have been allotted for the speech. It is better to develop each idea fully enough to be convincing than to present many ideas that are weakly developed and therefore not fully accepted or understood by the audience.

How is an idea communicated? First, it must be stated in a brief but clear and interesting way. Then the idea should be developed by explanation and illustration. Finally, the idea should be summarized.

Among the techniques available to the speaker for developing ideas are those in the following list. Which techniques the speaker selects will depend upon the nature of the data to be presented.

Giving examples.
Making comparisons.
Quoting statistics.
Quoting testimony of a recognized authority.
Repeating the idea in different words.
Defining terms used in stating the idea.
Using descriptive language that makes the listener "see" the situation.

Using narration to relate a story connected with the idea.
Using audio and visual aids.

Here is an example of how one idea used in a speech might be communicated, following several of the suggestions that have been presented. Suppose a speech is intended to convince an audience of business executives that their companies should purchase their own small airplanes for business use.

Principal Idea

A business saves both time and money by owning its own airplane.

Development

1. Tell the story of two business firms in the same city whose executives frequently travel by air from their place of business to cities about 200 to 300 miles away. One executive used the local airline service and had to spend two nights in a hotel away from home to complete the business transaction. The other executive had her own plane and was able to return home the same day as she left.
2. Show on a comparative chart the cost of using public air transportation over a one-year period as compared with the cost of using one's own plane for the same period of time and covering about the same total mileage.
3. Give several examples of travel time between your city and another heavily visited city nearby, making comparisons in time using public airline service and one's own private plane.
4. Quote executives of leading companies in your area who own their own planes and who are convinced that the convenience, as well as the saving of time and money, makes it essential that every company conducting business hundreds of miles away have its own plane.

Many speakers use such audiovisual materials as charts, slides, filmstrips, overhead projectors (with transparencies), videotapes, and motion pictures to enrich their presentations. Before deciding to use a visual aid, be certain that you have determined whether or not the material will be visible to the entire audience. The size of the audience and the type of room in which you make your presentation will be the principal determinants. Good visual aids can make your presentation more interesting by providing a change of pace. Talks dealing with figures can be made clearer and much more effective by using well-prepared charts and diagrams. If the situation is such, however, that mechanical means would prove ineffective, then consider the possibility of using duplicated handout materials.

Motion pictures and videotapes should be previewed to determine whether they are appropriate. Above all, facilities and equipment should be checked before the presentation so that there will be no delays after the talk has started.

The Conclusion

The conclusion of a speech should be brief and to the point. A summary of the major points made in the speech and a plea for action, if applicable, are all that are needed. The summary may repeat key words or expressions already used or may restate the principal ideas in different words. Sometimes an example, a comparison, or an effective quotation serves as an appropriate summary. In any case, the final statement should tell the listeners very specifically what they should do, believe, or understand as a result of the presentation.

PRACTICING THE SPEECH

The inexperienced speaker should write the entire speech from the outline developed, *not* for the purpose of reading the speech but for refining expressions, improving the choice of words, and timing the presentation. By recording this preliminary speech and then playing it back, the speaker can determine how the words will sound to the audience. Appropriate changes can then be made.

After you have refined the speech, have read it through several times, and have timed the reading, you should prepare an outline on index cards. This outline should include phrases, quotations, and statistics. If possible, it should be prepared in large, clear handwriting or in jumbo typewriter type so that you can refer to the notes casually from a distance of two or three feet. Supplementary materials should be keyed into the outline in some way (underlining, solid capitals, or color) that will make them stand out.

Using the final outline, you should practice delivering your speech and should try to anticipate the conditions of the actual talk. A beginning speaker often finds the following practice suggestions helpful. Stand erect—before a mirror if possible—and imagine your audience before you. Watch your posture, facial expressions, and gestures as you deliver the speech. If you can practice before an audience of family or friends who will be sympathetic but frank in their analysis, so much the better. If you can record your presentation, you will be able to hear how clearly you speak and to judge the overall effectiveness of your presentation.

DELIVERING THE SPEECH

Though *what* you say in your speech is extremely important, *how* you say it is equally important. The best talk ever written can put an audience to sleep if it is poorly delivered. On the other hand, an average speech can bring an audience to its feet if the speaker is poised, dynamic, and persuasive. To deliver a speech effectively, you must possess the following important characteristics: confidence in your ability to deliver an effective message, a pleasing personal appearance, and good stage presence and delivery.

Confidence

"I don't have a knack for public speaking." "Speakers are born, not made." "I'll make a fool of myself if I try to give a speech." "I'll get stage fright and forget everything I'm supposed to say." These are typical reactions of a novice speaker. If you believe any of these statements, then you, like so many other people, underestimate yourself. You're better than you think!

When you are talking to an audience, pretend that you are carrying on a face-to-face conversation with just one person. Remember that the audience is just as eager for you to perform well as you are to do so. Don't be upset if you are nervous—even experienced speakers and actors are. Feeling nervous is a result of anxiety about doing a good job, and most authorities feel that a little stage fright provides needed tension. However, try not to show the audience any signs of your nervousness.

One way to develop confidence is to make sure that the conditions under which you are going to speak are as favorable as you can make them. Try to arrive fifteen or twenty minutes before you are scheduled to speak. If you speak best standing behind a lectern—and most people do—ask your host to provide one. Even an improvised lectern, such as a cardboard box covered with a cloth and set on a table, is better than no lectern at all. If possible, get the feel beforehand of the space you are going to occupy when you do address the group. Know in advance how you will approach the podium. If you think your approach will be awkward for you or for others on the stage or distracting to the audience, ask your host to change the arrangement. Check the ventilation, the lighting, the public address system, and the seating arrangement. In short, make all the advance preparations you can to assure a feeling of familiarity with your surroundings. This is another big step in building confidence.

Appearance

One of the most important elements that will contribute to your confidence as a speaker is your appearance. If you can eliminate any concern about how you look to the audience, then you can concentrate on other aspects of your presentation. In preparing for your speech, spend a little extra time on personal grooming and the selection of clothing to assure yourself that your appearance will be as good as it can be. Clothing should be freshly cleaned and pressed, and shoes should be polished and in good repair.

Special advice to women speakers:

Choose jewelry that is tasteful and that will not be distracting. Above all, avoid jewelry that makes a distracting jangling noise when you move your hands and arms.

Choose makeup suitable to your appearance, and apply it skill-fully.

Although a touch of bright color is appropriate—even desirable—be careful not to overwhelm your audience with bizarre color combinations or dazzling prints or stripes. You want the audience's attention on what you are saying—not on what you are wearing.

Special advice to men speakers:

Wear a dress shirt and appropriate tie. Make certain that the style and color are currently acceptable.

At least one button of the suit coat should be fastened, whether or not a vest is worn.

Because in most cases the speaker is seated before the audience while waiting to be introduced, wear long socks, even if you do not ordinarily wear them, so that at no time are bare shins visible. Make sure that your socks harmonize with your suit.

Don't be too conservative with the necktie you choose—some experts recommend bright flecks of color.

Knowing that you are immaculately and tastefully groomed builds confidence in yourself and establishes the audience's confidence in you.

Good Stage Presence and Delivery

SPEAK OUT. You have a responsibility to make sure that you are heard by each person in the audience. Any person who can't hear will become uninterested, bored, and annoyed. If possible, before you deliver a speech, check the volume of your voice in the room where you will speak.

Keep your chin up when speaking so that your words will be directed out to the audience rather than down to the floor. Vary the pitch of your voice so that the audience is not lulled to sleep by a monotone. When you want to emphasize a point, raise your voice; when you wish to stir emotions, drop your voice so that it is barely audible to the audience. Either extreme of tone, of course, will lose its desired effect if prolonged.

BE POISED. If you have stage fright, take a deep breath before you begin to speak; this will relax your vocal cords. Stand with your weight distributed evenly on both feet, and don't shift from one foot to the other excessively. Don't stand too stiffly or too leisurely—appear alert but at ease. If your listeners think that *you* are comfortable, then they are more likely to be comfortable.

REVEAL AWARENESS OF THE AUDIENCE. An effective speaker must be aware of the audience at all times, not only in selecting and preparing the topic but also in giving the speech. This audience awareness must be transmitted in some way to the listeners. They respond much more favorably when the speaker talks directly to them or smiles at them occasionally. The speaker who looks at the ceiling, at notes, or into space throughout much of the speech, on the other hand, quickly loses rapport with the audience.

As you speak, look slowly back and forth over the entire audience, and pause here and there to "take in" a particular segment of the crowd. Smile frequently. Train yourself to watch the audience carefully and to be sensitive to its changing moods. If, as you are talking, you see blank or uninterested expressions on the faces of your listeners, you will know that your talk is dragging and that the audience has tuned you out. This situation may call for an amusing story, a personal anecdote, or merely a change in the pitch of your voice. If you are using visual aids, you might direct the audience's attention to a chart or other illustration when the talk seems to pall.

If your audience seems tired because the hour is late or too many speakers have preceded you, be quick to sense its boredom. If you aren't sure you can reawaken its interest with a sparkling performance, cut your talk to the bare essentials. Usually it is better to omit a portion of your speech than to run the risk of boring an already weary audience. The audience will be grateful to you.

AVOID OBJECTIONABLE MANNERISMS. A good speaker avoids objectionable mannerisms. When you talk, for example, do you toy with an object such as a paper clip, rubber band, or watch? Do you clear your throat, wet your lips, or remove your eyeglasses frequently? Do you punctuate your remarks frequently with an "uh," "ya know," "okay," or "anda"? Do you have pet expressions or slang that you overuse? If you are not aware that you have any such mannerisms, ask some of your friends to listen to a rehearsal and to criticize. A speaker who has even one annoying habit cannot give a completely successful talk, for mannerisms distract an audience.

DON'T READ OR MEMORIZE. Never recite your speech from memory or read it to the audience. Only a gifted actor or actress can make a memorized speech sound natural, and nothing is more boring to an audience than a singsong recitation. In addition, if you memorize your speech, you may become so flustered when you forget a line that you will find it difficult to continue. A memorized speech often does not follow a logical order because a speaker has omitted something important or has mixed up the parts.

Reading a speech so that the ideas sound convincing is also difficult. If you try to read your speech, you will lose eye contact with your audience every time you refer to your notes.

Instead of reciting or reading your speech, become sufficiently familiar with your material so that all you need is a brief outline with key words and phrases to make your speech flow in logical sequence. Use a conversational tone. Imagine that you are conversing with your audience, not giving an oration. Your voice should reflect the warm, easy tone that you would use if you were talking to a group of very good friends.

USE NOTES. Most speakers—even the most experienced—rely on notes to guide them in their presentations. There is nothing wrong with using notes. It is a greater crime for a speaker to dispense with notes and to give a rambling, disorganized speech than to use notes and to present an organized speech. Even if the notes are not actually used, having them on hand gives you confidence because you know you have something to fall back on if you should have a temporary lapse of memory.

Look at your notes only when absolutely necessary, and return your attention quickly to your audience after each glance at your notes. Keep your notes out of sight as much as possible while you are giving your talk, and turn the pages or cards as inconspicuously as you can. An audience is quickly discouraged by a large, slowly dwindling stack of notes.

PLAN DISTRIBUTION OF MATERIAL. Often the speaker will have duplicated material to distribute to the audience. As a general rule, such material should not be distributed at the beginning of a speech. If it is, the audience will be too busy examining the "giveaway" to pay attention to the speaker. The important points of a speech should be made before any material is distributed to the audience.

USE STORIES AND ANECDOTES DISCREETLY. Nearly every speech of any length is brightened considerably by touches of humor and by human interest narratives. Of course, such stories should not dominate the speech. Observe the following rules in using humor and human interest stories:

1. Make sure they are relevant. Use stories and jokes that are related to the topic, that add interest to the subject, or that illustrate a particular point.
2. Make sure they have a punch line. The story you tell should have a point. Before telling a joke to an audience, test it first on friends. Many stories and jokes fall flat because they are too subtle for a mass audience, because they are told poorly, or because they have weak punch lines.
3. Make sure they are in good taste. You should make certain that any story or joke you tell will not offend or embarrass the audience. Avoid risqué stories or jokes that make fun of physical handicaps, religious convictions, or ethnic groups.
4. Make sure they are short. A story or joke that lasts more than a minute or two is likely to fall flat because the audience loses interest or forgets the details that lead up to the punch line. Only the most skillful storyteller can get by with longer tales. Rehearse stories carefully before delivering them, and time them to make sure that they are not too long.

INTRODUCING A SPEAKER

One of the most important speaking assignments is introducing a speaker. A good introduction sets the stage for the main address. If the introducer does an outstanding job, the main speaker's task is greatly simplified. In introducing a speaker, observe the following points.

Use an Appropriate, Brief Introduction

The audience has come to hear the speaker, not the person who is introducing the speaker. Therefore, keep the introduction short—not more than two or three minutes in length.

When you are introducing a speaker, avoid such trite expressions as "The speaker for this evening needs no introduction," "I give you Ms. Lily Roberts," or "Without further ado, I present Dr. Adam King."

Set the Stage for the Speaker

Do some research on the speaker. Find out from the speaker's friends, associates, or secretary some personal traits or achievements that do not appear in the usual sources. A human interest story about the speaker's hobby, family, or generosity will warm the audience. Although you should have complete details about the speaker's experience, education, and attainments, you do not need to use them all. An audience is quickly bored, and sometimes a speaker is embarrassed, by a straight biographical presentation, no matter how impressive the speaker's background is. Only the most significant dates, positions, and accomplishments should be given. You need only to convince the audience that the speaker is qualified to speak on the topic assigned, is worth knowing, and has something important to say.

Keep Your Eyes on the Audience

Do not turn from the audience to face the speaker you are introducing—always face the audience and keep your eyes on them. Then, after you have made the introduction, wait until the speaker has reached the lectern before seating yourself.

End With the Name

Many successful toastmasters recommend that you not mention the speaker's name until the very end of the introduction. During the introduction refer only to "our speaker." Then, at the end of the introduction, say something like: "It is my pleasure to present Professor Anne Lincoln."

Make Closing Remarks Brief and Appropriate

At the end of the speaker's remarks, someone on the platform or at the speaker's table should assume the responsibility for closing the meeting. If the speech was a particularly effective one, you may say with sincerity, "Thank you, Professor Lincoln, for your most enlightening and inspiring message. We are most appreciative. Ladies and gentlemen, the meeting is adjourned." On the other hand, if the speech has been average or even disappointing, as indicated by the audience reaction, you may close by merely saying, "Thank you, Mr. Jones, for giving us your ideas on how to improve office procedures. Thank you for coming to our meeting tonight, ladies and gentlemen, and good night."

Under no circumstances should you prolong the closing remarks. If the speech was a good one, there is nothing more you can contribute to its effectiveness. If the speech was a poor one, the audience is probably tired and is anxious to leave.

COMMUNICATION PROJECTS

Practical Application

A. List three topics about which you feel qualified to speak. For each topic, give two reasons you feel qualified to speak on this topic. Indicate one audiovisual aid that you might use in presenting each topic before a group. For each topic, suggest one attention-getting title for a twenty-minute speech.

B. Select one of the topics you listed in Application A for a five- or six-minute presentation before the class. Prepare an outline for this speech, following the format suggested on page 548.

C. After your outline has been approved by the instructor, write your speech in full. Then read, refine, and time the speech. Finally, following the suggestions made in the text, make an outline of the speech on no more than four 5- by 3-inch index cards.

D. Suggest two ways that a beginning public speaker can overcome the common problems enumerated below:

1. Excessive verbalizing (using "uh," "ya know," "okay," "anda," and so on).
2. Nervousness.

E. Based on your ultimate career goal, prepare an outline for a five-minute talk on "Why Choosing a Career in the Field of _____ Is a Must for the Nineties." Be prepared to give this talk to the class.

F. You will be the master of ceremonies at your college convocation. The principal speaker will be the dean of the School of Business, and you will introduce him or her. Gather as much information as you can about the dean's background and compose an appropriate introduction. You may supply any additional details about the speaker that you feel will add interest to the introduction. The topic of the presentation will be "Making the Most of Your Business Education."

G. Compose two different closing statements that would be appropriate at the conclusion of the dean's presentation.

Editing Practice

The Editorial Supervisor. Edit and rewrite the following paragraph.

Enclosed please find a copy of the treasurers report. I am enclosing a check herewith in the amount of $75. Kindly acknowledge receipt of the same due to the fact that a previous check transmitted through the mails was lost. Please advise at an early date if their will be any changes necessary in the report herewith submitted.

Case Problem

Playing Fair. Judy, a coworker and friend, confides to you, "I don't think Ms. Gordon likes me. I was late twice this week and only fifteen minutes each time, but she warned me that if I'm late just one more time, she will deduct an hour's wages from my salary check." Your experience with Ms. Gordon (who is also your supervisor) has led you to believe that she has always been fair to the employees and that she was merely carrying out her responsibility in seeing that employees report to work on time. In discussing the matter with your friend, however, you don't want to appear to be on Ms. Gordon's side.

1. Do you think Ms. Gordon played fair with your coworker?
2. What would you say to Judy?

CHAPTER TWELVE

COMMUNICATING FOR JOB RESULTS

57

COMMUNICATING TO GET A JOB

You are attending school in order to prepare yourself with the appropriate skills and knowledge in a particular field, such as accounting, word processing, secretarial work, marketing, or management. In addition, this course in communication in which you are currently enrolled should prepare you to handle the reading, writing, listening, and speaking requirements of most jobs in the business world. One of the first business uses you will make of your communication skills will be to look for a job.

SOURCES OF JOBS

When you are ready to obtain a position in your chosen field or to advance yourself within that field, how do you determine what jobs are available?

Family and Friends

Through members of your own family and from your own friends who are employed in business, you may find out what job opportunities are available in their firms. Businesses often feel that their own employees are good sources of job applicants for new positions. Therefore, when you are in the market for a job, check first with members of your own family, their friends, and your own friends.

Newspaper Advertisements

The classified advertisement sections of newspapers are usually filled every day with announcements of job openings in many types of business positions. When you locate a position that sounds appealing to you and for which you meet the stated requirements, you should follow up on that advertisement to find out more about the available position. Your follow-up will be either in the form of a telephone call arranging for a personal interview or in the form of a letter of application accompanied by a résumé (see pages 563 and 572).

You may also use the classified advertisement section of a newspaper in another way. If you are seeking a position, you may advertise your availability in the "Situations Wanted" section of the newspaper. In preparing such an advertisement, you should clearly indicate the type of position you seek and briefly state the most important qualifications you possess. Above all, make it easy for employers to contact you. The following is an example of a "Situations Wanted" advertisement:

ADMINISTRATIVE ASSISTANT, dictation 140 wam, typing 65 wam, 6+ yrs. exper., supervise 3 employees, wd. proc. exper., wants position dwntn, 1500+ mo., 555-4366 after 5 p.m.

Interested employers will ask you to come for a personal interview or may request first that you write them a letter of application with a résumé. Some employers will send you one of their application forms and will ask you to complete it and return it to them before they ask you to come in for a personal interview.

Placement Offices and Employment Agencies

Most educational institutions have a placement office in which they maintain files of student applicants. If your school has a placement office, you should complete an application form and supply a list of three references—people who know about your education, your personal character, and your business experience. The procedure for acquiring references is discussed on page 570.

In addition to school placement services, your state employment office may be a good source for jobs. Check your telephone directory for the state employment office near you; then call to find out the procedure for registering your name and to ask any questions that you may have.

Private employment agencies are numerous in most cities. They may place applicants in part-time as well as full-time positions. For placing an applicant in a full-time position, the agency charges a fee, which is usually a percentage of the annual salary for the position. The fee may be paid by the applicant, or it may be paid by the employer. Many private agencies focus on only one area of employment—secretarial, accounting, editorial, production, and so on. Do some research to find out which agencies in your area specialize in your field of interest as well as to determine financial arrangements.

Direct Application

If you wish to work for a particular firm, you may apply for a position directly, either by calling in person at the firm's employment or personnel office (and completing an application form) or by sending a letter of application and a résumé. If your application makes a good impression and you possess the qualifications for a position the firm has available, you may then be called in for a personal interview.

USING YOUR COMMUNICATION SKILLS TO ACQUIRE A JOB

You can readily see that you will use all your communication skills in seeking a position. Your communication skills will prove of even greater importance in actually acquiring the position you desire. The impression made by the application form you complete or by the letter of application and résumé you send will determine whether you reach the next step—the personal interview. Therefore, follow the advice in the remainder of this section regarding application forms, application letters, résumés, and other employment letters.

THE JOB APPLICATION FORM

Every company requires a prospective employee to complete some kind of application form for its files. Sometimes this form is completed by the applicant while at the company office, and sometimes it is completed at home. In either case, the application will require accurate and up-to-date information (dates, names, addresses, and telephone numbers) regarding your educational background and work experience. Therefore, when you go to a job interview, you should carry a "pocket résumé" instead of relying upon your memory. Unless you are certain that a typewriter will be available for your use in completing the application form, carry one or two pens with you and make certain that the pens write well. If you are permitted to complete the form at home, use a typewriter. In all instances, complete the form neatly, leaving no questions blank. For questions that do not pertain to you, either write "n/a" (not applicable) or insert a dash (—) in the available space to indicate that you have not accidentally overlooked that item. Always reread your application form before submitting it in order to make certain that it is complete and correct.

THE RÉSUMÉ

A résumé, sometimes called a "data sheet," is an outline or summary of a job applicant's background and qualifications for a job. The care with which it is prepared and the information that it supplies often help determine whether the applicant will be requested to appear for a personal interview. Poorly prepared résumés usually wind up in the wastebasket. Therefore, your résumé should be prepared with great care and should emphasize your qualifications that best meet the requirements of the job you are seeking. During the interview, the résumé may serve as an agenda of topics to be discussed. Prepare a cover letter or letter of application to mail with your résumé. (The letter of application is discussed later in this section.)

```
                    Marika Gilbert
                    8739 Bellevue Avenue
                    Hyattsville, Maryland 20781
                    (301) 555-1570


POSITION APPLIED FOR    Secretary with opportunity for advancement to
                        Executive Secretary or Administrative Assis-
                        tant.

WORK EXPERIENCE

  June 1986 to          Strony Lighting Fixtures, 889 Main Street,
  Present               Hyattsville, Maryland--Secretary

                        Duties:  General secretarial work in office,
                        including taking and transcribing dictation;
                        accounting; filing; and operating word
                        processing equipment

  September 1984 to     St. Joseph's Hospital, 89 Liberty Avenue,
  June 1986             Hyattsville, Maryland--Part-time Office Clerk

                        Duties:  Typing, filing, transcribing, and
                        operating switchboard; occasionally served as
                        receptionist.  Worked afternoons and evenings
                        while attending school.

EDUCATION

  1984-1986             Colora Community College, Colora, Maryland--
                        Associate in Secretarial Science degree.

  1980-1984             Berwick High School, Rooneyville, Maryland--
                        Graduated cum laude, business education major.

REFERENCES              Mr. Carl Strony, President
                        Strony Lighting Fixtures Company
                        889 Main Street
                        Hyattsville, Maryland 20781
                        (301) 555-2750

                        Dr. Marvin Brody, Chairperson
                        Secretarial Administration Department
                        Colora Community College
                        Colora, Maryland 21917
                        (301) 555-1200

                        Mrs. Anne T. Modarick
                        124 South Elm Street
                        Hyattsville, Maryland 20781
                        (301) 555-3612
```

The format of a résumé helps to make it more effective. Note how the all-capital side headings and the use of underscores emphasize various aspects of this résumé.

Because you may apply for several job openings, it may not be practical to type an original copy of a résumé for each job. On the other hand, a carbon copy or an ordinary photocopy does not look professional and will give the reader a poor impression of you. However, you may inexpensively reproduce as many copies as you need through a letter-quality photocopier or the offset printing process using good-quality bond paper. In every city fast-copy services are available that will print copies at a very reasonable cost. All you have to do is prepare the original copy exactly as you wish it reproduced. Suggestions are provided in the next paragraph.

Format

Although one résumé may vary from another in organization and layout, most are commonly divided into these sections: (1) work experience, (2) education, (3) personal information, and (4) references. Each section should be arranged to show clearly the qualifications of the applicant. The typing should be clean and even, the margins should be well balanced and uncrowded, and the headings should stand out. In choosing a format, try to select one that best fits the information you will include. In doing so, keep in mind these points:

1. State the facts; leave interpretation of these facts to the reader.
2. Be sure the facts are complete. For example, say *when* you were graduated and from *where; when* you resigned from a position and *why.*
3. Be neat and orderly; there should be no typographical errors, smudges, or other evidence of sloppy work.
4. Within each section of your résumé, list the most recent information first.
5. Use brief phrases rather than complete sentences. For example, say "Took legal dictation" rather than "I took legal dictation each day from Mrs. Ortega, an attorney."
6. Limit the résumé to one page if possible. By doing so you will be forced to organize the information and to list only important details.
7. Stress your strengths by beginning with them—whether education or work experience.

An effective résumé is illustrated on page 563. Notice the prominence of the name, address, and telephone number of the applicant. Notice also the use of capitalized side headings and the use of underscoring to make certain aspects of the résumé stand out clearly.

Work Experience

Although the most important job qualification for a new graduate is educational preparation, do not underestimate the value of any kind of work experience, part-time or full-time. Almost everyone has held some type of job during vacations or on a part-time basis after

(Continued on page 569.)

The leader of a group discussion must prepare thoroughly to ensure its success.

To make an effective speech, gathering and organizing the data is an essential step.

Since a job interview may be the most critical factor in whether you are hired, you should prepare carefully for it.

Getting a job involves all your communication skills—reading, writing, listening, and speaking.

school. Such jobs as paper carrier, cashier, filling-station attendant, filing clerk, gardener, or even baby-sitter are experiences that speak well for the young man or woman seeking a job. Such experiences should be reported; they demonstrate that the applicant is industrious, has initiative, and is dependable. If you worked to pay for your education, state this fact.

In preparing the work experience section of your résumé, list the most recent work experience first. For each job, give inclusive dates, as well as a brief description of your responsibilities. For example, an applicant might write an entry as follows: "Hargood's Department Store, June 1985–September 1985, Sales Clerk. Sold sporting goods and athletic wear."

If you lack work experience in the type of work for which you are applying, you should not emphasize this on your résumé. Instead, when you write your letter of application to accompany your résumé, you can show how your knowledge of the job for which you are applying will compensate for your lack of experience. Furthermore, whatever kind of jobs you have performed will reveal the kind of work habits you are likely to bring to the job for which you are now applying.

Education

Your educational background will count very heavily in job hunting. Make the most of your presentation by including the following facts. First, list any colleges you have attended and the dates of attendance. List any degrees or diplomas you have obtained. Detail information such as the following:

Your major course of study (accounting, secretarial administration, advertising).

Special subjects you have had that will enhance your value as an employee. For example, a course in computer programming or business communication will be of interest to the prospective employer even though you are applying for a job in the accounting department. Be specific about subject titles. "Accounting IV" tells the employer nothing; "Financial Accounting" is more specific.

Second, name the high school from which you were graduated and the date of graduation. If you took subjects that relate to your qualifications for the position, list them.

Stress leadership qualifications, extracurricular activities, and special honors such as scholarships and awards. Business managers want employees with a wide range of interests; they want people with social poise and with leadership potential. Therefore, in listing both hobbies and interests, show that you have varied interests and that you have developed social graces and leadership qualities through extracurricular activities.

Personal Information

Federal law prohibits employers from asking the age, sex, marital status, religion, or race of applicants for positions. Therefore, supplying such information is optional. If you consider any of this data an asset, you can provide the information on your résumé. To decide, try to view yourself through the eyes of an employer.

References

To avoid making your résumé too long, limit your references to three persons. You should be prepared to supply additional references should the prospective employer request them. If you have had little or no job experience, include the names of instructors who know your potential as a business employee. However, if you have had any kind of work experience, list former employers who can attest to the quality of your work. Always include the job title of each person you list. For instance, write "Ms. Arlene Zimmerman, Office Manager," or "Dr. J. C. Cobb, Professor of Economics." Give the complete address and telephone number of each person, as illustrated in the résumé on page 563.

If you are registered with a school placement office, you may not need to list your references on your résumé. Instead, you can assemble a reference file for the placement office and, at the bottom of your résumé, state "References on file with City College Placement Office are available upon request." In this way, your references will not be bothered by telephone calls and letters; they will complete one letter for your file. Of course, you benefit too: you save space on your résumé, and you can easily keep an up-to-date reference file.

You should always obtain permission—in person, by telephone, or by letter—from each person whose name you use as a reference. Answering inquiries for prospective employers is a time-consuming task, and the people who agree to perform this task on your behalf do so because they have confidence in you, like you, and want you to succeed. Therefore, you owe them the courtesy of keeping them informed about your progress in getting a job.

THE LETTER OF APPLICATION

After you have prepared your résumé and you can see clearly how your qualifications fit the job you seek, you are in a good position to organize a cover letter or letter of application. The letter of application is your sales message. However, when the résumé accompanies the application letter, the letter should not merely repeat the data in the résumé. The function, then, of the letter is to highlight your most important qualifications to make the employer eager to learn more about you and grant you a personal interview. The résumé will help the employer determine whether you have the education and skills required for the job; the letter should convince the employer that you should get the job because you will be an asset to the company. In other words, the résumé is factual and rather formal; the application letter is a personalized sales message. Study the letter on this page and the following guidelines to help you in writing a letter of application.

Get to the Point Immediately

The first paragraph of the application letter should state the following:

Your intent to apply for the position.
The position for which you are applying.
The source from which you learned about the vacancy (if it is not a "blind" application).

There is no one "best" opening for a letter of application. The following opening sentences are suggestions that have been used successfully.

For newspaper ads:

Please consider me an applicant for the position of management trainee, as advertised in the June 25 issue of the *Tribune.*

I am applying for the position of accounting clerk that was advertised in the *Kansas City Star and Times* on Sunday, May 15.

The position of assistant buyer, which you advertised in the April 1 issue of the *Examiner,* is one for which I feel well-qualified. Please consider me an applicant for this position.

I am interested in the position of word processing supervisor advertised in the Help Wanted section of the June 12 *New Orleans Times-Picayune.* I should like to apply for that position.

For referrals:

A mutual friend, Marcus Leibman, has suggested that I write you concerning a position as secretary in your company.

Your company has been recommended to me by Mrs. Anita Flores, the placement director of Royal College, as one with exceptional opportunities for those interested in advertising. I should like to inquire about a possible opening in the copy department.

Attorney Albert Goldman, a friend of my family, has told me of an opening as associate editor of your company magazine. I would like to be considered for this position. (Mr. Goldman is a member of the law firm used by the employer.)

```
                                        389 Golden Place
                                        Duluth, Minnesota 55801
                                        May 10, 198-



Mr. Gerald Levine
Executive Editor
Chandler Newspapers, Inc.
43 Ibsen Drive
Duluth, Minnesota 55802

Dear Mr. Levine:

I am applying for the position of administrative assistant that was
called to my attention by the Placement Office of Venture College.  I
am confident you will find that my qualifications for this position
merit your serious consideration.

A summary of my qualifications is enclosed.  You will find that my
college training provides an excellent foundation for the position for
which I am applying.  I have always been interested in writing, and I
have concentrated heavily on English and the communication arts.  I
have held editorial positions on newspapers in both high school and
college.  Furthermore, my skill in shorthand and word processing has
been used in these positions, as well as in part-time jobs I held
while attending college.

As an administrative assistant, I would welcome the opportunity to
assist in an editorial capacity as well as to use my secretarial
skills in performing my duties as your assistant.  I have had
experience in both proofreading and layout.  My secretarial skills are
well above average, and I enjoy working with others.  You will find
that I am eager to learn and happiest when I keep busy.

I can be reached at 555-8700, Extension 34, between 3 and 5:30 p.m.
any weekday.  I would be pleased to come to your office at your
convenience.

                                Sincerely yours,

                                (Ms.) Georgette Slater
                                Georgette Slater


Enclosure
```

The letter of application is a personalized sales message.

For "blind" applications. A "blind" application is made directly to a company, whether or not a position is open.

> I believe my qualifications for a position as insurance adjuster will interest you.

> I have chosen your company's personnel department as one in which I would like to work. Therefore, I hope you will be interested in my skills and abilities.

> Here are five reasons why I think you will be interested in interviewing me for the position of traffic supervisor in your company.

Tell Why You Should Be Considered

The second paragraph of your letter should convince the employer that you are a desirable candidate for the position referred to in the first paragraph. Don't be afraid to brag. For example:

> Undoubtedly, Ms. Ryan, you want a secretary who can take dictation and transcribe rapidly and accurately, a secretary who has a thorough grasp of secretarial procedures—filing, telephone duties, letter writing, and mail routines. My training at Atlantic College (detailed on the enclosed résumé) has prepared me to handle all aspects of secretarial work competently and confidently.

Here is another example of a second paragraph in which you demonstrate your qualifications:

> A summary of my qualifications is enclosed. As you will see, my training at Carlton Business College was very comprehensive. Not only did I complete all the accounting courses offered by the college, but I also studied personnel management, economics, business psychology, office procedures and management, word processing, and statistics. In all my courses, I consistently ranked in the upper 25 percent of the class.

Of course, the nature of the second paragraph will depend on what you have to sell. If your business experience is limited and unlikely to impress the employer, you will have to emphasize your educational background. In such a case, you might follow the above paragraph with a statement such as this:

> Of particular interest to me in the accounting course was computerized accounting systems. In this class we learned the applications of accounting theory to automated procedures and equipment. I am especially eager to work in a large organization, such as yours, where data processing is used on a wide scale.

Here is another example of capitalizing on achievements in school:

> You will notice from my résumé that economics and business communication were among my best subjects. In addi-

tion, I was a member of the debating team, was on the school newspaper staff, and was president of our speech club. You will find my written and oral communication skills well above average.

The writer of the following paragraph lacks business experience but compensates for this by showing interest and enthusiasm.

I am very interested in your bank and in the work your tellers do. Several times during the past year, I have talked with Larry Hamilton, who started his teller training with you a year ago, about the interesting duties he performs and the pleasant working conditions. He is very enthusiastic about the opportunities for advancement. These discussions make me even more certain that banking is the kind of work I want to do and that your bank is the one in which I would like to work. I know that within a short period of time, I can learn to perform effectively as one of your tellers.

If you have had business experience that is related to the position for which you are applying, make the most of it.

I am particularly interested in accounting systems in which automated equipment and procedures are employed. Last summer I was a temporary employee in the systems department of Laskey-Brent Corporation, where I had an opportunity to become acquainted with information processing techniques. This experience was valuable, and I have decided to do further study in the field in evening school after I have obtained a position.

Show Willingness to Work and Learn

The employer who hires you is taking a risk—a risk that you may not be fitted for the position. One of the best assurances you can give that you are a safe risk is your willingness to learn and your genuine interest in the job. For example:

Obviously, there will be many routines and procedures that will be new to me. You will find me eager to learn and to improve.

I shall bring to the job a willingness to work and an eagerness to improve. Let me prove this to you.

I am not afraid of hard work; in fact, I enjoy it.

I pride myself on my punctuality, accuracy, and dependability.

I learn fast and I remember what I learn.

Make It Easy for the Employer to Ask You for an Interview

The last paragraph of your letter of application should be the action-getting paragraph—aimed at obtaining an invitation for an interview. Make it easy for the employer to contact you.

I can come to your office for an interview between 9 a.m. and 5 p.m. on any weekday. My telephone number is 555-7613. If you would prefer to write, please use the address at the top of this letter.

Some job hunters are more direct; they prefer to follow up on the letter rather than wait for the employer. For example:

I can come to your office for an interview between 9 a.m. and 5 p.m. any weekday. After you have had a chance to review my qualifications, I shall call your secretary for an appointment.

Some successful applicants enclose a postage-paid return card for employers to complete. For example:

Dear Ms. Stern:

Please come to my office on _____ at
(Date)

_____ for an interview.
(Time)

Very truly yours,

If a postal card is enclosed, you might include the following statement in your letter.

Would you complete the enclosed postal card and ask your secretary to drop it in the mail. I am available at any time that is convenient for you. If you would prefer to telephone, my number is 555-2518.

Send the application letter in an envelope of the same good-quality bond paper as that on which the letter is written. Here again, the rules for neatness, good style, and placement apply. Choose a plain (unprinted) white business envelope such as a No. 10 (4⅛ by 9½ inches). Include your return address in the upper left corner of the front of the envelope.

OTHER EMPLOYMENT LETTERS
Requesting Permission to Use Someone's Name as Reference

You should never use someone's name as a reference without first requesting permission to do so. Although permission may be requested by telephone or in person, it is often requested in writing:

As you may know, I was recently graduated from the City College of Business, and I am making application at several firms in the Baltimore area for a position as legal secretary. May I list your name as a reference on my application forms? I should be most grateful for this privilege.

You may answer at the bottom of this letter and return your reply in the enclosed envelope.

Thank you.

Thanking Your References

After you accept a job, you should personally thank each person who helped you to get the job—and you should do so by writing a letter or a brief note.

> You will be pleased, I am certain, to learn that I have accepted a position as legal secretary with Mumford, Hayes, and Richards, one of the largest law firms in Baltimore. I start to work next week, and I am looking forward eagerly to my new position. The job is exactly what I was looking for.
>
> Thank you very much for allowing me to use your name as a reference. I am sure that your recommendation was instrumental in my being hired.

Interview Follow-Up Letters

After you have been interviewed, it is good strategy (as well as courtesy) to write to the interviewer, especially if you have reason to expect that a decision will not be made in a short time. Your thank-you letter gives you another opportunity to do a selling job. The letter might follow this form:

> I enjoyed meeting you and talking with you on Thursday. Certainly, I came away with a much clearer picture of the work of a mail room supervisor in your corporation. The work sounds very exciting and challenging, and I am more convinced than ever that it is something I would like to do.
>
> Thank you for your time and the many courtesies you showed me. I was especially glad to meet Mrs. Wallin; please convey my best wishes to her.

Accepting the Position

If you have been notified that you have been chosen for a position, it is wise to accept in writing, especially if the firm is out of town or if your reporting date is a week or two away. You might use the style illustrated in the following letter.

> I am pleased to accept the position as your secretary. I know that I shall enjoy working with you in the field of public relations and communications. The salary of $225 a week, plus benefits, is quite satisfactory to me.
>
> As you requested, I shall report to work on Monday, July 5, at 8:30 a.m. Thank you for giving me this opportunity.

Declining a Position

Occasionally it is necessary to decline a job after it has been accepted. Naturally, you need solid, justifiable reasons for doing so. In such an event, give the reasons for your action. The following example illustrates an acceptable reason for declining a job.

> This morning I was offered a position by another firm at a much higher salary, and I regret that I have to decline the fine job you offered me.

COMMUNICATION PROJECTS

Practical Application

A. For the career field of your choice, what are likely to be the best sources of information regarding job openings?

B. For each of the sources you indicated in Application A, write an appropriate opening paragraph for a letter of application.

C. From the "Help Wanted" advertisements in your local newspaper, select a position that appeals to you and for which you are qualified (or will be upon graduation). Write a letter of application answering the ad, and attach a résumé you have prepared specifically for this job.

D. Write a letter to one of the people listed as a reference on your résumé (Application C) to ask permission to use his or her name.

E. As a result of your application for the position in C above, you have been called for a personal interview. Write an appropriate interview follow-up letter, supplying all the necessary information.

F. Assume that you have accepted the position for which you applied in C above. Write a letter of notification and thanks to one of the people who served as a reference for you.

G. Although you accepted the position for which you applied in C above and are scheduled to start work next week, yesterday you were offered a better position with the firm's chief competitor. This position has greater potential for advancement, a higher starting salary, and considerably better fringe benefits. Therefore, you decide to accept the better offer. Write a letter to the other employer, whose position you had already accepted, explaining why you must decline the position.

Editing Practice

Editors' Alert. Here are more sentences on which you can sharpen your editing skills. Try to develop an all-seeing eye that doesn't miss a detail. If necessary, rewrite the sentences.

1. Witch of the 2 manuals was the best?
2. Who's book did you use, there's or mine?
3. Its my judgement that you should expedite the delivery.
4. Having planned the develope a new proceedure, the meeting was called for Febuary 1.
5. It's well-known that the personal department is very efficient.

Case Problem

Practical vs. Ethical. Reread Application G. Be prepared to discuss your feelings, pro or con, regarding the applicant's rejection of an offer that had already been accepted.

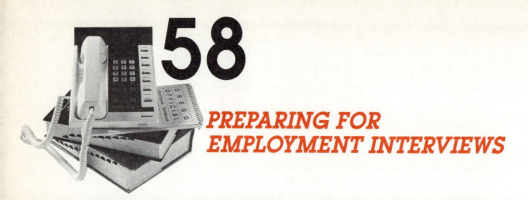

58

PREPARING FOR EMPLOYMENT INTERVIEWS

The job interview is one of the most important aspects of the job-seeking process and may be the critical determinant of whether or not you are hired. Therefore, it is essential that you prepare yourself adequately and perfect your oral communication skills. No matter how skillful and knowledgeable you may be, how impressive your résumé is, or how persuasive your letter of application may be, you may fail to be hired if you cannot "sell" yourself when you meet a prospective employer face to face.

In an interview, every time you speak you have an opportunity to sell yourself. Your response to questions, your description of experiences and situations, your explanation of procedures and methods—all contribute either favorably or unfavorably to the interviewer's impression of you. Therefore, you must prepare adequately for the interview and make plans far in advance. As a result of the type of planning you do, the interview may be either a frightening or an enjoyable experience.

HOW TO PLAN FOR THE INTERVIEW

Although you were not conscious of it at the time, preparation for the interview actually began quite some time ago. A number of years ago you had to choose the type of work you wanted to do. Then you had to obtain the necessary education and training required in this type of work. Ahead of you lies the job of selecting the type of company for which you want to work, compiling a résumé, writing a letter of application, and obtaining the interview. Such long-range planning is necessary, of course. The following discussion will be helpful in preparing for the job interview itself.

Know What You Have to Offer

Good sales representatives know their products thoroughly—better than anyone else does. They have analyzed their products from every conceivable angle; they know their strengths and their weaknesses. They understand fully what features of their products are most likely to appeal to prospective buyers, and these are the features they emphasize in their sales presentations.

As a job applicant, you are a sales representative, and your product is yourself. Preparing a résumé gives you an opportunity to put on paper what you have to sell—to see your strong points and compare them with those that your competitors for the position may have. The items emphasized on the résumé are those every employer is interested in—education, experience, and special interests and skills. You should know these qualifications so well that you can communicate them orally without hesitation.

The first step in planning for the interview, therefore, is to anticipate questions that you may be asked about your education, experience, and personal qualities. Here are examples of some of these questions:

What subjects did you concentrate on while attending college?

Which of these subjects did you like best? Why?

Tell me something about your course in _____ (personnel administration, business communications, office management, or other subjects).

I see by your application that you worked at Randolph's for two summers. What kind of work did you do? What did you like most about your job? What did you like least?

What do you most enjoy doing outside of working hours— hobbies and other activities?

Were you active in school organizations? Which ones?

Do you consider your skills (a) about average? (b) above average? (c) below average?

Do you like to write? Do you consider yourself strong in English?

Answers to such probing questions will tell the interviewer a great deal about you and about how well you would fit the position, how quickly you would adjust to the job and to the people around you, and what your potential is for growth. In preparing for a job interview, then, you might ask yourself this question: What would I want to know about me if I were the interviewer?

Make a Positive First Impression

As you plan for the interview, ask yourself, "What can I do to make a positive first impression upon the interviewer?" First, you must be on time for the interview. Arise early enough to allow sufficient time to perform all the necessary grooming chores and to provide for any delays in traveling to the interview. Wouldn't it be better to arrive a half hour early for the interview than to arrive five minutes late?

On no other occasion is it more important to look your best than at an employment interview. The impression you make when you walk into the room will very likely influence the interviewer's attitude toward you throughout the entire interview. Plan ahead, therefore, to make the most of your appearance. Furthermore, *knowing* that you look good will help to make you feel more at ease. If possible, determine in advance if there are any company rules regarding grooming and dress; for example, ask any employees whom you know. If you really want to be employed by this firm, prepare accordingly.

Regardless of any specific grooming and dress rules that may exist, there are two characteristics that you can be certain will affect that first impression you make—neatness and cleanliness. Clean hair, clean hands, clean fingernails, clean shoes, and clean clothing are "musts." Clothing should be pressed, should be clean, should be color-coordinated, and should lean more toward the conservative than the extreme. Remember, you are trying to give the interviewer the impression that you are businesslike and that you will convey a businesslike impression to the customers of that business. Will wearing casual clothing convey that impression?

Plan What You Will Say

Interviewers operate in different ways. Some will do most of the talking and will ask only a few questions about your education and experience. Others will draw you out as much as possible and say very little. Be prepared for such general statements or questions from the interviewer as these:

Tell me about yourself. (This request will give you a chance to emphasize your most salable features. The interviewer doesn't want to know about your childhood but wants you to answer such questions as these: What do you do best? What do you like best?)

Review your college work and your experience. (Here you will emphasize the college courses that will best implement your qualifications for this particular job. The same is true of your experience.)

What do you think your strongest points are? your weakest?

Tell me why you think you should be hired for this position.

What job would you like to have five years from now?

Anticipate some personal questions, such as:

What kind of person do you think you are?

Do you like to work?

What do you enjoy doing in your leisure time?

Do you read a great deal?

Where do you live?

What salary do you expect?

Are you punctual in your appointments?

Although you should anticipate the questions you are likely to be asked, it's a good idea also to think of questions you would like to ask the interviewer. Not only will you receive information, but asking questions also will show the interviewer that you have given careful thought to the position. Be prepared, therefore, to ask such questions as:

What duties are required in this position?

Does the company provide opportunities for further education?

What are the opportunities for advancement?

Anticipate the Salary Question

More often than not, the salary paid for a position—at least the general range—is known to the applicant before the interview. If the salary is not known, however, and the interviewer has not mentioned it, you should say, near the end of the interview, "I understand that the beginning salary for this position is $_____ a week. Is this correct?" (Base the figure you mention on knowledge, not whim. Find out from employment agencies or newspaper ads what the salary is for the jobs you apply for—before you apply.)

Sometimes information about the salary is withheld, or the salary is listed as *open*. This means that the company has set a general salary range for the job, but the specific amount paid will depend upon the qualifications of the applicant.

If the interviewer asks you "What salary do you expect?" be prepared to give an honest, straightforward answer. Find out in advance what similar jobs are paying; then say something like this: "I understand that similar jobs in this area range from $_____ to $_____ a week. I had expected to receive about $_____." (Mention a figure somewhere in the middle or, if you consider yourself unusually well qualified, near the top.)

Plan What You Will Take With You

Every applicant for a position should take the following items:

A good pen.
A pencil with a good eraser.
A résumé. (This may be put in a plain folder, in a large envelope, or in a special acetate folder. The résumé should never be folded and put in a pocket or purse.)
A small pad on which to take notes.
Information about references.

Applicants for stenographic positions are usually given a typewriting and shorthand test. In addition to the items listed above, they should also take a clean stenographer's notebook. Although these items are usually supplied by the company, it is well to be prepared in case they are not.

If you are applying for a position in which samples of your work would be helpful, take some along. Put them in a folder or in a clean envelope.

On the day of the interview, give yourself plenty of time to arrive at the interviewer's office on schedule. Take no chances on traffic jams and delayed trains, taxis, or buses; start early. Last-minute dashes to make an appointment are likely to leave you disheveled and breathless. Plan your schedule so that you can walk into the receptionist's office with calm assurance.

You'll usually be asked to fill out an official application form, and arriving ten or fifteen minutes early will give you a head start on this task. You will want to complete the application blank slowly and carefully (it will be part of your permanent record if you get the job). Try to get a copy of this application blank before arriving for the interview. In this way, you can be sure to give it the attention it deserves.

Find Out All You Can About the Company

There are two main reasons for finding out in advance all you can about the company. First, knowing something about the organization will help you to decide whether it is a place in which you would like to work. Second, you should have a strong answer to the often-asked question, "Why did you choose our company?" Too many applicants have no ready answer to that question beyond "I just heard it is a nice place to work," or "It's close to my home." It is much more effective to say, "I have always been interested in investments, and I know that your company is one of the leading investment firms in this area."

How should you research facts about a company? You might talk to the person, such as your placement counselor, who referred you to the organization. You might ask this person or an instructor for the name of an acquaintance who works there; then talk to the employee. If you have an opportunity, pick up copies of employee magazines, booklets, or advertising brochures. Above all, learn the exact spelling of the name of the person who is to interview you. If you are not absolutely sure, telephone the interviewer's secretary or speak to the company receptionist.

THE INTERVIEW

When you arrive at the office, you will be greeted by a receptionist. Give your name and the purpose of your visit. "I'm (your name). I have an appointment at nine with Mr. Nakama." If you have to wait a few minutes, review your résumé, check the completed application blank, read the literature that will probably be available in the reception office, or otherwise occupy yourself. Don't engage in conversation with the receptionist unless you are invited to do so.

When you are ushered into the interviewer's office, try to be relaxed (though not casual or arrogant) and to look pleasant. Do not extend your hand unless the interviewer does so first. It is enough to say, "How do you do, Mr. Nakama." You do not need to give your name; the secretary or receptionist will have announced your arrival.

Seat yourself only when you are invited to do so. Keep with you the materials you have brought. Don't place anything on the interviewer's desk unless you are invited to do so. The interviewer may or may not ask to see the application blank and the résumé. The moment will come, however, when you are asked about your education and experience. This is the time to give the interviewer your résumé if you haven't already done so. Say something like this: "Here is my résumé, on which that information is summarized. I also have completed the application blank." (Hand both to the interviewer.) Wait for the interviewer to make the first move. You will know at once how the interview will be conducted—whether the interviewer is going to ask most of the questions or prefers that you take the initiative. Usually the interviewer will direct the proceedings.

Don't smoke. Even if you are a smoker, it is probably best to refuse a cigarette if it is offered to you. Say simply, "No, thank you, not just now." If you are a nonsmoker, you merely decline with "No, thank you."

Face and speak directly to the interviewer. Don't stare at the floor or out the window while either of you is talking. Of course, you should take your eyes from the interviewer's occasionally, but leave no doubt that you are talking and listening to him or her. Speak slowly and enunciate carefully. Give your answers and statements in a straightforward manner; show that you have thought them through and that you can speak with precision. Give short answers; the interviewer doesn't want your life story or your complete personal philosophy in answer to every question. At the same time, a mere "Yes" or "No" is not sufficient. For example, if you are asked this question "I see you had one course in accounting. Did you like it?" it is not enough simply to say "Yes" (assuming that is how you actually feel). You might add, "I enjoyed the course very much, and I plan to take more accounting in evening school."

Be specific about your special qualifications. If you are asked about your skills in shorthand and typewriting, give the results of your last tests. Say something like this: "I can write shorthand at 100 words a minute fairly consistently on new material. My typing speed on the last few tests was in the upper 60s." Or "My accounting courses consisted of principles, cost, intermediate, and departmental. In the departmental course we were introduced to automation as it relates to accounting, and I especially enjoyed that." Or "I consistently made top grades in communication courses, and I particularly liked writing letters." Or "One of the most interesting things I did during my summers at Randolph's was to verify cash balance each day. It wasn't easy to make everything balance, since we had so many people handling the cash, but I was successful at it and learned a lot from the experience."

On the other hand, be noncommittal about controversial matters. If you are asked what you thought of Randolph's as a place to work and your opinion isn't especially favorable, say something like this: "My work there gave me some valuable experience, and I enjoyed much of it." If you are asked for your opinions about people for whom you have worked and for whom you feel no special fondness, say something like this: "Ms. Lincoln was often helpful to me; I believe I profited from working with her."

The interviewer will usually be interested in why you left other positions, especially when you have indicated on your application blank that you left because of unsatisfactory working conditions or for other negative reasons. If you complain to the interviewer about the people or about the company policies, however, you may give the impression that you are a chronic complainer. Try to be objective and to say something like this: "I found it difficult to adjust to some of the procedures and to the unusual hours at Randolph's. Many of the people were extremely pleasant and helpful. There were some with whom I didn't have much rapport, but I'm sure some of the fault was mine." The interviewer will appreciate your frankness as well as your discretion.

Try to be at ease; smile occasionally. Remember that the interviewer needs someone to fill a position that is open and is just as eager to make a decision in your favor as you are to get the job. Most interviewers are pleasant, friendly, and understanding. Try to display an air of confidence. Above all, don't fidget. Nervousness often shows up in such habits as brushing imaginary lint off clothing, straightening and restraightening a tie, fussing with hair, toying with an object such as a purse or a paper clip, and putting hands to the face. Avoid such habits; give your attention to the interviewer.

The interviewer will let you know when the interview is over. The usual sign is to rise. As soon as the interviewer does so, you should also rise. The exchange that takes place might be something like the following conversation.

Interviewer	
(rising):	I enjoyed meeting and talking with you.
You (rising):	Thank you, Mr. Nakama. I appreciate the time you have given me.

Interviewer:	We have your telephone number, and we will call you just as soon as we have reached a decision.
You:	Thank you. I shall look forward to hearing from you.
Interviewer:	Good-bye.
You:	Good-bye.

Leave quickly and thank the secretary and the receptionist as you leave.

FOLLOWING UP THE INTERVIEW

As soon as possible after the interview, make a written summary from notes and memory of the facts you learned in the interview and the opinions you have formed about the company and about the job for which you were interviewed. If you are being interviewed for jobs in several different companies, this written summary will prove an excellent way to refresh your memory about the interview when you are trying later to make your final job choice.

Whether or not you follow up the interview with a thank-you letter to the interviewer will depend on how much you want the job. If the position is an especially desirable one, you will want to thank the interviewer for his or her time and to reemphasize some of your special qualifications. For other suggestions relating to follow-up letters after interviews, refer to Section 57.

COMMUNICATION PROJECTS

Practical Application

A. Prepare written answers to each of the following questions and statements likely to come up in an employment interview.

1. Why do you wish to work for our company?
2. What kind of work do you enjoy doing most?
3. What kind of work do you enjoy doing least?
4. What salary do you expect?
5. What are your job goals for the next five-year period?
6. Why have you selected this type of work?
7. Tell me about yourself.
8. Why did you leave your last position?
9. How do you spend your spare time?
10. What do you do in the summer?

B. List ten suggestions (in the form of "Dos" and "Don'ts") for *preparing* for a job interview. Then list ten suggestions to be observed *during* the interview.

C. Make a list of the questions you might like to ask the interviewer about the position for which you are applying or the company for which you will be working.

D. Assume your interviewer says, "I notice that your department supervisor at Landow's was Karl Gustafson. I've heard that Gustafson is a tough person to get along with. Did you like working with him?" Compose the answer you would give your interviewer. (Assume that what he heard about Karl Gustafson is true, insofar as you are concerned.)

E. Answer the following questions:

1. Why do you think that you should thank the secretary and the receptionist when you leave the interviewer's office?
2. It is suggested that you take a small notebook along with you to the interview. What notes might you want to make?
3. Why is it important to choose carefully the company for which you would like to work?
4. In large companies, the applicant for a position is interviewed at least twice; first by a personnel specialist, and later on by the person for whom the applicant will work. What do you think is the main purpose of the first interview? How might the two interviews differ?

F. Assume that you have been interviewed for a position with the Hamilton Investment Company (for which you are well qualified and in which you are very much interested). The interviewer, Ms. Gladys Robbins, was very pleasant and was favorably impressed with your qualifications. However, she told you that she plans to interview several other applicants before making a decision regarding who should be hired. Write a letter to Ms. Robbins to thank her for the interview. In the letter, emphasize special qualifications you possess or present any additional facts that may improve your chances for being hired for the position.

Editing Practice

The Rewrite Desk. Edit and rewrite the following paragraph.

Your cashier's check dated Febuary 6 arrived to late for you to take advantage of our offer advertised in "The Accounting Journal." It occured to us that you might wish to mark your calender now for our forthcoming sale on April 6 and 7.

Case Problem

Introductions and Courtesy. Lolita Estrella is the new secretary assigned to the workstation next to yours. When Lolita first reports for work, the office manager is at a meeting and is therefore unable to introduce Lolita to you and to the other employees in the office.

1. What should you do to make Lolita feel welcome?
2. In the event that you do nothing, what might Lolita do?

59

HANDLING COMMUNICATION ACTIVITIES EFFECTIVELY

You already know that communication is so fundamental to any business operation that little would be accomplished in business without it. Among those business workers whose duties are almost exclusively involved with communication are secretaries, executive secretaries, and administrative assistants. Without these people, the flow of information would cease in most offices.

It is, therefore, especially important for all business workers to understand the duties of these specialists, and these duties are discussed in this section. If you plan to pursue a secretarial career, then this section will be of obvious interest to you. But even if you do not plan to pursue a secretarial career, you should pay special attention to this section, because it will help you to work more effectively *with* your secretary.

RESPONSIBILITIES RELATED TO INCOMING MAIL

Executives should give the incoming mail their first attention each day. Therefore, the efficient secretary opens and sorts the mail so that it is on the executive's desk as soon as possible.

Opening the Mail

Use a letter opener for opening mail. Never rip envelopes open or cut them open with scissors, because you may damage the contents. After removing the contents, check each envelope carefully for unremoved enclosures.

If the mail contains checks or other important papers, slit open the envelope on three sides (so that it opens as a flat sheet of paper) to make sure that you do not overlook the enclosures. Also, because addresses frequently are written only on the envelope, make certain that the address appears on the correspondence or you have a record of it before destroying the envelope.

Sorting the Mail

In a small office, all incoming mail may be picked up and distributed by whoever arrives at the office first: the secretary, the receptionist, an office assistant, even the boss. In a large office where a great deal of mail is received, the mail is picked up and distributed by a special staff in a central mail room. In either case, letters addressed to individuals or to departments are usually delivered unopened. Letters addressed to the company without specific reference to individuals or to departments are opened, read, and then routed to the appropriate persons.

Usually, the secretary is responsible for receiving and opening the employer's mail. The mail is handled in the following manner:

Letters marked "Personal" are placed *unopened* in the executive's in-basket or on the desk.

All other letters are opened, read carefully by the secretary, and placed on top of the executive's desk or in the in-basket. If passersby can look into the office, place the letters inside a folder so that they cannot be seen.

The mail should be arranged in order of importance. A commonly accepted arrangement is as follows (in order from top to bottom):

Telegrams and other "fast service" communications
Letters marked "Personal"
Other first-class mail
Circulars and advertisements
Magazines and newspapers

If there is a great deal of mail, it may be separated into three folders marked "Telegrams," "First-Class Mail," and "Other Mail." Some secretaries separate the mail according to the urgency with which it must be handled (some telegrams are not important, while a particular newspaper item or a circular may be). In this case, folders are labeled "First Priority," "Second Priority," "For Reading Only—No Action," and so on. Of course, the secretary must know enough about the employer's business to know which pieces of mail are in most urgent need of attention.

In addition to opening and sorting the daily mail for the executive, the administrative assistant usually takes on the following duties.

Reading the Mail

Usually the administrative assistant is expected to read the mail before placing it on the employer's desk. There are two important reasons for reading the mail: (1) to keep informed of matters that have a bearing on the executive's work and (2) to make the executive's job of answering the mail an easier one.

Suppose an executive receives a letter from Gordon Lee, a business acquaintance in another city. Mr. Lee writes that he will be visiting the city on a certain date and hopes to see the executive. The assistant reads the letter, checks the executive's calendar, and makes the following notation on Mr. Lee's letter: "You will be in New Orleans that week." Or suppose the executive receives a letter from Ms. Eileen Mack, a supplier, in which Ms. Mack refers to a specification sheet she received from the executive. The assistant attaches to Ms. Mack's letter a copy of the specification sheet referred to so that the executive will have on hand the information needed to reply to Ms. Mack. The assistant may also be called on to perform the following tasks in order to ease the load of the executive:

Underline or highlight important dates, amounts, or statements on incoming letters. Place notations in the margin of incoming letters, such as "I will answer this request" or "He refers to a telephone call from Mr. Allison" or "She means June 11 (instead of June 10)."

Place a routing slip on letters that probably should be handled by another department. Of course, if the letter is addressed to the executive, he or she should be given the opportunity to read it even though someone else will reply. The routing slip, however, makes it easier to handle the letter if the executive agrees with the recommendation to route it elsewhere.

Read and note for the executive's attention magazine or newspaper articles of special interest. This may be done by clipping to the publication a memo slip containing a notation such as "See pages 43, 44, and 76."

The busy executive who receives a large amount of correspondence may expect an assistant to prepare digests (summaries) of important messages. An executive who is planning to be away on an extended business trip may ask the assistant to send summaries once a week or perhaps more often.

Digest of Important Mail Received May 4

Ms. Kim Priebe	Would like you to visit Troy branch office sometime in June. Give her a firm date for your visit.
Mr. Wendell Ashe	Can you speak at the July 7 Rotary meeting? Select your own topic.
Mrs. Lupe Ricardo	Enclosed outline for summer advertising program. Would like your approval and suggestions.
IRS	Refund check enclosed.

RESPONSIBILITIES RELATED TO OUTGOING MAIL

Since busy executives have many communication responsibilities related to outgoing mail, secretaries should be able to accept some of these duties to free their bosses for other tasks. By taking responsibility for as many of the following outgoing mail duties as possible, secretaries will be valuable to the firm—and to their bosses.

Dictation and Transcription

Techniques of taking and transcribing dictation are not within the scope of this book. Certainly the secretary prepared to enter the business world has acquired and perfected these skills. Most employers look for more than these basic skills; they expect their secretaries to know the finer points of grammar, punctuation, capitalization, and spelling. Many executives rely on their secretaries to edit and correct their dictation; some also expect their secretaries to verify the facts, figures, and names used in their dictation.

EDITING.   How much editing should the secretary do on the letters the boss dictates? That depends almost entirely on the boss. Some administrators dictate very methodically, indicating punctuation, unusual spellings, and new paragraphs. Usually these executives are so sure of themselves that they want very little editing done. Others dictate only the barest outline of a letter and say to the secretary, "Fix it up." Most bosses, however, are somewhere between these two extremes; if the dictator makes errors in grammar and punctuation, the secretary usually can feel free to make the necessary changes. Obviously, the secretary must be positive of the correction before proceeding. If not, the secretary may say to the executive, "You mentioned June 22 as the first day of the meeting. Did you mean June 2?" or "In my notes I have 'I don't want to set any precedents in this decision.' I believe you actually said, 'I don't want to set *a precedent.*'"

FINISHED LETTERS.   After transcribing the letters, the secretary should proofread them carefully. A letter that is not correct or that contains unclear sentences should not be placed on the employer's desk for signature. The secretary should never try to pass over an error or a garbled sentence.

Transcribed letters should be accompanied by the addressed envelope and the enclosures when the letters are presented for signature. Place the envelope over the letterhead so that the flap faces the letterhead; by so doing, you won't obscure the message. If the executive is not in the office when the letters are brought in to be signed, the letters should be placed on the desk, face down or inside a folder.

PREPARATION FOR MAILING.   The secretary's responsibility for outgoing letters does not end when the letters are placed on the executive's desk for signature. First, the secretary should make certain that the executive knows that the letters *are* ready to be signed so that they will be mailed that day. Check to see that every letter is signed and that any enclosure mentioned in a letter is actually with that letter. And, double-check to see that each letter goes into its proper envelope. Nothing is more embarrassing than to have one person receive a letter that should have gone to someone else.

After preparing the letters for mailing, the secretary should make sure that the mail goes out on that day. If the outgoing mail collection has been missed, the secretary should either deliver the mail to the mail room or drop it into a mailbox after the office closes.

Letter Writing

Your preparation in this course should enable you to lighten your employer's work load by taking the responsibility for writing routine letters. Tactfully suggest that you undertake the job of writing routine letters: reservation letters, requests, referrals, thank-yous and acknowledgments, letters about appointments, and transmittal letters. Many of these letters are discussed in Chapter 9. However, some are so important to the secretary and administrative assistant that they receive additional emphasis here.

RESERVATION LETTERS. For letters making hotel and travel reservations, either the employer's signature or the secretary's signature may be used. Refer to Chapter 9 for additional information on writing reservation letters. The letter that follows has been written for the employer's signature.

> Please reserve a single room with bath for me for November 15 and 16, at a rate not to exceed $65.
>
> I shall arrive about 5 p.m. on November 15 and expect to check out before 2 p.m. on November 17. Please send me a confirmation of this reservation.

REQUEST LETTERS. Request letters, too, may be written either for the employer's or for the secretary's signature. Here is an example of a request letter written for the secretary's signature.

> Jessica Frey, the supervisor of our word processing center, attended your session on word processing at the convention of the American Executive's Institute last week in Des Moines.
>
> Ms. Frey indicated that your firm has available a unique layout for your center that contributes to a very efficient operation. She indicated that attendees interested in this layout would receive a copy of the layout and a description of the procedures followed if they would write a letter requesting these materials.
>
> We should very much like to have a copy of the layout and procedures. We should also like permission to reproduce a

sufficient number of copies for our branch offices. We would be happy to pay for any expenses incurred in sending a copy to us.

REFERRAL LETTERS.   Often executives may not be able to give personal attention to letters sent to them but really meant for someone else. In such cases, secretaries usually write an acknowledgment letter for their own signature and attend to any necessary follow-through. The following letter would be sent in answer to the request; at the same time, a copy of the original letter and a copy of the reply would be sent to the person who can fulfill the request.

> Thank you for requesting 100 copies of our booklet, Job Application Advice, for distribution to the seniors in your school. We are pleased that you feel our booklet will be useful to your students.
>
> Unfortunately, our supply of this booklet has been depleted. Therefore, I am referring your request to our Detroit office, where this booklet was prepared. You should receive your 100 copies within two weeks.

LETTERS WHILE THE BOSS IS AWAY.   Even though the secretary may not be requested to write letters while the boss is in the office, while the boss is away, the secretary may be expected to acknowledge important letters received and to explain any delays caused by the boss's absence. Letters written for these reasons are usually brief, courteous, and noncommittal—that is, the letter does not reveal private company business such as where the boss is or why the boss is away.

Sometimes the correspondence cannot await your employer's return. Such letters are referred to someone else in the company. Only urgent or highly important letters are routed in this way.

> Thank you for your April 5 letter to Mrs. King.
>
> Since Mrs. King will be out of the office for a month, I am referring your letter to Mr. James Corey, our credit manager. Mr. Corey will write you just as soon as he has had an opportunity to review your request.

After writing this reply, the secretary should write a memorandum to Mr. Corey, transmitting the letter to him.

> TO: Mr. James Corey   FROM: Carol West
> Secretary to Mrs. King
> SUBJECT: Attached Letter   DATE: April 7, 19—
> From Lee Sims
>
> The attached letter requires a further response by April 15, and as you know, Mrs. King is on leave until May 2. I have also attached a copy of my letter to Mr. Sims. I know Mrs. King would want you to handle Mr. Sims' request.

I would be grateful if you will send me a blind carbon of your letter to Mr. Sims for our files.

CW

When you answer a letter for your employer, do not express opinions that could disagree with those of your employer or that may prove embarrassing. For example, if a letter applying for a job was sent to a personnel director who will be away from the office for some time, the personnel director's secretary would *not* write:

Thank you for your application for a management trainee position. Your qualifications are excellent, and I know Mrs. Gordon will be favorably impressed.

The personnel director may feel differently about the applicant or may not have an opening at the present time. Therefore, a noncommittal letter like the following would be more appropriate.

Thank you for your application for a management trainee position. Mrs. Laura Gordon, the personnel director, is out of the office until June 15. She will write you shortly after she returns.

This letter makes no commitment beyond indicating that a reply will be forthcoming. Note, too, that the letter does not provide any confidential information regarding Mrs. Gordon's whereabouts.

Here is a summary of procedures to follow while the executive is away.

1. If the boss will be away for more than two or three days, acknowledge all letters to which a correspondent might reasonably expect a prompt answer. An example of such an acknowledgment letter is the letter just illustrated.
2. Forward mail to a knowledgeable person in the company if the incoming letter indicates that some action must be taken immediately.
3. If the employer is on an extended trip, send copies of letters requiring action before he or she is expected to return to the office. Be certain to send any necessary supporting materials.
4. Answer all letters that you would be expected to handle if your boss were in the office.
5. Place in folders all mail received—letters awaiting the executive's attention, photocopies of letters forwarded to others for reply, copies of letters that you or others have answered, advertising mail, newspapers, and so on.

OTHER LETTERS. In addition to the preceding letters, the secretary or administrative assistant may compose other letters on behalf of an executive or follow up on those that require future action. The initiative for writing letters for the executive may come from the assistant or from the employer, who might write on an incoming letter a notation such as "Tell him I'll see him next week." The assistant who takes the initiative may do one of the following:

1. Write a rough-draft reply and attach it to the incoming letter for the boss's approval.
2. Make such notations on incoming letters as "I'll answer" or "Will send today" or "Will say you'll be away that week."

There is no hard-and-fast rule about the duties of the administrative assistant in handling the employer's correspondence. Whether the assistant writes letters for the employer depends entirely on the executive's wishes and the assistant's ability. In any event, the assistant should never be presumptuous. The assistant should turn over *all* incoming letters, routine or not, until the employer decides that the assistant is able to originate correspondence.

COMMUNICATION FOLLOW-UP. The efficient administrative assistant assumes responsibility for following up on the employer's communication activities. For example, if certain letters must be answered by a specific date, the assistant should remind the employer when an answer is due. The assistant can either maintain a tickler file—a file of items needing follow-up—or record reminder notes on a desk calendar pad.

Follow-up is needed, for example, for incoming letters that arrive with enclosures omitted, for outgoing letters that request appointments and that have not been answered, for materials requested that have not arrived, or for some other action referred to in incoming or outgoing correspondence that has not materialized after a reasonable time. Here are some examples of such follow-up letters:

We received your May 6 letter indicating that you will be glad to accept the speaking assignment at the convention of the International Executives' Society in Geneva on July 8.

We would appreciate your sending by the end of this month the title of your presentation, a brief biographical outline, and a list of any equipment you would like to use in conjunction with your presentation.

Mr. Hajas left this morning on an extended trip to our major marketing centers. He would like to arrange a meeting with you for about an hour while he is in Washington on October 15. Would any time between 11 a.m. and 2 p.m. be convenient for you?

I must telephone Mr. Hajas before he leaves New York City on October 13. Therefore, would you please wire or telephone me collect (555-8798) before that date to let me know if you can see Mr. Hajas and at what time?

Signing Letters

When your boss is away or is in a hurry to leave the office, you may be asked to sign his or her name to dictated letters. Or you may be asked to sign all routine correspondence, even when your boss is in the office. If such is the case, write your initials immediately below your boss's "signature," as shown here:

Cordially,

Laura Ashton

(Miss) Laura Ashton

Some employers prefer that their signatures be imitated when the letter is written to people whom they do not know personally.

An administrative assistant sometimes writes letters for his or her own signature, as shown in the following examples:

Very truly yours,

Anne Roth

(Ms.) Anne Roth
Administrative Assistant
to Erik A. Torgeson

Cordially yours,

Gerald M. Hoover

Gerald M. Hoover
Assistant to the President

Messages

Whenever the employer is out of the office or in conference, the secretary should make written notations of all telephone calls received or in-person visits. Written messages do not rely on the secretary's memory and have the added advantage of reminding the employer to follow through. By keeping a copy of all messages, the secretary can advise the employer in advance if a telephone call is to be returned or if some other task is to be performed.

The illustration shown on page 596 is typical of the message forms used in most offices. Notice that only a few words are used in the message, yet the message is clear and complete.

MEETINGS AND CONFERENCES

Although a very informal meeting may require little preparation, the success of most meetings depends upon careful planning. To prepare for meetings, an assistant should be able to attend to these details: (1) reserve and set up the meeting room and restore it to order after the meeting; (2) prepare an agenda (a list of topics to be discussed at the meeting); (3) make definite assignments for each participant; and (4) take notes and prepare minutes of the meeting.

The Meeting Room

Make certain there is a sufficient number of chairs for participants and a few extra chairs for unexpected guests. If possible, conference members should be seated around an oval table in order to take the stiffness out of a meeting and to give everybody an opportunity to

Telephone Message

To: *Nina Rossi*

Here is a Message for You

Mr. Otto Kempel

of *Darik Designs, Inc.*

Phone No. *(301) 555-2791* Ext. _____

☒ Telephoned   ☐ Will Call Again
☐ Returned Your Call   ☐ Came To See You
☒ Please Phone   ☐ Wants To See You

Has several questions on the packaging proposal.

Taken By	Date	Time
J. S.	*9/3*	*10:40*

Taking clear telephone messages for employers and coworkers contributes to the efficiency with which a business or organization is run.

see, hear, and concentrate on the contributions of each participant.

Place a copy of the agenda, several pencils, and a writing pad on the table for each participant. Don't forget to provide ashtrays and drinking water. If audiovisual aids or computers are to be used, make certain that the proper facilities are available, including an operator if one is needed to run the equipment.

After the meeting is over, make certain that all equipment and unused supplies are returned and that the meeting room is restored to its original order. Report any problems involving borrowed equipment. Check all seating locations to be sure that no personal possessions have been left behind.

The Agenda

An agenda of a meeting is usually sent in advance to all participants so that they will have time to prepare their comments, suggestions, or questions. A copy of the agenda should be available for each participant at the meeting room in case someone misplaces an agenda or forgets to bring it to the meeting. The agenda below is typical for an informal meeting.

Agenda
Committee on Magnetic Data Storage
July 10, 19—
11:15 a.m.—Boardroom

1. Call to Order.
2. Minutes Previous Meeting.
3. Discussion of Magnetic Data Storage Problems—Fred Somis.
4. Suggested Solutions to Storage Problems—Anne Inacker.
5. Film Presentation—Cora Thomas.
6. Plans for Feasibility Study—Archie Leach.
7. Assignment of Committee Responsibilities—Harry Browne.
8. Selection of Next Meeting Date.
9. Adjournment.

The Notes and Minutes

A record should be made of what took place at the meeting, preferably in a stenographic notebook because the center rule on each page can separate the names of the speakers from their remarks. The notes should be transcribed as soon as possible. Section 50 gives specific suggestions for preparing minutes.

RESEARCH ACTIVITIES

Executives often are required to do some kind of research and usually expect a secretary or administrative assistant to help. The research work may consist merely of looking up information in the department's own files, telephoning and writing to other departments to gather facts and figures, or consulting one or more periodicals or reference books. On the other hand, some executives are engaged in activities that require more formal research, or they serve as editors of company publications. Many executives write articles for magazines—some may even write books. Furthermore, executives are often asked to deliver speeches. You can make yourself useful to your boss in these research capacities. Therefore, you should be able to make use of library facilities, since your responsibilities may encompass referring to basic reference sources and reading current periodicals.

Basic References

Every assistant to an executive should be familiar with such basic reference resources as the following:

A GOOD DICTIONARY.   The dictionary is probably the most frequently used reference source. For most writing purposes, a dictionary such as *Webster's Ninth New Collegiate Dictionary* (Merriam-Webster Inc.) or *The American Heritage Dictionary of the English Language* (American Heritage Publishing Company, Inc., and Houghton Mifflin Company) is sufficient. Executives who do a great deal of writing or editing should have available an unabridged dictionary.

A BUSINESS WRITER'S HANDBOOK.   A business writer's handbook contains such information as the following: rules for the use of English grammar, capitalization, spelling, punctuation; guides for transcribing, mailing, and filing business correspondence; aids to proofreading; styles and formats for typing; and information relating to postal, express, and telegraphic services.

Such handbooks provide useful sources for secretaries. Several are available. Among the most popular are *Standard Handbook for Secretaries,* by Lois Hutchinson, and *The Gregg Reference Manual,* 6th edition, by William A. Sabin (both, McGraw-Hill Book Company).

A RELIABLE FACT BOOK.   Most assistants find frequent use for a fact book such as *The World Almanac and Book of Facts* (World Almanac). This fact book contains such varied information as names and addresses of colleges and universities, population figures, baseball records, names of members of Congress, senators, Academy Award winners, and much, much more.

Special References

An executive assistant needs special references that pertain to the business of the executive. For example, the assistant who works for a lawyer may need a good law dictionary, such as *Black's Law Dictionary* (West Publishing Company), and a handbook for the legal secretary, such as *Legal Office Procedures,* by Marjorie Dunlap Bate and Mary C. Casey (McGraw-Hill Book Company). Other examples of special references follow:

Administrative assistant to a doctor. A medical dictionary, such as *Blakiston's Gould Medical Dictionary*, edited by A. Osol and C. C. Francis (McGraw-Hill Book Company); a medical secretary's handbook, such as *Medical Office Procedures*, by Miriam Bredow (McGraw-Hill Book Company).

Administrative assistant to a publisher. Various stylebooks, such as *A Manual of Style* (University of Chicago Press); *Writer's Guide and Index to English*, by Wilma R. Ebbitt and

David R. Ebbitt (Scott, Foresman and Company); *Style Manual for Writers*, by Pat Collins and Mary E. Pitts (Metro TN); *Words Into Type* (Prentice-Hall, Inc.); *Roget's International Thesaurus*, by P. M. Roget (Thomas Y. Crowell Company).

Administrative assistant to a chemist. *Lange's Handbook of Chemistry*, compiled and edited by J. A. Dean (McGraw-Hill Book Company).

Administrative assistant to an accountant. *Accountant's Handbook*, by L. J. Seidler and D. R. Carmichael (John A. Wiley & Sons); *Office Management*, by J. C. Denyer (International Ideas, Inc.).

Use of the Library

To use library facilities efficiently, you should become acquainted with the librarian and should seek the librarian's help. The librarian will be able to point out the available sources of information and special reference works as well as the library's auxiliary services, such as the interlibrary loan system, data base searches, and the library's reference services. Often, too, when you are not acquainted with the titles of books or articles or the names of authors, the librarian's help is a great time-saver.

Once you have found all the references you need, you should follow these practical suggestions for recording the information.

1. Be systematic and orderly in all notetaking. Most researchers use index cards for this purpose.
2. Always check to make sure you have the latest edition of the book.
3. Be careful to record for each reference the author's full name, the title of the book or periodical, the title of the article (if a periodical reference), the volume and number (if applicable), the publisher's name, the date and place of publication, and all page numbers referred to.
4. Write on only one side of the card and limit each card to one subject. (See Section 49 for further suggestions for taking notes.)

Reading and Writing Reports

Because your boss may spend a large portion of the day reading reports, you should be prepared to read and summarize reports. Be skillful in summarizing so that no important aspects are omitted and no facts misrepresented. To avoid misinterpretation, cite the page of important items.

Powers offers three important ways to reduce the communication costs of our company. (See page 23.)

Using the training provided in Sections 48 and 49, you should be able to write a report if you are called upon to do so.

Contributing Ideas

To be promoted to higher levels of management, you must be someone with imagination, someone who can make constructive suggestions. The illustration on page 601 is a proposal for saving time and materials that might well come from a secretary or administrative assistant.

GETTING ALONG WITH OTHERS

Anyone who works with an executive reflects the "voice, mind, and personality" of that executive because other workers look upon this assistant as a representative of the employer's point of view. By observing the following guides to good human relations, you will help set a desirable tone in the office and contribute to the morale of your coworkers. As a result, you will reveal your ability to supervise others and place yourself in a better position for promotion.

Be Discreet

Because you are working with an executive, you will be in a position to learn about many confidential matters regarding salaries, personal feelings about employees, company plans for changes in policies or procedures, and personal family matters. Information regarding these confidential matters should never be revealed to other employees, regardless of their rank. Statements like "That's a confidential matter I can't reveal," "I'm not free to reveal such information," or "You'll have to ask _____ (your boss)" will help you to keep confidences.

Be Impartial

An executive's assistant can't afford to show partiality. Your actions and attitudes toward other employees must, therefore, be based on facts rather than on emotions. By not becoming too friendly with others in the same department and by not gossiping, you will find it easier to remain impartial.

Be Loyal

Keeping confidences is one way of demonstrating loyalty. If your boss is being criticized, whether justly or unjustly, you can demonstrate loyalty by coming to the executive's defense or by saying nothing.

It is equally important that you show loyalty to coworkers. Because of your position, they may share many confidences with you regarding such matters as their health, pet dislikes, love affairs, feelings toward the company, or family arguments. These confidences should be kept—even from the boss. You will jeopardize office morale if you carry everything to the boss, and teamwork will then be difficult to obtain.

WINCHESTER RECORDS, INC.

INTEROFFICE MEMORANDUM

To: Alan Malden   From: Miriam Grafton

Subject: Computer Purchase   Date: March 24, 19--

I suggest that we purchase a computer for word processing, similar to the A-111 described in the enclosed brochure. As you can determine from the description on page 3, the A-111 can handle many of our routine writing projects in much less time than it takes us at present. Among the routine tasks that the A-111 can simplify are the following:

1. The revision of our Product Information Sheets. Over the past ten months we have paid more than $2500 to Allied Typing Service for revising our Product Information Sheets. Although a sheet may have only a minor correction, the entire sheet is always retyped. With a machine similar to the A-111, we could update our Product Information Sheets daily right here in our office. Each correction would take only a few minutes, and we would always have up-to-date Product Information Sheets.

2. The updating of our Weekly Production Status Report. The average length of the Production Status Report is 30 pages every week. Of course, it is critical that we complete the report and send it to headquarters on time. With the A-111, we could revise our Weekly Production Status Report in less than one hour.

In addition, there are many more projects for which we could use the A-111 advantageously. The machine would pay for itself within one year; more importantly, we could be sure that our Product Information Sheets are always up to date and that our production reports are sent to headquarters on time.

Of course, there are many other computers available on the market. Some may be less expensive and/or better-suited to our needs than the A-111. In any case, I believe we should explore the possibility of improving our productivity with an efficient computer for word processing.

If you would like to discuss this suggestion further, please telephone me on extension 6534.

MG

MG

Enclosure

Sharing constructive suggestions with management often helps employees advance on the job.

Be Businesslike

A higher degree of morale exists in offices where there are satisfied, productive workers. By being businesslike in your attitude toward the job and toward all other workers, you will indicate that you are aware that there is a job to be done and that the job demands hard work and efficient methods. The following "don'ts" will contribute to your businesslike attitude:

1. Don't visit among employees for social purposes. Remain at your desk unless you have business to attend to elsewhere.
2. Remember that the telephone is a business instrument—not a social one. If friends persist in calling you at the office, tell them that you are too busy to talk and that you will telephone them in the evening.
3. Don't joke about business matters or about office "characters." It is easy to take business matters—and some employees—lightly. Joking about company matters destroys purpose and takes away the genuine satisfaction that employees receive from doing their jobs well.
4. Don't let employees monopolize your time. Some employees like to visit and are constantly finding excuses to come to the assistant's desk (they may really want to see what the boss is doing). Show by your businesslike attitude that employee visits should be completed quickly.
5. Avoid extremes in clothing and accessories. Dress for business.

But Be Pleasant

Following the suggestions for getting along with others does not mean that you have to be disagreeable or even indifferent. You should smile easily and should be friendly toward everyone. Never let a bad mood show. Be cool, calm, and collected in all situations. Remember, you often set the tone for the atmosphere of the whole office as well as for job performance. Being pleasant and friendly is just as important to good human relations as being businesslike is to productivity.

COMMUNICATION PROJECTS

Practical Application

Assuming that you are the administrative assistant in each of the following situations, write the appropriate letters for your employer, Edward M. Goldman, Vice President, Modern Solar Products, Inc.

A. A letter from Gaylord Dorman requests a decision within ten days regarding Mr. Dorman's proposed study of the company's billing procedures. Since your employer is out of the country and cannot be reached, you are unable to make a firm commitment. Therefore, you refer this letter to Erwin Breyer, the auditor, for a reply. Write an appropriate letter to Mr. Dorman to let him know what you have done.

B.   Before Mr. Goldman left on his overseas trip, he asked that you write a letter to Maryanne Kassel, president of the local chamber of commerce. She had asked permission to submit Mr. Goldman's name as a candidate for president of the chamber. Mr. Goldman is unable to accept at the present time because of pressing problems in the business that will require his doing considerable travel during the next six months or more. Therefore, he feels he would not be able to give proper attention to the duties involved in the presidency.

C.   Your company has prepared a colorful brochure, *Getting the Most From Solar Power,* and you are responsible for handling requests for this brochure. Send personal letters under Mr. Goldman's signature in answer to the following requests:

1.   "Please send me information on solar power." Lillian McGruder, 23 Breeder's Lane, Covington, KY 41018.
2.   "I have seen a copy of your excellent booklet on solar power and would like 150 copies to send to my customers." Ronald Ewing, Ewing Heating and Air Conditioning, 17 Peachtree Street, NW, Atlanta, GA 30301. (This request must be refused because of a limited supply. The maximum you can send is ten copies.)
3.   "May I have permission to duplicate pages 23–26 of your brochure on solar power. I want to make this information showing comparative costs of power sources available to my customers. I will give you credit for authorship." Ralph Ingersoll, I & K Corporation, 2 Oliver Street, Bridgeport, CT 06611. (Permission is granted.)

D.   Compose a memorandum for Mr. Goldman, addressed to all department heads of the company. Recently your company purchased a 30-minute videocassette entitled *Power From the Sun.* You are to coordinate the use of this film and preview it for department supervisors only at 2:15 p.m. on Thursday, February 2, in the conference room. This showing is to be followed by a discussion regarding how to best use the cassette as a means of assisting employees to better understand solar power.

Editing Practice

The Supervising Editor.   The following sentences lack writing polish. Edit and rewrite them.

1.   Nothing should be done to change the procedure. You must see to it that it doesn't.

2. The ruling which takes affect today is the one concerning tardiness.
3. The reason Mel was late is because he had to pick up a report from another branch.
4. I have difficulty in distinguishing one to the other.
5. Under the last line in the return address on the envelope is to be printed his name and title.

Case Problem

Signing for the Boss. Sometimes employers are not available to sign letters when the letters are ready to be mailed. Three different suggestions for handling this situation were made by the following employers to their secretaries:

Employer A says: "Sign my name and put your initials below the signature."

Employer B says: "Just sign my name; don't bother to initial because no one will know the difference."

Employer C says: "Do not sign my name but instead type below the typewritten signature, 'Dictated but not read.'"

What are the advantages and disadvantages of each of these methods?

ELECTRONIC OFFICE GLOSSARY

ACCESS To retrieve information from a computer system.

APPLICATION Specific purpose for which a computer is used, such as word processing or accounts receivable.

ARCHIVE Storage of duplicate text, usually on a diskette. Generally refers to data that is infrequently used or that is stored as backup material.

BACKUP Storage of duplicate text on a diskette as a safety measure in the event the original stored item is damaged or lost.

BOILERPLATE Text that can be retrieved from storage in a word processing system to be reused without being keyboarded again. Boilerplate is usually used in combination with variable information that is newly keyboarded, but some documents are assembled entirely of boilerplate.

BYTE A unit of measurement in computer storage, roughly equivalent to one printed character.

COMPUTER A machine that performs calculations or otherwise manipulates information automatically by interpreting electrical impulses.

COMPUTER-BASED MESSAGE SYSTEM A system of communications that uses linked computers. Messages can be composed on the screen.

COMPUTER GRAPHICS The automated creation of charts, graphs, or pictures by a computer program from verbal or numeric information.

COMPUTER SECURITY The control of access to information in a computer system, usually to prevent unauthorized persons from obtaining confidential information. *Computer security* also refers to the protection of hardware.

CONFERENCE CALL Communication by telephone among three or more people in different locations.

CONTINUOUS-FORM PAPER Connected sheets of paper that have strips of sprocket holes along their sides to permit automatic feeding through a printer. The edges of the sheets are perforated so that they can be separated easily from each other and from the sprocket-hold strips.

DAISY WHEEL A type element for a word processing printer, serving the same function as the type ball of a typewriter. A daisy wheel is so named because it resembles a daisy, with the characters at the ends of the "petals."

DATA; DATA PROCESSING Although *data* is just another word for facts, in the electronic office it generally means numeric information. *Data processing* refers to the use of computers to perform calculations or other numeric operations (as opposed to *word processing*, which refers to the manipulation of text).

DATA BANK A collection of data bases.

DATA BASE A collection of related information that is organized to be used for more than one application. Examples are periodicals, indexes, and court decisions.

DEDICATED WORD PROCESSOR Electronic equipment designed specifically and only for word processing.

DISK; DISKETTE A circular piece of magnetic material that retains information by recording the electrical impulses generated by a computer or word processor. Disks, which are about as big as long-playing phonograph records, can store hundreds of pages of text or numbers and are usually used with big computer systems. Personal computers generally use diskettes, which are smaller and can store as much as 100 pages of information.

DOCUMENT Any printed business communication such as a letter, memo, or form.

EDITING The process of changing text by inserting, deleting, replacing, rearranging, and reformatting.

ELECTRONIC COPIER/PRINTER A copying machine that is faster than conventional photocopiers and can be linked with other electronic equipment.

ELECTRONIC FILES; ELECTRONIC FILING Documents that are stored in an information processing system are called *electronic files*. *Electronic filing* refers to recording these documents on storage disks or retrieving them from the disks for viewing, editing, or printing.

ELECTRONIC MAIL The electronic transmission of correspondence between video display terminals rather than through the use of paper.

ELECTRONIC OFFICE An office that uses information processing equipment to perform tasks such as word processing, financial projections, and so on.

EXECUTIVE WORKSTATION The information processing equipment, such as a personal computer, in a manager's office.

FACSIMILE; FACSIMILE TRANSMISSION A facsimile is a copy of a printed document. Facsimile transmission is the use of electronic equipment to transmit copies between distant points. Facsimile transmission involves the use of one device to scan the original electronically and another device to print the copy. These devices are connected over telephone lines or by other electronic means.

FILE A storage area in a computer's memory.

FLOPPY DISK; FLOPPY DISKETTE See **Disk; Diskette.**

FLOW CHART A chart showing the flow of work from start to finish, with symbols that represent operations and pieces of equipment.

FORMAT The page margin, depth, spacing, and indentation requirements of a document.

GLOBAL SEARCH A word processing function that electronically finds a word (or any string of characters) everywhere that it appears in a document.

HARD COPY A printed copy of a document produced by an information processing system. See also **Printout.**

HARDWARE The physical components of an information processing system: the computer, the keyboard, and so on.

INFORMATION PROCESSING A term that includes both word processing and data processing and refers to all operations that can be performed by a computer.

INPUT The transfer of text or data into an information processing system. *Input* can also refer to the text or data itself.

INTERFACE An electrical connector that permits a piece of equipment, such as a printer, to be attached to another piece of equipment, such as a microcomputer.

KEYBOARDING Using the keyboard of a computer or word processor to put information into a computer system.

LASER A device that transmits an extremely narrow beam of light. Laser technology is increasingly being used to store, transmit, and print documents in information processing systems. The word *laser* is an acronym for *l*ight *a*pplication by *s*imulated *e*mission of *r*adiation.

LOG ON; LOG OFF To key the code that tells a computer or word processor when you are using the system or when you have finished. Logging on may require that you use a password identifying yourself as an authorized user.

MENU A list of tasks or functions displayed on a video display terminal from which the operator selects the appropriate one to perform a particular task.

MERGE A command to create one document by combining text that is stored in two different locations. For example, many word processors can merge the standard text of a form letter with a mailing list to produce a batch of letters with a different name, address, and salutation on each letter.

MICROCOMPUTER A small and relatively inexpensive computer system commonly consisting of a display screen, a keyboard, a central processing unit, one or more disk drives, and a printer. See also **Personal Computer.**

MICROFICHE A sheet of microfilm about the size of an index card, on which dozens of documents can be stored photographically.

MODEM A device that enables personal computers to communicate over long distances. A modem converts electrical impulses from a computer into signals that can be transmitted over telephone wires, then converts them back to electrical impulses for the receiving computer.

NETWORK; NETWORKING The use of cables, telephone lines, satellites, and other technologies to allow communication among pieces of electronic equipment, sometimes over long distances.

OPTICAL CHARACTER READER (OCR) A device that scans printed pages and converts them into electrical signals for input into an information processing system so that they do not have to be rekeyboarded.

OUTPUT The final printing of text or information produced by a computer.

PASSWORD An identification code known only to authorized users of a computer system.

PERSONAL COMPUTER A microcomputer for personal or office use. See **Microcomputer.**

PHOTOCOMPOSITION The use of computers and photographic film, rather than metal type, for typesetting.

PRINTER The component of an information processing system that electronically prints copies of text or data that is stored in the system. The printer is operated by keyboarding commands to the system's computer.

PRINTOUT A paper copy, or hard copy, of information that is stored in an information processing system. See also **Hard Copy.**

PROGRAM A set of instructions, also called *software,* that tells a computer how to perform a task. Some programs are mass-produced and sold for use with personal computers, while others are written for specific systems. See also **Software.**

REPROGRAPHICS The reproduction of printed documents.

RETRIEVE; RETRIEVAL The process of taking a document out of storage. In word processing, retrieval usually means calling a document from a storage disk onto a video display terminal so that it can be read, edited, or printed.

SOFT COPY The text or data that is displayed on a video display terminal, as opposed to text or data that is printed.

SOFTWARE Instructions that tell a computer how to perform a task. See also **Program.**

STORAGE The electronic recording of documents so that they can be read, edited, or printed later. See also **Disk; Diskette.**

SYSTEMS ANALYSIS; SYSTEMS ANALYST The process of designing and developing information processing systems is known as *systems analysis,* and the people who do this are called *systems analysts.*

SYSTEMS MANAGER The person who oversees the design and operation of an information processing system.

TELECOMMUNICATIONS The transmission and reception of information over long distances, usually by means of telephone lines.

TELECOMMUTING Working at home or at a site other than at the traditional workplace on a personal computer that is connected with a company's information processing system.

TELECONFERENCE A "meeting" in which several participants at distant locations use telecommunications equipment to exchange documents, converse, and perhaps see each other on television screens.

TELETYPEWRITER A keyboard terminal used in the transmission of text over telecommunications lines.

TELEX An automatic switching service provided on a worldwide basis by various common carriers by which information is transmitted over telecommunications lines between teletypewriters.

TWX (TELETYPEWRITER EXCHANGE SERVICE) A system operated by Western Union in which teletypewriter stations are provided with lines to a central office for access to other such stations throughout the United States, Canada, and Mexico.

ULTRAFICHE A sheet of microfilm containing images that have been reduced to one-ninetieth of their original size. See also **Microfiche.**

VARIABLE Information in a form document that changes each time the document is produced. A common variable is the addressee in a form letter.

VIDEO DISPLAY TERMINAL (VDT) A televisionlike screen on which information being keyed into an information processing system, or already stored there, is displayed for reading or editing.

VOICE MAIL A technology by which voice messages can be recorded, stored electronically, and delivered at designated times.

WORD PROCESSING The use of electronic equipment to create, edit, store, print, or transmit documents electronically.

WORD PROCESSING CENTER; WORD PROCESSING OPERATOR An organization's *word processing center* is responsible for preparing finished documents from rough drafts or dictation provided by authors throughout the organization. The people who work in the center are called *word processing operators*.

WORD PROCESSOR A computer, either independent or part of a larger system, that performs word processing. A word processor generally consists of a keyboard, a video display terminal, a storage unit, an internal processor (or computer), and a printer.

WORKSTATION A computer terminal used for information processing. A workstation consists at least of a video display terminal and a keyboard. The storage unit, processor, and printer may be located at the workstation or elsewhere.

INDEX

off, from, 174
Office, traditional vs. electronic, 13–15
Omissions, commas for, 228–229
one another, each other, 154–155
opposite to, 174
or, subjects joined by, 145
Oral communication, 501–507, 509–515 (see also Speeches)
  appearance, physical, and, 510–512, 552–553, 580
  effective business relationships through, 505–506
  forms of, in business, 504–505
  group discussions, 535–543
  importance of, in business, 502
  interviews, job, 578–585
  one-to-one, 526–533
  role of, in business, 503–504
  speech qualities, 512–515, 518–523, 553
Ordinal numbers, 264–265, 267, 268
Organizational structure of office, 14–15
Origin of words, 277
our, are, 113
Out-of-date words, 287–288, 380–381
Outlines
  capitalization in, 244
  for reports, 462, 475
  of speeches, 548, 551
outside, 173
Overused terms, 53, 288–289

Paragraphs
  boilerplate, 449, 453; illus., 454
  length of, 314, 340–342
  main idea in, 339–340
  in news releases, 494
  as report form, 461–462
  transitional expressions in, 340–341
Parallel structure, 333–336
  with coordinating conjunctions, 183
  with correlative conjunctions, 184
Parentheses, 238–240
  letters or numbers in, 190–191
Parenthetic elements, commas with, 220
Part, portion, amount subjects, 139–140
part from, part with, 171
Participial phrases, 214
Participles, 81
  of transitive verbs, 93
Parts, principal, of verbs, 81
  irregular verbs, 88–90, 94
Parts of speech (see also Adjectives; Adverbs; Conjunctions; Nouns; Prepositions; Pronouns; Verbs)

Parts of speech (continued)
  interjections, 64
Passive vs. active voice, 332
Passive listening, 20–21
Past perfect tense, 84–85
Past progressive tense, 85
Past tense, 84
  of to be, 90
Percentages, expressing, 268
Perfect tenses, 84–85
Period fault, 192
Periods, 189–192
  with abbreviations, 254, 255, 257
  vs. colon, 201
  with quotation marks, 234, 236
Personal-business letter format, 378; illus., 379
Phrases
  gerund, 214
  infinitive, 68, 213
  introductory, 213–214
  participial, 214
  prepositional, 68, 168–169, 214
    vs. infinitives, 69
  in thought units, 319–320
  verb, 69, 82–83, 91
Physical factors
  in listening, 22–23
  in oral communication
    appearance, 510–512, 552–553, 580
    mouth, use of, 521–523
  in reading, 30
Physical needs, defined, 10
Pitch of voice, 513–514
Place names
  abbreviations in, 257
  capitalization of, 247
Placement offices, 561
Plurals of nouns, 98–105
  with apostrophes, 101
  common, basic rules for, 98–100, 296
  compound, 99
  ending in f or fe, 103
  ending in o, 102–103
  ending in y, 99–100, 296
  foreign, 104
  with only one form, 104–105
  possessive forms of, 109
  proper, 99–101
  with special changes, 101–102
  with titles, 100–101
Poetry, capitalization in, 244
Portion, amount, part subjects, 139–140
Positive attitude, 11
  listening with, 23–24
Positive degree, 152
Positive statements in response letters, 404, 407–408
Positive words, 329
Possessive adjectives, 150
Possessive forms of nouns, 108–111

Possessive pronouns, 112–113
Post office box numbers, 257
Posture of speaker, 510–511
Predicates, 66
  agreement of, with subject (see Agreement, subject-predicate)
  in sentence order, 76, 133
  separating subject from, 223
Prefixes
  in antonyms, 291
  in names, 246
  spelling pitfalls, 302
Prepositional phrases, 68, 168–169, 214
  vs. infinitives, 69
Prepositions, 63, 168–174
  balancing, 335
  vs. conjunctions, 182
  identifying, 168–169
  idiomatic use of, 169–172
  pitfalls in use of, 172–174
Present perfect tense, 84
Present progressive tense, 85
Present tense, 83–84
  of to be, 90
Principal parts of verbs, 80–81
  irregular verbs, 88–90, 94
Printed responses, 395
Product names, capitalization of, 250
Productivity, 11
  office, 14, 15
Progress reports, 482–483
Progressive tenses, 85
Promotions, congratulations letters for, 435, 440; illus., 436, 437
Pronouns, 60
  agreement of, with subject, 132
    with common-gender nouns, 134
  in appositives, 127–128
  case forms of
    nominative, 117–118
    objective, 118–119
    possessive, 112–113
    problems with, 119–120, 124–125, 127–128
  indefinite references with, 323–325
  relative, clauses with, 145–146, 181, 223, 321–322
  self-ending, 126–127
  who, whom, whoever, whomever, 124–125
Pronunciation, 276, 283
  and enunciation, 518–523
Proofreading, 47–50
Proper adjectives, 150, 248
Proper nouns, 246–248, 250
  plurals of, 99–101
Pseudohomonyms, 284–285
Public relations, 422–431
  news releases for, 489, 492
  oral communication and, 506
Punctuation (see also Commas; Periods; Semicolons)